Masters and Slaves of Modern Religion

Geoffrey Hebdon, Editor

GHB

Glass House Books

Publisher: Glass House Books, an imprint of Interactive Publications Pty Ltd
Cover design: UxByDesign, LLC. (USA)

ISBN: 9781922332622 (PB); 9781922332639 (eBk)

A percentage of the proceeds from this book will be donated to nominated
wildlife sanctuaries in Kenya, which are registered members of the Kenya Wildlife
Conservation Association as decided by the management committee of the MTC
International Foundation.

Psalms 119:109 informs us, "I hold my life in my palm constantly".

This book is dedicated to the memory of Edward Dunlap and Raymond Franz, two of the most courageous Bible students who ever lived.

Contents

Introduction & Editorial Note

This book is the first of a series of books under the theme, Masters and Slaves and the additional topics to be covered and currently being researched by our dedicated team will be released in the near future. Additional themes presently being investigated and published in the near future are, Masters and Slaves of Modern Marriage © and Masters and Slaves of the Corporate World ©. Additional subjects will be added in due course as they become relevant to assisting our many readers in finding answers related to these current important issues on a global level.

This narrative is related to modern religion and is published as a contribution to the need for openness, truth and honesty regarding religious cults and the dangers associated with mind control and how these cults operate. Many of these events and descriptions contained in this book have been reproduced, confirmed and acknowledged using information freely provided from the reliable non-profit organization Wikipedia, which we have extensively used, plus other numerous external sources. Our team of researchers have independently checked and verified as far as humanly possible all these details for accuracy and authenticity. Much of the information in this report was gleaned from the archives of the sources acknowledged, most of which is available to the general public; other sources are only available by special permission. Material related to the religions and cults covered, is also available in the public domain, but in all cases we have acknowledged the sources wherever possible.

We are grateful to The Corpus Vitrearum Medii Aevi (CVMA) of Great Britain, plus the Kings College of London and the British Academy. The JANET Network and JISC, plus the National Education & Research Network (NREN). We especially thank our friends, associates and students of the History Department of the University of Utah in Salt Lake City, USA, who wish to remain nameless but who volunteered and provided much of their time, plus the valuable material related to the background history of the various religions analyzed. We express appreciation to Marci Hamilton and Cambridge University Press and their brilliant reference work, God vs. The Gavel: Religion and the Rule of Law. We also acknowledge the excellent material and feedback submitted by forensic scientists and fellow researchers at Cambridge University in England. Without the help and cooperation of the above list of sources, this book could not have been published. We are certain that we have missed listing many other individuals and sources that have provided valuable material to support our research in various ways and if not named, we wish to apologize. To those who requested, they remain anonymous but also provided material and help in our research in many ways, our sincere thanks.

We also gratefully acknowledge the over 39 inspired writers of the 66 books of God's Word the Holy Scriptures. These men, who of course are no longer alive on earth today, consisted of scribes, prophets, priests and truthful co-writers of God's Word, were all Hebrews and accordingly members of the group identified in the Bible, "For in the first place the Jews were entrusted with the oracles of God." (Romans 3:2) Eight of these men were Christian Jews who personally knew Jesus Christ or knew of his words though his faithful apostles. Without the assistance and support of these men through their writings, this narrative could not have been published.

Most of the images and diagrams used in this narrative are in the public domain. Many of the photos used were taken by the editor or associates and these also are now in the public domain, a few other photos have been used after a request was made for permission from the copyright owners and these have been acknowledged accordingly. We also thank Wikipedia, the free online encyclopedia, created and edited by volunteers around the world and hosted by the Wikimedia Foundation and especially their ShareAlike 4.0 International and Creative Commons (CC By-SA 4.0) service. Additional images have been provided by courtesy of the Library of Congress.

All quotations from the Holy Bible are from *The New Revised Standard Version* (NRSV), which is an English translation of the Bible published in 1989 by the National Council of Churches. It is a revision of the Revised Standard Version, which was itself an update of the *American Standard Version*. This is our favorite and preferred translation of the Holy Scriptures above all others.

We are grateful to the voluntary staff of the non-profit charity, the MTC International Foundation, who read and commented on the various drafts. Their painstaking efforts eliminated many grammatical mistakes, improved exposition and also added important insights. All other errors in the text are mine alone as the editor. All references, quotations, opinions and views expressed in this narrative based on our research, are not necessarily those of the individual members of our research team or the editor. The personal names of many of our sources of information have been withheld at the contributor's request. Plus, our editorial staff has decided regarding the contributors who are now deceased to also withhold their names out of respect for their families with a few requested exceptions.

Most of the individuals we interviewed during our research are still active in modern day religions either for personal or family reasons, some of which we cover in our book, especially those connected to the Mormons and Jehovah's Witnesses. To our surprise many also expressed the opinion that they did not necessarily believe that their chosen religion was the only true religion on earth and many courageously displayed open-mindedness and a genuine tolerance for other religious groups and organizations. Many also openly acknowledged that they believe that there are genuine, sincere Christians in other religions of Christendom besides the one they profess, but they all had one common thread and that their desire was for their spiritual leaders and shepherds to always speak the truth.

Also, many of the individuals interviewed by our reporters and research team were not always bitter screwed-up ex-members of one of these religious cults with a chip on their shoulders; holding a personal grudge or grievance, but some were in fact still active members as they claimed they still loved and personally benefitted from belonging to their particular religion. Their hope was that by remaining an integral member and part of the group that they could perhaps help somehow in bringing about necessary improvements, changes and corrections of any misleading, negative or misguided beliefs, but doing so from within. Therefore, many of the comments brought together by the editor are genuine sincere opinions expressed by these serious-minded individuals, so whether you agree with this philosophy and tactic or not we must respect the decision of these sincere individuals. The editor has also made additional comments, where necessary, to expand on the related facts recorded. It must also be pointed out that the primary role and duty of the editor was to comb through the 1,000s of pages of information that came across his desk related to the subject of cults and religions. His duty and responsibility was to decide along with his team of able assistants what to include in this book and what best represents to our readers, facts and details related to modern-day religions, sects and cults, plus some of the dangers associated thereto.

Chapter Three of our book is about the Watchtower Society. As the longest chapter and the most candid in this narrative it is particularly important, as our research team gleaned information primarily from friends and associates who are or have been prominent members of this religion. These reliable facts and details about the Watchtower Society, also known as Jehovah's Witnesses, have previously never been exposed but many individuals expressed their desire to lay bare this information as a contribution to the real truth and of benefit to their fellow men and women. This religion, its past leaders and current Governing Body has also been identified as the most destructive cult in existence today and one that must be exposed and identified at all costs.

For example, we have the recent case that personifies the feelings of many as expressed in the recent book called, *My Beloved Religion* – And The Governing Body by Rolf Furuli of Larvik, Norway. The first words of the introduction of his book are:

> This book is not an attack on Jehovah's Witnesses. On the contrary! My beloved religion is the religion of Jehovah's Witnesses. And I have invested my whole soul in this religion for 59 years. However, the book represents a strong correction of those who have been members of the Governing Body of Jehovah's Witnesses in the 21st century.

Of interest to our readers, this sincere, genuine member of Jehovah's Witnesses has subsequently been expelled from his beloved religion but he still attends their public meetings whenever possible, but like many others is now strictly limited due to the current COVID-19 virus restrictions. From a report by an associate of Rolf's he stoically sits on an isolated seat at the rear of the Kingdom Hall and he is completely ignored by his many long-standing friends and associates as they have to obey the rules of the Governing Body of this religion and they treat him like a leper. Rolf is now identified as an apostate[1] despite all of his sincere attempts to offer meaningful, constructive suggestions on how the current misguided Governing Body and his beloved religion could be improved.

By not being open and truthful, many of these religious leaders walk into the trap of being deceitful, and they should remind themselves of this quotation by Sir Walter Scott (1771-1832) the Scottish poet and writer, "Oh what a tangled web we weave, when first we practice to deceive." Most individuals we interviewed also stressed that their leaders should be completely open about the so-called doctrines and historical facts that are claimed to exist and that are frequently used to try and prove that their religion is the only true religion on the planet. They all agreed with the words and sentiment expressed in the Bible, "So Jesus said to the Jews who had believed him: If you abide in my word, you are truly my disciples, and you will know the truth, and the truth will set you free." (John 8:32)

In a recent group discussion by our research team the question was raised, Is there such a thing as religious slavery, especially in the 21st century? As a result of this discussion an in-depth analysis was prepared as a series of reports, press releases and articles. We are pleased to announce that this information is now correlated and published as a complete volume for all genuine enquirers to read about this vital and important subject.

---

[1] Apostasy in Christianity is the rejection of Christianity by someone who formerly was a Christian or who wishes to administratively be removed from a formal registry of church members. It can also mean a defection or revolt against God and Jesus Christ. The term apostasy comes from the Greek word *apostasia* (ἀποστασία) meaning defection, departure, revolt or rebellion.

This issue of religious cults and the extreme demands made upon the individuals who are trapped or enslaved in such an organization by the leaders of these religions is so serious and truly cannot be simply viewed with a laissez-faire attitude. This subject must be met face on and this powerful report and exposé is the contribution that our team of researchers is making to ensure the facts are laid bare and the full disclosure of these damaging and dangerous religious cults. Who of us today is prepared to speak up and expose these religious cults for what they are and that creates such damage to the lives of people who try and sincerely serve their Creator as Christians under the leadership of their true Master, the Lord Jesus Christ? Our research team, one and all expressed the sentiments of the words recorded at Isaiah 6:8, "Then I heard the voice of the Lord saying, Whom shall I send, and who will go for us? And I said, Here am I; send me."

***

What is a cult? In modern English, the term cult has come to usually refer to a social group defined by its unusual religious, spiritual, or philosophical beliefs, or its common interest in a particular personality, object or goal. This sense of the term is controversial and it has divergent definitions in both popular culture and academia and it also has been an ongoing source of contention among scholars across several fields of study. Beginning in the 1930s, cults became the object of sociological study in the context of the study of religious behavior. From the 1940s the Christian counter-cult movement has opposed some sects and new religious movements, and it labeled them as cults for their un-Christian unorthodox beliefs. The secular anti-cult movement began in the 1970s and it opposed certain groups, often charging them with mind control and partly motivated in reaction to acts of violence committed by some of their members. Some of the claims and actions of the anti-cult movement have been disputed by scholars and by the news media, leading to further public controversy.

On his website, Carm.org, Matt Slick offers this comment.

> There are many non-Christian religions and cults in America:
> Mormonism, Jehovah's Witnesses, Christian Science, Unity,
> The Way International, Unitarianism, Islam, Hinduism, etc.

They all claim special revelation and privilege and those
that use the Bible invariably interpret it in disharmony with
standard biblical understanding. And groups especially like
the Mormons and Jehovah's Witnesses object to being labeled
a "cult" because it often gets an emotional reaction as well as
is a label they want to avoid. Another common denominator
among the Cults is their methods for twisting scripture. Some
of the errors they commit in interpreting Scripture are: 1)
taking Scripture out of context; 2) reading into the Scriptures
information that is not there; 3) picking and choosing only the
Scriptures that suit their needs; 4) ignoring other explanations;
5) combining scriptures that don't have anything to do with
each other; 6) quoting a verse without giving its location; 7)
incorrect definitions of key words; and 8) mistranslations. These
are only a few of the many ways cults misuse Scripture.

The Christian Apologetics Research Ministry (CARM) also written by
Matt Slick includes the following observations. For a group to be a cult
in the social sense, many of the following characteristics would have to
be present. For a group to be a cult in the doctrinal sense, essentials (*in
this case of the Christian faith*) would have to be violated. Some of the
characteristics are listed below by kind permission of CARM.

Submission: Complete, almost unquestioned trust in the
leadership. Leaders are often seen as prophets, apostles, or
special individuals with unusual connections to God. This
helps a person give themselves over psychologically to trusting
someone else for their spiritual welfare. Increased submission to
the leadership is rewarded with additional responsibilities and/
or roles, and/or praises, increasing the importance of the person
within the group.

Exclusivity: Their group is the only true religious system, or
one of the few true remnants of Gods people.

Persecution complex: Us against them mentality. Therefore,
when someone (inside or outside of the group) corrects
the group in doctrine and/or behavior, it is interpreted as
persecution, which then is interpreted as validation.

Control: Control of members' actions and thinking through
repeated indoctrination and/or threats of loss of salvation, or a
place to live, or receiving curses from God, etc.

Isolation: Minimizing contact of church members with those outside the group. This facilitates a further control over the thinking and practices of the members by the leadership.

Love Bombing: Showing great attention and love to a person in the group by others in the group, to help transfer emotional dependence to the group.

Special Knowledge: Instructions and/or knowledge are sometimes said to be received by a leader(s) from God. This leader then informs the members. The Special Knowledge can be received through visions, dreams, or new interpretations of sacred scriptures such as the Bible.

Indoctrination: The teachings of the group are repeatedly drilled into the members, but the indoctrination usually occurs around Special Knowledge.

Salvation: Salvation from the judgment of God is maintained through association and/or submission with the group, its authority, and/or its Special Knowledge.

Group Think: The group's coherence is maintained by the observance to policies handed down from those in authority. There is an internal enforcement of policies by members who reward proper behavior, and those who perform properly are rewarded with further inclusion and acceptance by the group.

Cognitive Dissonance: Avoidance of critical thinking and/or maintaining logically impossible beliefs and/or beliefs that are inconsistent with other beliefs held by the group. Avoidance of and/or denial of any facts that might contradict the group's belief system.

Shunning: Those who do not keep in step with group policies are shunned and/or expelled.

Gender Roles: Control of gender roles and its definitions. Severe control of gender roles sometimes leads to sexual exploitation.

Appearance Standards: Often a common appearance is required and maintained. For instance, women might wear prairie dresses, and/or their hair in buns, and/or no makeup,

and/or the men might all wear white short-sleeved shirts, and/
or without beards, or all wear beards.

The term new religious movement refers to religions which have
appeared since the mid-1800s. Many, but not all of them, have been
considered to be cults. Sub-categories of cults include: Doomsday
cults, personality cults, political cults, destructive cults, racist cults,
polygamist cults, and terrorist cults. Various national governments have
reacted to cult-related issues in different ways, and this has sometimes
led to controversy. English-speakers originally used the word cult not
to describe a group of religionists, but to refer to the act of worship
or to a religious ceremony. The English term originated in the early
17th century, borrowed via the French culte, from the Latin noun cultus
(worship). The word ultimately derived from the Latin adjective cultus
(inhabited, cultivated, worshipped), based on the verb colere (to care, to
cultivate).

While the literal original sense of the word in the English language
remains in use, a derived sense of excessive devotion arose in the 19th
century. The terms *cult* and *cultist* came into use in medical literature
in the United States in the 1930s for what would now be termed faith
healing, especially as practiced in the American Holiness movement.

This usage experienced a surge of popularity at the time, and extended
to other forms of alternative medicine as well. In the English-speaking
world the word cult often carries derogatory connotations. It has
always been controversial because it is (*in a pejorative sense*) considered
a subjective term, used as an ad hominem attack against groups with
differing doctrines or practices.

A new religious movement (NRM) is a religious community or
spiritual group of modern origins (since the mid-1800s), which has a
peripheral place within its society's dominant religious culture. NRMs
can be novel in origin or part of a wider religion, in which case they
are distinct from pre-existing denominations. In 1999 Eileen Barker[2]
estimated that NRMs, of which some but not all have been labeled

---

[2] Eileen Vartan Barker is the chairperson and founder of the Information Network
Focus on Religious Movements (INFORM) and has written extensive studies about
groups she defines as cults and new religious movements.

as cults, number in the tens of thousands worldwide, most of which originated in Asia or Africa; and that the great majority of which have only a few members, some have thousands and only very few have more than a million. In 2007 the religious scholar Elijah Siegler commented that, although no NRM had become the dominant faith in any country, many of the concepts which they had first introduced (often referred to as New Age ideas) have become part of worldwide mainstream culture.

In their Theory of Religion (1996) American sociologists Rodney Stark and William Sims Bainbridge propose that the formation of cults can be explained through the rational choice theory. In *The Future of Religion* they comment, in the beginning, all religions are obscure, tiny, deviant cult movements. According to Marc Galanter, Professor of Psychiatry at NYU, typical reasons why people join cults include a search for a community and a spiritual quest. Stark and Bainbridge, in discussing the process by which individuals join new religious groups, have even questioned the utility of the concept of conversion, suggesting that affiliation is a more useful concept.

Christian cults are new religious movements that have a Christian background but are considered to be theologically deviant by members of other Christian churches. In his influential book, *The Kingdom of the Cults*, Christian scholar Walter Martin defines Christian cults as groups that follow the personal interpretation of an individual, rather than the understanding of the Bible accepted by mainstream Christianity. He mentions The Church of Jesus Christ of Latter-day Saints (Mormons), Christian Science, Jehovah's Witnesses (Watchtower Society), Unitarian Universalism, and Unity as examples.

However the bulk of our research material – Chapters Two, Three and Four – centers on the Mormons, Scientology and the Watchtower Society, as these are indentified as the three most dangerous cults on earth today and they seriously affect the happiness and personal, private lives of millions of their slave like followers.

The following is a concise definition of a cult, by Dr Robert Lifton's Criteria of Cultic Mind Control: "A cult is any group that sets itself up as the supreme authority between God and Man. Cults claim the following:

- The Bible is seen as an insufficient guide for spiritual truth. Cult members are told to use the cult's literature for the proper understanding of God's truth.

- Group leaders are seen as God's channel of communication to man. They equate loyalty to the group as loyalty to God.

- They foster a, we/they mentality to the world, claiming that only inside the group can one find truth and ultimate salvation, and that outside the group is Satan's world.

- Doubt and criticism of the group or leaders are disallowed. They often claim that independent thinking is evidence of pride, and is seen as questioning God and His arrangement for life.

- Adherents dispense personal identity for the group mold and take on the personality and characteristics of the totalistic environment of the cult."

The definition of a follower of a cult is any blind, unthinking, unquestioning follower of a philosophy. To a lesser degree we have other groups like the Moonies. Moonie is a pejorative term sometimes used to refer to members of the Unification Church. It is derived from the name of the church's founder Sun Myung Moon, and was first used in 1974 by the American media and believe it or not, is now a popular religious cult in the USA, being established in the 1960s. The sole searching question related to the theme of our final chapter is posed, Are the followers of these cults actually religious slaves and if so will these cults increase in number and also in power, influence and strength; or will they ever be exposed for what they really are?

An enlightening article in the Atlantic (2014), created a list of six ways to recognize the difference between a religious community and a cult. Written down, the signs seem clear:

- Opposing critical thinking.

- Isolating members and penalizing them for leaving.

- Emphasizing special doctrines outside scripture.

- Seeking inappropriate loyalty to their leaders.

- Dishonoring the family unit.

- Crossing Biblical boundaries of behavior (versus sexual purity and personal ownership).

Chapter One: The Peoples Temple

The research undertaken by our team initially reveals perhaps the most glaring example of mind control by a religious cult, being named the Peoples Temple. (Full name being Peoples Temple of the Disciples of Christ). Our researchers came across the appalling case of Jim Jones and his cult known as the Peoples Temple and the mass murder (or suicide) of his followers. A brilliant book was written about this disastrous event by Tim Reiterman, *The Untold Story of Rev. Jim Jones*, which we have quoted sections below.

> The Peoples Temple Agricultural Project, better known by its informal name Jonestown, was a remote settlement established by the Peoples Temple, an American cult under the leadership of Reverend Jim Jones, in north Guyana, South America. It became internationally known when, on November 18, 1978, 918 people died in the settlement, at the nearby airstrip in Port Kaituma and at a Temple-run building in Georgetown, Guyanas capital city. The name of the settlement became synonymous with the incidents at those locations. In total, 909 individuals died in Jonestown, all but two from apparent cyanide poisoning, in an event termed revolutionary suicide by Jones and some members on an audio tape of the event and in prior discussions. The poisonings in Jonestown followed the murder of five others by Temple members at Port Kaituma, including United States Congressman Leo Ryan, an act that Jones ordered. Four other Temple members committed murder-suicide in Georgetown at Jones command.

While some refer to the events in Jonestown as mass suicide, many others, including Jonestown survivors, regard them as mass murder. As many as 70 people may have been injected with poison, and a third of the victims (304) were minors. It was the largest such event in modern history and resulted in the largest single loss of American civilian life in a deliberate act until September 11, 2001, the 9/11 destruction of the World Trade Center of New York City.

The Peoples Temple was formed in Indianapolis, Indiana, USA in 1955. Though its roots and teachings shared more with biblical church and Christian revival movements than with Marxism, it purported to practice what it called apostolic socialism. In doing so, the Temple preached that those who remained drugged with the opiate of religion had to be brought to enlightenment – socialism. In the early 1960s, Jones visited Guyana in South America – then a British colony – while on his way to establishing a short-lived Temple mission in Brazil.

Logo for the Peoples Temple (1955-1978), courtesy of Creative Commons

The initial 500 members began the construction of Jonestown; the Temple leadership encouraged more to relocate to the settlement. Jones saw Jonestown as both a socialist paradise and a sanctuary from media scrutiny. In 1976, the government of Guyana finally approved the lease it had negotiated (retroactive to April 1974) with the Temple for the over 3,000 acres (1,200 ha) of land in northwest Guyana on which Jonestown was located. In 1974, Guyanese officials granted the Temple permission to import certain items duty free. Later payoffs and bribes helped safeguard shipments of firearms and drugs through Guyanese customs. Jones reached an agreement to guarantee that Guyana would permit Temple members mass migration. To do so, Jones stated that they were skilled and progressive, showed off an envelope he claimed contained $500,000, and stated that he would invest most of the group's assets in Guyana.

According to escaped Temple member Odell Rhodes, the first to take the poison were Ruletta Paul and her one-year-old infant. A syringe without a needle fitted was used to squirt poison into the infants mouth, after which Paul squirted another syringe into her own mouth. Stanley Clayton also witnessed mothers with their babies first approach the tub containing the poison. Clayton said that Jones approached people to encourage them to drink the poison and that, after adults saw the poison begin to take effect, they showed a reluctance to die.

The poison caused death within five minutes. After consuming the poison, according to Rhodes, people were then escorted away down a wooden walkway leading outside the pavilion. It is not clear if some initially thought the exercise was another White Night rehearsal. Rhodes reported being in close contact with dying children. In response to reactions of seeing the poison take effect on others, Jones counseled, "Die with a degree of dignity. Lay down your life with dignity; don't lay down with tears and agony." He also said, "I tell you, I don't care how many screams you hear, I don't care how many anguished cries...death is a million times preferable to 10 more days of this life. If you knew what was ahead of you –you'd be glad to be stepping over tonight." Rhodes stated that while the poison was squirted in some childrens mouths, there was no panic or emotional outburst and the assembled Temple members looked like they were in a trance. This statement is contradicted by the cries and screams of children heard throughout the majority of the tape. Is this religious slavery or not?

***

The Cult Awareness Network, (CAN) a group aimed at deprogramming members of cults, was formed soon after the Jonestown deaths. After a slew of legal and fiscal issues, CAN disbanded in 1996 but since that date other organizations have taken up the role of exposing mind control groups that make mental slaves of their followers, outstanding is the current International Cultic Studies Association (ICSA). The group, which included American Congressman Ryan's daughter Patricia, was involved in various personal, social and legal battles with a range of religious organizations, from The Family International and Scientology to David Koreshs Branch Davidians, where they were found to be influential on law enforcements concerns for children in the eventual disastrous Waco siege. Although Jones used poisoned Flavor Aid, the drink mix was also commonly (mistakenly) referred to as Kool-Aid. This has led to the phrase drinking the Kool-Aid, referring to a person or group holding an unquestioned belief, argument, or philosophy without critical examination.

There are of course additional smaller organizations and groups that offer support and help to victims of cult-like religions who promote slave like adherence to their teachings and rules. For example, International Cultic Studies Association (ICSA) was founded in 1979 in Massachusetts as the American Family Foundation (AFF) one of several dozen disparate parents groups founded in the late 1970s by concerned parents. For a time it was affiliated with the Citizens Freedom Foundation (CFF) which later became the Cult Awareness Network (CAN). It also developed links with Evangelical Christian counter-cult movements such as the Christian Research Institute. ICSA is a non-profit organization, with a stated mission to study psychological manipulation, especially as it manifests in cultic and related groups. Michael Langone, ICSA's Executive Director, defines a cult as:

> A group or movement exhibiting a great or excessive devotion or dedication to some person, idea, or thing, and employing unethically manipulative techniques of persuasion and control designed to advance the goals of the group's leaders, to the actual or possible detriment of members, their families, or the community.

A recently formed very successful support group under the direction of Jon Atack, called Open Minds Foundation, whose mission states in part:

> Undue Influence happens when a predatory individual or totalistic group takes control over a person's beliefs, interests, thoughts, feelings, legal or medical rights, possessions, finances or behavior without that person's knowledge and consent,

usually under false pretenses. It is a legal term which has been used in courts for centuries, defining the state of control which exists when a person or group wields too much control over someone, thereby cancelling out that person's free will and autonomy. We want to show young people how they can resist being drawn into a coercive relationship, whether that be with an individual or with a group. Coercive control exists throughout society, whether it's in intimate relationships, in organizations that are sometimes called cults, in radicalization, in the white supremacist groups which are now on the rise. Even in business and multi-level marketing – you find the same dynamics and the same techniques being used.

As expressed by one survivor of the Jamestown incident. No one willingly joins a cult. No one joins something they think is going to hurt them. You join a religious organization, you join a political organization, and you join with people you really like and admire.

In the original Cult Awareness Network (CAN), which closed its doors in 1996, it listed over 200 mind control groups, amongst those listed were, The Family International (TFI), which is a cult that started in 1968 in Huntington Beach, California, USA. It was originally called Teens for Christ and later gained notoriety as The Children of God (COG). It was later renamed and reorganized as The Family of Love, which was eventually shortened to The Family. It is currently called The Family International. Also listed was Scientology, which is a body of religious beliefs and practices, launched in May, 1952 by American science fiction author L. Ron Hubbard. Hubbard initially developed a program of ideas called Dianetics, which was distributed through the Dianetics Foundation.

A third cult was also indentified; The Branch Davidians that are a religious group that originated in 1955 from a schism among the Shepherd's Rod/Davidians. The 'Branch' group was initially led by Benjamin Roden (an American religious leader and the prime organizer of the Branch Davidian Seventh-day Adventist Association who died in 1978). Branch Davidians are identified and associated with the Waco, Texas, siege of 1993, which involved David Koresh with most of his captives (slaves) after accidently burned after the government mishandling the whole affair of the siege.

This quote from *Rolling Stone* magazine provides more details.

> Although this extremist sect of the Seventh Day Adventists has been active since the 1950s, the Branch Davidians are best known for the 1993 standoff in Waco, Texas. David Koresh, the leader at the time, believed he was the Messiah and declared all women – including those underage or already married – "his spiritual wives". The group believed the apocalypse was imminent and, fearing its arrival, locked themselves into a sprawling compound. On February 28th, 1993, agents from the Department of Alcohol, Firearms and Tobacco raided the Waco compound on the suspicion that Koresh was stockpiling weapons. What started as a shootout soon turned into a standoff between the Branch Davidians and the FBI. It lasted 51 days, and eventually ended when tanks were brought in: the compound was filled with tear gas and caught on fire, leaving more than 80 people dead.

A truly sad end for the misguided followers who were chained to a religious cult that ultimately led to their death!

Chapter Two: Scientology

Scientology is a body of religious beliefs and practices launched in May 1952, by American author L. Ron Hubbard (1911–1986).[3] Hubbard initially developed a program of ideas called Dianetics, which was distributed through the Dianetics Foundation. The foundation soon entered bankruptcy, and Hubbard lost the rights to his seminal publication, Dianetics: The Modern Science of Mental Health in 1952. He then re-characterized the subject as a religion and renamed it Scientology, retaining the terminology, doctrines, the E-meter, and the practice of auditing. Within a year, he regained the rights to Dianetics and retained both subjects under the umbrella of the Church of Scientology.

Hubbard describes the etymology of the word Scientology as coming from the Latin word *scio*, meaning know or distinguish, and the Greek word *logos*, meaning the word or outward form by which the inward thought is expressed and made known. Hubbard writes, thus, Scientology means knowing about knowing, or science of knowledge.

Hubbard's groups have encountered considerable opposition and controversy. In January 1951, the New Jersey Board of Medical Examiners brought proceedings against Dianetics Foundation on the charge of teaching medicine without a license. Hubbard's followers engaged in a program of criminal infiltration of the U.S. government. Hubbard-inspired organizations and their classification are often a point of contention. Germany classifies Scientology groups as an anti-constitutional sect. In France, they have been classified as a dangerous cult by some parliamentary reports.

---

[3] Lafayette Ronald Hubbard (1911-1986), was an American author and the founder of the Church of Scientology. After establishing a career as a writer of science fiction and fantasy stories, in 1950 he published a *"branch of self-help psychology"* called Dianetics. Hubbard subsequently developed his ideas into a new religious movement that he called Scientology

In April 1938, Hubbard reportedly reacted to a drug used in a dental procedure. According to his account, this triggered a revelatory near-death experience. Allegedly inspired by this experience, Hubbard composed a manuscript, which was never published, with the working titles of The One Command or Excalibur. The contents of *Excalibur* formed the basis for some of his later publications. Arthur J. Burks, who read the work in 1938, later recalled it discussed the one command: to survive. This theme would be revisited in Dianetics, the set of ideas and practices regarding the metaphysical relationship between the mind and body which became the central philosophy of Scientology. Hubbard later cited Excalibur as an early version of Dianetics.

In August 1945, Hubbard moved into the Pasadena, California, mansion of John Whiteside Parsons, an avid occultist and Thelemite[4] follower of the English ceremonial magician Aleister Crowley and leader of a lodge of Crowley's magical order, Ordo Templi Orientis (OTO). Parsons and Hubbard collaborated on the Babalon Working, a sex magic ritual intended to summon an incarnation of Babalon, the supreme Thelemite Goddess. The Church of Scientology admits to Hubbard's involvement with Parsons while claiming that it was for the purpose of naval intelligence only. In the late 1940s, Hubbard practiced as a hypnotist and he worked in Hollywood posing as a swami (an ascetic or yogi who has been initiated into a religious monastic order). The Church says that Hubbard's experience with hypnosis led him to create Dianetics.

Hubbard's publication of *Dianetics: The Modern Science of Mental Health* was considered the seminal event of the century by Scientologists. Dianetics uses a counseling technique known as auditing in which an auditor assists a subject in conscious recall of traumatic events in the individual's past. It was originally intended to be a new psychotherapy and was not expected to become the foundation for a new religion. Hubbard variously defined Dianetics as a spiritual healing technology and an organized science of thought. The stated intent is to free individuals of the influence of past traumas by systematic exposure and removal of the engrams (painful memories) these events have

---

[4] Thelemic mysticism is a complex mystical path designed to do two interrelated things: to learn one's unique 'True Will' and to achieve union with the 'All'.

left behind, a process called *clearing*. Shortly after the introduction of Dianetics, Hubbard introduced the concept of the thetan (or soul) which he claimed to have discovered. Dianetics was organized and centralized to consolidate power under Hubbard, and groups that were previously recruited were no longer permitted to organize autonomously.

Dianetics amazingly appealed to a broad range of people who used instructions from the book and applied the method to each other, becoming practitioners themselves. Dianetics soon met with criticism. In 1955, Hubbard established the Founding Church of Scientology in Washington, D.C. The group declared that the Founding Church, as written in the certificate of incorporation for the Founding Church of Scientology in the District of Columbia, was to act as a parent church for the religious faith known as Scientology and to act as a church for the religious worship of the faith. In the course of developing Scientology, Hubbard presented rapidly changing teachings that some have seen as often self-contradictory.

According to Charles Lindholm, who wrote extensively about Scientology, said for the inner cadre of Scientologists in that period, involvement depended not so much on belief in a particular doctrine but on unquestioning faith and total dedication to Hubbard. Many Scientologists avoid using the words belief or faith to describe how Hubbards teachings impact their lives. They perceive that Scientology is based on verifiable technologies, speaking to Hubbard's original scientific objectives for Dianetics, based on the quantifiability of auditing on the E-meter. Scientologists call Dianetics and Scientology as technologies because of their claim of their scientific precision and workability.

***

Scientology is vehemently opposed to psychiatry and psychology. Hubbard criticized psychiatry as a *barbaric and corrupt profession*. Hubbard taught that psychiatrists were responsible for a great many wrongs in the world, saying that psychiatry has at various times offered itself as a tool of political suppression and that psychiatry spawned the ideology which fired Hitler's mania, turned the Nazis into mass murderers, and created the Holocaust. The internal structure of the

Scientology organization is strongly bureaucratic with a focus on statistics-based management. Organizational operating budgets are performance-related and subject to frequent reviews. A 2001 survey estimated that 55,000 people in the United States claimed to be Scientologists. Worldwide estimates of Scientology's core practicing membership ranges between 100,000 and 200,000, mostly in the U.S., Europe, the white population of South Africa and Australia. In 2011, high-level defector Jeff Hawkins estimated there were 40,000 Scientologists worldwide. Although the Church of Scientology claims to be the fastest growing religious movement on Earth, the church estimates of its membership numbers are reportedly significantly exaggerated and are actually decreasing.

The Church of Scientology is one of the most controversial religious organizations in the world. A first point of controversy was its challenge of the psychotherapeutic establishment. Another was a 1991 when the *Time* magazine article that attacked the church, which responded with a major lawsuit that was rejected by the courts as baseless early in 1992. And a third is its religious status in the United States, formalized when the IRS granted the organization tax-exempt status in 1993. It has been in conflict with the governments and police forces of many countries (including the United States, the United Kingdom, Canada, France and Germany). It has been one of the most litigious religious movements in history, filing countless lawsuits against governments, organizations and individuals. Reports and allegations have been made, by journalists, courts, and governmental bodies of several countries, that the Church of Scientology is an unscrupulous commercial enterprise that harasses its critics and brutally exploits its members. A considerable amount of investigation has been aimed at the church, by groups ranging from the media to governmental agencies.

Journalists, politicians, former Scientologists and various anti-cult groups have made accusations of wrongdoing against Scientology since the 1960s, and Scientology has targeted these critics – almost without exception – for retaliation, in the form of lawsuits and public counter-accusations of personal wrongdoing. Many of Scientology's critics have also reported they were subject to threats and harassment in their private lives. During his lifetime, Hubbard was accused of using religion as a façade for Scientology to maintain tax-exempt status and avoid prosecution for false medical claims. The IRS cited a statement frequently attributed to Hubbard, that the way to get rich was to found a religion, though some claim the statement is unsubstantiated.

This quote in *Time*, from a book written by Richard Behar titled *The Thriving Cult of Greed and Power*, perhaps summarizes everything about Scientology.

> The Church of Scientology, started by science-fiction writer L. Ron Hubbard to clear people of unhappiness, portrays itself as a religion. In reality the church is a hugely profitable global racket that survives by intimidating members and critics in a Mafia-like manner. At times during the past decade, prosecutions against Scientology seemed to be curbing its menace. Eleven top Scientologists, including Hubbard's wife, were sent to prison in the early 1980s for infiltrating, burglarizing and wiretapping more than 100 private and government agencies in attempts to block their investigations. In recent years hundreds of longtime Scientology adherents -- many charging that they were mentally or physically abused -- have quit the church and criticized it at their own risk. Some have sued the church and won; others have settled for amounts in excess of $500,000. In various cases judges have labeled the church schizophrenic and paranoid and corrupt, sinister and dangerous.

> The church's most fearsome advocates are its lawyers. Hubbard warned his followers in writing to beware of attorneys who tell you not to sue ... the purpose of the suit is to harass and discourage rather than to win. Result: Scientology has brought hundreds of suits against its perceived enemies and today pays an estimated $20 million annually to more than 100 lawyers. One legal goal of Scientology is to bankrupt the opposition or bury it under paper. The church today has 71 active lawsuits against the IRS alone. One of them, Miscavige vs. IRS, has required the U.S. to produce an index of 52,000 pages of documents. Boston attorney Michael Flynn, who helped Scientology victims from 1979 to 1987, personally endured 14 frivolous lawsuits, all of them dismissed. Another lawyer, Joseph Yanny, believes the church has so subverted justice and the judicial system that it should be barred from seeking equity

in any court. He should know: Yanny represented the cult until 1987, when, he says, he was asked to help church officials steal medical records to blackmail an opposing attorney (who was allegedly beaten up instead). Since Yanny quit representing the church, he has been the target of death threats, burglaries, lawsuits and other harassment.

Scientology's critics contend that the U.S. needs to crack down on the church in a major, organized way. I want to know, where is our government? demands Toby Plevin, a Los Angeles attorney who handles victims. It shouldn't be left to private litigators, because God knows most of us are afraid to get involved. But law-enforcement agents are also wary. Every investigator is very cautious, walking on eggshells when it comes to the church, says a Florida police detective who has tracked the cult since 1988. It will take a federal effort with lots of money and manpower. So far the agency giving Scientology the most grief is the IRS, whose officials have implied that Hubbard's successors may be looting the church's coffers. Since 1988, when the U.S. Supreme Court upheld the revocation of the cult's tax-exempt status, a massive IRS probe of church centers across the country has been under way. An IRS agent, Marcus Owens, has estimated that thousands of IRS employees have been involved. Another agent, in an internal IRS memorandum, spoke hopefully of the ultimate disintegration of the church. A small but helpful beacon shone last June when a federal appeals court ruled that two cassette tapes featuring conversations between church officials and their lawyers are evidence of a plan to commit future frauds against the IRS.

The IRS and FBI have been debriefing Scientology defectors for the past three years, in part to gain evidence for a major racketeering case that appears to have stalled last summer. Federal agents complain that the Justice Department is unwilling to spend the money needed to endure a drawn-out war with Scientology or to fend off the cult's notorious jihads against individual agents. "In my opinion the church has one of the most effective intelligence operations in the U.S., rivaling even that of the FBI," says Ted Gunderson, a former head of the FBIs Los Angeles office.

What is the wealth of the Church of Scientology? According to this report from the Fortune magazine this cult is registered as a non-profit, tax exempt organization. When the IRS finally granted the church tax-exempt status in 1993, after an unconventional meeting between the then-commissioner Fred T. Goldberg and Scientology's current leader, multimillionaire, David Miscavige, the financial ramifications were felt far and wide. Not only did the IRS stop demanding income taxes from the church, but local governments and states followed suit and granted the organization tax-exempt status.

Regardless of how the church managed to win recognition as a tax-exempt religious organization, that prize is worth hard cash. According to Jeffrey Augustine, author of the blog The Scientology Money Project, the church has a book value of $1.75 billion, about $1.5 billion of which is tied up in real estate, mostly at its headquarters in Clearwater, Florida and in Hollywood, California. The Church also owns property in Seattle, London, and New York, among other places. As for revenue, Augustine estimates that the church collects annual receipts of about $200 million, which he bases on conversations with former Scientology officials who have since left the organization. (Augustine is married to Karen de la Carriere, a former member of the church.) He says about $125 million comes from the sale of auditing services to its followers, while the remainder comes from donations. How much of that revenue would actually be subject to income tax is difficult to say; however, Augustine estimates that much of the money that comes in is spent on legal defense of the church.

Much more significant than income taxes, however, are property taxes. Most states and localities exempt religious organizations from paying property taxes on buildings that are primarily used for purveying religious services. [Most cults like Scientology, the Watchtower Society and the Mormons all benefit from this tax exemption and exploit it to the full extent of the law.] The church has managed to remain tax exempt because governments don't have much to gain from fighting the idea. The average person (Joe Public) are the people who really lose out, if you are to believe the testimonies of former members and numerous journalistic investigations are those who fall sway to its philosophy. But these are folks who tend to be in search of some higher power, not those who have much power themselves. Newly leaked 2015, 990-T forms for the Church of Scientology International and the Church of Spiritual Technology show that the organizations combined book value, or the value of their total assets, is $1.7 billion. Once again; we point out to our readers, this cult is displaying the typical characteristics of the masters and slaves of modern religion.

The Sea Organization (Sea Org) is a Scientology organization, which the Church of Scientology describes as a fraternal religious order, comprising the church's most dedicated members. All Scientology management organizations are controlled exclusively by members of the Sea Org. David Miscavige, the current de facto leader of Scientology, is the highest-ranking Sea Org officer, holding the rank of captain. The Sea Org has been described as a paramilitary organization and as a private naval force, having operated several vessels in its past and displaying a maritime tradition. Some ex-members and scholars have described the Sea Org as a totalitarian organization marked by intensive surveillance and a lack of freedom. The Sea Org has also been compared to a monastic organization.

In a 1992 memorandum by the Church of Scientology International, the following information was provided to the Internal Revenue Service (IRS) in the United States with regards to the nature of the Sea Org:

> The Sea Org does not have an ecclesiastical organizing board or command channels chart or secular existence such as an incorporated or unincorporated association. ... Although there is no such organization as the Sea Organization, the term Sea Org has a colloquial usage which implies that there is. There are general recruitment posters and literature for The Sea Org which implies that people will be employed by the Sea Org when in reality they will join, making the billion year commitment, at some church that is staffed by Sea Org members and become employees of that church corporation. ... The Sea Org exists as a spiritual commitment that is factually beyond the full understanding of the Service or any other but a trained and audited Scientologist.

The Sea Org was established on August 12, 1967 by L. Ron Hubbard, the founder of Dianetics and Scientology, initially on board three ships, the Diana, the Athena, and the Apollo, with the latter serving as flagship. In 1971, the Sea Org assumed responsibility for the ecclesiastical development of the church, and in particular the delivery of the upper levels of its auditing and training, known as the Operating Thetan or OT levels. In 1981, under the aegis of the Commodores Messenger Organization led by David Miscavige, the Sea Org dissolved the Guardians Office (GO) and assumed full responsibility for the international management of the Church, later reassigning the duties of the GO to the Office of Special Affairs in 1983 during the corporate restructuring of the Church.

It moved to land-based organizations in 1975, though maritime customs persist, with many members wearing naval-style uniforms and addressing both male and female officers as sir. In 1987, they purchased a ship, La Bohème, which they renamed Freewinds. OT VIII, the highest auditing level of Scientology currently available, is exclusive to the Freewinds and can only be undertaken there. The ship also hosts various courses, seminars, conventions and events throughout the year. The ship, Freewinds, which docks in Curaçao in the southern Caribbean is used as a religious retreat and training center, staffed entirely by Sea Org members. Sea Org members make a lifetime commitment to Scientology by signing a billion-year contract that is officially described as a symbolic pledge. In exchange, members are given free room and board, and a small weekly allowance. Sea Org members agree to strict codes of discipline, such as disavowing premarital sex, working long hours (on average at least 100 hours per week) and living in communal housing, referred to as berthings. They are allowed to marry, but must relinquish their membership if they have or want to raise children.

This recent report by the news channel, CNN, revealed the following:

> Once upon a time, Scientology had a fleet of ships, the church says, which were manned by its Sea Organization. The ships and crew helped Scientology founder L. Ron Hubbard with research and supervised church functions around the world, according to the church. Scientologists compare the Sea Org to members of a religious order, like monks and nuns, who devote their lives to the faith, often working long hours for no pay and living communally. The Freewinds is entirely staffed by the Sea Org, the church says, who dress in spiffy naval uniforms. But

there was another reason for Scientologists' seafaring ways, say scholars who have studied the church. In the late 1960s several countries, including the United States, started scrutinizing Hubbard's new movement. He had been kicked out of England in 1968, according to Hugh Urban, author of The Church of Scientology: A History of a New Religion. Thus Hubbard's shift to a sea-based organization during these years was clearly in part a response to his inability to operate freely in many nations such as the USA and UK.

CNN has reached out to the Church of Scientology but has not heard back from its communications department. On the high seas, Scientologists were pretty much free do what they wanted, and the floating religious retreat centers eventually became an essential part of their practice. In 1985, the church reportedly purchased the Finnish-built Freewinds, which once entertained tourists on the Commodore Cruise Line. The ship has since become its flagship, spiritually speaking, and its mission is pretty ambitious: The Freewinds is like no other place on Earth. It truly marks the beginning of a voyage to all eternity, the church says in its news release.

One former member, Gerry Armstrong, said that during his time in the Sea Org in the 1970s he spent over two years banished to the RPF as a punishment. The Rehabilitation Project Force (RPF) was created in January 1974 as a system of work camps set up by the Sea Org, intended to isolate and rehabilitate members who have not lived up to the church's expectations; have failed security checks, or have violated certain policies. Dr. Gordon Melton in his brilliant book, *The Church of Scientology,* writes that the RPF areas are located within Sea Org facilities, and that there are no locks on the doors.

It was essentially a prison to which crew who were considered non-producers, security risks, or just wanted to leave the Sea Org, were assigned. Hubbard's RPF policies established the conditions. RPF members were segregated and not allowed to communicate to anyone else. They had their own spaces and were not allowed in normal crew areas of the ship. They ate after normal crew had eaten, and only whatever was left over from the crew meal. Their berthing was the worst on board, in a roach-infested, filthy and unventilated cargo hold. They wore black boiler-suits, even in the hottest weather. They were required to run everywhere. Discipline was harsh and bizarre, with running laps of the ship assigned for the slightest infraction like failing to address a senior with Sir. Work was hard and the schedule rigid with seven hours sleep time from lights out to lights on, short meal breaks, no liberties and no free time.

When you read Chapter Three of this book related to the Watchtower Society, plus the special report in the Appendix, by Australian Philip Rees, a lifetime member of the Watchtower Society, you will recognize many similarities between these two groups and they are both identified as cults. According to scholar Susan Raine, Hubbard created the Sea Org as a kind of space navy, melding SF (science fiction) space ideas with Earthbound naval ones. Hubbard biographer Jon Atack recalled a confidential command within Sea Org that claimed that governments of the world were on the verge of collapse and the Sea Org (Scientology) would survive and pick up the pieces and then rule the world and the Universe.

Chapter Three: The Watchtower Society

The Cult Awareness Network (CAN) also listed additional mainstream religious groups or cults and originally listed amongst the over 200 cults indentified was, the Watchtower Society also known as Jehovah's Witnesses. This religion is a millenarian restorationist Christian denomination with a known record of many failed forecasts of the ending of the world and the pending Battle of Armageddon mentioned in the Bible; with some forecasts dating back to 1878 and especially their latest prediction of 1975 being the year and the resultant fiasco. This incorrect forecast resulted in a later apology to all members from the Watchtower Society's leadership. However Jehovah's Witnesses are mainly known for their attempted explanation and definition of the Bible text, which says "abstain from blood" (Acts 15:28, 29) and this interpretation being taken completely out of context, which is usually the sign of a cult and is the basis for members of this religion being instructed to refuse blood transfusions and in addition foods that may contain blood or if ignored then they face serious consequences imposed by the elders or leaders of this religion, as from 1961 it became a disfellowshipping or excommunicating offence.

> *Editor's Note*: This warning not to eat foods that contained blood or extracts of blood lead to a Pharisee type attitude developing within this cult (Matthew, Chapter 23) where the followers began religiously and carefully checking all the labels of food products they bought from their local stores. Most products provide a list of contents using descriptions and technical terms that a layman could not understand in any event. If a product or food was suspect then this news was then quickly spread abroad to the other members of this religion and soon a boycott was declared against certain nutritious and well-known beneficial foods, often without any foundation. These included certain brands of sausages, baby food and even pet food, and were advised by their leaders to write to the food manufacturers to verify that their products were blood-free and this soon became a cult-like practice by many members.

The use of this isolated phrase in the Bible, abstain from blood is a clear example of the use of a Bible text taken completely out of context, manipulated and misused to support a private interpretation of the Bible. Unbiased and knowledgeable students of the Bible understand this efficacious tactic used by the Watchtower Society, plus other cults and point out what the context and true explanation of this phrase really means, as recorded in the inspired Bible book of Acts of the Apostles 15:1-29. The four issues covered in this chapter of the Bible are, (a.) you abstain from what has been sacrificed to idols, and (b.) from drinking or eating blood, and (c.) from what is strangled, and (d.) from fornication. Blood transfusions and the knowledge of the various blood groups had not even been discovered or identified back in the first century and in fact the practice of bloodletting was used up until about the 19th century. Bloodletting is the withdrawal of blood from a patient to prevent or cure illness and disease. Bloodletting whether by a physician or by leeches and was based on an ancient system of medicine. It is claimed to have been the most common medical practice performed by surgeons from antiquity until the late 19th century.

This quote by Bible researcher and author Matthew Henry (1662-1714) in his excellent six volumes of *Bible Commentary of the Old and New Testaments* (1706-1710), clarifies this Bible text about blood.

> The dispute raised in the *Acts of the Apostles* Chapter 15 by Judaizing teachers was that some from Judea taught the Gentile (non-Jewish) converts to Christianity at Antioch that they could not be saved, unless they observed the whole ceremonial law as given by Moses; and thus they sought to destroy Christian liberty. There is a strange proneness in us is to think that all others do wrong who do not act just as we do. Their doctrine was very discouraging. Wise and good men desire to avoid contests and disputes as far as they can; yet when false teachers oppose the main truths of the gospel, or try to bring in hurtful doctrines, we must not decline to oppose them. We see from the words "purifying their hearts by faith", and the address of the Apostle Peter, that justification by faith, and sanctification by the Holy Spirit, cannot be separated; and that both are the gift of God.

May we have that faith which the great Searcher of hearts approves, and attests by the seal of the Holy Spirit? Then our hearts and consciences will be purified from the guilt of sin, and we shall be freed from the burdens some try to lay upon the Disciples of Christ. Paul and Barnabas showed by plain matters of fact, that God owned the preaching of the pure gospel to the Gentiles without the Law of Moses; therefore to press that law upon them, was to undo what God had done. The opinion of James was that the Gentile converts ought not to be troubled about Jewish rites, but that they should abstain from meats offered to idols, so that they might show their hatred of idolatry. Also, that they should be cautioned against fornication, which was not abhorred by the Gentiles as it should be, and even sometimes formed a part of some of their rituals. They were counseled to abstain from things strangled, and from eating blood; this was forbidden by the Law of Moses, and also here, from reverence to the blood of the sacrifices, which being then still offered, it would needlessly grieve the Jewish converts, and further prejudice the unconverted Jews. But as this reason has long ceased, we are left free in this, as in the like matters. Let converts be warned to avoid all appearances of the evils which they formerly practiced, or are likely to be tempted to; and caution them to use Christian liberty with moderation and prudence.

Why does the Watchtower Society continue to ban blood transfusions for members of their religion when there is so much clear evidence available to contradict their distortion and misuse of the words of Acts 15:29, abstain from blood as the commentary by knowledgeable Bible student Matthew Henry (1662-1714) clearly explains? In addition numerous other diligent Bible students confirm the identical opinion of Henry, especially during the 19th and 20th centuries. This Bible commentary clearly establishes that the quote from Acts 15:28, 29, is referring back to the many hundreds of other restrictions laid down by the Mosaic Law related to food, drink, health and sexual conduct covered in the Pentateuch (sometimes called the Torah by Jews) being the first five books of the Bible. The Christian Greek Scriptures (New Testament) makes it quite clear that Christians today are not under the Mosaic Law, including the rules and regulations regarding the use of blood. According to the inspired writings of the Apostle Paul this truth is stated in no uncertain terms and in various ways (see Romans 6:14; 7:1-14; Galatians 3:10-13, 24-25; 4:21; 5:1, 13; and 2 Corinthians 3:7-18), but in spite of this fact, the Watchtower Society still tries to prove that the mosaic law, abstain from blood, still applies to Christians today. They are the only religion and group that believes this folly and they stand alone in their stupidity and ignorance over the true meaning of the Word of God.

We are puzzled and no doubt you as an intelligent reader of this book are likewise puzzled, so we encourage all of our readers to use their God given intelligence and think for themselves and not to be duped by cults or religious leaders who have ulterior motives.

A member of our research team and who once belonged to this religion, commented that many sincere members gave up their precious lives by obeying this rule and instruction from their Governing Body, by literally sacrificing their lives or the lives of their minor children based on this rule and their loyalty to the cause by refusing vital, necessary, lifesaving blood transfusions. It is quite understandable that many are confused by the position taken by the Watchtower Society today with respect to the various blood components or blood products like albumin, erythropoietins, vaccines, immunoglobulins, and hemophiliac treatments. It does not seem possible to explain why it is a violation of God's law to accept plasma, platelets, red and white cells when all the fractions of these are permitted by this religion. However, because of increasing confusion there are now strong indications that the Watchtower Society may significantly modify their blood policy or abandon it altogether at some point in the near future, as they have in the past with other controversial issues and gross misleading and misinterpretations of the Bible, for example the Egyptian Pyramid fiasco and the Beth Sarim mansion scam, which are covered later in this chapter. However, if and when this change of Bible interpretation takes place, which it will, we still have to live with the memory of the thousands of lives lost and wasted because followers of this religion blindly and unnecessarily obeyed the mosaic law of abstaining from blood. In addition, the now confused and misguided Governing Body of this religion has to carry the blood guilt of causing this sad loss of human life.

Based on the recent development of the global pandemic COVID-19 during 2020, Jehovah's Witnesses have been directed that they are forbidden from accepting Convalescent Plasma Therapy, a new treatment that appears to offer hope for patients stricken with the corona virus. A leaked memo from a Jehovah's Witness Circuit Overseer instructs elders in his circuit that accepting plasma treatments to ward off COVID-19 is unacceptable. While these instructions are in harmony with current Witness teachings on blood and are for dissemination among a limited number of congregations, the material emphasizes the organization's willingness to place their theology above the need to preserve life. The recent development and use of vaccines is also being criticized in view of the fact that the preparation and manufacturing of a powerful vaccine to fight against the COVID-19 virus is also being investigated by the Watchtower Society as these vaccines, although claimed by the manufacturers do not contain blood, but may have been prepared using the plasma from the blood of animals, thus creating even more confusion to Jehovah's Witnesses. Also cited is the November 2006 Witness newsletter Our Kingdom Ministry in which Witnesses were advised that they might choose to accept certain fractionalized derivatives of blood, but under no circumstances would they accept the four primary components of blood, including plasma.

The informative website, JW Survey, interviewed former Witness clergyman Lee Elder, the founder of Advocates for Jehovah's Witness Reform on Blood. Elder said that the irony is that Watchtower policy permits the use of 100% of all blood fractions – just not simultaneously. Fractions of blood have been a hot topic among Jehovah's Witnesses since the technology became available to separate human blood into individual components. The spinning of vials of blood, called blood fractionation, results in multiple component layers inside test tubes, including red cells, white cells, and plasma.

Elder's comments reinforce the paradox where Jehovah's Witnesses are presently permitted to accept certain minor derivatives of blood, but are forbidden from donating their own blood to save the lives of fellow citizens. The Watchtower Organization has coercively prevented more than 8 million people from contributing to global blood banks, thus disabling the charitable aspirations of members who would otherwise be willing to help save lives. And then there is the obvious threat to the personal well-being of each member of the Jehovah's Witness Organization, which has made it clear that Convalescent Plasma Therapy is not an option. As Paul Grundy, ex-Jehovah's Witness, an associate researcher, points out on his website, although it is known that blood transfusions have sometimes caused the spread of disease and illnesses such as Hepatitis B (HBV), Hepatitis C (HCV), Human Immunodeficiency Virus (HIV) and AIDS, but with modern screening this problem has been largely eliminated. Do not put your life at risk due to unwarranted faith in the Governing Body. Conduct your own research on the best ways to prevent infection and treatments available in your community, unencumbered by sectarian dogma.

Of course, there are additional reasons why some individuals prefer not to have a blood transfusion other than it being prohibited by their religious leaders and that is the small risk of a 'transfusion transmissible infection' (TTI). This is any infection that is transmissible from person- to-person through parenteral administration of blood or blood products. Examples of known TTIs include: Hepatitis A, B, C, D and G, HIV, HTLV I and II, West Nile Virus, syphilis, cytomegalovirus, and malaria. This small risk has led to what is now known as bloodless surgery. In the *British Journal of Anesthesia (BJA)* (2015), the following remark was made about blood transfusions:

> Treatment of Jehovah's Witnesses during the past 50 years has led to a greater awareness of blood conservation and advances in bloodless surgery. Their beliefs regarding blood and transfusion raise various ethical and legal points, knowledge of which is essential. Evidence suggests that while there is no universally applicable treatment strategy, successful care requires a holistic approach focusing on pre-optimization, referral to an appropriate environment for surgery, and perioperative blood-conservation techniques.

In addition, as medical science advances many medical centers now use Transfusion-Free Medicine sometimes called bloodless medicine and uses medications and medical techniques to avoid the need for a blood transfusion.

The Watchtower Society has in the past also banned members from accepting organ transplants. Regarding the ban of transplants, called cannibalism by the leaders of the Watchtower Society, which was then later changed, once again showing the inconsistency of this sect. We cannot do better than quote once again from the website of the Australian ex-Witness, Paul Grundy, JW Facts.org.

> Transplants are a relatively new procedure and the rise in popularity during the 20th century led to the Society needing to provide a ruling on whether this conflicted with God's Holy requirements. When the Governing Body prayed for Jehovah to guide them on his standard, what was their conclusion? Is there anything in the Bible against giving one's eyes (after death) to be transplanted to some living person? Question by Watchtower reader, L. C., United States. The following was the official answer, 'the question of placing one's body or parts of one's body at the disposal of men of science or doctors at one's death for purposes of scientific experimentation or replacement in others is frowned upon by certain religious bodies. However, it does not seem that any Scriptural principle or law is involved. It therefore is something that each individual must decide for himself.' *Watchtower* 1961, Aug 1, p. 480, Questions from Readers.

> It did not take long for the Watchtower to change their mind on this life saving procedure. "Sustaining one's life by means of the body or part of the body of another human ... would be cannibalism, a practice abhorrent to all civilized people. ... It is not our place to decide whether such operations are advisable from a scientific or medical standpoint... Christians who have been enlightened by God's Word do not need to make these decisions based simply on the basis of personal whim or emotion. They can consider the divine principles and use these in making personal decisions as they look to God for direction, trusting him and putting their confidence in the future that he has in store for those who love him." *Watchtower* 1967, Nov 15 pp. 702-704.

> This article used the full force of God's name mixed with a touch of guilt to persuade the followers, look to God, love him, be enlightened by God's Word and don't have a transplant. Any Witness that had a transplant had engaged in cannibalism

and was a person without trust in Jehovah, somebody the congregations found necessary to disfellowship from amongst their midst. Watchtower reached for its usual method of using fear to convince members. Transplants were said to involve demonic influence, referring to quotes that a spirit guided the first heart transplant. In this regard the weekly, *Scope*, magazine went on to say; did a spirit guide Dr. Chris Barnard's hand during the historic heart transplant operation several weeks ago?... A former member of Dr. Barnard's heart surgery team ... had often seen a spirit figure standing behind Dr. Barnard during operations in the hospital theatre. ... But that is Klein Oupatjkie, Chris Barnhard's late father was the immediate reaction. *Awake!* (1968 June 22, p. 15.)

A further fear tactic was to warn that a transplant could change the personality of the recipient. A peculiar factor sometimes noted is a so-called personality transplant. That is, the recipient in some cases has seemed to adopt certain personality factors of the person from whom the organ came. (*Watchtower*, 1975, Sept 1, p.519). This pronouncement meant that a Jehovah's Witness could not accept a kidney transplant, a cornea transplant, bone marrow, skin, or anything else taken from another person. This has led to loss of lives that simple operations could have saved. It was reiterated in 1968 *Awake!* June 8, in which almost the entire magazine was devoted to the *Watchtower* view of medical procedures.

This edict on transplants, a disfellowshipping directive enlightened by God's Word lasted only thirteen years. There is no Biblical command pointedly forbidding the taking in of other human tissue ... It is a matter for personal decision. (*Watchtower*, 1980 Mar 15 p 31) The Watchtower has gone even further now, commending transplants for the way they have helped people. (*Awake!* 1989 Aug 22 p. 6) What is shameful in all this is that it was never stated that the view had changed. The *Watchtower* Index does not reference the 1967 article in regards to transplants. No apology has been published for the sake of those that were wrongfully disfellowshipped and those that unnecessarily lost their lives. How must this make a Witness feel that lost a loved one over this issue during the 1970s? The sad reality is that Witnesses as a whole do not even know that their teachings have changed. Many are willing to lay their lives on the line without an understanding of the issues at hand and how they differ from a not too distant past. The Society has blood on its hands when its incorrect use of the Name of God results in the death of misled members.

***

The Watchtower Society also practices the strict rule of disfellowshipping or excommunicating individual members if they refuse to toe the line or if they level genuine criticism, many of these being sincere positive suggestions, against its leaders or teachings, but still being described as apostasy by the masters of this religion. They are also well known for their strict rules regarding their followers not being permitted to celebrate birthdays or Christmas, which they claim that these prohibitions are based on clear, irrefutable Biblical instructions and state without any substantial basis that they are of pagan origins. The disfellowship dictum is such an extreme and cruel rule, and Witnesses are expected to uphold it even when it comes to very close friends and family members. Many Witnesses who are disfellowshipped never hear from their families ever again.

So strict is this organizational rule, which is confirmed in their official journal, *The Watchtower*. If a publisher refuses to do this and ignores the prohibition on associating with the disfellowshipped one, that publisher is rebelling against the congregation of Jehovah, and rebellion is as the sin of witchcraft and stubbornness is as idolatry and teraphim. If after sufficient warning the publisher persists in associating with the disfellowshipped person instead of aligning himself with Jehovah's organization he also should be disfellowshipped. (*Watchtower*, Oct.1, 1955)

This opinion piece received by one of our researchers explains why members of Jehovah's Witnesses truly fear and dread the very thought of ever being disfellowshipped, which is one of the most powerful tools that the Watchtower Society holds over its followers to keep them strictly in line regarding their teachings and rules.

> Witnesses are pretty socially isolated outside of fellow Witnesses. They don't really interact socially with outsiders

much. So the prospect of being disfellowshipped is a threat of losing all of their friends, their entire social support system, even members of their own families. In addition, assuming they believe in the religion of which they are members, being disfellowshipped represents their failure to live a life as they think God has commanded them to do, so that's also very hard to handle. Mostly, though, it's that being a Witness is their whole life, everything they do relates to it somehow, everyone they know on a personal level and spend time with is a Witness, and being disfellowshipped means being humiliated in a way, in front of everyone they know. If they want to be reinstated it will mean a difficult period of probation going to meetings etc., even though no one there will talk to you or acknowledge your presence, and there's a certain amount of shame that usually attaches to it even once they are eventually let back in. It's hard for most people to understand the extent to which being a Witness is woven into every aspect of their lives. It's not something they just do on Sunday and then go on to live the rest of their normal life for the remainder of the week.

This policy of disfellowshipping or excommunicating is now becoming a very serious legal issue for the Watchtower Society. In recent years certain countries are now ruling that this action is a violation of the law by inciting discrimination and hatred or violence against former members. This report from *Brussels Times* reveals the decision of a recent court in Belgium:

> The Jehovah's Witnesses in Belgium must pay a €12,000 fine for the systematic and disturbing exclusion of ex-members who have left the organisation, the Ghent correctional court ruled on Tuesday. The court ruled that the non-profit association behind Jehovah's Witnesses is guilty of inciting discrimination and hatred or violence against former members, reports the Belga news agency. The Jehovah's Witnesses' shunning policy cuts to the very core of relationships, and the victims suffer both physical and psychological consequences, one of the lawyers of the civil parties said during the trial last month.
>
> In 2015, an ex-member took the organisation to the Ghent public prosecutor's office for slander and defamation, insults and violation of the discrimination law. He claimed that once

the members had left the group, they were disowned and completely isolated socially, by order of the organisation. The Ghent public prosecutor's office summoned the Jehovah's Witnesses for four charges: incitement to discrimination on the basis of religious belief against a person, and against a group, as well as incitement to hatred or violence against a person, and against a group.

Belgium's Interfederal Equal Opportunities Centre (UNIA) and some fifteen individuals had taken up civil action, with the victims' lawyers emphasising the far-reaching consequences of the shunning policy, reports De Morgen. Jehovah's Witnesses state that ex-members should be shunned like the plague, said lawyer Pieter-Bram Lagae, who assists the ex-witness who started the case. He used to sit on the Jehovah's Judicial Committee and help decide on exclusions, until he realised it was going too far, Lagae said. We act, for example, for a man whose wife is still a member, and he is ignored in his own home. Or a woman who has never seen her father since the exclusion. This is just the start, former Jehovah's Witnesses member Patrick Haeck told Het Nieuwsblad. We are going to the European Court. This has to stop everywhere.

A report by Andrew Holden of Lancaster University, England, in his paper, "Peering Through the Watchtower," revealed the following. The Watchtower Society dismisses all other religious creeds as heresy, plus their loyalty is first and foremost to the organization right or wrong. Also contained in his report was the following observation, when people convert to the Watchtower movement they defer unquestionably to the authority of the Governing Body, a small number of presidential officials in America. They see themselves, not just as members of a religious movement, but one that monopolizes truth.

The Watchtower Society employs various levels of congregational discipline as strict formal controls administered by the congregation elders. Members who engage in conduct that is considered inappropriate may be counseled privately by elders and congregational responsibilities and privileges may be withheld or restricted. If initial counsel is not accepted, elders may present a talk to the congregation about the type of behavior, alerting other members already aware of the individuals conduct to limit social interaction with that person. Hearings involving serious sin are performed by formal *judicial committees*, in which guilt and repentance are determined by a tribunal of elders. A variety of controls can be enforced, from reproof and restriction of congregational duties to excommunication, known as disfellowshipping, which includes shunning by the entire congregation and even members of their own family. Members who persist in a course considered scripturally wrong after repeated counsel by elders, but who are not considered guilty of something for which they could be disfellowshipped, can be marked, based on Jehovah's Witnesses' interpretation of 2 Thessalonians 3:14. Actions for which an individual may be marked include dating a non-member, being considered lazy, critical, dirty, meddling, or taking material advantage of others or indulging in improper entertainment in the personal opinion of the judicial elders.

This enlightening report from the International Cultic Studies Association (ICSA) made the following observation:

> Members who choose to leave because of disagreement over doctrine, or who are forced out of the organization because of nonconformist behavior, are subject to the procedure of disfellowshipping, a form of shunning that does not allow any current member to associate with the disfellowshipped person. The Watchtower states: Baptized servants of Jehovah who deliberately follow a wicked course and refuse to change must be viewed as unrepentant and thus unfit for Christian fellowship... They must be expelled... it removes from their midst one who could exercise a bad influence on them. It also protects the purity of the congregation. If the disfellowshipped person disagrees publicly in any way with WTS teachings, he or she automatically becomes an apostate. Since members are not allowed to associate with disfellowshipped members, information potentially critical of WTS is handily kept out of members reach by not allowing them to discourse with former members about their reasons for leaving the organization.

Since its formation in the 1870s, the Watchtower Bible and Tract Society, also known as the International Bible Students Association (IBSA) has claimed that God has chosen this organization from among all the churches in the world to fill a special role in the consummation of prophetic history. Charles Taze Russell, a prolific writer and founder of the Bible Student movement, viewed himself as a mouthpiece of God and later as the actual embodiment of the faithful and wise (discreet) servant or slave of the parable of Matthew 24:45-47. The Watchtower Society is now the legal and administrative arm of Jehovah's Witnesses. Its representatives and leaders, a so-called Governing Body, still assert today that they have been given special insight into the true meaning of the Bible and the unique ability to discern the signs of Christ's second coming and also claim this small group of men; the number ranging from 7 to 18 over the years, [as of 2019 there are 8 men with no women allowed on this body] who are all based in New York and all claim they are directly appointed by God. This group of men, consisting the so-called Governing Body of this religion also claims they are now the current faithful and discreet slave and have been personally appointed by Jesus Christ, appointed over all the Lord's belongings as mentioned in the Bible. These same men are also professing to be the self-proclaimed omnipotent power authorized by God to operate the Watchtower Society that claims to be the only true religion on earth.

A number of schisms developed within the congregations of the Bible Students associated with the Watchtower Society between 1909 and 1932. The most significant split began in 1917 following the election of Joseph Franklin Rutherford as 2nd president of the Watchtower Society two months after Russell's death. The schism began with Rutherford's controversial replacement of four of the seven members of the Society's board of directors and the publication of a book called *The Finished Mystery*. This book was claimed to have been written by Charles Russell as the (prophetic and symbolic) 7th Volume of his *Studies in the Scriptures* series, but it clearly displayed that it was edited by Clayton J. Woodworth and George H. Fisher. It was advertised as the posthumous work of Pastor Charles Taze Russell but was actually written and not merely edited by C. J. Woodworth and George Fisher and later authorized for publication by Joseph Rutherford personally, now acting as the autocratic, 2nd President of the Watchtower Society.

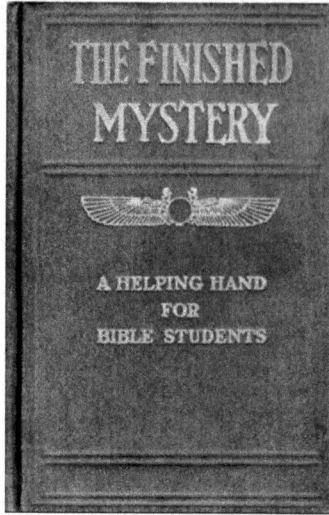

The controversial book, *The Finished Mystery* (1917),
courtesy of Creative Commons and Getty Images

This quote from the publication of 1993 by the Watchtower Society, *Jehovah's Witnesses – Proclaimers of God's Kingdom*, which is the current 749-page history book of the Watchtower Society, replacing the previous book, Jehovah's Witnesses in the Divine Purpose published in 1959 and provides a vivid, short review of the life of Clayton Woodworth.

> Clayton J. Woodworth (1870-1951). Friends of the truth throughout the earth will be interested to learn of the death of one who played a prominent part in the affairs of the Watch Tower Bible & Tract Society for many years, Clayton J. Woodworth. An editor and textbook writer before coming into the Society's service; he first became a member of the Brooklyn Bethel family in 1912, renewing this membership after a necessary interruption August 1, 1919. He was the writer of the commentary on The Revelation contained in the noted *The Finished Mystery,* which the Society published in 1917. For his part in this and other Society matters he was one of the seven brothers, including the Society's then president, J. F. Rutherford, who were sent to Atlanta Federal Penitentiary on false charges at the climax of World War I in 1918 but were released in 1919 and exonerated thereafter.
>
> Clayton J. Woodworth faithfully served as editor of *The Golden Age* and its successor *Consolation* (published from October 6,

1937, through July 31, 1946, inclusive). Because of advancing years, he was relieved of this work when the new journal *Awake* replaced *Consolation*, with the issue of August 22, 1946. However, Brother Woodworth remained faithful at other duties in God's service until his death, on December 18, 1951, at eighty-one years of age.

However, Woodworth will also be remembered for other aspects of the Watchtower teachings. A number of bizarre pieces of medical advice were issued during the days of the *Golden Age* magazine, later renamed *Consolation, 1919-1946*. This journal was under the editorship of Clayton J Woodworth who was instrumental in the introduction of the Watchtower laws against blood in consultation with Fred Franz and Joseph Rutherford as part of a campaign to set the Witnesses apart and in turn receive more criticism, translated into persecution by this religion. The stated purpose of Consolation has changed over time and was renamed the *Awake!* as of August 22, 1946. From 1982 to 1995, each issue of the magazine included a mission statement which read, "This magazine builds confidence in the Creator's promise of a peaceful and secure new order before the generation that <u>saw</u> 1914 passes away." [underline by the editor] This mission statement was later removed and does not now appear in this magazine as it had become a misnomer and very misleading mission statement now that we are in the year 2019 as the generation that <u>saw</u> 1914 are all now in the grave.

Charles Taze Russell had written six volumes of his books called Millennial Dawn, or later re-named Studies in the Scriptures, but often he spoke about writing a seventh volume. "Whenever I find the key," said he, "I will write the Seventh Volume; and if the Lord gives the key to someone else, he can write it." Russell's six book set of Studies in the Scriptures eventually sold over 20 million copies (truly a world bestseller), distributed worldwide through his loyal and devoted slave-like followers (book sales people). The Watchtower Society officers, now under the direct and complete control of autocrat Joseph Rutherford arranged to have these two Bible Students, Clayton J. Woodworth and George H. Fisher, compile this book, the Seventh Volume, consisting of commentaries on the Bible books of Revelation, The Song of Solomon and Ezekiel.

Copy of an advertisement of the *Studies in the Scriptures* by Charles Russell, courtesy of the MTC International Foundation, Creative Commons and Getty Images

These two co-editors therefore assembled material from Brother Russell's past writings, especially using the two now priceless famous books (copies of these two books were donated to our research team) *What Pastor Russell Taught-On the Covenants, Mediator, Ransom, Sin Offering and Atonement*, written and published by Leslie W. Jones, M.D. of Chicago in 1919, plus the companion book *What Pastor Russell Said – His Answers to Hundreds of Questions*, published and released by the Bible Students Book Store in 1917, and then submitted this information to Rutherford for his approval and then this was published under the provocative title, *The Finished Mystery* as the manipulative symbolic seventh volume of Studies in the Scriptures. Containing largely the thinking and past comments of C. T. Russell, and it was termed the posthumous work of Pastor Russell. This was a clear deceptive attempt to try and use the secret meanings of the symbolic use of the word seven, used extensively in the Bible, particularly in the book of Revelation. According to the Watchtower Society's interpretation of the number seven in the Bible, they state in their literature, that the number seven signified spiritual completeness or a complete cycle of things as established or allowed by God.

This expression and sentiment was contributed by one of our researchers, a now disfellowshipped member of the Watchtower Society.

> The words of Jesus Christ in the book of Matthew 18:22 also emphasized that these words related to the number seven included much more than Charles Russell's books. The Bible says, "I tell you, forgive not only seven times, but up to seventy-seven times." If only the Governing Body of the Watchtower Society followed these words of Jesus and how they treated me, labeling me as an apostate in their autocratic, dictatorial ruling of this religious cult as masters of modern religion. If only they could remember and also practice the Bible text, "He who is without sin, let him throw the first stone." (John 8:7)

The Watchtower Society ceased publication and distribution of Russell's books and writings in 1927, as personally authorized and decided by autocratic President Rutherford as he now had private ambitious plans already in place for many more books, this time written under his name as the author so as to take full credit, but these books were actually written by subjective ghost writers. Rutherford had schemed and planned for some years to produce his own books blazoned with his name to replace the successful books by Charles Russell, to be printed and to be sold by the already successful, well established, infrastructure of the existing group of colporteurs (book sellers), who served as slaves being loyal members of the Watchtower Society.

Charles Russell's books, especially the six-volume set of *Studies in the Scriptures* are still amazingly published and distributed even today in 2019 by several small independent Bible groups, and mainly offered free of charge as their contribution to the truth of the Bible. However, Rutherford, being a shrewd lawyer and businessman, obviously by this time in 1916 had delved into and observed the successful accomplishments of the Watchtower Society especially the massive sales established by Charles Russell's books. Rutherford immediately saw the ongoing potential of this brilliant money-making scheme of being a commercial enterprise for making profits by printing, publishing and selling literature that attracted people who were interested in the Bible, which had the potential market of most of the world's population.

Rutherford had already realized in his legal scheming mind of the potential profits to be made and realized under this already established existing system, plus recently being appointed as the new President of the Watchtower Society, he now had total, absolute and complete control of the buildings, factory, printing presses, plus a staff of volunteers who worked for a monthly pittance plus free bed and board in dormitories, and had an already established sales infrastructure consisting of colporteurs (book peddlers), so what could he lose, it was clearly a win-win situation. Rutherford claimed in all of his 21 books; from his first book that displayed his name and title, Judge Rutherford[5] *The Harp of God* published in 1921 a few years after he took complete control of the Watchtower Society, claiming that he was the author, but it was known by some in the Bethel headquarters that all of these 21 books were actually written by a ghost writer, probably at one time a very subjective, humble, simplistic Frederick Franz, a Bible researcher and writer. After Rutherford's death in 1942 the Watchtower Society claimed that they had sold over 400 million copies of Rutherford's books between the years 1926 to 1942.

Charles Russell had taught his followers that October of 1914 was indentified in the Bible as the end of a harvest period that would culminate in the beginning of Armageddon (the end of the world in Bible prophesy), manifested by the emergence of worldwide anarchy and the decline and destruction of civilized society. Various concepts promoted by Russell and his associates are still taught today by the Bible Student movements and also Jehovah's Witnesses, including a completely inaccurate and manipulated 2,520-year period, supposedly

---

[5] Rutherford who was a court recorder was appointed as a Special Judge in the Eighth Judicial Circuit Court of Missouri, sitting as a substitute judge at least once when a regular judge was unable to hold court because of illness. As a result of this appointment, he became known by the sobriquet or nickname "Judge" Rutherford, which of course delighted his ego.

that had been prophetically calculated from the Bible book of Daniel, Chapter 4 and termed the Gentile Times that was predicted to have started in the year 607 BC and ended in the year 1914 AD. The actual words 'gentile times' do not appear in the Bible, but the Watchtower Society claims by one single verse that the words of the Bible book, Luke 21:24, proves they existed, "And they will fall by the edge of the sword and be led captive into all the nations; and Jerusalem will be trampled on by the nations until the appointed times of the nations are fulfilled."

In 1881, Zion's Watch Tower Tract Society was formed as an unincorporated administrative agency for the purpose of disseminating tracts, papers, doctrinal treatises and Bibles, with Russell as secretary and William Henry Conley as president. Three years later, on December 15, 1884, Russell became president of the Society when it was legally incorporated in Pennsylvania. This society was later renamed Watch Tower Bible and Tract Society in September, 1896. Russell wrote many articles, books, pamphlets and sermons, which by his death totaled 50,000 printed pages. In 1886, he wrote the first of what would become a six-volume Bible textbook series called *Millennial Dawn*, later renamed Studies in the Scriptures, which presented his interpretation of fundamental doctrines. As a consequence, the Bible Students were sometimes called Millennial Dawnists. Russell died on October 31, 1916, in Pampa, Texas, during a cross-country preaching trip. On January 6, 1917, board member and Watchtower Society legal counsel Joseph Franklin Rutherford was elected president of the Watchtower Society, unopposed, at the Pittsburgh convention. Rutherford had been a member of Russell's movement since 1906 and was appointed as legal counsel in 1907 and had now obviously made a very quick advancement toward successful total control, plus an eventual takeover.

Rutherford later announced the publication of *The Finished Mystery*, which he then claimed was a posthumous volume of Russell's *Studies in the Scriptures*. By-laws passed by both the Pittsburgh convention and the board of directors stated that the new President Rutherford would be the executive officer and general manager of the society, giving him full charge, power and complete control of its affairs worldwide. Rutherford had obviously seen the potential of securing complete control of the Watchtower Society and had the same mental outlook as Ron Hubbard, who later started Scientology, if you want to get rich, you start a religion. However, Rutherford had no need to start a new religion, as by means of his tactics and legal manipulative mind he simply took over a leaderless religion when Charles Russell died in 1916.

This quote from the *Christian Research Institute Journal* explains how the scheming Rutherford managed the take over of this leaderless religion.

> According to instructions Russell left behind, his successor to the presidency would share power with the Watch Tower Corporations board of directors, whom Russell had appointed for life. But former vice president Joseph Franklin (Judge) Rutherford noted that the formality of re-electing the directors at an annual meeting of the corporation had been omitted, and he used this technicality to unseat the majority of the Watch Tower directors without calling a membership vote. He even had a subordinate summon the police into the Societys Brooklyn headquarters offices to break up their board meeting and evict them from the premises. After securing the headquarters complex and the sect's corporate entities, Rutherford turned his attention to the rest of the organization. By gradually replacing locally elected elders with his own appointees, he managed to transform a loose collection of semi-autonomous, democratically run congregations into a tight-knit organizational machine controlled from his office.

This new and very strictly controlled new arrangement of ruling the congregations and their members, Rutherford called a Theocratic (God ruled) arrangement that replaced the then existing and successful democratic method of managing the congregations and members. Immediately one wonders how the Great Theocrat (Jehovah or Yahweh) who resides in the unseen heavenly realm could now rule and operate a visible human organization, but Rutherford came up with the perfect solution and convinced most of the members of this religion that the Lord needed a visible organization to represent him on earth and Rutherford was the perfect solution.

Firstly, Rutherford reinforced the claim that the Almighty had appointed the Governing Body of the Watchtower Society as his representative on Earth, including of course Rutherford himself who was appointed President for life. He then introduced and expanded a previously insignificant arrangement that had been used by Russell his predecessor, namely for male volunteers (called pilgrims) to visit the congregations to offer support and guidance. The direct appointments of these pilgrims were now to be made by Rutherford personally and the so-called Governing Body, the Board of Directors; a group of men and appointees made directly from the Watchtower Headquarters. These appointees were called pilgrims and named because of their work, the definition of a pilgrim, according to *Websters Dictionary*, is a person who journeys to a sacred place for religious reasons, but from 1924 they were expected to also now work as door-to-door salesmen of Rutherford's books and magazines in addition to their other more public profile and prominent duty of giving lectures and chart talks. It appears that certain members of the pilgrims apparently resented the change, so they left the traveling work, some disgruntled ones even forming their own religious spin-off cults. The next step in slowly taking away the control of the democratically elected servants in each congregation, Rutherford in 1932 introduced a direct appointment selected by himself and the Society an appointee to be known as a service director to assist the local service committee, who were still elected democratically by the local brothers in each congregation.

Chart talks were basically lectures but using a large wall chart that had originally been used in Charles Russell's first volume of his series of books called *Studies in the Scriptures*, which was also called *The Plan of the Ages*. These lectures or talks used this complex; impressive but highly speculative chart to try and indentify the various stages of mankind's development from the creation of Adam in 4026 BC, and that 1874 AD was the end of 6000 years of man's existence. The chart also including the claimed appointed times of the nations (the gentile times) of 2520 years from 607 BC to 1914 AD and then on to the Messianic Age of a thousand years (also called the Third Dispensation) to begin before the ending of the human generation that witnessed the year 1914. These charts also used Russell's interpretations of the Great Pyramid of Giza in Egypt and were supported by the books and writings of John and Morton Edgar from Scotland, two very successful businessmen who were prominent members and financial supporters of this religious movement. Russell had first stated that 1874 was derived from a measurement of 3416 pyramid inches. In the early 1920s, the significance of the pyramidological predictions for 1914 was re-interpreted to mean that the old evil order began to pass away in 1914. Russell and his colleagues also used the Bible text in Isaiah 19:19 (AV) to try and prove their use of the pyramid of Giza in the explanation of the chart, "In that day there will be an altar to the Lord in the heart of Egypt, and a monument to the Lord at its border. It will be a sign and witness to the LORD Almighty in the land of Egypt."

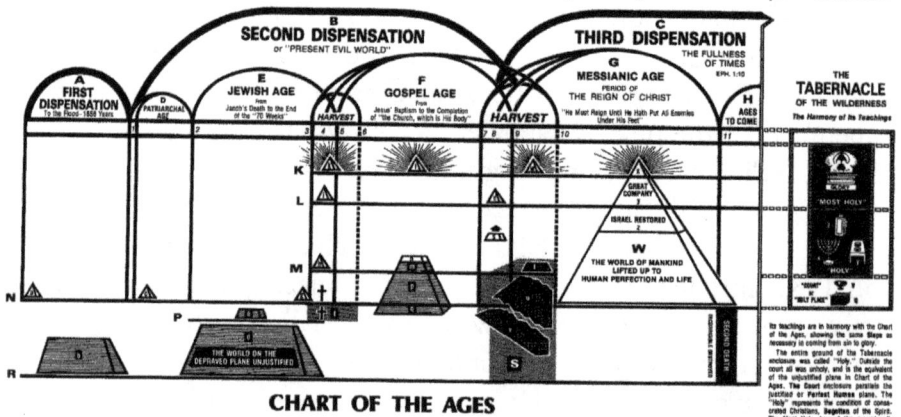

Photo of the famous Chart of the Ages courtesy of *Wikipedia* and Creative Commons

In 1924, an issue of the Watchtower Society's *Golden Age* magazine referred to the Great Pyramid as the Scientific Bible and added that measurements on the Grand Gallery inside the Great Pyramid accurately confirmed the dates 1874, 1914 and 1925 in Bible history. These chart talks by the travelling pilgrims operated from approximately 1917 to the mid 1920s and resulted in many gullible listeners actually becoming converted to the Watchtower religion, (probably being blinded by science) so this program was called a great success by Rutherford and his Society and a fulfillment of the Bible text at Matthew 24:14, "And this good news of the kingdom will be proclaimed throughout the world, as a testimony to all the nations; and then the end will come."

The Watchtower Society throughout its history still promotes and stubbornly tries to establish records to prove the coming end of the world, for example this quote from one of their journals. According to reliable Bible chronology, Adam and Eve were created in 4026 BC, so this is another way that helps confirm the fact that we are living in the final few years of this time of the end. (Daniel 12:9) The Bible shows that we are nearing the end of a full 6,000 years of human history. What significance does this have? ... When God gave his laws to ancient Israel, one of those laws involved keeping the Sabbath day holy. On the seventh day of the week there was to be no labor ... How fitting it would be for God, following this pattern, to end man's misery after six thousand years of human rule and follow it with His glorious Kingdom rule for a thousand years! (*Awake!* Oct.8, 1968, pp. 14-15)

Owing to the fact that the world did not come to an end in 1914, it was in the year 1920 that Rutherford commenced his famous lecture entitled, Millions Now Living Will Never Die and surreptitiously hinted that this year 1925 could now be the year. But alas another disappointment for the members of this cult, and reports show that the attendance at the Bible Students yearly Memorial celebration fell sharply again, dropping from 90,434 in 1925 to 17,380 in 1928. Rutherford simply dismissed their defection as the Lord shaking out the unfaithful.

A poster advertising the famous lecture by Joseph Rutherford in 1925,
courtesy of Creative Commons and Getty Images

Today the Watchtower Society has stated that its early leaders promoted incomplete, even inaccurate concepts of the Bible. In 1928, the belief that the Great Pyramid contained a prophetic blueprint of biblical chronology was rejected by the Governing Body of this religion and the Pyramid was now seen as having been built under the direction of Satan the Devil. This is one very clear example of the dangers and confusion of following the leaders of a cult and their crazy personal explanation and private interpretation of the Bible.

No matter how sincere Charles Russell and his fellow Bible students were, we have to recognize today that this ridiculous and insane interpretation of the pyramid of Giza and its measurements and using certain dates and periods of time, plus trying to relate it to the actual Bible records was the foundation and major building block of this religion. One of our readers rightfully asked the question, how did this religion keep operating and growing under the direction of its leaders from Rutherford until today and now claiming approximately six million followers? The answer is quite simple; it is because this established religion is nothing more than a cult with its manipulative associated powers. Analyzing the tried and tested techniques of a cult it is easy to see how this can happen. We therefore, to make crystal clear once again we repeat below (repetition for emphasis) and refer our readers to the notes in our introduction and the question, what is a cult?

Matt Slick on his website, Carm.org, offers this comment:

There are many non-Christian religions and cults in America: Mormonism, Jehovah's Witnesses, Christian Science, Unity, The Way International, Unitarianism, Islam, Hinduism, etc. They all claim special revelation and privilege and those that use the Bible invariably interpret it in disharmony with standard biblical understanding. And groups especially like the Mormons and Jehovah's Witnesses object to being labeled a cult because it often gets an emotional reaction as well as is a label they want to avoid. Another common denominator among the Cults is their methods for twisting scripture. Some of the errors they commit in interpreting Scripture are: 1) taking Scripture out of context; 2) reading into the Scriptures information that is not there; 3) picking and choosing only the Scriptures that suit their needs; 4) ignoring other explanations; 5) combining scriptures that don't have anything to do with each other; 6) quoting a verse without giving its location; 7) incorrect definitions of key words; and 8) mistranslations. These are only a few of the many ways Cults misuse Scripture.

Christian cults are new religious movements, which have a Christian background but are considered to be theologically deviant by members of other Christian churches. In his influential book The Kingdom of the Cults, Christian scholar Walter Martin defines Christian cults as groups that follow the personal interpretation of an individual, rather than the understanding of the Bible accepted by mainstream Christianity. The definition of a follower of a cult is any blind, unthinking, unquestioning follower of a philosophy.

The question thus posed to our research team was, why do people join or are attracted to a religious cult? The answer provided by one insightful member of our team from Cambridge University was the following,

"The process of joining a religious cult is usually because it attracts individuals from amongst those who are experiencing sociologically or psychologically unsettled circumstances in their lives and they look to the security and therapy of a group identity."

The final stage of taking over complete and direct control of the growing expanding congregations of Jehovah's Witnesses by Joseph Rutherford came about in June, 1938, when all congregations throughout the world had to adopt a resolution to pass complete control of the local congregation to the Headquarters in New York. The resolution drawn up by Rutherford himself, reads:

> We, the company [congregation] of God's people taken out for
> his name, and now at [name of the congregation] recognize
> that God's government is a pure theocracy and that Jesus Christ
> is at the temple and in full charge and control of the visible
> organization of Jehovah…and that The Society is the visible
> representation of the Lord on earth, and we therefore request
> The Society to organize this company [congregation] for service
> and to henceforth appoint the various servants thereof, so that
> all of us may work together in peace, righteousness, harmony
> and complete unity. We attach hereto a list of names of persons
> in this company [congregation] that to us appear more fully
> mature and who therefore appear more best suited to fill the
> respective positions designated for service. (*The Watchtower*,
> June 15, 1938)

> *Editor's Note*: Each congregation was left with a certain
> amount of freedom and liberty to name their own preferred
> local leaders, but these men were bound by this Resolution to
> implicitly follow all instructions and orders that came from
> the Head Office of the Watchtower Society, alias Joseph
> Rutherford. Not all congregations accepted this new rule
> of control introduced by Rutherford so quite a number of
> congregations simply broke away and formed their own splinter
> groups.

Referring back to the publishing of the *Finished Mystery* supposedly the 7th Volume of Russell's books, according to the article by Barbara Anderson in her Watchtower Documents, by 1918, there were only 3,868 persons actively announcing the Bible Student's message in the entire world. One of the reasons for the decrease in supporters was the disenchantment with the information presented in *The Finished Mystery*. Plus J. F. Rutherford and his seven associates were in Federal prison in Atlanta, Georgia, because of so-called anti-war statements in the book that Rutherford expected would bring the Lords blessed favor.

> *Editor's Note*: Barbara Anderson was a member of Jehovah's Witnesses from 1954 through 1997. She worked at Watchtower's headquarters in Brooklyn, New York, from 1982 to 1992 where during her last four years there, she researched the movement's official history (published in 1993). While working in the organization's Writing Department, Barbara discovered that the Watchtower organization covered up child sexual molestation committed by Jehovah's Witnesses. This issue caused her to exit the religion and eventually become an outspoken critic of Jehovah's Witnesses' sexual abuse policies. In 2007, Barbara appeared on NBC *Nightly News* with Brian Williams to report on the Watchtower's secret settlement of $12.5 million with sixteen victims of molestation by leading Watchtower men.

By June 1918, four of the seven Watchtower Society directors – Robert H. Hirsh, Alfred I. Ritchie, Isaac F. Hoskins and James D. Wright – had decided they had made a mistake in endorsing Rutherford's expanded powers of management, claiming Rutherford had now become extremely autocratic and narcissistic. In June of 1918 Hirsh attempted to rescind the new by-laws and to reclaim the powers of management from the president, but Rutherford later claimed he had by then detected a conspiracy among the directors to seize control of the Society and its assets. In July, Rutherford gained a legal opinion from a Philadelphia corporation lawyer that the four were not legally directors of the Society. On July 12, Rutherford filled what he claimed were four vacancies on the board, appointing his personal friends, Alexander H. Macmillan and Pennsylvania Bible Students, W. E. Spill, John A. Bohnet and George H. Fisher as directors. Between August and November of 1918 the Watchtower Society and the four ousted directors published a series of pamphlets, with each side accusing the other of ambitious, disruptive and dishonest conduct. The former directors also claimed Rutherford had required all headquarters workers to sign a petition supporting him and threatened dismissal for any who refused to sign. Police forcibly escorted the former directors from the Brooklyn headquarters on August 8, 1918.

Alexander Hugh Macmillan (1877-1966), also referred to as A. H. Macmillan, was an important member of the Bible Students, and later, of Jehovah's Witnesses. He became a board member of the Watch Tower Bible and Tract Society in 1918, appointed by Rutherford. He presented a somewhat biased history plus a number of inaccurate facts of the religious movement in his book *Faith on the March* (1957). He believed he had finally found biblical truth and later used the publications as a basis for his theory that he and others would be taken home to heaven in 1914. Macmillan was a very naïve and subjective individual. In the decades prior to 1914, Watchtower Society publications claimed that Armageddon would take place in 1914.

As the year 1914 approached, their publications stated that October 1914 would mark the end of the Gentile Times and the beginning of Christ's kingship. Many Bible Students believed they would be sent or called to heaven in 1914. At a convention at Saratoga Springs, New York, on September 27-30, 1914, Macmillan, believing that the church was going home in October, he announced that, this is probably the last public address I shall ever deliver because we shall be going home soon. Later in the same year, at a December meeting he was compelled to speak once again. Those present laughed about Macmillan's previous announcement of his last public address; so in the subsequent talk, Macmillan acknowledged, some of us had been a bit too hasty in thinking that we were going to heaven right away. Yet he was still convinced of the world's end coming soon, and in Macmillan's address to a meeting of Bible Students as proposing a new date for the coming Millennium and end of the world in the year 1925.

By mid-1919 about one in seven Bible Students had chosen to leave this religion rather than accept Rutherford's leadership, forming independent groups such as, the Stand Fast Movement, Paul Johnson Movement, and the Pastoral Bible Institute of Brooklyn. It is estimated that as many as three-quarters of the Bible Students associating in 1919 left the movement by 1931, mainly in protest against Rutherford's rejection of some of Pastor Russell's teachings. To reduce public confusion regarding the existence of several groups of Bible Students no longer associated with the Watchtower Society, Rutherfords faction of the Bible Students adopted the name *Jehovah's witnesses* on July 26, 1931, at a convention in Columbus, Ohio (note that witnesses was not capitalized at that time, we will explain why, later in our report.)

Our researchers also looked further into the financial affairs of the Watchtower Society as controlled by the manipulative lawyer Joseph Rutherford and revealed that there were many suspicious activities according to reports compiled at the time, even ownership of a private Gold Mine called Soda Lake in California registered in the personal name of Charles Russell. Plus, a press article reported the purchase of the building for the new Headquarters in New York in 1909 when it moved from Pittsburg, but the article did not mention, as it was hidden by Rutherford; the secret purchase of other buildings, the report later revealed that the theater building was worth nearly a half million dollars. Actually, in 1915, the assessed value of the theater building was $220,000.00, and the assessed value of the adjacent former hotel building was only $105,000.00. Those two large Manhattan properties were taken over by the new President Judge Rutherford after Russell's death, in 1917 valued at $330,000.00 (roughly $7,250,000.00 in 2019 dollars).

Russell and Rutherford also formed several other private, lucrative and profitable companies, which would act as agencies for the newly formed Watchtower, Bible and Tract Society of New York, Inc., and the Peoples Pulpit Association established in 1909, which both had been incorporated as non-profit and supported mainly by the door-to-door sales of Russell's famous books, *Studies in the Scriptures* plus subscriptions to *Zion's Watchtower* magazine and the generous donations from the sincere followers of this religion. The other private companies that Rutherford incorporated were, for example, the Mena Film Company, Inc., Pyramid Film Company, Inc., Packers Box Company, Inc., National Shippers Association, Inc., Angelica, Inc., and the Perfection Advertising Company, Inc., and the ownership plus the stock and resultant income was held jointly by Russell, Rutherford and a few nominees who were investors and leading wealthy members of this religion. This type of information was and still is unknown of course to the rank and file of the local somewhat naïve members of this religion. When Russell died in 1916 the memorandum of these lucrative private companies, prepared by Rutherford himself, made the provision that total ownership would then revert to Rutherford, who then became sole owner of these lucrative business ventures for the remainder of his life.

Upon the death of Russell, Joseph Rutherford in 1916 legally took over these lucrative businesses and private companies owned by himself, the late Charles Russell and other wealthy members of the Society being shareholders in these lucrative private ventures and enterprises. However, many of these shareholders, also being members of this religion, became quite concerned regarding his cronyism and nepotistic attitude now that Rutherford was also the all-powerful President and not just the Watchtower lawyer. In an effort to explain his increasing powers he sent a private letter to these investors and shareholders that was discovered in the archived files at the Watchtower headquarters. Rutherford claimed in the Watchtower magazine in order to justify his role of being the all powerful leader of this cult, "It was my duty to use the power the Lord had <u>put into my hands</u> to support the interests of the shareholders and all others interested in the Truth throughout the world ... to be unfaithful to them would be unfaithful to the Lord." [underlining is ours] Try and explain away this feeble excuse for exercising such blatant, scurrilous power over the subjective followers of this religion.

This extract below from the *Watchtower* of 1ˢᵗ September, 1916, explains the official policy of the Watchtower Society regarding the suspicion by some members of this religion based on rumors of these extra curricular investments and this statement is in part true but is also totally deceptive and misleading in order to throw off the persistent bloodhounds. This religion thought it expedient at the time and felt compelled to try and head off these serious questions regarding the external and private financial interests of Russell and Rutherford. Quote from the *Watchtower* magazine of 1916:

> Brethren write us from time to time respecting inventions, patents, mining claims, etc., desiring that THE WATCH TOWER BIBLE AND TRACT SOCIETY should join

with them in the development of these -- kindly offering the principal portion of all the profits. We greatly appreciate these kind offers, the generous hearts behind them, and the love for the Truth and its service thus manifested. But we are obliged to refuse all such offers, because the Society engages in no kind of business for profit. It confines its business transactions to financiering the Pilgrim Work, publishing the SCRIPTURE STUDIES, etc., and supplying them at cost or below cost; publishing THE WATCH TOWER, publishing the BIBLE STUDENTS MONTHLY, etc., and in the presentation, and formerly in the showing, of the PHOTO-DRAMA OF CREATION. The Society engages in no kind of mining or patent business or speculations. The money under its control comes from the Lord's consecrated people, and often represents hard-earned funds and self-sacrificing economy; it is used strictly and only for the forwarding of the Truth according to the best judgment of the executive officers.

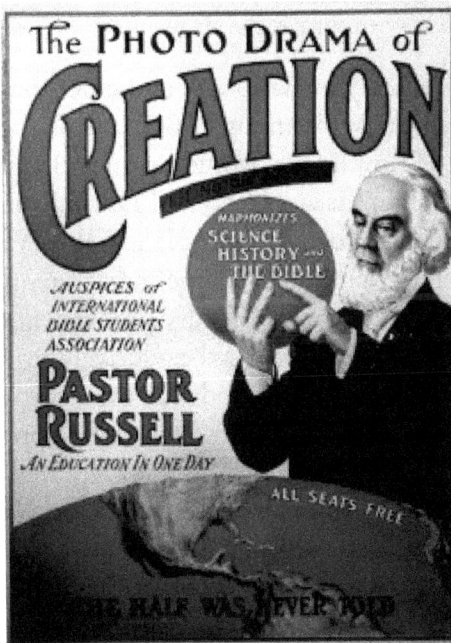

Cover of the famous film and slides produced by Charles Russell in 1914, courtesy of Creative Commons and Getty Images

There are many other cases that have been diligently investigated by other researchers regarding the questionable and sometimes unscrupulous financial activities of Charles Russell and Joseph Rutherford but space does not allow us to include all of these in this chapter of our book. Thousands of members left the congregations of Bible Students associated with the Watchtower Society throughout the 1920s, prompted in part by Rutherford's (and later Frederick Franz) failed predictions for the year 1925, increasing disillusionment with his on-going doctrinal and organizational changes, and his campaign for centralized head office control of the movement under himself as life-time appointed President, plus rumors of his very suspicious private financial dealings. William Schnell, author of the book, *30 Years a Watchtower Slave and former Jehovah's Witness*, claims that three-quarters of the original Bible Students who had been associating with the Watchtower Society in 1921 had left by 1931. In 1930 Rutherford stated and admitted that the total number of those who have withdrawn from the Society... is comparatively large.

Rutherford or more likely his visionary and chief theologian Frederick Franz predicted that the Millennium (1,000 year reign of Christ foretold in the Bible book of Revelation) would begin in 1925 and that biblical figures such as Abraham, Isaac, Jacob and David, would be resurrected back to earth to rule as princes of our planet. The Watchtower Society even bought a property and built a large mansion, named Beth Sarim, in California for their return. This luxury property in an expensive area of beautiful San Diego was later used exclusively by Rutherford as his home up until his death in 1942 and was then conveniently sold and forgotten by the Watchtower Society. This quote appeared in the *Time Magazine* of March 31, 1930, "Judge Joseph Frederick Rutherford, aged 60, lives in a ten bed-roomed Spanish mansion, No 4440 Braeburn Rd, San Diego, Calif. Last week he deeded No 4440 Braeburn Road, and adjacent two car garage and a pair of automobiles to King David, Gideon, Barak, Samson, Jephthae, Samuel and sundry other mighties of ancient Palestine. Positive is he that they are shortly to reappear on earth, Said he: I have purposely landscaped the place with palm and olive trees so that these princes of the universe will feel at home." This *Time Magazine* article was accompanied by two photographs, one showing Rutherford standing on the front steps of his new palatial mansion and the other with Rutherford with an arrogant pose standing between his two new luxury vehicles he had just purchased, a Fisher Fleetwood Cadillac coupe, plus a second one being a convertible. This type of vehicle is usually only purchased by multi-millionaires or gangsters, as they are the only ones who can afford them.

Alighting on Ohio Soil after His Drive from the Headquarters of the Society in New York City.

July 25, 1931, *Messenger* Magazine showing J.F. Rutherford (Judge Rutherford) with one of his 16-cylinder Cadillac cars, courtesy of Creative Commons and Getty Images

Between 1918 and 1929, as previously mentioned, several factions formed their own independent fellowships, including the Stand Fast Movement, the Pastoral Bible Institute, the Laymens Home Missionary Movement founded by Paul Johnson, and the Dawn Bible Students Association. These groups range from conservative; claiming to be Russell's true followers, to more liberal, claiming that Russells role is not as important as once believed. Rutherfords faction of the movement however had retained control of the Watchtower Society and its assets, plus later adopted the new name Jehovah's Witnesses in July 1931. By the end of the 20th century, Jehovah's Witnesses claimed a membership of about six million, while other independent splinter Bible Student groups were estimated to total less than 75,000. This was as a direct result of who had retained and controlled the assets of the original

Watchtower Society, namely the headquarters, the buildings, printing presses and the shipping facilities plus the existing infrastructure of the slave like followers, who obediently sold the Watchtower publications from door-to-door. The members of this religion sincerely believed this to be a sincere, direct expression of their faith as belonging to the only true religion and loyally following the firm and rigid instructions of their leaders and masters, the Governing Body.

As an example of the modus operandi of the Watchtower Society that clearly illustrates that it was more of a commercial enterprise with greedy, power crazy men, vying for control and authority, rather than operating as a Christian organization engaged in the work of promoting the Gospel of Jesus Christ. Plus, the examples of men like Paul Johnson, Jesse Hemery and Joseph Rutherford, being three very prominent influential leaders in the ranks of the Watchtower Society, were nothing but thieves and rascals, men who are now ignored as though they never lived and are preferred to be forgotten by the current Governing Body of this religion. These same three men who all claimed to be chosen by God, as do the current Governing Body of the Watchtower Society and specially selected members of the so-called Little Flock of the 144,000 of heavenly chosen ones to rule with Christ in Heaven, plus the behavior of these three men is so revealing and disgusting, plus it is an exposure of the hypocrisy of this religion at the highest level.

Based on archived legal records of the Watchtower Society, filed in the headquarters in New York, and also partially reported in the 1973 Year Book of Jehovah's Witnesses, but not presenting the full facts, details and background of this sordid and squalid account. The following details are revealed. On November 7, 1916, a cable (presumably under instruction from Rutherford) from Brooklyn headquarters advised the London Branch office that Brother Paul S. L. Johnson was about to leave for Britain. The purpose of his visit was to look into the difficulties involving the managers of the Society and the London Tabernacle. His real power in Britain would be no greater than that of any of the other pilgrim brothers who had come to these shores, and of this he was made perfectly acquainted before leaving the Brooklyn office. He made a tour of Britain, addressing public meetings on the subject, Britain's Fallen Heroes – Comfort for Their Bereaved. He recommended that congregations set up Schools of the Prophets to train brothers in public speaking. Backed by papers that appeared to give him plenipotentiary powers, he made a considerable impression in the congregations. With this newly acquired background he returned to London, and there his real aims soon became apparent.

On Sunday, February 4, 1917, the secretary of the London congregation read a letter from Paul Johnson that announced that Brothers Shearn and Crawford were no longer managers of the Society. Johnson as a Special Representative of the Watch Tower Bible and Tract Society took it upon himself to instruct the bank to reject the signatures of Shearn and Crawford and honor checks countersigned by Ebenezer Housden and Alexander Kirkwood. Then Johnson cabled J. F. Rutherford, who had recently become president of the Watchtower Society: Situation intolerable. Shearn, Crawford dismissed. As soon as President Rutherford heard of Johnson's dismissal of the two managers, he sent a cable calling for their reinstatement. They, however, refused to be reinstated. At the same time Brother Rutherford appointed a commission to look into the trouble. Unknown to Rutherford, one of the members of that commission, Ebenezer Housden, was involved in the whole situation, being one of the new check signatories.

Meantime, Johnson was quite undisturbed about Rutherford's reaction. He was satisfied that Rutherford was undoubtedly the victim of a cablegram campaign engineered by Shearn and Crawford. Johnson therefore began one himself. His first cable ran to eighty-five words, later eclipsed by others, including a one-hundred-and-fifteen-word effort. The first cablegram identified himself and others with characters in Esther, Nehemiah and other Bible books. He himself was likened to Ezra, Nehemiah and Mordecai. He invited the president of the Society to be his right-hand man. In the meantime Johnson had instructed Hemery urgently to lay in stocks of food and store them in a place safe from men and from rats. He suggested a false ceiling lined with tin. Wheat and peanuts, he said, were specially needed. He based his demands, he said, on Elisha's predictions of famine. About this time Jesse Hemery cabled Rutherford: Johnson claims full control of everything. Next day, Rutherford cabled Johnson:

Your work finished London; return America, important. And to Hemery, Rutherford cabled: Johnson demented. Has no powers. Credentials issued to procure passport. Return him America. On March 7, Johnson, in an eighty-seven-word cable to Vice-President A. I. Ritchie and W. E. Van Amburgh, repudiated Rutherford's authority to recall him to America, claimed full support of the London congregation as against Shearn and Crawford, and appealed to the Society against Rutherford, who, he said, was not elected to the presidential position. Johnson launched a campaign against the bank, threatening proceedings if they honored checks legally drawn and demanding recognition of his own nominees. He underlined his own plenipotentiary powers, withdrew authority from Alexander Kirkwood, suspended Hemery in a document formally witnessed by Ebenezer Housden, and made it known generally that he, Johnson, should have been the Society's president but had declined to accept.

Johnson, resisted by Hemery, the remaining manager in the London office, co-opted Housden as his accomplice, obtained the keys of the London office and forcibly took possession. He confiscated the mail, opened the safe and took money belonging to the Society, and then instituted a lawsuit in the High Court of Chancery in London, in the name of the Society by himself as special representative, against the manager of the London office and against the bank where the Society's funds were deposited. Acting through solicitors, Johnson obtained an injunction restraining the defendants from drawing on the funds of the Society. At this point Hemery wired Rutherford once again: Johnson rampaging. He and Housden seizing mails and cash. Hasten sealed cancellation authority. Solicitor recommends Johnson's forcible ejection. In reply Rutherford cabled: Resist Johnsons injunction. Does not represent Society. Restrain him. Written cancellation of Johnson's appointment came over the signature of the president, the stamp and seal of the Watch Tower Bible and Tract Society and attested by W. E. Van Amburgh. Formal annulment of all Johnson's acts and deeds accompanied the revocation of his authority. Johnson's lawsuit, for which he employed counsel, failed. His rebellion and attempt to seize the funds of the Society failed also. On March 10 Rutherford cabled Hemery to take full control. Hemery went immediately to the bank to safeguard £800 on deposit there. He was none too soon. Johnson arrived immediately after to use his letters from the head office to gain control of the money. A verbal and legal fight ensued. Frustrated, Johnson pursued his legal action. When the case came before the judge, Johnson's counsel decided, after reading Hemery's affidavit, not to proceed with his action. These developments, of course, deflated Johnson, and he was quiet for a time, but not for long. His illusions of grandeur revived. It soon became evident that his purpose was more than that of taking control of the office. He aimed to take control of the whole British field and its resources, and of the running of a separate edition of the Watch Tower magazine.

Johnson, balked and furious, conferred long with his fellow conspirator, Housden. On Wednesday, both went early to bed in their separate rooms. Hemery recruited Brother Cronk and four others. Two crept to Johnson's room and silently but firmly secured the door. Hemery, Cronk and the other two tiptoed to Housden's room and with some difficulty obtained the keys. Quickly, Hemery and Cronk went to the safe, unlocked it and swung the door. The money was gone. Johnson and Housden had scooped a deposit of £50 in gold, £190 in currency and the receipts from the mail during the days they held it. Besides this sum, a check for £350 was missing.

Hemery and Cronk made another trip to Housden's room, but this time not on tiptoe. Where is the money? demanded Hemery. Housden refused to divulge any information, even under close interrogation. But he did promise he would help Johnson no more. In the course of the questioning Hemery pointed out the possibility of bringing in the police. At 11:30 p.m. the doorbell rang. There on the step was a police officer. He wanted an explanation of a violation of the very stringent London lighting regulations. An upstairs window was brightly lighted and had no blackout. The officer insisted on seeing those responsible and Hemery took him to the offending room and knocked. The door opened and there, framed in the doorway, was a man whose urge to meet policemen had never been at a lower ebb. This, said Hemery to the officer, is

Mr. Housden.

Next morning at six o'clock the Bethel family awoke to sounds
of violence. A banging and pounding and a final thud gave
evidence that Johnson was not a man to be restricted by a door
wedged with a sizable chunk of wood. Cronk warned Johnson
that, though he could go to the bathroom if he wanted, he
could not have things his own way. Cronk mentioned that a
police officer had been up to see Housden the previous night,
though no mention was made of the reason for the visit. So
Johnson paid a visit to Housden's room. But Housden, shaken
by the events of the night, would not come out or even converse
with him through the door. Johnson began then to share the
worry that was clearly afflicting Housden. Desirable as he
once regarded these premises, it now appeared to him to be
time to leave, and that without delay. He returned to his room,
one flight up, and dressed. Leaving his baggage open, he went
out on the balcony overlooking Craven Terrace, climbed the
balustrade and hung suspended for a moment before working
his way down the face of the building. As the front door of the
Bethel was open, some might have thought there were easier
ways of reaching the street than the way Johnson chose, and
they would have been right. But had Johnson chosen the easy
way, the milkman that morning would have missed a sight that
made his day that of a silk-hatted, frock-coated city gent, feet
shod with rubber overshoes shinning down a drainpipe.

During that day Housden delivered to Brother Gentle a
package containing about £220 in gold, treasury notes and
other paper. Gentle phoned Hemery to say that he, Gentle,
would have to hold the money until a note from Johnson's
solicitors sanctioned its surrender. Hemery shocked Gentle
by pointing out that he was handling stolen property. By
evening Hemery received the cash. But the needed statement
of finances was still missing. Though President Rutherford
all along took a strong and emphatic line with Johnson, he
advocated with equal emphasis the need to deal with him in a
kindly way. In seeking to find some reason for the tremendous
disruption that had come upon the London branch and on the
work generally in Britain, he advanced the view that the years
of discord between the three managers was itself an inducing

factor, Jehovah having permitted the adversary to enter. On March 16, 1917, Rutherford sent copies of new rules for the London branch and invited the three managers to go over them together and then, if agreeable, sign and return a copy to Brooklyn headquarters. The rules vested due authority in Hemery as the president's representative.

The findings of the commission appointed to look into the troubles in London reached this country together with the president's conclusions. Rutherford's covering letter, however, gave the text of a cable from Housden to Brother Van Amburgh, which read: JOHNSON UNEARTHED COLOSSAL EFFORT BY HEMERY SHEARN CRAWFORD DEFRAUD WATCH TOWER OF FINANCIAL CONTROL. RUTHERFORD'S CABLEGRAMS ENCOURAGING THEM. HAVE BOARD SILENCE HIM. Signed HOUSDEN. This cable was dated March 18, 1917. As soon as it came to hand Van Amburgh turned it over to Rutherford. When the report of the commission reached Rutherford, he searched it in vain for information about this fresh conspiracy. Housden, a member of the commission and a signatory of the report, for reasons then not clear, had kept silent. Meantime the mystery of Johnson's whereabouts following his unorthodox exit of the British branch office, was not cleared up until April 1917, by which time he was halfway to America. It is true that following his hasty departure there were one or two strange telephoned messages received at the Bethel home, and it was concluded that Johnson was standing beside the mystery caller on each occasion trying to get some information about his friend Housden. Later, after two long sessions, Rutherford established that Johnson was perfectly sane on every point save one, namely, himself. Johnson contended strongly that he must return to Great Britain. President Rutherford's reaction: We will see to it that he does not return there. Instead it was recommended that Hemery arrange a tour to explain matters to the congregations. The idea was for Brother Kirkwood to assist with this tour, Hemery himself visiting the larger congregations.

This comment by an unnamed researcher into the history of the Watchtower Society in his article secretly published in the *Christian*

Reformer, a British religious magazine some years ago said:

> Johnson saw himself in scripture, similar to Elijah or Nehemiah and he wanted to be Russell's replacement. This might be why the majority of Bible Students did not want anything to do with him or his new sect at the time as they were in fear of the powerful Joseph Rutherford. Johnson saw types and anti-types in everything, as one Bible student sarcastically put it: If Moses farted in the wilderness; Paul Johnson would find an anti-type for it. Johnson lost the battle with Rutherford over the leadership of the Watchtower Society, so he simply started his own faction. It is fairly evident that Jesse Hemery was banking on Shearn and Crawford, the principal advocates of the freedom proposal, being eliminated by Johnson so that upon the latter's return to the United States Jesse would be left in supreme control of the British Branch of the Bible Students. By late February, however, Johnson announced that he, and not Rutherford, was the true successor to Pastor Russell and that he himself was to fulfill the role of the Steward in the Parable of the Penny. To the unbiased mind at the time the root of the trouble was obvious. Here were three men, Rutherford, Johnson and Hemery, each convinced that he, and he alone, was the best man to rule and direct the brethren, ambitious enough to attempt achievement of that coveted position, and blind to the harm they were causing.

Paul Samuel Leo Johnson (1873-1950) left the Watchtower Society when Joseph F. Rutherford finally took over the legal control of its future direction after Russell's death. He then founded the splinter group, Laymens Home Missionary Movement in 1920, and served on its board of directors from 1920 until his death on October 22, 1950, and this small religious group still has a few supporters even to this day. He authored 17 volumes of religious writings titled Epiphany Studies in the Scriptures, and published two magazines from about 1918 until his death in 1950.

> *Editor's Note*: It is ironic, but Jesse Hemery who was appointed overseer of the Watchtower Society's British Isles branch office by Charles Russell in 1901, holding that post until 1946 when Welshman Pryce Hughes took over, until he was also replaced in 1963 by Wilfred Gooch. Jesse Hemery had lived rent free

and using Watchtower funds for many years while operating his clandestine scheme out of the Watchtower offices at Craven Terrace in London. Hemery, who had also been privately writing his own literature, primarily against Rutherford and the changes he was making to erase or amend many of Russell's teachings, and Hemery went on and founded another splinter group, the now defunct Goshen Fellowship after he was personally disfellowshipped in 1951 by authoritarian President Nathan Knorr. Note that this was an arbitrary decision by Knorr without the benefit of a judicial committee to hear the case, another example of an asinine claimed Theocracy or more likely a Dictatorship in operation. As our intelligent readers reflect on this sordid, disgusting account of these greedy, power crazy men, vying for control and authority within the ranks of the Watchtower Society, how can one possibly believe that this religion was under the guidance of God's Holy Spirit when it simply reflects the division and dysfunction that takes place within this cult? As the Apostle Paul plainly warns us in answer to the question, "Does Christ exist divided?" at First Corinthians 1:10, the Apostle Paul continues, "Now I appeal to you, brothers and sisters, by the name of our Lord Jesus Christ, that all of you be in agreement and that there be no divisions among you, but that you be united in the same mind and the same purpose."

Members of Jehovah's Witnesses today are instructed by the Governing Body that they are to devote as much time as possible to their ministry to the Lord, mainly door-to-door selling of their literature, and are required to submit an individual monthly Field Service Report in which they reported total hours spent, plus books and magazines sold. Baptized members who fail to report a month of preaching are termed irregular in their service and may be counseled by the elders; those who do not submit reports for six consecutive months are termed inactive (or sarcastically referred to by many elders; being placed in the dead file.) One creative congregation secretary in one of the Birmingham, England, congregations of Jehovah's Witnesses, according to our reporter who verified this account as being absolutely true and accurate, which displayed a sad twist of mind. The secretary created a small cardboard box in the shape of a coffin and painted it black, in which to place these now defunct record cards of the inactive publishers, no doubt done with a weird sense of humor. Of course, when this was discovered by the visiting circuit servant, who after ruefully smiling to himself, he quickly intervened and was compelled to reprimanded this individual and put a stop to the now problematic situation, plus he had no choice but to recommended to the Branch Office the removal of this secretary and rescind his God given appointment in the congregation.

According to The Association of Religion Data Archive (ARDA), only about half the number who self-identified as Jehovah's Witnesses in independent demographic studies is considered active by the faith itself. It is also claimed by the Watchtower Society that only individuals who are approved and active as publishers are officially counted as members.

To illustrate the powerful control and regimentation that this religion has over its members, we refer to the following rules that they enforce. According to the instructions on page 274 of the 2019 Watchtower publication *Shepherd the Flock of God*:

> The Congregation's Publisher Records (S-21) belong to the local congregation [not the individual member whose name appears at the top of the card]. Each branch office provides direction to bodies of elders on whether to retain the records electronically or in printed form. If the records are retained electronically, the body of elders decides whether to use the form provided by the branch office or some other method that displays the same information in the same format. The congregation's field service records should contain at least 13 months of activity but no more than 36 months. (pp. 77-78) The file is divided into two sections – Active and Inactive. The section for active publishers should be arranged alphabetically, with the records subdivided into sections for (1) regular and special pioneers and field missionaries and (2) all other publishers. The section for all other publishers should be arranged by field service group. Additionally, three separate Congregation's Publisher Records should be filled out to reflect the combined monthly totals for (1) all regular and special pioneers and field missionaries, (2) all auxiliary pioneers, and (3) all other publishers. All of the records are also kept on a computer.

The latest trend by the Watchtower Society during the year 2020 is that as they have had to abandon these door-to-door visitations, in which they offer their literature for free or in return for donations, being a direct result of the world wide COVID-19 virus. They are now encouraging the writing of letters instead and let the Post Office be the messengers of the Good News, so be prepared for more junk mail in your post box. Plus they are using the internet and phone calls to try and spread the Good News of God's Kingdom. They have also told their members that they can still report the time spent writing these letters as field service in order to keep their record cards up to date as regular publishers and not be placed in the dead file. From a private comment by one of the leading helpers of the Governing Body, which he made to one of our contacts in the New York Bethel headquarters, he intimated that the door-to-door ministry will probably never be re-introduced again as there are now more practical and successful ways of spreading the good news than the futile task of knocking on doors, especially with the use of modern media and the newly planned Watchtower TV network and video studios already in the pipeline. This leading member of the Watchtower Society cryptically and also disgustingly said to a fellow elder, Maybe the Lord is using this virus in pointing out to his organization a new direction for the preaching work.

We are sure that no doubt, despite the hyperbole from their leaders, based on our research, to most members of Jehovah's Witnesses today, this will indeed be very good news about the door-to-door ministry and they will be relieved, if and when these wasteful and burdensome hours of knocking on doors is finally ended, as it will contribute to a large saving of their valuable time and energy. So, the members patiently wait for an official letter to be issued by the Governing Body to that effect. They maybe can then use the opportunity of redirecting this saved time and what it represents, to further develop a Bible trained conscience and undertake more private study of the scriptures and also remembering the scripture at Ephesians 5:16, "Making the most of the time, because the days are evil" (read also Hebrews 5:14). These sincere Christians can then discover that if they let the Bible speak for itself, they will really learn the full truth about Jesus Christ, and his father Jehovah (Yahweh) and the ransom that was paid on their behalf. They will enjoy the Grace of God and also experience the inspirational words of the

Apostle Paul at the Philippians 4:6, 7: "Do not worry about anything, but in everything by prayer and supplication with thanksgiving let your requests be made known to God. And the peace of God, which surpasses all understanding, will guard your hearts and your minds in Christ Jesus." Applying this biblical advice and counsel of Paul may prove to be one of the first steps to break free from the chains of a religious cult.

Returning to the subject of members of this religion having to report their monthly service to the Lord, a comment made by a fellow researcher into the history of Jehovah's Witnesses reported the following and is worth noting.

> When the Circuit overseer makes his regular visits to a congregation, on Tuesday during the day he meets with at least some of the Body of Elders and carefully goes over each publisher's record card. Now he will be able to do so online before he arrives. As we know, its all about streamlining and especially about control, control, control, as today all private and personal details of each and every Witness is now retained on a computer server. One thing that is obvious is that field service is not what it used to be, the majority of the reported activity is just fake service, such as hours or literature that is now just given away to avoid sales tax, the actual cost being covered by the members themselves by making donations when they collect the books and magazines from the literature department in their local Kingdom Hall. Also remember that the original reporting system started many years ago by Charles Russell was just a simple straight forward way for the colporteurs [peddlers of books] to report their sales, claim commission earned and request new supplies.

Interestingly, in the early years, full-time evangelists among these Bible Students (now known as Jehovah's Witnesses) were called colporteurs. Later, the term was discontinued, as it was claimed that it did not accurately describe the prime objective of their work, being Bible education. Moreover, the term did not represent the not-for-profit nature of their activities. Hence, today full-time ministers of Jehovah's Witnesses are called pioneers or missionaries. The potential of using and expanding this method of acting like a watchdog over all members now being required to submit a weekly or monthly report of their activity was further developed in 1919 under the personal supervision of Rutherford, a brilliant manipulative lawyer. He exploited the then existing simple system into the current highly controlled method of monitoring and controlling the individual members of the congregations, regarding their activity and level of dedication to the organization. One prominent member of the Bethel who still works in this religion's writing department and a past district overseer plus a graduate of the 10-month Gilead course for Branch overseers and special individuals, personally stated to one of our researchers; he said, that based on his long experience and observations, this field service reporting system is a modern-day curse against the organization, these are his exact words.

This unnamed individual, long-time friend of the editor along with his late dear wife Lynne from South Africa, provided this very honest and open opinion about the field service reporting system being a modern day curse, he was also one of the greatest proponents of 1975 as being the year and was personally interviewed on the BBC, which today he sadly regrets, he later stated, as he made such a fool of himself as did his fellow worker, the late Phil Rees, former Branch Servant of Australia and the former Assistant Branch Servant of Britain. Also on his LinkedIn page on the Internet, this unnamed individual now describes himself as writing consultant at Watchtower, the reason being is because he now has an exclusive private suite in the British Bethel home with all the comforts of a luxury hotel, fully paid for by the sincere donations of the members of this religion. He also still keeps himself occupied doing some research and writes short articles for the now almost defunct Awake! magazine. As one of his fellow workers in the London Bethel stated to our reporter, with some sarcasm in his voice, he has landed with his bum in the butter. [This is a phrase chiefly used in Britain and Australia that refers to being in a very fortunate or advantageous situation or position, alluding to a soft landing.] This individual; friend of the editor, has also made several important contributions to the material in this chapter of our book plus on *Wikipedia* related to the history of Jehovah's Witnesses, for which we are extremely grateful. Recently the Governing Body released a short video in 2017 of our dear, never to be forgotten, elderly friend, now aged 91 years old, under the title An Organization Second to None, in which he portrays his life story from when he converted to this religion at the age of 17 years of age. Publicly he still remains or at least portrays himself as a convinced member of Jehovah's Witnesses as being the only true religion on earth for very obvious personal reasons, despite all of his serious private misgivings about their policies and teachings. As he said recently to a close personal friend, Bethel is my home and I have nowhere else to go to.

James Penton in *Apocalypse Delayed*, states the following:

> Jehovah's Witnesses is a religion based on the business of selling books and magazines. That is why the term Publisher is used when they refer to a fellow member. Businesses collect data on sales to help make decisions. Jehovah's Witnesses literally were door-to-door salesmen for the Watchtower Bible and Tract Society. That was until the 1990s. Fears over losing their religious tax exempt status in the U.S. [prompted by the notorious Jimmy Swaggart Ministries scandal and the US Supreme Court ruling regarding sales tax] caused the Watchtower to change its model. Instead of selling their printed products, publishers were to place them with interested ones and then make sure that the person is fully aware of the donation process supporting the World Wide Work. This model failed as a business plan. As a result we saw many changes come and come quickly. Hardbound books were replaced with paperbacks. *Watchtower* and *Awake* magazines were reduced in the number of issues published and the number of pages. A new digital format has been adopted requiring members to download publications on their own electronic devices. Why the change again? For legal reasons, as I see the same being true with maintaining records on members with the recent privacy laws being passed in Europe. I could see members having to log into an account and report their activities with the servers being based in the headquarters in New York.

> Many of the old-timers might remember that in the distant past the success of the preaching work was measured by placements [sales]. There was a large information board in the lobby of the Kingdom Hall and service figures were listed there on a weekly basis, no different than any other sales organization.

At the Conventions the juiciest experiences were of the people that had the best numbers of placements (*sales*). All of this collapsed with start of the voluntary contributions, the service work has never recovered from that. They may be worried that data protection laws will harm them in future if they continue to collect this information. Plus they obviously realised that trends indicate they are entering a period of decline, and they see no advantage to continuing to collect and publish this data in these circumstances.

Plus there is a more basic point, that the Watchtower has often justified reporting time and placements on the basis that this information allows the organisation to plan their publishing activity efficiently. As they move away from print media altogether they may simply be facing up to the logic of their traditional rationale for reporting preaching and concluding that it is no longer necessary. Having said all this, I think this change has the potential to have a huge impact on the organization far beyond what the Governing Body may anticipate. It could deflate morale and accelerate the ongoing collapse of the organization. Individual reporting of time and sales of literature has been used for many years as a tool of control and judgment of spirituality. Do not forget that the bulk of Watchtower profit came from selling special and luxury items to actual members of the religion itself and not the public, for example insight books, deluxe Bibles, tapes, videos, yearbooks, Kingdom Interlinear, concordance, calendars, daily text, bound volumes, Bible stories book, and individual magazine subscriptions. I think we tend to forget just how huge Watchtower publishing used to be, and just how many items they sold to the members, before you even begin to factor in sales to the public. The profit on each item may not have been massive, but they certainly weren't selling at a loss, and with a captive market of millions it's easy to see how Watchtower Society was rolling in the money until the 1990s when the cutbacks began.

According to the current instruction book printed by the Watchtower Society called *Ministers of the Good News*, the following instructions and rules are clearly listed and obviously slanted in favor of the organization to allow them to monitor individual members.

Your individual field service report for each month is recorded on a *Congregation's Publisher Record* card. These cards are <u>not</u> personal property. If you plan to move to another congregation, be sure to inform your congregation elders. The secretary of your new congregation will request that your *Congregation's Publisher Record* card(s) be forwarded. If the secretary of your former congregation knows the name of the congregation to which you relocate, he can take the initiative in sending the record card(s) along with a letter of introduction (probably containing confidential information about your character and level of devotion to the organization). Consequently, the elders of your new congregation will be in a better position to welcome you and give you needed spiritual assistance. The latest publishers record card lists under publications placed, both printed and electronic plus video showings made [italics are added by the editor].

In order to justify this system of reporting and recording one's worship, praise and veneration of Almighty God, and then being required to report this worship by submitting a record on paper of ones genuflect, directly to the organization; the following weak argument is also included in this instruction book, *Ministers of the Good News*.

Some have asked since Jehovah knows what I am doing in his service, why do I need to put in a report to the congregation. True, Jehovah knows what we are doing, and he knows whether our service is whole-souled or just a token of what we are really able to do. Remember, however, that Jehovah recorded the number of days that Noah spent in the ark and the number of years that the Israelites journeyed in the wilderness. God kept account of the number of those who were faithful and of those who disobeyed. He recorded the progressive conquest of the land of Canaan and the accomplishments of the faithful judges of Israel. Yes, he recorded many details regarding the activities of his servants. He inspired this written record of what took place, making clear to us his view of keeping accurate records. Reports of increases help us to get an overall view of the expansion of Jehovah's organization. Experiences warm our hearts and fill us with zeal, moving us to have a fuller share in the preaching work. Our cooperation in turning in field service reports is important and shows our concern for the brothers everywhere. In this small way, we demonstrate our submission to Jehovah's organizational arrangement.

Editor's Note: This system of requiring all members of this religion to make monthly reports of their service to the Lord has evolved into a highly sophisticated system of keeping control of the movement and activity of its members, both positive and negative. This record card also included such data related to, if you claimed to be one of the anointed (heavenly chosen ones) or one of the other sheep (with the hope of living forever on the earth), plus the date you were baptized and the usual personal details, such as date of birth, married or single, etc.

An additional factor that was uncovered by our research team was related to the rules and regulations that the publishers had to follow that relate to their door-to-door sales of the Watchtower literature. Each congregation is allocated a map of the local area for which they are directly responsible to preach the good news and of a copy of this map was cut up into section and pasted on cards and called territory maps and then placed in an envelope specially designed and printed for this purpose. This territory map was accompanied by a control card that recorded the date the map was issued plus the name of the member who was now responsible for its care and both cards were placed in a box file. This was then controlled and supervised by one of the ministerial servants who was known as the territory servant and it was his task to issue these maps to the publisher or pioneer who requested one or maybe a field service leader who was supervising a group of members. This very efficient control system made sure that no local area was omitted or neglected in receiving the Message of the Kingdom. Of course, other local ministerial servants had other duties, such as the literature servant who controlled the book room in each Kingdom Hall and kept inventory and sales to local members. Plus, he had to complete a stock taking report every six months, which had to be forwarded to the branch office for double checking. As most of this literature sent out to congregations was on credit and if any shortfall of the stock occurred or accounts did not balance, then the local congregation had to cover the loss.

An additional strictly regulated practice was the way each baptized member received a copy of an instruction booklet titled *Preaching and Teaching In Peace and Unity*, which he or she had to sign and date under the specified line on page one, that displayed the words, "This booklet has been issued to" and in addition was a space for the signature of a witness, usually the senior member of the Service Committee known as the Assistant Congregation Servant, later renamed Congregation Secretary or Field Overseer. This signing procedure then became and was viewed as a legally binding commitment by the publisher to obey the suggestions and recommendations of the Watchtower Society. Upon the release of this new booklet in the 1960s, the Governing Body sent a confidential covering letter to all service committees that consisted in those days of the Congregation Servant, Assistant Congregation Servant and the Bible Study Servant; the letter stated that this booklet was simply suggestions and recommendations of the Society. This was another clear case and example of the very deceptive manipulative statements made by the Governing Body of this religion, as the use of this phrase suggestions and recommendations was nothing more than the expedient and clever use of words, as this new booklet was nothing more than a rule book. This confidential covering letter also gave instructions that all members had to always bring their personal copy of their booklet, (rule book) to the weekly Service Meeting along with their monthly copy of the bulletin or newsletter called the *Informant* but later renamed the Kingdom Ministry.

What illustrates the erratic behavior and inconsistency of the head office and Governing Body of this religion is how they frequently, by yo-yoing around, changed the name of this monthly newsletter. It was originally known as the Bulletin from the early years and then in 1936 renamed, The Informant and then again in 1956 as Kingdom Ministry. A few years later it was changed to Our Kingdom Ministry then along came 1976, another change, Our Kingdom Service and then in 1982 back again to Our Kingdom Ministry. There was nothing cryptic, inimical or harmful in this regular change of the name of this free four-page information sheet, as our contact in the Watchtower head office scrupulously checked the minutes of the Governing Body meetings for each of these years and confirmed that these changes were made by unanimous vote and the only comment they made, according to the official records was, this change of name is more appropriate. However, one member of the Governing Body, who is named as Lyman Swingle, had suggested and was unanimously adopted, according to the minutes of the 1956 meeting, he thought the title Informant suggested a political slant and sounded like some kind of undercover operation and maybe confuse the public about what the duties of the members of Jehovah's Witness performed, perhaps secretly under the table. We need to remind ourselves that Lyman Swingle, referred to in other sections of this chapter, was of a German background and he still had in his vivid memory, Nazi Germany and their treatment of the Jews and the practice of informing on their fellow Jews in return for favors.

One ex-member who worked in the writing department of Watchtower Society told our reporter that the change to Service from Ministry was brought about by Ray Franz of the Governing Body, but, as Ray was now labeled an apostate, they changed the name back again to Ministry. Our informant after checking the minutes of the meeting in 1976 when this change took place, he could find no record of this remark or any suggestion by Raymond Franz. Another comment was made by another source in the head office of the Watchtower Society who told us that the word Service was not emphasizing the preaching work enough, so they returned to using the word Ministry in 1982 and was not related to Raymond Franz being excommunicated in 1981. In a private letter dated January, 1982 from the Governing Body to all Branch Offices they stated the following:

> Dear Brothers: How we rejoiced over the article on God's Ministers in the March 15, 1981, issue of *The Watchtower*! As stated on page 18: All dedicated and baptized Christians, regardless of sex or age, can be proclaimers, preachers, ministers ... provided they give proof thereof by their conduct and their witnessing. As the apostle Paul did, we, too, desire to glorify our ministry? Is that not the way you feel about it? In harmony with the information recently published on this subject, it is most appropriate that the title of this publication now appears as Our Kingdom Ministry.

We believe this monthly newsletter; *Our Kingdom Ministry*, has now been abandoned completely. This was brought about after the closure of the Theocratic Ministry School in 2015 and the remaining Service Meeting was renamed as, Our Christian Life and Ministry Meeting with the following instructions:

> This meeting will proceed as outlined in the Our Christian Life and Ministry Meeting Workbook and according to the instructions that follow. All publishers should be invited to make themselves available to present student assignments. Others who are actively associating with the congregation may participate if they agree with the teachings of the Bible and their life is in harmony with Christian principles.

This new meeting, its new title and workbook was an amalgamation of the now defunct Congregation Book Study meeting, classified as being dangerous and encouraged private speculation and prospective apostates, plus also the now defunct Theocratic Ministry School, classified by the Governing Body as unnecessary, as all teaching and instructing was now to be provided by themselves and their helpers by means of videos and film.

In this new booklet *Preaching and Teaching In Peace and Unity*, the publisher was given clear instructions and rules on how to use a special form provided, known as the House-to-House Report Form (S-8), plus other forms that he or she had to complete and record, as part of their duties as an active member of this religion. To illustrate how the control and regimentation of this religion is strictly monitored you can simply view and search on Google under forms of the Watchtower Society and, listed there by some dedicated individual, are the names and reference codes of hundreds upon hundreds of required forms and documentation to enable the Watchtower Society to tightly operate and control this religion. Special holders for these S-8 forms can still by bought at Etsy online sales company, described as: this is a House-to-House Record Holder in ENGLISH, with ten different colors to choose from. These products were available at least up until the latest and final abandonment in 2020 of the door-to-door visitation work by the Watchtower Society. These record holders were privately manufactured by one enterprising member of this religion, but of course are now no longer needed. One satisfied customer wrote on the Etsy website, "exactly what I needed! I never had a pen, when I needed one or couldn't remember where I put my House-to-House records, this holder has eliminated those issues. Great product, great quality and fast shipping!"

The recording of the time spent preaching and selling the Watchtower literature was recorded on a Field Service Report (S-4) and one ex-circuit servant confessed that on many occasions it was suspect as to how accurate these records were. Apart from the fact that in many cases it was fake time just to keep the elders happy or to keep the elders out of their hair, so to speak, and there was often confusion as to how the time was to be recorded or counted. Did you start counting your time from the minute you knocked in the first door? Or did you count your time from the minute you left home for field service activity, even though it took you perhaps one hour to get the location of the territory map? Some members who were instructed to do street work simply stood on a street corner and called out "Stay Awake" by reading the *Awake* and never spoke to anyone or sold a single magazine, but they recorded this as time spent in their so-called ministry and service to the Lord. He also pointed that some engaged in the so-called street work and spent their time wandering or strolling up and down the sidewalks trying to accost passers-by with their magazines, but being rebuffed 99% of the time by the irritated public. Was this really worship of God or simply the blind obedience to the masters of this organization in order to display their dedication to the Almighty? These members were still instructed to record all of this time spent as worship and recorded on their monthly field service report.

So the Watchtower Society never really knew what figures were accurate or not, although they were proudly published in the Annual Year Book in any event and proclaimed as a sign of Gods blessing on the organization. This same ex-circuit servant also regretfully confessed that he had on occasions advised some special pioneers under his supervision that if they could not meet their required goal of 150 hours for any particular month because of circumstances beyond their control, which was a prerequisite for them to receive their small monthly payment from the Society treasury to help them survive. He suggested that they just enter the figure 150 hours, sign their report and request form and leave this decision between themselves, their conscience and Jehovah. To many sincere and honest Christians this might appear to be a clear case of fraud and dishonesty that these special pioneers were compelled to commit, because of these strict rules laid down by their religion. It is also worth noting that these regular and special pioneers could buy their literature supplies from their local congregation at a huge discounted price so that when they sold the literature to the public, they could pocket the huge profits made. This discrepancy was then made up by head office, but the Watchtower Society was not losing out, as the actual price of producing this literature in the first place was in the pennies, as the entire staff of the workers in the printery was on a voluntary basis.

To the credit of the Watchtower Society, they developed the most sophisticated and efficient methods of managing, controlling and recording sales of their literature and were envied by many secular marketing and sales companies. In fact, some businesses even studied and adopted the same techniques with great success. The use of the psychological tactic of setting goals and targets, as secular sales companies employed, was also successfully exploited. It became the standard goal of all active publishers to try and meet the target of personally achieving ten hours each month in field service, six return visits (back-calls they were known as) and at least one home Bible study each month. Meeting these goals was used by the branch office as an important barometer in deciding who could qualify as a regular, special pioneer or missionary, and in the case of male members it was used as a touch stone of their spiritual qualifications for those who could qualify as a ministerial servant and the ultimate desired goal of all male members, that of being appointed as an elder or overseer. The motivation and task of achieving, plus striving to meet these goals by the publishers was often the major content and theme of many lectures and service talks given by the leaders of the organization, lectures that had very little spiritual content, except they would use God's name and how pleased he was to see such wonderful statistics and figures being accomplished. Each congregation had a weekly meeting dedicated to discussing methods and techniques of how to improve and increase the sales of the Watchtower literature. This weekly meeting, usually held every Thursday evening, was at that time named the Service Meeting.

One of our research team came across a fascinating story about the use of the House-to-House Record Form (S-8) being used by the publishers and pioneers. This form allows space to record any useful information regarding the call made at each home, for example what religion the householder belonged to, if a Mezuzah or crucifix was displayed on the door frame, what subjects were of interest to them, not interested, etc., this kind of information was useful when planning to make a return visit, or a back call. The form even had abbreviated codes at the top, for example NH (not home), NI (not interested) plus of course the main use was to personally record the number of magazines or books sold that was later transferred to their weekly or monthly service report. On some occasions if the home owner tended to be volatile or offensive and strongly resented these calls, or they had a dangerous dog, this was entered on the S-8 form and slipped into the territory card envelope. On one occasion as a loyal publisher left the gateway to a dwelling in London; the householder to whom he had just presented the literature, became extremely irritated, which was a frequent occurrence, the householder came storming down the pathway and demanded to see what the publisher was recording in his house-to-house record form. Much to the embarrassment of this particular publisher and to the bitter anger of the householder, as he vehemently claimed it was a violation of privacy, as the publisher had written on his S-8 form, 'appears to be an atheist', which the householder definitely was not.

Another example of keeping records, much to the detriment of this religion and that has created some concerns for the Governing Body of this cult are the records of their financial dealings. For instance, external scrutiny of the Watchtower Society bank accounts and financial records by government departments are of concern, as this religion is registered as a non-profit. These records may reveal that certain individuals involved with the leadership of this religion or by the use of front companies benefitted financially from their relationship with the Watchtower Society in ways that may appear unfair, unscrupulous or even corrupt and downright illegal. In the case of Russell and Rutherford during the early years of this cult there is no question about this unethical practice based on accurate records uncovered, so we have no reason but to assume that this same modus operandi continues today amongst some of the leaders of this religion. Our research team uncovered and also received quite a number of first-hand reports of suspected cases of blatant misuse of their position by leading members of this religion involving mercenary and venal actions, but we were unable to obtain or uncover sufficient irrefutable records and evidence, so we decided to omit these reported cases from this narrative based on the principle of 'curia advisari vult' (Latin meaning still under consideration).

Raymond Franz; ex-member of this religions Governing Body, in his book, Crisis of Conscience, spoke about the report card as a means of exerting pressure on publishers and prospective full-time workers, those hoping to advance in their career in the Watchtower organization. When the possibility was discussed by the Governing Body about ending the obligation to report time and sales, some of the Governing Body members were worried that this would result in publishers doing nothing and as a result dramatically reduce the income of the Organization. He also mentioned and emphasized that the essential purpose of the preaching work, which was to sell and distribute the Societies literature. Raymond Franz also suggested that many monitory transactions made by the organization looked suspicious and was probably illegal, which will be analyzed later in this report.

It is interesting to note that the older publisher record cards (S-21) had the option of the congregation secretary, or field service servant (also known as the Assistant Congregation Servant) ticking one of two boxes, one indicating Anointed, the other box Jonadab, the later record cards changed this to Anointed (AN) or Other Sheep (OS). The term, Jonadab or Jehonadab class was an invention of Frederick Franz based on one of his crazy and wild interpretations of the Bible, referring to the record of King Jehu of Israel and his non-Israelite supporter Jehonadab. This erroneous interpretation invented by Frederick Franz under his heading of types and antitypes was used in his many books; acting as ghost writer for Rutherford, but has now been secretly dropped in recent years so you now find that the current Governing Body very rarely uses this term. Today, you will also not find the term, Jonadab class, used in their current literature as most of these obscure interpretations of types and anti-types promulgated by Frederick Franz from way back have been dropped for obvious reasons.

***

One of last books that Frederick Franz wrote, or was at least intricately involved with its contents, was called *Your Will Be Done on Earth*, published in 1958 by the Watchtower Society. It presented the most ludicrous interpretation of the Prophet Daniel's records in the Bible related to the world powers at his time in history, being 618 BC to 536 BC. Fred Franz transposed these events from this ancient time into his claim of them being simply types and more important in the 20th century the anti-types, according to his interpretation, stating that the king of the north was now Russia and the king of the south was America. The members of this religion have to accept this rubbish or hog-wash as it was presented to them and diligently studied by them at their Bible meetings, supposedly provided by the Governing Body claiming to be under divine guidance and inspiration. It has also been claimed that much of this material by Fred Franz was plagiarized or adapted from the older writings in the 1930s of Herbert Armstrong of the Radio Church of God and his *Plain Truth* magazine.

Quoting from *Wikipedia*: "Witnesses believe that exactly 144,000 men and women will reign with Jesus Christ in heaven, out of all Christians who have died since Jesus' resurrection. They refer to these as the anointed or spiritual Israel, and those still living are referred to as the remnant. Witnesses believe that, in a similar manner to Jehonadab, as a non-Jew, assisting Jehu, the Jonadab class assists spiritual Israel."

The August 15, 1934 *The Watchtower* stated:

> The Jonadab class are of those who 'hear' the message of truth and who must say to those in their hearing: Come. "And let him that heareth say, Come. And let him that is athirst come. And whosoever will, let him take the water of life freely." (Rev. 22:17) Those of the Jonadab class must go along with those who are of the antitypical Jehu company, that is, the anointed ones, and announce the message of the kingdom, even though they are not of the anointed witnesses of Jehovah and not allowed to partake of the bread and wine at the annual memorial.

Pastor Charles Russell had advertised for 1,000 preachers in 1881, two years after he started publishing his *Zion's Watchtower Magazine*, also very quickly filling these positions of service and he arranged to pay them a commission for selling his magazine and soon to be published book *The Divine Plan of the Ages*. This was the beginning of the main focus of the Watchtower Society and the primary purpose of its function of being a publisher, printer and seller of Bible literature and the introduction of these colporteurs (book peddlers). These 1,000 recruits plus the others who quickly joined the ranks were not in fact preachers in the true sense of the word but simply book sales people and this has been the modus operandi of the Watchtower Society even up into the 21st century. Russell also encouraged all who were members of the body of Christ to preach to their neighbors, in order to gather the remnant of the little flock of 144,000 saints, while the vast majority of mankind would be given the opportunity to gain salvation during Christ's coming 1,000-year reign due to start very soon he claimed. Russell's supporters gathered as autonomous congregations to study the Bible and his writings. Russell rejected the concept of a formal organization as wholly unnecessary for his followers and declared that his group had no record of its member's names, no creeds, and no sectarian name. He wrote in February 1884: "By whatsoever names men may call us, it matters not to us... we call ourselves simply Christians."

Elders and deacons were elected democratically by individual congregations and Russell tolerated great latitude of belief among members. He opposed formal disciplinary procedures by congregation elders, claiming this was beyond their authority, instead recommending that an individual who continued in a wrong course be judged by the entire congregation, which could ultimately withdraw from him its fellowship if the undesirable behavior continued. Disfellowshipping did not mean the wrongdoer was to be shunned in all social circumstances or by all Bible Students, though fellowship would be limited. From 1895, Russell encouraged congregations to study his Bible textbook series, Studies in the Scriptures, paragraph by paragraph to properly discern God's plan for humanity. In 1905 he recommended replacing verse-by-verse Bible studies with what he called the Berean Studies of topics he chose. The Watchtower Society meantime opened overseas branches in London (1900), Germany (1903), and Australia and Switzerland (1904). The Society's headquarters were also transferred from Pittsburg, Pennsylvania to Brooklyn, New York in 1909 under the advisement of their newly appointed legal counsel Joseph Rutherford.

This new Bible edition known as the Berean Bible produced by the Watchtower Society included the King James Version of the Bible but with added notes directly referring to Russell's articles in his various publications and became a valuable asset to his followers. According to the Bible, Acts of the Apostles 17:11, the apostle Paul and Silas had preached at Berea, Macedonia and the inhabitants had, received the word with all readiness of mind, and searched the scriptures daily, whether those things were so. A new Protestant Christian group began in the 1850s in the United States under the tutelage of Dr. John Thomas. The name Christadelphian was chosen as it is believed that those who believe and obey the Commandments of Christ and the Bible as the inspired word of God are Brethren in Christ. The original group split, with one group continuing with the name The Christadelphians and the second group adding the word Berean to become the Berean Christadelphians (see Chapter Six).

A member of our research team received a donated copy of the Berean Bible, being the Bible Students Edition of the Holy Bible (King James Version) printed by W. H. Bagster and Phelps, dated 1909. This Bible also contained the large section known as the Berean Bible Teachers Manual of approximately 481 pages. This masterful production is a great tool for serious researchers into the history of the original teachings of Charles Russell who founded the Watchtower Society in 1879. The Manual is in 4 parts, plus an Index.

Part I. *Zion's Watch Tower & Dawn Series* & 6 Volumes of *Studies in the Scriptures* personally edited by C. J. Woodworth.

Part II. *Instructors Guide* edited by G. W. Seibert

Part III. *Berean Topical Index* edited by G. W. Seibert

Part IV. *Difficult Texts Explained* edited by C. J. Woodworth

Index to Scripture. Citations in the *Watch Tower* magazine (From Jan. 1, 1908 to Jan. 1, 1916, incl.), plus a very useful concordance.

An advert related to the *Berean Bible*,
courtesy of the MTC International Foundation
and Getty Images

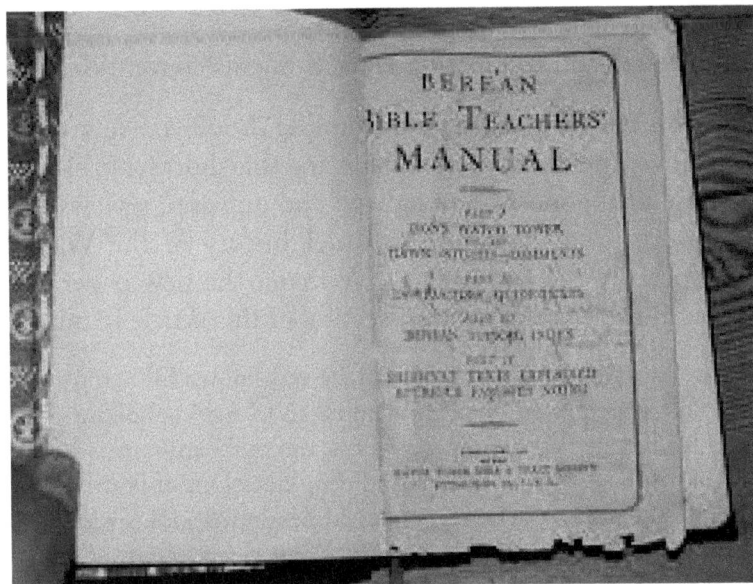

Inside of the *Berean Bible*, the section, *Berean Bible Teachers Manual*, courtesy of the MTC International Foundation

In 1910 Russell introduced the name, International Bible Students Association (IBSA) as a means of identifying his worldwide community of Bible study groups. He wrote: Now in the Lord's providence we have thought of a title suitable, we believe, to the Lord's people everywhere, and free from objection, we believe, on every score – the title at the head of this article (IBSA). It fairly represents our sentiments and endeavors. We are Bible students. We welcome all of God's people to join with us in the study. We believe that the result of such studies is blessed and unifying. We recommend therefore that the little classes everywhere and the larger ones adopt this unobjectionable style and that they use it in the advertising columns of their newspapers. Thus, friends everywhere will know how to recognize them when visiting strange cities. Russell also explained that the Association (IBSA) would be directed and managed by the Peoples Pulpit Association, which in turn, represented the Watch Tower Bible & Tract Society, Inc. All Bible Student classes using Watchtower Society publications could consider themselves identified with the Association and were authorized to use the name International Bible Students Association

(IBSA) in connection with their meetings. The name was also used when advertising and conducting Bible Students conventions.

We quote this enlightening extract from the Brooklyn, New York, news archives source, The Brownstoner Daily, and this short synopsis probably provides one of the most unprejudiced and unbiased reviews available today regarding the origins and a brief history of the Watchtower Society, especially the early years. We thank the newspaper for their permission to use a small, relevant section of this article in our book.

> Russell was an intense young man, he was known for being very interested in religion, and had taken to writing hellfire and brimstone Bible verses on fences and billboards around town. But he had very serious and deep questions of faith. Before the age of 20, he had changed denominations several times and investigated other religions, but never found satisfactory answers to his questions. In 1870, he and other fellow seekers began a Bible study group. They concluded that modern Christianity had strayed from true Biblical teachings, due to incorrect translations of important Bible verses and cultural pollution. Russell joined Nelson Barbour, who had predicted Christ's physical return in April of 1878. Russell sold his haberdashery business for a sizable sum of money, and spent two years of his life spreading the word of the Second Coming. When Barbours prophesy did not come to pass, many followers left him. But Russell was positive that Barbour had only miscalculated the date, not the event. He searched the Scriptures and came up with a new timetable: Christ would definitely return in 1914.
>
> Nelson H. Barbour (1824 -1905) was an influential Adventist writer and publisher, best known for his association with and later opposition to Charles Taze Russell. Adventists in the Geneseo area [a town in Livingston County in the Finger Lakes region of New York] met in Springwater to await the second coming of Christ in 1843. Their disappointment was profound, and Barbour suffered a crisis of faith. He later wrote: We held together until the autumn of 1844. Then, as if a raft floating in deep water should suddenly disappear from under its living burden, so our platform went from under us, and we made for shore in every direction; but our unity was gone, and,

like drowning men, we caught at straws. As 1873 approached, various religious groups began advocating it as significant. Jonas Wendell led one, another centered on the magazine The Watchman's Cry and the rest were associated with Barbour. British Barbourites were represented by Elias H. Tuckett, a clergyman based in Knightsbridge, London. Many gathered at Terry Island, New York to await the return of Christ in late 1873. Barbour and others looked to the next year, which also proved disappointing.

Led by Benjamin Wallace Keith, an associate of Barbours since 1867, the group adopted the belief in a two-stage, initially an invisible presence. They believed that Christ had indeed come invisibly in 1874 and would soon become visible for judgments.

Editor's Note: Forty years later in 1914 according to Russell's calculations mentioned many times in Scripture, the number 40 generally symbolizes a period of testing, trial or probation. Also, it often relates to the description of a generation in the Bible]. Barbour started a magazine in the fall of 1873 to promote his views, calling it *The Midnight Cry*. It was first issued as a pamphlet, with no apparent expectation of becoming a periodical. He quickly changed the name to *Herald of the Morning*, issuing it monthly from January, 1874. In December, 1875, Charles Taze Russell, then a businessman from Allegheny, received a copy of *Herald of the Morning*. He met the principals in the Barbourite movement and arranged for Barbour to speak in Philadelphia in 1876. Barbour and Russell began their association, during which Barbour wrote the book *Three Worlds* (1877) and published a small booklet by Russell entitled *Object and Manner of Our Lord's Return*.

Charles Taze Russell taken in 1911, aged 59 years old,
courtesy of *The Brownstoner Daily* and Creative Commons

The article in *The Brownstoner Daily* continues.

In a May 22, 1879 letter to Barbour, Russell explicitly resigned: Now I leave the Herald with you. I withdraw entirely from it, asking nothing from you ... Please announce in next No. of the Herald the dissolution and withdraw my name (as assistant editor on the masthead). In July 1879, Russell began publishing *Zion's Watch Tower & Herald of Christ's Presence*, the principal journal of the Bible Student movement. Several years after Russell's death, the magazine became associated with Jehovah's Witnesses and was renamed simply as *The Watchtower*.

Editor's Note: They removed the word Zion from the title as the increasing use of this word was associated with the now worldwide powerful Zionist movement of the Jewish people demanding a return of their claimed homeland from the Palestinians, then known as Palestine, under British rule, which they eventually succeeded in 1948 by United Nations mandate and became modern day Israel.

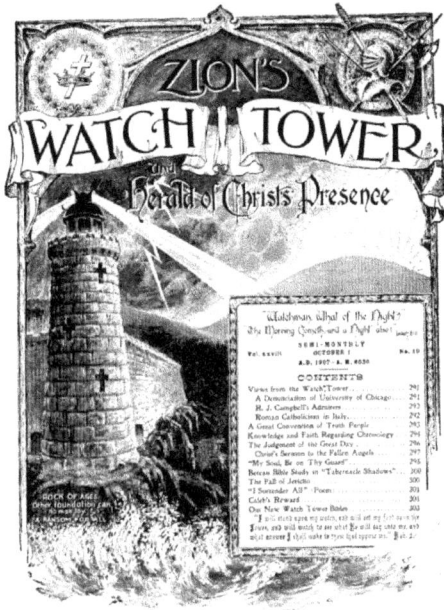

Cover of *Zion's Watch Tower and Herald of Christ's Presence*, October 1, 1907,
courtesy of *The Brownstoner Daily* and Creative Commons
(Note the cross & crown and the title *Zion's*)

In 1908, the Watchtower Bible and Tract Society had outgrown
Allegheny in Pennsylvania and decided to move everything to
Brooklyn, New York, and set up its headquarters and printing
operations here. Brooklyn was chosen because it was a large,
well-known city – the City of Churches, with a large religious
middle class. Newspapers at the time printed and syndicated
the sermons of Brooklyn's best pastors, and Russell was
determined to be one of them. After all, there wasn't much
time to waste. As the *Watchtower* published in 1908, Brooklyn
was "our most suitable center for the harvest work during the
few remaining years (underlining is by the Editor). Russellites
believed Jesus was sent from God, but he was not God. After
death the soul went to sleep. The faithful would be awakened
to join God's heavenly kingdom on earth. And that day was
coming soon – in 1914.

The Eagles newspaper of Brooklyn focused on a campaign to discredit this new religion founded by Russell. To say *The Eagles* management did not like Russell would be an understatement. From the beginning, they called the Society a sect and a cult, not a church. In 1911, *The Eagles* reported that Russell was bilking the public with Miracle Wheat. The Virginia grain was developed to be superior to regular wheat. Russell packaged it for sale as Miracle Wheat. It wasn't!

The Eagles newspaper printed a number of scathing articles and cartoons. Russell was furious, and in 1911 sued *The Eagles* for slander and libel. The resulting trial brought up not only the issues with the wheat, but Russell's personal life, the Society's theology and its finances. (Including the sordid details of the divorce trial instituted by his wife and also her claims for half ownership of the Watchtower valuable assets). *The Eagles* newspaper boasted on the eve of trial that the case would show that Pastor Russells cult was little more than a money-making scheme. After a very long trial, Russell lost the case. *The Eagles* danced at his defeat. Even in the very beginning, the Watchtower Society relied on volunteers to operate the presses and staff shipping rooms. These volunteers dedicated years to their work and were paid only pennies, while living in dormitories and group housing. Many observers saw this as a sure sign of cult behavior even as far back as 1910.

The Brooklyn Eagle, August 14, 1909 also reported, his wife, whom he married 30 years ago, when she was Maria F. Ackley, obtained a limited divorce from him in Pittsburg on the ground of cruelty. The judge who decided for Mrs. Russell granted her $100 per month alimony. Pastor Russell was always slow in coming to the front with payments and finally stopped paying alimony altogether. An order was issued for the pastor's arrest in Pittsburg, but Brooklyn is a comfortable enough place and Pastor Russell didn't like going back to Pittsburg where a yawning prison awaited him. He said that his friends had paid the alimony, anyhow, and that he was purged of contempt of court thereby. (In a further newspaper report of the day it stated, his wife divorced him in 1897 on charges of adultery with two different women, a stenographer and a housemaid; and that the judge flayed him, after granting the divorce, for his general ill-treatment of his wife. To avoid payment of the alimony ordered by the court, Russell promptly transferred his property and wealth, worth over $240,000, to the Watch Tower Bible and Tract Society.

In 1912, a minister in Hamilton, Ontario, sued Russell for defrauding the public and denounced his qualifications and legitimacy as a pastor. Russell countersued for libel. The case brought out more discrepancies in Russell's claims as a religious scholar: Russell re-translated the New Testament, yet neither spoke nor read Greek? The case ended with no decision and no award. Russell went back to Brooklyn. 1914 arrived. The faithful waited for Christ's return, but were instead greeted with the beginning of World War I. Russell then interpreted this to mean that the Last Days were indeed approaching. There was no time! He took to the road, preaching across the country. He was gone so often that his congregation in Brooklyn rarely heard him preach. Other leaders, especially Joseph Rutherford, began taking a more active role. Russell was burning the candle at both ends. He got sick but kept going. As he passed through Texas on a train heading home to Brooklyn, he died on October 31, 1916. He was buried in Pittsburgh. He was only 64 years old, but with his Biblical long white beard he looked much older. Joseph Rutherford was voted to succeed Pastor Russell. He transformed the Watchtower Society's beliefs and practices so significantly that he changed the group's name to Jehovah's Witnesses to separate them from the teachings of the Russellites.

Editor's Note: According to the research by Barbara Anderson in her report, Watchtower Documents she revealed the following: Mrs. Russell (1850-1938) was awarded the divorce because the court believed Pastor Russell was guilty of the many indignities she claimed he heaped upon her. She proved she was not guilty of the malicious rumors her husband spread: that she was a supporter of women's rights (dirty words in those days); that her object was to obtain control of the Watch Tower magazine, and that she parted from him because of her desire for personal prominence. Further, while reading the account of the death of Charles Taze Russell in the December 1, 1916 Watch Tower, I discovered Charles Taze Russell and his wife had a celibate marriage. This really took me by surprise. When I inquired whether this obscure fact was going to be published in the new (*Watchtower*) history book, the answer was, "No, the Governing Body decided the information might cause many of the flock to stumble."

The Pyramid monument to Charles Taze Russell next to his grave in Rosemont, Pittsburg, courtesy of C. Baile and Creative Commons (note the cross & crown on the face of this pedestal)

The *Watchtower* magazine of January 15, 1955, presented a watered-down version of this serious issue between Russell and his wife. Quoting from the *Watchtower* and referring to this relationship we read.

> The former Maria Frances Ackley, [wife of Charles Russell], who had become a co-laborer and a contributor of articles to the *Watch Tower* magazine. They came to have no children. Nearly eighteen years later, in 1897, due to Watchtower Society members objecting to a woman teaching and being a member of the board of directors contrary to 1 Timothy 2:12, Russell and his wife disagreed about the management of the journal, *Zion's Watch Tower*. Thereupon she voluntarily separated herself.

> This separation was despite the public statement by Charles Russell in his article that appeared in 1894. C.T. Russell, A Conspiracy Exposed, *Zion's Watch Tower Extra* edition, April 25, 1894, pp. 55-60, The affairs of the Society are so arranged that its entire control rests in the care of Brother and Sister Russell as long as they shall live. The fact is that, by the grace of God, Sister R. and myself have been enabled not only to give our own time without charge to the service of the truth, in writing and overseeing, but also to contribute more money to the Tract Society's fund for the scattering of the good tidings, than all others combined.

The report found in *Wikipedia* provides more information and background about Charles Russell and his control of the Watchtower Society and the private advice he received from his now very shrewd, influential, manipulative newly appointed legal counsel, Joseph Rutherford, who was now already secretly planning to eventually take over complete control of this religion when the opportunity arose. Rutherford was also fully aware of Charles Russell's debilitating personal problems, his divorce and his deteriorating health, which is confirmed from existing records. The advice, guidance, directions and strategy provided by Joseph Rutherford, being legal counsel to the somewhat naïve President of the Watchtower Society Charles Russell, are clearly and unmistakably seen from the tactics and planning by this scheming lawyer Rutherford from 1907 onward.

Quoting from *Wikipedia*:

> From 1908 Russell required the directors to write out resignations when they were appointed, so Russell could dismiss them by simply filling in the date.[6] In 1909, Russell requested legal counsel Joseph Franklin Rutherford to determine whether the society's headquarters could be moved to Brooklyn, New York. Rutherford reported that because it had been established under Pennsylvania law, the corporation could not be registered in New York State, but suggested that a new corporation be registered there to do the society's work. Rutherford subsequently organized the formation of the People's Pulpit Association, which was incorporated on February 23, 1909, and Rutherford conveniently wrote the charter, which gave the president [current or future] to be elected for life at the first meeting with absolute power and control of its activities in New York. The society then sold its buildings in Pittsburgh and moved all staff to its new base in Brooklyn.

Although all the New York property was bought in the name of the New York Corporation and all legal affairs of the society done in its name, Russell insisted on the continued use of the Watch Tower Bible and Tract Society of Pennsylvania name on all correspondence and publications. The move from Pennsylvania to New York occurred during court proceedings over the breakdown of Russell's marriage. His wife Maria had been granted a limited divorce[7] on March 4, 1908, but in 1909 returned to court in Pittsburgh to request an increase in alimony, which her former husband had refused. Authors and researchers Barbara Grizzuti Harrison and Edmond C. Gruss have claimed Russell's move to Brooklyn was motivated by his desire to transfer from the jurisdiction of the Pennsylvania courts. They claim he transferred all his assets to the Watchtower Society so he could declare himself bankrupt and avoid being jailed for failure to pay alimony, no doubt under advisement by his scheming lawyer Rutherford.

---

[6] This practice was both illegal and unethical but was no doubt a tactic recommended and employed by his scheming lawyer Joseph Rutherford.

[7] A limited divorce in America is a legal action where a couple's separation is supervised by the court. A limited divorce does not end the marriage. A limited divorce is generally used by people who: do not yet have grounds for absolute divorce; need financial relief; and are unable to settle their differences privately.

This plan and scheme now left Charles Russell without any personal wealth, which had been quite substantial, as it was all transferred to the bank account of the Watchtower Society. Russell was of course still the President and still had some measure of control over these funds, however when he died a few years later these funds remained in the bank account of the Watchtower Society and now would fall under the direct control of its new President for life, whoever that person was to be voted into that office, plus to a limited extent the other directors. Indeed, a brilliant plot and scheme that this ambitious lawyer Joseph Rutherford had firmly set in place for when he took over absolute control a few years later in 1916.

***

At the outset of this section of our research regarding religious slavery and the specific mentioning of these two religious groups, the Mormons and Jehovah's Witnesses by the Cult Awareness Network, we are fully aware that there are many other religious groups that have a modus operandi very similar to these two religions. Therefore our observations and recommendation to all our readers, is to carefully check by using a modicum of common sense that our personal religious beliefs and loyalties, plus that our Bible based conscience is not being manipulated or controlled by a religion organization and its leaders. Many of these men may try to dictate what you are to believe with respect to Bible doctrine and how your personal conscience is to react to certain given situations in life, in other words, avoid becoming a religious slave! These actions are also viewed as nothing more than brain washing by some individuals. Brainwashing, also known as mind control, menticide, coercive persuasion, thought control, thought reform, and re-education is the concept that the human mind can be altered or controlled by certain psychological techniques. Brainwashing is said to reduce its subject's ability to think critically or independently, to allow the introduction of new, unwanted thoughts and ideas into the subject's mind, as well as to change his or her attitudes, values, and beliefs.

Does the local rank and file of Jehovah's Witnesses require all these rules and regulations or can they trust their own Bible trained conscience? This comment by highly respected Randy Watters, ex-Witness and past leading member of the New York headquarters makes a valid point in answer to this question.

> Milton Herschel, a member of the Governing Body, once said over another matter of conscience. "If we let the brothers do this, there is no telling how far they will go." This is in direct conflict with the Apostle Paul's words at Romans 7:6 and Galatians 2:16-21; 3:10, so the Governing Body deemed it necessary to lay down rules to keep the brothers in line. Over and over I would hear it echoed among those in positions of responsibility at Bethel. "You just can't trust the brothers to themselves." In other words, the average JWs love for Jehovah was seemingly not able to keep him out of trouble; he needed to have rules, curfews and restrictions to govern all aspects of his life.

This statement by a leading member of the Governing Body of the Watchtower Society clearly requires that the followers of Jehovah's Witnesses need to be kept in chains and led along as slaves on the so-called right path, for their own good and protection. The following expression by a leading member of our research group is worth noting, "My own personal observations are based on spending many years of intense study of the scriptures of the Holy Bible and my investigation of many religious groups; some still successfully operating but many others having failed their members and have gone by the wayside. No matter what title a religious leader may display; be it Priest, Right Reverend, Doctor of Divinity, Vicar, Overseer, Elder or Bishop, we are also reminded that although many members of religious groups feel a measure of security and protection by being under the supervision of these so-called shepherds of the flock. But we must always remember that the Creator still endowed us with the intelligence and Bible based conscience and therefore a free will to decide our acceptance or rejection of certain doctrines and beliefs promulgated by these religious leaders."

Members of our research team, having had personal first-hand experience of the Mormons, Jehovah's Witnesses, Scientology plus a few other minor religious groups submitted a report on their findings, which we are now willing to share with our readers. The following report was submitted to our research team, by a long serving but now ex-member of the Watchtower Society, who also requested that his name be withheld for family reasons.

When Rutherford, by manipulation gained total control of the Watchtower Society and its assets after the early death of Pastor Russell, he had other plans and schemes in mind besides changing the name of this religion from Russellites or Bible Students. He also created in his legal mind, by brilliant psychological maneuvers, auto-suggestion and a skilled technique to change some of the minor teachings and doctrines of the Watchtower Society, mainly to try and separate, plus distance the religion away from the old Russellites and the many splinter groups, plus the established system of Christendom and its nominal churches.

For example, Rutherford used the common, popular and accepted issue of celebrating birthdays and Christmas practiced by most of the world. Pastor Russell and his associates, although somewhat misguided at the time on many issues, but who were also very sincere, dedicated Christians with a deep knowledge of the Bible; far deeper than Joseph Rutherford, who was simply a clever, scheming lawyer with very little Bible knowledge, and they had openly celebrated these events without any problem related to their personal conscience or biblical teachings up until Rutherford took over control of this organization. There is available a copyrighted photograph taken in 1926 of a Christmas Tree being prominently displayed in the lobby of the Watchtower headquarters in Brooklyn, New York, plus a photo, (displayed below) of the Watchtower staff celebrating Christmas dinner, including Rutherford and Frederick Franz. In addition Rutherford had by this time been now searching for a new name for his religion, now completely and totally under his autocratic, narcissistic control and he found one with the assistance of his guru prophet Frederick Franz.

The last time Christmas celebrated at the Brooklyn Bethel of the Watchtower Society in 1926, courtesy of Creative Commons

This new name for the Bible Students was created by Rutherford and his prophetic guru Fred Franz after searching the Bible for a creative sounding new title and they came across the verse in Isaiah 43:12, which say in the King James Authorized Version, "Ye are my witnesses, says the utterance of the Lord." In several other translations of the Bible, the title Lord is substituted by the Hebrew name of God, Yahweh or in English, Jehovah. It is of interest to our readers that we provide a little background to this new name adopted by the Watchtower Society in 1931.

This name of the Hebrew God, represented in Hebrew by the Tetragrammaton (four letters) יהוה (Yod Heh Vav Heh), which was transliterated into Roman script as Y H W H. Because it was considered blasphemous to utter the name of God, it was only written and never spoken, which resulted in the original pronunciation becoming lost. The name may have originally been derived from the old Semitic root הוה (hawah) meaning to be or to become. Yahweh, the god of the Israelites, whose name was revealed to Moses as four Hebrew consonants (YHWH) was called the tetragrammaton. After the Babylonian Exile (6th century BC), and especially from the 3rd century BC on, Jews ceased to use the name Yahweh or Jehovah for two reasons. As Judaism became a universal rather than merely a local religion in the Middle East, the more common noun Elohim, meaning God, tended to replace Yahweh to demonstrate the universal sovereignty of Israel's God over all others. At the same time, the divine name was increasingly regarded as too sacred to be uttered; it was thus replaced vocally in the language of the Jewish faith.

A window featuring the Hebrew Tetragrammaton יְהֹוִי,
courtesy of Creative Commons

From a confidential insider report by a past member of the Watchtower headquarters Bethel family in New York during the late 1920s, this information was passed along by his son to our team of researchers regarding the choice of this new name for the Watchtower Society. Rutherford and Fred Franz during the years running up to 1931 had considered many alternate names to identify this sect and separate themselves from the many other splinter groups based on the Russellites and Adventists. Both Rutherford and Franz of course totally ignored the established Jewish holy tradition and respect of not using the divine name in their terminology. For example they were definite in their decision to not use the word church in the new name due to its association with mainstream Christianity or Christendom. Our informant told our researchers that they would have preferred using the term, Jesus Christ in the new name, but as the Mormons had already jumped in and used that term in the naming of their cult, Fred Franz rejected that idea as they did not want to be confused or related to that sect by using a similar name. Plus both Franz and Rutherford rejected the simple name of Christian as is was too generic and was not enticing or magnetic enough in their supercilious opinion, so they simply ignored the inspired words of the Bible at Acts 11:26, "It was first in Antioch that the disciples were by <u>divine providence</u> called Christians."

Firstly, this text in Isaiah 43:12 (AV), "Ye are my witnesses, says the utterance of the Lord," is taken completely out of context by this religion, as the words are part of a Biblical historic record that portrays a Heavenly court where Israel has been conquered and oppressed by the empire of Babylon and the Creator, Almighty God indicates that the false gods of Babylon will not prevail and requests that they produce witnesses to confirm that their gods and possessed power are the real thing and more powerful than the God of Israel. In return, this imaginary court then calls for the nation of Israel to produce their witnesses, who will testify that the nation of Jeshuren (honorary title for Israel) will be restored again and its capital and temple will be rebuilt in Jerusalem. This is exactly what did happen later in history, as in the year 537 BC after Cyrus the Persian released the Jews from Babylonian captivity and refers mainly to the promised deliverance from Babylon. In this section of Isaiah, Chapter 43, the language of a trial returns with the demand for Israel to bear witness to Yahweh's deeds, to declare the incomparability of Yahweh and commands the hearers not to remember the former things, as they will pale into insignificance before the new thing (Isaiah 42:18) that Yahweh will do for the nation of Israel in the future with his saving power.

This historic account in the Bible book of Isaiah does not apply to the 20th century, even though some religions try to claim that this historical event of Israel being freed from Babylon in 537 BC was simply a type and portrayed an event today being that of an anti-type that is spiritual Israel (The Christian Congregation) being released from Babylon the Great (False religion) as portrayed in the Bible at Revelation Chapters 17 and 18, with the words, "Then I heard another voice from heaven saying, Come out of her, my people, so that you do not take part in her sins, and so that you do not share in her plagues." The use of this name Jehovah's Witnesses does not give liberty to any religious group to take this expression you are my witnesses out of context and create a modern day term and the license to apply it as a name for a religious cult, as it specifically applies only to the Jews back in 537 BC. The only name that is authorized for followers and believers in Almighty God and His son Jesus Christ is the one recorded at Acts 11:26, "It was first in Antioch that the disciples were by divine providence called Christians." [Divine providence, or simply providence, is God's intervention in the Universe and the protective care of God or of nature as a spiritual power.]

The idea of using the name Elisha in their new title was even considered, as Fred Franz was obsessed with this Bible character and he imagined; fantasized and even fashioned his life style after this Bible prophet and even privately claimed that the official cloak of the prophet Elijah had been passed down to him by means of Elisha and the Holy Spirit. (2 Kings 2:9-15) According to a rumor, but not confirmed by any eye witness we could locate, it was also reported at the time that Fred Franz was displaying early signs of insanity or religious mania and was discovered in his private suite in the New York Watchtower headquarters, totally naked and wandering around his rooms with an old multi-colored blanket around his shoulders that he claimed he had inherited. It appears however that Rutherford, the all-powerful autocrat and a law to himself, eventually won the day, ignoring all tradition plus the Bible injunction at Acts 11:26, he decided on this new name for his religion, Jehovah's witnesses.

Editor's Note: Freddy Franz was well known as an eccentric individual with very peculiar habits, but he was tolerated because of his role as head of the Watchtower's writing department. According to the report, published by The Watchtower Documents researched by Barbara Anderson. A reporter who worked for *Time* magazine and interviewed Franz when he became president of the Watchtower Society in 1977 (he had previously been vice-president). That interview actually resulted in a story appearing in the July 11, 1977 issue of *Time* magazine. After the interview, the reporter told a colleague privately that in all his years of interviewing important people, after spending an hour with Fred Franz, he was pretty sure that Franz was certifiably insane.

Ralph Miller, in *Jehovah's Witnesses – Victim of Deception* provides valuable material about the eccentric Fred Franz who became the 4th President from 1972-1992 after the death of Nathan Knorr and refers to the experience of a former Witness he interviewed called Paul Blizzard.

Years later, when my wife and I became Christians, we discovered the truth about Franz. I can now look back and see the deception of Satan on this man and the "spirit of delusion" that blinded him to the truth of the Gospel. Knowing also that he was the principal architect of Watchtower teachings for more than 70 years, I realize how demonically controlled he was. I recall Franz having an aura about him. He was the only one at Bethel, to my knowledge, who roomed alone. All other single people had roommates. I recall one occasion where a message was to be delivered to Franz's room. I volunteered to deliver it. I was stopped by a personal friend of Franz who said, don't bother him. We'll just send it through the mail. He may be in there getting some revelation. We raised our eyebrows then, thinking that Jehovah God had a special connection with him. I know now that a demon controlled Franz, not the Spirit of God. Taking the exams to qualify for a scholarship is a far cry from Macmillan's claims that he carried away the honors at the University of Cincinnati and was offered the privilege of going to Oxford or Cambridge in England under the Rhodes plan. Franz himself continued this deception, I appreciated that I had measured up to the requirements for gaining the scholarship.

Where did Macmillan get his information for his 1957 book, *Faith on the March?* Undoubtedly from Franz himself. When writing his autobiography, Franz probably never imagined that his 1911 transcript would surface. Again, the transcript proved him a liar. First, compare Macmillan's claims of Franz's linguistic knowledge with the transcript. Macmillan wrote: Franz has a fluent knowledge of Portuguese and German and is conversant with French. He is also a scholar of Hebrew and Greek as well as Syriac and Latin. Again, irrefutable evidence is revealed in Franz's college transcript. Franz's major language studies were in classical Greek, in which he accumulated 21 semester hours. There was only one course in biblical Greek offered then at the University of Cincinnati. According to the 1911 catalog, page 119, the course is titled *The New Testament – A course in grammar and translation.* Franz took this two-hour course, which is nothing more than a survey of New Testament Greek. The Greek Franz studied has a different grammar system from that of biblical Greek. The claims to his being a scholar of Hebrew, Syriac and Latin are lies. Hebrew and Syriac were not offered at the University of Cincinnati. Franz only took 15 hours of Latin, which would hardly qualify anyone as a scholar.

When this new name created by Rutherford for his religion and was first adopted in 1931 by the Watchtower Society perhaps in a sincere attempt to glorify God's personal name in Hebrew, being Yahweh or Jehovah in English. However, in the 1950s the Watchtower Society under the leadership of Nathan Knorr, 3rd President, changed their policy and in their literature now capitalized both words, as Jehovah's Witnesses thus giving the emphasis now on the name of a sect rather than the Hebrew sacred name of Almighty God the Creator. Many researchers into the history of the Watchtower Society have remarked that this drastic change that went unnoticed by the majority of the followers was possibly the start of the spiritual decline of this religion, with a greater concentration on their door-to-door book and magazine selling techniques that was now being aggressively promoted as the primary and only way to demonstrate the members loyalty, dedication and service to God.

Although it was common knowledge that Rutherford was an abuser of alcohol, if not an actual alcoholic, but when sober he still had a brilliant manipulative legal mind and as a lawyer he knew the power of persuasion and how to distort facts. I don't want to engage in character assassination, our informer said, but it was also known by a few of us in Bethel, but definitely unknown by the majority of the loyal followers of the Watchtower Society, that Rutherford was a married man, scripturally responsible for his family and had a wife called Mary (1869-1962) and a son, Malcolm Cameron (1892-1989) who both lived in Los Angeles, Southern California, who he supported financially with funds donated to the Watchtower Society, as they had all lived separate lives from 1916 onward. Today Rutherford would not even qualify as an elder or ministerial servant in any congregation of Jehovah's Witnesses, but here he was, claiming to have been appointed by Jesus Christ, now being the autocratic, narcissistic leader of a worldwide group of a growing, expanding religion, which claimed to be the only true religion on earth. But Rutherford now owned the Watchtower Society so he cared very little what other subordinates thought about his character and life style, as he would remain in power no matter what.

Rutherford reasoned and adopted the stratagem, that as the Bible states that true Christians would be persecuted and this was thus a clear sign of being the true religion, so he calculatingly took the action of creating additional steps and manipulated a situation that would obviously be very unpopular and bring about criticism from other religions and strong critics of the Watchtower Society and its members. In turn when this criticism grew and grew to eventually become a stark reality, which he already knew from past experience would occur, and the slave like members were feeling the heat of following these controversial new beliefs and doctrines that Rutherford had introduced and also had convinced the members of the religion to practice through his publications, claiming that this was divine revelation and that they were now being persecuted for righteousness sake as a result.

Most of the simplistic, gullible followers unknowingly accepted this scheme and tactic of Rutherford and as a result thus believed and were convinced they were now members of the only true religion on earth. Over time other changes and implementation of controversial doctrines and teachings under the label of new revelations were introduced by the Watchtower Society, for example abstaining from blood, which also brought about even more persecution. In 1928 the celebrating of Christmas and birthdays was discontinued after the Governing Body (Rutherford and Franz) informed the members that these were pagan celebrations and this brought about even more persecution. Plus the issue of saluting the flag, singing and standing for the national anthems, were listed as acts of apostasy by true Christians. According to the research by Barbara Anderson in her report, Watchtower Documents, she revealed the following.

> One thing was plain from my research of the Rutherford years – Rutherford deliberately stirred up trouble by attacking religions and governments and baiting the clergy, thereby inciting acts of retribution against individual Bible Students. This frequently resulted in Rutherford howling, Persecution!

For conscientious cussedness on the grand scale, wrote America's *Saturday Evening Post*, when dealing with this subject.

> No other aggregation of Americans is a match for Jehovah's Witnesses. Defiance of what others cherish is their daily meat. They hate all religions – and say so from the house-tops. They hate all Governments with an enthusiasm that is equally unconcealed ... For being generally offensive they have been getting their heads cracked, their meetings broken up, their meeting-houses pillaged and themselves thrown in jail. The leaders argue that the persistence of the Witnesses in spite of severest persecution, mobbings, beatings, tar and feather outrages, imprisonment and even death, is nothing less than miraculous and a sure proof of their divine mission.

Rutherford was also known for his intense dislike of women, even though he was a married man and had sexually used his wife Mary at least once, as she produced a son, Malcolm, born in 1892. He often used the expression that women were nothing more than a bag of bones and a hank of hair; proudly quoting from Rudyard Kipling's poem.

Photo of Joseph Rutherford taken a few years before his death
while sitting in his private office at Beth Sarim in San Diego,
courtesy of Creative Commons

About Joseph Rutherford's personal life, not much is known, and in our research we uncovered more about his son Malcolm than father Joseph. According to the Watchtower Press Office, Mary and her son Malcolm had been residing (from about 1920) in southern California, where the climate was better for her health. Mary M. Rutherford died December 17, 1962, at the age of 93. Notice of her death, appearing in the Monrovia, California, *Daily News-Post,* stating: "Until poor health confined her to her home, she took an active part in the ministerial work of Jehovah's Witnesses. Mary Rutherford, however, remained a loyal Jehovah's Witness until she died. They had one son, Malcolm, born in Cleveland, Ohio on November 10, 1892 before Rutherford and his wife Mary joined the Russellites, later known as Jehovah's Witnesses and Malcolm who reportedly never really joined his father's religious movement and only attended the meetings to please his mother and also declined to be interviewed about his father."

Joseph Rutherford was married to Mary Rutherford before becoming a Russellite, but sometime after Rutherford became President of the Watchtower Society they quietly separated. James Penton in his book, Apocalypse Delayed, speculates that perhaps his choleric temper or his serious alcoholism may have influenced this split. It appears however that young Malcolm had been brought up by his mother as a member of Jehovah's Witnesses in the Los Angeles area but later quit this religion as soon as he could, which is understandable in the light of the checkered, notorious reputation of his father, Joseph Rutherford.

According to the 1920 US census, Joseph Rutherford was no longer living with his wife. He appears on the roster for 124 Columbia Heights, Brooklyn, New York, and his job title is given as Minister -- Bible Society. Mary Rutherford, 50, born in Missouri (whose father was recorded as being born in Germany and whose mother was indicated as born in France) she also indicated on the census form as still being married and she was not otherwise employed and lived at 128 N. Eastlake Avenue, Los Angeles, California. Malcolm her son, meanwhile lived a few houses down on the same street at 124 N. Eastlake Avenue, Los Angeles, California. According to the census forms it records that Malcolm Rutherford, 26, born in Missouri and who was employed as an Attorney-at-Law and his wife Pauline Rutherford, 23, who was also born in Missouri. There was one final registration in 1946, when Malcolm C. Rutherford of 2207 Laverna Avenue, Los Angeles, California registered as a Republican. Since Bible Students did not take part in politics, this data indicates that Malcolm ceased being a Bible Student sometime between 1917 and 1924.

Meanwhile, according to the 1930 US census, Malcolm C. Rutherford, 37, and Pauline S. Rutherford, 33, resided at 6246 Drexel Avenue, Los Angeles, California. Malcolm indicated that his job was Clerk – Superior Court. As far as Pauline is concerned, the government records indicate that her full name was Pauline Short Rutherford, her mother's maiden name was Reed, she was born on 8/12/1896 in Missouri, and she died in Los Angeles on 8/29/1948. Malcolm Rutherford died in 1989, and was in his 90s. He never spoke of his involvement with the Watchtower Society. In fact, he split as soon as he could after his father became the President. He lived a hermit's life, moving around from place to place so that apostates could not find him. He hated his father from what we were told from those who knew him personally. Our source who knew a few Bible Students in the Los Angeles area who grew up with him said at the time he died, he was living alone and renting a room in a private home. A few days later after he died, apostates went to visit the home and tried to gain access to his personal belongings. The owner of the house told them she would contact them after she went through his things. She donated everything to goodwill. A friend of ours eventually found his Bible in a used bookstore. In it was the name of Judge Rutherford, as it was his personal copy. Poor guy just wanted to be left alone! Though Mary accompanied her husband Joseph on several European tours before World War I, (1914-1918) she was not included in the Judge's post war entourage. As Mary told her friend, when Joe would come out to visit in California, he would spend his time at his home Beth Sarim with his mistress and would never visit his wife, who lived just 100 miles away from the San Diego mansion.

Malcolm Cameron Rutherford, 24, filled out his WWI Draft Card, at which time he lived at 128 N. Eastlake Avenue, Los Angeles, California. He states that he was born on 11/10/1892 in Boonville, Missouri. Malcolm was then a bookkeeper and clerk for H. G. Pangborn and Co. in Los Angeles. Significantly, he claimed an exemption from the draft as Member of Bible Students Association, so he was still a Bible Student at the time. Malcolm obviously became inactive and no longer associated with Jehovah's Witnesses. In our research, we have found a few current elderly Bible students that used to be associated with Malcolm and his mother Mary back in the early 30s. They both used to attend the Los Angeles congregation of Jehovah's Witnesses, part of this ecclesia split off and continue to this day in Burbank, California as the Los Angeles Bible Students.

This useful snippet of information was gleaned by a member of our research team that reveals the travel information of Joseph Rutherford around the early 20th century. The first appearance of the Rutherfords in an extant passenger manifest is in the list for the ship Prinz Friedrich Wilhelm, departing Southampton on 11/2/1913, which mentions Joseph Rutherford, 43, born on 11/8/1869 [sic] in Versailles, Missouri, and Mary Rutherford, born on 8/17/1871 [sic] in Hornville, Missouri. Both were residents of 10 Orange Street, Brooklyn, New York. The second reference to them can be found on the manifest for the S. S. Mauretania, departing Liverpool, England, on 9/19/1914, wherein we find Joseph F. Rutherford, 44, born in Versailles, Missouri, on 11/8/1969 (sic), his wife Mary M. Rutherford, born in Hornville, Missouri, on 8/17/1871 (sic), and their son Malcolm C. Rutherford, 22, born on 11/10/1892 (sic). Joseph Rutherford thereafter appears in 18 more ship manifests, but never with his wife and only once more with his son Malcolm. On 5/16/1938, Malcolm Rutherford, aged 48, and his wife Pauline Rutherford, aged 41, were listed as passengers arriving in Los Angeles, California aboard the *SS Mariposa*,[8] along with Joseph F. Rutherford after they had all been on a world cruise.

> *Editor's Note:* Jan Haugland from Norway, a freelance historian, provided the above information in 2016, a brilliant biography of Joseph Rutherford and a brief history of the Watchtower Society in his article published on the website *Medium.com* under the title, The Successor Problem and is well worth reading. Jan provided much of the above information about Joseph Rutherford and his family and Jan's notes were part of his Masters Thesis, at the University of Bergen, Norway.

This enlightening report from the International Cultic Studies Association (ICSA) provided the following information:

> The Watchtower Society, commonly referred to as Jehovah's Witnesses, exerts a great deal of control over the everyday life of its members. Women, in particular, suffer from psychological stresses in this high-control environment, as it is also a culture where patriarchal attitudes limit women's personal power and predominate in their relationships with men. Women in the WTS occupy a position of decreased personal power relative to men in the group. Women are commonly exhorted to remain in submission to their husbands, and are banned from instructing baptized male members about spiritual matters and from addressing the congregation from the pulpit. A woman is regarded as a weaker vessel who should manage her household under her husband's approval and direction, owing to her duty of submission to her husband. (Watchtower Society, 1971).

---

[8] *SS Mariposa* was a very large luxury ocean liner launched in 1931; one of four ships in the Matson Lines White Fleet which also included *SS Monterey, SS Malolo* and *SS Lurline*, and was frequently used by millionaires for their annual vacations.

The seminal WTS text just cited goes on to define a wifes role as caring for the family, prepare nutritious meals, keep the home clean and neat and share in instructing their children – subjecting themselves to their own husbands (p. 242). In addition to a relative lack of power compared to their male compatriots in the congregation and in relationship with their husbands in the home, women as well as men must cope with a community gestalt that discourages independent thinking, mistrusts higher education, controls access to information critical of the group, restricts members from expressing doubts, discourages diversity, and severely punishes nonconformists.

> In a patriarchal society, men are the holders of power. Patriarchy is defined as a male dominated social system, with descent through the male line (*Oxford Dictionary of Current English*, 1992, p. 653). Patriarchy is thought to have arisen in conjunction with the concept of private property and the need to pass property on to an heir (Engels, 1972), usually male. In a traditional patriarchal society, women usually do not earn wages by working outside the home, which places them in a financially dependent position to their male partner and eliminates or decreases outside contacts and information about the world at large. In a patriarchal society, women generally do not hold positions of power or influence in the community. It is the men who sit on the village counsel, who vote, instruct, police, and guide the community. A woman's primary role is to provide care and nurturance to her husband and children. Without financial resources and with little community recognition or power, a woman in this kind of society either adapts to her role and fits in, or struggles against the order of things and becomes a problem, or, if possible, leaves in search of a society with more egalitarian values. Women are relatively powerless in a male-dominated society. Feelings of hopelessness, helplessness, worthlessness, futility and suppressed rage, the major ingredients of depression, are the emotional responses of anyone in a permanently subordinate position.

> Having survived into the 20th century, WTS still maintains its 19th century attitudes toward women. Women are told to be in submission and to maintain a state of wifely subjection to their husbands. They are not allowed to address the congregation

directly as a man does, and may not religiously instruct a baptized male member. All of the leaders, from the Governing Body, which runs the worldwide organization, down to Elders and Ministerial Servants of the local congregation, are all male. According to the Watchtower Society, the woman, in God's arrangement for the family was always to be in subjection to her husband and not to usurp his authority. Also, in the Christian congregation, the woman is not to teach other dedicated men, nor to exercise authority over them.

This opinion by fellow researcher David Tatro is of interest regarding the role of women in the religion of Jehovah's Witnesses.

> The *Jehovah's Witness Bible*, the *New World Translation of the Holy Scriptures*, uses terminology that seems odd or strange to the general public. One of these peculiar terms is found at 1 Timothy 3:8, which the *NWT* renders: "Ministerial servants should likewise be serious, not double-tongued, not giving themselves to a lot of wine." The Greek word that the *NWT* translates as ministerial servants is diakonoi, which literally means servants. Most modern Bible translations use the term deacon as it describes a ministry in the church. The Jehovah's Witnesses apply the term ministerial servants to their secondary church officers. Now don't get me wrong; the Witnesses can call their clergy any name they want to. But the term ministerial servants is redundant. It is almost like saying serving servants.
>
> However, when the Greek word diakonoi appears in the singular at Romans 16:1, the *NWT* renders it minister. No doubt that is because at Romans 16:1 the word is used in reference to Phoebe, a woman, and due to the Witness church's bias against a female clergy the *NWT* translator couldn't use the term ministerial servant to describe a woman. The *New Revised Standard Bible* calls Phoebe a deacon, and the New Jerusalem Bible uses the term deaconess at Romans 16:1. It is very interesting when one reads 1 Timothy 3:1-13 [*Revised English Bible*]. In these verses St. Paul lists the requisites for bishops and deacons. In verse 11 he says: "Women in this office must likewise be dignified, not scandal mongers, but sober, and trustworthy in every way." For the benefit of the Jehovah's Witnesses who are more familiar with their own Bible version,

the *NWT* says, "Women should likewise be serious, not slanderous, moderate in habits, faithful in all things."

St. Paul's instruction needs to be considered in light of the time and the place. In his instructions to Timothy Paul wasn't denying women the office of deacon, but in the instance of a house church, so as not to appear subversive, women should learn in silence. In a different setting a deaconess could teach and hold a position of influence in the church. However, the Jehovah's Witnesses take St. Paul's instructions out of context in order to justify the denial of leadership positions for women in their religion. Nevertheless, there is considerable evidence from the Scriptures, from scholars, and from history that women held leadership positions in the ancient church. If a religion is truly Bible based there can be no justification for treating women as second-class Christians. There is nothing to fear but much to gain with women in leadership roles. Christians will be especially blessed and enriched when women are restored to full equality in today's church.

The weird anomaly promulgated by the Governing Body of the Watchtower Society that women are not allowed any position of authority within their organization, is that women are permitted to partake in the annual memorial celebration (the Lord's evening meal originally started by Jesus Christ and his eleven faithful apostles; all men) by sharing in eating and drinking the unleavened bread and red wine, (expressions of sharing in the symbolic body and blood of Jesus) which is their heart felt personal expression, claiming to be part of the remnant of the so-called little flock of 144,000. This is in line with the current teachings of the Watchtower Society, that these women truly believe they will rule in heaven as sexless Kings and Priests with Jesus Christ when they die, along with and equal to, their fellow males in the congregation who claim likewise. (Matthew 22:30, plus Revelation, Chapter 7 and 14.) Yet these same women are not permitted, while still on this earth awaiting their heavenly reward, to have any involvement with the decision making of the Governing Body or for that matter in any position of authority, responsibility or contribution verbal or written, all occupied by men throughout the many congregations of Jehovah's Witnesses worldwide. How does one explain this weird teaching and obvious contradiction?

An additional issue that Rutherford and the Governing Body introduced and once again quickly turned to criticism, directly coming from most other religions leveled against the Watchtower Society and their claim that Jesus did not die on a cross but on a simple tree or upright stake. The Governing Body then manipulated this criticism, once again, into being another sign that true Christians were being persecuted for righteousness's sake. The Cross and Crown (a cross passing through a crown) is a Christian symbol used by various Christian denominations, particularly the Bible Student movement and in the past by the Watchtower Society. It has also been used in heraldry and by the Free-Masons plus Knights Templar, a fraternal order affiliated with Freemasonry. The emblem is often interpreted as symbolizing the reward in heaven (the crown) coming after the trials in this life on earth (the cross).

The cross and crown with wreath of laurel leaves,
courtesy of *Wikipedia* & Creative Commons

This symbol was also prominently featured in the early publications and memorabilia of the International Bible Students Association (IBSA). First appearing on the cover of the January, 1881 issue of *Zion's Watch Tower*, the cross and crown were surrounded by a wreath of laurel leaves, and the symbol was also used on lapel badges, pins and buttons (metal and celluloid that could only be bought from the Watchtower Society at a highly inflated price and that had been manufactured by one of Russell's and Rutherford's private companies) and these pendants of various designs that members proudly displayed. However, not all of its uses by the I.B.S.A. included the wreath of laurel leaves. Although Charles Russell's gravesite is marked by a pyramid memorial erected by the Watchtower Bible and Tract Society, using donated funds, with an illustration of the Cross and Crown symbol, the Watchtower Society discontinued using the cross and crown some years later, under direct instructions from Joseph Rutherford, viewing it as a pagan symbol.

The doctrine of the Watchtower Society has now been for some time that Jesus was executed not on a cross but on an upright stake. In 1936 the symbol of the cross and crown was discontinued on the cover of the official Watchtower journal that had been prominently displayed since its first copy of 1879. This issue of whether Jesus Christ was put to death by the Roman centurions on a cross; an upright stake with a cross bar at the top or a simple upright stake or tree is an ongoing major issue to be disputed by sincere Bible scholars and is beyond the scope of this book to debate. However we encourage our readers that if they wish to pursue their interest in the subject of whether Jesus was executed and put to death on a stake or wooden cross that they read the enlightening book by the MTC International Foundation and the late Philip Rees, a leading Watchtower official. This soon to be published book is titled *Error 404-The Mystery of the Man Who Never Was or The Greatest Man Who Ever Lived©*. This brilliantly researched book provides extensive historical material related to this important subject plus intimate details of the life of Jesus Christ and his earthly sojourn.

Regarding Jehovah's Witnesses and their controversial doctrines, as reported by a member of our research team, which was based on an interview with a prominent past leader in this religious organization, he submitted the following. I will not reveal the name of the person I interviewed, out of respect and deference for his family, as he is now deceased, but he did reveal certain facts, based on his extensive experience of being at one time a prominent member of the leadership of the Watchtower Society. He personally knew individual members of the Governing Body, and he pointed out that there was and still is continuous strife amongst the current leaders, based mainly on how to handle the fact that some of their major doctrines that have been the very core and prime beliefs of this religion since as far back as when the *Watchtower* magazine was first published in 1879 and founded by its first President, Charles Taze Russell (1852-1916). In addition, the current attempted explanations by the Governing Body as to why changes are unnecessary are seriously being questioned by many of the more intelligent members of this religion. The *Watchtower* magazine is the primary communication channel of the Governing Body of this religion and remains so today and its contents plus instructions are viewed as a divine guide to be strictly obeyed and followed by all dedicated members.

According to the member of our research team, he reported that his interview continued with the following answers to his in-depth questions related to the existing strife, conflict and confusion amongst the Governing Body, which appertain primarily to two major doctrines currently promoted by the Watchtower Society.

One issue is connected to the interpretation of the term generation that will witness the end of the world (system of things) as mentioned in the Bible book of Matthew, Chapter 24, "This generation will not pass away until all these things occur." Our unnamed source clarified that over the years the explanation of how long is a generation, which has always been linked to the pivotal year 1914, had become a very serious issue. According to the current doctrines of the Watchtower Society and because over 100 years have now passed since 1914, they have in recent issues of their official journal put forward the most obscure and controversial explanation in an updated interpretation and meaning, primarily in an attempt and effort to try and explain the word generation in the Bible. Many intelligent current members of this religion have privately questioned this interpretation and rationalization of this new revelation that has been put forward by the Governing Body. Plus, some have privately commented, if perhaps the interpretation of this Bible text currently put forward by their leaders (who are only human after all) is possibly incorrect, as the Bible text at Matthew 24:36 confirms, "concerning that day or hour nobody knows, neither the angels in the heavens nor the Son, but only the father." Plus, one stupid, senseless remark made by a leading member of this religion when discussing 1975 and who claimed he represented the Governing Body told his audience after quoting this scripture at Matthew 24:36, said, "Ah ah, but note my brothers, that this inspired text does not mention the year, but only the day or hour are secret to the father, but today we now know the year as it has been revealed by the Father to the Governing Body." Pause for a moment, try and digest that sort of reasoning by the leaders of this religion that takes place in the headquarters of the Watchtower Society.

Governing Body member, Albert Schroeder held an enclosed meeting with high-ranking Jehovah's Witnesses representatives from European Watchtower branch offices back in 1977. At that meeting, he told the exclusive audience that there was a campaign going on both inside the organization and from outside to have the Society's 607 BCE (before our Common Era) – 1914 CE (Common Era) chronology and the understanding of the last generation be overthrown. The Society, however, had no intention of ever, ever abandoning it, he emphatically stated. Of course, Schroeder is now dead, buried and almost forgotten, but the identical attitude is still being shown by the existing members of the Governing Body today. One is compelled to ask the question, why? when there is so much excellent and accurate research material available today that proves this original erroneous teaching of 1914, and the 2,520-year period from 607 BC to 1914 AD, and called the gentile times that was introduced by Charles Russell back in the 19th century, with his very limited access to modern chronology and the latest resources, cannot possible be true, accurate or correct.

This statement was made in a Watchtower article as recently as 2016 that indicates their stubborn reluctance to change their private interpretation of the year 1914.

> A crucial time was drawing close. In 1876 the Bible student Charles Taze Russell contributed the article, Gentile Times: When Do They End? to the *Bible Examiner*, published in Brooklyn, New York, which said on page 27 of its October issue, "The gentile times will end in A.D.1914." The Gentile Times is the period referred to in another Bible translation as the appointed times of the nations. (Luke 21:24) Not all that

was expected to happen in 1914 did happen, but it did mark the end of the Gentile Times and was a year of special significance. Many historians and commentators agree that 1914 was a turning point in human history.

This enlightening quote by Paul Grundy on his website, JW Facts.com is of value.

A key factor to the growth in number of Jehovah's Witnesses is the promise that this system will end at any moment. The shorter the expected time left, the higher the growth. (Immediately prior to dates the end was specifically expected, such as 1914, 1925 and 1975, growth increased to as high as 20%.) When there has been no specific date set, the concept that this generation will by no means pass away has been used to stimulate urgency. Looking retrospectively, it is remarkable to see the number of changes to the generation teaching, in order to make each decade in the 1900s appear to be the decade Armageddon would come.

The second major doctrine that is currently being faced by the very frustrated and confused Governing Body of the Watchtower Society is related to the claim that only a certain exclusive number of their members can be classified as a little flock numbering exactly 144,000, and this strictly limited number are the only ones who, when they die, will immediately ascend to heaven and sit at the right hand of Jesus as Kings and Priests and the remainder of the members must be satisfied with the possible hope of a resurrection back from the grave to this planet earth at some time in the unknown future. This claim of an exclusive group of 144,000 is based on a Bible text in the book of Revelation, Chapter 7 and 14; a revelation by Jesus Christ [to the apostle John] and he sent forth his angel and presented it in signs. This original doctrine and claim that the 144,000 mentioned in the Bible is a literal number was one of the basic cornerstones of this new religion that was started by Charles Russell and his associates back in the 1860s and they believed that this exclusive group of Christians had been slowly and gradually gathered over the centuries from the days of Jesus, when he lived on the earth in the first century, up until the last days and the end of the world, which Russell claimed started in 1914. It was then claimed that as only a few members of this group remained to be gathered, therefore the phrase was coined, the remnant of the little flock, who of course are claimed today to be all members of Jehovah's Witnesses.

Our informative and confidential source reflected on the years around 1931-1935, when the then new powerful leader of the Watchtower Society, Joseph Rutherford (1869-1942), who became the second president of The Society under questionable circumstances after Russell died in 1916. Rutherford and his associated guru, also sarcastically known as the visionary and oracle who was now primarily responsible for the organization's interpretation of the Bible, and who was also the primary ghost writer for Rutherford's 21 religious books and 86 booklets, namely Fredrick Franz (1893-1992). This literature published and then was publicly sold by the members of the Watchtower Society from house to house totaling millions of copies. Between Rutherford and Frederick Franz, they directed and completely controlled the beliefs and doctrines of the Watchtower Society. At that time in the history of this religion, they stubbornly stuck to the claim that the number of 144,000 was a literal number, when all serious and knowledgeable students of the Bible know and clearly understand that the Book of Revelation is mostly, if not entirely symbolic in its contents and that this number referred to, namely 144,000, is in fact a symbolic number and definitely not a literal number.

Most people today think the Biblical book of Revelation is a doomsday account of the last days of our planet earth. Revelation's confusing symbols, strange characters, and rash of plagues leads people to stay away from it. This is understandable. Most knowledgeable Bible scholars have concluded that the book of Revelation is entirely symbolic in its content, for example in Revelation 6:1-11 in which the breaking of seven seals and the four horsemen of the apocalypse are vividly described as symbolizing, pestilence, war, famine and death and especially in Verse 11 the use of the term white robes and Jesus Christ being described as a lamb in Chapters 21 and 22.

Photograph from 1928 of Joseph Rutherford seated in his private office in New York, courtesy of Creative Commons (note the very large coal fired stove in the background, he was a man who insisted on his comforts)

Frederick Franz (1893-1992) who was the actual author and ghost writer of the many religious books credited to Joseph Rutherford that prominently and misleadingly displayed that he was the author, and according to our informer, they were mainly based on Fred's obscure, private interpretation of many Bible texts, which were so extreme that most have been abandoned by recent articles published by the Watchtower Society. In 2010, the Watchtower Society also redefined and asserted that the generation of 1914 regarded by Jehovah's Witnesses as the last generation before the battle of Armageddon (the end of the world) includes persons today whose lives overlap with the anointed that were on hand when the sign began to become evident in 1914. The Governing Body expediently had to make this major change in interpretation, as previously the Watchtower Society had always stated that the generation that was still living who had <u>witnessed</u> and was alive in the year 1914.

In 2015, the Watchtower Society in their official journal tried to explain and cited that Fred Franz was an example of one of the last members of the anointed who were alive in 1914. Franz would have been 21 years old in 1914 and it is recorded that he was baptized as a member of the Bible Students on November 30, 1913 or April 5, 1914, suggesting that the generation would now include any individuals who claimed they are of the anointed up until the death of Franz in 1992 at the earliest. So this now conveniently moves the generation up until at least the year 2062 or beyond, accepting the term generation being about 40-80 years as mentioned in the Bible at Psalms 90:10. This term generation of course now includes the eight men who today claim to be of the anointed and as such authorized to sit on the Governing Body of this religion, also claiming to be todays faithful and discreet slave appointed over all of the Lord's belongings described in the Gospel of Matthew.

This irrational change by the Watchtower Society in 2010 of the Biblical term, this generation, to an overlapping generation can be clearly seen as a desperate attempt to ignite urgency in the religion of Jehovah's Witnesses in order to preach more and to give more. The question being asked today is, can a religious organization that makes ongoing critical doctrinal errors rightfully claim to be directed by Almighty God and being under the influence and guidance of his Holy Spirit? We let you our intelligent readers decide for yourselves! Based on the ongoing research by our team, many members of this religion especially those who are beginning to think for themselves, are now seriously questioning this latest explanation by their leaders and this may create a backwash of more criticism from their more intelligent members.

According to the research by Barbara Anderson in her report, Watchtower Documents, she revealed the following. "And there was the time when I was going through a large file cabinet in the office of the fourth president of the Watchtower Society, Fred Franz, when he was frail and blind and no longer using his office, I found letters from President Rutherford addressed to Franz dated in the 1930s. One letter contained a question which Rutherford asked Franz to answer for a forthcoming issue of the *Watchtower* magazine. In every *Watchtower*, there was a column containing Rutherford's answer to a specific Bible question. The letter confirmed to me that Franz, who, in 1926, joined the editorial staff as a Bible researcher and writer for the Society's publications, wrote the answers to those questions, but Rutherford took the credit. The letter was specific. It did not ask Franz to research the question, but to answer it for a particular Watchtower column."

Between 1920 and Rutherford's death in 1942, the Watchtower organization grew to include thousands of new followers worldwide, mainly recruited by the door-to-door sale of the religious books and magazines, primarily accomplished through the slave like group of special pioneers (also known as colporteurs) who were paid a commission on books sold, plus a very small monthly allowance. Our source also revealed that when the number of members of the Watchtower Society kept increasing during the years around 1935 and was now quickly approaching the figure and actually exceeding this original literal number of 144,000 members as interpreted and claimed by Charles Russell. This was owing to the fact that many disillusioned members of nominal churches and religions of Christendom were abandoning their stale, boring and apathetic Catholic or Protestant religions. In addition, world affairs were deteriorating after the dreadful First World War (1914-1918) [the war to end all wars] and the spread of Nationalism; especially in Europe. In addition, the Nazi, Fascist movements in Europe[9] also contributed to the reason why many sincere religious people were looking for support from some kind of religion that offered hope or salvation from the now worsening conditions in the world.

Our well informed source continued that these sincere individuals were looking for a more fundamental, stimulating and personal type of religion without the claptrap of the traditional churches, plus he quoted from an article he had recently read by Quirinus Munters, in Sage Publications, that they wanted to find a religion that had definite commitments to moral value and a firm authority structure and the

---

[9] Eugenio Pacelli, former nuncio to Germany, became Pope Pius XII on the eve of the 2nd World War. His legacy is contested. As Vatican Secretary of State, he advocated détente via the Reichskonkordat and hoped to build trust and respect in Hitler's government. Although Pius XII publicly affirmed the supposed Vatican neutrality, he maintained links with the German government. Controversy about his reluctance to speak publicly and explicitly about Nazi crimes, however, has continued to this day.

Watchtower Society plus the Mormon Church appeared to fulfill that need in the case of many sincere Bible loving Christians. Also, as pointed out by our source, the interpretation of the little flock was now becoming a misnomer, as all members of Jehovah's Witnesses at that time, 1931-1935 partook of the bread and wine symbolizing the body and blood of Jesus Christ, a memorial celebrated annually around the Jewish Passover each year and thus indicating they were members of this exclusive little flock with a heavenly calling, as that was the custom and current belief of the day.

The number now partaking of the bread and wine around 1935 was wildly exceeding being just a little flock, so the interpretation of this original doctrine created by Russell and his associates back in 1879 had to be quickly amended and changed somehow, as our source said in his own words, as he was an Australian (we stress, not the words of our research team member), they now found that they had their knickers in a twist! (A slang phrase or idiom and it basically mean becoming upset or agitated). Therefore a new doctrine was quickly introduced by the Governing Body (basically Rutherford and Fredrick Franz) in late 1934 and early 1935 by means of the bold interpretation that many of the current and definitely all new members could not claim to be of this special and unique little flock, but rather came under another newly created Biblical category[10] or title, claimed to be members of a great crowd of other sheep of unnumbered individuals and could therefore not rightfully partake of the bread and wine, which was now reserved exclusively for the remnant and members of the so-called little flock.

This new category and new doctrine of the other sheep was based on the Bible text at John 10:16 and was interpreted in its modern form by the Watchtower magazine, when in fact as most serious students of the Bible know, that this text is directly referring to the Gentile (non-Jewish) nations being allowed to become followers of Christ; becoming Christians, in addition to the Jewish people who had become followers of Christ and believers back in the first century of

---

[10] This was a clear, irrefutable case of using two completely unrelated Bible texts, taking them out of context and creating a new Biblical phrase as though it was directly from the Bible and that they are God's own sacred words, a true and clear indication of the modus operandi of a cult.

the Christian era and they were to become one flock. Previous to the year 1935, the Watchtower Society still promoted and believed in the original teachings of Charles Russell that the Great Crowd or Great Company was in fact a secondary heavenly class referred to in the Bible book of Revelation as a great crowd which no man was able to number and standing before the throne and the Lamb of God. The Governing Body at that time stated that this Great Company of Revelation 7:9, 14, was identified as a secondary spiritual class who have insufficient zeal for the Lord, the Truth and the brethren who are granted heavenly life, but on a lower spiritual plane. Even though they were invited to live in heaven when they died they were to serve as servants rather than kings and priests.

In the blog, Beroean Pickets of 2014, the article "Going Beyond the Things Written," writer and researcher, Meleti Vivlas, said: "Can there be any doubt that the entire doctrine of the other sheep – as Christians who are not anointed with God's spirit; who do not have a heavenly calling; who are not to partake of the emblems; who do not have Jesus as their mediator; who are not children of God; who only achieve an approved state before God at the end of the thousand years – is entirely based on Rutherford's [or rather Frederick Franz, this comment is made by a member of our research team] concocted, inconsistent and wholly unscriptural belief."

Today, these two major doctrines are creating very serious problems for the current Governing Body and leaders of the Watchtower Society; our source informed us, and they know that these two doctrines being at the very core of the foundation of this religion since 1879, that if they made such a dramatic change of interpretation, they take the very real risk of many intelligent members becoming disillusioned and perhaps viewing the Governing Body as being false prophets for over 100 years as warned in the Bible. (Matthew 24:4, 5, 23, 24) Of course on many previous occasions the Governing Body has changed their interpretation of other lesser important doctrines, these new explanations being tolerated and accepted by the rank and file of their followers, and the Watchtower Society have usually used a Bible text, taken out of context as usual, "But the path of the righteous is like the light of dawn, that shines brighter and brighter until the full day" (Proverbs 4:18), and to justify such changes as being new light or enlightenment based on prayer and divine guidance. The organization's earlier literature has included claims that its predictions about dates such as 1925 were indisputable, absolutely and unqualifiedly correct and bearing the stamp of approval of Almighty God, but the modern Governing Body, which was established later, being reported to now stating privately behind the scenes, but not yet publicly, that its teachings are neither infallible nor divinely inspired.

The question now being faced by the Governing Body of this religion, is how they can now admit that their past interpretations of the Bible are in fact erroneous and how can they really take the risk of informing the now millions of followers regarding these facts; letting the full truth be known; only time will tell according to our unnamed source. He also added that the Governing Body is also fully aware, from past history, that a large falling away of followers would seriously affect the massive income of millions of dollars received each year by the Watchtower Society; donations made by sincere God loving members as voluntary contributions to the Lord's Work. Major events of falling away had taken place in the past when prophetic forecasts had failed and the Governing Body is no doubt fully aware of this reality.

The following report about Rutherford's exploits during 1925 to 1942 proves very enlightening and reveals details about the motives and tactics of Rutherford and the Watchtower Society during this period. In 1918, Watchtower publications began predicting, under the direction of Rutherford, that Old Testament patriarchs or princes would be resurrected back to earthly life in 1925 or soon thereafter. This erroneous prediction proved to be one of the biggest scams and embarrassment in religious history. It was taught that these princes would become earth's new leaders and rulers and that their resurrection would be a prelude to the inauguration of a new earthly society and the abolition of death under the banner of Rutherford's famous booklet and speech, *Millions Now Living Will Never Die*. In Rutherford's final book these words are revealed: Hence those faithful men of old may be expected back from the dead any day now. The Scriptures give good reason to believe that it shall be shortly before Armageddon breaks. In this expectation the house at San Diego, California, which house has been much publicized with malicious intent by the religious enemy, was built, in 1930, and named Beth-Sarim meaning House of the Princes. It is now held in trust for the occupancy of those princes on their return (*The New World*, p. 104).

During this time period, Rutherford spent most of his time living in San Diego, California, supposedly for health reasons, and the Watchtower openly reported, which is a very misleading statement: In time, a direct contribution was made for the purpose of constructing a house in San Diego for Brother Rutherford's use. The property and land of approximately 100 acres in the most beautiful part of San Diego was acquired in October, 1929 by a loyal cult member, Robert J Marten and was given to Rutherford in December for the nominal fee of $10. A brand-new luxury mansion was then built within that year using Watchtower donated funds. Rutherford named the property, Beth-Sarim and dedicated it for the use of the returning to earth, Old Testament princes, (all men; we are not sure about their wives or concubines, as no mention is made in this divine revelation claimed to have been received by the Governing Body (i.e. Rutherford and Fred Franz) who were now expected to be headquartered in San Diego, California, instead as previously claimed, in Jerusalem, Palestine, as had in the past been interpreted by the Governing Body of the Watchtower Society. The title deed for Beth Sarim; written and drawn up by Rutherford himself, said: that the property was to be held perpetually in trust (by himself) for these Old Testament princes and was to be surrendered to them once they soon arrived back on earth. However, there was a conditional clause placed in the title deed and extracted from the title deed of this property, dated 24 December 1929, and related to the expected tenants, King David, Abraham, Moses or someone else arrived. The title deed clearly stated, the said Joseph F. Rutherford in such lease or other paper writing shall have the right and privilege of residing on said premises until the same be taken possession of by David or some of the other men herein named and this property and premises being dedicated to Jehovah and the use of his kingdom it shall be used as such for ever.

Beth Sarim was located in the Kensington Heights section of San Diego with over an area of about 100 acres, landscaped with olive, date, and palm trees so that the princes would feel at home. The 5,100 square feet (470 m²) prestigious residence, designed by San Diego architect Richard S. Requa, is a ten-bedroom Spanish mansion, complete with a swimming pool and with an adjacent two-car garage. The building costs at the time were about $25,000 (millions in today's value). Writing in the book Salvation in 1939, Rutherford (or more likely, Frederick Franz) explained that Beth Sarim would forever be used by the resurrected princes when they returned.

Beth Sarim mansion, courtesy of Wikipedia & Creative Commons

Of course, these historic Bible characters never did appear back on earth in 1925, or at any time thereafter and this was just another of the many false, misleading, erroneous predictions by the Governing Body of the Watchtower Society, so the large luxury mansion in southern California was to stand vacant, or was it? But it appears that Rutherford had already been planning a permanent move to a more suitable climate to live and to still operate and retain absolute, total control of the Watchtower Society and its funds as he was the President for life. He wanted to move away from the extreme heat and cold of the east coast of America. So, he moved into this palatial home himself on the temperate west coast with his essential staff, both male and female, which he claimed were necessary for his responsibilities and to care for his 'comforts'.

Editor's Note: Our researchers came across many additional disturbing articles and reports that are displayed in the public domain about the claimed private life, debauched morals and personal conduct of Joseph Rutherford apart from his excessive drinking, especially his immoral behavior related to his two constant female companions, Bonnie Boyd and Berta Peale. If these stories were included in this book it would have been censored and banned for being X-rated. But as our reporters could not authenticate and establish these very troubling reports as being totally accurate or truthful, we have not included them in this chapter about the Watchtower Society. This decision is in line with the mission of the MTC International Foundation, sponsor of this book, to only report what is confirmed and known to be factually true.

These comments made by a research website into the history of the Watchtower Society made the following observations. Rutherford's imagination that Jehovah was going to resurrect the Princes to live in California shared the American centric views of similar religions such as the Mormons. The *Messenger* magazine (a now defunct publication of the Watchtower Society) of 1931 explains that San Diego was chosen, (instead of the Brooklyn headquarters on the east coast of America) for its climate. The climate is the same as that of Palestine. The place is planted with date and palm trees, such as would be familiar and pleasing sights to these resurrected men.

In 1942 the House of Princes (Beth Sarim) was sold after the death of Rutherford, proving false the statement that it would be for perpetuity and forever at the disposal of the aforementioned princes. Why did the Watchtower board of directors decide to sell Beth Sarim? The *Watchtower* magazine of 1947, December 15th explained, without any apology regarding the waste of money that was regularly donated by the sincere supporters of this religion, funds dedicated to the work of the Lord and advancement of spreading the gospel. The *Watchtower* stated:

It had fully served its purpose and was now only serving as a monument quite expensive to keep; our faith in the return of the men of old time whom the King Christ Jesus will make princes in ALL the earth (not merely in California) is based, not upon that house named Beth Sarim, but upon God's Word of promise.

Editor's Note: Whoever wrote those words that appeared in the Watchtower Magazine in 1947 must have done so with tongue in cheek, as it is one of the most blatant, deceptive claims ever made by this religion and is simply another testimony to their status as a cult.

Rutherford had of course moved into the mansion, Beth Sarim in early 1930 soon after its completion and served as caretaker of the property while still awaiting the resurrection of the princes. Newspapers of the time reported on Rutherford's lavish lifestyle, which included a 16-cylinder *Fisher Fleetwood Cadillac* coupe[11] plus an inordinate regular supply of liquor. After Rutherford's death, the Watchtower Society maintained Beth Sarim for a few years, before selling the property in 1942. The belief that the princes would be resurrected before Armageddon was abandoned in 1950 by the Governing Body of this religion. In 1954, when asked at a trial in Scotland why the property was sold, Fredrick Franz, then vice-president of the Watchtower Society explained (accompanied by loud laughter by the spectators in the public gallery) in court records: Because it was there, and the prophets had not yet come back to occupy it, to make use of it, and the Society had no use for it at the time, it was in charge of a caretaker, and it was causing great expense, and our understanding of the Scriptures opened up more and more concerning the Princes, which will include those prophets, and so the property was sold as it was serving no present purpose.

This quote from a review of the Watchtower Society in the book *Apocalypse Delayed* by James Penton, reveals:

A. H. Macmillan (1877-1966) a member of the Governing

---

[11] To place the value of this automobile in perspective, a new Ford auto in 1931 cost approximately $600. A 16-cylinder Cadillac cost between $5,400 and $9,200, depending on style and Rutherford owned two of these extravagant vehicles for personal and private use.

Body is on record as saying that the real reason for building Beth-Sarim was for no purpose other than to get the drunken and declining Rutherford out of Brooklyn. Even Hayden Cooper Covington (1911-1978), a high-ranking Watchtower Society official and famous defender of the legal rights of Jehovah's Witnesses in the United States, plus also a member of the Governing Body (also Vice-President) for a short period of time (1942-1945), said that Fred Franz had stated, They built the judge a house out in California just to get him out of Bethel in New York. That's ironic, since Covington was a practicing alcoholic himself and was once disfellowshipped for it.

Quoting from the website JW Survey that reflects on the serious issue of this building constructed exclusively for Joseph Rutherford:

The funding of Beth Sarim is one of the murkier aspects of this story – and the most difficult to get a full picture of. Watchtower literature repeatedly evades the suggestion that Beth Sarim was built directly out of Society funds. Beth Sarim was built with funds that were a direct contribution for that purpose, asserts the *Proclaimers* book [Official history book of Jehovah's' Witnesses]. No money has been drawn from the funds of the Watch Tower Bible & Tract Society, or any affiliated association… for the purpose of erecting, purchasing or acquiring the possession of any building or real estate in San Diego, California, insisted the Society Treasurer (W. E. Van Amburgh) at the time. Irrespective of how the builders were paid, the facts are that a luxury residence was built for the exclusive use of the President of the Watchtower Society using contributed money, to be held in trust by the Society [according to the deeds]. Moreover, the deeds stipulated that Beth Sarim would belong to the Watchtower Society on Rutherford's death, and it was the Society who pocketed the proceeds from its eventual sale. Beth Sarim was therefore as much a Watchtower property as any other. Donated funds were used for the personal gain of one man, albeit quite likely under false pretenses. Beth Sarim in San Diego still stands today as a monument to the folly of unfounded expectation and privileged seclusion. (Proverbs 18:1) The greatest sadness in this entire story is that Rutherford's modern-day successors, the Governing Body, refuse to fully acknowledge this important chapter in

Watchtower's history and learn from it. Instead, they repeat the exact same errors that Rutherford made – isolating themselves from reality in their plush offices and conference rooms, and allowing fanciful interpretations of scripture to dictate the lives of millions.

Rutherford was not the only person in America expecting resurrected leaders from Bible history and would want to live with them in America. Genevieve Ludlow Griscom, member of another cult, Outer Court of the Order of the Living Christ, had similar delusions of grandeur. In 1928, a year earlier than Beth Sarim, Griscom built a similarly opulent property at 360 W. 253rd Street in Riverdale, New York, for Jesus Christ to live after his second coming, also expected <u>very soon.</u>

The Governing Body of Jehovah's Witnesses today is the ruling council of the religion known as Jehovah's Witnesses, consisting of a small group of <u>men</u> (no women allowed) who all live, work and are based in the group's luxury, brand new headquarters in the United States of America and view themselves as the humble faithful and discreet slave of Matthew 24:45-47. This body formulates doctrines, oversees the production of written material for publications and conventions, production of very effective and professionally directed videos, and administers the group's worldwide operations. This quote from another research team investigating the facts about Jehovah's Witnesses and the truthfulness of the term, faithful and discreet slave reveals the following instruction regarding obeying and following this body of leaders: "A mature Christian does not advocate or insist on personal opinions or harbor private ideas when it comes to Bible understanding. Rather, he has complete confidence in the truth as it is revealed by Jehovah God through his Son, Jesus Christ, and the faithful and discreet slave." (*Watchtower,* 2001, August 1, p. 14.) The biblical term faithful and discreet slave is now synonymous, according to recently claimed inspired revelations by the Watchtower Society, with the existing eight elderly male members of the Governing Body of this religion who are based in New York, USA.

For many decades the Watchtower Society believed that, the Faithful and Discreet Slave class included all so-called anointed (heavenly called) Witnesses, wherever they lived on earth, but from 2009 the Governing

Body began making statements to increase its own exclusive authority. Finally, during the 2012 Annual Meeting, the Governing Body publicly announced it had now assumed the role of the Slave solely upon them only.

> The evidence points to the following conclusion: The faithful and discreet slave was appointed over Jesus' domestics in 1919. That slave is the small, composite group of anointed brothers serving at world headquarters during Christ's presence who are directly involved in preparing and dispensing spiritual food. When this group works together as the Governing Body, they act as the faithful and discreet slave. *(Watchtower,* July 15th 2013)

To illustrate the extreme power of this Governing Body, even to the point of dictating the private sexual conduct of married people, and one of our researchers submitted this short report. In their official mouthpiece the *Watchtower* magazine in the section, Questions from Readers, the following was recorded.

> In the past some comments have appeared in this magazine in connection with certain unusual sex practices, such as oral sex within marriage and these were equated with gross sexual immorality. On this basis the conclusion was reached that those engaging in such sex practices were subject to disfellowshipping if unrepentant. The view was taken that it was within the authority of congregational elders to investigate and act in a judicial capacity regarding such practices in the conjugal relationship.

It is a known fact from the hidden files of the Watchtower Society that a number of suicides resulted from individual members, especially females, after being excommunicated for these so-called unnatural sexual practices notably allowing their husbands to have anal sex with them to avoid becoming pregnant. A few years later the Watchtower Society rescinded this strict death dealing rule but ignored the fact that they had blood on their hands for enforcing this strict rule in the first place and intruding into the private lives of their members. Members were even encouraged to spy on one another. Read this quote from the *Watchtower* magazine of 2012: "So if we know that a brother or a sister has fallen into such wrongdoing, we should encourage that one to approach the elders and seek their help. (James 5:13-15) If he or she does not do so within a reasonable period of time, though, we should report the wrongdoing to the elders."

According to the words of Paul Grundy published on his informative website, JW Facts and who researched this controversial topic, he also reported the following.

- The *Watchtower* defines fornication to include oral and anal sex. As such, Jehovah's Witnesses are not to participate in oral or anal sex, even if married and both parties consent. If found out, the couple will be stripped of any privileges they hold in the congregation. They can be disfellowshipped for these practices if they refuse to stop participating in them. Though hard to imagine, Witnesses do admit to such practices due to being told to confess such sins.

- Oral or anal sex between married couples was classified as a disfellowshipping offence, 1974.

- No longer a disfellowshipping offence, 1978.

- Once again a disfellowshipping offence, 1983.

- Since 2011, very vague.

Since 2007, *Watchtower* has been silent on whether these practices are forbidden in marriage, with reference to them being specific to unmarried people. The 2011 Elder's handbook *Shepherd the Flock of God* uses wording that could be taken two ways, but seems to imply that oral and anal sex is only 'porneia' (The Greek word porneia refers to prostitution, with the related terms 'porne' and 'pornos' referring to female and male prostitutes) when practiced between unmarried people, and it seems the Watchtower Society wants to let this topic go away without being specific on the leadership's opinion.

In 1980, serious dissent arose among members of the Governing Body especially regarding the significance of the year 1914 in Jehovah's Witnesses doctrines. According to former Witnesses, James Penton and Gary Botting, internal dissatisfaction with official doctrines continued to grow, leading to a series of secret investigations and judicial hearings.

Consequently, dissenting members were expelled from the Brooklyn, New York headquarters staff in the same year. At the same time of these judicial hearings, Raymond Franz, a leading member of the Governing Body was also keelhauled before a special committee, but was not excommunicated despite the fact he was accused of spreading false teachings; in other words, apostasy. However he was ordered to vacate his position and along with his wife Cynthia, after spending almost 20 years in their very comfortable home at the headquarters of the Watchtower Society in New York, they were forced to leave in the year 1980.

This copy of an emotional letter from a current unnamed member of this religion was received by our editorial staff and we feel it deserves mentioning in our report.

> Raymond Franz set a fine example, and despite he was in very responsible position within the organization, he still had the courage to fearlessly speak out regarding some of the obvious errors in the current doctrines and teaching carried forward from the days of Charles Russell, Joseph Rutherford and Frederick Franz. Raymond's love for the truth of the scriptures motivated his bold decision to speak out and we respect him so much for that sacrifice. It is a great pity that other members of the Governing Body do not follow his fine example and also admit that Raymond Franz spoke the truth and exposed the lies and errors and that they have a similar responsibility to do likewise, to openly admit this, despite the costs involved.

> After Raymond Franz was forced to withdraw from his position on the Governing Body of this religion and move out of Bethel in New York, he still continued displaying an honorable spiritual attitude and when he could, he answered letters from sincere members and ex-members of Jehovah's Witnesses. This is a portion of one of the letters that Raymond wrote, by courtesy of a Christian witness called Daniel: I am sure you appreciate the need for patience during a time of transition. I feel that there is no experience that cannot bring some benefit, if we are willing to work to that end. Some of those experiences we characterize as negative and unpleasant can often teach more than those we view as pleasurable. At the same time that does not excuse from responsibility those who contributed to

our making decisions that we would probably not have made had we not been misinformed. It was probably the rather cavalier, insensitive spirit so often manifest in Governing Body discussions that most disturbed me.

Our informant revealed that the one single member of the Governing Body who tried to defend the genuine, sincere sentiments of Raymond Franz, who had previously always having expressed quite openly with his colleagues on the Governing Body at their regular weekly meetings and without any deceptive secrecy by Raymond and based on his deep research of Bible history, was Lyman Swingle (1910-2001). Lyman also said that the other members on the Governing Body appeared to be callously and totally indifferent to the developing very serious situation. Lyman was also putting his head in a noose as he was fully aware of the dictates revealed in the official journal and rules of the Society.

> We should meekly go along with the Lord's theocratic organization and wait for further clarification, rather than balk at the first mention of a thought unpalatable to us and proceed to quibble and mouth our criticisms and opinions as though they were worth more than the slave's provision of spiritual food. Theocratic ones will appreciate the Lord's visible organization and not be so foolish as to pit against Jehovah's channel their own human reasoning and sentiment and personal feelings. (*Watchtower*, Feb.1, 1952, p. 80)

Lyman Swingle was a descendant of German immigrants to America with a personality that displayed a very severe, aggressive, forceful tendency at times, and he had volunteered to work in the headquarters of the Watchtower Society in New York when he moved from his home in Salt Lake City, Utah, in the year 1930, and he was eventually elected to the seven member Governing Body in 1945; replacing Hayden Covington (see side note on Covington) who the Watchtower Society falsely claimed had resigned, but more likely was forcibly removed under extreme pressure, manipulation and subterfuge by Nathan Knorr and his fellow subordinate members on the Governing Body.

Many of the members of the family of Lyman Swingle and their peers are still active, very sincere Christians and a few are also still adherents of the Watchtower Society in Salt Lake City, Utah, USA, plus a few others are also now active members of the Mormon Church and they all willingly answered many of our questions about his life and sincere commitment to Jesus Christ as a devout Christian. Although to give a fair and balanced representation to other researchers who are unrelated to our Foundation, another report we received but that we have been unable to fully authenticate, by ex-member of Jehovah's Witnesses and former worker in the New York headquarters, self-confessed homosexual Howard (Howie) Rutledge Trans. Howie Trans who claims he worked closely and was intimately involved with certain unnamed members of the Governing Body of this religion and he stated in a public interview, "That Lyman Swingle, became such a foul mouthed, abusive drunk in his later years that ultimately no Bethelite could share a room with him, and that he had to be transferred to Bethel's medical rooms for 24 hour observation until he died."

If this report by Howie Trans is true or even partially true, which was hinted at by a close relative of Lyman Swingle from Salt Lake City, when he told our reporter that Lyman had some kind of a mental or emotional breakdown during the final years of his life and up until his eventual death in 2001, while he was still serving on the Governing Body and also still living in the New York Watchtower headquarters, where he had voluntarily worked and served for many years. Lyman had also recently lost his much loved, but sadly disabled wife Crystal in 1998 and he never fully recovered from that personal loss. Despite this claim by Howie Trans regarding the physical and mental state of Lyman in his final days, the leaked records in the archives of the Watchtower Society relate that Lyman Swingle on Wednesday, March 7, 2001, he attended the usual weekly meeting of the Governing Body of Jehovah's Witnesses of which he was a member. The following Tuesday his condition worsened, and at 4:26 a.m., March 14, he was pronounced dead by his doctor.

When our inside contact at the New York headquarters of the Watchtower Society, in checking the minutes of that weekly meeting of the Governing Body on March 7, 2001, which lasted approximately only 30 minutes, and no mention is made regarding the physical or mental condition of Lyman Swingle, in spite of this claim by Howie Trans that Lyman was in such a poor mental state of being required to be confined to a monitored hospital room and supervised as though he was insane or off his mind. Plus no mention is recorded in the minutes that Lyman made any comments or asked any questions, so it is possible that Lyman was in a wheel chair and under sedation by the use of some kind of medication or drug. According to the minutes of this weekly meeting no vote on any issue was considered, discussed or made, which was not unusual and the meeting followed the usual format, as this group of men had their own personal and individual agendas in any case.

The personal experience of Lyman Swingle was that he had seen first-hand one of his closest friends and fellow member of the Governing Body, Raymond Franz, who was a devout, sincere genuine Christian and a diligent, courageous Bible student but was now being crushed and destroyed by the powerful hierarchy of the Watchtower Society because he simply spoke the truth about the false doctrines, errors and teachings being forced down the throats of the members of this religion. No doubt Lyman was also having a personal crisis of conscience but did not have the strength of character to take a firm stand as did his dear friend Raymond Franz. This was probably because poor, vulnerable Lyman didn't or couldn't handle the trauma[12] and so as a result he paid a very heavy price for his human weakness. In this personal example of Lyman Swingle we have yet another clear indication of the sad consequences of being trapped, chained and enslaved by a religious cult. Always remember also, as this sad case of Lyman illustrates, that alcohol abuse is often used as self-medication to try and ward off or cope with stress and fear.

The following comment was also made by a fellow worker in the New York headquarters at the same time as when Raymond Franz was requested to resign from the Governing Body and move out of the Bethel headquarters in 1980.

> Lyman Swingle was one of the few, if only person who felt bad from the Governing Body about how Ray Franz was being treated. I remember in his biography Ray said that Lyman

---

[12] Trauma is damage to the mind that occurs as a result of a distressing event. Trauma is often the result of an overwhelming amount of stress that exceeds one's ability to cope, or integrate the emotions involved with that experience.

came up to Raymond Franz and his wife crying, feeling awful about what they were going through and that they had to leave Bethel. That speaks volumes right there about the man's view of justice.

Lyman Swingle was also described as generally open minded by his fellow workers in Bethel, which is a very rare quality indeed for a member of the Governing Body. In addition Lyman along with Raymond Franz, long before the run up to the final confrontation with the rest of Governing Body in 1980 regarding current doctrines, as some years earlier Lyman Swingle along with Raymond Franz had tried to pressure the other members of the Governing Body to abandon the so-called absolute date of 1914 AD and the so-called imaginary gentile times of 2,520 years, 607 BC to 1914 AD. They also pointed out to their colleagues on the Governing Body as these dates were erroneous and irrelevant in the light of many other external reliable sources of Bible research, they at least must agree to re-examine this date that had been an unsubstantiated core doctrine of this religion since the days of Charles Russell and his colleagues back in 1879, but the efforts of Ray Franz and Lyman Swingle were to no avail.

Some additional details are revealed in the Special Report No.6, about the life and death of Lyman Swingle, who was a very sincere but sadly misguided individual. A member of our research team provides some additional facts about his questionable relationship and marriage to Crystal Zicker, plus the role he played in excommunicating Edward Dunlap, being one of the most courageous Bible students who ever lived. Lyman was also one of the greatest proponents of the false doctrine taught by the Watchtower Society, of there being two separate classes of Christians in this religion, the so-called elite anointed ones and the other lesser group bearing the label, great crowd of other sheep.

This clear example is another warning to us today that as we observe from our reading plus study of the Bible and with our Bible trained conscience, if we see errors and misconduct by leaders of a religious cult then we must arouse the courage to speak out. In order to do so we may have to pray to our Heavenly Father for the strength to fearlessly and with boldness to accomplish this duty and responsibility, plus maybe also seek the help and support of our family and friends; if necessary and practicable. We have a responsibility to do this as the words of Psalms 119:109 instruct us, "I hold my life in my hand continually, but I do not forget your law." (This is clearly illustrated on the cover of our book) An interesting comment by a fellow Bible student reveals what this Bible text at Psalms 119:109 actually means. "Exposed to perpetual and extreme danger, as any precious and frail thing is which a man carries openly in his hand, whence it may easily fall or be snatched away by a violent hand being in the utmost jeopardy, and always exposed to danger and in continual peril of your life."

In addition, it helps to know that the promise of our Creator at Isaiah 41:10 is very real, which is that he will support us in our effort. "Do not fear, for I am with you, do not be afraid, for I am your God; I will strengthen you, I will help you, I will uphold you with my victorious right hand." We must remind ourselves of the inspired words of David in Psalms 31:1-24 and we invite you to read these expressive, powerful thoughts once again as you contemplate your personal dilemma on how to break free from the chains of a religious cult.

> *Side Note on Hayden Covington*: We have included this brief account kindly submitted by a contributing editor, as it illustrates the behind the scenes of a religious cult; its ambitious, manipulative leaders and its Governing Body, plus what in fact takes place unknown to the rank and file of its sincere, somewhat naïve members, which is nothing more than the avaricious greed for power and position within this cult. This is especially noted from what took place between headstrong rivals Nathan Knorr and Hayden Covington after autocrat, President Joseph Rutherford died on 8 January, 1942, and how Knorr cleverly used and manipulated a long entrenched, false doctrine and teaching originally introduced by this religions founder Charles Russell way back in 1879 and which is totally unsupported by the Bible. Quoting from *The Watchtower*, which is accepted as the inspired word by members of this religion, is the following statement.

Jehovah has established a limited number, 144,000, to make up the little flock, and he has been gathering it since Pentecost 33 C.E. Logically, the calling of the little flock would draw to a close when the number was nearing completion, and the evidence is that

the general gathering of these specially blessed ones ended in 1935.
(*Watchtower*, Feb.15, 1995)

An additional motive for including this information in our account regarding Hayden Covington is because the Watchtower Society makes virtually no mention in their literature of this very serious and vicious feud and battle for power between Knorr and Covington and is nothing more than another sordid episode of their history that they prefer to ignore and try to forget. Neither of these men had an impeccable reputation regarding their personal conduct, so this contest and struggle for power very quickly became very nasty and squalid.

This erroneous idea that was aggressively promoted by Knorr was regarding the claim he made that only members of the so-called heavenly class of specially chosen ones, the literal 144,000 Kings and Priests of the book of Revelation mentioned in the Bible being allowed to become a member of the Governing Body of the Watchtower Society. The outcome of this power struggle was that Covington was cleverly removed from the Governing Body and Knorr became firmly established and entrenched as the monarchial autocrat after the style of Rutherford and he often made important decisions; as did Rutherford, that affected the lives of millions without even discussing or obtaining the approval of the other six members of the Governing Body, the self appointed faithful and discreet slave of Matthew 24:45-47, supposedly taking care of all of the Lord's belongings. By the cunning and manipulative removal of his only rival, Knorr now had clearly established his path and way clear for self-aggrandizement for many years to come. Nathan Knorr now preened himself as he had achieved his life-long ambition and now occupied the throne, located and positioned in the President's Penthouse Office of the Watchtower Society overlooking downtown Manhattan in New York after successfully removing his despised and threatening rival Hayden Covington and sweeping his challenger to the throne to one side. But let us take a step or two back in time so we can better observe this struggle for power between these two ambitious men; how it started and the damage it created.

The Governing Body in the 1950s. Left to right: Lyman Swingle, Thomas Sullivan, Grant Suiter, Hugo Reimer, Nathan Knorr, Fred Franz and Milton Henschel, courtesy of *Wikipedia* and Creative Commons

Hayden Cooper Covington (January 19, 1911-November 21, 1978) was legal counsel for the Watch Tower Bible and Tract Society in the mid-20th century. He argued numerous cases before the United States Supreme Court in Washington D.C. on behalf of Jehovah's Witnesses in defense of their religious freedoms, winning most of them. In 1967, he also defended the then world heavyweight boxing champion Muhammad Ali (Cassius Clay) in his legal battle against the draft during the Vietnam War, earning himself a fat fee of $247,000.00 in the process. By this time when Covington took on the Muhammad Ali case he was approaching his sixties; had left the Watchtower headquarters and had been excommunicated from the religion of Jehovah's Witnesses because of his sins. From photographs of the time he was clearly showing signs of rapidly aging plus his health was beginning to wane especially his ongoing liver problems caused by his heavy drinking. For a full review of this very public and controversial court case of Muhammad Ali and his attorney Hayden Covington before the US Supreme Court, we invite you to read the special report No.5 in the Appendix, submitted by one of our researchers.

Our brief review of the life of Hayden Covington is based on leaked papers from his personnel file in the Watchtower Headquarters, plus oral information gleaned by our reporter from individuals who personally knew this man and his relationship with Joseph Rutherford, 2nd President of the Watchtower Society and the 3rd President, Nathan Knorr.

Covington was born in Texas and raised on a farm. An able student, Covington worked his way through law school in San Antonio, at the San Antonio Public School of Law, in its waning days before becoming St. Mary's University School of Law in 1934. Covington successfully passing the Texas bar exam, with an impressively high score, one year before graduation. He was admitted to the Texas Bar in 1933. He was well known as a very highly educated man and this superior erudite skill later created a serious problem with some of his fellow workers in the Watchtower headquarters plus with some of the narrow-minded leaders of Jehovah's Witnesses, especially the then Vice-President Nathan Knorr.

Hayden was formally baptized as a member of Jehovah's Witnesses in late 1934 and at that time there was ongoing confusion created by the teachings of the Watchtower Society and its Governing Body that all new members joining this religion around the years 1934 and 1935 could not claim to be members of the special, unique literal number of the remnant of 144,000, those personally chosen by God and were going to heaven when they died and becoming co-rulers of the Universe with Jesus Christ, as they claimed this number was now full. So it appears that Covington never partook of the emblems for that reason, despite the majority of the members of his local congregation already doing so; namely partaking of the bread and wine at the annual memorial that publicly indicated, plus claiming that one was a member of this unique group of chosen ones, selected by God himself to rule at the right hand of Jesus Christ. So, Hayden Covington humbly accepted his earthly destiny as a member of the so-called great crowd of other sheep in line with this new doctrine and teaching that was now being promoted by the organization at that time.

This was a new teaching and belief by this religion, urgently and officially revealed and introduced in 1934-1935 with the claim that, millions now living would never die or if they did die then their only hope for salvation was not heavenly paradise, as was the typical belief of most Christians, this new teaching made it clear that going to heaven immediately after death was reserved exclusively for the 144,000, but rather their only hope was to live on earth again sometime in the future, if they qualified for an earthly resurrection. The reasoning behind the urgent introduction of this new doctrine in 1935 by the Watchtower Society is that the number of members joining this religion had now dramatically exceeded the literal number of 144,000 and Armageddon had still not come as foretold, so some new light (Proverbs 4:18) had to be invented to explain this unexpected phenomenon and this serious misunderstanding of the scriptures and somehow had to be explained to their followers by trickery, smoke and mirrors. So, this new official doctrine became another effort by the Watchtower Society to display its neoteric wizardry to control, decide and manipulate the personal beliefs of their slave like followers without any solid Biblical evidence or support, which of course is another sign of a cult.

> *Editor's Note*: Read more about this weird teaching of there being two completely separate and distinct groups within the religion of the Watchtower Society in other sections of this chapter. Also note that many individuals who joined and were already baptized prior to 1935 and who had been sincerely partaking of the bread and wine each annual memorial date, as that was the then current belief and custom of all members believing they were part of the so-called remnant of the little flock that they had joined prior to 1935. But many of them stopped doing so after 1935 as they appear to have changed their minds about being selected to join Jesus Christ and maybe, perhaps to go to heaven when they died and the alternate idea of living on earth forever as humans in an earthly paradise looked even more appealing, so this fact also added to the confusion amongst the ranks of this religion. They had read the Bible text for themselves and sincerely believed that there will be a promised new earth and also the text that relates the inspired words of the Apostle John, "He will wipe every tear from their eyes. Death will be no more; mourning and crying and pain will be no more, for the former things have passed away." (Revelation 21:4)

One of our researchers who has interviewed many members of this religion over the years and especially those who were converted and got baptized about the same time as Nathan Knorr when he was a teenager in 1923, and long before this new light or claimed revelation of 1935 made by Rutherford and his prophetic guru Freddy Franz related to this new doctrine of the great crowd of other sheep was released. These individuals interviewed admitted that they only partook of the emblems of the bread and wine as a public display that they were of the remnant as that was the only choice they had when they were baptized, as it was the core belief of the organization at that time, but they had not experienced any divine revelation by means of the holy spirit that they were special, unique and had been personally selected by God or Jesus Christ to rule in heaven.

The belief and official doctrine of the Watchtower Society, as interpreted and revealed by founder Charles Russell at that time in 1879 and up until 1935 was that the great crowd of other sheep or the Great Company of Revelation 7: 9, 14, was identified as a secondary spiritual class who have, insufficient zeal for the Lord, the Truth and the brethren, and who are granted heavenly life, but on a lower spiritual plane. Even though they were invited to live in heaven they were to serve as servants rather than kings and priests. This new concept of the great crowd of other sheep or Great Company living on earth forever had not been invented at that time. So, it appears that we only have the personal word of any individual in the past, such as Nathan Knorr, who partook of the bread and wine from the age of 18, the year he was baptized, like every other baptized member in his local congregation, as it was the existing custom, they all sincerely and innocently believed, following the lead of Rutherford and the Organization at that time that they were all of the so-called heavenly class of 144,000.

In addition, we have the disquieting example of the man Theodore (Ted) Jaracz, who started to partake of the bread and wine in 1971 at the age of 50 years old so that he could be selected to join the Governing Body of this religion, as privately maneuvered and promised by his very close personal friend Nathan Knorr. (read this truly disturbing report later on in this chapter) In addition we also have reports of others even today in 2019 regarding men who verbally claim to be of this special class of 144,000 Kings and Priests to rule the Universe with Jesus Christ in heaven, so that they can serve on the powerful Governing Body of this religion, but offer no proof other than their own private claim and individual word and no other evidence can be presented, Biblically or otherwise. We encourage you to also read about the personal experience of Philip Rees, one time Watchtower Branch Servant of Australia and his private encounter with Nathan Knorr regarding his being invited to join the Governing Body of this religion and the steps he was requested to take in order to qualify, as related in Special Report No.1 in the Appendix of this book.

Joseph Rutherford, three years before his death, had invited Hayden Covington to be a leading member of the headquarters staff of the Watchtower Society in 1939 after only being an associate of this religion for less than five years. From reports at the time it appears that Covington was becoming more and more like the right-hand man of Rutherford, primarily being fellow attorneys and having similar legal minds and strategies. Hayden was chosen by Rutherford, not because of his spirituality or knowledge of the scriptures but because essentially it was based on his superior secular college education and his skill as a very successful defense attorney as he had already been personally appointed by Rutherford to handle several cases of defending draft dodgers who were prominent members of Jehovah's Witnesses. Covington was subsequently recognized as one of the greatest civil liberties attorneys in American history. During his tenure as the head of the Watchtower Society's legal department, he presented 111 petitions and appeals to the Supreme Court of the United States in Washington. He won exactly 37 (more than 80%) of the 44 cases he brought before the Court, involving issues including compulsory flag-salute statutes, public preaching and door-to-door literature sales and distribution.

Hayden Covington claimed that he had incontrovertible proof and evidence that Joseph Rutherford had told him privately and confidentially that he was to be prepared and to ready himself to take over as the next president of the organization when Rutherford eventually died, but our researchers could not locate any correspondence, written directive or record in the archived Watchtower files in the New York offices if this was the case. The Covington family refused to answer our calls enquiring if perhaps Hayden had kept copies of all of his correspondence and agreements with Rutherford, which one would expect being a lawyer, so we only have the personal word of Hayden himself. One fact we do know of course is that Rutherford also knew full well that Haydon did not claim or profess to be a member of this so-called little flock of kings and priests but simply a member of the so-called great crowd of other sheep class and it appears this was of little concern to Rutherford, he was just looking for the right man to take over complete control of his rapidly expanding religion and to keep it running smoothly and financially plus commercially successful after his soon to be expected death.

In our intensive research we found it most unusual, as both of these men, Rutherford and Covington were skilled, shrewd lawyers so one would automatically think, reason and expect that some sort of written instruction would have existed in the archived files at the Watchtower headquarters that contained this wish and desire of the autocrat Rutherford for Covington to be the next President, as numerous other agreements signed between Rutherford and Covington were archived, filed and located being of lesser importance and significance. It has been strongly suggested that such an important written instruction did actually exist in the files held in the headquarters in New York, but Nathan Knorr in his capacity as Vice-President personally took it upon himself and destroyed this document immediately after the death of Rutherford. But once again after our extensive research we have not discovered any actual proof of this unsettling claim other than that Knorr had spent his entire life, since he was 18 years old, devoted to Rutherford and his religion plus his compulsive, paranoid obsession was to inherit his throne. What we do know after studying the character and conduct of Knorr over his career with the Watchtower Society, is that Knorr was so obsessed with his grandiose ambition to be the next President of the Organization, plus his reputation of being relentless, ruthless and his louche behavior that he would do anything; literally anything, plus use about every trick in the book to realize his dream.

"Judge" Rutherford, center, with his bodyguards. A mighty messenger, he fell heir to the spiritual (and material) empire of Charles Taze (Pastor) Russell.

(left to right) Nathan Knorr, Joseph Rutherford and Hayden Covington taken in 1939, courtesy of the *Saturday Evening Post*

When Rutherford died of cancer of the rectum and colon in 1942, his death certificate states, rectal carcinoma and that is usually caused by homosexual activity, the then existing Vice-President Nathan Knorr took over and was officially elected by unanimous ballot as the new President by the existing board of directors and Hayden Covington was appointed as Vice-President to replace Knorr by the same board of directors after being a member of this religion for little over eight years. This was a shock to most long-standing members, as Hayden Covington did not even claim to be a member of the unique, so-called little flock as did all other members of the Governing Body. From internal reports Knorr privately never agreed with this appointment of Covington but the remaining members of the Governing Body outwitted him somehow, much to the bitterness of Knorr who was an autocrat after the fashion of his mentor Rutherford. So here was Hayden Covington, now a member of the Governing Body of this powerful, dramatically expanding and influential religion and he was not even a member of the so-called body of Christ the remnant of 144,000 and this truly irked Nathan Knorr as he already had displayed feelings of bitter resentment that Covington was so successful as a lawyer and making a prominent name for himself, so Knorr had to make a plan to get Covington out of the way somehow.

Covington and Knorr clashed from day one and their relationship was turbulent and very bitter to say the least. From a personal observation of this relationship gleaned by our reporter from a long-time serving member of the New York Bethel it appears that Nathan Knorr who had only received a minimum of education and just scraped through graduation from a small, backwoods, local High School when aged 18 years old; never went to college and had then been persuaded by his grandmother to volunteer and work in the printing (sweat shop) factory of the Watchtower Headquarters in New York. Knorr had been baptized in 1923 (personally by Fred Franz it is claimed, the same year he also entered the Watchtower Factory) as a member of the Bible Students Association; this name was used before Rutherford and Freddy Franz created the name Jehovah's Witnesses in 1931. Nathan Knorr, based on the tradition of this religion at the time he was baptized, this 18-year-old youth declared himself to be a member of this special heavenly anointed class, as this is what he was taught and no doubt personally believed that he was one of the so-called chosen ones of the remnant of the 144,000; personally selected by God to eventually rule with Jesus Christ in Heaven. This situation and state of affairs also created even more friction between himself and Hayden Covington as Knorr felt in his warped mind that Covington, although being a devout baptized Christian equal to Knorr, but by not publicly declaring himself as being a member of this exclusive heavenly class as Knorr claimed to be, that Covington was an imposter on the Governing Body. If it were not so serious this situation would be farcical or a paradox!

Also remember that Jehovah's Witnesses believe salvation is a reward and gift from God and only attained, firstly by being part of God's only true religious organization the Watchtower Society, and secondly, putting faith in Jesus' ransom sacrifice. However today they also now believe in different forms of a reward of a resurrection after death for these two groups of claimed Christians. One group, the remnant of the anointed (chosen ones), will definitely and immediately go to heaven when they die, while the other group, named and labeled the other sheep or the great crowd will live forever on earth if they are loyal to the Organization or maybe if they do die before the new earth foretold in the Bible (Revelation 21:1 and Isaiah 65:17) comes (sometime in the future) they will have to lie in the grave and maybe receive a resurrection back to earth, if they qualify, but with a new body, and using the Bible text at 1 Corinthians 15:12-57 as the basis for this theory.

Most of the existing, remaining directors of the Watchtower Society back in 1942 after the death of Rutherford; at least four out of the six wanted Covington, who being a very skilled and successful lawyer and was an ideal candidate to take over as the new leader and next President to replace Rutherford and they also appeared totally unconcerned that he was not of this so-called heavenly class; their view and desire was how to re-create and continue the existing success of their publishing and printing empire and keep the cash flowing in. But by introducing this controversial issue and the manipulative, clever tactic that to be on the Governing Body one has to be, according to the Bible, a member of the so-called heavenly class, so Knorr by subtle persuasion convinced the other weaker members of the Governing Body to change their minds and he ultimately stymied the more technically qualified Covington from his personal ambitious plan to take over from Rutherford as the next President of the Society. Hayden Covington had also claimed and made strong assertions that this was what Rutherford wanted in the first place; for Covington himself to become the next leader of this expanding, successful and lucrative religion and that Knorr was to continue as the Vice-President being responsible for the rapid expansion of the primary business of the Watchtower Society, being that of a commercial enterprise of printing millions of books and magazines that were then sold from door-to-door by the gullible followers of this cult, as this was Knorr's area of expertise.

Nathan Knorr had become the manager of the large and expanding printery when the existing manager Robert Martin died in 1937 of an undisclosed cause, but suggested in another report, of cancer of the colon. Robert Martin, by the way, was part of the group of Watchtower officials who were convicted and imprisoned for 40 years by the American government for espionage in 1918 but later released after the World War I (1914-1918) was over. Knorr was very young to have been assigned such a prominent position in the ranks of the Watchtower Society, but Rutherford overlooking many other older men, with much greater experience, so he must have thought that young Nathan Knorr was much better qualified to hold such a major responsibility of managing the rapidly expanding lucrative printing empire of the Watchtower Society or maybe perhaps for other surreptitious undisclosed reasons, as suggested by some. Fellow workers of Nathan Knorr who knew both Knorr and Rutherford quite well, and they had noticed that a very unhealthy, suspect relationship had developed between these two men and that this was probably the real reason why Knorr secured this very prominent important position at such a young age. In addition, Knorr appeared to be mesmerized by the powerful, overbearing character and ethos of Rutherford. Knorr was only 32 years old at the time, unmarried; still a virgin we presume and a very frustrated young man according to some of his friends and many of his co-workers commented that after his new appointment as factory manager by Rutherford in 1937, he gradually became an obnoxious and arrogant supervisor to serve under.

There are so many other reports that our researchers uncovered that relate directly to Nathan Knorr's obsession with homosexuality and masturbation, plus his attempts to expose, in his opinion and in his own words, as though he was speaking subconsciously about himself, "these filthy activities as being part of Satan's attempt to destroy the Watchtower Society from within." Many onlookers and listeners to Knorr and his tongue lashings before the New York Bethel family, was left with the clear impression from facial expressions and body language that when Knorr used this condemnatory phrase, he was including himself. This obsession with these so-called filthy activities was also particularly noticed when he lectured the new young men during their initiation procedures when they joined the New York Bethel headquarters staff as sincere and genuine volunteers.

A comment made by a person who once sat in on one of these series of eight introductory lectures, called new boy talks by Nathan Knorr, said that Knorr appeared to get some sort of perverted pleasure from this task of lecturing about masturbation to these new young innocent recruits and who were as green as grass.[13] Our source also sarcastically added that if these young men were not already practicing masturbation when they entered Bethel then they sure would be by the end of the week; purely out of curiosity! Knorr's extremely vivid; risqué and lurid descriptions of these activities could only have come from a person who was very familiar with the practice of homosexuality and masturbation. Knorr was no medical doctor, psychologist or psychiatrist but he appeared to have accumulated so much abundant knowledge regarding sex and its related practices. According to ex-Bethel worker Paul Blizzard in his blog, The Inside Story of a Former Third Generation Jehovah's Witness, he states, "One joke at Bethel went: If there's an article on sex, Knorr wrote it; if it is on the Bible, Franz wrote it."

In addition, whenever an announcement was made by Knorr to the Bethel family, usually at his podium during breakfast time at 7.00 am each morning; that is when he was in town and after he had been in his private shower for about 15 minutes, he often related and named certain members who were being excommunicated and kicked out of Bethel for being caught and convicted of homosexual or other considered immoral behavior and he would then use his old familiar phrase, these filthy activities as being part of Satan's attempt to destroy the Watchtower Society from within. Nathan Knorr spoke with such vehemence, fervor and passion at these early morning sessions, announcements and tongue lashings that it appeared to many observers that he was trying to whip himself by self-flagellation. Self-flagellation is the disciplinary and devotional practice of flogging oneself with whips or other instruments that inflict pain. Flagellation (Latin *flagellum*, whip), flogging, whipping or lashing is the act of beating the human body with special implements such as whips, lashes, rods, switches, the cat o' nine tails, the sjambok, the knout, etc. Typically, flogging is imposed on an

[13] This British idiom means that if someone is as green as grass, they have little experience or knowledge of something and trust what other people tell them too easily.

unwilling subject as a punishment; however, it can also be submitted to willingly, or performed on oneself, in religious or sadomasochistic contexts.

Also, it is on record that the female cleaning staff and volunteers in Bethel who were usually the very subjective wives or one of the few secret girlfriends of the frustrated leading male members of the organization, but who were faithfully and loyally carrying out the instructions of the Governing Body (as unto the Lord), which were also outlined, according to the very strict *Bethel In-House Manual*. These female cleaners were required to report any explicate female nude magazines such as *Playboy* found in the many bedrooms and dormitories, plus any soiled bed sheets and who were instructed by the Governing Body to report such findings, which seemed to happen on a regular basis. However the finding of bottles of liquor and alcohol was an accepted fact and need not to be reported.

These magazines, such as *Playboy, Penthouse, Hustler* and *Gay Times*, were to be sent to the incinerator to be destroyed but not before each of the older male members of the branch committee had checked these sex-magazines for establishing evidence of the danger of such magazines to the spiritual health of these vulnerable young brothers and take necessary action if and when required, as they claimed this close examination of these magazines was based on their official duty, as they had to carry out their theocratic responsibilities on behalf of the Governing Body. As pointed out by one sister who worked as a cleaner in the London Bethel and told our reporter, it was puzzling and difficult to explain as to why the brothers on the branch committee insisted on inspecting these sex magazines on a regular basis, as when you have seen one you have seen them all!

Meantime the Governing Body, just prior to the death of Rutherford and on into the 1950s, all fully realized that the massive income received each year by the organization came primarily from the lucrative business of the door-to-door sales of the millions of books and magazines, plus that Knorr was ideal in 1942 to continue the overall supervision of the very successful expanding printing factory and world-wide distribution of the Watchtower literature. They cared very little about the rumors or reports of the private, personal conduct of their colleagues, Nathan Knorr or Joseph Rutherford, they simply desired to make sure this massive income was maintained plus further increased and this probably motivated their strong feelings about attorney Covington becoming the next President and for Knorr to continue his current success in operating the printing and distribution of the literature.

It appears however that Nathan Knorr, now that he had successfully accomplished his claim to the throne as President of the Watchtower Society, using his growing clandestine and manipulative influence over the rest of the subjective and weaker Governing Body members, arbitrarily decided that as Covington was not of this unique, so-called heavenly class he therefore was not qualified to be a member of the Governing Body. As leader and chairman of the Governing Body, Knorr must have felt that by removing Covington he was acting on behalf of Almighty God and that he personally believed that God through his Holy Spirit wanted Covington removed and that Knorr actually believed he was God's instrument in accomplishing this task, this is how the Governing Body operated at that time. These are of course all signs of a true megalomaniac. A megalomaniac is a pathological egotist, that is, someone with a psychological disorder with symptoms like delusions of grandeur and an obsession with power. We also use the word megalomaniac more informally for people who behave as if they're convinced of their absolute power and greatness.

So eventually Nathan Knorr and the rest of the Governing Body members, now under his complete control, all of whom had previously approved of Hayden Covington being appointed as Vice-President and member of the Governing Body, and many of them had actually wanted to see Covington appointed as the 3rd President of the Watchtower Society in preference to Nathan Knorr. Together being now a unanimous group under Knorr's absolute control and direction, they requested that Covington must now resign after less than three years as Vice-President. In addition, it is reported that Knorr strongly objected to the heavy drinking of alcohol by Hayden Covington, which was a valid point and being almost as bad as his former friend and boss the late Joseph Rutherford, both being sarcastically referred to as the dynamic duo. Of course, Knorr had little cause to complain and condemn

Hayden Covington, as Knorr himself and some of his colleagues on the Governing Body were well known as very heavy drinkers, Knorr's favorite being the very expensive Bell's whisky directly imported at his insistence from Scotland, paid for out of the Watchtower donated funds allocated for food and sustenance for the various Bethel families. (Yes, our investigative reporters have seen the archived copies of these invoices, once under the control of the office of Grant Suiter, Secretary / Treasurer)

From real time accounts of this incident and conflict between Knorr and Covington coming to a head, it appears that Nathan Knorr was very envious of Covington's superior education, plus his lectures had a greater impact on the rank and file members of this religion as Covington transcended as a public speaker more than Nathan Knorr, the now officially appointed President and Covington was reported as a brilliant orator and eloquent public lecturer with a stentorian voice, which mesmerized his audiences. In turn this made Knorr insanely jealous as Knorr had a reputation of having a tepid, weak voice whenever he gave a lecture even though he tried, but unsuccessfully, to emulate Covington's speaking style. Here was Hayden Covington, and still speaking on behalf of the Governing Body (the claimed Faithful and Discreet Slave of the Bible) which truly riled Nathan Knorr and drove him to fits of anger. Knorr eventually won the day and further established his autocratic rule, so in one fell swoop he had Covington removed from his position as Vice-President; his position as one of the seven directors of the Watchtower Society and also from the Governing Body itself, which at that time was made up of the seven legally appointed directors.

From an unconfirmed report of a conversation between Hayden Covington and a personal friend of his in the Watchtower headquarters, he accused Knorr of being like a snake or serpent and the personification of Lucifer. Whether this claim is true or not, it is consistent with a later recorded interview with Covington when he likened Nathan Knorr to a cobra. For enlightened students of the Bible regarding the Bible character called Lucifer (Shining One), we recall that this was another name for Satan as used in Genesis 3:1; Job 1:6-12; Zechariah 3:1, 2; John 14:30; 1 Corinthians 5:2; 2 Corinthians 2:11; 1 Timothy 1:20;

Revelation 12:7-9; 20:1-3, 7-10, and especially the words of Isaiah 14:12-14, "I will ascend above the tops of the clouds; I will make myself like the Most High". Covington also said in this later recorded interview that Knorr connived him out of the presidency. The definition of conniving is someone who is prone to scheming in a harmful way, a person who is always scheming to take things that don't really belong to him is an example of someone who would be described as conniving. As reported by his unnamed personal friend, Hayden Covington believed an article that he had recently read in answer to the question about Lucifer or Satan and his demon angels influencing humans, especially those who were in positions of authority, such as religion, politics or commerce. Hayden had closely observed the conduct of Nathan Knorr and his actions of lying, deception, underhanded and sneaky, plus deliberately misleading others and Hayden genuinely and sincerely believed that Knorr was allowing himself to be used as a tool of Satan, as these were all characteristics of Lucifer (see the extract from the written article in the Appendix, Special Report No. 3).

Can one possibly imagine the free flow of God's pure Holy Spirit and blessing being poured out upon this religion when this sort of disgusting and corrupt behavior was being conducted behind the scenes by its so-called power-mad vicious leaders? (Ephesians 4:26-32) This is a religious organization that hypocritically claims to be Almighty God's only pure and holy organization on earth! You as an intelligent reader of this book about cults can easily draw you own conclusion over this very important and serious issue.

A very serious question was posed by one of our readers who is still an active member of Jehovah's Witnesses and an Elder in his local congregation, how did the Watchtower religion and organization prosper and expand if it did not have the blessing of God's Holy Spirit? Our simple comment is to refer to the religious cult of the Mormon Church now claiming to have 17 million followers and the Church of Scientology, how did they expand and prosper, being today two of the most powerful and influential religions on earth? How did the Roman Catholic Church, the largest religion in Christendom, claiming 1.3 billion members in 2018, expand and prosper over the almost 2000 years of apostasy from true Christianity; as originally established by our

Lord Jesus Christ in 33 AD? So, on reflection, this expansion of the Watchtower Society has nothing to do with the blessing of Almighty God but simply with the powers and the mechanical energy that the masters of these religions possess.

Referring back to the serious personal conflict for power between Nathan Knorr and Hayden Covington, Knorr also had Covington removed from his penthouse office in New York and arranged for his long standing personal friend, the pathetic and easily manipulated Freddy Franz appointed as Vice-President, who also now occupied the vacant penthouse office and Knorr also selected Lyman Swingle from Salt Lake City to replace Covington as one of the seven directors of the Watchtower Society and a permanent member of the Governing Body. Covington however still worked in the Watchtower headquarters for a short period of time to continue handling some unfinished legal cases on behalf of the organization. Hayden was transferred from his penthouse office and worked in a very small, cramped, windowless basement office for a couple of years, personally assigned to him according to an archived internal memo by his authoritarian boss Nathan Knorr, which no doubt gave Knorr a great feeling of power, plus superiority, dominance and personal satisfaction.

Even though it was unknown to many, including probably President Knorr himself, according to one source a rumor existed amongst the more strait-laced older members in the New York Bethel headquarters that Lyman Swingle was already personally involved in an unhealthy and possibly unscriptural relationship with a married sister in the New York area when he was appointed to the Governing Body by Knorr. From our research this married sister was a very attractive young woman of Polish descent, and a previous Roman Catholic before she converted to Jehovah's Witnesses. This was also claimed to be true in an interview, according to one of Swingle's relatives from Salt Lake City, who also said that, Lyman was only human after all. At first we hesitated in accepting information from this unnamed relative of Lyman Swingle, who submitted this story to our reporter, but finally agreed to include this detail in our chapter on the Watchtower Society as this informant had just recently quit the Watchtower Society and joined the Mormon Church for the basic underlying reason, he claimed, that he was stumbled by the numerous reports of the homosexuality and immoral conduct amongst the members of the Governing Body and many other brothers he personally knew in the Watchtower headquarters, which was true of course.

We could find no evidence that confirmed this rumor regarding Lyman Swingle being involved in an unscriptural relationship with a married woman back in 1945 when he was appointed to the Governing Body, except that eleven years later on June 8, 1956, Lyman Swingle married a recently widowed sister with two young children called Crystal Waldrop (née Zicher) who had been separated from her husband for many years, she also happened to be the same woman he was suspected of dating back in 1945 while she was still legally married. One of our researchers, when he heard this story regarding this relative of Lyman Swingle quitting the religion of the Watchtower Society and joining the Mormon Church, he sarcastically stated with a chuckle, this guy must be crazy as he was simply jumping out of the frying pan into the fire.

> *Editor's Note*: A friend of the editor, who still works in the London Bethel of the Watchtower Society, sarcastically said when he heard of this news about Swingle, "At last we know that at least one more member of the Governing Body who did not have homosexual tendencies."

This was another clear example of how Nathan Knorr was so focused and obsessed with his personal ambition and power as the autocratic leader of this religion that often he was not even aware or concerned about the secret and clandestine affairs of his fellow members on the Governing Body and the same mentality have been adopted by the current Governing Body especially about the notorious drinking habits and misuse of alcohol by some fellow members. Plus if anyone objected to their unscriptural teachings and practices they were crushed underfoot as being rebellious, disloyal and satanic. From our research, also supported by writer and fellow researcher Rolf Furuli, when he was still a devoted member of Jehovah's Witnesses, the same situation exists even today amongst the secretive Governing Body as they feel so powerful in their so-called God appointed positions as prospective Kings and Priests to jointly rule the Universe with Jesus Christ. And as pointed out by Rolf in his latest book, *My Beloved Religion and the Governing Body*, they simply operate in a separate fantasy world and as a law to themselves. By being a law unto themselves it means that they behave in an independent way, ignoring laws, rules, or conventional ways of doing things.

By the time this book is published, Rolf Furuli will have probably joined the long list of individuals who have been disfellowshipped for apostasy, remember that one is not allowed to offer sincere suggestions, honest opinions or positive criticism to the Governing Body of the Watchtower Society, who operate as the ruthless leaders of this religious cult. To try and justify the spiritual execution of these sincere Christians we once again quote from *Watchtower*, August 15, 1981, p. 25.

> From time to time, there have arisen from among the ranks of Jehovah's people those who, like the original Satan, have adopted an independent, faultfinding attitude. They do not want to serve shoulder to shoulder with the worldwide brotherhood. (Compare Ephesians 2:19-22.) Rather, they present a stubborn shoulder to Jehovah's word. (Zech. 7:11, 12) Reviling the pattern of the pure language that Jehovah has so graciously taught his people over the past century, these haughty ones try to draw the sheep away from the one international flock that Jesus has gathered in the earth. (John 10:7-10, 16) They try to sow doubts and to separate unsuspecting ones from the bounteous table of spiritual food spread at the Kingdom Halls of Jehovah's Witnesses, where truly there is nothing lacking. (Ps. 23:1-6)

This brief description and observation was submitted by a person who intimately knew this man Nathan Knorr, as reported in the book by James Penton, *Apocalypse Delayed - The Story of Jehovah's Witnesses.*

> Nathan Knorr was an organization man from the start. Often cold, ruthless and business-like and strongly disliked by a number of members of the headquarters for his quick turnabouts on policy and roughshod treatment of those opposed to his ideas.

Returning to the account of Hayden Covington, according to confirmed internal records held at the New York headquarters, Knorr personally originated written reports that described various reasons and excuses; belittling and using pejorative terms plus vitriolic comments, all officially put on record, regarding the ongoing claimed incompetence of Hayden Covington in caring for his duties as legal counsel for the organization, plus some reports directly referring to his drinking problem. This was part of Knorr's overall devilish plan as he was consumed with such hatred for this man and he would not be satisfied until he could get Hayden kicked out of Bethel altogether, and as the pressure increased this did nothing but drive poor Hayden Covington to drink more and more and eventually becoming a full-blown alcoholic. Hayden now realized with a sense of fatalism during this short period of time that his services on behalf of the Watchtower Society were now vilipend or worthless as Nathan Knorr personally humiliated Hayden in every way he possible could, and was extremely critical of his need to continue as the legal counsel to the Watchtower Society despite his personal and legal official appointment by Joseph Rutherford and based on a legally binding agreement drawn up back in 1939. So Knorr stubbornly and perversely set up his own legal department working directly under his personal control and supervision even though he was a total ignoramus in this field and area of expertise. He did so without the voluntary skill and services of the now sacked; fired and dismissed current legal counsel, being also one of the most brilliant attorneys in America (if not the whole world) and who had willingly served this religious organization for many years without payment of the usual expensive legal fees and Hayden Covington was still at that time a loyal member of Jehovah's Witnesses, although still struggling and battling with his own personal demons.

Hayden Covington finally left the Watchtower Headquarters and settled in Cincinnati, Ohio, with his wife Dorothy and their two young children, who were both born after Hayden left Bethel in New York and he hoped to resume a normal life as a father and family man. As reported by a friend of the family, as things turned out, all was not well for the Covington family after settling in Cincinnati. Dorothy being a very sincere, loyal follower of the Watchtower Society, brought up her two children in the principles of the Bible as best she knew how under the domineering instructions of the organization. She took them to all the meetings as instructed, five per week at that time, out in the field service selling the Watchtower literature on a regular basis as instructed, both Saturdays and Sundays, but she also burdened them with all the demanding overly strict rules and regulations imposed by this oppressive religion of Jehovah's Witnesses.

This unfortunately resulted in a very distressing experience for the Covington family down the line, when her only son Lane, in the prime of his life, could no longer handle this oppressive, demanding and dictatorial religious system. This young man Lane must have been fully aware of his father's famous experiences before he was born, especially while Hayden was serving under Joseph Rutherford and later under the ruthless Nathan Knorr and could easily blame his father's current mental and emotional condition on this religion, but he also knew that his father was not inexcusable. His father Hayden had displayed the same greed and lust for power within this religion, as many of these men at the top of this religion had done, and still do, and his father was now paying a heavy price. Dorothy had to cope with a marriage partner who was an alcoholic and as many of our readers will recognize and acknowledge is no easy task, as the whole of the family and its stability was seriously affected. As events unfolded, Hayden Covington was later disfellowshipped from this religion as an unrepentant alcoholic, an official decision made by the judicial committee of his local congregation in Cincinnati. This in turn created even more serious problems for the family as they now had to comply with a set of rules laid down by their masters of this religion that now prevented them from having any meaningful, loving relationship with the father and head of this family, this no doubt in turn created extreme stress and strain on this poor family of baptized Jehovah's Witnesses.

It has been suggested by one of our researchers who spoke to an ex-member of the Watchtower headquarters in New York and who was familiar with this terrible and embarrassing case of the rivalry between Knorr and Covington that Knorr himself was behind this disfellowshipping action. The report was that Nathan Knorr in the 1950s had made a private phone call to the local congregation servant of the Cincinnati congregation, who in those days was also the chairman of the local judicial committee, as it had been reported to Knorr by one of his spies, a district servant called James ***** that

Hayden Covington was now rumored to be a complete and outright alcoholic and was becoming an embarrassment to the organization. So it is claimed that Knorr stepped in and gave his private instructions to this judicial committee that they were to immediately hold a committee meeting and take the necessary steps to expel Hayden from the organization. We were unable to establish the full details of the account of this committee meeting and if Hayden actually voluntarily appeared before a judicial committee and hearing to try and defend himself, which would have been the usual procedure. But knowing how ruthless Nathan Knorr was and how consumed with hate for this man Hayden Covington, it would fit into his overall plan to finally destroy this now sad and pathetic individual Hayden Covington and expel him from the so-called Christian Congregation, which resulted in a letter and announcement being read out to the entire local congregation. So, in our opinion, in the light of all the evidence we have seen, this account is both acceptable and believable, but we will let you, as an intelligent reader of this report, draw your own conclusion.

When Knorr heard of this news of the final downfall of Covington, according to a writer in the New York headquarters who informed one of our researchers, Knorr experienced a frisson of delight and immediately notified his fellow members on the Governing Body, who no doubt also experienced a feeling of success and accomplishment. Also with some final relief, probably ignoring their guilty conscience in helping to carry out the wishes of their autocratic and demanding, ruthless leader, Nathan Knorr, in his successful action and quest of finally removing Hayden Covington from the organization of Jehovah's Witnesses. This final step of excommunication in turn was unquestionably used to justify all Knorr's previous malicious actions against Hayden Covington.

Nathan Knorr was also no doubt inwardly satisfied that he had finally accomplished what he set out to do, as confirmed and supported by his friend Freddy Franz and another confidential associate, his private secretary Milton Henschel, both now firmly entrenched on the Governing Body by Knorr. Both of these men were known for submitting to every whim of Knorr and in believing Knorr's actions were the necessary official duties in his role of being the now all-powerful, legally appointed President of the organization. Plus, of course, using his other underhanded tactics and acts of turpitude that he committed, and the steps he had taken, ethically or unethically in blocking Covington in his own private and personal ambitious bid for the Presidency of the organization in opposition to Knorr. To a limited extent, these actions that Knorr took and probably sincerely believed were considered necessary by him in order to protect the Watchtower Society as the claimed only true religion on earth, a so-called pure religion and the removal of an imposter by the name of Covington. In addition, these actions would also perhaps help to appease the conscience of Nathan Knorr when he prayed to Almighty God each night for being compelled; supposedly under the guidance of God's Holy Spirit, by having to instigate these extreme actions of removing Hayden Covington from his officially appointed position within the organization and from the powerful Governing Body, which Knorr now completely controlled.

It mattered not that in this procedure and personal vendetta he had destroyed the life and soul of a fellow man in the process; crushing the spirit of an individual who had believed that his service to the Watchtower Society as its legal counsel for many years and who also in fact sincerely believed to be his genuine vital service to Almighty God as a dedicated Christian and member of this religion, even though on reflection we all now know that he was obviously misguided. So Knorr had the personal experience that must have given him some sort of twisted and warped satisfaction that he; as a true psychopath[14] and as chairman of the Governing Body was acting on behalf of Almighty God as his personal representative on earth and had removed, plus totally destroyed this hated undesirable man; his enemy Hayden Covington a so-called imposter on the Governing Body, who was his long time bitter rival to the claim they both had made back in 1942. But Nathan

[14] Psychopathy (ASPD) is traditionally a personality disorder characterized by impaired empathy and remorse, being bold and showing egotistical traits. Plus displaying the use of cruelty to gain empowerment and referring to tough, aggressive or hostile tendencies with a grandiose sense of self-worth, plus being cunning and manipulative. A psychopath also shows a lack of ability to love or establish meaningful personal relationships, expresses extreme egocentricity, and demonstrates a failure to learn from experience and other behaviors associated with easily becoming angry, manipulating and does not care if they have hurt someone in the process.

Knorr, who personally believed that he, being appointed by God's Holy Spirit as the all-powerful 3rd President of the Watchtower Society, he had the right and authority to undertake this duty.

A friend of the Covington family commented that Hayden reached the lowest ebb of his life and even contemplated suicide; he realized that his career as a world renowned famous, leading defense attorney was now looking like a catastrophe. In addition, he slowly became a pathetic wreck of a man, primarily as a result of his experiences and run-in with ruthless Nathan Knorr; the powerful Watchtower Society and its Governing Body. From reports it appears that Hayden could not hold down a decent regular job, despite his past reputation of being a brilliant attorney and spent many hours each day in the local bars, this was also confirmed when his wife Dorothy Mae was interviewed for an article that appeared in a *Watchtower* journal. She also stood by him during those depressing times and she worked full time in a newspaper office to financially support the family. She is also on record a few years before she died in 2015, as she also said, "Hayden supported the freedoms that we sometimes take for granted. I think it is wonderful that he spent his life helping those who needed it – not just in the United States but in many other places."

In a report by J. Bergman Ph.D., who is an ex-member of Jehovah's Witnesses, he wrote an article called "Insight on Jehovah's Witnesses" that appeared in the journal published by Springer Publishing called *Review of Religious Research (1959-2016)*. This article included a personal interview with Hayden Covington in 1974, four years before his death, and he recorded the following.

> He (Covington) kept calling N.H. Knorr, the president then, a cobra. When I asked him why he said this, "Do you know what a cobra does? They'll slither behind you, and they'll strike viciously." It became apparent that he detested Knorr. This could be because his problems with the Society began when Knorr became president. Covington claimed that he, Covington, had the votes to become the next president to succeed Rutherford, but Knorr connived him out of the presidency.

For a more complete coverage of this report based on this interview by J Bergman with Hayden Covington, please see Appendix, Special Report No. 4.

Just months before he died in 1978, aged 67 years, Hayden Covington applied for reinstatement to this religion, based on his claimed repentance from his sins, which was granted by the local judicial committee of his wife's congregation in Cincinnati. This was one decision that autocrat Nathan Knorr could not overrule or interfere with as he was now dead and buried. Hayden was no doubt motivated by his loving and supportive wife of many years, plus the ominous coming end of the world and the imminent, just around the corner new world promised by the Watchtower Society to those who were in good standing according to their official religious records and he probably viewed his reinstatement as an insurance policy, just in case. After all what did he have to lose as he was approaching death himself because of very serious health problems as a result of his excessive drinking habit? His life became an epic example or pathos of what happens when one is captured and enslaved in a religious cult.

Hayden Covington and his wife Dorothy had two children, a daughter, Lynn Lee Covington born in 1959, and a son, Lane Christian Covington born in 1962. Daughter Lynn Covington Elfers gave an interview in 2018 for the Robert H. Jackson Center in New York, recounting her father's brilliant work as a voluntary lawyer on behalf of the Watchtower Society. She also cynically highlighted how her father worked for next to nothing and could have been earning millions in private practice, but no mention is made regarding his bitter rivalry with Nathan Knorr. According to Ohio public records, in 1988 at the age of 25, Lane Christian Covington committed suicide by hanging himself. So here we have once again clear examples of innocent lives being destroyed by the masters and power of a religious cult, although it is recorded that Dorothy the widow of Hayden Covington remained a loyal follower of this religion until the day she died aged 92 years in 2015, except for a short period in 1975-1977, when her loyalty to the organization waivered along with many others, because of the erroneous claim of the end of the system of things coming in October of 1975.

The official statement by the Watchtower Society in 1955 provided a much different watered down, very misleading and deceptive rendering of this serious incident of the tussle for power between Knorr and Covington, which article was nothing more than hypocrisy and false propaganda that stated, "On September 24, 1945, H. C. Covington graciously declined to serve further as a member of the board of directors and as vice-president of the Watch Tower Bible and Tract Society of Pennsylvania, not as an evasion of responsibilities, but rather as an effort to comply with what appeared to be the Lord's will for all the members of the directorate and the officers to be of the anointed ones [with a heavenly hope], since his hope was [earthly] as that of one of the other sheep."

According to a friend and co-worker of Hayden Covington he definitely did not graciously decline his appointment on the Governing Body but he was very bitter, resentful and angry that Knorr had finally got the better of him and out maneuvered him. In addition, Knorr had cleverly convinced, by means of lies and deceit, the other members of the Governing Body to agree with his underhanded scheme of removing Hayden from his prestigious position within the Organization. Knorr had already asked Covington to resign from the Governing Body, also being at that time the board of directors, but Hayden Covington had adamantly refused. Hayden Covington was still at that time a loyal believer in Jehovah's Witnesses and their teachings and he sincerely believed that his appointment as Vice-President and being a Member of the Governing Body was still in line with the will of God, even though he personally viewed Knorr as being a thief and stealing from him the rightful position of being the next President of the Watchtower Society when Rutherford died. So, Hayden would not abrogate his position in the so-called Lord's organization and he refused to resign. According to this friend of Hayden the next step that Knorr took was to call a special meeting of the Board of Directors and Knorr had pre-empted the other five members of his special resolution to remove Covington from the Board and appoint a replacement and this action was also confirmed by a relative of Lyman Swingle of Salt Lake City, as Lyman who did publicly claim he was of the so-called remnant of the anointed class had been told in advance of this plan by Nathan Knorr. Apparently, this special board meeting of six members was entirely legal and in compliance with the terms of the Memorandum, Charter and Articles of Establishment of the Watch Tower Bible and Tract Society of Pennsylvania, Inc.

Our inside contact at the New York headquarters of the Watchtower Society checked and confirmed that the minutes of that special board meeting held at 10am on Monday, September 24, 1945, clearly stipulated that a vote of all six directors, unanimously adopted a resolution by Nathan Homer Knorr and resolved to remove Hayden Covington as a director of the board of the Watchtower Society and appoint Lyman Swingle as a replacement. The reason for the removal is clearly cited in the minutes of that meeting and that the reason was because of his excessive drinking and use of alcohol and no mention is made whatsoever of the fact that Hayden Covington was not a member of the so-called remnant of the anointed heavenly class of 144,000.

This clearly proves that the statement in the *Watchtower* magazine of 1955 regarding Hayden Covington deciding to graciously decline his appointment is nothing more than a blatant lie inserted to mislead the local members of this religion and was probably instigated and personally instructed by the autocrat, President Nathan Knorr. What does the Bible say about those who are liars?

> "Truthful lips endure forever, but a lying tongue lasts only a moment." ~ Proverbs 12:19.

> "The getting of treasures by a lying tongue is a fleeting vapor and a snare of death." ~ Proverbs 21:6.

> "The way of the guilty is crooked, but the conduct of the pure is right." ~ Proverbs 21:8.

> "Lying lips conceal hatred, and whoever utters slander is a fool." ~ Proverbs 10:18.

(Read also Psalms 55:23 and 2 Peter 2:1-3)

> *Editor's Note*: This following self-condemnatory statement that appeared in the *Watchtower* magazine crystallizes the issue of telling lies and speaking the truth when it relates to modern religion. What will guide us in choosing the right religion? The *Encyclopedia Universalis* is correct when it highlights the

importance of truth. A religion that teaches lies cannot be true. (*Watchtower*, December 1, 1991, p. 7) During our research into this religion of Jehovah's Witnesses we came across many occasions that they used blatant lies to cover over their errors of judgment and incorrect interpretations of the Holy Scriptures, plus they completely ignore the words of the Apostle Paul at Romans 3:4, "Let God be found true, though every man be found a liar."

One final note submitted by our research team and is a clear lesson, from which we can all learn, that is if we feel that we are possibly enslaved or trapped in a religious cult. The lesson is that poor Hayden Covington was deluded into thinking that Almighty God would eventually put things right, as this is what he had been taught by the Watchtower Society. He reasoned as all members of cults do today, especially members of Jehovah's Witnesses, that if they wait upon the Lord he will correct matters for the sake and good of his Holy name. Of course as we learn from history, this did not happen in the case of Hayden Covington and his experiences with the Watchtower Society. Many today do not always agree with the teachings and current policies of this religion but they remain as members on the foolish belief that Almighty God has chosen this organization as the only true religion on earth today and is directing it and will make any necessary changes when required, so why be overly concerned. This is exactly what Hayden Covington believed, but look at what happened to him, he ended up a destroyed individual in every way possible; spiritually, emotionally, mentally and also physically.

It is clear that the Lord did not step in and make the changes that Hayden hoped and prayed for, as he waited upon the Lord. Almighty God did not move Knorr back again to the position of Vice-President and Covington to be promoted and appointed as the new President, as Rutherford wanted and probably left in his written instructions to be opened upon his death and this should be a powerful lesson for all members of religious cults today. No matter what the Governing Body of the Watchtower claims today, Almighty God, Yahweh is not directing or dealing directly with this religion or any other religious cult, he never has and never will, so this leaves members of a cult with a serious choice. Do they accept what is dished out to them in the various manipulative teachings and policies of a cult and remain as slaves chained to their religion and carry on as usual, or do they break free and remove themselves from this cult that is guaranteed to eventually ruin their lives, as it did the life of Hayden Covington.

It is not an easy choice but one that must be faced and thousands have succeeded, some with great difficulty, but they have resumed a normal life and found the strength to pick up their lives again and practice true Christianity as taught in the Bible and by Jesus Christ and not controlled by a cult that claims to be God's only spokesman and only communication channel between ourselves and God. These courageous Christians have done so and broken free of their chains by reminding themselves of one of the most powerful and encouraging Bible texts ever written, quoted below, and an important message sent to us by our Heavenly Father through his Holy Spirit and recorded in the inspired Holy Bible and not through a group of men who sit in a boardroom of a religious organization, gathered together in a New York compound of a religious cult, issuing instructions and directives to their slave like followers by means of videos and films over the internet.

These words are recorded by the Apostle Paul at Ephesians 3:14-19. "For this reason I bow my knees before the Father, from whom every family in heaven and on earth takes its name. I pray that, according to the riches of his glory, he may grant that you may be strengthened in your inner being with power through his Spirit, and that Christ may dwell in your hearts through faith, as you are being rooted and grounded in love. I pray that you may have the power to comprehend, with all the saints, what is the breadth and length and height and depth, and to know the love of Christ that surpasses knowledge, so that you may be filled with all the fullness of God."

***

We are privileged, by kind permission of Randy Watters of Manhattan Beach, California, to include a few extracts recorded in his several brilliant books, articles and website that relate the experience of a young man who served for a number of years in the New York headquarters and later in a senior position of the Watchtower Society, and his serious but also somewhat amusing recollections that help us to appreciate what these men had to experience and endure while serving as slaves to this Organization. Randy is an ex-witness and current CEO of the non-profit association, Free Minds, Inc, which is dedicated to helping people to escape from cult-like religions.

> In my first three years at Bethel I became aware of the moral short-fallings of many a Bethelite, from smoking to swearing, racial fights and so forth. Some managed to avoid going to the weekly meetings altogether! Their parents had shipped them off to Bethel like it was the military or something, a last chance to straighten them out. Bethel broke you: you either made the grade or ended up a nut job. A few even took the suicide route, it was so traumatic. Waking up early to bells, few females, 20 minutes to eat, often no dinner, not to mention living in New York City. I knew one guy that chickened out after the taxi ride from the airport to Bethel!
>
> One week Daniel Sydlik of the Governing Body came out to lecture the Bethel family and said that it was appropriate to be dressed up like you were going to a meeting when you come to the table (at least with a neck tie). That went over like a lead balloon, and the rebellion was met by none other than Fred Franz, who came to breakfast all next week in an old dirty white T-shirt that said, "Where in the hell is McCook, Nebraska?" There was no controlling him. We thought that it was so sad, as Freddy was idolized by many. To me he was like an old Baptist preacher with a dry sense of humor, but more than ten minutes of listening to him drove you up a wall. In some ways it was like living in an old folks' home. Brother Maxwell Friend liked to feed the pigeons (a no-no in NYC), and Brother Suiter of the Governing Body used the breakfast podium to lash out at him without mentioning names, "Those who feed the pigeons are not our friends." Plus there was no shortage of unintended humor, with George Gangas of the Governing Body thanking Jehovah for his shoelaces and Karl Klein also of the Governing Body giving a lecture in his prayers. I felt like a Catholic schoolgirl with the old nuns!
>
> The trouble began when a handful of brothers were commissioned to write the book *Aid To Bible Understanding*. In researching their chronological dating system for the last days,

historical research overwhelmingly indicated that their precious date of 1914 (supposedly the invisible return of Christ) was nothing more than the start of World War I. My overseer, Tom Cabeen, began to share this with me, a little each day in a hushed tone behind the printing presses. It was intriguing but dangerous! According to all historical records, Jerusalem was destroyed in 587-586 BC, a full 20 years later than the Witness date. Neither was there found any basis in the Bible for a 2520-year Gentile Times. Russell's dates and concepts had been constructed with inaccurate history.

Another member of the Governing Body, Lloyd Barry, said on May 29, 1980 in addressing the elders of the Bethel family: "When we talk about law, we talk about organization. With all our hearts we need to search after that law. Jehovah doesn't give individuals interpretation. We need a guide, and that is the faithful and discreet slave. We should not be getting together in a clique to discuss views contrary to the faithful and discreet slave. We must recognize the source of our instruction. We must be like an ass, be humble, and stay in the manger; and we won't get any poison."

I learned a lot about men and their power games from my time at Bethel. I learned that those who are seeking power will do anything to keep it, even sacrificing their common sense and the friendship of others. They will find ways to justify their actions through theological arguments. One thing should be clear if you study the history of the Watchtower Society: doctrine is irrelevant. It changes all the time, as the Governing Body rewrites their own history and rewrites themselves into the Bible, as if it was written to them and only them. You can study theology until you're blue in the face. You can know the Bible word for word. But unless you understand how they manipulate it to their own ends, you will remain clueless as to how to counter them. They will laugh at you. If you learn to call their bluff and expose their methodology, they will not challenge you further. Like the Wizard of Oz caught performing behind the curtain, they will pull the fabric of deception back in place. Learn their techniques more than their theology.

Was the Governing Body paranoid of losing their control due to the doctrinal questions of some Bethel family members in 1979? Perhaps, but I believe that they were not so much afraid or paranoid as they wanted to flex their muscles. This seemed obvious to me, because of their previous ploys for power, and their haughtiness and lack of shame in how they presented themselves. They acted like gloating hyenas just having made their kill. President Knorr was now out of the picture, and they were now in charge. I had to get out of there! Any respect I had for these leaders was lost within a few weeks of listening to their morning diatribes to the Bethelites, attacking the so-called apostates.

Below is a portion of the public testimony of our respected friend Randy Watters as expressed on his website, and whether you agree with his sentiments or not, we must respect his work and dedication to expose religious cults and for speaking the truth about the Watchtower Society and we have primarily included it for that reason alone.

> *By Randy Watters*: The crux of the matter is this: Jehovah's Witnesses are not allowed to interpret the Bible, but must rely on the ever-changing interpretations of 14 (eight in 2019) men in New York, none of whom are Greek or Hebrew scholars, and have no business translating a Bible, let alone controlling the lives of millions of people. Christianity is meant to be an experiential faith. You come to Christ as your mediator, ask forgiveness for your sins, and you receive the new birth (John 3:3-7). Christianity is God working through man, not man working for God. When I realized this in 1979 after a study of Romans and Galatians, it soon became obvious that "grace" is the key to a life in Christ.

What is the Grace of God or Divine Grace mentioned by Randy Watters? It is the love and mercy given to us by God because Yahweh desires us to have it, not necessarily because of anything we have done to earn it. Grace in Christianity is the free and unmerited favor of God as manifested in the salvation of sinners and the bestowing of blessings. Common Christian teaching is that grace is unmerited mercy (favor) that God gave to humanity by sending his Son, Jesus Christ, to die on a stake or cross, thus securing man's eternal salvation from sin. These words by the Apostle Paul recorded at Ephesians 2:8, 9, confirm this. "For by grace you have been saved through faith, and this is not your own doing; it is the gift of God not the result of works, so that no one may boast." (see also Romans 6:23, John 14:7; Acts 4:12; 1 Timothy 2:5, 6).

You will have noticed that the apostles (especially Paul) make it clear that we do not earn or by the result of works make our way to salvation by doing good deeds, acts of accomplishment or giving up sinful behavior. Our only hope is to place all our confidence, faith, and trust in the Lord Jesus Christ, the Savior who offered Himself up on the stake or cross to redeem us from sin. These words of Ephesians 2:8, 9, of course completely obliterate the theory and teaching of the Watchtower Society that one can earn their salvation and their total distortion and misuse of the Bible text at Philippians 2:12, 13. "Therefore, my beloved, just as you have always obeyed me, not only in my presence, but much more now in my absence, <u>work out your own salvation</u> with fear and trembling; or it is God who is at work in you, enabling you both to will and to work for his good pleasure."

The Governing Body of the Watchtower Society, as religious cults usually do, they expertly take a Bible text completely out of context and by manipulation apply this text to be implemented by their followers, implying that the number of hours they spend each month in the door-to-door sale of their literature, how many meetings they attend each week and most important of all, how much money they donate to the Watchtower Treasury and they point out to their followers that these are ways one can work out their salvation.

The Apostle Paul also gives this command using a strange and often misunderstood phrase: work out your own salvation with fear and trembling. This unique remark speaks of ongoing obedience to the Lord's instructions regarding our daily conduct for those of us already practicing Christianity and doing so with total awareness that Yahweh and his son Jesus Christ are watching and observing our behavior. It's important to note that Paul is not telling Christians to <u>work</u> for their salvation. This statement implies a need to <u>live out</u> – to practice, demonstrate, and exhibit – the salvation, which believers have in Christ.

Paul wanted the Christian believers in Philippi to live their personal lives with success, contentment and unity, as advised in Psalms 119:109, "I hold my life in my palm constantly, but I do not forget your law". Doing so without complaining, but being confident and courageous to speak the truth when it comes to religious cults that claim to be the exclusive spokesmen of Almighty God.

***

Returning to the experience of Raymond Franz in the late 1970s, Lyman Swingle had made his opinion forcefully known to the other fellow members of the Governing Body that the reason Raymond Franz dissented from the existing core teachings, namely the symbolic or literal number of the so-called little flock of 144,000; and the correct explanation and definition of who are the other sheep or great crowd mentioned in the Bible. Also, the so-called absolute date of 1914; plus the term this generation and it was all based on his genuine sincerity plus the honest, extensive, very accurate, exhaustive research by Raymond and his dedicated team of fellow Bible students. Plus Raymond Franz was very concerned about the current feedback of the negative results of many members being disillusioned with the failure of the world's last days coming to an end in 1975, which had been aggressively promoted by the Governing Body and their spokesmen, especially Frederick Franz (his uncle by the way) the most senior member of the Governing Body and was viewed by many as a divine prophet and was the originator of the claim that 1975 would be the year of Armageddon.

In addition, our informant who referred back to Raymond Franz and his experiences, also made a rather touching comment as he had personally met the member of the Governing Body, Lyman Swingle of Salt Lake City, and who was interviewed by the member of our research team regarding this well-loved man, Lyman. He said, "Lyman was well known for his lack of a sense of humor, his dour expression and being over serious, but behind his Germanic appearance he was a most gentle, compassionate soul and one of the most genuine Christians I have ever met."

This extract from the book, *Crisis of Conscience*, written by Raymond Franz, sheds some light on how this former member of the Governing

Body of the Watchtower Society discovered the importance of not being enslaved to the doctrines and teachings of the leaders and masters of a cult. This should also be taken as a very serious lesson to be learned by all of our readers, no matter which religious affiliation or leaning we profess. Raymond wrote:

> I began to appreciate more than ever before how vitally important context was in discerning the meaning of any part of Scripture, and that realization seemed to be true of others of the group who were working regularly on the Aid project. We also came to realize the need to let the Bible define its own terms rather than simply taking some previously held view or letting an English dictionary definition control. We began to make greater use of the Hebrew and Greek lexicons in the Bethel library, and concordances that were based on the original language words rather than on English translations.

Raymond Franz is also on record of admitting the following sentiments.

> It was an education and it was also very humbling, for we came to appreciate that our understanding of Scripture was far less than we had thought, that we were not the advanced Bible scholars we thought we were. I personally had been on such a treadmill of activity over the previous twenty-five years that, although reading through the Bible several times, I had never been able to do such serious, detailed research into the Scriptures, in fact never felt a great need to do so since it was assumed that others were doing it for me. Now having both time and access to the extra Bible helps, the lexicons, commentaries, Hebrew and Greek concordances, and so forth, was an aid. But above all it was seeing the need always to let the context guide, always to let the Scriptures themselves control, that made the major difference. There was no overnight change of viewpoint but, over a period of years, a gradual deepening of appreciation of the crucial need to let God's Word speak for itself to the fullest extent possible.

According to Raymond Franz's account, as revealed in *Crisis of Conscience*, on 21 May, 1980, he was called to a special Governing Body meeting, which was to be tape recorded. He agreed to participate, with the unambiguous stipulation that he be given a copy of the tape recording. He was verbally assured by the Governing Body that his request would be honored. He further states that this request was not honored. In other words, the Governing Body is dishonest and will lie, if it is expedient to do so. He was asked various questions about the organization and its teachings, rather than questions about the gossip that had been circulating throughout the New York Bethel headquarters and which had led to the disfellowshipping (excommunicating) of others who had been assisting him in his research, under the charges of apostasy. The questions pertained to the literal or symbolic number of the 144,000 mentioned in the Bible book of Revelation, the last days, the generation, the anointed remnant, the year 1975 and the role of the organization and its leaders as God's exclusive representatives on earth, etc.

The Governing Body under the chairmanship of Albert Schroeder was not satisfied with Raymond's answers, so they continued to question him. The majority of those men in attendance just sat and listened and made no comment and asked no questions, it appears that the aggressive and known hypocrite Bert Schroeder dominated the entire proceeding. After three hours, Raymond Franz was told he could go. The next morning, he was asked to make more recorded comments about a second tape recording, which related to additional Witnesses' hearsay and gossip about other members; he declined to comment on the unsubstantiated material.

On 22 May, 1980, Albert Schroeder, Chairman of the Governing Body, came to Raymond Franz's private room in Bethel and informed him that some of the Governing Body members wanted him immediately disfellowshipped regardless of the lack of evidence against him. This did not include the member and stalwart Lyman Swingle, according to the leaked records of those secret meetings received by our research team; Lyman appears to have accepted the honest and open answers by Raymond and was all for investigating further the findings of the accurate Bible research by Raymond Franz and his team of assistants. This suggestion by Lyman was in order to consider what steps, if any, the Governing Body could possibly take to further examine and correct these errors of doctrine, if they actually existed. Raymond Franz therefore assumed from this that they had failed to persuade a majority, so there would be no expulsion.

Schroeder said that the Governing Body however wanted Raymond Franz to immediately resign. Raymond chose to write a resignation letter, but he vehemently refused and was personally disgusted and offended by the Watchtower Society's offer of a private cash settlement and a monthly stipend, plus to become a member of the Infirm Special Pioneers list. This was a special fund which Raymond knew from experience was frequently and sometimes unethically misused for friends of leading members of this religion, plus it was also being financed by the voluntary donations of the many sincere members of this religion as contributions to the Lord's Work. It was primarily for this reason that Raymond refused this cash offer and preferred to stand with dignity on his own two feet. Raymond was well aware that this offer of cash and a monthly stipend was a subtle way and attempt to buy his silence, as they had done previously with two other men who were asked to resign from the Governing Body, namely the homosexual Ewart Chitty and pedophile Leo Greenlees, and the Governing Body was hoping that Raymond would just disappear and remain silent as these other two disgusting characters had done. Most of these cases recorded on the Infirm Special Pioneers List, based on confirmed records we researched in the Watchtower headquarters and various branch offices were not really physically infirmed at all, but rather victims of the result of the over use of alcohol and excessive use of over the counter and prescription drugs and medication. These individuals were often sad cases of simple, straightforward emotional and mental burnout or chronic stress created by their life style or personal guilty conscience, having been caused by misleading sincere people into believing the doctrines of this religion that they represented.

Remember the correct definition of infirm is of poor or deteriorated vitality, especially feeble from age, being weak of mind, will, or character, irresolute or vacillating. If the Governing Body thought for one minute that Raymond Franz would accept this cash offer, being simply nothing but hush money and that he was willing to be classified and dumped in this infirm category, then most of these stupid, boneheaded men themselves should have been found accountable and re-classified, no longer as members of the Governing Body but rather as members of the official Infirm Special Pioneer list of the Watchtower Society.

Raymond Franz, according to our reporter, also refused this private offer from the Watchtower Society for him to be added to the list of Infirm Special Pioneers, created and maintained by the Governing Body as he knew he would be living a lie, as he was in perfectly good health mentally, emotionally and physically; he was neither ill, sick, infirmed or addicted to alcohol as many of they were. But this clear deception, lying and unethical scheme to compel Raymond to live a lie for the rest of his life did not seem to concern the officials on the Governing Body, even though everyone familiar with this very disturbing, serious incident in the New York Bethel knew full well that Raymond was in very good physical and mental health. Plus Raymond's spiritual health was also extremely sound, in the opinion of many who worked in the Bethel at the time, plus many outside of Bethel who personally knew him, but who were unfortunately too cowardly and afraid of their masters to step forward and support his cause.

The reasoning of the powerful, arrogant Governing Body was that they had the god-given authority to offer this private cash settlement and ongoing monthly payment as they had done on many other occasions regarding friends of the leaders of this religion, using the donated funds of the numerous members who had sincerely contributed their hard-earned money to the work of the Lord. This offer of a cash settlement to Raymond Franz in these circumstances is yet another masterful use of lies and deceit, plus another clear example of this religious cult and its modus operandi of chicanery and duplicity used by this religion when it is expedient to do so.

Most of the members of the Governing Body just wanted to get Raymond out of the Bethel headquarters as soon as possible so that they would not have to look at his face each and every day, as he would simply remind them of the guilt they must have inwardly felt and now carried in their hearts regarding this ruthless action of requesting his resignation, simply because he was following his Bible trained conscience and his core values of honest Bible research. They were also very aware of the well-founded research that he and his fellow Bible students had presented to them, which provided solid evidence and clearly explained that many of the existing teachings of the Watchtower Society were actually incorrect interpretations of the

Bible. Of course, most of the Governing Body had already stubbornly decided that they would never ever change these old, long established teachings introduced by Russell, Rutherford and later Freddy Franz, even if they were incorrect,[15] as they could not risk a major falling away of their members and financial supporters if they made these dramatic and necessary changes. Also making these changes in the teachings and doctrines plus having to admit their errors and mistakes could easily upset many of the more intelligent members and perhaps producing a revolt and as a consequence losing the essential money, cash flow and donations regularly received from the flock that kept their luxurious life style intact.

The Governing Body had already taken the drastic steps of excommunicating and kicking out of the Bethel headquarters most of the fellow researchers and Bible students associated with Raymond Franz, so Raymond was now like a single thorn in their side and barb in their eyes. (Numbers 33:55) By taking this step of never having to see or hear from him ever again they obviously hoped it would help them erase the guilt they felt and experienced as a result of their action of trying to destroy a genuine Christian and honest man who had simply shown the necessary courage to speak up and expose the ruthless and extreme powers the Governing Body held as masters of this cult. Little did they know or foresee, as since this major controversial event in the ranks of the leaders of this religion, there has been a tidal wave of books; apart from Raymond's own book *Crisis of Conscience* (1983). Plus in addition today there are numerous articles, television programs and websites that have all made major contributions to exposing this hypocritical, deceptive and dangerous cult, especially the secret cover-up of child and sexual abuse that had been taking place within their ranks over the many years.

Raymond and his wife left the organization's headquarters in 1980 with a sigh of relief and personally experienced the feeling of being finally free from the chains of a religious cult.

---

[15] Remember it was Schroeder who said these words in 1977 as reported on page 94 of our book, "there was a campaign going on both inside the organization and from outside to have the Society's 607 BCE (before our Common Era) – 1914 CE (Common Era) chronology and the understanding of the 'last generation' be overthrown. The Society, however, had no intention of ever, ever abandoning it," he emphatically stated.

A close friend and fellow researcher working in the New York headquarters at the same time as Raymond Franz was also excommunicated because he sincerely questioned some of the erroneous teachings of the Governing Body (the masters). In an audio recording in two parts, Edward Dunlap himself speaks of the decades of full-time service and his devotion to the Watchtower Society. He tells of the serious problems he started to discover with the teachings from different articles of *The Watchtower* and what really happens in reality. Edward was head and the actual Registrar, also a senior lecturer for many years at the Watchtower Society's missionary school called Gilead. He explains what led him to be interrogated by some members of the Board of Directors, (Governing Body) from the moment when he started to present his personal points of view on different theological questions. He could not accept the doctrine about the remnant being the rest of the anointed class, according to his understanding of Romans 8:12-17, and the so-called little flock, also of the 144,000 mentioned in the Bible book of Revelation, Chapter 7 and 14, and this being a symbolic number and not literal as claimed by the Governing Body, which eventually led him to be also disfellowshipped for apostasy in 1980.

Edward Dunlap was well educated, which of course is not usually well thought of or respected by the Governing Body of this religion and with his many skills he took part in the modernization of all the printers of the Watchtower Society throughout the world. He had also written the excellent book *Commentary on the Letter of James,* copyrighted by the Watchtower Society as usual. This brilliant 224-page book was written by Edward Dunlap and released in 1979 and based on his deep research into this very important Bible book of James, which is the fifty-ninth book of the inspired word of God and originally composed by the fleshly half-brother of Jesus and was probably transcribed in 62 AD shortly before the death of James.

Why did the disciple James write this letter to the Christian congregation? One Bible commentary records the following. Christian standards were beginning to fall during the later half of the first century and the Christian brotherhood was being plagued with internal strife and contradiction and there was an urgent need for more faith, which was supported by works of faith? An additional review provided by our research team is: "The book of James looks a bit like the Old Testament book of Proverbs dressed up in New Testament clothes. Its consistent focus on practical action in the life of faith is reminiscent of the Wisdom Literature in the Old Testament, encouraging God's people to act like God's people." The pages of the Bible book of James are filled with direct commands to pursue a life of holiness. He makes no excuses for those who do not measure up. In the mind of this early church leader, Christians' evidence their faith by walking in certain ways and not others. For James, a faith that does not produce real life change is a faith that is worthless. The disciple James is also described in other Bible records as being a pillar in the early Christian congregation established by Jesus Christ in 33 AD.

Commentary on the Letter of James was proudly proclaimed by the Governing Body of the Watchtower Society that it would be the first in a new series of books described as commentaries on the various other books of the Holy Bible. This was an obvious and transparent plan to produce more and more printed books that would be bought and purchased by their loyal followers, which in turn of course would increase their revenue from their publications and printing empire. Other excellent publications already existed that served the very purpose of providing meaningful comments and observations on the contents of the various books of the Bible, for example, *All Scripture is Inspired of God and Beneficial*, published and released in 1963. Remember however that the Watchtower Society was in the business of printing and distributing books and magazines as this guaranteed at that time the massive income realized from their commercial enterprise, so more books to be written, sold and purchased by their followers, the more income they received.

Needless to say, that promise of more commentaries was quickly abandoned because of the now developing, very serious, so-called apostasy within the organization and some personal viewpoints being expressed as a result of the intensive research being undertaken by various members of the writing department of the Watchtower Society, plus many other brothers who were not part of the domineering Governing Body. One brother in the writing department, a friend of a member of our research team said,

Ed told me at the time (1978 or so) that he was hoping the society would do a book like James on each book of the New Testament over time and get away from the silly (stupid) stuff like Babylon the Great has Fallen, etc. He also stated, It was not by what Dunlap put IN the Commentary on James book that was wrong teaching, but by LEAVING OUT any distinction between the anointed and great crowd. This went unnoticed through proofreading and publishing simply because they all knew that there was nothing Biblically wrong with what the book said.

After its release in 1979 the Governing Body belatedly discovered certain phrases and terminology were used in this book with which they disagreed, so it appears that the Governing Body suddenly panicked over their failure to carry out their fiduciary duty and due diligence as the faithful and discreet slave under the so-called guidance of the Holy Spirit. They had failed in their duty to carefully and painstakingly check the content of this book, as was the usual practice in line with all current articles and material that was prepared by the writing department of the Watchtower Society, done so in order to make sure it was in line with current teachings and dogma. It seems they were getting sloppy in their duty as the faithful and discreet slave and were failing their responsibility, which they claim in the words of Jesus at Matthew 24:45, providing the (spiritual) food at the proper time. There was a feeble attempt after certain controversial phrases were discovered in this Bible commentary on the book of James and to make changes to the text of this book by sending out in the monthly *Kingdom Ministry* instruction bulletin to all the congregations, certain cut-out and paste-on changes to the wording of certain phrases used in this *Commentary* book. Also there was one sentence in the James book that could be interpreted as saying "All Christians have the heavenly hope" (and not only the literal 144,000). The Governing Body clarified that statement in a Question from Readers published in the *Watchtower* magazine in 1980, and admitted their error saying that the word anointed should have been inserted to avoid confusion.

This scheme of cut out and paste, which was the first time in the history of the *Watchtower* publications this had occurred, it also actually backfired as it simply brought attention and focus to the negligence of the Governing Body in allowing these so-called errors to be published in this new book by Edward Dunlap in the first place. But a few months later it was then quickly decided by the now confused and stubbornly recalcitrant Governing Body to withdraw this publication altogether and ban it from all theocratic libraries. They also told their followers who had in good faith purchased over two million copies of this book, using their hard-earned money and instructed them to throw the book away and put it in the garbage. They also took the extreme step of having Edward Dunlap, author of this new book, excommunicated for apostasy in order to avoid further embarrassment. Edward Dunlap was also part of the team of Jehovah's Witnesses who wrote the brilliant Bible encyclopedia, Aid to Bible Understanding. He also wrote many other articles in the publications of the Watchtower Society.

Quoting once again from Raymond Franz's *Crisis of Conscience*, the following is recorded regarding this loyal and faithful Christian Edward Dunlap. When being forced to leave the Brooklyn Bethel, Edward and Betty his wife went to Oklahoma City and had almost nothing else than their own clothes. Dunlap's brother, Marion, offered him a job and was therefore also excommunicated for having assisted someone who was disfellowshipped. Five other family members were also disfellowshipped at the same time for the same reason. Raymond Franz was a close friend of Dunlap and both often discussed together various biblical subjects. He says about Dunlap:

> I first met him in 1964 when attending a ten-month (special)
> course at Gilead School. He was then the Registrar of the
> School and one of its four instructors. Ed was of ordinary
> education but had the ability to take very difficult, complex
> subjects and put them in understandable language, whether
> it was the functions of the Mosaic Law or a scientific
> study of genetics. However, more important to me was his
> unpretentiousness. Aside from a penchant for loud ties, he was
> a basically low-key, low profile person, in appearance, demeanor
> and speech. He had always been thoroughly devoted to the
> organization; his full-time service record equaled mine in
> length, being 40 years of our life. So they disfellowshipped Ed
> Dunlap, and he was asked to leave what had been his home at
> the Bethel headquarters. He returned to Oklahoma City where

he had grown up and where, now 72 years of age, he supported himself and his wife by hanging wallpaper, a trade he had practiced before he began his 40 years of service as a full-time representative of the Watch Tower Bible and Tract Society.

Edward Dunlap died a few years later of a heart attack but he had retained his strong faith in the Divine Creator and his son Jesus Christ to the end, and he set a fine example for us today. He proved that being released from the chains of a religious cult does not mean the end of ones life as a genuine practicing Christian, but rather it opens up ones life and presents one with the freedom of expression of our personal beliefs in line with our Bible trained conscience. The traumatic events that were experienced by this man, Edward Dunlap are almost unbelievable if they were not true, but are now accurately recorded for posterity and prove that his life was not in vain. He experienced such emotionally disturbing events and incidents that were inflicted by the ruthless Governing Body of this religion that could only have come from the minds of individuals, who acting as a group, that were fiendish and wicked plus displayed a mephistophelian contempt, plus they flouted the very principles of true Christianity. What these so-called shepherds did to this man in the name of the Lord is inexcusable in any circumstances. The Governing Body finally decided to expel Edward from his beloved religion that had consumed most of his adult life and kick him out of the organization and this was a clear ploy on their part to cover over their own embarrassment and negligence of duty regarding this new publication that they had once fully and wholeheartedly approved *Commentary on the Letter of James*.

The Watchtower Society is a religious group that claims to be the exclusive organization on earth today that represents our Almighty Creator, Yahweh, who is a God that personifies love. "Beloved, let us love one another, because love is from God; everyone who loves is born of God and knows God. Whoever does not love does not know God, for God is love." (1 John 4:1 -21) How can this religion justify their actions and how they treated this humble and modest man Edward Dunlap? He committed no sin against the Holy Spirit, (Mark 3:28, 29) he was not an apostate, he was simply following his Bible based conscience founded on his many years of intensive Bible study and reading. He was a humble man and not once did he ever think more of himself than he ought to have done, (Romans 12:3; Proverbs 3:7) unlike many of the leaders of this religious cult. We encourage you to read the complete record of this enlightening experience of Edward Dunlap, ex-Jehovah's Witness, in Special Report No. 7 of the Appendix.

A leading member of the Watchtower Society also later pointed out to a member of our research team that one of the most blatant acts of hypocrisy that any religion could ever display is that of having double standards. In 1992, the Watchtower Society actually became an Associate NGO (Non-governmental Organization) member of the United Nations but the rank and file of Jehovah's Witnesses had no knowledge of this fact, it was simply expedient to hide and conceal this from the local naïve congregation members. This secret membership of the UNO was despite spending decades condemning the UNO as the scarlet-colored wild beast of Revelation and being part of Satan's organization.

As a result, when the facts were exposed many Jehovah's Witnesses severed ties with the Watchtower Society for what they considered a hypocritical and dishonest chapter of the religion's history. In 1991, the Watchtower Bible and Tract Society of New York had applied to be a Non-Governmental Organization (NGO) Associate Member of the United Nations Department of Public Information (UN DPI). This is the closest relationship a NGO can form with the United Nations. The application was renewed annually and is a matter of public record. The Watchtower Society remained an Associate Member until a few days after knowledge of this involvement became public through the release of breaking news, an exposé in *The Guardian* of 8ᵗʰ October, 2001.

> The United Nations is being asked to investigate why it has granted associate status to the Jehovah's Witnesses, the fundamentalist US-based Christian sect, which regards it as the scarlet beast predicted in the Book of Revelation. Disaffected members of the 6m-strong group, which has 130,000 followers in the UK, have accused the Witnesses' elderly Governing Body of hypocrisy in secretly accepting links with an organization that they continue to denounce in apocalyptic terms. The UN itself admitted yesterday that it was surprised that the sect,

whose formal name is the Watchtower Bible and Tract Society
of New York, had been accepted on its list of non-governmental
organizations for the last 10 years.

UNITED NATIONS   NATIONS UNIES

POSTAL ADDRESS—ADRESSE POSTALE UNITED NATIONS, N.Y. 10017
CABLE ADDRESS—ADRESSE TELEGRAPHIQUE UNATIONS NEWYORK

REFERENCE: 11 October 2001

To Whom It May Concern:

Recently the NGO Section had been receiving numerous inquiries regarding the
association of the Watchtower Bible and Tract Society of New York with the Department
of Public Information (DPI). This organization applied for association with DPI in 1991 and
was granted association in 1992. By accepting association with DPI, the organization agreed
to meet criteria for association, including support and respect of the principles of the
Charter of the United Nations and commitment and means to conduct effective
information programmes with its constituents and to a broader audience about UN
activities.

In October 2001, the Watchtower Bible and Tract Society of New York
requested termination of its association with DPI. Following this request, the DPI has made
a decision to disassociate the Watchtower Bible and Tract Society of New York as of 9
October 2001.

We appreciate your interest in the work of the United Nations.

Yours sincerely,

Paul Hoeffel
Chief
NGO Section
Department of Public Information

7

Letter dated 11 October, 2001 from the United Nations recognizing the belated
resignation of the Watchtower Society, courtesy of Creative Commons

To assist our readers we quote from the *Watchtower* magazine, the official
journal of Jehovah's Witnesses.

No, the UN is not a blessing, even though the religious clergy
of Christendom and the rabbis of Jewry pray heaven's blessing
upon that organization. It is really the image of the wild

beast, the visible political, commercial organization of the god of this system of things, Satan the Devil. So the UN will soon be destroyed along with that beastly organization (*The Watchtower* of 1984).

In addition, this quote from the *Watchtower*:

> So today we can see in actuality what the apostle John saw in symbol, that that scarlet-colored wild beast is full of blasphemous names. Those expressions of admiration for it turn false religionists, not to the worship of Jehovah God the Creator, but to idolatry of a man-made creation, the worship of a political image, the worship of an international organization for world peace and security. Rev. 17:3. (*Watchtower*, 1963).

This controversial issue was deeply researched by Paul Grundy on his website, JW Facts.com, and reveals the above and following facts. This website includes copies of confidential letters sent by the United Nations Press Office plus a copy of a secretive (leaked) letter sent by the Governing Body of the Jehovah's Witnesses to all branch office committees around the world in a feeble attempt to try and explain this hypocrisy by using more blatant lies regarding their claim of complete innocence of being a mistaken member of the United Nations for 10 years. We once again remind our readers that this type of chicanery, behavior of lying and deceit is typical of how a cult operates.

This observation was made by an ex-member of the New York Bethel who personally knew Edward Dunlap and Raymond Franz:

> Three principle brothers undertook the writing of the Watchtower Society publication *Aid to Bible Understanding* in 1969. This 1,696 page Bible encyclopedia and reference work was an enormous undertaking, representing many thousands of man-hours of intense study. It took three brothers working on it full time about five years to complete, and was released in 1971. It generated much enthusiasm and deep study of God's Word among Jehovah's Witnesses, and continues to do so to this day. The *Aid* book contained some of the finest explanations, illumination, and historical, archaeological reckoning of the scriptures ever written. A new version was released in 1988, adding many more maps and charts along with beautiful

colored pages and illustrations. It was also split into two
volumes and renamed Insight on the Scriptures.

It has been pointed out by a few members of our research team that
there are still some very misleading items of information in *Aid to Bible
Understanding* and its later revision, the *Insight on the Scriptures* book.
For example, comments regarding the Bible book of Ezekiel, Isaiah and
the prophet Daniel, plus the subject, Appointed Times of the Nations
and the date 607 BC, to mention just a few. This book published by the
Watchtower Society, although often used by members of our research
team and found to be very helpful, but is definitely not infallible or
inspired of God and his Holy Spirit and must be used with discretion
as a reference work only.

The passing of the year 1975 without incident left the Watchtower
Society open once again to new claims of prophetic failure and many
elderly members of long standing, based on their previous experiences,
had already warned their newer fellow members against being too
excited about this new forecast, as previous claims had also come to
nothing. Instead of trying to maintain the prophetic significance of
that year, however, the group's leaders embarked on a lengthy period of
denial and purge, blaming rank and file membership for misreading the
organization's interpretations. As Bryon Wilson said in his book *When
Prophesy Failed* (1978), "For people whose lives have become dominated
by one powerful expectation, and whose activities are dictated by what
that belief requires, abandonment of faith because of disappointment
about a date would usually be too traumatic an experience to
contemplate." This failure of the Governing Body of the Watchtower
Society and their forecast of events related to the year 1975 did not
create a massive falling away of the now millions of loyal followers of
this religion, as had been forecast by some of their critics, but many;
estimated being about 500,000 did leave the religion, some temporarily
and others permanently; being disillusioned by this failed claim of the
new system beginning in 1975. But it unfortunately did create in turn
a greater confidence in the power of the masters; the Governing Body,
and that they could maintain their slave like control that they now held
over their loyal, somewhat subjective and naïve adherents, no matter
what they claim or say.

According to our source; prior to 1975 many Witnesses sold all their possessions, postponed surgery or cashed in their insurance policies to prepare for Armageddon, it was also noted as a fact that many others also selfishly used this remaining short time and their funds to undertake extensive luxury overseas vacations, visiting places they had always dreamed of, as an excuse while they still could, before the world's chaotic end came in October of 1975. In May, 1974, the Watchtower Society told members:

> Reports are heard of brothers selling their homes and property and planning to finish out the rest of their days in this old system in the pioneer service. Certainly this is a fine way to spend the <u>short time remaining</u> before the wicked world's end.

One prominent spokesman of the Governing Body publicly stated with great zeal and enthusiasm:

> Many of us have suffered misery and sickness. You don't have to experience that any more. The new order is near ... Sell your house, sell everything you own and say, oh boy, how long can I carry on with my private means. That long? Get rid of things! Pioneer! Plan to shower people with magazines during these <u>last few months</u> of this dying system of things.

Barbara Anderson in her reports that are covered on her website Watchtower Documents states.

> Of course, Jehovah's Witnesses select certain scriptures to back up their dates. However, they sure ignore scriptures that don't. Notice what Ronald Fry, former Witness and now a leading critic went on to say about one such scripture: "It is appropriate to consider what Jesus Christ said in warning about those who would claim special knowledge about the time of his return: "Look out that you are not misled; for many will come on the basis of my name, saying "I am he." How can any date-setters – or even those who say, "The due time has approached" – ignore this warning? The Watchtower leaders have!" Ronald Fry is also on record as stating, "The pattern or modus operandi of the Watchtower Society has evolved over the years but has basically remained the same. The same magazine that counseled the Witnesses against looking to a date reaffirmed the strong

prediction that the generation of 1914 would not pass away until the end came. They have not learned from past failures and persist in their efforts to reveal what only God knows.

In his book, *The Small Sects in America,* Elmer T. Clark observes regarding the end of the world and second coming of Christ:

> It has been said that more than a hundred speculators predicted that the advent would occur within the decade following the end of the American Civil War. Of course, in that number was the small American sect directed at first by C. T. Russell and then by others under the direction of the Watchtower Society. During their tenures, four administrations of Watchtower leaders – Russell, Rutherford, Knorr, and currently a Governing Body made up of many members – loudly proclaimed three dates and softly offered to insiders other dates for the return of Jesus Christ during more than one hundred and thirty years. Now a fifth administration, for the most part, a different group of Governing Body members, is being more coy about date-setting, but reminds members over and over again that Jesus' second coming will be very, very soon.

Also in 1967 was the publication of a very controversial book by William and Paul Paddock, called *World Famine 1975* [16] that helped to support the Watchtower theory that 1975 was a critical year in world history. It became a global bestseller, primarily because almost every member of the religion of Jehovah's Witnesses bought a copy and they also recommended it in their door to door sales pitch and public talks. Some very naïve members actually carried a copy with them from door to door and used it in their sales presentation. According to the Canadian news source,*National Post*, the story of how the Paddocks brothers were certain that mass starvation would sweep the world, and destroy nations like India, is an important reminder to beware of experts who are sure they know what the future will bring.

Editor's Note: Meantime these two so-called expert writers and

---

[16] *World Famine 1975* analyzed the world's agricultural situation and the failure of smaller nations to encourage efficient food production and concluded that famine was inevitable throughout the world. William, an agronomist, and Paul, a retired Foreign Service officer, set forth that only this country, the USA, could avoid a world disaster.

researchers have gone into oblivion along with their lucrative royalty earnings in their bank accounts; cold cash earned through their publishers from this ridiculous and ludicrous book mainly bought by the gullible members of Jehovah's Witnesses and their free advertising of this publication to support the current theory of Freddy Franz that 1975 was to be the year.

In a research report by the Christian Research Institute Journal, it was pointed out how the date 1975 accomplished an upturn and increase in the number of converts to the Watchtower Society.

In the early 1960s Witness leaders became concerned over declining growth. Something had to be done to rejuvenate the movement. The decision was made to employ the technique used so successfully by Russell and Rutherford: prophetic speculation and date-setting to create great expectation of momentous events looming on the horizon. A series of books and articles [beginning in 1966 with *Life Everlasting in Freedom of the Sons of God*] rolled from the Brooklyn presses announcing that September 1975 would mark the end of 6000 years since the creation of Adam. It was clearly suggested time and again that the seventh millennium of mankind's existence could be expected to run parallel with the millennial reign of Christ. Readers were assured that they were living in the last days. The book, *The Truth That Leads to Eternal Life* [containing a chapter entitled,The Last Days of This Wicked System of Things] stated that these last days began in 1914 and will end within one generation. The warning is then given, "this means that only a short time is left before the end comes!" (p. 95) the result of these startling pronouncements was a phenomenal increase in activity and conversions. The number of world-wide baptisms went from 58,904 in 1966 to 295,073 in 1975. During those same years the number of publishers [Witnesses involved in preaching and literature selling activities] rose from 1,058,675 to 2,062,449.

A leading member of the current Governing Body is on record as saying, "Now it's true that the Faithful Slave, at times, has had wrong expectations throughout the decades. See, sometimes they've had wrong expectations, for example 1975. Many responsible ones at headquarters, they thought maybe, maybe Jehovah would bring the 1,000 year reign to begin in that year, but of course it didn't happen did it. They have learned from their mistakes that you really can't be specific about Jehovah's day." If you ask the Governing Body today regarding the 1975 claims, they prefer it be forgotten as they know that today most members of this religion, estimated at least about two-thirds have joined this religion since 1975 and most were not even born in 1975, so have no memory of that erroneous, ridiculous false claim. In the research by Paul Grundy on his brilliant website, JW facts.com, he points out the following, "From 1966 to 1975, the Watchtower regularly implied that Armageddon would arrive in 1975. However, ask one of Jehovah's Witnesses about this date and they will invariably deny there ever being such statements."

Plus, one leading representative of the Governing Body made this ludicrous public statement in 1967 at a large convention in California, "Well now, as Jehovah's Witnesses, as runners, even though some of us have become a little weary, it almost seems as though Jehovah has provided meat in due season, because he has now held up before all of us, a new goal, a new year. Something to reach out for and it just seems it has given all of us so much more energy and power in this final burst of speed to the finish line. And that's the year 1975. Well, we don't have to guess what the year 1975 means if we read the *Watchtower*. And don't wait 'till 1975. The door is going to be shut before then." The Watchtower Society even introduced instructions to the rank and file of their members, that if they started a private Bible study with a member of the public; usually using the small blue book, *The Truth That Leads to Eternal Life* (1968), they were to limit the study period to six months maximum in order to use their time wisely for the last few remaining months of the old system of things.

One long serving Witness, a special pioneer of over 25 years' experience that we interviewed, laughingly reported the occasion she was advised by her local, very heavy handed district overseer and aggressive proponent of 1975 as being the year, to make her door-to-door presentation more powerful by using the introduction, "This is probably the last time I will be offering you hope for salvation." This presentation to the householder actually backfired as she laughed out loud while remembering this stupid suggestion made by a representative of the Governing Body, as the straight forward solemn reply from the householder was, "Did I hear you say this would be the last time? Thank God, as we are getting really fed up with you people making these irritating visits trying to sell your magazines!"

This extract from the website, Witnesses for Jesus, by Anne Marie is very enlightening as related by a person who attended a Watchtower convention in 1966 and the date of 1975 was being aggressively promoted.

> This talk admitted to the many prophecies the Society had given in the past regarding the coming of God's battle of Armageddon that Jehovah's Witnesses believe will end world governments and usher in God's 1,000-year Kingdom rule under Jesus Christ. The speaker made a point of explaining that the reason that all of their past dates had failed was because they had not been properly based upon Bible chronology. The speaker spoke with such authority that there was no doubt that Armageddon was now certain to come "no later than the autumn of 1975"; that although the Watchtower had been wrong in the past, "this time we got it right!" The brother was emphatic about it! He explained that this new book would clearly show that the Watchtower Society's new claims were verified by Bible chronology through the five-page chart laid out in the first chapter of the book.
>
> As the following years progressed, the urgency to do even more Kingdom preaching work was continually stressed by the Watchtower organization. We were told that the salvation of mankind was our responsibility, and this was not to be taken lightly! The pressure was ever increasing to do more to prove our loyalty and faithfulness. As 1975 drew near, many Jehovah's Witnesses began to quit their jobs [and gave up their pensions] in order to devote more time to the door-to-door ministry. Many sold their homes and businesses, cashed in life insurance policies, rejected college education for themselves and their children, and even put off non-emergency medical or dental treatment in expectation of the end. All of these actions were commended by the Watchtower Society and hailed by the organization to the rank-and-file as good examples of what faithful Jehovah's Witnesses were to be.

Had not the Watchtower Society commended the brothers and sisters who had sold their homes and businesses in order to put more time into the Watchtower's preaching work? Had not the Society said, "Certainly this is a fine way to spend the short time remaining before the wicked world's end?" (*Kingdom Ministry,* May 1974, p. 3) And now they were telling us that our disappointment was our own fault for not heeding the words of Jesus? This kind of revisionist history was slowly fed to the masses so that what they had drummed into our heads about 1975, was somehow turned around, and they managed to convince the remaining Jehovah's Witnesses that the belief that Armageddon would come in 1975 had really been our own idea in the first place – that it had never been taught to us by the Watchtower Society. I heard stories of pioneers who had faithfully put in thousands of hours preaching the Watchtower message, throwing down their Watchtower book bags, saying, "I've had it!" and walking away from the Watchtower Organization.

When so many left and said that they didn't believe anything the Society taught anymore, the Watchtower organization turned around and used their example of leaving as an excuse to show why Armageddon hadn't come. They said that the prediction had been some type of test of loyalty and that Jehovah had been cleaning house to get rid of all those who He knew were not truly His people, even though they had looked good to the rest of us. This ploy worked quite well to keep the rest of us in! It even worked on me! It made us even more diligent to prove our loyalty to Jehovah.

We also quote some additional, rather distressing, but typical expressions we uncovered regarding the failed year of 1975. One leading district servant in Britain, representing the Governing Body, declared from the podium in front of an enthusiastic clapping crowd, "If Armageddon does not happen by 1975, then Jehovah's Witnesses will be the laughing stock of the world." Another member of the religion said, "I remember an elderly brother, a very kind man that everyone in the congregation loved. He was dying of cancer in 1974 and he would say, if only I can hold out till 1975, then I will be in the new system and cured of my sickness. The poor man died in 1975 still holding onto that false hope."

Our research team has many, many more expressions on record of the major disappointments and sadness regarding the failed year of 1975, far too many to include in this book, but they all illustrate the danger of following men who claim to be representatives and spokesmen of Almighty God.

In his recent book entitled, *Judgment Day Must Wait – Jehovah's Witnesses Between Idealism and Deceit*, Poul Bregninge exposes the new claim by the Watchtower Society that Armageddon may now come in 2034 based on recent articles published by the Watchtower Society. In a review of this brilliant book, which goes into greater detail about the Watchtower Society than our chapter does, our fellow researcher, Richard Kelly makes the following observations.

> For all that the Watchtower has done to champion freedom of religion; it does not practice what it preaches. Poul does a masterful job of showing readers just how difficult the Watchtower makes it for members today if they want to leave. The organization has become a giant without heart or sense. Members stay with the group because of family and social ties, the threat of severe shunning if they leave and a phobia-induced fear of Armageddon.

Bregninge's book clearly illustrates how foolish people can be when they too strongly and uncritically engage in a utopian idea. He concludes his story with:

> We now find ourselves in 2016, more than 100 years after the Day of Judgment failed to materialize. But in spite of it all, and once again, according to the Witnesses, we are nearing the end of the road; Armageddon is just around the corner.

An additional comment was made by a reader of this manuscript before publication, "It reveals the psychological and cult-like tactics used to brain-wash adherents. This book helps us to better understand how well-meaning people can become victims of delusion; suffer tragic personal consequences and ruin family relationships."

One thing we have seriously noted is the regular change in Watchtower doctrines and their interpretation of the Bible, for example the teaching that the Witnesses, when engaged in the preaching work, separate the sheep-like people from the goat-like people under the direction of the anointed class, who are in turn claim they are under the personal direction of Jesus Christ. This teaching and doctrine was used to drive and motivate the importance of the door-to-door preaching work and selling of their literature. This might appear to be a minor issue to many of our readers but this basic doctrine was changed in 1995 when the Watchtower Society explained that Jesus does the actual separating work when the entire wicked system of things ends at Armageddon (which is the same as Christendom has taught for 1900 years). The Holy Scriptures record the following: "When the Son of Man comes in his glory, and all the angels with him, then he will sit on the throne of his glory. All the nations will be gathered before him, and he will separate people one from another as a shepherd separates the sheep from the goats, and he will put the sheep at his right hand and the goats at the left." (Matthew 25: 31-46) The Governing Body had been incorrect regarding this teaching of Jesus for decades and their followers simply blindly followed and believed this false teaching and now suddenly they change their minds, why our sincere readers ask? Is this a sign of compromise and maybe a weakening of their aggressive position taken over this and many other controversial doctrines?

We now briefly return to the story of Raymond Franz, former member of the Governing Body of the Watchtower Society as recalled by one of our research team.

> The important knowledge gained by the in-depth, accurate research by Raymond Franz and his assistants was openly and regularly being shared with other members of the Governing Body and colleagues within the headquarters of the Society, especially regarding the year 1914 and 1975, plus other issues related to current Bible chronology. They did not keep it secret, hidden or concealed, as it had directly resulted from his team's intensive research while he was genuinely preparing material for the new Watchtower publication, the Bible Encyclopedia, Aid to Bible Understanding, doing so under direct instruction from the Governing Body. All of this important research and the contents of all publications had to be finally approved by the Governing Body in any case. Most of the other members of the Governing Body were truly rattled by his well-founded

research, plus could not mentally or emotionally handle the thought of such dramatic changes in major doctrines of their religion, so they have still stubbornly adhered to these core teachings even to this day. Why we asked; for what purpose, after realizing that the now obviously incorrect teachings and research that was originally introduced by the founder of this religion, Charles Russell and his sincere associates back in 1879 is no longer valid?

Not one of the members of the current Governing Body of the Watchtower Society has had the courage to openly come out with the admission that the original doctrine related to 1914 and the last generation of this system of things carried forward from Russell's day in 1879, could in fact be an error and today that they are still promoting this idea in this year of 2019, that is plainly and unquestionably a false misleading interpretation of the Bible. Our readers will no doubt be asking, why? This comment was made by a very intelligent associate of our research team, R.P. from Cambridge, England: "I guess that no one wants to be responsible for the dissolution of Jehovah's Witnesses as we know them, and so somehow 1914 must remain a core teaching."

For more information about the original history of Charles Taze Russell and the formation of the Watchtower Society, we recommend the brilliantly researched book (in two volumes) by B. W. Schulz and the late R. M. de Vienne, A Separate Identity: Organizational Identity Among Readers of *Zion's Watch Tower*, 1870-1887 (2014). A book review from Cambridge University stated:

> This is the first book about the early years of the group of people who eventually morphed into Jehovah's Witnesses. And, as historians, Schulz and the late, de Vienne have made a conscious effort not to get bogged down when it comes to the matter what may or may not be religious truth. They basically say one's choice of religion is in effect a personal decision while the job of a historian is to be accurate. Thus, the book is neither pro-Witness nor anti-Witness. Whether your personal beliefs match or differ from these men of 150 years ago, it will complete many pieces of a jigsaw that you likely never knew existed.

From October 1, 1972, adjustments began in the oversight of the local congregations of Jehovah's Witnesses. The writings and research of the new book and Bible encyclopedia, *Aid to Bible Understanding* that was primarily headed by the excellent research of the dedicated student of the Bible, Raymond Franz, then a leading member of the Governing Body, plus other additional notes submitted by other members of the organization, including a report from one of our leading researchers.[17] and this led to a new understanding of the Bible's mention of elders and older men and this seems to have been the catalyst for this religion to formally adjust its organizational structure once again.

> *Editor's Note*: As a point of interest, if you, as a member of Jehovah's Witnesses and today ever write to the Watchtower Society with a question regarding their policy or beliefs, you will never, ever receive a direct reply. Your letter and query will be simply sent to the Branch office of the country in which you reside and then the management team of the local Branch Office will investigate and trace your local congregation and forward your sincere letter and direct question to the Presiding Overseer or a judicial committee to handle. You have simply indentified yourself as a prospective apostate. (Is this the big brother system or not? Definition of big brother is monitors everyone's every single move). This modus operandi was tested recently and confirmed by a member of our research team who has a relative who works in the Bethel and Watchtower office of a prominent unnamed country and this is exactly what transpired.

This major revision of oversight and once again another change of policy by the Watchtower Society who claims to be directed by Almighty God who never changes, the words in the Watchtower Society's organizational manual of 1972, clearly explains these new adjustments of oversight in the individual congregations, based on their private interpretation of the Bible: "It is noteworthy that the Bible does not say that there was only one 'older man', one overseer, in each congregation. Rather, it indicates that there were a number of such. The members of such a body [or, assembly] of older men were all equal, having the

[17] These changes also affected the local branch offices and the permanent Branch Servant (Overseer) was replaced with a branch coordinator who headed a branch committee, all now claiming to being of equal status.

same official status, and none of them was the most important, most prominent, most powerful member in the congregation."

Based on this new interpretation, that was claimed to be new light received directly to the Governing Body from Jesus Christ through the Holy Spirit, there would no longer be one permanent congregation servant, or overseer, but rather a body of elders and ministerial servants and these newly appointed elders would have equal authority and share the responsibility for making decisions in the local congregations. Because of this dramatic change in policy by the Watchtower Society, supposedly under the guidance of Jesus Christ and the Holy Spirit our researchers discovered that in many cases there was chaos and confusion when this dramatic change was implemented. This major decision and revision regarding this dramatic change of policy was the Watchtower Society's alone and certainly Jesus Christ or his heavenly father Yahweh had not changed their minds as to how the true Christian Congregation was to be supervised. (Malachi 3:6) This is not supposed to be how the Holy Spirit works. "Now I appeal to you, brothers and sisters, by the name of our Lord Jesus Christ, that all of you be in agreement and that there be no divisions among you, but that you be united in the same mind and the same purpose" (1 Corinthians 1:10).

For example, in some cases that were revealed to our reporters related to this confusing change of policy of supervising the local congregations, the actual existing congregation servant who was authorized to act as chairman of this special meeting to recommend the new elders to the branch office for their appointment, did not himself qualify as an elder, being a joint decision made by the group of existing ministerial servants who reviewed the field service records, level of dedication to the organization and the reputation of each male member of the congregation. Naturally this caused some confusion and arguments amongst the group and, in some cases, we discovered the use of abusive speech and threats of violence. Sometimes the resulting confusion required the intervention of the local circuit servant to try and sort out the chaos but not always with success, resulting in some disgruntled ex-congregation servants left out in the cold and some even quitting this religion altogether. In other blood relation cases, for example physical brothers, fathers and sons and also favoritism and business relationships influenced the choices of the men recommended as new elders, once again creating jealousy, envy and bitterness by some. Our researchers even discovered that the use of bribery and blackmail was attempted and also actually used to try and influence their being selected as members of this newly created local body of elders.

We need to remind ourselves of course that these men are still imperfect humans and are tempted like all men in positions of responsibility connected to religion, politics and commerce, but they are still without any excuse for using blatant corrupt practices and mendacious lies, so we must be on our guard against such leaders of religious cults. Some men have even gone to the extreme in their conduct as to be party to sexual abuse of women and children in the congregations and hiding this behavior, and many of these men being actual appointed elders and leaders as pointed out in other sections of this narrative.

Later, the chairmanship of the Governing Body itself would also be affected by these changes, rotating each year in alphabetical order. In December 1975, the powerful position of leadership of Jehovah's Witnesses passed from the President of the Watchtower Society, to a collective Governing Body of Jehovah's Witnesses under its rotating chairman, whoever that happened to be. Former member of the governing body Raymond Franz, stated in Crisis of Conscience that the actions of presidents Russell, Rutherford and Knorr in overriding and failing to consult with other directors proved that the Bible Students and Jehovah's Witnesses had been under a monarchical (or dictatorial) rule until 1976, leaving no decisions to any joint Governing Body.

As a result of this so-called new light and revelation from God regarding organizational changes, the autocratic, very frustrated Nathan Knorr was not removed as the 3rd President of the Watchtower Society, but the position he occupied simply became a meaningless title or figurehead without any real authority. Up until 1975, whoever held the position of President, especially since the days of Joseph Rutherford, also acted as the all-powerful Chairman of the Governing Body, a position that narcissistic Nathan Knorr the protégé of Rutherford, personally inherited in 1942. As recorded earlier in this report, Knorr had skillfully by underhanded and questionable means removed his only competitor, the very successful Watchtower lawyer Hayden Covington, and Knorr now truly relished plus thrived upon his position and throne as a true autocrat being the new all-powerful President. The members of the re-organized Governing Body, now cleverly using its new two thirds majority rule introduced in 1975, again supposedly revealed to them by divine revelation they then by manipulation introduced this rotation of the Chairman of the Governing Body, thereby stripping Knorr of all of his power as an autocrat, much to his anger and bitterness and although he fought against this decision with his bellicose character, he had to finally accept his fate. They then appointed the now aging, almost blind, eccentric and mentally unstable, 84-year-old Freddy Franz as the new Chairman of the Governing Body, as from 1 January, 1976.

Nathan Knorr died aged 72 years old the following year on 8 June, 1977, a very sad, pathetic, disillusioned man and according to the official records, as a result of a cerebral tumor?[18] Another report however made by a long-standing member of the New York headquarters who had observed the rapid deterioration of Knorr; his health and his general demeanor and he claims his death was probably caused by inordinate, extreme stress accompanied with heavy drinking of alcohol over the last year of his life. Knorr was mainly secluded in his private suite in the Watchtower headquarters most of the time and as he now had no meaningful duties to perform for the so-called Lord's Organization and his life had now lost purpose and meaning, the result causing him great personal stress. Remember a year earlier he had been the powerful leader of a robust, expanding, successful religion, bringing in millions of Dollars each year from the sale of its literature and he travelled the world speaking like a prophet to the thousands of slave like followers. Plus, he had spent and dedicated his entire adult life in service to this religion. Knowing of other cases similar to Knorr, he must have felt he was being dumped on the scrap heap, meaning to completely discard someone or something as trash that is unwanted. The phrase also implies that the thing or individual being discarded is being treated as worthless, which

---

[18] Stress induces signals that cause cells to develop into tumors, Yale researchers have discovered. Stress symptoms can affect your body, your thoughts and feelings, and your behavior. In addition stress can prompt people to turn to unhealthy coping mechanisms, such as smoking, drinking excessive amounts of alcohol, or overeating.

is a dreadful, atrocious, depressing problem and especially a distressing personal experience for any person to cope with.

It must have been very difficult for Nathan Knorr to adjust and accept this dramatic change to the management of the Watchtower Society as he was replaced as Chairman of the Governing Body by a man who was labeled as certifiably insane by outside observers. Many others who worked in the headquarters also remarked that his successor Freddy Franz was already senile and mentally unstable when he took over this responsible position. Meantime, it is reported that Nathan Knorr became more and more depressed and spent most of his time in his private suite in the New York Watchtower headquarters drinking heavily. Also, his penthouse Office of the President that at one time was the very busy central hub and a hive of activity of this religion, but now it was rarely used, it stood dark and vacant, the telephone never rang and it echoed with an empty silence. By contrast, see the photograph on page 146.

There was some concern by many of the workers in the Watchtower headquarters and in addition by many of the rank-and-file members of this religion as to how Nathan Knorr was handling this problem of him being replaced as the powerful Chairman of the Governing Body. This was compounded by a wild rumor that was circulating in Europe, claimed to have been sourced from the London Branch Office of the Watchtower Society that Knorr had attempted to take his own life during the early part of 1976 and that he was now restricted and confined to his private suite in the New York headquarters and was under suicide watch. This serious issue was further aggravated by the reluctance of the Watchtower Press Office to provide a total denial plus any meaningful details about this wild rumor, also in addition was very cagey when asked about the physical and mental health of Nathan Knorr.

At the beginning of 1977 the Watchtower Society officials decided to move Knorr from his private suite in New York to live on the Watchtower Farm in Wallkill, Orange Country, upstate New York, approximately 57 miles outside New York City. Officially the move was reported and recorded as being for health reasons. Another private report goes on to say that the real reason for the move and relocation was to hide him away, as they had done with Joseph Rutherford, who was labeled by actual senior officials of the Watchtower Society as a debauched drunkard back in the 1940s, when he moved to live in the Watchtower Society owned mansion called Beth Sarim located in San Diego, California. Based on this private report it was the intension of the Governing Body to keep Knorr out of sight, away from prying eyes and inquisitive observers, some stating that Knorr was literally drinking himself to death. We could not verify this claim regarding his serious drinking problem actually causing his death, except he was known as a very heavy drinker while he was alive and would touch nothing else but his favorite 20-year-old very expensive 40% ABV (alcohol by volume) proof, Bell's whisky and sometimes consuming two or three bottles per day. Paid for, by the way, from donations sent in by the sincere followers of this religion as a contribution to the Lord's work. If his heavy drinking was not the actual cause of his death it did at least make a major contribution to his early demise.

Knorr's widow, Audrey Hyde; she had re-married another Watchtower worker very soon after Nathan's death and in her short life story and interview that appeared in the Watchtower magazine in 2004, she naturally never mentions the ongoing drinking problem of her late husband Nathan Knorr but appears to glorify their marriage as a normal, successful one. Also, in a later interview shortly before she died in 2014, Audrey claimed that Nathan never touched alcohol while he was living at Watchtower Farm during his final days, which we find hard to believe. It is a known fact that an alcoholic can easily find secret and surreptitious ways to obtain their supply of liquor and satisfy their insatiable appetite for a drink, using all kinds of tricks to hide their alcohol use, being mixed in various ways and being unnoticed by onlookers, including one's wife.

In addition, Audrey the wife of Knorr, who was approximately 20 years younger than Nathan, although she now also lived on the Watchtower Farm, it is reported she was very much distracted with an ongoing relationship she had formed with a new friend she had met who worked on the farm and who was of a similar age; a Jehovah's Witness called Glenn Hyde. According to Audrey in the record of her life story she appears so guileless and she innocently states that Glenn "was a very handsome, quiet, and gentle person". In our opinion the very opposite of the truculent, hard-nosed, Nathan Knorr and it is reported that Glenn was also moderate in his drinking habits, which would have been a bonus to Audrey. It is also suggested that by this time in her life, Audrey, as she was no fool, had learned that Nathan Knorr had only married her in the first place back in 1953 when she was only 32 years old, to try and hide his homosexuality from public scrutiny, along with several others on the Governing Body, and that the marriage had never been consummated.

Also, in a private conversation with a personal friend and uncovered by one of our dedicated researchers, Audrey actually stated that Nathan kindly wanted her to find a normal husband to share her future happiness, but Audrey wisely omitted this remark from her life story as it would definitely have upset the Governing Body and they would have banned her article indefinitely. Also, Audrey said to her friend that she felt real pity for Nathan despite him misleading her about his homosexuality, as she had seen and observed him mentally and emotionally deteriorate to such a level that he became a sniffling wreck of a man, drunk most of the time and totally disillusioned about his religion. Audrey Hyde continued in her dedication to the Watchtower Society until the day she died on 3 September, 2014, despite what she had seen and knew about this religion, as this was the religion she had been brought up in by her mother Nina Mock, who had joined the Bible Student Association in 1913, eight years before Audrey was born. This is what normally happens to individuals who have been born into and brought up as members of a religious cult and do not have the strength of character to break free.

Glenn Hyde was a little older than Audrey Knorr (née Mock) but they had so much in common and from reliable reports they spent a great deal of time together during the months of January through to June of 1977 while both living on the farm, so we believe she was not even aware, or more likely maybe by now didn't even care, regarding Knorr's ongoing serious drinking problem while they were living on the Watchtower Farm during those last few months of Knorr's life. Also, Audrey had found a new love in her life, probably for the first time, and she was fully aware that her husband Nathan was on his last legs, so to speak, and nearing the end of his life, so she had to look ahead to her future and put behind her the memories of the past 24 years spent as the legal wife of Nathan Knorr. In addition, Audrey was not too involved with the daily care of her very sick legal husband Nathan, as he had two private nurses assigned to supervise and assist him as his health was quickly diminishing. Although we were supplied with the names of these two male nurses by our contact who had gained access to the archived records in the New York headquarters of the Watchtower Society, we could not locate these individuals in order to ask them the direct questions of how Nathan Knorr was able to get access to his supply of alcohol, and why they did not prevent and restrict him from drinking, as he was a very sick man.

In addition, as these volunteer nurses assigned from the Watchtower headquarters were not officially registered nurses but simply volunteer medical aids, but according to records they did have the name of a local doctor to contact in case of emergency. These two men, medical aids, were probably so much in awe of Nathan Knorr who was still officially a member of the all-powerful Governing Body, that probably being subjective, simplistic individuals, as most of Jehovah's Witnesses are, they complied with Knorr's demands for his liquor. Nathan Knorr still being and acting as the official, but by now the powerless President of the Watchtower Society, but he was still trying to give orders up to his dying day. After extensive investigation and search for these nurses we came to the conclusion that they were both now probably deceased, so we did not continue our search to further establish an answer to this puzzling and perplexing situation.

One of the members of our research team from Salt Lake City made the sarcastic remark that these two male nurses caring for Knorr were perhaps gay and fearful of the aggressive Knorr, as was the case of the volunteer nurse called Howie Trans who worked in the Watchtower Society infirmary in New York. Trans was the self-confessed homosexual who had cared for Lyman Swingle, also of the Governing Body, during Lyman's last days spent in the medical rooms of the New York headquarters. Although the Watchtower Society is known to probe into the private lives of their members and followers, plus make copious notes and records regarding their personal behavior, for example the case of married couples and their private sexual conduct as referred to in other sections of this report. There is no exact known number or record of how many of the men working in the Watchtower Society complexes have homosexual tendencies, however we do know that it is an established fact there are indeed many in this almost all male environment. Let it be noted by our readers, especially those who are reading this book based on their interest and curiosity into the activities of the Watchtower Society, that based on many interviews with ex-members of Jehovah's Witnesses who had signed up and volunteered to work in the Watchtower headquarters or one of their branch offices, homosexuality was a very serious problem, this is a known fact.

When a young man filled out and completed his application form to join the volunteer staff of the Watchtower Society and work in Bethel, he was not asked the question, are you heterosexual, homosexual or bisexual? The Watchtower Society are hot on their demand for record keeping and asking personal questions, but they were more interested in how many hours per month were spent by the applicant in the field service selling the Watchtower literature, and these figures had to be confirmed by the local service committee of his congregation. This was used as a gauge for leveling and measuring his dedication to the organization. From many reports received, these young men were drawn into homosexual practices only after they joined the volunteer staff of this religion, as the essentially all male makeup of the personnel in this environment encouraged this sort of behavior.

It has been suggested that Nathan Knorr was actually aware of this budding relationship between his much younger wife Audrey and Glenn Hyde while living on the Watchtower Farm and reading between the lines of the interview with Audrey in 2004, that Knorr was also fully aware of his own expected and actually hoped for early death. In addition, with Audrey still being a reasonably young, healthy woman and only in her early 50s, also no doubt a frustrated woman after being married to Nathan Knorr for 24 years and who was a reputed homosexual. Despite what Audrey Hyde claims in her life story, and by her somewhat sentimental remarks about the years she spent legally married to Nathan Knorr, he actually verbally encouraged Audrey to plan for her future and in her life story of 2004 she emphasized these words that Nathan had said to her. "Look ahead, for there is where your reward is. Don't live in the past – although your memories will continue." These dying words of Nathan Knorr had so many hidden meanings and possible guilt but they must have at least reassured Audrey that she was doing the right thing regarding her current and future relationship with Glenn Hyde; otherwise, she would not have quoted them in her life story.

One member of the Governing Body, Lloyd Barry (1916-1999) from New Zealand and who worked in the Australian Branch Office of the Watchtower Society for a number of years, he also intimately knew Nathan and Audrey Knorr. Lloyd Barry, back in 1983 had confidentially discussed this manuscript of the of the life story of Audrey Hyde with Lyman Swingle, also of the Governing Body, a manuscript that Audrey had submitted to the Writing Department for preparation to be published in the *Watchtower* magazine. Lloyd Barry who was then in control of the Writing Department was invited to join the Governing Body by his friend Nathan Knorr in 1974 and from reports he was a very simplistic, naïve individual, which was the view of many who knew him at the Watchtower headquarters. In addition, some leading members had the opinion that Lloyd Barry was also simple minded based on some of his recent decisions and recommendations, plus he was also showing signs of perseveration, which is the act of repeating something, such as words or actions, over and over again and perseveration is a common symptom of Alzheimer's disease. This view was expressed by Harry Peloyan, plus a number of other leading members of the Watchtower staff in the New York headquarters. In addition, Lyman Swingle, who was an avid reader of the Superman Comics, also said according to his relative in Salt Lake City, that Lloyd Barry was no brainiac.

Lloyd Barry had suggested and claimed that Nathan Knorr by these final words as contained in Audrey's life story: "Look ahead, for there is where your reward is." Barry claimed he could see nothing unusual or hidden in this statement by Knorr to his wife Audrey shortly before he died. During this friendly argument, Swingle pointed out in answer to Barry's claim, that he was incorrect and Swingle believed that Audrey read in that statement her husband Nathan had made and by using the word future and this is emphasized in her life story, that her legal husband Nathan had basically given her the green light to go ahead and marry Glenn Hyde after Knorr's soon to be expected death.

Barry retorted that in his opinion, which was nothing but hyperbole, he believed that Nathan Knorr was simply referring to Audrey's future life in a paradise earth, sometime in the future as being her reward and not to her future life with her handsome friend Glenn Hyde. Plus, in the expression used by Nathan, "Don't live in the past – although your memories will continue," Lloyd Barry also claimed that her memories were of the years Audrey spent traveling the world and meeting with many fellow Jehovah's Witnesses along with her late husband, and that Nathan was not referring to the sad, distressing, continuing memories that Audrey must have experienced regarding her troubled life with a man who was an incurable alcoholic and lived a life as a secret, closeted homosexual, as suggested by Lyman Swingle. However, as both Nathan Knorr and Audrey Hyde are now dead and buried, we will never learn the full truth and real meaning behind these actual words exchanged between this married couple, so it is no use our speculating. Lloyd Barry of the Governing Body collapsed and died in 1999 aged 83 years old while delivering the final address at a district convention in Hawaii, and Lyman Swingle died in 2001 while being cared for in the Watchtower headquarters infirmary in New York after a total mental breakdown.

Audrey Knorr and Glenn Hyde were married in early 1978, within months of Nathan Knorr's death and a few of the more old fashioned and straight-laced members in the Watchtower headquarters felt this was inappropriate. However, Audrey Hyde in her life story also sadly states "In time, Glenn was stricken with Alzheimer's disease. After we had been married for ten years, Glenn died."

A most interesting and fascinating incident took place related to this article and life story by Audrey Knorr that eventually appeared in the *Watchtower* magazine of 2004. A few months before Grant Suiter died in 1983, he held a private function in his executive suite at the Watchtower headquarters and he invited a few friends, including other members of the Governing Body to celebrate the wedding anniversary of himself and his young Italian wife Edith. Wedding anniversaries are one of the few celebrations that members of Jehovah's Witnesses celebrate and are permitted by the Watchtower Society without the threat of being ostracized, expelled or shunned, whereas christenings, birthdays, Mother's Day, Father's Day, Valentine's Day, May Day, New Year's Day and Christmas are still banned. Why? The official answer by the Watchtower Society is, "because it draws attention to the individual and exalts humans, so is therefore ungodly."

During this private get-together, Grant Suiter and Milton Henschel began confidentially discussing between themselves this draft manuscript that Audrey Knorr had submitted to the Writing Department earlier in 1983, but which was only finally published in the *Watchtower* magazine in 2004. A heated debate ensued between these two men from the Governing Body and was witnessed by a third person, Lyman Swingle, who was also in attendance at this celebration function. Suiter and Henschel who apparently were a bit loose tongued, probably having had too much to drink, and they both strongly objected to a remark that Audrey Knorr had used in her manuscript. It is the fiduciary duty of the Governing Body to make sure that all material and articles that appeared in the *Watchtower* are truthful and accurate, although in actual fact they often and regularly fail in this duty. Their responsibility includes proof reading all content that comes from the Writing Department, including articles related to doctrines, new teaching and policy, articles that are always anonymous in the actual published and printed magazine. But occasionally a personal life story appears in the *Watchtower* and this article will contain the actual name of the writer, but is still checked for accuracy, honesty and truthfulness.

These two members of the Governing Body apparently objected to Audrey Hyde stating in her life story that her marriage to Nathan Knorr was a happy and successful one, they made the cogent argument and sullied her claim stating that these words she used were not true as she claimed, being "We've had a happy marriage. Many people never experience that. One thing that made our marriage happy was Nathan's thoughtfulness." Both Suiter and Henschel, who now apparently disliked Knorr, had personal knowledge of the character of Nathan Knorr and also of the background to this marriage, both of them knowing that Knorr was homosexual, so this naturally also influenced their negative opinion. They also objected to the remark made by Audrey: "That Nathan had told me that I could live in the past with my memories or that I could build a new life." Suiter and Henschel felt that Audrey had nefariously used these words of Nathan Knorr as an excuse to continue with her new close relationship with Glenn Hyde while Knorr was still alive, and then marrying Glenn within a few short months of Knorr's death, as intimated in her article, which these two members of the Governing Body privately criticized.

Both Suiter and Henschel knew that this claim by Audrey in her life story regarding her marriage being "happy and successful" was in fact not completely true and accurate as they both had personal knowledge that Nathan Knorr was a homosexual, as indeed they both were, and this marriage to Audrey had been a farce or cover up and used to hide Knorr's homosexuality, once again as their own marriages were. No doubt Audrey had gained some solace and consolation being married to Nathan Knorr and certainly benefitted from the extensive travels they made together, although still noticeably being accompanied by Knorr's private secretary Milton Henschel. Grant Suiter and Henschel later persuaded the rest of the Governing Body, including Lyman Swingle, to jointly decide together by holding back their approval plus the printing of this manuscript in the Watchtower magazine regarding the life story of Audrey Mock, the widow of Nathan Knorr. Of course, Suiter died in the December of 1983 and Henschel died later in 2003, so they could no longer block the issuing of this life story. The then current Governing Body of 2003 authorized its release with certain updates and minor amendments and it finally appeared in the May, 2004 issue of the *Watchtower*.

> *Editor's Note*: The above intriguing account, which was supposed to be a confidential conversation between two members of the Governing Body but was unethically passed on by Lyman Swingle of the Governing Body to one of his close relatives, who at that time was a member of the same religion and associated with the Holladay Congregation of Jehovah's Witnesses in Salt Lake City. This relative of Swingle, now an ex-Jehovah's Witness passed this account onto a member of our research team during a lengthy interview a few years ago and we have found no reason to doubt its authenticity.

The last time Nathan Knorr was seen in public was at the annual general meeting of the Watchtower Society, Inc., held on Friday, October 1, 1976 in Pittsburg, Pennsylvania and attended by the approximately 500 legally elected members (shareholders) of the Society. According to an eye witness he looked a total wreck of a man as he slouched along the handrail to the platform and had to be assisted up the steps to his seat on the board of directors by two Bethel assistants.

A brief glimpse into the life of Nathan Knorr helps us to understand what happens to a person who is chained to a religious cult. We have some compassion for this individual who had misguidedly spent his entire adult life, approximately 54 years, living and serving his beloved religion at their headquarters in New York City. From the day he was baptized at the age of 18 years after he left the Allentown High School as a young naïve man in 1923, he immediately left his home in a small town based in rural Pennsylvania and moved to the bustling metropolis of New York City to work full time in the Watchtower headquarters. His first job, according to the records, was in the rented Watchtower factory located in Concord Street, New York and he was assigned to sweep the floors of Printing Room No.1., in this old dirty factory but he was later transferred and promoted to the shipping department in the brand-new purpose-built Watchtower factory, being an eight-storey structure built in 1927 and located at 117, Adams Street, New York. Young Nathan remained focused on his life ambition, so as a result of his dedication to the organization, his hard work plus whatever other chicanery he had to use, as he was prepared to do anything it takes to get to the top of this religion, so his ambitious drive and motivation was eventually rewarded as he finally did make it to the top in 1942.

Nathan Knorr had been promoted to factory manager in September 1932. On January 11, 1934, at the age of 28, Knorr was elected as a director of the *Peoples Pulpit Association* (now Watchtower Bible and Tract Society of New York, Inc.), who also at that time made up the Governing Body and was made its Vice President the following year of 1935, eventually becoming the 3rd President of this powerful expanding religion in 1942 at the age of 37.

This short comment by ex-Witness James Penton, who knew this man, makes some valid observations.

> Nathan Homer Knorr. Well, he was an austere man. He came from a Dutch Calvinist background before he was converted to Jehovah's Witnesses, and he had acted as a sycophant when Rutherford was alive. Sometimes Rutherford would chastise him publicly. And he didn't like this, but when he became the president of the Watchtower Society, he did exactly what Rutherford had done to certain Witnesses who would not obey every order from him at the headquarters of the organization. He really was very severe with people, everyone otherwise had to stand to attention when he demanded that they do something. He was a hard man. He was single as long as Rutherford was alive, and for some time after. He did marry, which possibly showed he had a normal sex drive although some suspected that he also had homosexual feelings as well. The reason for saying this was that he developed what were called new boys talks at the headquarters of the Watchtower Society in Brooklyn, New York. And he would often describe homosexual relations, [plus the practice of masturbation] which took place at the headquarters of the Watchtower Society, doing so in very vivid ways. These were called the new boys talks.

Regarding the family history and background of the late Nathan Knorr our researcher checked with the Genealogy Department of the LDS Church in Salt Lake City and there it is recorded that his father was Donald Ellsworth Knorr and his mother is named as Estella Bloss and they were married in April of 1903 when Donald was aged 31 years and Estella was aged 20 years. The only other reference regarding Nathan's parents is that they were both American born and lived in Bethlehem, Pennsylvania when Nathan was born on 23 April, 1905. Our research also revealed that Donald Knorr was employed as the theater manager of the Pergola Movie Theatre in Hamilton Street, Allentown according to the 1940 US Census. There is a record of an older brother to Nathan named Robert E. Knorr and born about 1904 but no further information was discovered so it is possible he died young. Nathan also had a younger sister born in 1907 and named Isobel Estella Knorr, but little is known about her except that she probably never married and attended her brother's funeral in the Wallkill Kingdom Hall in 1977. Isabel Estella Knorr of 29th Street, Allentown, Pennsylvania died on 2 June, 1999, aged 92 years old and her funeral was held in the Parkway Congregation of Jehovah's Witnesses in Allentown.

The US Census forms of 1910 and 1920 both record Nathan as living in the household of Donald Knorr, but in the 1930 Census he is recorded as living in Brooklyn, New York. Also, on the US Government Draft Registry dated 16 October, 1940, Nathan Knorr surprisingly lists his next of kin as Grant Suiter of Brooklyn, New York, who was a very close personal friend and drinking partner, who was also a member of the Governing Body and Nathan's employer is listed as The Watchtower Bible and Tract Society. Regarding his next of kin, which is defined as being a person's closest living relative, this is most confusing and unusual, if not an actual falsehood, as it is known that Nathan had a younger sister Isobel who was still alive in 1940 and was still an active member of Jehovah's Witnesses. Also, his father Donald only died in 1964 so was also still alive in 1940, plus for most of Nathan Knorr's lifetime while he served in the New York headquarters, although his mother and grandmother had probably died by this time and he had no other known living relatives. It has also been suggested that as his father was an absent or disinterested father and that Nathan had very little contact with him throughout his lifetime. Nathan's father was probably not a member of Jehovah's Witnesses, so in the mind of Nathan Knorr his father was already figuratively dead, as it is a common view of fanatical members of this religion to view relatives who are not Jehovah's Witnesses and disagree with their beliefs are ultimately doomed for eternal destruction and already dead in God's sight.

We do know from accurate reports that Nathan was primarily brought up by his Grandmother, but we could not establish if she was his maternal or paternal grandmother only that she was of the very strict Dutch Calvinistic religion and background. There is no record if she actually legally adopted Nathan or just simply took on the duty and responsibility of bringing him up as a child, but it was she who actually chose his given name Nathan, who was a prominent Bible character. The prophet Nathan was a court prophet who lived in the time of King David (1035-970 BC) He was an advisor to David, with whom David reflects on the contrast between his own comfortable home and the tent in which the Ark of the Covenant is accommodated. The prophet Nathan then announced to David the covenant God was making with him (2 Samuel 7:4–17, a passage known as Nathan's Oracle), contrasting David's proposal to build a house (i.e. a building) for the Ark with God's plan to build a house (i.e. a dynasty) for David. Later, he came to David to reprimand him for committing adultery with Bathsheba while she was the wife of Uriah the Hittite, whose death and murder King David had also arranged to hide his previous transgression.

Regarding the choice of Nathan Knorr's middle name Homer, his grandmother probably chose this name also, as Homer was a common American name at the time being a reminder of the famous Greek author, poet and historian who lived around 850 BC. The name Homer means pledge as in dedication and is of Greek origin. This could have been the reason why Nathan Knorr's grandmother eventually persuaded Nathan to become baptized at the age of 18 years and then to offer himself to serve in the Watchtower headquarters for the rest of his life. Another interesting fact is that it is claimed that young Nathan Knorr was baptized personally by Fred Franz who had also given the baptism talk at the event of Nathan's baptism in 1923. Fred Franz was known as a religious nut so he may also have influenced Nathan to dedicate himself to the Bible Students religion, later known as the Watchtower Society. One interesting fact that came to light during our research of the life of Nathan Knorr is that without doubt Nathan Knorr had homosexual tendencies and according to our associate who holds a qualification in clinical psychology, this could have been caused by being brought up and strongly influenced by his very self-willed and overbearing grandmother.

An additional opinion was expressed to try and prove that an overbearing mother, or in Nathan's case grandmother, can create homosexual tendencies. In an article by Chuck Colson titled "Born Gay? A Parent's Guide," which asserted that the way parents relate to their male children, can create homosexuality. Colson quoted extensively from Joseph and Linda Nicolosi's book *A Parent's Guide to Preventing Homosexuality* as support for the view that weak or distant fathers and smothering mothers create gay males. According to Nicolosi, gay males suffered a "gender wound" in childhood and failed to identify properly with their fathers. These males remain tied to their mothers and reject masculine identification. Somehow, however, the "pre-homosexual male" becomes gay by falling in love with what he once rejected – masculinity – and seeks gay sex as a means to find it. This complex subject is covered more fully in the upcoming publication by the MTC International Foundation titled, Masters & Slaves of Modern Marriage, to be released in the near future.

When Nathan Knorr reached the end of his sad life in 1977, he had only one known living fleshly relative to attend his funeral and he had no children to mourn his passing, he only had his widow Audrey, his sister Isobel and a few members of this religious sect to which he had dedicated his entire life. Many who attended his small private funeral in the local Kingdom Hall in Wallkill, New York, being members of his religion did not really know him and other members disliked him. Other individuals who belonged to the group of ex-Jehovah's Witnesses utterly hated him and viewed him as a libertine, as he was partly responsible for introducing and enforcing the doctrine of the Watchtower Society pertaining to the banning of blood transfusions that caused the death of so many innocent victims. In addition, during his stewardship as leader of this cult he was responsible for enforcing the issue of excommunicating individuals, labeling them as apostates because of their Bible trained conscience and their sincere questions about the teachings of this religion. So here passed away the life of a man who had been chained to a religious cult for all of his adult life and is now almost forgotten and is just another name in history, plus a character in the checkered chronicles of the Watchtower Society.

To round out this brief review of the life of Nathan Knorr we include a sad story uncovered by one of our researchers that relates to the experience of one individual who also spent almost all of his entire adult life working in the Watchtower headquarters. This brief article was written by William (Bill) Cetnar, member of the New York headquarters of Jehovah's Witnesses for some years, but we warn our readers that this ex-Witness started a website in French that opposes and severely criticizes the Watchtower Society based on his own personal experiences. Cetnar also wrote *Questions for Jehovah's Witnesses*

(1983). We nevertheless include this article as it clearly illustrates the lack of compassion and love amongst the Watchtower Society leaders, especially Nathan Knorr, who was not a loving and caring person, according to many who knew him, and he displayed a very vindictive personality. The following is the English version of Bill Cetnar's article.

One tragic event that happened at the Watchtower Headquarters during my service there involves Charles de Wilda. Charlie, as we all called him, was a deserter from the Cavalry after the First World War and looking for employment, he came to Headquarters. He was told there was work available, but the salary was only twenty dollars a month with room and board. He accepted the offer and when I knew him, he had already worked there for more than thirty years. Now, Charlie was old, a little slower, but still a hard worker. President Knorr often praised him and used him as an example for the volume of work that one man could accomplish. Charlie was the best bookbinder on the fourth floor.

But, like everyone else who worked at Bethel, he was not allowed like everyone else to get married if he wanted to stay at Bethel. Knorr often repeated this rule, and that irritated Charlie. However, in 1952, violating his own rule, Knorr married Audrey Mock, one of the sisters at Bethel. A few years after the marriage, Charlie went to see Knorr, and told him he had broken his own law and he should resign. He added: "You preach love more than anyone else, but it is you that practice it the least."

The result of this confrontation, Charlie was not allowed his usual seat in the cafeteria, and was relegated to a distant corner at the back. The pretext for this is that he was rude. It was evident that he was being punished. He refused to remain put in his new seating place and returned to his former place. His life was made so bitter at Bethel; he took his few possessions and departed. Bethel was his whole life. He never even took his vacations. He did not know where to go, he never had any one to receive him, but for him, at the time, anything was better than Bethel. I met him later, and he slept at a flophouse for fifty cents a night. When he was short of money, he begged from Bethel workers and other Witnesses to give him some money to provide him with food. I gave him some for his needs. The Bethel workers were instructed to not give him money, and a letter was sent saying the same from the Bethel headquarters directed to the congregations in the area. I heard later, that eventually Charles de Wilda died on a park bench in a public park. That is how one rewards a man who after forty years of faithful service in God's organization because he denounced an evident anomaly. This was an example that revealed to me how little the love that exists at headquarters for the personnel who worked there.

Regarding the eventual removal of Knorr as Chairman of the Governing Body, this two-third majority rule used by the Governing Body of the Watchtower Society has been used in political and commercial circles for many years and is certainly not inspired by Almighty God as related to those organizations. A two-thirds vote, when unqualified, means two-thirds or more of the votes cast. This voting basis is equivalent to the number of votes in favor being at least twice the number of votes against. Abstentions and absences are excluded in calculating a two-thirds vote. The Watchtower Society by introducing this new rule in 1975 supposedly communicated to them by Almighty God as new light or a revelation makes mockery of their claim that this religion is free from the influences of this wicked satanic world! Pope Alexander III introduced the use of supermajority rule (two-thirds) for papal elections at the Third Lateran Council in 1179 AD. In the Democratic Party of the United States the determination of a presidential nominee once required the votes of two-thirds of delegates to the Democratic National Convention. Plus the United States Senate still enforces this rule even today in the Congress and parliamentary plus political parties of many other governments in the world also use this rule.

The definition of the two-thirds rule is the following: the two-thirds rule is used at all levels of government and in many social and political organizations to prevent the dominance of a small majority over large minority. Despite the claim by the Governing Body of the Watchtower Society that they had been informed by the Lord Jesus Christ through Holy Spirit to change their rule of voting, from the unanimous (all in total agreement) voting rule to this new revelation of now being only a two-thirds rule mechanism, is absolutely ludicrous and laughable. There is no such thing as a two-thirds rule in the Holy Scriptures as related to truth, honesty and lying; truth is truth (100%) (There is no such thing as a half-truth) and deceit and lying is just simply deceit and lying (100%) (There is also no such thing as a half-lie or white lie).

This above fact is an established principle of the Bible and true Christianity, and the Governing Body of the Watchtower Society should be complying with this principle of 100% truth as they claim and label their religion as "The Truth"[19] and they must desist from using tactics that are nothing more than deceit, dishonesty and hypocrisy. In addition, as a reminder to the leaders of this cult, the inspired Apostle Paul plainly says in 1 Corinthians 1:10, "Now I appeal to you, brothers and sisters, by the name of our Lord Jesus Christ, that all of you be in agreement and that there be no divisions among you, but that you be united in the same mind and the same purpose." Has the Governing Body forgotten what the Bible says and considered it expedient to just simply ignore these inspired words of the Apostle Paul and doing so to their own advantage?

> *Editor's Note*: This appointment of Freddy Franz in January of 1976 to his position as the new Chairman of the Governing Body and the removal of Nathan Knorr, now being the ex-chairman of the Governing Body, was by means of this new two-thirds rule. Most members of the Governing Body had grown to intensely dislike the aloof Knorr because of his autocratic, ruthless and dictatorial control, style and manner, so they were simply looking for a way to strip him of his power. The appointment of Freddy Franz brought about severe criticism from many senior members of this religion in the New York headquarters with the possibility of a major split developing. It was clear to all that this man Freddy Franz was not mentally or physically capable of handling such a prominent role so there was obviously another underhanded reason why Freddy was selected, apart from the obvious motive

[19] When a member of the Governing Body was asked why they call the religion of Jehovah's Witnesses, "The Truth", the following was his answer. "What do we mean by the term the truth? Generally, we use it to describe our beliefs, our way of worship, and our way of life. People who are "in the truth" know what the Bible teaches, and they live according to its principles. As a result, they are set free from religious falsehood and they enjoy the best life possible for imperfect humans."

of the calculating Governing Body in stripping Knorr of his autocratic rule of the Watchtower Society.

When President Knorr died in June of 1977, the Governing Body once again by the two thirds majority rule elected Freddy Franz as the new President of the Watchtower Society as from June, 1977, the position still being a meaningless and powerless role since 1976, a position Franz held for 16 years until his death in 1992 at the age of 99. The real controlling power of this religion was in the hands of the newly structured Governing Body. Freddy Franz after his death was then succeeded as President of the Watchtower Society by Milton G. Henschel (1920-2003) in 1992, the longtime personal friend and past private secretary of Nathan Knorr. According to this quote from the *Watchtower Documents* website:

> Reporting on the election, note how Franz was described in the August 1, 1977 *Watchtower*: "His outstanding reputation as an eminent Bible scholar and his tireless work in behalf of Kingdom interests has won him the confidence and loyal support of Jehovah's Witnesses everywhere." The report from Watchtower Documents continues, Really? – "Everywhere? Not exactly true! Harry Peloyan the Awake! Editor was furious that Freddy was elected president by the other members of the Governing Body as were many other insiders at headquarters. Peloyan went to see Lloyd Barry (of the Governing Body) to tell him of his resentment and that of other important staff members because it was Franz that came up with the 1975 fiasco that resulted in as many as 500,000 Witnesses leaving the faith and the near collapse of the organization.

> Donations were down. Subscriptions for the *Watchtower* and the *Awake!* magazines were few and far between. To many, electing Franz to the presidency looked as though he was rewarded for the 1975 debacle. Barry tried to defend the choice by saying Franz was next in line for the presidency, but that carried no weight with those who resented the choice that was made for the reasons given here and who believed Franz should have been skipped over and demoted. The sentiment among many at headquarters was that ineptness should not be rewarded.

Harry Peloyan was born in 1925 and had joined the headquarters staff of the Watchtower Society in 1957 plus being well educated and a graduate of Harvard University he quickly worked his way up the hierarchy of this religion, eventually becoming editor-in chief of one of the organization's leading journals. It is reported he was later removed as Editor of Awake! due to serious personal clashes with Theo (Ted) Jaracz, the most ruthless despot and sadistic member of the Governing Body. This serious conflict with Jaracz was primarily related to the hidden secret files containing the many cases held at the headquarters related of sexual abuse and child molestation that had been secretly collected and hidden away from public scrutiny. Harry did not really care one iota regarding this deceptive, ruthless man Jaracz and his attempt to hide the facts and secret files related to the many cases of sexual abuse of children, as Jaracz was so powerful he could not be challenged, but Harry felt that he had to do something to expose this criminal act by the Watchtower Society.

Harry Peloyan and many other sincere Christians working in the Writing Department of the Watchtower Society were already uniting in their attempt to expose this dreadful, disgusting situation, including his fellow worker and researcher Barbara Anderson who was later excommunicated from this religion for her bold and courageous actions. Harry Peloyan was never excommunicated, nor was he asked to resign or vacate his position in the New York headquarters, but from insider reports he was a changed man, as his spirit was now crushed under the powerful Governing Body, being influenced by the destructive, ruthless Theo Jaracz, (nicknamed 'iron fist' by some in the Bethel) and Harry simply withdrew into himself, especially after his dear wife Rose was diagnosed with cancer and her eventual death in 2005. This simplistic but sincere life story of Harry appeared in the *Watchtower* of 1 May, 2006, in which he describes how his wife of 54 years, Rose Marie died on 30 January, 2005, at their home in Brooklyn, New York, and in it he states. "I suffered the most crushing blow of my whole life. My dearest Rose Marie died and the suffering I experienced when my wife died has been far more intense and long lasting but among those brought back [in the resurrection] will be Rose Marie. What a welcome she will receive from her loved ones! How satisfying it will be at that time to live in a world where there is no suffering."

Many of our observant readers will have gathered from the above remarks by Harry Peloyan in his life story, which appeared in the *Watchtower* that he and his late wife erroneously believed they were members of this so-called earthly class of the great crowd of other sheep who do not go immediately to heaven when they die, unlike what the so-called unique anointed class claim when they die, including Harry's arch-enemy and adversary, Theo Jaracz. Harry and his wife had been taught by the Governing Body of this religion that they will have to wait for an earthly resurrection sometime in the unknown future with a new fleshly body, which will look similar to their previous old body so that they will be recognized, but only if they have been obedient to the organization. We are not sure what Harry believes today as he looks back over his many years of association with the Watchtower Society and whether he has changed his mind about this erroneous belief, but what we do know is the following.

It has come to light from our intensive research that many intelligent, long standing members of Jehovah's Witnesses are becoming disillusioned with the chaos and confusing status of the current Governing Body, they are also disillusioned with the new more involved, complicated, deceptive system of so-called helpers to the Governing Body and in addition with the Watchtower Society itself, regarding their incorrect private interpretation of numerous scriptures in the Bible. Plus the many questionable doctrines having been permanently fixed and entrenched in the minds of the Governing Body since this religion was founded way back in the 1880s by Charles Russell, which today they are reluctant to revise or even reconsider, this is also causing many members great concern. This is especially true regarding this claim of there being two separate classes of Christians on earth today, a belief that is unique to Jehovah's Witnesses, namely being the exclusive remnant (including all of the current members of the Governing Body) of a literal number of 144,000 and the so-called unnumbered great crowd of other sheep.

This subject is more fully discussed in other sections of this chapter. As a result, these far-sighted intelligent members of this religion, some actually being senior leaders in their local congregations, still remain in this religion for family or other personal reasons, especially the social aspect, but within their hearts they privately believe and follow their own Bible trained conscience that these erroneous doctrines are not accurate or Bible based. So, as a result, some now have their own private views on many current beliefs and doctrines of the Watchtower Society but don't publicly express them for fear of the consequences.

The current Governing Body of elderly men, all living in the lap of luxury at the brand new Watchtower headquarters based in Warwick, New York State, has now virtually passed overall control and the future direction of this religion to this much younger, brighter but also a very shrewd, calculating group of so-called helpers, (very similar as to how the Mormon Church operate today with their President, Twelve Apostles and group of assistants called the Seventy who actually carry out the day to day operations of this cult). This Watchtower Society group of helpers, (approximately 30 members at the latest count and divided up into six specific committees) on the surface appear to be working under the direction of the elderly, declining, current eight members of the Governing Body, but these helpers basically now operate and control the Watchtower Society today and formulates its future beliefs, plus the current confusing doctrines. They also formulate policies, legal and financial, sometimes using outside non-Witness expert wiz-kids who are their financial and property consultants and advisors.

What is the current role in the Watchtower hierarchy assigned to these helpers and what duties do they perform? This role is clearly implied in the *Watchtower* article of May, 2015, although with a clever attempt to hide the fact, and the claim that only the Governing Body makes final decisions. To quote from this article, "They attend the weekly meeting of the committee to which they are assigned, providing background information and offering suggestions. The Governing Body members make the final decisions." We now know from first hand reports that this is not true according to the facts, the committee, consisting of all helpers plus the chairman, if present, makes the final decision and not the Chairman supposedly representing the Governing Body. And the Governing Body simply gives their rubber stamp to what the committee has decided.

This was recently illustrated by the very clever underhanded Kingdom Hall scheme and the seizing of ownership of all these thousands of properties that once belonged to the local congregations of Jehovah's Witnesses, then in turn amalgamating congregations, closing down others and then selling off these now vacant and unused properties. In London, England, dozens of Kingdom Halls being sold to the local Muslim groups to be converted into Islamic Centers, with the Watchtower Society pocketing the proceeds of these sales, which is a diabolical financial scandal. It is possible that this new powerful controlling faction, the so-called helpers might soon come to their senses and realize that they will have to adapt or die in their management style and their current collection of unscriptural beliefs, practices and private interpretations of the Bible. That is if they survive the current massive growing list of legal cases and ongoing serious problem being faced by the Watchtower Society by being sued for billions of Dollars for sexual and child abuse. They must by now be very conscious and fully aware of what happened to the cult, The Worldwide Church of God and its successful magazine The Plain Truth that is covered in more detail later in this book. As we relate this account about the Watchtower Society today, we can see no evidence of any changes ever taking place.

According to the Watchtower Society's article in the May 2015 issue of their journal they try to feebly explain how these helpers operate.

> Since 1992, the Governing Body has appointed experienced, mature Christian elders to help its committees carry out their work. These helpers, from among the other sheep, provide valuable support to the Governing Body. They attend the weekly meeting of the committee to which they are assigned, providing background information and offering suggestions. The Governing Body members make the final decisions, but the helpers implement the committee's direction and carry out whatever assignments they are given. The helpers accompany Governing Body members to special and international conventions. They may also be assigned to visit branch offices as headquarters representatives.

However, the Governing Body had voted back in December of 1975 to establish these six operating committees to oversee the various administrative requirements of the organization's worldwide activities that formerly had been under the personal direction of the President, whoever that happened to be. But it took a number of years to arrange, organize and complete this dramatic new feature of management as some on the Governing Body used various delaying tactics as they were afraid of losing their personal powers, authority and benefits from their prestigious positions. This decision to create these special committees was made at the same time that they stripped Nathan Knorr of his autocratic powers as the President and also his role as permanent Chairman of the Governing Body and the introduction of a rotating Chairman from 1976 onward.

This article in the *Watchtower* referred to above, is once again a very misleading and deceptive one and is yet another surreptitious attempt to explain the role of these helpers and to reassure the rank and file of the members of this religion that the actual Governing Body was still in charge of the Organization, no matter how old they are, as each of these six committees is chaired by a member of the ageing Governing Body. But based on our inside information and further examination, these helpers follow the decision of the joint committee, not necessarily the ruling of the Chairman, as the *Watchtower* article claims, who is always a member of the elderly Governing Body. So despite what the article of 2015 states, namely that, "the Governing Body members make the final decisions", based on information from a fellow worker and personal friend of a member of this group of helpers, the helpers carry out the necessary work and instructions based on the joint decision of the committee. So, these committee meetings chaired by a single member of the elderly Governing Body, this man is simply a figure head or façade and the major decisions of this religion are now made by these committees consisting of these so-called helpers and not by the members of Governing Body as claimed. As previously stated, they simply act as figure heads to try and convince the rank-and-file members of this religion that they are still in charge. Anthony Morris, a member of this Governing Body actually admitted this to a fellow leading member of the headquarters staff back in 2017 and who related this fact to one of our researchers. Read more details later in this Chapter regarding Anthony Morris, member of the Governing Body and his open confession.

Based on a conversation between one of these helpers and a friend of one of our researchers from England who serves in the British Branch Office of the Watchtower Society and who was visiting the New York headquarters some years ago, the following enlightening details were revealed. It appears that after the new arrangement of the appointment of these helpers and the formation of the six special committees were introduced in 1992, a totally different management system of the Watchtower Society was implemented. These Governing Body Committees were listed as the Personnel, Publishing, Service, Teaching, Writing and Coordinator's Committees, each with between seven or eight members being designated as helpers. This unnamed helper was quite sincere and appeared genuine when he expressed that this new arrangement was a clear sign of the blessing and guidance of Jehovah on his organization. He also pointed out to our source that these committees acted like mini-governing bodies, as they had direct control and the power of decision making over clear specific areas of the workings of the organization. In addition, he stated, was one very important factor that impressed him and that was when the committee made a decision it had to be unanimous, and in full unison based on the scriptures, and not by the previous system of the worldly and political two-third majority rule, as had been the practice of the primary Governing Body over the years, and this had convinced him of the guidance of the Lord and his Holy Spirit.

It is now quite clear to intelligent observers of this change in management that it is this body of helpers who are now controlling the leadership, doctrines, policies and future direction of the Watchtower Society and Jehovah's Witnesses, and not as publicly claimed by the current eight elderly men who compose the current Governing Body. This fact has also been regrettably admitted by Anthony Jackson, a current member of the current Governing Body. This has now created some confusion amongst members of this religion, as the current Governing Body still claim to be the 'faithful and discreet slave' of Matthew 24:45-47 and are the ones who are providing the 'food at the proper time'. This change of management does not remove the current very serious problems facing this religion, whoever is in charge, as they still face the ever-increasing accusations of sexual abuse, the problem of shrinking funds and how to deal with the doctrines of this religion and the current resistance by many members who are now questioning the accuracy their teachings and private explanations of the Bible.

The article in the *Watchtower* of 2015 also clearly states that these helpers are all members of the so-called other sheep class, which is another misleading and deceptive remark. It is a known fact that this is not the case at all, as some of these younger men, for personal reasons seem to have changed their mind since they were baptized as members of the so-called other sheep class a few years ago and then were later invited to join this prestigious group of helpers, as some now claim they are members of the so-called anointed heavenly class of 144,000. Thereby now claiming that they have been personally selected by Almighty God and informed by Jesus Christ through the Holy Spirit that they are now to partake of the bread and wine at the annual Memorial as an indication of their now public claim they are of the special anointed ones with all the benefits that go along with this selection.

Why, you might ask, why do these helpers make this decision today when they know that this number of 144,000 was completed and filled over 80 years ago in 1935, as claimed at the time by the late Joseph Rutherford and Freddy Franz? The answer is quite obvious and is that to eventually be invited to join the powerful position on the exclusive Governing Body of this religion, who also claims to be the prophetic faithful and discreet slave of Matthew 24:45 that this is the only gateway in terms of current interpretations of the Bible by the Watchtower Society. This maneuver has already been successfully used and clearly demonstrated by the disgusting claim of the late Theo Jaracz in 1974 that he was one of the chosen ones so he could get onto the Governing Body, using the excuse that some members of the anointed had become unfaithful and lost their privileged place and thus created a vacancy in this Holy Spirit chosen remnant class. Read also the frustrating case of Philip Rees, one time Branch Servant of Australia and the manipulations of Nathan Knorr, the then President of the Watchtower Society, as pointed out later in this report.

One of our researchers wrote a sincere letter to the Governing Body requesting an explanation of why this article made the claim and stated that all of these helpers were of the so-called other sheep class when it is known that some of these helpers claim they are of the so-called anointed class of 144,000 and personally chosen by God to eventually rule the universe with Jesus Christ in heaven, as Kings and Priests when they eventually die. These much younger men, like some on the current Governing Body of eight men, who also later in life claimed they had been chosen as one of the anointed heavenly class. Take for example the case of Anthony Morris who was not even baptized as a Jehovah's Witness and one of the other sheep class until the year 1971. So, during the years between 1971 and 2005 Anthony Morris must have changed his mind and decided that he was now one the anointed heavenly class and he publicly started to partake of the bread and wine at the annual Memorial celebration. This now publicly displayed his new claim that he had been selected by Almighty God, so as a result he was invited to join the Governing Body in 2005.

In an attempt to explain why these younger men are now partaking of the emblems of bread and wine claiming to be of the anointed 144,000, and that Joseph Rutherford and Freddy Franz, who under supposed divine revelation were incorrect when they stated that this selection was completed in 1935, this article appeared in the May 1, 2007 *Watchtower*.

> As time has gone by, some Christians baptized after 1935 have had witness borne to them that they have the heavenly hope. (Romans 8:16, 17) Thus it appears that we cannot set a specific date for when the calling of Christians to the heavenly hope ends.

Several current members of the Governing Body were in fact previous members of this group of helpers but eventually were promoted to the Governing Body in line with current policy, but only if they claimed and displayed their sharing in the bread and wine ritual that they were members of the so-called little flock of 144,000. So the current group of helpers has a clear precedent and example to follow. By the way if you are curious, our researcher naturally did not receive a reply to his letter from the Governing Body, again just total silence and another cover up regarding one of the greatest and most serious issues now facing this misleading and deceptive religious cult.

Returning briefly once again to the account of Harry Peloyan, we discovered the following details. He was 79 years old at the time his wife tragically died, and, from unconfirmed reports, Harry now in his nineties still lives in their Brooklyn apartment in a building owned by the Watchtower Society but soon to be sold to the Kushner family, a New Jersey property company, for redevelopment. But for personal and emotional reasons Harry still remains a member of Jehovah's Witnesses notwithstanding all of his bitter experiences and conflicts with their policies and teachings. It is also reported that Harry was the author and head of the committee of the *Watchtower* publication of 1959, *Jehovah's Witnesses in the Divine Purpose*, a 316-page history of the Watchtower Society, a book that our research team has used in their duties and Harry was also a past instructor at the Watchtower missionary school of Gilead. So, he was no light-weight in the Watchtower hierarchy when he made this powerful outspoken criticism regarding Freddy Franz being incompetent and not qualified to be President of the Watchtower Society, plus his accusation of the criminal actions of the Governing Body in hiding the secret files from the authorities regarding sexual and child molestation by some of their leading members.

Harry commendably also made a vital contribution to the exposure of these many cases of child molestation by assisting ex-Witness Barbara Anderson in her ongoing campaign and dedication to expose these criminal actions by the Governing Body of the Watchtower Society. In a private letter to Barbara Anderson, reproduced by kind permission of Barbara, dated 1997, Harry stated, "But I wonder who is going to answer for the many Witness children who in the past five years of inaction have had their lives ruined by baptized Witness molesters." Of course, as we all now know, Barbara Anderson was excommunicated from the religion of Jehovah's Witnesses because of her continued insistence on exposed this criminal activity of the Watchtower Society related to sexual and child abuse, even appearing on the NBC *Nightly News Dateline* television program and relating the secret settlements of over $12.5 million with sixteen victims of molestation by leading men in the Watchtower religion. After Barbara was excommunicated, Harry Peloyan at that time still being a loyal member of Jehovah's Witnesses and in order to retain his position within the organization he blindly obeyed the letter of the law as instructed in the Watchtower literature and he cut off all direct communication with Barbara Anderson, doing so with full knowledge that her ongoing campaign to expose this criminal activity by the Watchtower Society and was Bible based and in full harmony with what the scriptures recommend. (Psalms 97:10;

Proverbs 6:16-19 and Galatians 6:1)

Also from insider reports, Harry also quickly lost personal interest in the need to continue investigating and exposing this criminal activity of the Watchtower Society related to sexual and child abuse. He probably reasoned as many have done, what's the use, one cannot change the Watchtower Society or the policy of the Governing Body no matter how hard one tries, it's like banging your head against a brick wall and to continue to try can quickly lead to one being labeled as an apostate and being disfellowshipped. Harry knew from first hand experience what had happened to his fellow Bethel workers, Raymond Franz and Edward Dunlap back in 1980s, so poor disillusioned Harry Peloyan simply faded into the background.

We have included this short intimate account of this life experience of Harry Peloyan, one-time leading member of the Watchtower Society, and based on a report from one our research team, as it clearly illustrates the dilemma currently facing 10,000s of Jehovah's Witnesses today. Do they remain as members of this religion and try to bring about reform of the many erroneous doctrines and teachings plus the draconian policies from <u>within</u> the Organization or do they leave this religion, breaking free from their 'chains' and try to bring about reform from <u>outside</u> the Organization? There is a price to be paid either way so this issue cannot be treated lightly, "there ain't no such thing as a free lunch" (an American idiom meaning one cannot get something for nothing)[20] even if something appears to be free there is always a cost to the person or to society as a whole. Harry chose the former and unfortunately paid a very heavy price! So if you as one of our current readers about religious cults face the same dilemma, you must by now be fully aware of the inner struggle you also now have to confront. One member of our research team submitted a brief account related to the dramatic change in the personality and character of Harry Peloyan and deserves mentioning in this report as it illustrates once again the danger of being chained to a religion and the damage that belonging to a cult can create.

---

[20] The term "free lunch" refers to the once-common tradition of saloons in the United States providing a "free" lunch to patrons who had purchased at least one drink. Many foods on offer were high in salt (e.g., ham, cheese, and salted crackers), so those who ate them ended up buying a lot of beer.

This member of our research team had reason to visit the New York headquarters of the Watchtower Society to discuss an article he had written for the Awake! magazine and he bumped into Harry Peloyan, as he had personally known him for a number of years but was somewhat shocked when he observed how Harry had dramatically changed from the last time he met him about eight years previous. He remembered Harry as a strong, forthright and outspoken personality with plenty of guts, the sort of man who would endure 'sweating blood and biting bullets' for the right cause, even going head-to-head with members of the Governing Body when he felt they were incorrect in their decisions. But meeting him again eight years later he now appeared to be a very fearful individual, timid in his speech and persona and nothing like the character he used to be.

Apparently, Harry had recently been invited to become a helper to the Governing Body, a very prominent and honorable role to play in the hierarchy of the Watchtower ranks. However it appears that the invitation was blocked by the member of the Governing Body; his adversary the sophomoric Theo Jaracz and this had caused Harry a great deal of personal grief, emotional pain and bitter disappointment. Harry was also still mentally and emotionally suffering from his failure to follow through, along with a few of his fellow workers in the headquarters Writing Department related to his previous role in helping to expose the criminal activity of Watchtower Society in hiding the secret files related to child and sexual abuse by Watchtower leaders. It was also known that Harry as previous editor-in-chief of Awake! had refused to allow articles exposing the sexual and child abuse by the Catholic Church as he felt it was hypocritical to do so when he personally knew what was going on behind the scenes in the ranks of the Watchtower Society.

So, at this latest meeting a few years ago, between our fellow researcher and Harry Peloyan, he appeared to be as frightened as a rabbit, was the phrase used by our reporter, and he had become a shadow of his former self. This experience of Harry Peloyan is recorded with the motive of showing what can happen to an individual who cannot or is unwilling or unable to break free from the restrictive chains of a religious cult. Harry made his choice and paid his price! Our dear friend Harry

Peloyan was fully aware that other members of this religion, including his one-time personal friend and fellow worker Barbara Anderson; they had all taken this bold and courageous step of exposing these hidden files of sexual and child abuse, as their conscience would not allow them to further support such hypocrisy of the Watchtower Society, but they also paid their price. But they were at least free from the chains of a religious cult and used their God given right as assured and clarified in Psalms 119:109: "I hold my life in my palm constantly, but I do not forget your law."

A question was raised by one member of Jehovah's Witnesses we interviewed, how does one actually become a member of the Governing Body? Apart from the personal experience of Philip Rees, the past Branch Servant of Australia; and please read the personal story of Philip in the Appendix and the secret offer he was made by autocrat Nathan Knorr. There are other examples of men suddenly partaking of the bread and wine, as a gateway to becoming members of the Governing Body, claiming they have been personally chosen by God and revealed to them privately by means of the Holy Spirit. One such glaring case was the man Theodore (Ted) Jaracz (1925-2010). The following brief report by ex-witness Barbara Anderson, in her *Watchtower Documents* stated:

> According to reports, around 1968, in California, Jaracz questioned many of those who professed to be of the anointed, asking, "How do you know when God is calling you to be of this group? What does it feel like to be called?" One anointed Witness told me that he responded, "If you were anointed, you wouldn't have to ask." The circuit overseer by the name of Wetzler, a witness to the conversation, remarked afterwards that Jaracz apparently <u>wanted</u> to partake. In and around 1969-70, Jaracz supposedly was transferred to Arizona to be district overseer, and by 1971, he was partaking even in light of the Watch Tower's teaching that by 1935, the door to heaven was closed because the number of anointed chosen by God was filled, although the Witnesses believed that, from time to time, a replacement would be needed if someone fell away. But it didn't sound like Jaracz was chosen to immediately fill the boots of someone who fell away in 1968 because he didn't start

to partake for yet another three years after he began asking questions.

The January 1, 1977 *Watchtower* stated,"To meet further demands of expansion, it was arranged in 1971 to increase the number of older men serving as the Governing Body of Jehovah's Witnesses from seven [the legal directors of the Watchtower Society] to a total of eleven members." [Further expansion to eighteen members took place late in 1974] And it was during the next year, 1975 that one of the most significant organizational readjustments in the 100-year history of the modern-day witnesses of Jehovah came under consideration. After discussions that continued through most of that year, the reorganization was approved on December 4, 1975, by a unanimous vote of the seventeen members of the Governing Body. It became operative from January 1, 1976.

Jaracz's decision to partake was timely, wasn't it, because around early 1974, he was asked to become part of the Bethel family, with an invitation in late 1974 to be a member of the Governing Body and to be a member of the Governing Body, one would have to be "anointed". I would not be surprised to find out that Ted Jaracz was told by his personal friend, Nathan Knorr, before 1971 that during 1971 the number of the GB was going to be increased, although Jaracz didn't become a member until 1974, but he had hopes and was preparing himself just in case he would be invited; hence he claimed to have heard the call to the heavenly kingdom and began to partake of the emblems. This is not an uneducated guess because I was told by a senior staff writer that it was Knorr who was responsible for inviting a scheming and fanatical Jaracz to Bethel with the intention of inviting him to be one of the GB to get even with the other "directors" for removing him from his "throne." After all, Knorr knew what Jaracz did at the Australian Branch that caused him to be removed, and knew full well what he was capable of. Jaracz became a member of the Governing Body at the end of 1974 and by the time January 1976 rolled around, he probably was responsible for much of the "... most significant organizational readjustments in the 100-year history of the modern-day witnesses of Jehovah..." that gave him powers that a man like him could only dream of having, especially when he was installed on two of the most powerful Governing Body committees, Service and Teaching, where decisions made would effect the lives of millions of people. It's no wonder one former JW, an acquaintance of Jaracz from California said Ted Jaracz was an "imposter".

With regards to the unknown reason why Jaracz was removed as branch overseer in Australia, one time in Brooklyn Bethel, one Bethelite was overheard telling a high-ranking member of the Bethel family that Ted was going to make sure he didn't mess things up again, referring to his problems in Australia. During the last two years I worked in the Writing Department, Jaracz's closed-mindedness over the child sexual abuse issue, mental health therapy and other topics brought anxious, stressful days upon compassionate staff members in the department. One well-respected writer, Lee Watters, said directly to me that Ted Jaracz was insane. He said, "Watch his eyes when he's speaking, and you'll see he's not normal." In conversations with others, Jaracz was said to be, "coldly calculating," "insolent," "caustic and sharp-tongued," "underhanded" and "devious". I heard tales of the many times Jaracz imposed his detrimental opinions on weaker GB (Governing Body) members through his forceful character.

Editor's Note: Read the complete first-hand account of this man Theo Jaracz on Barbara Anderson's website, Watchtower Documents under the title "Theocratic Life and Times of Theodore Jaracz" (Item 3024). Knowing and learning of the above facts about the Watchtower Society and the chaos, underhanded and devious schemes of the men that hold the position as masters and the Governing Body of this religion all underscores once again that this organization is nothing more than a cult.

Today the very idea of fellow members of this religion being able to sincerely contribute and suggest possible changes or improvements in the doctrines or teachings is anathema and has all but disappeared along with freeness of speech. (Proverbs 31:8, 9) This is especially true since the experience of Raymond Franz and his associated research staff back in the 1980s who spoke out with freedom of speech and this resulted and exposed the need for an even stricter and tighter control by the Governing Body as masters of this religion. This step has been taken to prevent another event similar to the Raymond Franz affair, which could cripple the power of the Governing Body if another such incident like that would ever take place in the future, so the laager (a group of wagons that were put into a circle in order to protect people in the middle) mentality of the Governing Body has developed. They have evolved into a secretive group of elusive untouchables, especially with the recent introduction of their broadcasting network and videos of the Governing Body acting like televangelists similar to Jimmy Swaggart, Jim and Tammy Bakker, Oral Roberts, plus the dozens of other weird characters who swamp the airwaves with their religious propaganda, especially in America.

The expression freeness of speech occurs 16 times in the text of the New Testament (Christian Greek Scriptures) of the Holy Bible. For example, see Ephesians 3:8-12, Philippians 1:20; 1 Timothy 3:13; Hebrews 3:6; Hebrews 10:35 and 1 John 3:21. According to Vine's Expository Dictionary of Old and New Testament Words, the Greek definition for the term freeness of speech denotes "freedom of expression, unreservedness of utterance . . . the absence of fear in speaking boldly; hence, confidence, cheerful courage, and boldness, without any connection necessarily with speech." Freeness of speech also involves remaining tactful while not allowing distressing circumstances or fear of man to inhibit our speech and should make us aware that no man or religion has the right to quell or squash our freedom of speech.

This awareness to curtail or control freedom of speech no doubt was the primary reasoning behind the Governing Body recently closing down the weekly Theocratic Ministry School in 2015 being conducted in all of the local congregations of Jehovah's Witnesses, which had been successfully used since its introduction back in 1943 to train the local brothers in teaching and public speaking skills. It was also self-proclaimed and self-adulated by the Watchtower Society as a brilliant weekly school and provided meaningful training to prepare their members for achieving (non-certified) qualifications even for secular employment, in preference to (certified) college education.

So why did the Governing Body close down and debunk this very successful weekly Theocratic Ministry School? The basic reason is very clear, it is control, control and even more, stricter control. Many long-standing members of Jehovah's Witnesses that we interviewed, a very large proportion expressed their bitter disappointment over this decision by the Governing Body to shut down the weekly *Theocratic Ministry School* as these members had benefitted so much on a personal level for many years by the excellent training they had received by means of this school and the material provided. The training involved covered the fields of how to express oneself with meaning and skill, how to use the power of speech to edify and educate one's audience, how to speak extemporaneously and how to confidently and freely express ones opinions and beliefs. Although as pointed out by one of our reporters, a great deal of the material used in these Watchtower texts books was blatantly plagiarized from other text books related to public speaking.

In the judgment of the Governing Body, as discussed amongst themselves, no doubt with some advice from their helpers, this once successful training program was now encroaching on an area that they wanted to retain complete and absolute control, so the decision was made to discontinue this program and function of allowing the local brothers to increase and exercise their ability to develop their speaking skills and flair or talent to express themselves. They also argued that perhaps this skill or appetency, as had been secretly reported by the local circuit servants, was also being used to detract from the actual written words of the Governing Body as related through their publications and perhaps allowing the more intelligent men in the local congregations to place their own personal slant or tilt on the words of the Governing Body. So the most direct and straight forward way forward was to stop and cancel this training facility once and for all time.

Another factor that influenced the decision for the Watchtower Society to close down this important Theocratic Ministry School is that they had seen the value of the dramatically improving communication technology. Under the advisement of their helpers who had made the suggestion to the reticent and taciturn Governing Body that the Watchtower Society should modernize and take advantage of this new technology of communication, especially the internet, so they moved ahead.

Up until recent years the Watchtower Society had viewed the use of the internet as dangerous to their loyal and obedient followers and was a tool of the devil, as it exposed them to outside opinions and information that was detrimental to the followers of this religion, especially from the new and expanding websites that were anti-Watchtower and anti-Witness. But it was brought to their attention by their helpers that other religions were using this tool of the devil to great advantage, especially the Mormon Church, so the elderly, conservative Governing Body had to bring the organization up to date. From inside information it took a great deal of persuasion of the Governing Body to begin using modern techniques to instruct the brothers by means of the internet and the use of videos, online lectures, and films, but the more modern minded and younger helpers finally had their way. The Governing Body was also reminded how successful the live dramas that were put on at the annual district assemblies, being now the highlight of the entire program, the live lectures and speeches being viewed as boring by most of the attendees, so why not expand this success of visual aids. This of course finally brought about the need to offer training to the local brothers to be teachers and lecturers obsolete, when the influential Governing Body and their helpers could all undertake this task themselves by means of videos, films, cartoons and the internet, so to continue with the training offered in the local congregation's Theocratic Ministry School was now outmoded, unnecessary and also too risky.

It was more important for the leaders of this sect to retain full control and expand that control over the local members of this religion, so the tried and tested method of modern technology was now the focus of the expanding Watchtower Society. We remind our readers that this religion demands that absolute obedience was; has always been and is still the requirement of the day and the local members not be allowed to use their freeness of speech or expressions and also not to use their own minds for thinking for themselves. One of the so-called helpers to the Governing Body, Robert Wallen who has been a leading member of this group of helpers since 2000 is on record as stating "I like to have someone tell me what I have to do." This man is totally ignoring the words of the Apostle Paul at Hebrews 5:13, 14: "But solid food is for the mature, for those whose faculties have been trained by practice to distinguish good from evil." In addition, Robert Wallen, in view of the circumstances in which he made this immature remark or statement, he certainly was not referring to the time when Jesus said to his disciples "Let the little children come to me, and do not stop them; for it is to such as these that the Kingdom of Heaven belongs."Wallen made this statement, "I like to have someone tell me what I have to do", because he expects all members of Jehovah's Witnesses to think likewise and to display the same frame of mind as himself.

This man Robert Wallen is also currently one of the most prominent leaders and decision makers of this religion and when he makes a statement like this on behalf of the Governing Body, he portrays himself as an immature child in desperate need of guidance and direction. Robert Wallen made the adult decision to get baptized as a member of Jehovah's Witnesses at the age of ten years old on July 1, 1939 and was a close personal friend of Theo (Ted) Jaracz, a very ambitious, aggressive, arrogant and destructive member of the Governing Body, and he was also personal executive secretary of Jaracz, which of course is another story. Wallen also faced a great deal of opprobrium and reproach from many concerned leading officials in the Watchtower headquarters over this relationship, but gives us a clue when we listen to the wise and mainly true saying "Show me who your friends are, and I'll tell you who you are."

Barbara Anderson a fellow researcher into the history of the Watchtower Society wrote a very enlightening, widely published article in 2010 about this man Theo (Ted) Jaracz called "The Theocratic Life and Times of Theodore Jaracz," a portion of which we quote with kind permission of Barbara.

> Why would I want to know more about this man? What did he do to deserve closer scrutiny? The fact is Ted Jaracz was directly responsible for an untold and immeasurable amount of grief or worse to an inestimable, but certainly, enormous number of people during his reign as a GB (Governing Body) member, if not before. His steadfast and unwavering grip on certain Watch Tower notions or opinions he claimed were taken from scripture, resulted in harm to too many followers, and for compelling countless Witnesses to forsake their religion, and, for some, to even renounce their belief in God.

The following information about Ted Jaracz is based on events
I personally observed and experienced, or heard about from
the mouths of credible informants. Some personal accounts
I kept to myself for many years as requested by people who
didn't want to be identified by Jaracz as the source of sensitive
information and subsequently be disfellowshipped. He certainly
had the power to order an investigation into leaks as he did in
2001 when he sent a Bethelite from the US Branch to the UK
Branch to hunt for leaks at a time when some at that branch
were sending confidential material to "apostates." [Including
a member of the Branch Committee who was and still is a
personal friend of the editor of this book] He also said, only the
GB [Governing Body] can state what a Christian conscience
is! He had not changed on this point from the time the GB
was discussing alternative (*military*) service back in 1978 when
he said, "We should have a united stand all over the world. We
should be decisive in this matter.... If we were to allow the
brothers this latitude we would have problems.... The brothers
need to have their consciences educated [*Crisis of Conscience*,
p. 139]. Of course, that meant consciences manipulated by the
GB. Now the "iron fist" Theodore Jaracz, is gone. We wait to
see if there will be action taken to demonstrate that the present
GB of Jehovah's Witnesses really do care about their flock by
removing the harmful organizational policies that a hard-liner
such as Jaracz supported or maneuvered into place, which have
been slowly destroying the organization he came to control, and
he did it all in the name of God.

One astute member of our research team reminded us once again of
the blatant contradictions of the Watchtower Society and one such
glaring example was promulgated by Robert Wallen and Theo Jaracz.
For example, in examining one of the Watchtower quotes, we find them
actually discouraging readers from the very policy that they themselves
clearly taught in their famous small blue text book *The Truth That
Leads to Eternal Life* (1968). According to the Watchtower Society, by
May 1987 this publication, now out of print, had reached 106,486,735
copies in 116 languages and is listed in the *Guinness Book of Records*.
They even use the same words in perfect contradiction of themselves.
Consider the following from the Truth book: "We need to examine...
what is taught by any religious organization with which we may be

associated... If we are lovers of the truth, there is <u>nothing to fear</u> from such an examination." And then in the year 1987, Robert Wallen stated, no doubt making reference to the recently released successful book by Raymond Franz, ex-member of the Governing Body of the Watchtower Society, Crisis of Conscience. Wallen stated, "We don't have to read apostate literature to know it's wrong" ... "You may even reason" ... "if we have the truth, we have <u>nothing to fear</u>" ... "In thinking this way, some have fed their minds upon apostate reasoning and have fallen prey to serious questioning and doubt." So try and work out that conundrum? [underlining is ours].

> *Editor's Note*: However we remind our readers that no matter what wrong decisions Robert Wallen has made in his life as a sincere Christian while doing his duty on behalf of the Watchtower Society, especially in the notorious, egregious case of the devout, courageous Bible student Edward Dunlap being excommunicated, or any erroneous statements Robert made in his capacity as part of the group of the Watchtower hierarchy, and his willing cooperation with the infamous and questionable Theo Jaracz, he is still one of God's children. And like every one of us, he is an imperfect human being with all of our inherited sins and depends, as we all do, on the forgiving sacrifice of Jesus Christ. As pointed out in other portions of this narrative, especially in the case of Anthony Morris, another misguided current member of the Governing Body. To quote: "Therefore in our humble opinion these leaders deserve our pity; our display of compassion and empathy plus to possibly try and help them to escape from these cults rather than our outright personal condemnation of them as imperfect, misguided individuals, as after all they are still children of God" (Philippians 2:14-16; 1 John 3:1-3).

It was the 5th President of the Watchtower Society, and member of the Governing Body, Milton Henschel, who was heard to say at a meeting of a group of senior officials of the Watchtower Society, "If we let the brothers do this, there is no telling how far they will go." He is also reported as saying, "You just can't trust the brothers to themselves." In addition, another member of the Governing Body, Lloyd Barry is on record as stating, "We should not be getting together in a clique to discuss views contrary to the 'faithful and discreet slave.' We must recognize the source of our instruction. We must be like an ass, be humble, and stay in the manger; and we won't get any poison."

> *Editor's Note*: Asses, also known as mules, donkeys or burros, have long been companion and work animals for humans. We are not sure exactly what 'simple minded' Lloyd Barry had in mind when he used that expression, "be like an ass" but it certainly highlighted two things; one that members of this religions must not think for themselves but simply obey their masters without question, and secondly, that the Governing Body view their subordinates simply as beasts of burden to carry out the work of their 'masters'. It is this type of thinking that goes on behind the inner workings of the Watchtower Society and the loyal followers are expected to have complete trust and confidence in this style of management and dimwitted insipience. This is another clear example of how religious cults operate.

Returning to the cancellation of the Theocratic Ministry School, from the leaked minutes of this meeting of a special committee, being one of the six committees that now appear to totally operate the Watchtower Society today, and being fully staffed by members of this group of helpers that made this unanimous decision, as a committee to disband the Theocratic Ministry School in 2015. This committee of eight named members, all so-called helpers, was chaired by a member of the Governing Body who is not named (he was either asleep, absent mentally or physically). It was then authorized by this committee to issue this supposed instruction from the Governing Body to now cancel this important organizational feature of the brilliant school that was started, ironically by Nathan Knorr back in 1943. A letter was then issued by the Governing Body to be read to all congregations dated October 4, 2015, the day after the Annual General Meeting had announced this closure and this now highlighted the new direction in which the organization was moving. Gone was the much-loved very successful Theocratic Ministry School, to be replaced by a 15-minute low-key session embodied in the weekly Service Meeting, for demonstrating simple preaching presentations and sales techniques of how to use the Watchtower literature they sold from door-to-door or on the streets.

One forthright member we interviewed stated, after being told by his local circuit servant that this decision was simply progress of Jehovah's Organization being lead by God's Holy Spirit, and he must be willing to accept it and not be so stubborn or ask questions, but simply obey whether the Governing Body is right or wrong. This Witness replied, "If this is progress then I no longer want to be a part of it," and a few months later he quit this religion altogether.

Many of these individuals we interviewed however agreed that the closing down of the weekly Congregation Book Study by the Governing Body, influenced once again by their helpers, usually held on Tuesday evenings, was perhaps justified as these informal small group meetings held in the private homes of a local Witness often devolved and deteriorated into debates and sometimes speculation about what the organization was doing, especially related to their teachings and this trend was causing great concern to the leaders of this religion. A confidential letter was sent out to all circuit and district servants, under instructions from the Governing Body, requesting feedback regarding the continuation of the Congregation Book Study meetings. This view was also confirmed by the reports and feedback submitted by a large number of the various circuit servants, plus two district servants who operated under the supervision of the London Branch office; confidential reports that were leaked to our reporter. Their comments were based on their regular visits to the various local congregations of Jehovah's Witnesses in the British Isles and they reported, almost unanimously, that this informal type of weekly gathering only encouraged more open talk, freedom of speech, which in turn then encouraged possible criticism or speculation. Of course, this tendency was the main primary worry and concern of the Governing Body, so they determinedly put a stop to this trend of group free speech. Shortly thereafter the Congregation Book Study was terminated and cancelled in all congregations of Jehovah's Witnesses and the recommendation made that as an alternative each Witness family was to individually use Monday evenings for a family home Bible study and family evening. No doubt this decision by the Governing Body was also based especially on reflection of the events of the late 1970s and 1980s related to members of the Writers Department of the Watchtower Society in New York and their small group gatherings and many having to be disfellowshipped for apostasy because of their private discussions and outspoken comments regarding the current teachings of the Watchtower Society.

By this time the Governing Body and their helpers have virtually taken over complete control of this role of instruction and teaching through the videos and broadcast service now being used at their local Kingdom Hall meetings and assemblies, so the need for local brothers to be able to develop the skills of public speaking had now fallen away. This of course now gives them even more control as masters over the flock and eliminates any possible private views being expressed publicly by local elders or ministerial servants. This new communications project and method is the perfect scenario for firmly establishing absolute and total control over the lives of the slave like followers of this religion, by reinforcing such a powerful and controlling system as envisaged by the now elderly modern day Governing Body and their appointed much younger, astute, calculating, ambitious helpers and assistants.

To illustrate the powers of this new Governing Body and their so-called helpers introduced after the removal of the autocratic Nathan Knorr from his throne, we quote from the book by Rolf Furuli, in which he also covers the history of Jehovah's Witnesses. There is on record a court case heard in the Supreme Court of the State of California, case # CIV 508137, in and for the Country of San Mateo, dated February, 2012, in which three local elders who had been discharged from their positions by the Governing Body of the Watchtower Society and they actually sued the Watchtower Society to try and legally enforce their reinstatement as elders.

> The attorney and counsel acting for Jehovah's Witnesses said, according to the court manuscript, in defense of the rights and power of this religious organization to remove these elders, he presented the following argument: "I say organization and I am general counsel for the National Organization of Jehovah's Witnesses out of Brooklyn, New York. Ordinary I would not be here but this is one of our 13,000 congregations in the United States. We are a hierarchal religion structured just like the Catholic Church. And when the order from the Pope comes down in the Church defrocking a priest and kicking him out, he no longer has any say in the matter or in the Parrish. The same is the situation in this case also." The crowd who were in the public gallery, according to a witness listening to this court case, gave out a loud gasp as they were so shocked and

had never heard before such self-condemnatory words from the mouth of a leading official of the Watchtower Society.

In order to firmly establish their power and further enhance their control over the members of this religion, according to the Times Herald-Record of 8 October, 2019, the success of taking over production of videos, films and media production, etc., to lead and teach the submissive followers has compelled the Governing Body of this religion to make plans to build a massive production studio, one of the largest in the world. Quoting from the *Times Herald-Record*:

> The Watchtower Bible and Tract Society announced plans to build an enormous audio-visual production center on land partly in Tuxedo but mostly in Ramapo. Members of the nonprofit group, better known as the Jehovah's Witnesses, plan to use the building to consolidate and expand various multi-media production offices, which they say will make materials about living a principled life. The new 1.5 million-square-foot facility would be almost as big as the Jehovah's Witnesses' newly built 1.6-million-square-foot headquarters, located two miles away in the Town of Warwick. As in Warwick, roughly 1,000 volunteers would live and staff the Ramapo media production center. Besides studio space, the complex would include offices, residences, underground parking, a fitness area and a visitor center for the public.

> The 155, Sterling Mine Road property consists of 242 acres in Ramapo and seven acres in the Town of Tuxedo. The project is currently in the environmental review phase following a July application submission to the Town of Ramapo Planning Board. Robert Zick, a Jehovah's Witnesses spokesman, estimated it could take two years for the group to finish planning the project and up to another four to build the complex. Zick was not readily able to say why the project had a six-year timeline, but he said the bio-diverse nature of the site might make it complex to develop. "We're ramping up production in response to heavy demand of audio-visual offerings," Zick said. "People find these materials to be useful, so we're putting more resources behind them, and we're putting everything under one roof." He also said the Jehovah's Witnesses have seen a swell of outside interest from the general

public in some of the group's audio-visual advice materials, including videos offering parenting advice. Among them are partially animated videos, in which a non-animated human hand quickly draws cartoons on a whiteboard, and a voice-over offers guidance.

This is another clear example and a clue of the true purpose of the Watchtower Society, or its planned subsidiary, in building this massive studio complex and becoming a world leading commercial enterprise in the field of television and video films.

This report in the *Times Herald-Record* is however very misleading as our reporter uncovered information that this new building project, studio complex plus television network will not be operated by the existing Watchtower Society, Inc., but a completely new legal business structure was in the making that will operate as a separate legal entity and independent from the main organization, which was established back in 1884 by Charles Russell. Also, in a report leaked to our investigator, one Watchtower official confirmed that this new massive studio complex will be used to house the planned Watchtower television network that will occupy most of the studios to produce programs in most major languages. This new television network will be part of a new and completely separate legal entity from the Watchtower organization and he claimed it would be financially self-supporting as the millions of dollars required to operate a new venture of this magnitude, would be covered by the pay-to-view network with world-wide distribution and will be supported by the millions of subscribers and also advertising revenue. He also emphasized that this new method of distributing the good news of God's Kingdom is far superior to the current books and magazines that are presently being given away for free and only partially covered by ever reducing donations.

What this official did not clarify to our reporter was how the over six million followers of this religion could be forced to become subscribers to this new pay-to-view television network in order to regularly receive their daily and weekly instructions, guidance and directions from their leaders and masters. However, although the number of members of Jehovah's Witnesses has all but stagnated, and these current figures are now certainly not used as a sign of God's blessing on this religion as previously claimed, it still leaves a captured audience of over six million who will be forced to use this new television network, by paid subscription. They will be compelled to subscribe in order to receive the programs that will contain the lectures and directions from their leaders, so it is a foregone conclusion that this new television network will be a financial success. Also, our reporter mentioned that he had noted in recent months a distinct toning down by the Watchtower officials and spokesmen in their press releases of not using the common terms, 'the impending end of this system of things' and 'last days of this world order' and other similar expressions, although these phrases are still used in their printed literature, but for how long? However, as books and magazines will eventually very soon be phased out and the latest instructions and material can only be read on iPads, laptops and large screens in their Kingdom Halls; is this an indication and clear sign of things to come?

The obvious question is asked once again by our readers who learned about selling all the New York and London properties for a massive profit and then building the new luxurious World headquarters of the Watchtower Society in Warwick, upstate New York, which houses the Governing Body and their helpers, plus the not so luxurious, based on first hand reports; the brand new British Headquarters on the Temple Farm scrap yard in Essex, plus in addition the now newly planned Watchtower Television Studio and Communications Center for 2027. They ask if the Governing Body truly believe that we are living in the last generation of this system of things, why do they still aggressively continue these exorbitant building projects. As a point of interest, Jehovah's Witnesses being registered as a nonprofit saved over $368 million in real estate taxes over the last year they were based in New York City, so likewise they will also be exempt from paying any taxes in their new location in Warwick, upstate New York.

We invite you to read this latest enlightening report from one of our investigative journalists. Our source of information, and we will now call him our whistleblower and he will remain nameless, as he still occupies a leading position within the headquarters of the Watchtower Society, Inc., in New York. He has assured our reporter that he will continue to update him with all further news and developments regarding this new ambitious venture, the Watchtower Television Network (WTN). This name has yet to be officially registered pending the outside lawyers involved setting up this new legal corporation and securing the required capital investments. It is also being considered by these shrewd lawyers that perhaps a completely different name be selected for this new Television Network so as to distance itself from the now disgraced names, Watchtower and Jehovah's Witnesses. They will still however, according to our whistleblower, probably try to weave in the claimed Biblical name of this sect, Jehovah's Witnesses as this name is now so well known, but this is still under discussion, so perhaps even that name will disappear also.

> *Editor's Note*: Fortunately and gratefully the personal Hebrew name of our Divine Creator, Yahweh in Hebrew or Jehovah in English will not disappear, but just the name of this religious sect, that has blatantly misused this precious name of our Creator to label their cult as being chosen by God, (Isaiah 43:12). So, this legally registered New York City corporate name, Jehovah's Witnesses will hopefully permanently disappear from the planet just as did the name Watchtower from the Brooklyn, New York skyline and buildings.

This newly planned venture of a television network and studio is under the control of a secret, clandestine group of prominent officials of the current Watchtower Society in New York and who almost act like the mafia. Our 'Foundation' based on our policy of honest and open reporting will of course pass on any developing or breaking news to the websites that faithfully and accurately carry the latest news regarding the sometimes dangerous cult-like activities of the Watchtower Society, websites such as Watchtower Documents, JW Survey, JW Facts, JW Watch, Faith Leaks.org, plus many others. These websites are of course hated by the official leaders of the Watchtower Society and managers of their official website, JW.org and are the subject of threats, current legal actions and litigation to sue the owners of these websites and attempt to close them down to prevent this vital information being known to the world and to silence these voices of reason. This opinion was also expressed by a fellow researcher: "The Watchtower Society is using its official website, jw.org to present a whitewashed image to the public, garnering trust through presentation of an attractive and professional looking layout, yet its feature articles are filled with dishonest and misleading information."

Although we do admit that sometimes these anti-Watchtower and anti-Jehovah's Witnesses websites go overboard and present material that is of no benefit to anyone, especially lovers of truth, honesty and openness. For example, in our research we saw an article some time ago regarding one of the leading members of the current Watchtower Society's Governing Body, the now elderly Anthony Morris. It appears that an unnamed reporter secretly followed this man as he visited his favorite liquor store to buy a large quantity of whiskey and the article portrayed him as a slovenly, decrepit, drop-out and being shabbily dressed, plus looking like a tramp, which is a distortion of the real facts and the actual truth regarding this man and was nothing more than capricious, derogative reporting. We point out that this sort of reporting is of absolutely no benefit to the many thousands of readers of these usually up-building, enlightening and constructive websites. These informative sources and websites, which are dedicated to exposing the truth about religious cults and definitely not about targeting individuals or personalities who could simply be misguided, unwitting victims of a cult, even though they occupy senior positions within a particular religion. Most of these individuals need our help and support to free themselves from the chains of a cult rather than condemning them outright and trying to destroy their lives and character. There is an old wise saying, "If one can't say anything good about a person then simply say nothing."

Our inside reporter and whistleblower informs us that the last time he met Tony Morris in the New York Bethel some months ago; he appeared to be an elderly, dignified gentleman, but also a very troubled and worried man in view of what was currently taking place regarding the Watchtower Society and their increasing financial woes. Tony Morris also admitted that most of the decisions these days are not made by the existing Governing Body but rather a much younger, aggressive management team of brilliant strategists who are now assisted by outside, high powered, very shrewd, experienced Wall Street lawyers and accountants.

Our reporter added that there is no doubt that these very same ruthless lawyers and accountants were also behind the new policy of the Watchtower Society, introduced in 2019 to seize ownership of all the thousands of Kingdom Hall properties throughout the world, now worth millions of dollars, seized or rather stolen from the many local congregations of Jehovah's Witnesses and their local Board of Trustees, referring to these properties in their letter of advice (secretly leaked to our reporter) "The Watchtower Society are sitting on an untapped gold mine." This latest scheme is probably now the last step the current Governing Body and their helpers can take in their devil-may-care attitude and their attempt to raise more desperately needed funds for their survival.

Another very important point we must consider when we see these high-ranking individuals and leaders of religious cults, for example, Tony Morris of the Watchtower Society, it is that they were probably not coverts but most being born into or brought up and indoctrinated from being very young children in these cults. They themselves are actual victims of the modus operandi of a cult, so it is the cult that we should be exposing and condemning, not necessarily the unfortunate victims who have been captured and enslaved in a religious cult. From our many years as researchers and investigative reporters we have met many leaders of various religious cults and organizations, most of whom had a timorous disposition, with some very glaring exceptions of course, and we have observed this reality and fact of life. In our humble opinion these leaders deserve our pity; our display of compassion and empathy, plus to possibly try and help them to escape from these cults rather than our outright personal condemnation of them as imperfect, misguided individuals, as after all they are still children of God (Philippians 2:14-16; 1 John 3:1-3).

Although Tony Morris, born in 1950, claims in his very emotional life story published in the Watchtower that he only became a convert as a young man in 1971, he also admits that his dear mother who was associated with the Witnesses when he was a child, also strongly influenced his decision to eventually become a dedicated member of Jehovah's Witnesses. It should also be noted that Tony Morris also now misguidedly claims that he is one of the Lord's special anointed chosen ones, being a member of the so called remnant of the 144,000 (claimed to be a literal number according to the Watchtower Society interpretation of the Bible) referred to in the Book of Revelation and to eventually rule the Universe as kings and priests while residing at the right hand of Jesus Christ in heaven. This claim is made even though back in 1935 Joseph Rutherford the 2nd President of the Watchtower Society, along with his guru prophet Fred Franz clearly and very plainly stated in their writings in the Watchtower literature that the selection of this literal number of 144,000 was completed in that year of 1935. No mention was made by Rutherford in his divine revelation at that time that there maybe or possibly some exceptions, he was very adamant about the number now being filled, the reason why is explained in other sections of this chapter. The Governing Body at that time, which was of course dominated by autocrat Rutherford, they all believed and accepted his new teaching that the number of 144,000 was filled and completed in 1935 and they had no revelation or conception of any additional individuals being called after that date.

So this very idea of some individuals being called to become a member of the so-called little flock of 144,000 after 1935, even up to the year of 2019, is a pure fabrication by the current Governing Body and was introduced by the past autocratic President Nathan Knorr, who especially dominated and laid down all dictates of the Governing Body of seven men from 1942 up until 1976, to conveniently suit their modern day requirements and personal manipulation of Bible texts. Of course Tony Morris, along with a few others of his colleagues now serving on the current Governing Body of the Watchtower Society sincerely claim they have been selected by Almighty God and Jesus Christ through God's Holy Spirit to replace former unfaithful or sinful members of this anointed class, as they all believe the erroneous idea that this number of 144,000 is actually a literal number, when all other knowledgeable students of the Bible know for a fact it is only a symbolic number that the Apostle John was visualizing in his book of Revelation. As ridiculous at it may sound they even claim that Jesus Christ has spoken to them privately by means of the Holy Spirit and personally informed them they have been chosen. To most of our intelligent readers this clearly explains the dangers of a cult and the ludicrous private interpretations of the Bible and doctrines plus beliefs passed down from the masters.

This manipulative tactic of others joining the anointed class after 1935 (the official closing date revealed to Rutherford by divine revelation?) and individuals now making claims that after that significant date, to have been personally informed by Almighty God that they had been chosen to join the remnant of the 144,000 to replace some 'bad apples' and then also having to renounce their past status when they first joined this religion and were baptized as one of the so-called great crowd of other sheep class. This crazy idea and teaching is in line with the ever changing current doctrines of this religion. But even more so in recent years; as in the past, especially in encouraging friends and acquaintances of the existing members of the Governing Body to make the personal claim to be one of the anointed (taking the bread and wine at the annual memorial celebration) and eventually as a result opening the gateway of being possibly invited and enlisted on the esteemed, select and powerful Governing Body of this religion. We cannot speak for the current members of this Governing Body as they must personally and individually answer to Almighty God if their claim to be members of the bride class to co-rule the Universe with Jesus Christ in heaven as Kings and Priests is perhaps illusionary, a fixation of their mind or a hallucination and a pure delusion of their power as masters of this religion.

For example, the successful case of Theodore (Ted) Jaracz, in 1971 suddenly claiming he had been chosen as one of the anointed and then being invited to join the Governing Body by his close personal friend Nathan Knorr. This case is already fully covered in this report and also the unsuccessful case of Philip Rees being invited to join the Governing Body is covered in Report No.1 of the Appendix. There were of course other private and personal reasons why certain individuals in this religion after 1935 claimed to be members of this so-called heavenly class, kings and priests of Revelation 5:10; 20:4 and 20:6, (read also Matthew 22:30) Please read especially the cases we covered regarding the friend of homosexual Ewart Chitty, member of the Governing Body and the two lesbian special pioneer girls from Ireland, plus numerous other cases we have on record leaked to us from the Watchtower headquarters in New York; unfortunately too many to list.

So, who is to know that today in the light of Rutherford's personal interpretation of the Bible; his claimed divine revelation and the 1935 cut-off date that the current Governing Body who all claim to be of the anointed are in fact all imposters? Of course, this possible consideration cannot be allowed by this religion or even discussed, so they now proclaim under the usual standby rule for making the regular, sometimes dramatic changes in their interpretation of the Bible, claiming to have received new light on the subject matter. (Proverbs 4:18) The Governing Body today therefore are quite within their rights on the basis of their claim of being the faithful and discreet slave described in the Bible book of Matthew, Chapters 24 and 25, to make any changes they wish to their claimed interpretation of the Bible including Rutherford's divine revelation of the year 1935. In addition, the Lord's belongings, as explained in the Watchtower literature, the so-called followers and subjective members of this religion must simply accept this new light as being the truth whether right or wrong, which again is another clear sign of a cult.

This truly insightful comment from a current website by fellow researcher, Sean of JW Changes.com, while examining the term Governing Body (GB) is of interest.

> In spite of the GB being a group of self-appointed men and having no Biblical authority for its existence, Jehovah's Witnesses have been misled to treat these men as though they were royalty. The truly disturbing part is that the Watchtower tells you they are royalty! According to Watchtower doctrine only they and the collective faithful slave are the kings and priests of Revelation 5:10; 20:4 and 20:6. These men ask more and more from the rank-and-file Witnesses and receive what I believe is borderline worship from the average JW. All the while they themselves do not have to contend with any of the things people in the real world must deal with. No wonder they can tell the friends not to worry about getting an education, work fewer hours, spend more time serving the organization, etc.

However, to play down this public criticism and theory of the Governing Body and those claiming to be part of the remnant of the 144,000 being like royalty, and receiving special messages from Jesus Christ by means of the Holy Sprit, the *Watchtower* of June 15, 2009, pp. 23-24 hypocritically stated:

They do not believe that their being of the anointed gives them special insights beyond what even some experienced members of the great crowd may have. They do not believe that they necessarily have more holy spirit than their companions of the other sheep have [this of course now includes the real controlling component of the Watchtower Society today, the powerful, younger and somewhat secretive group of so-called helpers, most who claim to be of this so-called other sheep class]. They do not expect special treatment; nor do they claim that their partaking of the emblems places them above the appointed elders in the congregation."

Referring back once again to the report regarding this planned television studio complex by Jehovah's Witnesses, we quote:

This new television network (WTN) will operate as a completely separate, legal, commercial venture and enterprise set apart from the existing Watchtower Bible and Tract Society, Inc., as the current New York or Pennsylvanian Corporations do not have the financial resources to set-up and operate a venture of this magnitude because of their existing dire financial state of affairs and it will of necessity be financed by outside investors, some who are currently well-known celebrities in the sports and entertainment fields and who have some affiliation with Jehovah's Witnesses.

Our whistleblower would not name these celebrities but hinted that the Wall Street lawyers are currently working on a scheme to divert a large sum of money, millions of Dollars, that the late pop idol 'Prince' Rogers Nelson (1958-2016), who has supposedly left a large portion of his fortune to the Watchtower Society but without a will or specific instructions on how this money is to be used, and is currently being fought out in court with other claimants, mainly by various members of the family of Prince. Our reporter contacted the agents of some of these well know celebrities, such as the family of the late Michael Jackson in Palm Springs, the tennis players of the Williams family in Los Angeles, Michelle Rodriguez-actor, Donald Glover-actor, Geri Halliwell-singer in the Spice Girls, Brian Bennett, Hank Marvin and Brian (Licorice) Locking, all ex-members of Cliff Richard's pop group, The Shadows. Also contacted were the agents of George Benson-singer, Naomi

Campbell-model and actress, plus Ja Rule-rapper, but all of their agents simply replied with the usual bland remark, "no comments at this stage."

Editor's Note: According to the news source, *USA Today* of April 2019, this report was provided. "But the most obvious lesson of the Prince tragedy still remains and it is utterly prosaic: If you die without a will, you might leave behind confusion. Prince's assumed massive estate, believed to be worth hundreds of millions, is still unsettled, still not officially valued and still not disbursed to the heirs, his six siblings. Instead, platoons of lawyers have been working on it for three years, racking up bills, arguing with each other, arguing with the heirs, arguing with consultants hired to advise on various estate matters, and filing blizzards of documents and paperwork with the Carver County probate court, which has made little progress in its mission to sort all this. The heirs' dissatisfaction with the estate administrators has grown, leading to their latest effort to gain more control over spending: So far, administrators have spent $45 million, including $10 million in legal fees, the heirs claim in documents."

Our whistleblower in the New York headquarters of Jehovah's Witnesses quickly pointed out once again that this new venture will be a completely separate legal entity from the existing Watchtower Society, Inc., (currently non-profit and tax free) and will be a stand-alone commercial enterprise and be self-financing plus will **NOT** operate as a non-profit organization and hopefully at a later stage also offer an IPO (Initial Public Offering) to the primary benefit of the investors. This new for-profit television network will include staff being employed who have the skills and expertise plus will be paid excellent salaries as producers, directors and engineers also the secret management team of the Watchtower Society has already authorized leading recruitment agencies to begin contacting staff working at Fox News, CNN and other leading television networks. The use of the code name WTN (the possible future Watch Tower Network) is still being secretly litigated by the lawyers acting for the new for-profit corporation, yet to be formed, by a new division of Jehovah's Witnesses. Currently the code name WTN is legally owned by Associated Press (AP) of London and known as Associated Press Television News Ltd. or AP Television News and was founded in 1994 as Associated Press Television or APTV. They moved to their present New York headquarters in 1999 when APTV bought out competitor, Worldwide Television News (WTN) and hired Roberto Soto as their first NYC Bureau Chief. The WTN building and facilities located in Broadway were deemed more suitable than the existing AP headquarters and Soto redesigned the newsroom, where APTN (NY) stayed until AP moved their operations to West 33rd Street in New York City, and later to 200 Liberty Street in New York City in 2017, where they remain today. Since its rebranding in 2005, the APTN name and logo has been dropped in favor of AP Television News, featuring the red AP logo of the Associated Press to emphasize its connection to the AP. However, many broadcasters still refer to the television organization as APTN.

The planned WTN (Watchtower Television Network) will offer, not only the usual televised material and their claimed continuing campaign to spread the gospel of Jesus Christ but also will attract audiences because of the planned program material such as dramas, soaps, cartoons, documentaries, plus other programs of general interest such as nature and environmental issues.[21] Also in view of the prospects of attracting more and more advertisers they hope that they will quickly be able to abandon the pay-to-view business model. Our source pointed out that although this was a massively ambitious project and may not come together, but take a look at the example of Oprah Winfrey and her television network, OWN (Oprah Winfrey Network) and remember all she had when it was launched in 2011 was her name plus of course some of her private wealth, but today it operates as a very successful network with an average of over 82 million regular viewers and reaches over 70% of American households.

However, it appears that the Mormon Church has already established a dominant lead over the Watchtower Society and their planned television network because the Mormon Church as of 2020 announced

---

[21] The Watchtower religion is already producing and selling *(the actual cost being covered by donations at this stage)* to the public, short video cartoons that are partially animated videos, in which a non-animated human hand quickly draws cartoons on a whiteboard, and a voice-over offers guidance on a selected theme, and is already generating substantial income for the new studio and is proving to be a successful, commercial enterprise.

the following related to their expanding television network, now called Church News-CN. As stated on their website:

> The imperative of Jesus to 'be one' inspires us to communicate with one voice. 'Newsroom' has long been an essential resource to the media, the general public and members. We believe this consolidation; now called 'Church News' provides a more unified online reading and viewing experience for Latter-Day Saints and interested observers of the faith.

Of course this new Watchtower Television Network (WTN) planned for 2027, being a completely separate legal corporate venture, this will guarantee its ongoing survival in case of the very likely event that soon and in the near future the original, main Watchtower Society, Inc., established in 1884, being primarily a printing and publishing business empire will eventually be forced to declare bankruptcy in view of the massive pile and long list of legal claims, totaling billions of dollars now being made against them because of sexual abuse and they will be forced to close their doors once and for all time. An additional report by Steve Lieberman of the news source, The Journal News stated the following, which was also confirmed by the Hudson Gateway Association of Realtors of White Plains, New York.

> The Jehovah's Witnesses are known for spreading their message by going door to door and handing out their pamphlets. Now the worldwide religious organization is planning a mega audio/video production center for religious materials, including dormitories for workers, outside Sloatsburg amid the woodlands along the town's western sector. The complex is located on 242 acres off 155 Sterling Mine Road with seven additional acres extending into the Orange County community of Tuxedo. The Jehovah Witnesses world headquarters sits two miles away in Warwick. Watchtower also owns nearly 750 acres on both sides of Route 22 in the Putnam County town of Patterson. The center is expected to be an integrated working and living facility designed to support the Christian denomination's increasing production of Bible-based audio and video programs, officials said.

> The organization estimates environmental review will take two years and another four years to build the facility. The group said

the project would take up less space than the approved housing development. Cady said the goal is to preserve the property's natural environment and habitat, minimally affecting the area's wetlands. He said plans call the installation of bio-retention ponds or rain gardens and storm water ponds to mitigate the impact of water runoff and preserve the biodiversity. This 1.5 million-square-foot complex is to be built at 155, Sterling Mine Road in Ramapo, 2 miles from Jehovah's Witnesses' World Headquarter. "Our organization goes to great lengths to share the Bible's message with others, free of charge," spokesman Keith Cady said. "Our printed publications are well known all over the world, but in recent years, we have greatly increased our production of audio programs and films. They are now central features of our official website."

When our reporter contacted spokesman Keith Cady, who works as a voluntary architect and project manager for the Watchtower Society, he replied that he had no further knowledge to add to this rumor of a new studio complex that was yet to be built and was only in the planning stage that would be owned and operated by a separate legal entity set apart from the current Watchtower Society, Inc. Cady also said we should contact the legal department, which as usual refused to return our telephone calls.

This experience of operating a broadcast facility is not new to the Watchtower Society as way back in 1924; Joseph Rutherford established a radio station WBBR based on Staten Island in New York. Its primary use was to broadcast the scathing lectures of Rutherford as he with his booming voice lambasted, berated and mocked the clergy of the day, especially the Catholic Church and labeled them as Babylon the Great and the personification of the filthy harlot riding on the back of the wild beast, as vividly described in the book of Revelation, Chapters 13 and 17, by the Apostle John. This was part of Rutherford's overall manipulative scheme to provoke the clergy so that in turn they in retaliation attacked Rutherford and his religion. For example as recorded on one disk, "they claim to be teachers of the Gospel and proudly display the initials D.D (Doctor of Divinity) after their names, but they are in reality D.D (Dumb Dogs) quoting from Isaiah 56:10 (KJV) "His watchmen are blind: they are all ignorant, they are all dumb dogs, they cannot bark;

sleeping, lying down, loving to slumber. Yea, they are greedy dogs which can never have enough, and they are shepherds that cannot understand: they all look to their own way, every one for his gain, from his quarter. Come ye, say they, I will fetch wine, and we will fill ourselves with strong drink; and tomorrow shall be as this day, and much more abundant."

The clergy of Christendom were naturally provoked and inflamed by these offensive remarks of Rutherford and made their feelings clearly known, which Rutherford then using to his own advantage, as in turn he told the rank and file of the Witnesses that they were now being targeted and being persecuted by other religions because of being members of the only true religion on earth and most followers of this religion swallowed this theory by Rutherford, hook, line and sinker. To once again quote from the brilliant website, Watchtower Documents, by Barbara Anderson:

> One thing was plain from my research of the Rutherford
> years – Rutherford deliberately stirred up trouble by attacking
> religions and governments and baiting the clergy, thereby
> inciting acts of retribution against individual Bible Students.
> This frequently resulted in Rutherford howling, "Persecution!"

This now extinct radio station, WBBR, at one time owned by the Watchtower Society also presented, according to our researcher, songs and vocals by the eccentric, tremulous tenor, Freddy Franz, who was accompanied by a voluntary quartet and orchestra. I was recently privileged to listen to one of these now rare recordings and one cannot help but ruefully smile at the stinging dialogue of Rutherford against the clergy and Satan's world and it supporters, and then the intermission of a recording of Freddy Franz pathetically in full song, vocally declaring sentiments about the coming world peace and blessings to mankind. These recordings are now viewed as priceless collector's items! Of course, this is the same Freddy Franz (1893-1992) claimed prophet and ghost writer of Rutherford's articles, books and the lectures that he gave over the radio and on phonograph records that were carried and played from door to door during the 1940s. This radio station also had a group of volunteer Witnesses who had formed what was known as the Kings Theatre and they presented on the airwaves, Bible dramas that included some very amateurish productions but they still nevertheless entertained their enslaved, captivated and dedicated listeners until the radio station was finally closed down in 1957.

Another early successful pioneer of radio and televangelism was a man called Herbert Armstrong, founder of the Radio Church of God. The experience of this arrogant, narcissistic individual, who was also a law unto himself, very similar to Joseph Rutherford, but his story still exists today as a clear example of ignoring the need of holding to the truth of God's written word the Holy Bible, and the danger of claiming personal revelations from God as related to wild interpretations of many historical records contained in the Bible, very similar to the modus operandi of the Watchtower Society.

This new religion, Radio Church of God floundered as it was not based on the truth of the Bible (John 17:17, see also Psalms 119:160) but singularly on the private and personal interpretations of its leader, so it became a dinosaur and eventually non-existent and disappeared. This cult is now no longer in existence or a danger to us today, plus it only lasted for a few short years, (1933-1986?) and therefore does not deserve a separate chapter in our book. However, it still needs to be highlighted as another clear example of the underhanded schemes and methods used by religious cults to try and control their members as we still try to live our lives as true Christians and as we follow our genuine Master Jesus Christ and his teachings, plus to be free of all cultish influences. This example also clearly indicates the dangers of following a religion that is controlled by the private interpretations of the Bible by its leaders and shows that without doubt it does not have the backing of God's Holy Spirit, and is controlled by men who can only verbally claim, without any proof whatsoever to be appointed and directed by Jesus Christ and the Holy Spirit. So let the members of Jehovah's Witnesses beware as they will see glaring similarities between these two cults!

Summary and brief history of the Worldwide Church of God

Herbert Wright Armstrong (July 31, 1892-January 16, 1986) was the founder of the Radio Church of God incorporated October 21, 1933 and later renamed Worldwide Church of God on June 1, 1968, and he also started Ambassador College in Pasadena, California on October 8, 1947, the first class having four students, all members of his own family. This attempted college venture was finally closed down in 1997 because of serious financial problems and probable tax fraud. Armstrong was an early pioneer of radio and televangelism, first taking to the airwaves on January 7, 1934 from the 100-watt station KORE in Eugene, Oregon. Armstrong preached what he claimed was the comprehensive combination of doctrines in the entire Bible, in the light of the New Covenant scriptures, which he maintained came directly to him from the Bible by means of the Holy Spirit. These theological doctrines and teachings have been referred to as Armstrongism by non-adherents. His teachings included the interpretation of biblical prophecy in the light of British Israelism and strictly required obedience and observance of parts of the Mosaic Law including the Law of the seventh-day Sabbath, dietary prohibitions, and the covenant laws related to Holy Days.

Armstrong often said that, like John the Baptist (the proclaimed second Elijah in Bible prophesy), he was a voice preaching in a spiritual wilderness of religious confusion. For this reason he was considered to be both an Apostle and the end-time Elijah (very similar to Freddy Franz of the Watchtower Society imagining himself as the reincarnated Elisha and wearing his cloak, 2 Kings 2:13) proclaiming as God's representative, the Gospel of God's Kingdom to the world before the return of Jesus Christ in the very near future. Through his autocratic role within his religion and his foundation, Armstrong and his advisers amazingly through manipulation of his skilled staff and helpers, held meetings with heads of governments in various nations, including Margaret Thatcher, Leader of the British Government, Emperor Hirohito of Japan, King Hussein of Jordan, and Indira Gandhi of India, for which he described himself as an ambassador without portfolio for world peace.

In February 1934, Armstrong began the publication of the magazine, *The Plain Truth*, which started out as a church bulletin. It was at this time that Armstrong began to make so-called prophetic claims and among them was the claim that Hitler and Mussolini were the prophesied Beast and False Prophet of the Book of Revelation who would deceive the nations for a short time just before the return of Jesus Christ.

This piqued the interest of his audience especially in Europe and America. The broadcast expanded to other cities, and in 1942 began to be broadcast nationwide from television network WHO of Des Moines, Iowa, a 50,000-watt superstation. Critics point to statements in his early writings that proved to be inaccurate, totally deceptive and misleading. For example, a statement from Armstrong in a lead article in the February, 1939 edition of *The Plain Truth*, about a coming world war, said this: "By way of brief review of previous articles, and radio messages, notice, first, that this war will involve ALL nations. It will be the first real world war. Secondly, it will center around Jerusalem.... And thirdly, this war will END with the Second Coming of Christ!" *The Plain Truth*, given away for free, continued to be published and circulated, even after the death of Armstrong, eventually reaching a monthly press run of eight million copies.

> *Editor's Note*: Fred Franz, head of the Writing Department being also the major source for the material published by the Watchtower Society, he often blatantly plagiarized and adapted entire sections from the Plain Truth, especially from the older copies and he used this material in his articles that he wrote in the Watchtower magazine on behalf of this religion. This material was then claimed to be direct revelations from Almighty God as revealed to the Governing Body.

In 1952 Armstrong published, *Does God Heal Today?* which explained and provided the details of his doctrine and teachings on physical healing and his total ban on doctors? Among his tenets were that only God heals and that medical science is of pagan origin and is ineffective. He believed that most illnesses were caused by faulty diet and that doctors should prescribe proper diet rather than medicine. He taught that members are not to go to doctors for healing but must trust in divine healing alone. This was his teaching despite his father's death in 1933 after an all-night vigil of prayer. This teaching has been the cause of much controversy as individuals influenced by such teachings came to ultimately die unnecessarily as a result. This teaching by Armstrong also created some confusion with the public as this ridiculous policy was also very similar to what Jehovah's Witnesses promoted at the same time, that of refusing blood transfusions plus organ transplants and needlessly dying as a result.

The United States and Britain in Prophecy was published in 1954. It became the most well-known and requested church publication, with over six million copies distributed, mainly being free to the public. In this book, Armstrong makes the claim that the peoples of the United States, the British Commonwealth nations, and the nations of Northwestern Europe are descendants of the Ten Lost Tribes of Israel. This belief, called British Israelism, formed the central basis of the theology of the Worldwide Church of God. Armstrong believed that a unified Europe, identified by him as a revived Roman Empire and as the first-mentioned beast of Revelation Chapter 13 and would oppose Jesus at his second coming in the battle at Armageddon. Furthermore, he stated repeatedly that a unified Europe would have previously defeated and enslaved the American and British peoples. He also often pointed to the European Common Market or European Community[22] as its precursor, but tended to refer to it as a kind of United States of Europe. Splinter groups (previously members of the Worldwide Church of God) today usually identify the current European Union as the unified Europe that Armstrong devoted much writing to. A closer look at many of his teachings and beliefs were typical of many other evangelical religions especially including the Watchtower Society and eventually proved to be inaccurate and incorrect.

As we have noted, on January 5, 1968, the Radio Church of God was renamed the Worldwide Church of God shortly before the church began to broadcast a television version of *The World Tomorrow*, which was a total rip-off from the BBC program *Tomorrows World* that ran from 1965 to 2003. This program by the Worldwide Church of God would eventually expand to 382 U.S. television stations and 36 television outlets internationally, dwarfing the excitable and sensational evangelists like Jerry Falwell (supporter of Apartheid), Jimmy (always full of artificial tears) Swaggart, Jim and (Glamorous?) Tammy Bakker, plus Oral Roberts (suspected gay). By this time, Garner Ted Armstrong, the son of Herbert W. Armstrong, was the voice and face of the program. It was speculated that with his charisma and personality, he was the logical successor to his father Herbert, but doctrinal disagreements and

---

[22] The European Community (EC) was an economic association formed by six European member countries in 1957, consisting of three communities that eventually were replaced by the European Union (EU) in 1993.

widespread reports of extramarital sex led to his suspension in 1972. After initially changing his behavior he returned, but these issues resurfaced, coupled with his challenging of his father's authority as Pastor General, resulting in him being permanently disfellowshipped (the church's term for excommunication) in 1978.

On April 15, 1967, Herbert Armstrong's wife Loma died, three and a half months before their 50th anniversary. Before she died Herbert sent a co-worker a letter that has often been criticized for its harsh tone to the failing of the rank and file of the members of his church and for its continuous calls for more money (does this sound familiar to members of the Jehovah's Witnesses?). There are many other stories discovered by our researchers about the morals and personal conduct of Herbert Armstrong but these are mainly based on rumors only. One incident of his personal conduct claimed to have been witnessed by several individuals, such as regularly having sex with his own young underage daughter (how warped can a man be if this is true), but we have not included most of these salacious accounts in this report.

During his latter years, Armstrong warned the Church that vultures were waiting for him to die. He was deeply concerned that some dangerous, liberal elements would enter in after his death and that the Church thought to then be of Philadelphia characteristics, "I know your works. Look, I have set before you an open door, which no one is able to shut. I know that you have but little power, and yet you have kept my word and have not denied my name." (Revelation 2:7-14) He also foretold that these new calculating, manipulative elements would become also like the congregation of Laodicea of whom Jesus said, "I am going to vomit you out of my mouth." (Revelation 3:15-22)

Almost until his final days, there was uncertainty about who would succeed Armstrong in the event of his death. The church's Advisory Council of Elders, acting on a clause in church by-laws added in 1981, was to select a successor only after his death, yet Armstrong reportedly worried about the ramifications if certain individuals were selected, such as his own son Garner or evangelist Roderick Meredith. Dr. R. Meredith had been appointed as Pastor General of the Worldwide Church of God in 1952 by Armstrong himself after he graduated from the now discredited Ambassador College in Pasadena but when he failed to take control of the Worldwide Church of God (WCG) founded by Armstrong he defected and later founded, The Living Church of God (LCG), which is one of hundreds of groups that formed after the death of Herbert W. Armstrong, when major doctrinal changes (causing turmoil and divisions) were occurring in the former Worldwide Church of God (WCG) during the 1990s.

On February 27, 2007, the Living Church of God (LCG) launched Living University, a nonprofit, online (distance-learning) institution. LCG also explored accreditation for Living University's undergraduate degrees, diplomas, and certificates, but Living University was never accredited by any agency recognized by the United States Department of Education. More and more states in America were blocking non-accredited colleges and universities from offering classes within their borders, so it was decided to close down and terminate Living University. So it closed its doors on May 14, 2018, after final commencement exercises for 30 students present and also provided an example of another failed venture of a religious cult.

In the years after Armstrong's death in 1986, Worldwide Church of God leaders came to the conclusion that many of his doctrines were not biblical but pure speculation and private interpretations. It was a different understanding regarding the nature of God specifically that caused this sect to entirely rewrite its doctrines. Those doctrines taught by the late Armstrong were subsequently rejected being considered to be aberrant and opprobrium. Today this vastly changed organization is in full agreement with the statement of faith of the National Association of Evangelicals.[23] In the light of these major doctrinal shifts made, in April 2009 the denomination also changed its name to Grace Communion International (GCI) to better reflect its New Testament, grace-centered teaching. Today, it is unrecognizable from the organization over which Herbert W. Armstrong once presided.

---

[23] The National Association of Evangelicals (NAE) is an association of evangelical denominations, organizations, schools, churches and individuals. The association represents more than 45,000 local churches from nearly 40 different denominations and serves a constituency of millions. The mission of the NAE is to honor God by connecting and representing evangelicals in the United States.

Editor's Note: Many of our readers of this Chapter related to the religion of Jehovah's Witnesses and their history will indentify many similarities between these two cults. Is this experience of the Worldwide Church of God and the Living Church of God and their downfall also a presage and warning of what will eventually happen to the Watchtower Society? They should also be reminded by the wise words of Jonathan Swift (1667-1745) the Anglo-Irish satirist, essayist and cleric who said, "You should never be ashamed to admit you have been wrong. It only proves you are wiser today than yesterday."

***

Meantime, Frederick Franz who later became the 4th President of the Watchtower Society, Inc., in 1977 up until his death in 1992, even though he was almost blind and mentally unbalanced and was simply used as a tool by other scheming members of this Governing Body to manipulate him and to use his vote in matters that were of primary importance to them personally.

The Watchtower radio station WBBR was eventually sold on 15 April, 1957, as stated by the Watchtower Press office, "It had served its purpose and the interests of God's Kingdom well, but was no longer needed". Also, the use of the phonograph and the playing of Rutherford's scurrilous lectures was also abandoned in 1944 after a 10-year period of use, as the local congregations had introduced a new very successful weekly program called the Theocratic Ministry School with two excellent text books, called *Theocratic Aid to Kingdom Publishers*, later replaced in 1955 with *Qualified to be Ministers and Equipped for Every Good Work*. Then later still in 2001, yet another text book being a replacement book released by the Watchtower Society was named *Benefit From Theocratic Ministry School Education*. They provided in their instructions that accompanied this latest new book, as though they were instructing children and not mature thinking adults, namely: "Remember number one, print your name in the space provided for it on the title page. Always bring the book with you when you attend the school. This textbook is also a workbook. When you read in it important points that you feel will help you, underline them. Use the generous margins to write down practical points that you learn during discussions at the school." All of these textbooks used in the Theocratic Ministry School are now out of print and no longer of any use or value to members of the Watchtower Society religion today.

In 1934 the Watchtower Society had introduced the portable phonograph (gramophone)[24] for use in their house-to-house ministry. Within about four years some 20,000 of these were supplied and in use in the field service. These clumsy contraptions all carried a serial number, for example, Serial Number 2000-W and were very inefficient machines and were a cheap imitation of the successful Edison Corporation's gramophone. The reason they bore a serial number is because these machines were out on loan to the special pioneers and local congregations that used them, but of course very few were ever returned as they were either broken or had been stolen. Today you can still buy one of these ancient phonographs manufactured by the Watchtower Society, or more likely a private company owned by Rutherford and a few secret investors, as a relic of memorabilia on eBay, but please be warned, you are probably buying stolen property!

Some Witnesses who were unaccustomed to speaking to strangers used a testimony card to introduce these recordings. More often, the individual Witness simply asked the householder to listen to the record, which often broke down during transmission, and having prepared the machine in advance, he would then put it on the door step or hold it on his arm to try and play the recording. Some local brothers using their ingenuity and creativity sometimes used baby perambulators (prams or baby carriages) to carry these heavy machines in the streets and market places. Others designed large audio horns and placed them on the top of motor vehicles and drove around the streets to declare Rutherford's aggressive and insulting messages against the churches and other religions resulting in numerous court cases of disturbing the peace. Sometimes the incensed public attacked these vehicles and overturned them causing injury to the poor Witnesses inside, once again labeled as persecution by Rutherford and the Governing Body.

[24] The phonograph work, according to the report in the 1938 Year Book showed that there were 430,000 discs available with lectures in sixteen languages all in use on 19,600 various sound machines including these phonographs. In 1937 there were reported on the accumulated field service reports, 10,368,569 listeners, and for 1938, 13,070,426.

This new, very successful program called the Theocratic Ministry School introduced in 1943 by Nathan Knorr was to train the members of the local congregations to become efficient in being able to personally present from door to door an oral sermon to the householders and then try and sell by means of a sales pitch, the product being Watchtower literature, very similar to the modern multi-marketing schemes that sell skincare products, jewelry and slimming diets, internet services, etc. But primarily, the School was for the male members to be qualified as teachers and speakers from the public platform in each local congregation. As pointed out elsewhere in this report, this practical and useful school; very successful in the opinion of most members we interviewed, was abandoned a few years ago as the masters of this religion, the Governing Body and their helpers now take upon themselves, for obvious reasons, all the teaching and instructions required in the congregations and local assemblies by means of videos, films and a direct communication network.

Our whistleblower also asked our reporter where the name MTC International Foundation came from, and what do the initials *MTC* stand for and represent. We were privileged to enlighten him with the following information. While teaching at a private non-profit, non-racial academy in South Africa during the Apartheid years, the head of the IT and Computer Department, plus a voluntary instructor in the Computer School, Ray Delaforce; who was also a brilliant computer programmer and sincere Christian evangelist, he often used this phrase to his students, "make today count" (MTC). Of interest to our readers, the Charter and Founding Statement of the non-profit, MTC International Foundation include the following words. "Our mission is threefold; we speak and report the truth, the whole truth and nothing but the truth, so help us God."

Thus, these initials *MTC* became a daily slogan. It developed into the name of the sponsors of this private academy, the MTC Training Foundation supported initially by the First National Bank (FNB) of South Africa, also by donations and grants from leading local businesses, including the Pick & Pay Foundation, managed by Wendy, the very concerned South African and spiritually minded wife of Raymond Ackerman. Later it evolved into its present name MTC International

Foundation. This phrase, Make Today Count, was later used as a title for a new book written by a friend of Ray's named John Maxwell and published in 2004.

Editor's Note: According to his biography, Hearing Grasshoppers Jump: The Story of Raymond Ackerman, Raymond Ackerman was a wealthy individual primarily due to his hard work. His JSE (Johannesburg Stock Exchange) listed Pick n' Pay Group as a supermarket chain with 870 stores in South Africa, Zimbabwe and Australia. In South Africa the group faces fierce competition from Shoprite and Woolworths. Ackerman built a strong reputation as a consumer champion, fighting supplier cartels in bread, petrol, cigarettes and many other industries. He no longer has executive responsibilities at Pick n' Pay, but he and his family still own about 48% of the stock. Raymond's grandfather Meyer Ackerman moved to South Africa from Lithuania at the end of the 19th century. His ostrich-feather business failed, but he later opened a grocery store in Cape Town called Ackerman's.

Raymond Ackerman and his wife Wendy were amongst a large group of white South Africans who detested apartheid and how this abhorrent system blocked many opportunities for the non-whites in the country from obtaining a decent education and career openings, which in turn provided exclusive opportunities to the white population only. Raymond and Wendy through their family trust fund used their wealth and assets to assist these disadvantaged students, especially the children of their employees and provided numerous bursaries for students attending this private academy owned by the MTC International Foundation. For more information on this horrific, satanic apartheid system in South Africa we recommend you read the new book *Zero Hour of the Apartheid Regime of Zuid Afrika*.

***

Returning to our story of the Watchtower Society, one of our research team remembers an incident when one of the more reasonable members of the Governing Body of the Watchtower Society many years ago was speaking to a captured, very attentive private audience. After going to great lengths to explain that the Watchtower magazine was the official line of communication between Almighty God and the members of the organization, he then discussed that he often had been personally asked, "Who writes the articles in the *Watchtower* magazine?" He shocked his listeners by making the bold statement to his audience, "You do!" He then went on to clarify that the Governing Body prepares the material, as they are appointed by Jesus Christ as the faithful and discreet slave over all the Lord's belongings, but they write these articles under the guidance of the Holy Spirit after research based on the many questions and queries that are regularly submitted to the headquarters by genuine sincere Christians from around the world. But today this clearly is now no longer the case, as your question or query will not even be acknowledged, despite a regular feature that used to appear in the private (members only) study portion of the Watchtower magazine, known as Questions from Readers.

Raymond Franz later wrote in his biographical book, Crisis of Conscience (1983) "I have since come to appreciate the rightness of a quotation I recently read, one made by a statesman, (John F. Kennedy) now dead, who said: "The great enemy of the truth is very often not the lie – deliberate, contrived and dishonest – but the myth – persistent, persuasive and unrealistic." I now began to realize how large a measure of what I had based my entire adult life course on was just that, a myth – persistent, persuasive and unrealistic." *Crisis of Conscience* presents the story of a struggle to prevent the erosion of a God-given freedom of conscience and the ensuing dilemma of choosing between loyalty to God and loyalty to one's religion. Former member of the Governing Body of Jehovah's Witnesses, Raymond Franz delivers a rare glimpse into the inner workings of the Watchtower Society. *Crisis of Conscience* offers a penetrating view of the supreme council of this organization, the Governing Body and their life altering power over human lives.

According to Raymond Franz, decisions of the Governing Body were supposedly required to be unanimous up until 1975, (thus the reason why autocrat Rutherford and later Nathan Knorr often made very important decisions without even consulting the Governing Body) after which a two-thirds majority of the full Governing Body was required, regardless of the number present and since 1975, the Governing Body has been the supreme ruling council of Jehovah's Witnesses. Lyman Swingle (also nicknamed Salty by some and Slim by others of his very close friends) was a farsighted individual and also a member of the Governing Body, especially when it came to the future survival of the Watchtower Society and is on record as saying, "We have always had all the money to do the things we needed to do…and if we didn't…we felt it was God's holy spirit telling us, namely it wasn't what we should be doing." Charles Russell, the founder of this religion also expressed the identical opinion in one of the first issues of the Watchtower magazine back in April, 1879, Russell said, "That it will continue as long as God provides the funds and if the funds ever dry up, it will mean God wants the Watchtower to stop." These in-depth wise opinions by sincere Christian members of the Watchtower Society have now been simply ignored by the current Governing Body. Why, we ask?

Realizing the donation of funds was gradually shrinking; the need for a continuous supply of funds became a very serious and focused issue to the Governing Body of the Watchtower Society in order to survive and continue to enjoy their privileged life style. How could they continue operating and functioning when they now faced this dramatically shrinking supply of donations and also were now facing massive legal challenges throughout the world, with the increasing court cases related to sexual harassment and abuse of children and single women in the organization, crimes that had been committed and convicted by their subordinate shepherds and leaders over many years? What was their solution and answer to this desperate situation after closing down many of their overseas branch offices and attempts to cut expenditure? After spending their dedicated time over the many years supposedly to caring for the so-called spiritual needs of the members of this religion under their oversight, they decided that it was more opportune, expedient and necessary to redirect their primary interests and concerns to the lucrative real estate market now existing under their direct control. You as an intelligent reader of our report can draw your own conclusions as to what happened next.

The following comments and update on the Watchtower Society selling their lucrative property holding in New York are based on current information available as of January, 2019.

It is reported that the Watchtower Society in 2014 had secured a staggering $375 million deal for six of its most well-known Brooklyn, New York, real estate holdings, but some were much run down and neglected properties, many bought years ago around 1909 by Russell and Rutherford. The deal, signed with property developers, Fuchs and Rosen that was formed in 1991 by two German, Jewish individuals, as the company began buying distressed assets from other agencies and also linked with the Kushner Property Companies. Kushner Companies are an American real estate developer in the New York City metropolitan area. Its founder, Charles Kushner, a Russian Jew, was convicted of tax evasion and witness tampering in 2005, and served time for his crimes in federal prison. As a result, he officially was forced to hand over the management of his company to his son, the young, very inexperienced Jared Kushner who is now married to Donald Trump's daughter Ivanka. Charles Kushner was still in total control however, even though he operated from a prison cell in New Jersey. Most of these new luxury apartments and offices, converted from these property holdings, previously owned by the Watchtower Society are now being sold to foreign nationals, many who use money (legally or illegally) that they have moved off-shore for tax avoidance or evasion reasons, including many prominent Russians, Arabs, Chinese, South Africans and Israelis.

Also removed from these buildings previously owned by Jehovah's Witnesses, now sold to the Kushner companies, were the slogans, Read God's Word the Bible Daily and the illuminated sign *Watchtower* erected in 1969, and after 49 years they have both now disappeared from the New York City skyline. The Watchtower sign had now been replaced with the sign Welcome in 15-foot-tall red letters. It remained there until 2017, when the building's new owners, a consortium of developers that includes LIVWRK and CIM Group of Los Angeles, dismantled it during construction on the new Panorama complex. A battle between the developers and the city over what, exactly, could replace the bright red beacon followed, with the Board of Standards and Appeals finally decreeing in 2018 that a new sign could be erected.

This article published in the *Brooklyn Daily Eagle* of 2013, sheds further light on the property dealings of the Watchtower Society.

Office and residential developers are waiting to see when the Jehovah's Witnesses will bring their next Brooklyn Heights and DUMBO (Down Under the Manhattan Bridge Overpass) properties to market now that they've finalized the sale of five DUMBO industrial buildings to the Kushner Cos. and RFR. They have 16 unsold properties – but the clock is ticking. In 2017, they expect to finish building their (luxury) new headquarters in upstate Warwick, where they are relocating, executives said last week. Also, a hotel at 90 Sands St. will remain occupied by the Witnesses until 2017 but will not be available for sale – Kushner and RFR have already agreed in advance to buy it. Starting in the 1980s, rapidly rising Heights real estate prices – and the high legal costs of taking properties off city tax rolls – gave pause to Watchtower elders, especially those living outside New York. But those objections were invariably over-ruled, a Watchtower honcho of that era told the Brooklyn Height Press – because whether it was a house or a hotel, whenever the group bought a property, the value was higher the very next day.

The Brooklyn Paper (2016) also reported the following.

> Donald Trump's son-in-law and campaign advisor, property developer Jared Kushner, bought the Jehovah's Witnesses' iconic Watchtower headquarters in Dumbo last Wednesday, which he plans on turning into a tremendous, classy office complex by September next year. "Over the next year, we'll begin transforming the property into one of the marquee urban office campuses anywhere in the country, let alone New York City," said Kushner, who is married to the Donald's daughter Ivanka Trump and is reportedly an incredibly influential figure in his Presidential bid.

Ivanka Trump is the daughter of Ivana Marie Trump (Née Zelníčková*)*, former Czech glamour model and one of Donald Trump's many divorced wives and girlfriends. Ivanka abandoned her Christian heritage passed down by her mother and joined the Jewish religion as required by her husband to be, Jared Kushner. Ivanka Trump and Jared Kushner are still involved with their massive property and business empires earning according to recent news articles, approximately $150 million per year, but both commendably also worked part-time on a voluntary basis in the West Wing of the White House in Washington as senior advisors to the former, one-term narcissistic President of America. Why, you might ask, and so do we, as they are both very rich and well established in business? What is their underlying ulterior motive?

In a new book about Jared Kushner, this review was received:

> Jared Kushner and Ivanka Trump are the self-styled Prince and Princess of America. Their swift, gilded rise to extraordinary power in Donald Trump's White House is unprecedented and dangerous. In her book Kushner, Inc., investigative journalist; a fellow Brit, Vicky Ward, digs beneath the myth the couple has created, depicting themselves as the voices of reason in an otherwise crazy presidency, and reveals that Jared and Ivanka are not just the President's chief enablers: they, like him, appear disdainful of rules, of laws, and of ethics. They are entitled inheritors of the worst kind; their combination of ignorance, arrogance, and an insatiable lust for power has caused havoc all over the world, and may threaten the very democracy of the United States. Author Vicky Ward follows their trajectory from New Jersey and New York City to the White House, where the couple's many forays into policy-making and national security have mocked long-standing U.S. policy and protocol. They have pursued an agenda that could increase their wealth while their actions have mostly gone unchecked. In Kushner, Inc., Ward holds Jared Kushner and Ivanka Trump accountable: she unveils the couple's self-serving transactional motivations and how those have propelled them into the highest levels of the US government where no one, the President included, has been able to stop them.

Our reporter also reminds us that in view of the latest news (March, 2019) about the greatest scandal in the history of the education system in the United States, the issue of being able to bribe officials in order to gain entry into top universities, as did Charles Kushner with his son Jared and this has once again raised queries of how the rich buy their under-achieving children's way into elite universities with massive, tax-deductible donations. Is this true democracy or corruption? Writer Daniel Golden published a book a few years ago called *The Price of Admission,* and he recently wrote an article in the *Guardian* newspaper regarding his successful book, which has now been revived in view of this recent scandal.

> My book exposed a grubby secret of American higher education: that the rich buy their under-achieving children's way into elite universities with massive, tax-deductible donations. I also quoted administrators at Jared's high school, who described him as a less than stellar student and expressed dismay at Harvard's decision. "There was no way anybody in the administrative office of the school thought he would on the merits get into Harvard," a former official at The Frisch School in Paramus, New Jersey, told me. "His GPA did not warrant it, his SAT scores did not warrant it. We thought for sure, there was no way this was going to happen. Then, lo and behold, Jared was accepted. It was a little bit disappointing because there were at the time other kids we thought should really get in on the merits, and they did not.

It reported that Russian Jew, New Jersey real estate developer and convicted criminal, Charles Kushner had pledged $2.5 million to Harvard University in 1998, not long before his son Jared was admitted to the prestigious Ivy League school. At the time, Harvard accepted about one of every nine applicants. Nowadays, it only takes one out of twenty.

The New York Times received in 2018 an anonymous letter that stated, "I work for the president but like-minded colleagues and I have vowed to thwart parts of his agenda and his worst inclinations." The newspaper also stated, "*The Times* is taking the rare step of publishing an anonymous Op-Ed essay. We have done so at the request of the author, a senior official in the Trump administration whose identity is known to us and whose job would be jeopardized by its disclosure. We believe publishing this essay anonymously is the only way to deliver an important perspective to our readers."

From inside information received and leaked to our reporter he believed that this Op-Ed was actually from Jared Kushner, who is privately making plans to have the Vice President, Mike Pence (known by the staff in the White House as a religious nut) temporarily take over as President of the United States after the very obvious, ultimate fall from grace of his father-in-law Donald Trump. It was later confirmed that the source of this critical Op-Ed was from Miles Taylor, ex-Homeland Security senior official and personal friend of Jared Kushner, who it is claimed knew about this Op-Ed by Taylor and actually encouraged him to write this Op-Ed to the Times. It is also known that Jared Kushner is a back-stabber in both business and politics as he hypocritically publicly praises his father-in-law-Donald but privately looks forward to his eventual demise. It is also claimed that Ivanka and Jared along with Mike Pence (a holy trinity of two Jews and a Christian fanatic) virtually run the chaotic White House. Plus, Jared and Ivanka also have personal ambitious future plans to become the ultimate leaders of the greatest nation in the world, the United States of America. As we now know from history and the recent election that Donald Trump, his family and friends have all now had to vacate their luxury rooms in the White House on Pennsylvania Avenue in Washington, D.C.

Michael D'Antonio, a CNN contributor and biographer who wrote The Truth About Trump, said in a new interview, "that Vice-President Pence believes God is calling him to function as a president-in-waiting." He further added, "Absolutely everything Mike Pence does is oriented toward him becoming president." D'Antonio also said this during an appearance on CNN on Tuesday in promotion of his new book *The Shadow President: The Truth About Mike Pence.* D'Antonio claimed. "By the time he had left high school, he had decided that he was going to be president of the United States. ... He thought God was calling him to that position, and now, be the Vice President and function as a president-in-waiting. We also see Donald Trump in this huge crisis, this rolling chaos," D'Antonio said. "And I think, with every day, Mike Pence imagines he's one day closer to the Oval Office." When asked by CNN host John Berman if he believes the vice-president is "maneuvering to get the top job" at the expense of Trump, D'Antonio also replied: "Oh, I think yes."

Our reporter also added "Mike Pence is well-known as a loser, a religious fanatic and a totally disillusioned, subjective man controlled by his influential, powerful wife, but the ambitious plans of Ivanka Trump and Jared Kushner are much more focused as they intend to eventually take over as "Emperor and Empress of the United States of

America". What greater ambition could one have? Can you envisage this scenario of two non-Christian, Jewish individuals being your next leaders and dictators? They both know; as they spend time every day with Ivanka's father Donald that the present leader of America is a dangerous, extremely narcissistic individual, has early signs of dementia and is mentally unbalanced, so their motives are probably pure. So let us all hope that their plans don't back-fire?"

Many of our readers will be asking, what are the true signs of a person with a narcissistic personality disorder (NPD)? For more enlightenment we invite you to read chapters Seven and Eight of the best-selling book, *The Delamere Saga – The Untold Story of Vale Royal Abbey*, which covers the world-famous character, Hugh Cholmondeley, 3rd Lord Delamere (1870-1931), who also had a very bad case of the narcissistic personality disorder. Also, another best-selling book recently published by Mary Trump, niece of Donald Trump, *Too Much and Never Enough: How My Family Created the World's Most Dangerous Man*, also reveals the narcissistic personality of Donald Trump.

> *Editor's Note*: As we are now aware, Donald Trump was soundly beaten in the General Election of 3 November, 2020 for the Presidency of the United States and his ambition to become 'King' of America had now evaporated. Also, he now witnesses his family dynasty crumbling around his 'tiny' feet. Ivana Marie "Ivanka" Trump his daughter and Jared Kushner have also vacated their Washington mansion and moved to Florida to be near her father and recently bought a piece of land for the sum of $30 million dollars in Miami on which they plan to build a new mansion. Ivanka and Jared probably used a small portion of the accumulated fortune they made while working as volunteers for four years in the White House, but meantime had unscrupulously made private business deals and contracts through their nepotistic connections. Jared Kushner and Joseph Rutherford of the Watchtower Society would have made great business partners, Jared with his Israeli and Arab-Muslim friends and business connections and Rutherford with his Nazi German connection. (Read the brilliant book by James Penton titled *Jehovah's Witnesses and the Third Reich*). This link between Kushner and Rutherford is ironic and satirical, apart from the fact that Kushner ended up purchasing all the

Watchtower properties in Brooklyn, New York, as according to the now bubbling rumors of the business dealings between the Watchtower Society and the Kushner Property Group are in big trouble, and based on information being currently uncovered by our reporters (please excuse my language) a lot more "shit will hit the fan."

Melania, the current wife of Donald Trump, is also now under scrutiny related to her private family from the Yugoslav Republic of Slovenia and the scandal of how they all managed to get the Green Card so quickly and become citizens of the United States through Melania's marriage to Donald Trump. The two sons of Trump, Donald, junior and Eric are also facing more scandals related to their domestic and financial dealings. In the case of Mike Pence, former 48th Vice-President, he is now riding off into the sunset and political oblivion and as he approaches the proverbial "three score years and ten", Psalms 90:10 (KJV) poor Mike, being a claimed born-again Christian is still trying to understand in his simple and confused mind, why God has not yet kept his private promise to Mike that one day he would be President of the United States of America.

***

Changing the subject back to the sale of the New York properties of the Watchtower Society, we continue with the report from our research team. "Also, it was pointed out by our reporter, that the *Watchtower Society* had already gained another $500 million from the sale of other run down property holdings in Brooklyn, New York, many with rent controlled tenants who refused to vacate and all sales were free of capital gains tax. This critical comment was made by another reporter, "For this reason, it was more lucrative to build a brand-new headquarters in the middle of nowhere on a disused toxic chemical waste site that nobody wanted, and go to the considerable trouble of relocating millions of dollars worth of equipment, if this means freeing up the Society's Brooklyn goldmine and pocketing a sorely needed cash windfall. It may seem that the Watchtower Society is flushed today with money as a result of these sales, now tallied at over one billion dollars, and indeed it may well be for the time being. However, this doesn't mean that everything is bright and rosy for the Watchtower's future aspirations. As organizational downsizing continues, necessitated by stagnating growth, don't be surprised if this cash windfall gets used up more quickly than anyone expects."

This vacant, disused property in upstate New York had been recently purchased for the new world headquarters of the Watchtower Society and was formerly owned by the International Nickel Company for various uses, including a head office and a research, development facility, from 1960 to 1987. After being unoccupied for about four years, the site was acquired by King's College, New York, with the intention of converting it into a college campus. That use of the site never came to fruition for financial reasons, and the property remained vacant for more than twenty-four years until the Watchtower Society purchased the property in 2009 though their property agents, Kushner, Inc., and their Russian associates. The Watchtower Society later found and discovered, after purchasing the site that it was polluted with chemicals and other hazardous materials, which were banned as far back as 1979 by the United States government. A court case is still pending under the clause of Caveat emptor, which is a Latin term that means let the buyer beware. Similar to the phrase, sold as is, this term means that the buyer assumes the risk that a product may fail to meet expectations or have defects. Our legal department comments that the Watchtower Society has no chance of winning this case, using the idiom, not a snowball in hell of a chance.

It is interesting to note that in December, 1994, Kings College of New York closed its doors, as a result of many years of declining enrollment, financial troubles, poor management, corruption and the deterioration of their Briarcliff campus. The college had purchased the large property in Warwick for a new campus in upstate New York with the help of several major investors, but was prevented from selling the Briarcliff campus in a timely fashion because of ongoing legal investigations regarding their suspicious financial records. The college then conveniently declared bankruptcy, owing more than $25 million to its creditors, loans arranged by the disreputable Deutsche Bank especially for the mortgage on the new campus purchased in Warwick. A private loan was also raised rumored to be held by an overseas company controlled by corrupt Russian oligarchs connected to New York attorney Rudolph Giuliani plus his client and silent business partner Donald Trump. Giuliani is currently under investigation by the FBI and the Attorney General of Southern New York for fraud, tax evasion and money laundering.

It is also rumored that the sale of the distressed property that Kings College now owned in Warwick, upstate New York, was handled by the property company, Fuchs & Rosen, who had very strong (under the table) connections with certain members of the Watchtower Real Estate and Investments office in Brooklyn. They also, by coincidence handled the sale to the Kushner Property Company, the numerous properties owned by the Watchtower Society in Brooklyn, New York thereby earning a massive, lucrative commission. Our legal guru who has also practiced as a real estate broker for many years also pointed out the common practice within the trade of paying a finder's fee. In the context of a real estate transaction, a finder's fee (also known as a referral fee) is a fee paid to a person for the introduction of a buyer to a seller that results in a successful sales transaction and is not illegal.

There are now very disturbing rumors regarding the relationship with the property brokers Fuchs and Rosen, who handled most of the sales of the Watchtower properties in New York and also the claim that they handled the purchase of the chemically polluted vacant land in Warwick, upstate New York for the Watchtower Society's new headquarters plus other large tracts of nearby unused land. Our reporter pointed out, that if, as it is rumored, certain individual members of the Watchtower Real Estate and Investment office had a private business relationship with these real estate agents, while it is not illegal to pay or accept a finder's fees, it is certainly unethical and a clear misuse of one's privileged position within the non-profit charitable Watchtower organization. Along with all matters related to religion, politics and commerce, the truth will eventually prevail and our research team is determined and dedicated that the truth will be revealed and fully exposed in due course as related to this serious matter. Our reporters and researchers relentlessly pursue the truth in line with their assigments.

According to the research by Barbara Anderson in her *Watchtower Documents*, the following as an example of the hypocrisy and ethics of property dealings by the Watchtower Society some years ago.

Unknown to the local Brooklyn community, including most
of the Watchtower staff, negotiations was already underway to
purchase an old Brooklyn factory located right next to the East
River on Furman Street. This neglected building was huge –
over a million square feet of space – where armored tanks were
built during WWII. Elevators were so large they could easily
carry a large truck up and down the 13-stories. Incidentally,
after many years of renovation by volunteer workers, the
building was sold in April 2004, making the Watchtower
Society an enormous profit. In addition, the rundown 12-story
Bossert Hotel, which opened in 1909 on Montague Street
in downtown Brooklyn Heights, a local historic district,
was secretly under consideration for purchase by 'Cohi
Towers Associates', an organization formed by a number of
wealthy Jehovah's Witnesses to purchase buildings for the
Watchtower's use. Using 'Cohi Towers Associates' to purchase
these buildings hid the Watchtower's involvement and kept
local opposition groups from knowing that another building
in the neighborhood would be removed off the tax rolls. The
'Cohi' organization then later signed over the building to the
Watchtower Society.

During May, 2015, Jehovah's Witnesses Broadcasting episode in which
the Governing Body member, Stephen Lett disclosed a very serious
shortfall between anticipated income and the current expenditure of
this religion, which was a clear admission that funds were very quickly
drying up. The very attentive members of Jehovah's Witnesses were then
urged to give up even more of their "valuable things" (Proverbs 3:9)
in order to offset this shortfall and make important new construction
projects possible. This manipulative appeal must have worked to
prompt the conscience of many of the sincere humble members of
this cult. The result was the construction of the new headquarters at
Warwick in upstate New York, built to house the over 800 full-time
staff of the Watchtower Society that was completed in 2017 and from
reports is a most lavish, expensive building complex and no expense
was spared in its construction. Even the drain covers, it would appear,
have been customized to feature the Watchtower logo. Donald Trump's
mega-million dollar luxury hotels and golf courses never went to that
extravagant expense.

A member of the Governing Body stated a few years ago: "Although we are not yet certain of Jehovah's will regarding Warwick, we are proceeding to develop the site with the intention of relocating the world headquarters of Jehovah's Witnesses there." A genuine sincere letter from a reader, asked, "Why are they building this elaborate place when the world is so near its end?" That question is on everybody's mind! The answer is simple in my humble opinion, as expressed by our informant. "It's because that the Governing Body, whoever they are today, does not really believe what they are preaching. They are trying to convince the whole world about the end being so near when they themselves do not believe that nonsense. When the followers of this religion run out of being squeezed out of their money then it will all be over."

As a repeat of the now very successful, financially shrewd and mercenary American project of moving away and selling their former, now very lucrative property holdings in Brooklyn, New York city, The International Bible Students Association (IBSA) – the British charity that manages Jehovah's Witnesses' printing, literature distribution and related administrative functions is now also relocating the Britain Branch Office from Watchtower House, Mill Hill, London, to a location called Temple Farm, Chelmsford in Essex, an existing polluted scrap yard full of rotting vehicles and rusty wrecks. The preparation works on the site have already begun in 2015 and the construction works already started by spring 2016. There is a local rumor from our contact in the London Bethel that this piece of land containing the scrap yard and formerly a large farm was donated to the Watchtower Society from a deceased estate of a local Witness, so it is possible that the land cost was absolutely nil and buckshee. Our inside contact in the London Bethel could not gain access to the files related to this property transaction as all these files are currently help in the private offices of a London solicitor while the transfer of all equipment, files and documents are being moved to the new premises at Temple Farm so we have been unable to factually confirm this claim from existing records.

From feedback, this change of plans to now sell Watchtower House and IBSA House in London has brought great disappointment to the many members in Britain, as the Mill Hill properties that were purposely designed and built with volunteers only a few years ago at great cost and sacrifice to them personally, and is located in the beautiful greenbelt area of north London. It now appears that the property prices in London, England, have sky-rocketed and this recently built Mill Hill project called Watchtower House, and the adjoining IBSA House (so loved and admired by the many members and volunteers of the Watchtower Society in the UK, being almost like a temple from the numerous visits and tours arranged) but has now become a massive illiquid asset. So it has now been decided by the Governing Body of the Watchtower Society that it became more lucrative to sell the buildings in London and to release the millions of tax free British Pounds (GBP) tied up in the property, as it was now a desirable project for Arabs to convert into a hotel and convention centre for their many Muslim clients and visitors from the Middle East, who are also buying up half of England, according to our reporter.

Meantime, many skilled volunteers, being sincere members of this religion, have once again – structural engineers, architects, interior designers, landscapers, solicitors, and so many more – are hard at work designing and building the new branch offices on this former derelict farm in Essex, England. Hundreds of brothers and sisters have worked for well over a year to get the project to its current stage. The first construction volunteers are now living on location. Hundreds more will be needed to transform this polluted site into the new Britain Branch Office and of course, as usual, another campaign is also now underway requesting more donations from the loyal flock to support this new project. This includes demolishing the derelict buildings of the former car breakers and wrecking business, trying to remove the resultant polluted soil, carrying out land drainage, archaeological investigation, plus setting up a residential support site and a main support site. According to an article in October, 2015 by the *Essex Chronicle*, "the old buildings and car breakers garages have been already demolished. Furthermore, the personnel support manager of the branch relocation department denies rumors that the relocation and construction project could collapse because of the recent urgent shortage of funds."

Editor's Note: It appears that the financial problem of shortage of funds was temporarily resolved for this new Temple Farm project as the Watchtower Society (British Branch) as they managed to finally secure a large loan from the JP Morgan Bank in Luxemburg on 11 December, 2019, using various properties as collateral or security. According to our contact in the London Bethel this loan was secured by a friend of one of the branch committee members and this referrer earned himself a nice fat referral fee in the process. No doubt this legal loan agreement with JP Morgan Bank included all the British Kingdom Hall properties that the Watchtower Society had recently seized from all the local congregations and which are now legally owned outright in the name of their own Watchtower Charity, instead of the local charities of each individual congregation.

One of our researchers interviewed a local resident in a nearby village to Temple Farm and she was very pleased about this dreadful site and ex-farm being redeveloped, as the smelly, polluted site after so many years was to be used for some other purpose. What she did not realize is that the new owners, the International Bible Students of Great Britain are registered as a non-profit organization and therefore will be exempt from all taxes and property rates and will financially contribute absolutely nothing to the local community, except perhaps the benefits of the thousands of members of this group visiting their new temple and maybe spending money in the local shops and restaurants. Our reporter had learned that two enterprising ex-Bethel brothers were quitting their assignment of service and ministry to the Lord and opening a for-profit Watchtower Souvenir shop in the local village so that will probably secure some income for the local residents.

For the identical underlying reasons, the decision was made by the Governing Body (supposedly and primarily being responsible for all spiritual matters) for selling all the lucrative properties in New York, they also decided to sell the London headquarters, a decision that is to now unlock the millions of dollars tied up in these valuable properties. A long serving member in the headquarters in London, who asked not to be named, expressed his great disappointment to our reporter as he pointed out that the London Headquarters on The Ridgeway in Mill Hill (formerly the site of the ancient Brittacy House originally built in 1827 but demolished when the Watchtower Society bought the site), was skillfully and carefully designed only a few years ago, with other major additions also having been recently constructed as a purpose built facility to care for all the future requirement of the London Bethel office staff, printing facilities, land for growing vegetables, etc., and in his opinion is still the perfect facility for handling the duties of the Watchtower Society in Britain until the new system arrives in the very near future.

He also was quick to add, that the decision has now been made and he has to go along with what the Governing Body decides, whether right or wrong (spoken like a true slave of modern religion). There is now another ongoing campaign to solicit more funds from followers of this religion to finance this new project on a derelict trash dump, a former Kent farm (full of rotting old car wrecks) notwithstanding the massive profits made from the sale of the Watchtower House and IBSA House properties in north London.

A self-proclaimed sales pitch was also declared and unashamedly released to the press.

> Watch Tower House is a purpose-built mixed use live/work development which combines residential, office, production and amenity space within an interconnected building. Originally designed and constructed in the early 1980s, the building has been adapted and enlarged during the intervening years. In its current configuration, residential floor space predominates, with around 170 bed spaces currently being provided. The total gross internal floor space is 10,120sq.m. The external footprint is 4,571sq.m. The plot size is 32,629sq.m (8 acres) adjacent to Watch Tower House and to the west is an open field which lies within the Green Belt. The field stretches from the rear gardens of houses in Rushden Gardens northwards to The Ridgeway where there is a dedicated access point from the road. In total, this area is some 8.3 acres. The combined area of the open field and Watch Tower House is some 16 acres. For further details of both this building and the open field, please contact our real estate brokers.

An additional *New York Times* news source revealed the following:

> Back in December 2015, the group continued its recent trend of unloading its valuable Brooklyn-based properties, by putting

its flagship Watchtower headquarters compound on the market, ending the New York borough's century-long term as the home of the Jehovah's Witness movement. A statement from the religion's Governing Body said that the ad-hoc way it had acquired property over the years had led to its campus being far too spread out and therefore difficult to manage, therefore it was selling off the properties and centralizing its organization in the town of Warwick, in upstate New York.

The *Daily Mail* newspaper also reported regarding the New York properties "That the sale should generate around $1 billion for the Witnesses." Regarding the London properties it also reported "Accounts ending August 2014 value the entire portfolio in London at £73 million, but the actual sales are expected to bring in funds well in excess of that. The whole sale of everything is projected to be completed by 2021 at the latest, by which time the Jehovah's Witnesses say it will be fully installed in a purpose-built facility in Chelmsford, Essex. In the meantime, IBSA is keen to point out that its building could be vacated quickly if buyers required."

Referring back to the report from our research associate regarding any possible change of major doctrines and policies of the Watchtower Society in order to maintain their income, our informant reflected that this is the underlying fear of the current Governing Body, that if membership keeps dropping through disillusioned members quitting, especially if caused by any dramatic changing of major core doctrines, established from way back when this religion was originally founded in 1879 and as a result the voluntary contributions start to dry up completely, the future of the Watchtower Society looks very bleak indeed. Thus the attempt to maintain at least the status quo, or create other modern means and techniques of collecting funds from their members in order to survive or finally collapse. On the other hand, the Mormon Church currently has a compulsory tithing system for their members and this could possibly ensure their wealth and power for many years to come.

> *Editor's Note:* This religious cult, the Mormon Church, also faces the fact that as their income from tithing is slowly diminishing and membership has stagnated they will ultimately have to

relax the strict rules over their followers and adapt or abandon their so-called divine revelations, and signs are already being seen that they are preparing to be just another mainstream religion in order to retain their followers. Read more about this master of modern religion in Chapter Four.

Our researcher went on: "The Watchtower Society has in the past also seriously considered introducing the biblical practice of tithing (10% of the income of each member) (Matthew 23:23) similar to the Mormon Church, but has so far been reluctant. The Governing Body in this case, today hypocritically claims that tithing was only applicable in terms of the Mosaic Law and does not apply to Christians today. At the very same time, compare this claim with their strict rule 'abstain from blood' covered earlier in our report that was also in terms of the Mosaic Law and this clearly displays the erratic inconsistency of the Governing Body of this religion."

Our researcher continued:

> But as a clever, shrewd alternative they have recently introduced what is now nicknamed stealth tithing. This newly acquired financial wizardry introduced by the Governing Body of Jehovah's Witnesses was condemned by many, including actual faithful long-standing members of the religion, as being not only unscriptural, but unscrupulous and unethical manipulation of the local congregations that amounted to nothing more than financially raiding the local subjective brothers and seizing their congregational assets. This new scheme of stealth tithing did however, when finally implemented and forced upon the local slave like members of the local congregations, who were powerless and could not really object to the rules and authority of the masters. This new scheme was supposed to create a guaranteed indefinite supply of money for the organization to continue their ever-expanding insatiable appetite and demand for funds, and thus allowed their ever-increasing operating costs and future anticipated large losses to be covered. The desperate need for these additional funds is not counting the rapidly accumulating list of legal cases involving billions of dollars that they now face over child and sexual abuse, plus the many cases having secretly been settled out of court, that the lowly, humble rank and file of the members of this religion

know nothing about; these settlements costing additional millions upon millions of dollars. If these new funds could not be obtained somehow by the masters of this cult and a new method or technique introduced that guaranteed their demand for funds to be covered for the foreseeable future, as the way that the existing financial support they received from voluntary donations were shrinking rapidly and they saw the end of their religion and their associated powers was possibly not far off. A desperate attempt was made to ensure their survival no matter what the cost, as they were facing big problems.

A question asked by one individual we interviewed who stated in confidence that the Watchtower Society proudly boasts and declares in their literature and adverts for their meetings and assemblies that they never solicit, ask, demand or beg for money. They claim that this is one of indications and signs that separate them from the nominal religions of Christendom and their passing of the collection plates or baskets. Does the Watchtower Society directly ask for money, of course they do, even though they officially deny that they do so and the facts nullify their erroneous claim. The following are extracts from leaked letters, sent to all Congregation Elders in the United Kingdom, which plainly states this fact. This letter to all Congregation Elders in Britain and Ireland, dated February 25, 2015 plainly states: "Looking ahead to the need to replace older vehicles in the coming year, we are again writing to invite you to contribute to this arrangement. We anticipate that the expenses can be covered if there is a contribution from each congregation in the amount of £3.00 (€3.75) per publisher. This does not mean that each publisher is expected to contribute this amount. Rather, the congregation as a whole can make the contribution, and all may help with the expense, as they are able. (Acts 11:29) We recommend that each congregation pass a resolution to contribute based upon the number of publishers". In addition, this letter of March 29, 2014 to all Elders: "All congregations are asked to establish a monthly resolved donation to support Kingdom Hall and Assembly Hall construction worldwide by no later than May 31, 2014." These requests or demands for money are as plain as it gets!

Christians are instructed in the Bible to voluntarily contribute according to what a person has and not being bound and tied to specific amounts (called pledges by some religions) determined or dictated by the leaders and masters of their religion. The words of the apostle Paul clearly point out this principle at 2 Corinthians 9:7, "Each of you must give as you have made up your mind, not reluctantly or under compulsion, for God loves a cheerful giver." See also the words at 2 Corinthians 8:12, "For if the eagerness is there, the gift is acceptable according to what one has – not according to what one does not have." Also, we need to remind ourselves that the definition of a pledge is very clear and is a "thing that is given as security for the fulfillment of a contract or the payment of a debt and is liable to forfeiture in the event of failure to pay".

One prominent elder and leader of the Watchtower Society who we interviewed, stated that if a vote was allowed democratically by the millions of the individual members of this religion, from gleaned information and feedback the vast majority would have resisted this decision by the Governing Body regarding this new financial arrangement and preferred the already successful existing arrangement be continued. But they have no vote or choice as this so-called theocratic (being a word used but simply means autocratic or dictatorial in practice) organization and its Governing Body and their helpers makes their official decisions and the members are instructed to obey without question. We remind our readers once again that to contradict or oppose the Governing Body is labeled as an act of apostasy and can lead to a member being excommunicated if they do not toe the line as clearly outlined in the secret instruction manual to all local elders and judicial committees, titled Shepherd the Flock of God, which again is another sign of a cult.

A leaked letter dated March 29, 2014, has been circulated to all elders advising of a huge shake-up in financing arrangements for all local Kingdom Hall and assembly hall construction and existing loans from the Watchtower Society. According to the leaked letter: "Congregation and Assembly Halls will no longer be asked to repay a loan." However, in the elders-only part of the letter, congregations are instructed that their new monthly compulsory pledge must be, "at least the same amount as the current monthly loan repayment" for congregations repaying loans for building work. In other words, if your congregation was paying off a time limited loan, probably a 10-15-year amortized loan from the

Watchtower Society for the Kingdom Hall build or refurbishment project, your loan repayments must now effectively continue indefinitely (for an unlimited period of time; namely forever). If a congregation isn't already making loan repayments, then a confidential survey is to be taken by passing out slips of paper to determine how much the local brothers are willing to pledge each month, once again to continue indefinitely and no longer on a simple ad hoc voluntary basis. But when you consider the Watchtower Society's apparent financial woes as evidenced by the unprecedented organizational downsizing, not to mention the increasing threat posed by the numerous child and sex abuse lawsuits, the Governing Body's assault on congregation coffers for extra cash is all too predictable.

To illustrate the consequences of the new financial instructions to all congregations issued by the Governing Body in 2014, we quote this experience that we received from one of our researchers. Our reporter spoke to the secretary of a local congregation in England, who had built their own Kingdom Hall out of their own funds and private donations by local members, plus a small bank loan that was repaid within a few short years, so they were debt free. The local congregation now had to pay this newly introduced compulsory monthly pledge to the Watchtower Society, which in fact was like paying rent for a building that they already owned, lock, stock and barrel; constructed and paid for by their own local funds and ownership was currently held by a board of trustees, being leading members of the local congregation. The local body of elders had no choice but to obey this latest instruction, order and directive from the Governing Body, but the secretary with an innocent, naïve smile on his face said, "at least we know that if times ever get tough and we cannot keep up with our monthly pledge then we know and feel reassured that the mother organization will not evict us." Little did he know!

Our researchers came across a case of a congregation on the south coast of England who stopped paying their monthly pledge (stealth tithe) to the branch office in London and the Watchtower Society took them to court and demanded an eviction order and for re-possession of the Kingdom Hall property, even though it had been built and paid for by the local brothers. Fortunately, in this case the court ruled in favor of the local congregation and against the greedy, ruthless and avaricious Watchtower Society. There are also other cases similar to this one in other countries and especially in the United States of America. No doubt this religion will create some other legal manipulative scheme of preventing this from ever happening again in the future. This incident of a breakaway congregation claiming ownership of their Kingdom Hall property paid for by themselves and actually winning the court case caused great consternation to the Watchtower Society financiers so they had to quickly create or devise, a new arrangement or scheme to prevent this from ever recurring again. Lo and behold, it did not take long for the leaders of this religion along with their shrewd, calculating legal advisors to introduce a new fool-proof arrangement to seize control of all of these valuable Kingdom Hall properties, now worth millions, that all local congregations were once again compelled to agree with this new theocratic arrangement, claimed to have been revealed to the Governing Body by the God's Holy Spirit.

In the latest update reported by the website JW Survey.org, it appears they have obtained leaked documents affirming that the Jehovah's Witness headquarters in the United Kingdom has orchestrated a systematic takeover bid of all Kingdom Hall properties located in England, Scotland and Wales. In a letter dated November 8, 2019, the London-based Kingdom Hall Trust announced that all UK congregations will dissolve their status as individual congregational charities and become branches of the KHT. The Kingdom Hall Trust (KHT) is a Jehovah's Witness Legal Corporation established in 1939 under instructions from Joseph Rutherford and Hayden Covington. From the archived records in the London Bethel, they were also assisted by the then corrupt British Branch Servant, Jesse Hemery, who served from 1901-1946. Hemery was eventually caught with his hand in the till and was excommunicated personally by Nathan Knorr, the 3rd President of the Watchtower Society in 1946.

This new corporation of 1939 was created under the registered name, London Company of Kingdom Witnesses. On June 30, 1978, it was officially registered as a charity in the UK. In 1994, the name was changed to the Kingdom Hall Trust. While the KHT was already engaged in the acquisition of property used by Jehovah's Witness church members, the latest directive proposes that all and every UK Congregation relinquish their individual charity status and operate under the blanket control of the single Kingdom Hall Trust charity, which in turn of course is conveniently owned and directly controlled by the Watchtower Society, Inc. We quote directly from JW Survey website: "Five documents were leaked, including a private letter to all elders, a separate letter to be read to congregations, and an FAQ document explaining the dissolution of the local congregation charities. Also included were the pre-formatted meeting minutes and congregation resolutions to be filled out, resolved, and returned to the KHT in London. According to the letter presented to individual congregations, the UK Charity Commission approved the merging of all UK congregations into the single Kingdom Hall Trust, with the premise that all congregations in the United Kingdom agree to these changes. While the Kingdom Hall Trust directors state that these changes are for purposes of simplification, the leaked documents suggest that permanent control of property and finances may be the true motivation. The November, 2019 letter to congregation members says: "However, because elders would no longer serve as trustees, your local donations would be administered by KHT as part of its general funds." This could mean that the Trustees (KHT) could decide to use your donations to support the Kingdom work elsewhere in the branch territory or throughout the world to meet the needs and requirements of the organization."

> The 2019 documents issued from London reveal much more than the mere transfer of Charity Commission responsibilities. They clearly state that individual congregations no longer own or control their own properties, many of which have been in operation for many years, Kingdom Halls built with private funds and labour provided by the local Witnesses. Aside from the necessary public filings, the Witnesses' handling of private donations is cloaked in secrecy, a fact which will not sit well with the Charity Commission of the UK, or the US-based Internal Revenue Service. The new policies may also not sit well with lifelong members of the Jehovah's Witness faith who spent decades backing their local congregations in a responsible manner. While most will no doubt support the transfer of property and finances to the JW headquarters, others may privately express misgivings. For this reason, it appears

that the Kingdom Hall Trust Corporation has instructed congregation elders to spin the merger edict in a positive light.

The letter to all of the Elders states: "We encourage the elders to speak positively of the proposal and help publishers understand the changes being proposed." These notable changes come amidst increasing scrutiny of Jehovah's Witnesses stemming from their controversial child abuse reporting policies. Significant financial judgments against the religion have fueled concerns worldwide. Whether the control and movement of these very large sums of money and assets now owned by Jehovah's Witnesses in a measure to minimize legal accountability, remains to be seen."

Our reporter also confirmed that this new ruling does not change in any way the original instruction given a couple of years ago that local congregations still have to pay rent being a monthly pledge or stealth tithe for the use of the property that they once owned, probably built by their own funds and hard work of voluntary labor, and has now been seized by the Headquarters of the Watchtower Society. Now that the Watchtower Society had underhandedly taken over ownership and control of the thousands of valuable local Kingdom Hall properties throughout the world and now own outright by their clever manipulation, what was their next plan?

They are in desperate need for more funds as the voluntary donations are shrinking by the month and their door-to-door sale of literature is now having to be given away to avoid having to charge and collect sales tax or VAT. With the guidance and creative advice of their manipulative legal, financial advisers and experts they have now come up with a scheme to consolidate local nearby congregations and then sell off their newly acquired surplus valuable properties, now being the unused and unneeded Kingdom Halls. Our reporter submitted the following information from *Watchtower Documents*:

> To underscore the reason for seizing ownership of all the local Kingdom Halls in many countries is that the Watchtower Society is now using this newly enforced financial scheme to sell off many of these newly acquired Kingdom Halls and then amalgamating local congregations to double up the using of

only one local place of worship for their meetings even if this involves extra expense of travelling greater distances for the local brothers to attend their Bible meetings, creating an extra financial burden on many.

According to our source, Jehovah's Witness congregations are merging and the redundant properties are being sold as part of a worldwide efficiency initiative that will free up additional funds for the church's so-called relief work in the U.S. and abroad; money that is desperately needed because in lieu of the offerings and tithes many other religious denominations receive. Remember that Jehovah's Witnesses currently receive only voluntary donations and pledges to help fund their missionary and relief work, which are now drying up rapidly. Also pointed out is that they are currently considering other schemes and methods of raising funds and are receiving advice from their Wall Street attorneys, therefore we have no idea what scheme (legal or illegal) they will introduce next as they once again are approaching desperation.

For example, in the USA, the very attractive Kingdom Hall on Applebutter Road in Pennsylvania was built only a few years ago and contains more than 7,300 square feet of space on two levels, one of which is an unfinished basement. According to information supplied, the property could easily be converted to a multitude of office or commercial uses including possibly a night club, strip club or entertainment center, in terms of local City zoning laws. A real estate listing for this newly marketed property now owned by the Watchtower Society (after its compulsory purchase from the local congregation) states: "features include dedicated parking for over 55 vehicles, two ADA (American Disabilities Act) restrooms, utility room, coat room, two viewing rooms and plenty of storage." The property was listed for $350,000 by commercial real estate agents in Allentown. The hall formerly housed the Hellertown congregation of Jehovah's Witnesses, which last year was closed down and became the Saucon Valley congregation and was merged with two other nearby congregations. Its members now meet at the much larger Emaus Avenue, Kingdom Hall (also now owned outright by the Watchtower Society since 2019 under their new manipulative scheme of compulsory purchase) in Salisbury Township. We have discovered that there is a compiled list of hundreds of Kingdom

Hall properties that are currently for sale or recently sold in the USA, totaling $20,574,699.00 worth of real estate, this is not counting the additional sales in other countries especially in Britain that will produce additional millions.

So, buildings once used and dedicated to the worship of Almighty God by the many sincere followers of Jehovah's Witnesses, will no doubt be increased in value through property sales, and thousands more local Kingdom Halls are now being placed on the open market to be sold in order to raise the now desperate funds required by this religious cult. Very few of these buildings will be purchased by other so-called Christian religions as places of worship owing to the fact that religion in general is on the decline in most countries of the world. These once proud buildings will end up being purchased and deployed for other worldly, mundane or commercial uses and possibly undesirable purposes by being converted into other uses without much concern by the shameless sellers, the now recently acquired new owners, the Watchtower Society. In Brazil it is reported in 2019 that there are now over 600 Kingdom Halls for sale there and in London, England, five top quality Kingdom Halls in South London, have now become Islamic Centers and Mosques. A recent report, still under investigation, reveals that as the London Bethel headquarters of the Watchtower Society in Mill Hill, North London, and related buildings that included an attached dedicated Kingdom Hall has been successfully sold to a Saudi Arabian company and the Kingdom Hall will now be converted into a Mosque.

One Kingdom Hall sold in Sedona, Arizona, USA, for $825,000.00 has been purchased by a new age religious organization that is based in spiritism and offers meta-physical courses under the leadership of a guru, plus also advertises a magical labyrinth, this labyrinth is also a yantra or living mandala, wherein one enters and experiences a sacred space dedicated to housing spirit and spiritual energies. How low can the Governing Body and their helpers go to get their hands on more cash? In addition, there are now hundreds of more Kingdom Halls now up for sale through-out the USA. However, this way of raising capital to help out with their cash flow problem must be fast coming to an end as the Watchtower Society continue to sell off the Kingdom Halls; the high value ones are nearly all now sold so they are left with a stock of unused Kingdom Halls at a much lower value, thus creating a shrinking supply of money.

> *Editor's Note*: A fellow researcher, Paul Grundy of JW Facts.org calculated that over $450 million dollars' worth of Watchtower property has been found listed for sale at online real estate websites between 2006 and 2020, comprising Kingdom Halls, Assembly Halls and Branch Offices. This figure is the value of only around 500 properties that have been found advertised online for sale during a 15-year period. Kingdom Halls are being sold in Britain, Australia and USA ranging from around $1 million at the higher end down to $100,000 in countries with lower property prices, such as Poland. A rough estimate of the total value of Kingdom Halls now owned outright by the Watchtower Society is over $US15 billion. The Watchtower Society, since its scheme of changing the ownership of Kingdom Halls from local congregations and their local board of trustees to Watchtower ownership they removed financial liabilities from some congregations, but by gaining direct control of a far greater value of their assets and properties, which has proved to be an act of financial wizardry. Whilst the above changes are financially obscure and possibly unknown to the average Jehovah's Witness, the follow-on affect is causing discontent. The transfer of Kingdom Hall ownership has been followed by the consolidation of congregations and sale of Kingdom Halls. This can be traumatizing for people that donated to and helped construct a Hall that Watchtower has subsequently sold and directed the congregation members to be split up and designated to another congregation meeting in a different Kingdom Hall often some distance away.

Based on an inside report from the New York headquarters of the Watchtower Society, they are now entering into a serious panic mode regarding the shrinking funds and the desperate need to realize their existing assets and somehow get their hands on more cash. We thought it expedient to include this report submitted by one of our reporters. He reviews the drastic steps taken to date by the Governing Body of this religion, their helpers and their financial wiz-kids in order to realize more income and funds to cover their dramatically increasing costs, especially now including the millions of dollars involved in the pending court cases for child molestation and sexual abuse.

It is reported, but would not be official confirmed by the Press Office of the Watchtower Society, that during the year of 2020 they have requested hundreds of their volunteer workers to return home or go and stay with relatives, as the demand for literature and other material used in their preaching work has dropped dramatically and, as a result, they do not have the finances to even feed or pay them their meager monthly allowance and support these once willing volunteers. One individual who suffered this lay-off told our reporter that he had been informed of this decision by his supervisors, as there was no work for them to do in the printing factory but not to worry and that it was only temporary until the Corona Virus pandemic was over, and he added that the Watchtower facilities at Patterson and Wallkill, New York is beginning to look like a ghost town. This sudden downturn in demand for literature is no doubt caused as a result of the severe restrictions enforced by the general rules laid down to prevent the spread of this deadly COVID-19 virus, and with regard to the Watchtower Society it could not have come at a worse time as they are already being seriously affected by a dramatic shrinkage of donations. Also, the door-to-door distribution of their literature is now at a standstill and as a dramatic attempt to create a demand for their literature they have come up with this temporary scheme of swamping the public with letters, emails, social media, telephone calls and posting the *Watchtower* magazine online for free if requested.

One of our research team has already received a spam email that was automatically dumped into his junk mail box. According to a release from the Watchtower Press Office the following information was provided:

> During the month of November 2020, Jehovah's Witnesses
> worldwide will be participating in a global campaign. You won't
> see them preaching door-to-door due to local health guidance
> related to the COVID-19 pandemic, but instead, sharing a
> special edition magazine online, through letter writing, and
> by making phone calls to their neighbors. During this global
> campaign that began Sunday, Nov. 1, the Witnesses are

distributing an electronic and print edition of their *Watchtower* magazine entitled "What Is God's Kingdom?" Jehovah's Witnesses feel the answer to that question has been of interest to people of many different faiths for centuries, so they will deliver this magazine free of charge to the general public, business owners, and government and court officials, according to the press release announcement. An electronic copy is currently available online in over 300 languages on the official website of Jehovah's Witnesses at JW.org under the library, magazine section.

The general consensus is that this latest campaign by the Watchtower Society launched in November 2020, within a few short weeks is already looking like a failed venture and business model by this religion and publishing empire in their attempt to give away their literature, and will no doubt be just another nail in their coffin. In their attempt to use the internet and other modern technology to promote this new campaign, by the use of social media, emails and private websites of their members, they have clearly underestimated the current power of the internet and the developing skills and responsibility of blocking information, advertising material and other spam. Most of the leading search engines, providers of social media and finely tuned computer servers are currently blocking this campaign as propaganda. In addition, modern telephone services quickly identify calls from unknown numbers and classify them as potential spam calls. From our inside source in the Watchtower headquarters, the IT guys who work under the direction of the Governing Body and their helpers are already scratching their heads as what to do next.

This sad situation has created a very difficult problem for this religion and many are beginning to wonder if it will ever recover. Of course, the entire world economy has been affected creating massive unemployment and closure of small businesses, also donations to non-profits has almost evaporated and the Watchtower Society is no exception. This additional shortage of funds has contributed to the dramatic downturn in the activities of the Watchtower Society apart from the sad unfortunate deaths of many members; this report was received from a fellow researcher: "As of the end of November 2020, a Watchtower announcement advised that over 7,000 Jehovah's

Witnesses had died from COVID-19, a tragedy for all those affected by such loss. It highlights God does not afford Jehovah's Witnesses protection, and that the Governing Body are not enlightened to protect their followers. They have simply directed them to abide by the guidance of local governments, which varies in effectiveness by country."

Also, most Kingdom Hall meetings are now a thing of the past until further notice, these religious meeting are curtailed along with other religions, also the door-to-door distribution of their literature is now almost at a standstill, so voluntary donations have now all but ceased, either from the public or the local publishers who normally donated the money to obtain this literature from their local Kingdom Hall that was then distributed free of charge. Currently there is an attempt to keep in contact with their followers by means of the internet, social media and communication software like Zoom, this of course is totally unsatisfactory but they have no choice under present circumstances. The Watchtower Society has been affected just as much as the rest of the world and this has created drastic changes by the various branch offices of this religion; their administration and religious meetings and of course the door-to-door distribution of their literature.

One additional serious issue that was leaked by the Treasury Department of the London Bethel of the Watchtower Society is that all local congregations are tied up with legal agreements as explained in other sections of this book, as they are obligated to pay a stealth tithe or rent for their local Kingdom Halls that they once owned, which is now owned outright by the Watchtower Society since the new financial arrangement was introduced in 2019. The dilemma now being faced, as many local congregations are now in default with their monthly pledge, does the Society that has the legal prerogative to ignore the problem or begin to start legal action for eviction as they have previously done. We are aware that this situation in Britain has also spilled over into most developed countries of the world, and a similar trend is being experienced especially in North America where the headquarters of this religion is located. As 2020 closes we are not sure if these defaults in payments to the Watchtower Society are just isolated cases or if they are increasing, so we will wait and see if tolerance and compassion prevails or will the desperate need for more money force their hand?

The following extract is from a press release that was sent out by the MTC International Foundation in early 2020 and some of the details and circumstances may have changed owing to the dramatic effect of the world-wide pandemic of the COVID-19 virus since March, 2020.

As a result of having to cease selling their literature from door-to-door and now being compelled to give it away for free in order to avoid sales tax, plus the expected voluntary donations for their literature did not materialize as expected and was a failed business decision. Owing to shrinking funds they then introduced the new scheme known as stealth tithing in which the local congregations were compelled to make compulsory monthly donations, also known as pledges and payments by many congregations are now in default because of worsening financial conditions in the world. This manipulative scheme has also not produced the desired increase in funds that they expected. The Governing Body and their helpers have already taken steps to cut back and close down many of their branch offices and as they owned the actual property that held these Branches, they sold off these commercial properties for reasonable profits, but this also did not cover their increasing insatiable demand for funds. Our inside contact in the accounts department at the London Bethel in the UK reported that many congregations are now in serious default with their monthly compulsory pledges because of increasing unemployment as a result of the recent pandemic COVID-19 sweeping the world. So, we are not sure at this stage how the Governing Body will handle all these cases of non-payment, will they sue or simply accept the de-facto situation, either way they are in big trouble.

They have now also sold off their nest egg, the numerous now lucrative properties that they owned in New York City, most of which were bought many years ago when property prices were very cheap. The Watchtower Society realized over one billion dollars from the sale of these properties but had to use a large slice to build their new luxury headquarters in Warwick, upstate New York, built on a disused toxic waste site. The remaining balance was put toward current expenses, but this amount also fell far short of the cash they desperately needed. So what was the next step?

They then sold the recently built luxury Branch Offices in London, England, in order to realize more funds, as that property, which they legally owned outright but had actually been built by the local British brothers by means of their voluntary labor and donations. This property had increased so much in value in a few short years that they took advantage of the rocketing real estate market in north London and used some of the proceeds to build a new British branch office on an old farm that was being used as a scrap yard for rotting vehicles and is rumored to have been donated to the Watchtower Society from a deceased estate of a loyal local member of this religion. The quality of these new branch office buildings being constructed on the new compound at Temple Farm in Kent, are of a much reduced standard when compared to the previous luxury premises in Mill Hill, North London, plus the recently built Headquarters complex in the USA, but the Watchtower Society did receive a green building award along with their other compound in Warwick, New York state, which is commendable. The very large balance of the proceeds from the sale of the Mill Hill properties in London was then sent to the head office in the USA, or more likely transferred to one of their secret offshore bank accounts. Once again this was still not enough to cover the insatiable demand for more funds.

Editor's Note: One is sometimes blinded with the distorted claims of the Watchtower Society in advancing the green building philosophy and environmental considerations, when building their new private compounds, such as the new British complex, but we must seriously remind ourselves that they are using funds that have been stolen or deceptively donated from their humble and very sincere members. Also these funds are being used to advance their cause and ambition as being the only true religion on earth and to provide exclusive isolated accommodation for their leaders and helpers who claim to have been appointed by Almighty God, which is another sign of a cult very similar to the Church of Scientology. If the current members are happy with this philosophy and conduct, plus continue giving their donations to the so-called Lord's Work, then so be it and then the future will decide. As we are reminded of the wise words of the Bible, "For everything there is a season, and a time for every matter under heaven." (Ecclesiastes 3:1-9)

Our readers will have noted that we have used the term compound when describing these two major building projects built by the Watchtower Society on Temple Farm in England and the Warwick project in New York State, and there is a specific reason for this. One of the basic definitions of the word compound is the following, "a compound is an enclosed area of land that is used for a particular purpose." However, it also brings up a more serious subtle underlying meaning. One of our researchers is preparing the thesis for his PhD at Cambridge University, England, and extensively researched this subject of a religious compound and has graciously allowed us to use some of his valuable material, which our readers will find to be both fascinating and disturbing. We have of course already mentioned the 3,000-acre religious compound constructed by the cult, Peoples Temple under the control of Jim Jones at Jonestown in Guyana in Chapter One of this book. Also mentioned is the cult called The Branch Davidians and their religious compound constructed in Waco, Texas in the USA, by their cult leader David Koresh.

One of the clear signs of a cult as mentioned in the introduction of this book is to isolate themselves from the urban community, and although the Watchtower Society tries to justify selling all their properties in densely populated New York and London as they were becoming too difficult to manage as the various facilities were too spread out in these cities. The building of these two new religious compounds perfectly match their desire to be isolated as they are constructed in outlying abandoned rural areas with a very small population.

We include this extract from the notes of one of our researchers and contributor from Cambridge, England. This quotation taken from the notes of the webpage of *Online Psychology Degree Guide* and reveals an interesting observation. Both terrifying and utterly fascinating, cults have a tendency to capture the attention of just about everyone. Questions abound: Where do these people come from? What are they really doing inside those secluded compounds? Most interesting, perhaps, are the psychological components of cult life, questions such as: Who in the world would fall for that? Why is the desire for isolation so important? In an effort to answer these questions and more, we've listed various things to know related to the psychology of cults.

Quotation from Cambridge University:

What is the primary purpose of constructing a religious compound? Historically cults have always been with us and they continue to be a part of the world today. The word cult can be broadly defined as formal religious veneration, a system of religious beliefs and its body of adherents. It also refers to a religion regarded as unorthodox or spurious, great devotion to a person or idea as well as persons united by devotion or allegiance to an artistic or intellectual movement or figure. American history is particularly rife with religious groups that can be seen as cults, such as the devoted followers of Mary Baker Eddy, the founder of Christian Science, or the Mormons being united through their devotion to Joseph Smith. Plus the Watchtower Society also known as Jehovah's Witnesses and their recent trend to isolate themselves from urban communities and their leaders, the Governing Body, constructing isolated private compounds to undertake their work of directing and controlling their subjective followers. All of these religious groups were at one time also regarded by many as "unorthodox or spurious".

I include this extract from an article by Tara Isabella Burton who writes about religion and culture and her work has appeared in *National Geographic, The Wall Street Journal* and *The Atlantic,* among others. She is a Clarendon Scholar at Trinity College, Oxford, working on a doctorate in theology. "Cults, generally speaking, are a lot like pornography: you know them when you see them. It would be hard to avoid the label on encountering (as I did, carrying out field work last year) 20 people toiling unpaid on a Christian farming compound in rural Wisconsin – people who venerated their leader as the closest thing to God's representative on Earth. Of course, they argued vehemently that they were not a cult. Ditto for the 2,000-member church I visited outside Nashville, whose parishioners had been convinced by an ostensibly Christian diet programme to sell their houses and move to the one square mile of the New Jerusalem promised by their charismatic church leader. Here they could eat – and live – in accordance with God and their leader's commands. It's easy enough, as an outsider, to say, instinctively: yes, this is a cult."

An equal and no less fervent network of what became known as counter-cult activists emerged among Christians who opposed cults on theological grounds, and who were as worried about the state of adherent's souls as of their psyches. The Baptist pastor Walter Ralston Martin was sufficiently disturbed by the proliferation of religious pluralism in the US to write, *The Kingdom of the Cults* (1965), which delineated in detail the theologies of those religious movements that Martin identified as toxic, and provided Biblical avenues for the enterprising mainstream Christian minister to oppose them. With more than half a million copies sold, it was one of the top-selling spiritual books of the era. Writing the history of cults in the US, therefore, is also writing the history of a discourse of fear: of the unknown, of the decline in mainstream institutions.

The construction and building today of private religious compounds is similar to what was known as a hermitage. A hermitage can either be a place where a hermit lives in seclusion from the world, or a building or settlement where a person or a group of people lived religiously, in seclusion and separate from urban communities. When included in the name of continental European properties or churches, any meaning is often imprecise, and may refer to some distant period of the history of what is today a property that is either a normal parish church, or ceased to have any religious function some time ago. Secondary churches or establishments run from a monastery were often called hermitages. In the 18th century, some owners of English country houses equipped their gardens with a hermitage, sometimes a Gothic ruin, but sometimes, as at Painshill Park, a romantic hut which a hermit was recruited to occupy. The so-called Ermita de San Pelayo y San Isidoro is the ruins of a Romanesque church from Ávila, Spain, that eventually ended several hundred miles away, as a garden feature in the Buen Retiro Park in Madrid.

Another example of cults and the building of private compounds to house their leaders is the case of the cult called The Branch Davidians and their religious compound constructed in Waco, Texas in the USA by their cult leader David Koresh.

The Branch Davidian compound built in 1950s, courtesy of the FBI,
University of Cambridge and Creative Commons

Mount Carmel Center near Wako, Texas, engulfed in flames on April 19, 1993,
courtesy of the FBI, University of Cambridge and Creative Commons

This was one of the most terrible and horrific experiences
related to a religious compound ever recorded and created

great controversy. The Branch Davidians were founded by
Ben Roden in 1959 as an offshoot of the Davidian Seventh-
Day Adventist Church, which had been established by Victor
Houteff several decades earlier. Houteff's group eventually
moved to a farm some 10 miles east of Waco, Texas, but by
1962 Roden and his followers had taken possession of the
settlement, which was known as Mt. Carmel. There the Branch
Davidians lived a simple life, preparing for the imminent
return of Jesus. However, in the mid-1980s the group became
embroiled in a power struggle, and by the end of the decade
Vernon Howell (later called David Koresh) had become head
of the Mt. Carmel community. He soon began taking spiritual
wives, several of whom were reportedly as young as 11 years old.
Allegations of child abuse and Koresh's launch of a retail gun
business attracted the attention of legal authorities. Believing
that the group was illegally stockpiling weapons, the U.S.
Bureau of Alcohol, Tobacco and Firearms (ATF) obtained
both an arrest warrant for Koresh and a search warrant for the
compound. On February 28, 1993, more than 70 ATF agents
raided the complex. Gunfire erupted – though it is uncertain
who fired first – and during the two-hour battle, four federal
agents were killed and more than a dozen injured. In addition,
six Davidians reportedly died. Nearly 900 law-enforcement
officials subsequently descended on the compound,
including FBI hostage negotiators.

During phone calls, Koresh engaged in Bible babble and threatened
violence, though he stated that neither he nor his followers were
suicidal. Partly in exchange for various supplies – including milk that
was delivered in cartons with listening devices – Koresh allowed more
than 30 followers to leave. However, it was thought that some 100
remained in the compound. As talks stalled – at one point Koresh
said that he would surrender if one of his sermons was broadcast on
national radio, but then failed to do so when it aired – agents tried
various strategies, including turning off the compound's electricity,
playing Tibetan chants over loudspeakers, and shining spotlights
on the complex to disrupt sleep. Convinced that Koresh would not
surrender, U.S. Attorney General Janet Reno gave permission for
the FBI to raid the compound with disastrous results illustrated in the
photo above.

***

Returning to our account regarding the desperate need for more funds by the Watchtower Society, the next step that was considered, as pointed out by the financial advisers to the Governing Body and their helpers was that they were actually sitting on an untapped gold mine, being the local Kingdom Halls of Jehovah's Witnesses, most of which were currently owned by the more than 100,000 individual congregations throughout the world. It was the traditional method that local Kingdom Halls were built by the local brothers by means of their own donations, volunteer labor, plus sometimes small secured bank or personal loans and the ownership of the building was held by a local board of trustees made up of leading members of each individual congregation. The Governing Body was advised by their financial gurus that if only there was a way that the ownership of these thousands of Kingdom Halls, which must be valued in the millions, could somehow be transferred to the Head Office of the Watchtower Society, they would be home and dry.

The scheme that was then enforced was that each congregation was to dissolve their local board of trustees and transfer these properties to a central board of trustees, which in turn was owned and controlled by the Watchtower Society itself. It is one thing taking over ownership of a property, but was of no use except to facilitate as collateral, maybe for further equity loans, which would be impossible especially in view of the financial status and condition of the Watchtower Society. Inc., plus all the additional pending legal cases in the pipeline. Also, it was a known fact that because of the increasing public knowledge of the dire straits of their financial headaches; ongoing problems and downsizing, plus the rapidly increasing legal cases pending against them for sexual and child abuse, the banking institutions viewed the Watchtower Society under the category, very high risk and now labeled them as anathema. So this underhanded scheme was followed up with stage two of their plans by making the decision to close down many congregations and amalgamate them with other nearby congregations thus freeing up surplus Kingdom Hall buildings and property. In turn, these now vacant properties could then be placed on the open market for sale and thus release further funds to pour into their bottomless bucket. As already pointed out in this report, this scheme has already been successfully employed and the first Kingdom Halls are now for sale or have been sold, but as this type of building would only attract a certain limited market so it would be truly a buyer's market only. So it remains to be seen if this last phase of these attempts to raise the desperately needed funds will be a success or not.

What the Governing Body of the Watchtower Society must have now come to realize that they have now used about every trick in the book to raise these desperately needed funds and there really is now no other source of funding they can turn too, thus the reason why they are now in panic mode. They must also now be fully aware of what their founder, Charles Russell foretold over one hundred years ago, as this self-fulfilling prophesy is now clearly taking place. As early as the second issue of the *Watchtower*, in August 1879, Brother Russell stated: "*Zion's Watch Tower* has, we believe, JEHOVAH for its backer, and while this is the case it will never, ever neither beg nor petition men for support. When He who says: "All the gold and silver of the mountains are mine", fails to provide the necessary funds, we will understand it to be time to suspend the publication." Consistent with that scripture, there is no begging for money in the literature of Jehovah's Witnesses. (Watchtower publication, *Jehovah's Witnesses Proclaimers of God's Kingdom*, Chap. 21, p. 340.)

Charles Taze Russell refused to imitate the churches of Christendom. He wrote: "It is our judgment that money raised by the various begging devices in the name of our Lord is offensive, unacceptable to him, and does not bring his blessing either upon the givers or the work accomplished." We once again repeat the prophetic words of the founder of this religion, "When God fails to provide the necessary funds we will understand it to be time to suspend the publication of the Watchtower magazine." Will the current leaders of this religion accept this stark fact and reality or continue to bury their heads in the sand and wallow in self-pity?

A typical modest Kingdom Hall in England, paid for and owned by the local congregation, courtesy of the MTC International Foundation and *Coventry Evening Telegraph*©

When the secretary of the local congregation in England was discussing with our reporter that the Watchtower Society would never evict the local congregation from their Kingdom Hall if they ever defaulted in their monthly pledge, he used the term mother organization as being synonymous with the Watchtower Society and the Governing Body. In further explanation of the term mother organization frequently used by Jehovah's Witnesses we once again quote from the official Watchtower magazine in the article "Show Respect for Jehovah's Organization" that appeared in their 1 May, 1957 issue and included this quote under the sub-heading, Identifying the Mother Organization. Remember the *Watchtower* magazine is claimed to be the official channel between God and Jehovah's Witnesses world wide and they are expected to accept this information as divine revelation through the Governing Body, the faithful and discreet slave (Matthew 24:45) and to obey and believe everything they read without question. The following is a direct quote from the 1957 *Watchtower* article that used the theme scripture of Proverbs 6:20, "My son, keep your father's commandment, and forsake not your mother's teaching. For the commandment is a lamp and the teaching a light, and the reproofs of discipline are the way of life".

According to the *Watchtower* article:

> If we are to walk in the light of truth we must recognize not only Jehovah God as our Father but his organization as our mother. This foretells the birth of more children, but this time on earth. This occurred in 1919. The land that is born is the restored condition on earth of Jehovah's anointed remnant in a New World society, a condition free for Jehovah's worship and for organized service, theocratically. The new nation is the remnant of spiritual Israel delivered from Babylon and now under the established newborn Kingdom. Those of this nation inhabit the theocratic land on earth, the delivered, restored condition of the remnant of Christ's joint heirs. But since these children of Zion above have a heavenly destiny to reign with Christ, they also become a part of the universal organization that is God's wife, and will, with Christ, form the capital city of that organization. So God's woman Zion or Jerusalem above is his universal organization, with one hundred and forty-four thousand members. Being so closely associated with the mother organization, Christ's bride would certainly resemble her mother in all respects, as would even those Christians still on earth in the flesh who are engaged to be married to Christ. These would serve as her representatives and would therefore be easily recognizable by their conformity to God's requirements for his visible channel of communication.

The view in the MM Outreach website, whose sole purpose seeks to help people find Jesus by exposing the false doctrine of the cults and aberrant movements, adroitly stated regarding this controversial article and is worth considering.

> Truly, the majority of Jehovah's Witnesses, no matter how duped in other ways, cannot really believe that Jehovah's wife

includes the 144,000, who are also children of this same wife! It's a perversion of what is natural, a breaking of all God's laws on marriage. The whole concept is in violation of God's plain statements on the sanctity of marriage, of the God-given rules regarding fathers, mothers, wives, and children. Now we come to the crux of the matter, under the subheading, "Identifying the Mother Organization". To my surprise, they begin by saying, "The real mother of Christians is not and cannot be an earthly organization". They quoted Galatians 4:26, "The Jerusalem above is free, and she is our mother". Jumping to Isaiah 54:5, 6, (and using their ever-present dots to remove the parts that don't fit) they said: "Thy Maker is thy husband; Jehovah of hosts is his name; and the Holy One of Israel is thy Redeemer...For Jehovah hath called thee as a wife forsaken and grieved in spirit." In this way Paul identifies Jehovah's wife as His invisible universal organization, the mother of Christ and of his joint heirs".

This description of the term Mother Organization and its associated explanation by the Governing Body of the Watchtower Society will no doubt appear to most of our readers as being one of the weirdest and extreme, fanatical descriptions of the relationship of Jesus Christ; his heavenly father Yahweh, plus the angelic heavenly realm that they will ever read. This article in the *Watchtower* magazine was written by someone, and claiming to represent Almighty God, he used the most warped, exaggerated, hyperbolic imagination ever recorded, and one of our experienced researchers who interviewed a person who had spent time working in the Writing Department of the Watchtower Society for many years claims that the style of writing of that article could have come from no other person than the guru, prophet and seer of the Watchtower Society at the time, the eccentric, peculiar, mentally unbalanced and deranged Fredrick Franz who was head of the Writing Department, who was also the ghost writer for most of Joseph Rutherford's books, articles and lectures and later Franz became the 4th President of the Watchtower Society. Also stated in that same Watchtower article the following is noted, which perhaps is one of the most blasphemous statements ever made by this religion, to try and place a man-made religious earthly organization on the same level as our heavenly Divine Creator, Almighty God. "The Society is identified as our mother and Jehovah God as our Father. If we are to walk in the light of truth we must recognize not only Jehovah God as our Father but his organization as our mother...Today, also, God requires and exacts from his children obedience honor and respect. These must be rendered, not only to the living God himself, but to his wifely organization as well" (*Watchtower*, May 1, 1957, p. 274).

Our research team seriously considered if the Watchtower Society and the Mormon Church have private or secret connections, as there are so many similarities? Or is it just the American way of operating a successful lucrative religious movement? Are they in collusion, as the Mormons have general conference twice a year where the prophet, apostles and quorum of the seventy give televised addresses to the worldwide members? In recent years the annual general meeting of the Watchtower Society, including talks by Governing Body members, has been televised for Jehovah's Witnesses worldwide. On the other hand, the Witnesses don't copy the Mormons in supporting or encouraging education, and they could sure learn a great deal about raising money. Our researcher continued.

> I knew the characters, the history, the events, the Joseph Smith stories, the religion's history, etc., and I long suspected even then that the Watchtower Society has been copying certain things from the LDS church. For example, the first thing I noticed was when the Tuesday night book study was dropped by the Watchtower Society because it encouraged private discussions of current doctrine, trends plus speculations, in other words it was not so easily controlled by the masters and then family worship evening was started. The Mormons have been doing Home Family Evening for decades before the JWs started this feature. The Mormons also had a slick, brilliant website with all their books and resources professionally displayed on there. Next thing you know, JW.Org comes along and their setup is almost identical.

However, with the increasing threat of legal cases now pending and possibly now involving billions of dollars in damages, especially regarding child and sexual abuse being awarded against the Watchtower Society, they have no doubt taken specialized legal advice on how to protect their massive wealth. The Watchtower Society is registered as a non-profit organization and is therefore tax exempt. But they still have billions of dollars in assets, plus still receive additional millions in tax free donations each year from its loyal members; albeit shrinking, so it is now reported that they are putting their money under dozens of different names registered in tax-free off-shore countries, known as post-box firms, such as Panama and Cayman Islands; much like the big celebrities and corrupt politicians have been doing to avoid paying taxes on their wealth. The Watchtower Society could be involved in money laundering (a criminal act), because Raymond Franz, previous member of the Governing Body, hinted in Crisis of Conscience that some currency transactions, in his opinion were not legal. Of course, money laundering seems to be easy these days, but even major world banks and their officials and crony, corrupt politicians, usually eventually getting caught, or maybe not if they are personal friends of the United States President and receiving a pardon, so perhaps this trap will also expose the Watchtower Society and their hidden billions.

In the United States, The Watchtower Bible and Tract Society listed the book value of its assets as $1,451,217,000.00 on its 2015, IRS Form 990-T. This places the Jehovah's Witnesses into the same billion dollars plus cult status as the Church of Scientology. But in view of the secret Panama Leak papers, which were leaked out during 2008, it appears that the Watchtower has many more cash assets in overseas accounts. The $1.45 billion listed on the Watchtower's 2015, 990-T form is only the money we know about in the USA. Who knows how much the Watchtower Society has hidden away since it began doing business in 1884? But in view of the secret Panama Papers, the Offshore Leaks, the Bahamas Leaks and the Paradise Papers investigations, which were leaked out during 2016, it appears that the Watchtower Society has many more cash assets in overseas accounts. The $1.45 billion listed on the Watchtower's 2015 990-T is the only money we know about, based on the records of the official Internal Revenue Service (IRS) of the USA.

This quote by a fellow researcher into the Watchtower Society, a writer for the Scientology Money Project also commented and confirms the above: "It is worth noting that on Line H of these 990-T's the Watch Tower Bible and Tract Society lists its primary unrelated business activity as Investment Activities. So, while the rank-and-file Witnesses are striving to please Jehovah, the big boys at the top have sold over $700 million in prime real estate and plowed that cash into undisclosed investment activities."

The ICIJ (The International Consortium of Investigative Journalists) a non-profit group, of which the MTC International Foundation is a supporter, their database contains information on more than 785,000 offshore entities that are part of the Panama Papers, the Offshore Leaks, the Bahamas Leaks and the Paradise Papers investigations. The data covers nearly 80 years up to 2016 and links to people and companies in more than 200 countries and territories. The secret registry includes names of many well-known Watchtower officials who stupidly, foolishly and some unfortunately naively allowed their names to be used as vehicles of fraud and money laundering, under the guise of service to the Lord. Most of their names will not be revealed in this book out of respect for the past friendship that many of these vulnerable, very sincere Christian (although sadly misled) men who had connections with some of the leading members of our research team. But we now know of at least three of these innocents have since resigned their official position within the Watchtower ranks for personal reasons or more likely in view of their pending exposure in the forthcoming leaked papers. Others are deceased or have committed suicide.

This extract from a report by ICIJ (The International Consortium of Investigative Journalists) records:

> The U.K. government measure, which will force overseas territories to make public the owners (or individuals) of all their registered companies by the end of 2020, was set out in a proposed amendment to a government anti-money laundering bill, which is currently before parliament. The point is made eloquently but passively by the Panama and Paradise papers: it is only by openness and scrutiny – by allowing charities, NGOs and the media to join up the dots – that we can expose this dirty money and the people standing behind it, and closed registers do not begin to allow us to do that.

On March 9, 2016, employees of Mossack Fonseca, a Panamanian law firm that for decades had kept the financial secrets of global celebrities, oligarchs and criminals, including many so-called non-profit groups, made a stomach-churning discovery. Someone had copied huge amounts of data from its computers. Emails, contracts, banking statements – 11.5 million documents of the firm's most sensitive client records, a staggering 2.6 terabytes of data – had been taken. Included in this leaked information was this extract of the International Bible Students Association (the British equivalent to the Watchtower Society in America). Our researcher revealed the following extract from these secret financial records that have been used to hide financial assets off-shore, either to avoid paying taxes or shielding this cash from being seized in compensation for fines and court awards, as for example the numerous child and sexual abuse cases now being faced by the Watchtower Society. The report by The International Consortium of Investigative Journalists (ICIJ) continues:

INTERNATIONAL BIBLE STUDENTS ASSOCIATION
Connected to one address. Connected to six officers.
Incorporated: 11-DEC-1986. Registered in: Barbados Linked countries: United Kingdom Data from: Paradise Papers - Barbados corporate registry Barbados corporate registry data is current through 2016
CONNECTIONS

Officer	Role	From To Data
From		
ANDREWS JOHN STUART	Director -Paradise Papers -	
Barbados corporate registry		
BELL PETER PHILIP	Director - Paradise Papers -	
Barbados corporate registry		
DUTTON JOHN DENNIS	Director - Paradise Papers -	
Barbados corporate registry		
HARDY STEPHEN ALBERT	Director - Paradise Papers -	
Barbados corporate registry		
PAPPS STEPHEN	Director - Paradise Papers -	

Barbados corporate registry
WYNN JOHN ALFRED Director - Paradise Papers - Barbados corporate registry Address Data From
IBSA HOUSE, THE RIDGEWAY, LONDON, NW7 1RP, ENGLAND

***

To support the power of the master, the Governing Body in 2009 disclosed in *The Watchtower* and indicated that any future dissemination of any new spiritual light is the responsibility of only a limited number of the slave class, asking: "Are all these anointed ones throughout the earth part of a global network that is somehow involved in revealing new spiritual truths from God? No!"

In 2010 the Watchtower Society also said that deep truths were discerned by responsible representatives of the faithful and discreet slave class at the group headquarters in America, and then considered by the entire Governing Body (eleven men at that time, also who all conveniently lived in America) before making doctrinal decisions. In August, 2011, the Governing Body even cast doubt on other member's claims of being anointed as members of this so-called heavenly class as the number partaking of the bread and wine was increasing dramatically each year causing some confusion. They stated "A number of factors – including past religious beliefs or even mental or emotional imbalance – might cause some to assume mistakenly that they have the heavenly calling." The Governing Body also stated that "we have no way of knowing the exact number of anointed ones on earth; nor do we need to know" and that it "does not maintain a global network of anointed ones." At the 2012 Annual Meeting of the Watchtower Society, the faithful and discreet slave mentioned in the Bible book of Matthew was redefined as referring to the Governing Body only, and the terms are now synonymous. It is also stated in black and white that the Governing Body (eight men in 2019) are the only ones on earth today who hold the divine right to interpret the Bible. "All who want to understand the Bible should appreciate that the greatly diversified wisdom of God can become known only through Jehovah's channel of communication, the faithful and discreet slave." (*Watchtower*, Oct. 1, 1994, p. 8.)

Regarding not knowing the exact number of those claiming to be members of the so-called remnant of the anointed little flock of 144,000, this is a somewhat deliberate misleading statement by the Governing Body regarding not knowing the number of partakers of the bread and wine, indicating they are of this so-called anointed class. Each time the annual Memorial was celebrated, the attending Elders of each congregation were instructed to make a secret count of those who partook of the bread and wine and this figure was then passed along to the Governing Body, otherwise how would they have known that the figure was increasing or decreasing year by year and causing such great concern. It is obvious to a reasoning mind that the Governing Body must keep some sort of record, otherwise how did they know that the number of partakers still keeps rising dramatically year after year. To avoid embarrassment and diffuse the many questions being regularly asked regarding this number of 144,000 being literal or symbolic and this exclusive group are the only ones allowed into heaven when they die, and the fact that the number claiming to be of the remnant or remainder of this exclusive group kept increasing by the year, they ceased making the figure public knowledge some years ago.

Fellow researcher based in Australia, Paul Grundy, expressed on his website, JW Facts:

This means long standing Witnesses who have been in the organization for some time have begun to reject the doctrine of a paradise earth. Instead, as time passes by and Jehovah's Witnesses' ever-imminent Armageddon is delaying from generation to generation, it is likely that more and more Jehovah's Witnesses are considering the possibility that paradise is really in heaven. This is a view that almost all other Christian denominations hold. It's likely that some Jehovah's Witnesses do not want to leave the religion for various personal reasons. Instead, they have taken the choice to remain as a Jehovah's Witness but have embraced the biblical teaching that paradise is actually in heaven.

The correct interpretation and use of the word paradise in the Bible has been disputed and discussed by many Bible students, therefore in order to assist our readers some meaningful research was supplied by a leading Bible scholar, plus the enlightening private, archived notes of the late Edward Dunlap, one time senior lecturer at the Watchtower Bible School of Gilead and arguably one of the world's leading students of the Bible. Edward Dunlap was a most knowledgeable and courageous Bible student and later he was excommunicated as an apostate by the Governing Body of the Watchtower Society simply because Edward had genuinely and sincerely exposed many of the hypocritical and deliberate misinterpretations of the Holy Scriptures by this religion, in

tion, tion

order to dupe their followers into believing certain Bible text that were used to support their false doctrines and teachings. To clarify; the word paradise is used three times in the New Testament (Greek Scriptures) at Luke 23:43; 2 Corinthians 12:4 and Revelation 2:7, and on each occasion implies a heavenly location. In addition, the Old Testament (Hebrew Scriptures) in the book of Genesis refers to the Garden of Eden as paradise, being the original home of mankind on earth after the creation of Adam and Eve in the Middle East, but is now no longer in existence. Please read the Special Report No.6 in the Appendix for more information that includes some extracts from the notes of Edward Dunlap.

***

Prior to 1971, the various named Watchtower Society legally appointed directors were informally identified as members of the Governing Body. Jehovah's Witnesses publications began capitalizing Governing Body as a proper noun in 1971; *The Watchtower* that year also announced, "The present Governing Body comprises eleven anointed witnesses (all men) of Jehovah." Over the years this number of men has fluctuated as a result of deaths; resignations; two of these individual resignations, mainly because of accusations that they were homosexuals or pedophiles, neither of these two men, Ewart Chitty and Leo Greenlees was ever excommunicated and they were simply re-assigned or closeted away. Plus a few new members have been added over the years (personally called by God they claim) to be replacements for previously sinful members of the anointed ones and members of the Governing Body.

There has never in modern times ever been a woman on the Governing Body of the Watchtower Society, not since Maria Russell (1850-1938) the wife of Charles Russell (1st President) served as a director of the Watchtower Society and she served as its secretary and treasurer for some years (1879-1897). She also was a regular contributor to the columns of *Zion's Watch Tower* and for a time was an associate editor of the journal. The Watchtower Society, along with the Catholic Church, the Mormons and along with some other conservative, evangelical religious sects disqualify all women from holding positions of authority simply because of their sex (not brains, skills, intelligence, intuition, devotion or spirituality, which has often excelled over many male leaders of these religions). And this is based on the personal interpretation of the Bible by these religions recorded in 1 Timothy 2:12. "I do not permit a woman to teach or to assume authority over a man; she must be quiet."

Editor's Note: This is another difficult Biblical passage to interpret, and there are many opinions about its appropriate meaning and application. In the middle of the passage, however, it is one verse that has been referenced throughout the history of Christendom and used as a clear mandate to restrict women from teaching, adding their valued point of view or opinion, leading, or even speaking during worship gatherings. Based on the feedback from numerous very intelligent female members of the Jehovah's Witnesses that we interviewed, many sisters have chafed and felt personally humiliated and insulted by this enforced restriction placed upon them by the all-male Governing Body.

For readers who wish to obtain more information on this religion or cult we recommend reading the informative book by this former member of the Governing Body of the Watchtower Society, the late Raymond Franz (1922 - 2010), who was excommunicated from this religion after he had been a sincere dedicated Christian, avid student of the Bible and a member for most of his life. His *Crisis of Conscience* is a biographical narrative, written in 1983, three years after his expulsion from the Jehovah's Witnesses religion. In 1965 Franz became a member of the religions headquarters staff in Brooklyn, New York, where he was assigned to help in essential research and to edit the new Bible encyclopedia, *Aid to Bible Understanding*. In 1971 Raymond was appointed as a member of the religion's Governing Body. He left the Governing Body in 1980 after a high-level inquiry was launched into allegations that several headquarters staff, including Raymond Franz, was spreading wrong teachings.

This brilliant *Aid to Bible Understanding* was published under the name of the Watchtower Society, but it later became public knowledge in 1983 that in fact it was prepared under the editorship of Raymond Franz. Raymond had worked under the clear instructions of the combined Governing Body that the material was to be based purely on known facts and accurate research, including outside sources and not necessarily influenced by any current Biblical interpretations that appeared in the Watchtower publications over the years. As a result of the expulsion of Franz, the Governing Body immediately withdrew this publication, but a few years later published a replacement book in two volumes named Insight on the Scriptures, which had been expanded with the addition of many more maps and illustrations. These two volumes originally released in 1988 have been amended and revised on several occasions the latest being 26 November, 2018. Ironically this new publication still retained much of the excellent research material from the previous; now withdrawn book, Aid to Bible Understanding, prepared by the dedication and hard work of sincere Bible students under the supervision of Raymond Franz, who were now all considered as apostates and Raymond and his fellow Bible researchers had by this time been excommunicated from the Watchtower Society.

Aid to Bible Understanding was released by the Watchtower Society, and this 1,696-page volume was circulated, distributed and was then purchased by the millions of members of this religion, in the English language. The book had to be translated into other languages, such as Spanish, French and German, but this created some serious issues after it was withdrawn in 1983. Our researcher, who had a personal friend who was in a senior position in the German Bethel of the Watchtower Society, explained that after taking many months in translating this book and planning to release it in five or six separate, smaller volumes to allow the German Witnesses to have immediate access to this brilliant material, and who had willingly and sincerely purchased the first volume of this book (letters A to E), but were suddenly told to dump it in the garbage, as there would be no more volumes being released. The official in the German Bethel was angry as hell, in the words of Phillip Rees, who managed the printing department and was a senior member of the London Bethel. What a waste, and also a clear indication of the extreme powers of the ruling Governing Body over their slave like followers and the drastic, destructive decisions they make to maintain their powerful control as masters.

The member of our research team reported that her unnamed source had shown her a copy of a letter from the Governing Body dated 1980 to all congregations, with this extract, "We are saddened to report at this time that five members of the Bethel family, and a few others in the New York city area have recently been disfellowshipped. There has been some apostasy against the organization and the promoting of sectarian divisions in some of the congregations of God's people." The Watchtower Society has never retracted or denied the contents of *Crisis of Conscience,* but they have secretly instructed congregation leaders that if any member has a copy of this book, they are committing an act of apostasy and must be dwelt with accordingly. For the enlightenment of our many readers, our researcher provided this information from *Wikipedia* and her confidential source referred to some extracts, which could be of interest. Italics in the following quote are by the editor.

> *Crisis of Conscience* provided an abject view of the Watchtower Society leadership and its requirements of its members, plus it gave Franz's perspective on failed expectations among the Witness community that Armageddon would take place in 1975 (as claimed for many years as a defining date by the organization and innocently believed by the majority of the religious members, resulting in many disillusioned members making the most extreme detrimental decisions regarding their private life style and future plans, and eventually leading to many of them quitting the religion). The book also expressed the private views of Raymond Franz, based on his research regarding fundamental Witness teachings, especially on the significance of the year 1914 (again another date that has been promoted since 1879 with definitions as to its significance being changed many times over the years, but still promoted in their literature as an absolute date) and the continued expectations of Armageddon (the end of the world) coming soon. His expulsion was reported by Time magazine in February 1982.

Time stated:

> For 40 years Raymond Franz devoted his whole being to the Jehovah's Witnesses. The religion responded by raising him to the very top, as a member of its worldwide Governing Body. But it was a difficult period for the leadership. In 1975 the sect

faced a debacle: the present world did not vanish as Witness publications had all but guaranteed. In a faith in which doubt is not tolerated, questions inevitably arose in the minds of some believers.

A leading member of the current Governing Body of the Watchtower Society is on record as facetiously saying:

> Now it's true that the Faithful Slave, at times, has had wrong expectations throughout the decades. See, sometimes they've had wrong expectations, for example 1975. Many responsible ones at headquarters, they thought maybe, maybe Jehovah would bring the 1,000-year reign to begin in that year, but of course it didn't happen did it. They have learned from their mistakes that you really can't be specific about Jehovah's day.

The Watchtower Society has often boldly made claims in their literature as being factual when in reality these claims have been erroneous and nothing more than blatant lies. For example, "If you are a young person, you also need to face the fact that you will never grow old in this present system of things." *Awake!* May 22, 1969, p. 15 (underlining is ours). This is only one of the many examples that we uncovered in our research of the Watchtower Society literature.

Raymond Franz claimed that he declined repeated requests over the next two years for further media interviews about the workings and insight of the Watchtower Society, but in 1983 he decided to end his silence after a number of Watchtower articles criticized the motives, character and conduct of both current and former Witnesses who conscientiously disagreed with the organization and its interpretation of certain scriptures. One article described these sincere dissidents as being like ... Satan, independent, faultfinding, stubborn, reviling, haughty, apostate and lawless. Franz also claimed that many Jehovah's Witnesses who choose to leave because they cannot honestly agree with all the organization's teachings or policies and are subsequently disfellowshipped, or formally expelled, and shunned as apostates. He wrote that he sincerely hoped his book might prompt members of Jehovah's Witnesses to consider the conscientious stand of defectors with a more open mind. He hoped that a discussion of deliberations and decisions of the Governing Body during his term would illustrate fundamental problems and serious issues within the organization: "They demonstrate the extremes to which loyalty to an organization can lead, how it is that basically kind, well-intentioned persons can be led to make decisions and take actions that are both unkind and unjust, even cruel."

Our researcher came across this article in *The Watchtower*, August 15, 1981, p. 25:

> From time to time, there have arisen from among the ranks of Jehovah's people those who, like the original Satan, have adopted an independent, faultfinding attitude. They do not want to serve shoulder to shoulder with the worldwide brotherhood. (Compare Ephesians 2:19-22.) Rather, they present a stubborn shoulder to Jehovah's word. (Zech. 7:11, 12) Reviling the pattern of the pure language that Jehovah has so graciously taught his people over the past century, these haughty ones try to draw the sheep away from the one international flock that Jesus has gathered in the earth. (John 10:7-10, 16) They try to sow doubts and to separate unsuspecting ones from the bounteous table of spiritual food spread at the Kingdom Halls of Jehovah's Witnesses, where truly there is nothing lacking. (Ps. 23:1-6) They (the so-called apostates) say that it is sufficient to read the Bible exclusively, either alone or in small groups at home. But, strangely, through such Bible reading they have reverted right back to the apostate doctrines that commentaries by Christendom's clergy were teaching 100 years ago, and some have even returned to celebrating Christendom's festivals again, such as the Roman Saturnalia of December 25th (Christmas) and Jesus and his apostles warned against such lawless ones.

Critics have accused the Watchtower Society of being authoritarian, controlling and coercive in its dealings with the local members of the Witnesses. Raymond Franz, being a former Governing Body member, has claimed the Watchtower Society's emphasis of the term theocratic (God-ruled) organization to describe the authority structure of Jehovah's Witnesses, which places God at the apex of its organization, is designed to exercise control over every aspect of the lives of Jehovah's Witnesses and conditions them to think it is wrong for them to question anything the society publishes as truth as it comes directly from God. The Watchtower Society has been accused of employing techniques of mind control on Witnesses including the direction to avoid reading criticism of the organization, using frequent and tightly controlled indoctrination meetings, regimentation, social alienation and elaborate promises of future rewards. Apart from a few personal life stories, the authors of all Watchtower Society magazine articles and other publications are anonymous and correspondence from the society does not typically indicate a specific author or personal signature.

To the average uninformed member of Jehovah's Witnesses, they are totally unaware as to what actually goes on behind the scenes and the internal workings of this cult. They are also unaware that many of the high-ranking individuals that control this organization are also guilty as in many other institutions, religious, commercial or political of the misuse of their authority and powers plus using the principle and tool of quid pro quo. This is a 14th-century Latin term for something for something, and describes when two parties engage in a mutual agreement to exchange goods or services. In business, religion or politics and in a legal context, quid pro quo conveys that an item or service has been exchanged for something of equal or similar value.

Our researchers came across several cases of the gross misuse of this power of quid pro quo by the officials of the Watchtower Society. For example, there is on record a case where an elderly sister who had recently become a widow and her family owned a large piece of land that had previously been used as a farm. She instructed her attorney to enter into her last will and testament that this large tract of land was to be bequeathed to the Watchtower Society upon her death. Shortly after this document was lodged with the Branch Office, her son who was satisfactorily and contentedly serving as a lowly, humble regular pioneer in a local congregation was suddenly given a senior position of authority within the organization. He was appointed as a Circuit Servant along with all the secret financial perks enjoyed by those in these elevated positions, even though he was ill-equipped spiritually, emotionally or physically to handle such an assignment and he sadly soon had to quit his appointment because of a serious nervous breakdown.

Many other cases similar to this one are known by those who have worked in the headquarters and various branch offices of the Watchtower Society throughout the world. We also have on record from leaked files, of this sort of underhanded activity taking place especially in the London branch office of the Watchtower Society when the Head of the Service Department for many years was a man called John Alfred Wynn who often acted as a law to himself. John Wynn was particularly well known as being skillful and regularly using this technique of quid pro quo and was known to have promoted certain men to more senior positions within the local organization when they were not really fully qualified or had insufficient experience. However, being the sons of individuals and businessmen who had rendered some vital service to help the branch office with their urgent printing needs, or other necessary business requirements, so Wynn adopted and used the principle of quid pro quo. Using this technique and arrangement of quid pro quo is not unscriptural, per se, but is certainly unethical in this context but it was found to be expedient, self-serving and useful to all parties involved.

The Watchtower Society today now has an ever-increasing team of aggressive and apparently sometimes very ruthless lawyers to handle the large number of cases currently being launched against them for child and sexual abusive. In addition these same aggressive lawyers are now very quick to sue any individual or group that publishes derogatory remarks regarding the factual and proven activities of the Watchtower officials; they have now adopted this tactic in imitation of the notorious, sue crazy Scientology cult. This quote from the website Avoid JW.org reveals an interesting step taken by the Watchtower Society in order to further control its members.

> In an attempt to further control its members beginning in 2018, JW.org [The official Watchtower website] will implement a program in which every single JW will be assigned a database number and their information will be in the JW.org's global database. All Jehovah's Witnesses will be given a number and tracked unless we can stop this invasion of privacy here in the US and around the world. The Watch Tower is very upset and concerned about all the leaks coming from their headquarters. They use Office 365 now and embed data into PDF files in

an attempt to track where the leaks are coming from. They have been issuing subpoenas from the Southern District of New York to various internet providers in the US, along with Google, Inc., in an attempt to track down the source of the leaks and identify the individuals involved in leaking their literature and videos. Watch Tower demands their freedom of speech but attempts to deny it to those sharing their publicly available materials which, by the way, are not being distributed for any monetary gain.

As quoted in Chapter Two of our report, the Church of Scientology has been involved in court disputes in several countries for many years. In some cases, when the Church has initiated the dispute, questions have been raised as to its motives. The Church says that its use of the legal system is necessary to protect its intellectual property and its right to freedom of religion. Critics say that most of the Church's claims are designed to harass Suppressive Persons, people who impede the progress of the Scientology movement. It is abundantly clear that this religion, as plaintiffs, sought to harass the individual defendants and destroy the church defendants through massive over-litigation and other highly questionable litigation tactics. This same modus operandi is now being used and employed by the Watchtower Society group of lawyers.

Barbara Anderson, in *Watchtower Documents*, reveals.

> Jehovah's Witnesses are discouraged from doing extensive personal research into their modern-day history. Such action can cause a truth-seeking Witness to be labeled *apostate* and be shunned by family and friends. Yet, scrutiny of ancient Biblical history is allowable and thought to be important. So why can't the same standard apply to Witnesses' modern-day history which reaches back approximately one hundred and thirty years at the very most? Based on the premise that these days are the last few gasps of a dying world, and salvation or eternal destruction depend upon Witnesses having all the information necessary *to prove whether or not they really ARE the one and only true religion*, one would think the more proof discovered, the better.

***

One of the most flagrant misuses of the writing department of the Watchtower Society was the publishing of a completely new translation of God's Holy Bible to primarily suit their personal doctrines, interpretations and beliefs. It is called the *New World Translation of the Holy Scriptures (NWT)* and was originally released in six separate volumes from 1950-1960 but described as rendered from the original languages by the New World Translation Committee. It is known by many that this actual distorted translation was the work of Frederick Franz, so-called prophet of this religion that he began in the year 1947. Franz was also known as the chief theologian of the Watchtower Society. Frederick Franz was also the ghost writer for Joseph Rutherford's numerous books and articles, plus also the originator of many of the religions most peculiar teachings, especially the foretold resurrection of the biblical prophets of old (ancient worthies) returning to earth sometime after 1925, plus the theory, calculations and using complex charts, of the year 1975 and the world's end. According to researcher James Penton, he wrote, "to all intents and purposes the New World Translation is the work of one man, Frederick Franz." Franz afterwards became the President of this organization, from 1977 to 1992, and was no doubt responsible for all of the numerous amendments, revisions and changes.

During a court trial in Scotland in 1954, Frederick Franz was asked by the Government lawyer just who the translators of this new Bible version were. Franz replied under oath: "That is an absolute secret. It will never be revealed now or even after death." Only someone with something to hide would be so intent on secrecy. He was also asked: "What happens if somebody submits a translation. Does the committee examine it?" Mr. Franz in reply, said: "No. I give it my O.K.; then the President, Mr. N. H. Knorr, has the last word." He was further asked to explain how "translations and interpretations of the Bible were made." Franz replied that they emanated from God and then added: "passed to the Holy Spirit who, invisible, communicates with Jehovah's Witnesses – and the publicity department" (Franz was the head of the Publicity Department also called Writing Department).

The actual 762-page court transcript of this controversial trial was not even publicly acknowledged by the Watchtower Society until 18 years later, as the answers to many questions presented by the State barristers and because of the shocking answers, under oath, by the leading representatives of the Watchtower Society, including the brilliant Watchtower lawyer Hayden Covington. These answers made it quite clear that the members of Jehovah's Witnesses had no personal choice in believing or accepting without question what was taught by the Governing Body, otherwise they would be excommunicated. This was a straightforward, undeniable example of the role of masters and slaves of modern religion. This famous 7-day trial of 1954 was a test case related to a young full-time pioneer brother called Douglas Walsh, who was the presiding overseer (congregation servant) of Dumbarton, a small local congregation in Scotland and regarding his claim of being exempt from military service as a minister of religion. This case eventually went up to the House of Lords in the British Parliament.

Editor's Note: The following is an extract retrieved from the archives of the Scottish Record Office under the title, *Pusuers Proof of Douglas Walsh VS. The Right Honourable James Laytham Clyde, M.P.* and taken from the records of this 1954 court case in Scotland during the trial of Douglas Walsh. The Barrister representing the State asked these questions and the exact answers are supplied by Covington and Fred Franz. This is a brief extract from selected pages of the Court transcript, kindly supplied by a member of our research team who has read the entire trial notes and records. (see http://www.uniset.ca/other/cs5/19561WLR1002.html)

HAYDEN C COVINGTON – Former Lawyer for the Watchtower Society – is in the Witness Box and is being cross examined by the State Barrister.

Q. Is it not vital to speak the truth on religious matters?

A. It certainly is.

Q. You have promulgated – forgive the word – false prophecy?

A. We have. I do not think we have promulgated false prophecy, there have been statements that were erroneous, that is the way I put it, and mistaken.

Q. It was promulgated as a matter which must be believed by all members of Jehovah's Witnesses that the Lord's Second

Coming took place in 1874?

A. Yes.

[A short discussion of the evidence given by Fred W Franz about 1874 takes place here.]

Q. That was the publication of false prophecy?

A. Yes. That was the publication of a false prophecy; it was a false statement or an erroneous statement in fulfillment of a prophecy that was false or erroneous.

Q. And that had to be believed by the whole of Jehovah's Witnesses?

A. Yes, because you must understand, we must have unity, we cannot have disunity with a lot of people going every way, an army is supposed to march in step.

Q. Back to the point now, a false prophecy was promulgated?

A. I agree to that.

Q. It had to be accepted by Jehovah's Witnesses?

A. That is correct.

Q. If a member of Jehovah's Witnesses took the view himself that that prophecy was wrong, and said so, would he be disfellowshipped?

A. Yes, if he said so, and kept on persisting in creating trouble, because if the whole organisation believes one thing, even though it be erroneous, and somebody else starts on his own trying to put his ideas across, then there is a disunity and trouble, there cannot be harmony, there cannot be marching .... Our purpose is to have unity.

Q. Unity at all costs?

A. Unity at all costs, because we believe and are sure that Jehovah God is using our organisation, the governing body of our organisation, to direct it, even though mistakes are made from time to time.

Q. A unity based on an enforced acceptance of false prophecy?

A. That is conceded to be true.

Q. And the person, who expresses his view, as you say, that it was wrong, and was disfellowshipped, would be in breach of the covenant, if he was baptised?

A. That is correct.

Q. And as you said yesterday expressly, would be worthy of death?

A. I think....

Q. Would you say yes or no?

A. I will answer yes, unhesitatingly.

Q. Do you call that religion?

A. It certainly is.

Q. Do you call that Christianity?

A. I certainly do.

[FRED FRANZ – Vice-President of the Watchtower Society – also answered questions submitted by the Barrister.]

Q. In addition to these regular publications do you prepare and issue a number of theological pamphlets and books from time to time?

A. Yes.

Q. Can you tell me this; are these theological publications and the semi-monthly periodicals used for discussion of statements of doctrine?

A. Yes.

Q. Are these statements of doctrine held to be authoritative within the Society?

A. Yes.

Q. Is their acceptance a matter of choice, or is it obligatory on all those who wish to be and remain members of the Society?

A. It is obligatory.

[The British Government Barrister then directed attention to certain teachings that the Watchtower Society had in time rejected, including some involving specific dates.]

Q. Did Pastor Russell not fix 1874 as some other crucial date?

A. 1874 used to be understood as the date of Jesus' Second Coming spiritually.

Q. Do you say, used to be understood?

A. That is right.

Q. That was issued as a fact, which was to be accepted by all who were Jehovah's Witnesses?

A. Yes.

Q. That is no longer now accepted, is it?

A. No.

Q. But it was a calculation, which is now no longer accepted by the Board of Directors of the Society?

A. That is correct.

Q. So that I am correct, I am just anxious to canvas the position; it became the bound duty of the Witnesses to accept this miscalculation?

A. Yes

Q. So that what is published as the truth today by the Society may have to be admitted to be wrong in a few years?

A. We have to wait and see.

Q. And in the meantime, the body of Jehovah's Witnesses has been following an error?

A. They have been following misconstructions on the Scriptures.

Q. Error?

A. Well, error. These Watchtower Society books give an exposition on the whole Scriptures.

Q. But an authoritative exposition?

A. They submit the Bible or the statements that are therein made, and the individual examines the statement and then the Scripture to see that the statement is scripturally supported.

Q. He what?

A. He examines the Scripture to see whether the statement is supported by the Scripture.

Q. I understood the position to be and do please correct me if I am wrong that a member of the Jehovah's Witnesses must accept as a true Scripture and interpretation what is given in the books I referred you to?

A. Yes, but he does not compulsorily do so, he is given his Christian right of examining the Scriptures to confirm that this is scripturally sustained.

Q. And if he finds that the Scripture is not sustained by the books, or vice versa, what does he do?

A. The Scripture is there in support of the statement, that is why it is put there.

Q. What does a man do if he finds a disharmony between the Scripture and those books?

A. You will have to produce me a man who does find that, then I can answer, or he will answer.

Q. Did you imply that the individual member has the right of reading the books and the Bible and forming his own view as to the proper interpretation of Holy Writ?

A. He comes – – –

Q. Would you say yes or no, and then qualify?

A. No. Do you want me to qualify now?

Q. Yes, if you wish?

A. The Scripture is there given in support of the statement, and therefore the individual when he looks up the Scripture and thereby verifies the statement, then he comes to the Scriptural view of the matter.

Q. A Witness has no alternative, has he, to accept as authoritative and to obey instructions issued in the Watchtower or the Informant or Awake?

A. He must accept those.

Returning to the account of the new translation of the Holy Bible, it is also significant that this *New World Translation* has been amended and revised on numerous occasions since its original release some years ago, actually so many times, that our researcher was unable to actually count the number of changes, therefore asked the question, "did God and the Holy Spirit make mistakes while passing this recent translation on to Jehovah's Witnesses, as claimed by Fred Franz representing the Governing Body?" Franz had studied classical Greek, part-time for two years at the University of Cincinnati, but dropped out after his sophomore year. When asked in a Scotland courtroom if he could translate Genesis 2:4 into Hebrew, Franz replied that he could not. The truth is that Franz was unable to translate Hebrew or Greek. The *NWT* is so extremely biased and perverted; it is questionable if any Hebrew or Greek scholars worked on it. It is nothing more than a sectarian paraphrase in modern language, not a translation. In addition, no one else on the planet ever uses this distorted translation, except Jehovah's Witnesses or maybe a few ex-Jehovah's Witnesses in their research.

In the foreword of the 1961 edition of the *New World Translation* (now in one volume), the committee claim that they have, "translated the words, thoughts and sayings of the heavenly Author of this scared library of sixty-six books; Jehovah God, which holy men of long ago put down in writing under inspiration. So we have as a responsibility to transmit as far as possible his thoughts and declarations. This does not mean that earlier renderings or translation was now being replaced or rejected but rather the purpose was to attain a closer conformity to the original reading in the original languages." You as the reader of these comments by this translation committee can use your own intelligence and easily see through these naïve and deliberately misleading remarks.

Dr. Bruce M. Metzger, professor of New Testament at Princeton University, calls the *NWT* a frightful mistranslation, erroneous and pernicious, reprehensible. If the Jehovah's Witnesses take this translation seriously, they are polytheists.

Professor of New Testament Language and Literature, Dr. William Barclay, a leading Greek scholar, also said, "It is abundantly clear that a sect who can translate the New Testament like that is intellectually dishonest." Samuel Haas, in his review of the *New World Translation*, in the *Journal of Biblical Literature*, states: "This work indicates a great deal of effort and thought as well as considerable scholarship, it is to be regretted that religious bias was allowed to colour many passages. Their work is a highly biased attempt to justify some of their non-biblical doctrines. In terms of scholarship, the *New World Translation* leaves much to be desired and is characterized by their own biased interpretations."

In 1963, Anthony A. Hoekema wrote: "Their *New World Translation* of the Bible is by no means an objective rendering of the sacred text into modern English, but is a biased translation in which many of the peculiar teachings of the Watchtower Society are smuggled into the text of the Bible itself." Julius R. Mantey, co-author of A Manual Grammar of the Greek New Testament, and also A Hellenistic Greek Reader, said about the New Testament of the *NWT* that it's "a distortion not a translation."

***

In recent years the Watchtower Society has faced an additional very serious problem related to the shepherds of the flock, being legally and criminally charged with child molestation and sexual abuse, which has taken place over many, many years but previously been secretly hidden or covered over. Of course, this is not on the same scale as the many Priests and Cardinals being likewise charged in the Catholic Church, or the Mormon Church and their connections with the Boy Scout Movement of America but it nevertheless is dramatically increasing. This very serious issue of sexual abuse by Jehovah's Witnesses is being exposed more and more by the day. A recent report of March, 2019 supplied by attorneys Wagner-Reese of Indianapolis, USA, who are handling and exposing many of these crimes, revealed that the Watchtower Bible and Tract Society of New York, the parent corporation of the Jehovah's Witnesses compiled and maintained a database of up to tens of thousands of accused pedophiles within Jehovah's Witnesses. The database, which contains detailed reports of allegations of sexual abuse, has been kept secret for decades.

Quoting from Wagner-Reese's website:

> In 1997, a letter was sent by the Watchtower Bible and
> Tract Society, which instructed all congregation leaders to
> report all known sexual perpetrators to headquarters without
> telling anyone else. The reports were reportedly compiled
> to create a database comprising hundreds of alleged sexual
> abusers. However, this information was never shared with
> the authorities. While the allegations were reported to the
> leaders of the Jehovah's Witnesses, nothing happened to the

perpetrators who remained in the congregation. In addition to not reporting pedophiles to the police, victims were also kept silent by the Jehovah's Witnesses with harsh policies for those that make sexual assault accusations. Jehovah's Witnesses maintain a two-witness rule, which requires an accuser to have two eyewitnesses before the church would begin an investigation. If another witness could not be produced, they were sometimes accused of providing a false accusation. In some cases, this could lead to the member being excommunicated from the church for lying. This is not the first time Jehovah's Witnesses have hidden allegations of sexual abuse. In 2016, a royal commission was established in Australia investigating the church's mishandling of sexual abuse. It was discovered that the Church failed to report over 1,000 accused sexual abusers over the course of almost 60 years.

Former Jehovah's Witness elder, William Bowen who today campaigns against what he says is a sect policy that protects sexual abusers of children, he also says sect leaders have disfellowshipped over 60 members or abuse victims who have gone public with their criticism. Bowen founded Silent Lambs, Inc., which monitors allegations of sexual abuse by Jehovah's Witnesses. He says thousands of people have contacted his organization with credible reports of sexual abuse by leading members of this religion. If you take the time to read the many cases covered on this website, you will want to vomit over the filthy lies and conduct of these men, many in leading positions within the ranks of the Watchtower Society, who were discovered, arrested and convicted over their crimes involving young children. Many of these cases were actually known and recorded in the files of the Watchtower Society, but secretly hidden from the authorities by the Governing Body of this religion.

According to a recent newspaper report from Lake County, Montana, USA, on September 26, 2018, a Montana jury of seven men and two women handed down the largest-ever punitive damages award for a single abuse victim. The Watchtower Bible and Tract Society of New York, together with the Christian Congregation of Jehovah's Witnesses were found guilty of both negligence and malice in connection with the intentional failure to file police reports on behalf of plaintiff Alexis

Nunez and two additional victims. A combined total of 35 million dollars was assessed following detailed instructions given to the jury by Judge James A. Manley. This report that appeared in the *Daily Mail* of 25 March, 2019 stated:

> The Governing Body of the Jehovah's Witness Christian denomination has been accused of maintaining a secret database of child molesters within the group and failing to share that information with law enforcement agencies. The Watchtower Bible and Tract Society, which serves as the head of the Jehovah's Witness organization, have reportedly paid millions of dollars in court fines and settlements over the years rather than unseal its files containing the names and addresses of the accused.

What is causing some concern and resistance by the over 6 million members of this religion is that they willingly make regular voluntary contributions under the heading, Contributions to the Lord's Work (apart from the monthly compulsory pledges) and then they hear of such massive amounts, previously kept secret, such as $35 million dollars of these contribution going toward settlement of court cases in the form of damages and compensation as a result of the behavior of their spiritual leaders, this is not counting the many additional court cases involving millions of dollars, being settled out of court that the local brothers know nothing about. Also, with so many more court cases in various countries still pending, with amounts now totaling billions of dollars being claimed for sexual abuse, especially of children and single women, and attempted cover up of these cases by the leaders of the Watchtower Society, this is creating great concern for the future survival of this religion.

This serious issue of sexual abuse and molestation of children amongst the Watchtower Society is increasing so rapidly that we have heard reports of legal firms (nicknamed ambulance chasers) are now being formed and focused, one recently in San Diego, USA, with a specialized staff of over 35 lawyers and interns all ready and willing to sue the Watchtower Society for legal claims and damages. They boast that they have already collected to date (2018) over $500 million on behalf of their clients, being members or ex-members of Jehovah's Witnesses. So, if you as a reader of this Chapter, are a sincere member of this religion and you would like to know where your modest contribution or donation to the Lord's work of spreading the Good News of God's Kingdom is being used by the Governing Body, it was probably part of this over $500 million paid in fines, damages, compensation and fees to these lawyers, plus the unknown millions settled out of court by the Watchtower Society. This current problem facing the Watchtower Society is the ever-increasing number of cases of sexual abuse of children. This report, (below) by Paul Grundy, who is an experienced researcher into the activities of the Watchtower Society and who recently appeared on the Australian, ABC News channel. Paul, who is the editor of the website, JW Facts.com, along with many other ex-Witnesses have sincerely dedicated theirs lives to the service of mankind and to making sure that the full and complete facts are fully exposed about the practices and deceptions by the Watchtower Society. The following report was submitted:

> But the Royal Commission highlighted a number of areas that are flawed within the religion, particularly around the handling of child abuse victims. These include:
>
> The two-witness rule. A rule within the religion that states officials cannot accept an accusation of child abuse unless there was a second person who also witnessed the abuse – something that rarely happens.
>
> Women's role (or lack of) in the congregation and judicial committee process. As a patriarchal religion, women are to view men as their head. They cannot be part of a judicial committee. In practise this means a young female victim must go into graphic details of her abuse alone in front of three older men.
>
> The expectation that the victim confront the perpetrator as part of the process.
>
> Not making it mandatory for elders to report accusation of abuse. While not being obliged to report accusations may be legally acceptable in some states, the Royal Commission identified that the judicial committee process meant that often elders would uncover actual proof of a crime, even a confession, but still not report it. At this stage, where it had moved from

an allegation to proof of a crime, there was a legal obligation to report.

Not reporting allegations to the police. This practise was to protect Jehovah's name, and was due to a general mistrust of people in "the world". According to Watchtower: "While some contact with worldly people is unavoidable – at work, at school, and otherwise – we must be vigilant so as to keep from being sucked back into the death-dealing atmosphere of this world."

Fear of psychologists, based on the belief that they may give advice that is not in line with Watchtower principles.

The Royal Commission also highlighted that because of Jehovah Witnesses' insistence on separation from worldly society; they were unwilling to join other organisations in any sort of redress scheme for victims. Evidence given at the commission also contradicted the claim from those within the religion that child sex abuse was very rare. The commission heard there were almost 300 cases in Australia alone during the last 10 years, and Toole [Watchtower lawyer] testified that for the past two years he had received three or four calls a month about new cases. For such a relatively small organisation, that's a huge problem. What's more, this only includes reported cases, and not the many people that no doubt remain silent.

In March of 2019, the police in the Netherlands actually had to raid and make a forced entry into the Amsterdam Bethel office because the Watchtower Society had stubbornly refused to hand over sealed records of the many cases of sexual abuse in that country that they had secretly filed away. This also included many cases of actual leading personnel in the Bethel headquarters.

One of our researches was asked the question in view of these compounding court cases, "How much wealth does the Watchtower Society actually have in order to cover these escalating costs?" This was the answer from one contributor. "The actual worth is difficult to estimate, the value of land and property will of course sky rocket as we get more overcrowded in this world. They have an awful lot of both! According to Diane Wilson in *Awakening of a Jehovah's Witness* they budgeted $50 million for the refurbishment of a building project in

New York a few years ago, this doubled (despite all the free labor), "give to Jehovah" they said, and one of the leading officials said to her "No matter how much we spend the amount we have in the bank never decreases. It's wonderful to see how Jehovah provides."

Diane Wilson wrote this observation in her book *Awakening of a Jehovah's Witness* that covers her 25 years of membership. A review in *Psychology Today*, December, 2002, commented:

> Who are those polite, well-scrubbed Jehovah's Witnesses who appear at our doors to hand out leaflets and offer to discuss the Bible? Diane Wilson, made vulnerable by a childhood of psychological abuse, succumbed to the group's charms and remained a member for 25 years. Wilson describes the indoctrination process, the hypocrisy, and the gradual suppression of individuality. Much of what she describes might be said of any cult, and members of mainstream religions may come to see the dangers of fanaticism in their own faiths.

> So they have significant resources of cash. Where from? The magazines and books were sold for seemingly a pittance or actually now given away for free. The WTS has the largest printing press in the world and with buying in such bulk - are sure to be laughing all the way to the bank. There was a report (New York's richest companies) – where their yearly net income (Brooklyn) was listed as just short of a BILLION dollars – and they have 3,340 staff - remember all volunteers! Then count all their business interests, which they try to deny having! Plus, how many of the faithful donate to the Society in their will and are encouraged to make donations of land and beneficiaries. JWs are one of the richest religions around, and size for size, I would argue the richest in the world! If you take into consideration all of the Kingdom Halls, all of their branch offices plus printing facilities, all of their stock market shares, and their bank accounts. I would imagine anywhere from $200 Billion to a trillion.

Anders Andersen, a financial expert, said in his blog:

> Although the members of the Governing Body of Jehovah's Witnesses, on the surface don't receive much money for their services, it's mistaken to think they do not have any monetary benefits at all.

They receive:

Free housing (modest to some but of a very high standard)

Free medical and dental care

Free meal service

Free house keeping service

Free tailor, laundry service, hair dresser, beauty shop and masseur

A little pocket money (and I mean: really just a little)

Free travelling around the world to conventions in a lot of countries

Voluntary monetary gifts from adherents they meet on their travels (a very important factor to consider)

They receive all of the above for life, so effectively they also receive their pension and retirement home for free. Take out your calculator and figure out what you are paying for the services listed above. It is most of your income, isn't it? So, they do have monetary benefits with their position. They just aren't getting rich from it (that is, what we know about)

Editor's Note: Please read the personal experience in the Appendix regarding Philip Rees, one time Branch servant of Australia, as he exposes this hidden secret and never discussed perk.

According to inside information provided to our research team, growth in membership of this religion has all but stagnated and in many countries has actually decreased. This has compelled the Governing Body to close many of their branch offices in a number of countries and dispose of their property holdings in order to raise more funds. Any growth in membership is now only taking place; not by new coverts, but rather the adding of new members from the birth of children born into this religion, especially in Africa and South America where birth control is virtually non-existent. Plus these new members from these regions of the world are unable to make important meaningful voluntary or compulsory financial contributions to the Lord's organization. This stagnation in growth and funds has now of course affected the bottom line and brought about the selling of their lucrative property holdings, especially in New York and London, plus severe cut backs in any new and future projects.

This quote by writer and researcher John Redwood (ex-Watchtower member and active critic) in his somewhat cynical but believable article on his website sums up the feelings of many:

> The level of secrecy, Orwellian control, and the recent organizational dependence on technology and legal support appears to have overshadowed the fundamental concept of Christianity. The gap between rank-and-file members of the organization and those who pull the corporate strings has become a massive chasm. The average Witness knows little or nothing of these things. They simply trust. While millions of dollars in donated funds are dispensed to satisfy the rising number of child abuse lawsuits, Jehovah's Witnesses' legal department has curiously found the time and finances to aggressively tackle any suspected current or former member who shares their content. The notion of "received free, give free" does not apply to the Jehovah's Witness corporate empire. The Biblical image of a poor, but spiritually rich savior has been replaced with real estate holdings, printeries, lawyers, and an insulated, self-anointed, self-appointed board of directors." John Redwood is also on record as making this comment, "Now that books and magazines are being abandoned in favor of videos, the governing body members are front and center in the public eye, more so than ever before. Nothing says "cult" better than eight men and their helpers preaching from their televangelistic network in New York, controlling the lives of eight million followers.

The full facts will have to be faced one day in the very near future, regarding the validity of the core teachings of the Watchtower Society, but the feckless, inept Governing Body meantime currently still stubbornly sticks to these basic teachings promulgated by Charles Russell and Joseph Rutherford passed down from the 19th century. But by using the principles of the Bible texts, "Make sure of all things" (1 Thessalonians 5:21) "Let God be found true" (Romans 3:4) "Do not believe every inspired expression, but test the inspired expressions to see whether they originate with God" (1 John 4:1). "Carefully examining the scriptures daily as to whether these things were so" (Acts 17:11) these Biblical instructions will eventually bring about the changes required, otherwise this religion and cult will eventually implode.

The current doctrines, such as the year 1914 being a pivotal year in Bible chronology that started the beginning of the last days; the correct biblical understanding of the term generation that will not pass away until all things are fulfilled (Matthew 24:34). Plus, the interpretation that the little flock of anointed ones mentioned in the Bible and the number of 144,000 is actually a symbolic number and not literal as currently claimed and that the term great crowd of other sheep is a misnomer and corrupted Bible phrase and is not a separate group of mankind set apart from a disconnected little flock or heavenly class. It is now known of course by our readers that the interpretation of the Watchtower Society regarding this so-called little flock of 144,000 anointed ones is unique to the Watchtower organization and is now simply used as a tool and means to promulgate and maintain the power that the existing Governing Body, all claiming to be anointed ones, holds as masters of this religion as clarified in this research report.

The current Governing Body and their helpers is fully aware that they are still promoting fallacious teachings and doctrines but do not have the courage to take a firm stand and display their integrity and honesty plus inform the rank and file of the members of this religion of their confusion, so they continue to writhe with pain in their inner consciences over this dilemma. This will ultimately mean that there will be increasing, inexorable pressure toward being forced to make necessary changes to their teachings and beliefs in order to retain the loyalty and support of the millions of their followers. So we will wait and see if this ever occurs. Or as one of our researchers expressed, maybe they are too disinterested to be even concerned about this important pending issue of future survival, as these eight elderly men, with an average age of being in their late 70s, consisting the existing Governing Body and they all currently enjoy such a comfortable position and life style, relishing the unique benefits of being the masters of this religion. So their philosophy is probably pass the buck and to let the next generation of the Governing Body take care of this problem of having to change and handle the serious issues currently being faced, such as child molestation, erroneous doctrines and teachings, plus being exposed over their financial dealings.

The hypocrisy of the Watchtower Society is well expressed in one of their own leading publications:

> We need to examine, not only what we personally believe, but also what is taught by <u>any religious organization</u> with which we may be associated. Are its teachings in full harmony with God's Word, or are they based on the traditions of men? If we are lovers of the truth, there is nothing to fear from such an examination." – *The Truth that Leads to Eternal Life*, Watch Tower Bible & Tract Society, 1968, p. 13

We sincerely hope this famous quote by James Faust (1920-2007) will inspire our readers to become more involved in making sure that all religious cults are exposed for what they are. "Honesty is more than not lying. It is truth telling, truth speaking, truth living, and truth loving. The truth no matter how hard it is to bear must be accepted and confronted head on, because it is real."

> *Editor's Note*: A final word regarding the question of the massive wealth connected to the leading religious cults in the world. A whistleblower from the Watchtower Society and the Mormon Church has expressed the fact that both of these religious organizations have secretly amassed billions of dollars over the years, which is unknown to the rank and file of their sincere members. So the question has now been raised, should a church or religion be allowed to amass $100 billion even though they claim to be a non-profit or not-for-gain institution and therefore free of the payment of any taxes?

During our research of religious cults the issue of these cults using various methods to acquire funds, either through compulsory tithing, appeals for contributions or written pledges (also now known as stealth tithing) was carefully examined. The question was raised on many occasions by the individuals we interviewed, why do these religions need to amass such large holdings of cash, what is the gross value of these secret holdings and who has access to these secret funds and what are they used for? This opinion was expressed by Sam Brunson, Law professor at Loyola University:

In the first instance, that's not a new question; I was at a conference a couple of months ago that asked that same question about private foundations and donor-advised funds. And it's been a big question in the university context: Harvard has been described as a hedge fund with a university attached. According to the story in the *Post*, the Harvard endowment is worth almost $50 billion. That $50 billion supports or, if it were used, would support at least about 23,000 students and another 16,000 staff and faculty. I don't think you'll find anyone (well, virtually anyone) who argues that tax-exempt organizations shouldn't be able to accumulate any assets. After all, charitable giving is at least moderately cyclical, while need is countercyclical. In a downturn, there is more need for charitable support, while donors often can't give as generously.

On the other hand, $100 billion is a lot of money. That's plenty to fund a lot of rainy days. Is it too much? Probably! What is the appropriate size for an endowment for the Mormon Church, with it's X million members and large non-investment real estate holdings that are self-insured? I don't know. It's definitely something north of zero. And ultimately, as we engage, we need to understand that there's not a right and a wrong answer to this. All we have is grey, and we will swim in the ambiguity of grey. But as we talk and argue and fight over the amount, maybe we'll start to engage questions of the relationship of money and religion, of what the purpose of money is for a church, of how we (as stakeholders) want to see the church use the money that we help contribute.

Chapter Four: The Mormons

Another group listed in the Cult Awareness Network as a dangerous cult is the Mormon Church, also known as The Church of Jesus Christ of Latter-Day Saints (LDS). In the Word of Wisdom (equal to the Bible by Mormon followers) they are told that fruits, vegetables, and grains are nutritious and helpful to our bodies; they are also encouraged to eat meat sparingly. God also counsels them in this law; so they claim, to avoid a handful of harmful and addictive substances, including coffee, tea, alcoholic beverages, and tobacco, which all display very sound thinking and in itself attracted many members, especially women and the ultimate banning of alcohol and tobacco by this religious sect.

According to the website, Cult Definition this comment is made regarding the Mormon Church:

> A comparison with historic, Bible-based Christianity, shows that the Mormon Church rejects, changes or adds to the central doctrines of the Christian faith to such an extent that Mormonism must be regarded as having separated itself from the faith it claims to represent, and instead having established a new religion that is not compatible with Christianity.

The Church of Jesus Christ of Latter-day Saints (LDS) the official name of the Mormon Church, claims to be not only:

a) Christian in nature, but also

b) The only true expression of historical Christianity.

In reality, the teachings and practices of the LDS church as well as the documented history of Christianity, shows that Mormonism has plagiarized and usurped Christian terminology and scriptures, creating a new religion that is different from Christianity in key doctrines and practices. Similar to the Watchtower Society they also believe in excommunicating followers if they do not toe the line or if they level criticism against its leaders, also described as apostasy. The

Mormon Church teaches that direct revelation from God continues today, directly through the Church leaders so accordingly these revelations to direct the entire church comes direct from God to the President of the Church, whoever that happens to be. At the time of writing, Russell M. Nelson was appointed as the 17th president and prophet of The Church of Jesus Christ of Latter-day Saints on Sunday, January 14, 2018, in the upper room of the Salt Lake Temple.

The LDS Church has been characterized by its members as a family-centered religion and has been one the world's leading promoters of the Boy Scout movement.[25] The church teaches that every being that ever lived upon the earth initially had a spirit body and that all were born to Heavenly Parents in a pre-mortal existence. The leader of the church is the President of the Church, and church members regard him as a prophet, seer and revelator. He is often referred to by members of the church as the Prophet because the President is thought to hold the same divine calling as biblical prophets. The President's responsibility is primarily over the church as a whole. Church members believe his stewardship also extends to all humanity (including you our reader) as the Lord's chosen mouthpiece. He is entitled to guide the church and the entire world through revelation, acting as God's spokesman.

---

[25] This policy of supporting the Boy Scout movement has been dramatically changed as from 2020 as they have now severed all ties owing to the claims that now exist and proven of sexual abuse of these young men. To date almost 100,000 individual cases have been filed by these abused young men.

The first presidents of the Church of Jesus Christ of the Latter-day Saints.
Lithograph by Currier & Ives, c. 1879, courtesy of the Library of Congress

Our researcher pointed out that many Mormon men have been abusively using their power as masters over these youngsters who belonged to the Boy Scouts of America. This quote from the CNN newswire revealed this year:

> The Boy Scouts of America (BSA) believed more than 7,800 of its former leaders were involved in sexually abusing children over the course of 72 years, according to newly exposed court testimony – about 2,800 more leaders than previously known publicly. The Boy Scouts identified more than 12,000 alleged victims in that time period, from 1944 through 2016, according to the testimony, which was publicized Tuesday by attorney Jeff Anderson, who specializes in representing sexual abuse victims.

This extract from the article by Dr. Michael Brown that appeared in the news source, GOPUSA, reveals the shocking conduct by the Boy Scouts of America, and will no doubt also have serious repercussions on the Mormon Church:

> The open secret is no secret anymore. The tragedy is being uncovered for the world to see. As headlines now announce, "Sexual abuse scandal rocks the Boy Scouts of America as it is revealed more than 12,000 members were victims of perpetrators who will soon be revealed in perversion files." This is shocking and terribly painful. But it is not surprising in the least. It has been reported for years that the Boy Scouts of America (BSA) was covering up this sexual scandal, whether by hook or by crook. As reported by the *LA Times* in January 2015, "Settlement in sex abuse case keeps Scouts 'perversion files' closed." Now, at last, this horrific story is coming to the light of day. But who can calculate the damage that was done? How much emotional blood does the BSA have on its hands? How many lives have been marred or even destroyed?
>
> There are now of course many pending cases regarding this offensive activity and abusing young boys for sexual pleasure and to quote just one item from the Fox News channel. "Five men who say they were sexually abused as kids while in the Boy Scouts of America are suing the organization and the Mormon Church because they say both groups fraudulently presented the Boy Scouts as a safe, wholesome activity for boys. The men

filed the lawsuit Monday in Boise's U.S. District Court. They contend that the Boy Scouts of America and The Church of Jesus Christ of Latter-day Saints knew that there were child molesters in the Boy Scouts, but they covered up the danger instead of letting parents and children know about the risk.

The Mormon Church, said in its announcement that it has "increasingly felt the need to create and implement a uniform youth leadership and development program that serves its members globally." The two organizations jointly determined that as of December 31, 2019, the Church will no longer be a chartered partner of the Scouts, it said in a joint statement with the Boy Scouts. The Church of Jesus Christ of Latter-day Saints publicly said it will sever all ties with the Boy Scouts of America, ending a century-old tradition deeply ingrained in the religious life of Mormon boys. For 105 years, the relationship between the Boy Scouts and the Mormon Church has been important to both groups. Any boy who is part of a Mormon congregation automatically becomes part of the Boy Scouts. The Mormon Church has been the largest participant in the Boy Scouts in the United States, making up nearly 20 percent of all of the Boy Scouts 2.3 million youth members. Church officials did not cite specific Scouts' policy changes that spurred the split, but the two groups have increasingly clashed over values in recent years, particularly following the Boy Scouts' move to include openly gay troop leaders.

One member of our research team, who was born into and brought up in the Mormon Church, also submitted his report regarding the dangers of claiming to be the only true religion and that all other religions are considered to be unacceptable to God and therefore on the path to eventual destruction and eternal damnation. The Church of Jesus Christ of Latter-Day Saints (LDS Church) has always been the subject of criticism since it was founded by American religious leader Joseph Smith in 1830. The most controversial, and in fact a key reason for Joseph Smith's murder in 1844, is the claim that plural marriage [as defenders call it] or polygamy [as attackers call it] is Biblically authorized. Under heavy pressure the territory of Utah would not be accepted as a state in America if polygamy was still practiced, thus the church formally and publicly renounced the practice in 1890.

Utah's statehood soon followed. However, plural marriage remains a controversial and divisive issue, as despite the official renunciation of 1890, it still has sympathizers, defenders, and semi-secret practitioners.

More recent criticism has focused on questions of historical revisionism, homophobia, racism, sexist policies and misogyny, inadequate financial disclosure, and the historical authenticity of the *Book of Mormon*. In recent years, the Internet has provided a new forum for critics of the Mormon Church, very similar also to the sect of Jehovah's Witnesses. Clicking on leading search engines on the Internet, the sites that are listed first are not directly related to these religions but rather to all the anti-religious websites. In the past the use of the Internet and social media was strongly discouraged by both of these cults in order to prevent their followers from reading and discovering negative news about their religion (talk about mind control), plus they warned that it was a dangerous practice and detrimental to the spiritual health of their adherents. The term a tool of Satan was the phrase used by the elders of both cults. In recent years however, expediently and hypocritically there has been an about face and both religions now actively use the Internet to promote their ideologies, teachings and propaganda.

Soon after the Mormon Church officially suspended the practice of polygamy, the US federal government reduced its legal efforts to seize church property. Despite this step, Mormon leaders after 1890 continued to sanction and participate in plural marriages in secret, albeit in smaller numbers, both in America and in Mexico, for a period better measured in decades than years. One historian said that polygamy completely demoralizes good men and makes bad men correspondingly worse. As for the women – well, God help them! First wives it renders desperate, or else heart-broken, mean-spirited creatures. For example, Sarah Pratt ended her marriage to husband Orson Pratt in 1868 because of his obsession with marrying younger women. Pratt was one of the leading members of the Mormon Church and claimed his position of being of the quorum of the twelve apostles of the Mormon Church and at the age of 57 years old, Orson Pratt married a sixteen-year-old girl, his tenth wife, younger than his daughter Celestia. Sarah Pratt lashed out at Orson in an 1877 interview, stating: "Here was my husband, gray headed, taking to his bed young girls in mockery of marriage. Of course, there could be no joy for him in such an intercourse except for the indulgence of his fanaticism and of something else, perhaps, which I hesitate to mention." Orson Pratt remained a leading member of this cult and influenced many of the most unusual doctrines promulgated by this religious sect over the years up until his death in 1881.

This religion also teaches that a living person, acting as proxy, can be baptized by immersion on behalf of a deceased person, citing 1 Corinthians 15:29, Malachi 4:5, 6; John 5:25 and 1 Peter 4:6 for doctrinal support. This is another typical example of a cult taking a Bible text out of context and twisting it to suit a particular belief or teaching. These baptisms for the dead are performed in their temples. Floyd C. McElveen and the Institute for Religious Research state that verses to support baptism for the dead are not justified by contextual exegesis of the Bible. In 2008, the Vatican of Rome issued a statement calling the practice erroneous and directing its dioceses to keep parish records away from Mormons performing genealogical research.

Holocaust survivors and other Jewish groups criticized the LDS Church in 1995, after discovering that the church had so-called baptized more than 300,000 Jewish holocaust victims. After that criticism, church leaders put a policy in place to stop the practice, with an exception for baptisms specifically requested or approved by victims' relatives. Jewish organizations again criticized the church in 2002, 2004, and 2008 stating that the church failed to honor the 1995 agreement. However, Jewish and Mormon leaders subsequently acknowledged in a joint statement in 2010 that concerns between members of both groups... have been eliminated.

Reacting to accusations of sexual abuse by teachers, Boy Scout leaders, clergy, etc., social welfare activists have campaigned for more robust measures toward greater prevention of abuse of individuals served by counselors and other professionals, advocating greater transparency and quicker referral of allegations to criminal investigators. Many argue that the LDS Church treats women as inferior to men, the same as Jehovah's Witnesses. The Cult Awareness and Information Centre also point to comments such as those made by church leader Bruce R. McConkie, who wrote in 1966 that a "woman's primary place is in the home, where she is to rear children and abide by the righteous counsel of her husband." An additional comment was made that women will never get into the celestial kingdom, except her husband receives her, if she is worthy to have a husband; and if not, somebody will receive her as a <u>servant</u>. In Mormon doctrine, celestial marriage is a prerequisite for exaltation for members of either gender.

***

A major issue with critics is that this religion received by divine providence a text book which they claim is equal to the Bible and was discovered on golden plates by a young boy called Joseph Smith. The *Book of Mormon* is a sacred text of the Latter-Day Saint movement, which adherents believe contains writings of ancient prophets who lived on the American continent from approximately 2200 BC to 421 AD. It was first published in March, 1830 by Joseph Smith as An Account Written by the Hand of Mormon upon Plates Taken from the Plates of Nephi.

According to Smith's account and the book's narrative, the *Book of Mormon* was originally written in otherwise unknown characters referred to as reformed Egyptian engraved on golden plates. Smith said that the last prophet to contribute to the book, a man named Moroni, buried it in the Hill Cumorah in present-day Manchester, New York, USA, before his death, and then returned to Earth in 1827 as an angel, revealing the location of the plates to Smith, and instructing him to translate the plates into English for use in the restoration of Christ's true church in the latter days. Critics claim that it was authored by Smith, drawing on material and ideas from contemporary 19th-century works rather than translating an ancient record. Differences between the original and printer's manuscript, the 1830 printed version, and modern versions of the *Book of Mormon* have led some critics to claim that evidence has been systematically removed that could have proved that Smith fabricated the *Book of Mormon*, or are attempts to hide embarrassing aspects of the church's past with Mormon scholars viewing the changes as superficial, done to clarify the meaning of the text.

There are several theories as to the origin of the *Book of Mormon*. Most adherents to the Latter-Day Saint movement view the book as a work of inspired scripture. The most common belief of adherents is that promoted by Joseph Smith himself, who said he translated ancient golden plates inscribed by prophets. Smith claimed the angel Moroni, a prophet in the *Book of Mormon*, directed him in the 1820s to a hill near his home in Palmyra, New York, where the plates were buried. Besides Smith himself, there were at least 11 witnesses who said they saw the plates in 1829, and three also claiming to have been visited by an angel. Critics have explored a number of issues, including (1) whether Joseph Smith actually had golden plates, or whether the text of the *Book of Mormon* originated in his mind (imaginary) or through inspiration; (2) whether it was Smith himself who composed the book's text or a very clever associate of Smith's, such as Oliver Cowdery or Sidney Rigdon; and (3) whether the book was based on prior works, such as the View of the Hebrews, the Spalding Manuscript, or the King James Version of the Bible. The Smithsonian Institution issues a standard reply to requests for their opinion regarding the *Book of Mormon* as an archaeological or scientific guide. Prior to 1998, the statement denied any evidence for pre-Columbian contact between Old and New Worlds: "Certainly there was no contact with the ancient Egyptians, Hebrews or other peoples of Western Asia or the Near East." In 1998, the Smithsonian began issuing a shorter letter without the detailed response found in the first letter, and limited its comment to briefly deny any use of the *Book of Mormon* as an archaeological guide by the institution.

Many members of the Latter-Day Saint movement claim historical authenticity of the *Book of Mormon*. Most, but not all, Mormons hold the book's connection to ancient American history as an article of their faith. This view finds no acceptance outside of Mormonism and is unique to this cult. The theory that the *Book of Mormon* is an ancient American history is not considered scientifically credible by anyone except the Mormon Church. Mormon apologists have proposed multiple theories to explain apparent inconsistencies with the archaeological, genetic, linguistic and other records. The *Book of Mormon* gives an account of two civilizations formed by families who supposedly migrated to the Americas. One group of families came from Jerusalem in 600 BC and afterward separated into two nations, known as the Nephites and the Lamanites. Another group came much earlier, when God confounded the tongues at the Tower of Babel (Genesis 11:5-9) and that group is known as the Jaredites. After thousands of years, all were destroyed except the Lamanites. Latter-Day Saints claim that these Lamanites are among the ancestors of the current Native Americans. The dominant and widely accepted view among Latter-Day Saints is that the *Book of Mormon* is a true and accurate account of these ancient American civilizations whose religious history it documents.

Joseph Smith, whom most Latter-Day Saints believe to have translated the work, stated, "I told the brethren that the *Book of Mormon* was the most correct of any book on earth, and the keystone of our religion, and a man would get nearer to God by abiding by its precepts, than by any other book." Unresolved issues of the book's historicity and the lack of supporting archaeological evidence have led some adherents to adopt the position that the *Book of Mormon* may have been the creation of Smith, but that it was nevertheless divinely inspired. Between these two views is the view held by some Latter-Day Saints that the *Book of Mormon* is a divine work of a spiritual nature, written in ancient America, but that its purpose is to teach of Christ and not to be used as a guide for history, geology, archaeology, or anthropology.

One comment made by a researcher of truth said:

> The author labored to give his words and phrases the quaint, old-fashioned sound and structure of our King James's translation of the Scriptures; and the result is a mongrel – half modern glibness, and half ancient simplicity and gravity. The latter is awkward and constrained; the former natural, but grotesque by the contrast. Whenever he found his speech growing too modern -- which was about every sentence or two – he ladled in a few such Scriptural phrases as "exceeding sore," "and it came to pass," etc., and made things satisfactory again. "And it came to pass" was his pet. If he had left that out, his Bible would have been only a pamphlet.

After interviewing a large number of adherents of the Mormon Church, one member of our research team discovered that many did not actually believe in the original story of young Joseph Smith as recorded in the journals of the Mormon Church, namely Smith having a visitation and meeting with God, Jesus Christ and the angels, plus being directed to the discovery of golden plates on a hill called Cumorah near Palmyra, New York State, USA, where he lived with his parents. They however still felt that they had benefitted from being members of the Church because of the support and help of their local congregation (Stake), both financially and by food banks, plus socially and family connections and would never, ever abandon their religion for these reasons alone, whether it is the true religion or not was irrelevant to them. Plus, they accepted the story of Joseph Smith as it was instructed and written down by the Church as an article of faith similar to the Ten Commandments written down by Moses in the Bible.

Joseph Smith said that he found the golden plates on September 22, 1823 on a hill, near his home in Manchester, New York, after the angel Moroni directed him to a buried stone box. He said that the angel prevented him from taking the plates but instructed him to return to the same location one year later. He returned to that site every single year, but it was not until September 1827 that he recovered the plates on his fourth annual attempt to retrieve them. He returned home with a heavy object wrapped in a frock, which he then put in a box. He allowed others to lift the box but said that the angel had forbidden him to show the plates to anyone until they had been translated from their original reformed Egyptian language. Smith dictated the text of the *Book of Mormon*, claiming that it was a translation of the plates.

Many members of the Mormon Church interviewed were very intelligent, well-educated individuals and said that they could not really accept or believe this miraculous account of young Joseph Smith as officially claimed by the Mormon Church, but they did acknowledge and accept it as an 'article of faith' as one described. They also likewise accepted as an additional article of faith that Jesus of Nazareth was the son of God and was transferred from heaven to be born on earth in Bethlehem from a young Jewish virgin girl called Mary, but there is no proof of this event either, they said. This article of faith regarding the miraculous birth of Jesus Christ is well documented in the four gospels of the Holy Bible and is accepted by most modern Christian religions, even including the cult of Jehovah's Witnesses. Within the Latter-Day Saint movement, the 13 Articles of Faith is a statement of beliefs composed by Joseph Smith and first published in the Mormon newspaper *Times and Seasons*. It is a concise listing of thirteen fundamental doctrines of Mormonism. Most Latter-Day Saint denominations view the articles as an authoritative statement of basic theology. Some denominations, such as The Church of Jesus Christ of Latter-day Saints (LDS Church), have adopted the articles as scripture (see Pearl of Great Price).

A question posed by a member of our research team, how did this religious sect become so popular and today claim to have over 15 million members worldwide? The following information will perhaps explain this phenomenon. Joseph Smith the founder and leader of the Latter-Day Saint movement, and his brother Hyrum Smith were killed by a mob in Carthage, Illinois, on June 27, 1844. The two brothers had been in jail awaiting trial when an armed mob of about 200 men stormed the facility, their faces painted black with wet gunpowder. Hyrum was killed first, having been shot in the face. As he fell, Hyrum shouted, "I'm a dead man, Joseph!" After emptying the pistol with which he tried to defend himself, Joseph was then shot several times while trying to escape from a second-story window and fell from that window as he died.

Joseph Smith, as mayor of the town of Nauvoo, Illinois, had ordered the destruction of the facilities producing the Nauvoo Expositor, a newly established newspaper set up by a group of non-Mormons and people who had seceded from the church. The newspaper's first (and only) issue was deeply critical of Smith and other church leaders – reporting that Smith was practicing polygamy and claiming he intended to set himself up as a theocratic king. In response, Smith declared the paper a public nuisance and ordered its press destroyed. The destruction of the press led to charges of riot against the Smith brothers and other members of the Nauvoo City Council. Warrants for his arrest were dismissed by Nauvoo courts. Joseph Smith declared martial law in Nauvoo and called on the Nauvoo Legion to protect Nauvoo. The brothers voluntarily traveled to the county seat at Carthage and surrendered to the authorities to face the charges. After surrendering, the brothers were also charged with treason against the State of Illinois for declaring martial law. The brothers were in the Carthage jail awaiting trial when the mob attacked.

Five men were indicted for the killings but were acquitted at a jury trial. At the time of his death, Joseph Smith was also running for President of the United States; crazy as it may sound. Smith's death marked a turning point for the church, and since then, members of the Latter-Day Saint movement have generally viewed that the two men were murdered in cold blood and were religious martyrs (similar to Jesus Christ). Joseph Smith, now being classified as a martyr, this no doubt inspired the few loyal followers and this religion eventually grew to a current membership of approximately 15 million worldwide.

To present a fair and balanced view of the martyrdom of Joseph Smith, this quote below; direct from the LDS Church press office is both enlightening and touching. We also hope this information will help our readers to become more aware of the dangers of religious slavery and how to free themselves. When we speak of the mob that killed Joseph and Hyrum Smith in Carthage Jail, we sometimes forget that each of these men had names and lives. One of these men, from the militia in the neighboring town of Warsaw, Illinois, commemorated his participation in the killings engraved on this horn, which carried his gunpowder: "Warsaw Regulators, The end of the Polygamist Joseph Smith kilt at Carthage Jail June 27, 1844." While we do not know the name of the man who owned this powder horn, we do know the names of several men who helped organize and carry out the plan to kill the Prophet Joseph. As two commentators have stated:

> The murder of Joseph and Hyrum Smith at Carthage, Illinois, was not a spontaneous, impulsive act by a few personal enemies of the Mormon leaders, but a deliberate political assassination, committed or condoned by some of the leading citizens in Hancock County [Illinois].

> Joseph Smith had faced opposition, suspicion, and persecution most of his life, from the time he first saw God the Father and His Son, Jesus Christ, at age 14. As the Church grew, opposition shifted from mockery of the religious beliefs of Church members to distrust and fear of the Church's – and Joseph Smith's – growing political power. In Nauvoo, Illinois, conflict that had simmered for years came to a boil when Joseph and the city council ordered the destruction of the *Nauvoo Expositor* press. The *Nauvoo Expositor* was a newspaper

published by apostate members of the Church who were
opposed to plural marriage, a practice that had been growing in
Nauvoo. The paper argued that Joseph Smith, "had too much
power, that polygamy was whoredom in disguise, and that the
Nauvoo charter should be unconditionally repealed."

While many people hoped that the death of Joseph Smith would also
mean the end of the Mormons, today millions of Church members
around the world join in singing,

> Hail to the Prophet, ascended to heaven!
> Traitors and tyrants now fight him in vain.
> Mingling with Gods, he can plan for his brethren;
> Death cannot conquer the hero again.

After the assassination of the original founder and leader of the
Mormon Church, Joseph Smith, Brigham Young became the new
leader in 1838. Brigham was born to John Young and Abigail Nabby
Howe, a farming family in Whitingham, Vermont, and worked as
a travelling carpenter and blacksmith, among other trades. Young
was first married in 1824 to Miriam Angeline Works. Though he
had converted to the Methodist faith in 1823, Young was drawn
to Mormonism after reading the Book of Mormon shortly after its
publication in 1830. He officially joined the new church in 1832 and
traveled to Upper Canada as a missionary. After his wife died in 1832,
Young joined many Mormons in establishing a community in Kirtland,
Ohio. Young was then ordained a member of the original Quorum of
the Twelve Apostles in 1835, and he assumed a leadership role within
that organization in taking Mormonism to the United Kingdom and
organizing the exodus of Latter-Day Saints from Missouri in 1838.
Young was the longest-serving President of the LDS Church in history,
having served for 29 years. (To read more about this enigmatic character,
Brigham Young, and what he accomplished in Salt Lake City, please
read our Special Report No. 2, in the Appendix.)

Shortly after the arrival in what is now known as the State of Utah, in
the United States of America, Young and his pioneers, established the
new Mormon colonies and were incorporated into the United States
through the Mexican Cession of 1848. Young petitioned the U.S.
Congress to create the State of Deseret. *The Compromise of 1850* instead

carved out Utah Territory and Young was installed as governor. As governor and church president, Young directed both religious and economic matters, which is a most powerful position for any man to occupy. He encouraged independence and self-sufficiency. Many cities and towns in Utah, and some in neighboring states, were founded under Young's direction. Young's leadership style has been viewed as autocratic. The Republic of Texas was a sovereign state in North America that existed from March 2, 1836, to February 19, 1846. It was bordered by Mexico to the west and southwest, the Gulf of Mexico to the southeast, the two U.S. states of Louisiana and Arkansas to the east and northeast, and United States territories encompassing parts of the current U.S. state of Oklahoma, Kansas, Colorado, Wyoming, and New Mexico to the north and west.

When federal officials received reports of widespread and systematic obstruction of federal officials in Utah (most notably judges), American President James Buchanan (1791-1868) decided to install a non-Mormon governor. Buchanan accepted the reports of the judges without any further investigation, and the new non-sectarian governor was accompanied by troops sent to garrison forts in the new territory. When Young received word that federal troops were headed to Utah with his replacement, he called out his militia to ambush the federal force. During the defense of Utah, now called the Utah War, Young held the U.S. Army at bay for a whole winter by taking their cattle and burning supply wagons. The Mormon forces were largely successful thanks to a man called Lot Smith. However Young eventually relented and agreed to step down as governor. He later received a full pardon from President Buchanan. Relations between Young and future governors and U.S. Presidents were mixed.

Over time the Mormon Church and Jehovah's Witnesses will be forced to relax their slave like control of their members in order to retain membership and prevent further falling away of their followers. In a news release (April, 2019), the Mormon Church said it would allow children of LGBTQ (lesbian, gay, bisexual, and transgender) parents to be baptized and blessed in the church. It will also update its handbook to no longer categorize same-sex marriage as an act of apostasy, or abandonment of the church and its values. According to the release, church President Dallin H. Oaks said the changes will be effective immediately. Previously, the church faced backlash after enacting a policy barring children of LGBTQ parents from joining the church until they turned 18 and leave their parents' home. The church has altered its teachings on LGBTQ relationships in recent years, saying it no longer considers same-sex attraction a sin. No doubt the Watchtower Society is fully aware of these changes by the Mormons and from rumors they will also perhaps relax their strict rules regarding this issue.

***

Finances of The Church of Jesus Christ of Latter-day Saints are similar to other non-profit and religious organizations, in that their funding comes from the donations of its members and the principal expense is in constructing and maintaining facilities, plus other unrecorded expenses. When the LDS Church takes in more donations than it pays out in period expenses, it uses the surplus to build a reserve for capital expenditures and for future years when period expenses may exceed donations. The church invests its reserve to maintain the principal and generate a reasonable return and directs its investments into income-producing assets. The LDS Church has not publicly disclosed its financial statements in the United States since 1959. The Mormon Church at the time said the estimates were grossly exaggerated, but a recent investigation by Reuters in collaboration with sociology Professor Cragun estimates that the LDS Church is likely worth $40 billion today and collects up to $8 billion in tithing each year, very similar to the Watchtower Society's received contributions. The Church of Jesus Christ of Latter-day Saints is about to become one of Florida's largest private landowners in a move that is drawing speculation and even concern among some conservation and environmental groups as they have heard reports that a large compound for the exclusive use of Mormons is being planned similar to the Watchtower Society and their recently built compounds. The LDS Church has connections to or owns U.S. stock market holdings valued at least $32 billion according to information gathered from an independent website.

In a report that appeared in the *Washington Post* of January 16, 2020 it revealed the source of this whistleblower and the complaint about a massive $100 billion the Mormon Church was hoarding:

Growing up in a Mormon family of 10 children, David and Lars Nielsen had a special bond. They were Science Olympiad partners in high school in Modesto, Calif., and chemistry lab partners at Brigham Young University in Provo, Utah. They helped each other through prestigious MBA programs and, as fathers, took their kids to ride motorcycles in the Black Hills of South Dakota. When David, a former investment manager for the Church of Jesus Christ of Latter-day Saints, made the dramatic decision last fall to file a confidential whistleblower complaint, he turned to a trustworthy, familiar partner: his twin, Lars. The 41-year-olds began spending 10-hour days working on a project they called "the Mormon Giga-church," Lars said.

The brothers decided to compile the complaint after each had come to question aspects of the religion their family had practiced since the earliest days of the church, according to interviews with Lars and correspondence from his brother that Lars provided to *The Washington Post*. But it was Lars, acting alone, who decided to go public with the complaint. And after a lifetime of shared aims, that decision has opened a rift between the twins so deep that they stopped speaking to each other. The trove of documents the brothers submitted to the Internal Revenue Service in November alleges that the church has amassed about $100 billion in accounts intended for charitable purposes. Their report accuses church leaders of misleading members – and possibly breaching federal tax rules – by stockpiling surplus donations instead of using them for charitable works. It also accuses church leaders of using the tax-exempt donations to prop up a pair of local businesses.

It truly boggles the mind when one reviews the list of investment companies the Mormon Church owns and controls as a non-profit organization and the following list from the website Mormon Leaks provides the following details regarding the billions of dollars in LLC company assets.

Mormon Leaks provided the names of at least the 13 LLC companies:

Ashmore Wealth Management LLC, valued at $1,918,532,000.0

Argyll Research LLC, valued at $446,327,000.00

Clifton Park Capital Management, LLC, valued at $880,518,000.00

Cortland Advisers LLC, valued at 2,177,742,000.00

Elkfork Partners LLC, valued at $3,687,774,000.00

Flinton Capital Management LLC, valued at $2,943,847,000.00

Glen Harbor Capital Management LLC, valued at $4,407,275,000.00

Green Valley Investors LLC, valued at $2,098,464,000.00

Meadow Creek Investment Management LLC, valued at $4,603,236,000.00

Neuburgh Advisers LLC, valued at $2,791,122,000.00

Riverhead Capital Management LLC, valued at $2,361,388,000.00

Tiverton Asset Management LLC, valued at $1,598,252,000.00

Tyers Asset Management, valued at $2,855,436,000.00

These companies have a combined value of $32,769,914,000.00.

In fairness to our readers and the policy of the MTC International Foundation, we have included the official statement from the LDS Church in a press release:

> We take seriously the responsibility to care for the tithes and donations received from members. The vast majority of these funds are used immediately to meet the needs of the growing Church including more meetinghouses, temples, education, humanitarian work and missionary efforts throughout the world. Over many years, a portion is methodically safeguarded through wise financial management and the building of a prudent reserve for the future. This is a sound doctrinal and financial principle taught by the Savior in the Parable of the Talents and lived by the Church and its members. All Church funds exist for no other reason than to support the Church's divinely appointed mission. Claims being currently circulated are based on a narrow perspective and limited information. The Church complies with all applicable laws governing our

donations, investments, taxes, and reserves. We continue to
welcome the opportunity to work with officials to address
questions they may have.

The LDS Church supplied the following information to our research
team in May 2018, which is more than we could obtain from the
Watchtower Society officials and their cash holdings.

- While many might think the widespread influence and real estate
  assets of the Church indicate that it is a financially profitable
  organization, the current prosperity of the Church only reflects
  and is measured by the faith of its members as they observe the
  law of tithing and follow principles for provident living and self-
  reliance. Buildings owned by the Church are only maintained
  and updated by the ongoing support of the Church's faithful
  members.

- The Church pays all taxes required by law. This is true worldwide
  as the Church follows the laws required by each nation in which
  it has a presence. Church-affiliated entities that are organized as
  for-profit corporations pay all required taxes on their net income.

- In order to prevent any misuse of funds, Church leadership
  ensures all expenditures are approved by the First Presidency, the
  Quorum of the Twelve Apostles, and the Presiding Bishopric.
  Certified professionals also perform regular audits to ensure
  practices adhere to Church policies and principles.

- Following the principle of preparing for the future, the
  Church maintains diversified reserves, including stocks, bonds,
  commercial and residential real estate, and agricultural properties.
  All funds are invested solely to support the Church's mission and
  help prepare for the Lord's Second Coming. The Church carefully
  chooses its investments with the help of certified professional
  financial advisers. The majority of the Church's reserves are
  funded through the sacred tithes and offerings given by members.
  Reserve funds of the Church have historically been used when
  resources have been scarce or when Church growth has deemed
  extra resources necessary. These funds provide for the future and
  ensure necessary resources will continue to be available as the
  Church grows.

- Recognizing an increasing need for welfare and humanitarian needs around the world, the Church has spent billions of dollars to help meet these needs over the past few years. Church-affiliated entities also contribute to these funds and give regularly to various charitable causes. Many Church members donate their own time and resources to also help in these efforts. The Church dedicates significant resources to educational and humanitarian efforts aimed to help people rise out of poverty and achieve self-reliance. As the Church grows, increasing financial means are needed to continue to preach the message of Jesus Christ. The Church continues to maintain and build its reserves in anticipation of this growth.

- Church members donate 10 percent of their income to the Church as tithing. It is through this spiritual principle that the Lord funds His Church. Members believe promised spiritual and temporal blessings follow those who obey God's commandments.

In a recent article by reporter Sam Brunson that appeared on the website, By Common Consent (BCC) he reported regarding this $100 billion bank account:

> Has it really been nearly a year and three months since Lars Nielson released his brother's whistleblower complaint against the church? What felt like the story that would dominate news of Mormonism in 2020 was quickly buried by Trumpian scandals and then the worldwide pandemic? Like most people, I've only thought about the $100 billion endowment fleetingly over the last year or so; I've been more wrapped up in translating my job to my home, helping my kids become at-home students, and playing the saxophone. Monday, though, a court decision came across my desk that made me think of Ensign Peak Advisors and Lars Nielson. See, one reason his brother filed a complaint with the IRS was in hopes of getting a whistleblower award. Statutorily, whistleblowers are entitled to receive between 15 and 30% of the amount the IRS collects as a result of their complaint.
>
> Now I'm not trying to suggest that the Nielsons are similarly going to try to compel the IRS to pursue an investigation of Ensign Peak Advisors. But it is worth noting that the courts have made it very clear that they cannot force the IRS to

pursue an investigation it doesn't want to and that the IRS has no obligation to pay a whistleblower claim unless it decides to follow through on the complaint.

In the 2019 list of the world's wealthiest religious organization, the LDS Church comes out at No.1 with a net worth of $67 billion with the Watchtower Society coming in No.2. Questions persist today in 2019, inside and outside the Church of Jesus Christ of Latter-Day Saints about the now claimed $100 billion reserve the faith has amassed in an investment account. In the Mormon Land podcast, historian D. Michael Quinn says the church's reserves are actually much steeper than has been reported. But, he adds, so are its expenses, especially in supporting its global presence.

Dennis Michael Quinn (born March 26, 1944) is an American historian who has focused on the history of the Church of Jesus Christ of Latter-day Saints (LDS Church). He was a professor at Brigham Young University (BYU) in Provo, Utah, from 1976 until he resigned in 1988. At the time, his work concerned church involvement with plural marriage after the 1890 Manifesto, when new polygamous marriages were officially prohibited. He was excommunicated from the church as one of the September Six and is now openly gay. His three most influential books, each of which is the focal point of intense controversy, are Early Mormonism and the Magic World View, The Mormon Hierarchy: Origins of Power, and The Mormon Hierarchy: Extensions of Power.

The *Salt Lake Tribune* of 20 March, 2020 reported that Ensign Peak Advisors, the investment arm of the LDS Church, reported a total of $38.7 billion of holdings in the U.S. stock market. Truth & Transparency website first reported on this topic in May, 2018 by uncovering $32 billion traded by 13 shell companies connected to the Church, and again last month when revealing the increased value of those shell companies as well as venture capital investments made by another shell company connected to the Church. Last month, in another unprecedented move, the Church gave an exclusive interview to the *Wall Street Journal* discussing the portfolio, admitting to having intentionally obfuscated the paper trail with the shell companies discovered by Truth & Transparency. They feared that members would reduce their tithing donations to the Church.

This story from the *Salt Lake Tribune* implies that this $38 billion is in addition to the money already reported by Truth & Transparency saying that Ensign Peak's portfolio is more diversified than any of those smaller funds. However, closer analysis of the data suggests otherwise. This money is obviously a fraction of the $100 billion known to be controlled by the Church, as originally reported by the *Washington Post*, and simply the only amount discovered through public records. While it is likely that only a small portion of the $38 billion reported by the *Salt Lake Tribune* wasn't already known, the Church is obviously making strides in becoming more financially transparent. Time will tell if the behavior is the new norm or a one-time attempt to silence critics.

Court cases are now being filed against the Mormon Church for their blatant misuse of these funds received by tithing. For example, in 2020 a member of a leading Mormon family, the very wealthy Huntsman family of Salt Lake City included the following statement in their court filing according to the *Salt Lake Tribune*.

> For decades, in a fraudulent effort to elicit the donation of tithing funds from Mr. Huntsman and other devout Church members, the LDS Corporation repeatedly and publicly lied about the intended use of those funds, promising that they would be used for purely non-commercial purposes consistent with the Church's stated priorities namely, to fund missionary work, member indoctrination, temple work, and other educational and charitable activities. Behind the scenes, however, rather than using tithing funds for the true purpose they lined their own pockets by using these funds to develop a multi-billion-dollar real estate and insurance empire that had nothing to do with charity.

The following report was submitted to our team of researchers and underlines the power of the masters of modern religion. The comments are equally applicable to the masters of the Watchtower Society as both of these cults operate on the similar lines of autocratic control. This quote is from the *Midwest Book Review*:

> The Mormon Church today is led by an elite group of older men, nearly three-quarters of whom are related to current or past general church authorities. This dynastic hierarchy meets

in private; neither its minutes nor the church's finances are available for public review. Members are reassured by public relations spokesmen that all is well and that harmony prevails among the brethren. But by interviewing former church aides, examining hundreds of diaries, and drawing from his own past experience as an insider within the Latter-day Saint historical department, Michael Quinn presents a fuller view. His extensive research documents how the governing apostles, seventies, and presiding bishops are strong-willed, independent men (much like the directors of a large corporation) who lobby their colleagues, forge alliances, out-maneuver opponents, and broker compromises. Quinn's *The Mormon Hierarchy: Extensions Of Power* reveals clandestine political activities, investigative and punitive actions by church security forces, personal loans from church coffers (later written off as bad debts), and other privileged power-vested activities. *The Mormon Hierarchy* considers the changing role and attitude of the leadership toward visionary experiences, the momentous events which have shaped quorum protocol and doctrine, and day-to-day bureaucratic intrigue from the time of Brigham Young to the dawn of the twenty-first century.

Growth of this cult is also now stagnating and actually decreasing in many areas of the world to the great disappointment of its leaders and masters. Wilfred Decoo reported:

Last week the church reported 16,565,036 members. What did some foresee a quarter of a century ago for 2020? In the *Ensign* magazine of August 1993, an analysis of church growth concluded: "If growth rates for the past decade remain constant, membership will increase to 12 million by the year 2000, to 35 million by 2020, and to 157 million by the mid-twenty-first century. By 2020 a majority of all church members will reside in Latin America with less than one-fourth in North America, a near reversal of the 1995 pattern in just twenty-five years."

A similar projection in 1996 was reported in the quarterly journal, *Dialogue: A Journal of Mormon Thought*. The editor wrote based on various factors but with plenty of reservations, leading to a cautious:

The First Presidency in 2020 will preside over no more than about 35 million members. However, their most positive projections, based on regional dynamics goes on to say, generate forecasts which cumulatively project much higher growth rates than those based on the combined population. Thus, the cumulative membership size for the Series 1 projections [based on regional growth rates between 1980 and 1990] in 2020 comes to 121 million.

There are quite a few factors that may influence church growth. For conversion: changing attitudes toward organized religion, credibility of the message, tolerability to the claim of exclusive truth, international distinctness of the church's name in languages around the world, missionary volume and effectiveness, public relations efficiency, countries' political openness, migration impact, and more. Within the church, programs, activity rate, retention, fundamentalization or not, changing fertility, generational shifts, and more, play their role. I would also refer to the more recent analyses by Ryan Cragun and Ronald Lawson. They do not predict numerical developments, but come to sobering conclusions as to the future by examining the membership data for comparable proselytizing groups – Mormons, Jehovah's Witnesses, and Seventh-Day Adventists. A main reason for the much lower result than most projections anticipated is probably to be found in the secular transition related to the level of economic development in each country.

[Their conclusion:] The single largest predictor of growth is growth momentum – once a religious group starts to grow in a country, it continues to grow. However, that growth eventually slows due to a variety of factors, including reaching a saturation point and reduced demand. Aside from momentum, both supply and demand factors are important. However, of these, the most prominent is level of economic development. It appears that once that these countries reach a moderately high level of economic development, the same three groups experience very little to no growth. Whether that is due to modernization generally or social safety nets specifically, we cannot say. Future research should attempt to discern which of the two (it may be both) actually causes the secular transition.

Either way, it is clear that once that point is reached, the future of these proselytizing religious groups in those countries is very gloomy.

According to the latest news from the Mormon Church, they are also on the decline just like the Watchtower Society. The Church discontinued at least two large congregations in California during 2020. Part of a long-term trend of Church decline, the Church in California has struggled for decades to achieve measurable growth due to high rates of member relocation to other states. The number of congregations in California has decreased from an all-time high of 162 in 1995 to 151 at present, with likely several more consolidations in the near future.

This autocratic and domineering religion, the Mormon Church, also admit that they have made serious mistakes in the past but will not openly admit at this stage that currently they are viewed as a cult of the worst kind, but this may change as they integrate into the more conventional religious movements and just become another sect of Christendom. The so-called Apostle Dieter F. Uchtdorf's October 2013 speech in which he conceded that church leaders have simply made mistakes and said or done [things] that were not in harmony with our values, principles or doctrine. We openly acknowledge this fact, Uchtdorf also said, "that in nearly 200 years of church history, along with an uninterrupted line of inspired, honorable and divine events there have been some things said and done that could cause people to question."

> *Editor's Note*: Is there a hidden message to the Watchtower Society somewhere in these words of Uchtdorf? We are sure that at this present time the Governing Body and their helpers are experiencing a similar problem of should they admit their mistakes also?

In conclusion, we refer to writer Ron Rhodes and what he said in his book about Mormons that hints at a possible compromise of claiming to be the exclusive church of Almighty God and some of its more stringent teachings. "The Mormon church has in recent years sought to downplay its exclusivism as the restored church. Indeed, the Mormon church has increasingly become involved with the interfaith movement, joining with various Christian denominations in various charities." So, this fact alone may be the future of this religious cult, but we patiently wait and see!

Chapter Five: Christian Science

The next three chapters of our book, cover religious cults that are now slowly sliding into oblivion, which illustrates the basic principle that this is what happens to cults when their solicited funds start to dry up, usually accompanied with a shrinking membership.

We have included some details that our researchers uncovered but not to the same depth as the cults covered in Chapter 2, 3 and 4, as these religious cults are the most dangerous and treacherous in modern times. These religions may slowly weaken and water down their strict teachings, doctrines, rules and policies in order to retain membership and keep the cash flow coming in. A clear example of this relaxing of strict policy is the Mormon Church who up until recently strongly resisted any change in their view of the LGBT community, but as from 2019 they now accept them as members of their church. It has been distinctly noted in our research, the Watchtower Society very often copies and imitates what the Mormon Church does, and there has been suggestions that at times there have been secret meetings and collusion between these two groups. So perhaps we will also soon see a weakening of some of the strict rules of the Watchtower Society in order to keep their membership from sliding further downwards. If these changes continue then both of these religions will eventually simply become conformists and operate very similar to the many other conventional religions throughout the world.

Christian Science is a set of beliefs and practices belonging to the metaphysical family of new religious movements. Metaphysics is the branch of philosophy that examines the fundamental nature of reality, including the relationship between mind and matter, between substance and attribute, and between potentiality and actuality. It was developed in 19th-century New England by Mary Baker Eddy, who argued in her 1875 book *Science and Health* that sickness is an illusion that can be corrected by prayer alone. The book became Christian Science's central text, along with the Bible, and by 2001 had sold over nine million copies.

Mary Eddy Baker (1953), courtesy of Creative Commons and Getty Images

Mary Baker Eddy and 26 followers were granted a charter in 1879 to found the Church of Christ, Scientist, and in 1894 the Mother Church, The First Church of Christ, Scientist, was built in Boston, Massachusetts. Christian Science became the fastest growing religion in the United States, with nearly 270,000 members by 1936, a figure that had declined by 1990 to just over 100,000. The church is known for its newspaper, the *Christian Science Monitor*, which won seven Pulitzer Prizes between 1950 and 2002, and for its public Reading Rooms around the world.

Christian Science Seal, courtesy of Creative Commons. (note the similarity to the
Watchtower Society symbol used for many years on their official journal,
the *Watchtower*)

Mary Eddy described Christian Science as a return to primitive
Christianity and its lost element of healing. There are key differences
between Christian Science theology and that of other branches of
Christianity. In particular, adherents subscribe to a radical form of
philosophical idealism, believing that reality is purely spiritual and
the material world an illusion. This includes the view that disease is a
mental error rather than physical disorder, and that the sick should be
treated not by medicine, but by a form of prayer that seeks to correct the
beliefs responsible for the illusion of ill health.

The church does not require that Christian Scientists avoid all medical
care – adherents use dentists, optometrists, obstetricians, physicians for
broken bones, and vaccination when required by law – but maintains
that Christian-Science prayer is most effective when not combined
with medicine. Between the 1880s and 1990s, the avoidance of medical
treatment led to the deaths of many adherents and their children.[26]
Parents and others were prosecuted for, and in a few cases convicted of,
manslaughter or neglect.

Several periods of Protestant Christian revival nurtured a proliferation
of new religious movements in the United States, as for example the

---

[26] Many uninformed individuals sometimes get confused between the Christian
Science movement refusing medical treatment and the Watchtower Society
movement refusing blood transfusions.

Mormons and Jehovah's Witnesses. In the latter half of the 19th century these included what came to be known as the metaphysical family: groups such as Christian Science, Divine Science, the Unity School of Christianity and later in 1927 the United Church of Religious Science. In 1927, Ernest Holmes (1887–1960) established the Institute of Religious Science and Philosophy in Los Angeles to teach his principles and belief in the power of the mind for healing and fulfillment of life. From the 1890s the liberal section of the movement became known as New Thought, in part to distinguish it from the more authoritarian Christian Science.

This quote from the *Encyclopedia Britannica* sheds some light on additional interesting facts about the background of Christian Science religion.

> In the history of religion, Christian Science is a small movement, but it has had significance out of proportion to its size. It is one of several lasting movements from 19th-century America and reflects the interest of many religious groups in the revitalization of primitive Christianity. Yet Christian Science has aroused considerable controversy as well as misunderstanding as a result of its view of creation as wholly spiritual, a view that breaks decisively with traditional Christian cosmology and scientific materialism. Eddy's view of the material world and the practices that stemmed from it distinguished Christian Science from similar movements.
>
> While she shared much with the tradition of philosophical idealism (which also stresses the role of the spirit in understanding the world), especially with transcendentalism, her emphasis on healing differentiates Christian Science from forms of idealism that interpret experience but do not attempt to affect it. In Christian Science the cure of disease through prayer is seen as a necessary element in the process of redemption.
>
> Eddy's teachings have led to a complex relationship between church members and the medical establishment. Christian Scientists are not compelled by the church to practice faith healing, and they generally employ the services of dentists and optometrists for care of teeth and eyes, respectively, and

often those of physicians for setting broken bones or delivering babies. The church also encourages members to scrupulously obey public health laws, including quarantine regulations and immunization requirements, when religious exemptions are not provided. Officials of The Mother Church, on the other hand, have worked diligently for the enactment of laws in the United States to accommodate Christian Science practice. Christian Scientists needing nursing care are encouraged to go to a Christian Science sanitarium or to seek home care from a Christian Science nurse.

Although it offers a unique theology, Christian Science's major impact on the world has come from its ministry of spiritual healing. Many of the more than 50,000 testimonials of healing reported by the church since the beginning of the 20th century concern undiagnosed disorders, emotional problems, and psychosomatic illnesses. On the other hand, a substantial number of healings involve conditions diagnosed by physicians as congenital, degenerative, or terminal, though there has been little systematic evaluation of such healings. Furthermore, Eddy's emphasis on healing had a direct influence on the revival of interest in spiritual healing in mainstream Protestantism.

The healing performed in the Pentecostal and Holiness churches and in healing movements including the Order of St. Luke (Episcopal Church) was inspired by the ministry of two of Eddy's contemporaries, Charles Cullis and the Reverend Elwood Worcester. While not a feminist, Eddy was clearly liberated, assigned strong females to key leadership positions, and taught that the spiritual equality of men and women must have political and social effects. A report by the U.S. Bureau of the Census in 1936 listed The Mother Church membership in the United States at about 269,000. Following this dramatic early growth, there was a period of leveling off in the 1930s and '40s and steady decline since then.

The term metaphysical referred to the movement's philosophical idealism, is a belief in the primacy of the mental world. Adherents believed that material phenomena were the result of mental states, a view expressed as life is consciousness and God is mind. The metaphysical groups became known as the mind-cure movement because of their strong focus on healing. Medical practice was in its infancy, and patients regularly fared better without it. This provided fertile soil for the mind-cure groups, who argued that sickness was an absence of right thinking or failure to connect to Divine Mind. The movement traced its roots in the United States to Phineas Parkhurst Quimby (1802–1866), a New England clockmaker turned mental healer, and whose motto was the truth is the cure. Mary Baker Eddy had been a patient of his; leading to debate about how much of Christian Science was based on his ideas. Most significantly, she dismissed the material world as an illusion, rather than as merely subordinate to Mind, leading her to reject the use of medicine, or *materia medica*, and making Christian Science the most controversial of the metaphysical groups. Reality for Eddy was purely spiritual.

At the core of Eddy's theology is the view that the spiritual world is the only reality and is entirely good, and that the material world, with its evil, sickness and death, is an illusion. Eddy saw humanity as an idea of Mind that is perfect, eternal, unlimited, and reflects the divine, according to Bryan Wilson; what she called mortal man is simply humanity's distorted view of itself. Despite her view of the non-existence of evil, an important element of Christian Science theology is that evil thought, in the form of malicious animal magnetism, can cause harm, even if the harm is only apparent. Eddy viewed God not as a person but as All-in-all. Although she often described God in the language of personhood – she used the term Father-Mother God (as did Ann Lee, the founder of Shakerism), and in the third edition of *Science and Health* she referred to God as she – God is mostly represented in Christian Science by the synonyms, Mind, Spirit, Soul, Principle, Life, Truth, Love.

Eddy's view on life after death was vague and, according to Bryan Wilson in his excellent book *Cults & Religion*, there is no doctrine of the soul in Christian Science: "After death, the individual continues his probationary state until he has worked out his own salvation by proving the truths of Christian Science." Eddy did not believe that the dead and living could communicate. In 1907, Mark Twain described the appeal of the new religion:

She has delivered to them a religion which has revolutionized their lives, banished the glooms that shadowed them, and filled them and flooded them with sunshine and gladness and peace; a religion which has no hell; a religion whose heaven is not put off to another time, with a break and a gulf between, but begins here and now, and melts into eternity as fancies of the waking day melt into the dreams of sleep. They believe it is a Christianity that is in the New Testament; that it has always been there, that in the drift of ages it was lost through disuse and neglect, and that this benefactor has found it and given it back to men, turning the night of life into day, its terrors into myths, its lamentations into songs of emancipation and rejoicing.

Science and Health expanded on Eddy's view that sickness was a mental error. People said that simply reading *Science and Health* had healed them; cures were claimed for everything from cancer to blindness. Eddy wrote in the *New York Sun* in December, 1898, in an article called, To the Christian World, that she had personally healed tuberculosis, diphtheria and said:

At one visit a cancer that had eaten the flesh of the neck and exposed the jugular vein so that it stood out like a cord. I have physically restored sight to the blind, hearing to the deaf, speech to the dumb, and have made the lame walk.

Eddy wrote that her views had derived, in part, from having witnessed the apparent recovery of patients she had treated with homeopathic remedies so diluted they were drinking plain water. She concluded that Divine Mind was the healer: The author has attenuated Natrum muriaticum (common table-salt) until there was not a single saline property left ... and yet, with one drop of that attenuation in a goblet of water, and a teaspoonful of the water administered at intervals of three hours, she has cured a patient sinking in the last stage of typhoid fever. The highest attenuation of homeopathy, and the most potent rises above matter into mind. This discovery leads to more light. From it may be learned that either human faith or the divine Mind is the healer and that there is no efficacy in a drug.

Rodney Stark writes that a key to Christian Science's appeal at the time was that its success rate compared favorably with that of physicians, particularly when it came to women's medical and emotional health. Most doctors had not been to medical school, there were no antibiotics, and surgical practices were poor. By comparison the placebo effect (not being treated at all, no matter what the treatment was) worked well. Stark argues that the very elaborate and intensely psychological Christian Science treatments maximize such effects, while having the advantage of not causing further harm. Stark has proposed in his book The Rise of Christianity that Christianity grew through gradual individual conversions via social networks of family, friends and colleagues. His main contribution, by comparing documented evidence of Christianity's spread in the Roman Empire with the history of the LDS church (and the Watchtower Society) in the 19th and 20th centuries, was to illustrate that a sustained and continuous growth could lead to huge growth within 200 years. This use of exponential growth as a driver to explain the growth of the church without the need for mass conversions (deemed necessary by historians until then) is now widely accepted.

Stark has suggested that Christianity only grew because it treated women better than the pagan religions.

> *Editor's Note*: In numerous cases from my experience of many years as a Christian husband and father, plus as editor of this report, women have long been the driving force of mankind, mainly in discreetly protecting and humbly advancing the role of their husbands; also protecting them from making fools of themselves and also taking care of their precious children.

Rodney Stark also suggested that making Christianity the state religion of the Roman Empire weakened the faithfulness of the Christian community by bringing in people who did not really believe or had a weaker belief. This is consistent with Stark's published observations of contemporary religious movements, where once-successful faith movements gradually decline in fervor due to the free rider problem. This report by ex-members of this cult, Christian Scientists, on their website, The Ex-Christian Scientist, said of this cult and its leader:

> When Mary Eddy died in 1910 her estate was assessed at

approximately three million dollars. According to the U.S. Bureau of Labor Statistics inflation calculator, that's roughly equivalent to $73 million in 2016 terms. We know that Eddy invested in real estate and mortgages, so her equivalent net worth in 2016 dollars is probably much higher than $73 million. There are only two pathways to that kind of wealth: you can either be a successful entrepreneur or an investor. Mary Baker Eddy was both.

Sales of her book *Science and Health with Key to the Scriptures* provided another long-term income stream. [does this sound familiar?] The so-called Christian Science 'textbook' was indeed priced like a textbook, approaching $100 in 2016 terms. Eddy revised it constantly (over 400 revisions), and she insisted that students should always have the most recent edition [clever marketing]. Consequently, sales never declined with passing years – even if students upgraded only at major revisions. According to her publisher's accounts, she was paid $45,000 in royalties for the three years sales ending in 1895, well over $1 million in today's dollars. In my experience as an accountant and auditor, I have found the old adage follow the money to be useful in shedding light on an individual's motivations. As Jesus so aptly put it; where your treasure is there will your heart be also. In light of what we know of Mary Baker Eddy's financial history, it is clear that accumulating wealth was a priority for her, as with all leaders and 'masters' of modern religions. She succeeded because she marketed Christian Science brilliantly and invested shrewdly. It is ironic to note however, that although she made a lot of money by *marketing* healing, she didn't necessary practice healing, at least not too much. In fact, she adamantly refused to take patients – even the case of her own gravely ill grandchild. The critic Gillian Gill wrote in 1998, from a feminist perspective we suppose, admires Eddy's financial acumen. But Mark Twain, when he called her, "that shameless old swindler," is closer to my sentiment.

Mark Twain was a prominent contemporaneous critic of Eddy's. His first article about Christian Science was published in *Cosmopolitan* in October 1899. Another three appeared in 1902–1903 in *North American Review*, then a book, *Christian Science* (1907). He also wrote

The Secret History of Eddypus, the World Empire (1901-1902), in which Christian Science replaces Christianity and Eddy becomes the Pope. Twain described Eddy as, "grasping, sordid, penurious, famishing for everything she sees – money, power, glory – vain, untruthful, jealous, despotic, arrogant, insolent, pitiless where thinkers and hypnotists are concerned, illiterate, shallow, incapable of reasoning outside of commercial lines, immeasurably selfish." One of our researchers after reading Mark Twain's opinions of Christian Science and Mary Eddy posed the question; we wonder what Mark Twain would have thought about the Watchtower Society and the Mormons today, if he reviewed their history and modus operandi with such acumen and insight?

Mark Twain called *Science and Health* strange and frantic and incomprehensible and uninterpretable, and argued that Eddy had not written it herself. "There is nothing in Christian Science that is not explicable," he wrote, "for God is one, time is one, individuality is one, and may be one of a series, one of many, as an individual man, individual horse; whereas God is one, not one of a series, but one alone and without an equal." Mary Eddy apart, Mark Twain felt ambivalent toward mind-cure, arguing that the thing back of it is wholly gracious and beautiful. His daughter Clara Clemens became a Christian Scientist and wrote a book about it, *Awake to a Perfect Day*.

A census at the height of the religion's popularity in 1936 counted approximately 268,915 Christian Scientists members in the United States. With the movement in decline, the church has sold buildings to free up funds; it closed 23 of its churches in Los Angeles between 1960 and 1995, and in 2004 it sold the First Church of Christ, Scientist, Manhattan, to the Crenshaw Christian Center for $14 million. (The building was sold again in 2014 to be converted into condominiums.) Our readers will recognize the same pattern with the Watchtower Society covered in Chapter 3 of our narrative.

There were an estimated 106,000 Scientists in the United States in 1990, according to Rodney Stark. In 2009 the church said that for the first time more new members had been admitted from Africa than from the United States, although it offered no numbers. While the *Manual of the Mother Church* prohibits the church from publishing membership figures, the church does provide the names of Christian Science practitioners (members trained to offer Christian Science prayer on behalf of others). In 1941 there were 11,200 practitioners in the United States, against 965 in 2015 (1,249 worldwide). Stark writes that clusters of practitioners listed in the *Christian Science Journal* in 1998 were living in the same retirement communities.

From the very informative website, Evidence Unseen, this observation was made.

> Critics have noticed clear plagiarisms of her work from others who wrote before her. Few Christian Scientists realize that Mrs. Eddy's writings... also bristle with plagiarisms. Quite aside from what she stole from Quimby's papers, and from early books on mind healing, she copied shamelessly, often word for word, from John Ruskin, Thomas Carlyle, Charles Kingsley, Swiss critic Henri Amiel, and from other authors... not once did she credit her sources or even suggest to readers that she was cribbing.

The church also publishes the weekly *Christian Science Sentinel*, the monthly *Christian Science Journal*, and the *Herald of Christian Science*, a non-English publication. In April 2012, JSH-Online made back issues of the *Journal, Sentinel* and Herald available online to subscribers. The church faced internal dissent in 1991 over its decision to publish The *Destiny of The Mother Church*. Written and privately printed in 1943 by Bliss Knapp, former president of the Mother Church, the book suggested that Eddy was the Woman [the Harlot] of the Apocalypse of the Bible's New Testament book of Revelation. Knapp and his family bequeathed $98 million to the church on condition that it publish and authorize the book by 1993; otherwise, the money would go to Stanford University and the Los Angeles County Museum of Art. The church published and made the book available in Christian Science reading rooms. One senior employee was fired for failing to support the church's decision, and 18 of the 21 editorial staff of the religious journals resigned. In the end the other parties disputed that making the book available in Reading Rooms constituted authorization, and the bequest was split three ways.

Professor Charles Braden in his article of 1963 said:

Mary Baker Eddy pushed the postulates of positive thinking to their absolute limit. ... She proposed not merely that the spiritual overshadows the material, but that the material world does not exist. The world of our senses is but an illusion of our minds. If the material world causes us pain, grief, danger and even death, then that can be changed by changing our thoughts.

Caroline Fraser, Ph. D, formerly on the editorial staff of the *New Yorker*, her also had work in *The Atlantic Monthly* and New York Review of Books, among others. She is the author of *God's Perfect Child: Living and Dying in the Christian Science Church*. Written by a former Christian Scientist, and is the first unvarnished account of one of America's most controversial and least understood religious movements. Amazingly quite a few well-known Americans, from Lady Nancy Astor to Carol Burnett, George Getty to Jean Harlow, Ginger Rogers, Doris Day, Mary Pickford, and Robert Duvall, have all been touched by the teachings of the Church of Christ, Scientist.

In *God's Perfect Child*, Fraser examines the strange life and psychology of Mary Baker Eddy, who lived in dread of a kind of witchcraft she called Malicious Animal Magnetism. She takes us into the closed world of Eddy's followers, who refuse to acknowledge the existence of illness and death and reject modern medicine even at the cost of their children's lives. She reveals just how Scientists have managed to gain extraordinary legal and congressional sanction for the Church's dubious practices, explaining how the Church has won insurance coverage for their faith-healing treatments and Medicare reimbursements for religious services in their nursing homes. She also tracks the faith's enormous influence on New Age beliefs and other modern healing cults, including Scientology, Therapeutic Touch, and the movement based on A Course in Miracles. This book is a passionate expose of religious zealotry; telling one of the most dramatic and least-known stories in American religious history.

Chapter Six: Christadelphians

The Christadelphians are a millenarian Christian group who hold a view of Biblical Unitarianism. There are approximately 50,000 Christadelphians in around 120 countries. The movement developed in the United Kingdom and North America in the 19th century around the teachings of John Thomas, who coined the name Christadelphian from the Greek language for Brethren in Christ.

Claiming to base their beliefs solely on the Bible, Christadelphians differ from mainstream Christianity in a number of doctrinal areas. For example, they reject the Trinity and the immortality of the soul, believing these to be corruptions of original Christian teaching. They were initially found predominantly in the developed English-speaking world, but expanded in developing countries after the Second World War. Congregations are traditionally referred to as ecclesias and would not use the word church due to its association with mainstream Christianity, although today it is more acceptable.

The Christadelphians are a small Christian denomination. They might best be described as a conservative Christian movement which differs from conventional denominations in their beliefs concerning the nature of God, Jesus Christ, the Holy Spirit and Satan. Some conservative Christians in the Counter-Cult Movement (CCM) consider the Christadelphians to be a cult. This information from the news source, Stem Publishing, written by A. J. Pollock, is also useful:

> Its founder was Dr. John Thomas M.D., who was born in
> London in 1805 and died in New Jersey, U.S.A., in 1871.
> Though a medical man, he practiced medicine very little. At one
> time he took to farming, but made no success of it. The most of
> his life was spent in promulgating his strange doctrines by word
> of mouth, and the aid of a busy voluminous pen.

When twenty-seven years of age Dr. Thomas emigrated to the United States of America, and got into touch with and joined a religious sect named Campbellites, so called after the chief propagandist of the system. Baptism, as essential to salvation, is one of their chief doctrines. After some time, Dr. Thomas began to teach the non-immortality of the soul, to deny eternal punishment, etc., and indeed was beginning to shape what became in time known as Christadelphianism. When about thirty-three years old the divergence between Thomas and Campbell became acute, and occasioned a very wordy warfare on paper. It makes sad reading. Bitter personalities were indulged in on both sides. It ended in their parting. Laboring often under great disappointments and reverses, Dr. Thomas founded the sect that bears the name of Christadelphian. Dr. Thomas visited Great Britain three times, and finding his propaganda more prosperous in this country, decided to reside in England, went to the States to arrange his change of residence, but died before it could be carried into effect. We glean the accounts of how this sect originated from a biography of Dr. Thomas written by Mr. Robert Roberts.

Our research team discovered the following highlights about this cult. Their leaders are classified as lecturing brethren, managing brethren and presiding brethren. All are male volunteers who are elected to their posts. In common with many conservative Christian denominations, women are excluded from positions of authority. However, they are given equal voting rights. They have no paid clergy or church hierarchy. Members do not vote, run for political office, or go to war. Many members read the Bible daily; some use a reading plan which completes the Old Testament once per year and the New Testament twice. Some Christadelphians discourage their members having fellowship with Christians from other denominations.

Quoting from *All About Cults*:

> Christadelphians, a religious sect, was founded by Dr. John Thomas, the son of a British Congregationalist minister. During Thomas immigration to the United States in 1832, the ship encountered several violent storms. Thomas vowed that he would devote his life to the study of religion if God would spare his life. Shortly after his arrival in the United States, Thomas briefly associated himself with the Cambellites, while sharing their belief that Jesus Christ would return to earth in 1866.

But as he continued to study with the Cambellites, he soon disagreed with their teachings, left the group, and began his own sect called the Brethren of Christ.

Numerous religious movements in the middle 1800s began as an outgrowth of religious unrest -- Mormonism, Jehovah's Witnesses, Christian Science, Seventh Day Adventism, and Spiritism. Each sect tried to discover truth through a new revelation or by combining some truth with their own opinions. When the Civil War began, Thomas, along with his followers, believed that the war marked the beginning of the Battle of Armageddon (Revelation 16:16). The group embraced pacifism, refusing to participate in war. To be recognized as a religious group exempted from fighting, Thomas renamed his followers Christadelphians (1848) -- Greek for Brethren of Christ. Thomas visited England to introduce his new-found religion and then discovered the soil fertile for his beliefs on prophesy and the coming Kingdom. He returned to America again. His subsequent visits (1862 and 1869) to lecture in England helped anchor Christadelphianism in England. Because of his efforts, England has the largest number (20,000) of members in the world.

The Christadelphian religious group traces its origins to John Thomas (1805–1871), who immigrated to North America from England in 1832. Following a near shipwreck he vowed to find out the truth about life and God through personal Biblical study. Initially he sought to avoid the kind of sectarianism he had seen in England. In this he found sympathy with the rapidly emerging Restoration Movement in the US at the time, including other sects like the Mormons and the Watchtower Society. This movement sought a reform based upon the Bible alone as a sufficient guide and rejected all creeds. However, this liberality eventually led to dissent as John Thomas developed his personal beliefs and began to question mainstream orthodox Christian beliefs. While the Restoration Movement accepted Thomas's right to have his own beliefs, when he started preaching that they were essential to salvation, it led to a fierce series of debates with a notable leader of the movement, Alexander Campbell. John Thomas believed that scripture, as God's word, did not support a multiplicity of differing beliefs, and challenged the leaders to continue with the process of restoring 1st-century Christian beliefs and correct interpretation through a process of debate. The history of this process appears in the book, Dr. Thomas, His Life and Work by a fellow Christadelphian, Robert Roberts.

During this period of formulating his ideas John Thomas was baptized twice, the second time after renouncing the beliefs he previously held. He based his new position on a new appreciation for the reign of Christ on David's throne. The abjuration of his former beliefs eventually led to the Restoration Movement, disfellowshipping him when he toured England and they became aware of his abjuration in the United States of America.

Although the Christadelphian movement originated through the activities of John Thomas, he never saw himself as making his own disciples. He believed rather that he had rediscovered first century beliefs from the Bible alone, and sought to prove that belief through a process of challenge, debate and writing journals. Through that process a number of people became convinced and set up various fellowships that had sympathy with that position. Groups associated with John Thomas met under various names, including Believers, Baptized Believers, the Royal Association of Believers, Baptised Believers in the Kingdom of God, Nazarines (or Nazarenes), and The Antipas, until the time of the American Civil War (1861–1865). At that time, church affiliation was required in the United States and in the Confederacy in order to register for conscientious objector status, and in 1864 Thomas chose for registration purposes the name Christadelphian.

Initially, the denomination grew in the English-speaking world, particularly in the English Midlands and in parts of North America. In the early days after the death of John Thomas, the group could have moved in a number of directions. Doctrinal issues arose, debates took place, and statements of faith were created and amended as other issues arose. These attempts were felt necessary by many to both settle and define a doctrinal stance for the newly emerging denomination and to keep out error. As a result of these debates, several groups separated from the main body of Christadelphians, most notably the Suffolk Street fellowship and the Unamended fellowship. Due to the way the Christadelphian body is organized there is no central authority to establish and maintain a standardized set of beliefs and it depends upon what statement of faith is adhered to and how liberal the ecclesia is, but there are core doctrines most Christadelphians would accept. In the formal statements of faith a more complete list is found. In the Central fellowship, the BASF, the standard statement of faith has 30 doctrines to be accepted and 35 to be rejected.

Christadelphians state that their beliefs are based wholly on the Bible, and they do not see or view other works as inspired by God. They regard the Bible alone as being inspired by God and, therefore, believe that in its original form, it is error free and errors in later copies are due to errors of transcription or translation. Based on this, Christadelphians teach what they believe as true all of the Bible teachings. Christadelphians also believe that Jesus is the promised Jewish Messiah, in whom the prophecies and promises of the Old Testament find their fulfillment. They believe he is the Son of Man, in that he inherited human nature (with its inclination to sin) from his mother and the Son of God by virtue of his miraculous conception by the power of God. Christadelphians however reject the doctrine of Christ's pre-existence in heaven as the archangel Michael. They teach that he was part of God's plans from the beginning and was foreshadowed in the Old Testament, but was no independent creature prior to his earthly birth. Although he was tempted, Jesus committed no sin, and was therefore a perfect representative sacrifice to bring salvation to sinful humankind.

They also believe that God raised Jesus from the dead and gave him immortality, and he ascended to Heaven, God's dwelling place. Christadelphians believe that he will return to the earth in person to set up the Kingdom of God in fulfillment of the promises made to Abraham and David. This includes the belief that the coming Kingdom will be the restoration of God's first Kingdom of Israel, which was under David and Solomon. For Christadelphians, this is the focal point of the gospel taught by Jesus and the apostles. Christadelphians believe that the Kingdom of God will be located on the Earth, with Jerusalem as its capital. Our readers will note that the Watchtower Society also believed this idea as one of their core doctrines from the days of Charles Russell the founder of the Watchtower Society in 1879, up until Rutherford made drastic changes to their beliefs during the

1920s and 1930s to separate this religion from other splinter groups of the Russellites.

Quoting from the official website of the Christadelphian religion we learn that:

> The Christadelphians believe that the Holy Bible (all 66 books) is the inspired word of God, complete and self-sufficient to instruct us in the way of salvation. We do not believe that any Christadelphian, past or present, has received any type of special revelation. It is only through sustained and prayerful reading of the Scriptures that we come to an understanding of the purpose of God in our lives, and how He would have us conduct ourselves day to day. We have no central organization telling us what to do and believe. Neither are we some fringe group following a charismatic leader or some internal text. Rather, we are tied together everywhere by our zeal for reading God's Holy Scriptures and our understanding of His plan and purpose as He has revealed to everyone therein. Israel, as the literal descendants of Abraham, will always have a place in the plans of God. This is not through any particular righteousness of theirs; on the contrary, both the Bible and history have shown them to be a stubborn and willful people (much like us all). However, God is bound by his promise to Abraham his friend to care for his descendants for ever.

Christadelphians are a non-liturgical denomination. Christadelphian ecclesias (congregations) are autonomous and free to adopt whatever pattern of worship they choose. However, in the English-speaking world, there tends to be a great deal of uniformity in order of service and hymnody. Christadelphians understand the Bible to teach that male and female believers are equal in God's sight, and also that there is a distinction between the roles of male and female members. Women are typically not eligible to teach in formal gatherings of the ecclesia when male believers are present, are expected to cover their heads (using hat or scarf, etc.) during formal services, and do not sit on the main ecclesial arranging (organizing) committees. They do, however: participate in other ecclesial and inter-ecclesial committees; participate in discussions; teach children in Sunday Schools as well as at home, teach other women and non-members; perform music; discuss and vote on business matters; and engage in the majority of other activities. Generally, at formal ecclesial and inter-ecclesial meetings the women wear head coverings when there are acts of worship and prayer.

This extract from *The Dangers of Cults* by Michael Ashton, adds more information regarding the subject of cults:

> There are news reports containing shocking information about individuals or groups that have come under the sinister control of organisations that claim to be religious. Dependence on the leader is encouraged by a series of complex games with rules imposed by the leader. Gradually members are conditioned to stop thinking for themselves and are strongly encouraged to accept unquestioningly the leader's decisions and teachings. As a community, Christadelphians do not engage in tithing – donating a tenth of one's income – nor do they expect it of any of their converts. They are not therefore a wealthy community, with the problems of greed and corruption that large funds can cause, and they do not have paid ministers. By contrast, the term cult is normally associated with those groups regarded as distinctly dangerous – because of the implications of their beliefs and the methods used to attract and control their members. Cult is a more sinister term with overtones of persuading individuals against their will and against their better judgment. It must not be confused with simply holding different beliefs.

> There are ecclesially-accountable committees for coordinated preaching, youth and Sunday School work, conscientious objection issues, care of the elderly, and humanitarian work. These do not have any legislative authority, and are wholly dependent upon ecclesial support. Ecclesias in an area may regularly hold joint activities combining youth groups, fellowship, preaching, and Bible study. Only baptised [by complete immersion in water] believers are considered members of the ecclesia. Ordinarily, baptism follows someone making a good confession of their faith before two or three nominated elders of the ecclesia they are seeking to join. The good confession has to demonstrate a basic understanding of the main elements – first principles – of the faith of the community. The children of members are encouraged to attend

Christadelphian Sunday Schools and youth groups. Interaction between youth from different ecclesias is encouraged through regional and national youth gatherings. Many ecclesias organise holidays for young people, the most popular form in the UK being camping holidays and Youth Weekends such as Swanwick and others locally organised by different ecclesias.

The differences in belief between the amended and un-amended groups led to a schism in the movement within North America. In the rest of the world, Christadelphians follow the Amended belief system. During the 1970s, an unsuccessful attempt was made to merge the two groups in the US. They were unable to find a consensus on the matter of the resurrection responsibility. They remain separate to this day. There are currently about 90 un-amended and 80 amended congregations in the US. Worldwide, the two groups have some 850 congregations located in Africa, Australia, New Zealand, North America, South East Asia and throughout Europe.

Chapter Seven: Exclusive Brethren

Another group that displays most of the high control characteristics of the Watchtower Society and the Mormons are the Exclusive Brethren, who teach these are the last days and the world's end is pending, and separation from worldly people and that Satan controls this world. They also practice strict shunning, even of members of their own family.

The Exclusive Brethren are a subset of the Christian evangelical movement generally described as the Plymouth Brethren. They are distinguished from the Open Brethren from whom they separated in 1848. The Exclusive Brethren are now divided into a number of groups, most of which differ on minor points of doctrine or practice. Perhaps the best-known of these, mainly through media attention, is the Raven-Taylor-Hales group, now known as the Plymouth Brethren Christian Church, which maintains the doctrine of uncompromising separation from the world based on their interpretation of Second Corinthians, Chapter 6 and Second Timothy, Chapter 2, believing that attendance at the Communion Service, the Lord's Supper, governs and strictly limits their relationship with others, even other Brethren groups. The Plymouth Brethren Christian Church have some fellowships in nineteen countries – including France, Germany, Spain, Italy, Denmark, the Netherlands, Switzerland, Sweden, Egypt, and Argentina, but they are more numerous in Australia, New Zealand, the United Kingdom, and North America, where they are referred to just as the Exclusive Brethren.

The Plymouth Brethren split into Exclusive and Open Brethren in 1848 when George Müller refused to accept John Nelson Darby's view of the relationship between local assemblies following difficulties in the Plymouth meeting. Brethren that held Muller's congregational view became known as Open, those holding Darby's connexional view, became known as Exclusive or Darbyite Brethren. Darby's circular on 26 August 1848, cutting off not only the Bethesda faction of the Brethren but all assemblies who received anyone who had ever attended

Bethesda, was to define the essential characteristic of exclusivism that he was to pursue for the rest of his life. He set it out in detail in a pamphlet he issued in 1853 entitled, Separation from Evil – God's Principle of Unity. But a tension had existed since the earliest times, as set out in a letter from Anthony Norris Groves in 1836 to Darby (who was not a believer in adult baptism).

The history of the Exclusive Brethren is not only one of division. Eventually several of the groups realized that the divisions caused by personalities clashes or ecclesiastical issues were no longer relevant and reunions occurred. The Kelly and Lowe groups reunited in 1926 to form the Lowe-Kelly group, in 1940 with most of the British Groups, the Tunbridge Wells group and in 1974 with the Glanton division and are sometimes known as Reunited Brethren, though there was a further split in 2000 and their ageing congregations have often not been replenished and are dwindling rapidly. Most of the Grant party threw in their lot with the Open Brethren in 1932. There are common threads throughout all Plymouth Brethren groups, most notably the centrality of the Lord's Supper (Holy Communion of unleavened bread and wine) in the weekly calendar as well as the format of meetings and worship: the distinctions between the many groups are generally not well understood by non-members. The adjective exclusive has been applied to the groups by others, partially due to their determination to separate from and exclude what they believe to be evil. Exclusive Brethren usually disown any name and simply refer to themselves as Christians and brethren, those with whom we walk, those in fellowship with us, or the saints. However, the Raven/Taylor/Hales group being the most universally identifiable has attracted the term Exclusive Brethren and accepted its application to themselves as meaning, the exclusion of, or withdrawal from, evil.

Most Exclusive Brethren groups have no formal leadership structure. In many assemblies matters up for debate may be discussed at special meetings attended solely by adult males (no women permitted) called, in some groups, Brothers Meetings. As a result, schisms can occur in the Brethren over disagreements about church discipline and whether other sister groups in other locations have authority to intervene in these disagreements. There are often global family connections due to the emphasis among members to marry within the Exclusive Brethren ("Marry only in the Lord", 1 Corinthians 7:39), and family connections often influences which side of the issue members will take. The PBCC (Plymouth Brethren Christian Church) avoid this trend by having a structured leadership with a central authority figure which has maintained unity through the upholding of a universal standard. Some Exclusive Brethren assemblies commend men who are dedicated to the work of preaching. Although they usually do not receive a salary, gifts of cash are often given to them by the separate assemblies where they preach and teach.

It is difficult to number the Exclusive Brethren, with the exception of the Raven/Taylor/Hales group, of which there are approximately 46,000 meeting in 300 church assemblies in 19 countries, with strongest representation in Australia, New Zealand, Great Britain, and North America. Other Exclusive groups now number only 23,000 in the UK but there are larger numbers on the European continent and also in North America. Some have suggested that the Plymouth Brethren Christian Church (PBCC), the subgroup of the Exclusive Brethren that has attracted the most media coverage, can be categorized as a cult because of its policy of separating itself from other orthodox denominations and because it prohibits radio and television, limits the use of computers and discourages socializing with people outside the movement. Critics of the PBCC have accused it of using cult techniques by controlling all aspects of its members' lives. The group's control over its members is such that many who have left the group have had trouble adjusting to life outside. To help with this problem, several websites have been set up to assist people who have left the church to adjust into mainstream society.

From the official website of the Plymouth Brethren Christian Church:

> As members of the Plymouth Brethren Christian Church, we strongly believe that the family is of particular importance. We live, work and pray as Brethren – a community of families held together by our common Christian belief. We congregate every Sunday in simple Meeting Rooms (Gospel Halls) to

celebrate the Lord's Supper (Holy Communion) and to preach the Gospel. We also gather daily for Bible readings and prayers. We ask for privacy as a congregation for the celebration of the Lord's Supper and other special occasions which are by invitation.

Members of the Exclusive Brethren church are encouraged to have large families. However, their children live quite separate lives from other children. They are not allowed to form friendships with people outside the church, who are known as worldlies.

This cult is quick to sue if they consider a past member is discrediting them, very similar to the view that the Mormons, Scientology and The Watchtower Society also take. According to the Sydney Morning Herald of January, 2019:

> An Australian arm of the fundamental Christian sect the Exclusive Brethren is suing a Scottish academic for hundreds of thousands of dollars, in a move that former members of the sect say is an attempt to silence him and other critics of the group. The sect claims Ian McKay, a former lecturer at Glasgow University who left the Brethren in 1969, has breached their copyright by quoting from its *Ministries* and by scanning copies of a church address book. Legal documents filed in a Scottish court and seen by the *Sydney Morning Herald* and *The Age Newspaper* reveal that an Australian business and a UK charity, both linked to the Brethren, have demanded more than a quarter of a million pounds – around half a million dollars – in costs and damages from McKay.
>
> The secretive Brethren, now known as the Plymouth Brethren Christian Church, are a Christian-based religious sect led by multi-millionaire Sydney businessman Bruce D. Hales. According to the court documents it claims to have 17,000 members in the UK and 14,000 in Australia. Former members call it a cult. McKay has been part of an online effort by many former members to throw light on the group's activities. But in September last year he was hit with two legal actions in the Scottish Court of Session.
>
> The first action, from the Bible and Gospel Trust, the sect's printing arm registered as a tax-free charity in the UK, seeks

£100,000 in damages ($182,000) for publishing online at least 15 quotes from church publications known as the Helpful Ministries. He acquired and made use of the Helpful Ministries in a furtive manner," the Trust claimed, "in the full knowledge that he was doing so against the wishes of the [PBCC]".

The extracts that McKay allegedly published, include revelations such as Bruce Hales' list of 27 places where Exclusive Brethren should not go, including the newsagent, the cinema, football or cricket matches, restaurants, hotels and bars, fireworks displays, swimming pools, universities or the zoo. He also quoted text from a Brethren publication by John S Hales, Bruce's father, talking about terrible influences that are coming from the devil about equality of women and calling women's liberation a falsehood.

The Trust claimed it was unable to quantify the damage it has suffered until it had found out the full extent of McKay's copyright breach, but was also seeking damages for the moral prejudice that it has suffered by reason of the infringements. It also asked the court to order McKay to reveal who provided him with the sermons – and to name anyone he had shown them to.

The second legal action is by Universal Business Team, a Brethren-controlled Sydney business that, according to the documents, compiles and produces books for the PBCC. It seeks £181,000 pounds in damages. The books include the names and other personal details of PBCC members around the world. According to the legal documents McKay offered to scan some address books belonging to another former Brethren member, and then sent a link to the scanned PDFs back to that member. McKay is accused of authorising others to make further copies of the PDFs, and issuing them to the public.

This, the company claimed, amounted to a large-scale copyright infringement that led to complaints regarding a subsequent edition from people who did not want their names in the address books any more. *The Sydney Morning Herald* and *The Age* attempted to contact the Trust for comment. McKay, he said he was unable to comment on the case as it was before the courts. Jill Aebi-Mytton, a former Brethren member and a friend of McKay, said he was extremely anxious about the legal action.

This true-life experience by ex-member Rosie Strode in 2007 and recorded by the BBC and also published by the *Guardian* provides an inside glimpse of this cult:

Growing up in the Exclusive Brethren meant missing out on a lot of things other children took for granted. It meant no TV, radio or recorded music, no pets, parties, school outings, plays or sports, no cinema, novels, magazines, no make-up or haircuts, and strict clothing rules. I was used to living a life different from those of my friends. Even so, it struck me as strange; one morning when I was eight years old, that Mum wasn't trying to get me ready for school. Instead she was frantically stuffing clothes into cases. She told me I was going away. Downstairs I saw my elderly grandmother wringing her hands and protesting, but she was ignored as I was pushed through the front door and my hand taken by one of the Brethren from our local Meeting. He led me to a van in which was several other Brethren, including one of my uncles.

After what seemed like hours, we arrived at the suburban home of the Brother, his three spinster sisters, bachelor brother and ancient mother. I was taken down to the basement, which was to be my home for the foreseeable future. I felt anxious - where was Mum? She would be along later. Where was Dad? He was unclean; I should not wish to be with him. Later, as I was tucked up on an old settee, I tried not to cry. One of the sisters read me Bible stories to help me fall asleep. A few days later Mum arrived. She told me that the Brethren were rescuing me because Dad had left them after a disagreement over doctrine. The Ministry from the latest leader, Jim Taylor Jr. in the US, stated Brethren could no longer eat or drink with outsiders. Dad thought it wrong that he could not share even a cup of tea with his elderly widowed mother, who lived with us but belonged to a milder sect. When he stood up in the Meeting and said he disagreed, he was excommunicated.

As the weeks passed, I missed my father dreadfully. Unknown to me, he had made me a ward of court, so the family became uneasy at giving us refuge and eventually Mum took me home. I can remember Dad returning early from work, bringing a punnet of strawberries to welcome me back. I sat on his lap and sobbed. The nightmare was not over, though. For the next decade, life carried on much as before, but with one big difference: Mum would not eat or sleep with Dad and would barely speak to him. I was often used as an intermediary, with each trying to persuade me the other was wrong. My best friend comforted me when I was desperate with worry that my mother would die during her fasts, when she didn't eat for days in the hope that the Lord would answer her prayers and bring Dad back to the path of righteousness.

My worldly, unclean school friends were very sympathetic and tried to bridge the gaps in my experience by carefully recounting theirs. Sometimes I secretly watched TV or listened to records with them on the way home from school. Once they daringly arranged for me to see a film – *To Kill A Mockingbird* – at the local cinema during school hours.

Meanwhile Jim Taylor Jnr's edicts became increasingly bizarre - Sisters had to wear their hair hanging down their backs, covered in a headscarf; all adult Brethren must be married - and then he started to go to bed with married Sisters, supposedly showing how pure he was. Eventually, in 1970, at a Meeting in Aberdeen, he appeared drunk and stated that his word was of such consequence that the Bible was no longer necessary - a bombshell that caused a number of clearer-sighted Brethren to protest and break away. By this time, it was too late for me to care. I was in my late teens and, to the horror of my family, left for university shortly afterwards. There I ate chips and curry for the first time, openly read newspapers and novels, drank wine, wore normal clothes, listened to pop music and cut my hair. Being unclean was delicious.

My mother may have disapproved but she, too, left the Taylorites then, joining instead the same sect as my father and grandmother. She is still alive, still strictly religious, but she does not shut me out of her life. In the cult I left behind, Taylor died an alcoholic. Another Universal Leader stepped into his shoes, and the Brethren now even run their own schools. My heart bleeds for those children.

A review of Michael Bachelard's book, *Behind the Exclusive Brethren*, was submitted to our research team.

Michael uncovered the facts about this secretive sect for more than two years while working as an investigative reporter at *The Age. The Age*, a daily newspaper, has been published in Melbourne, Victoria, Australia, since 1854 and is owned and published by a company called Nine. *The Age* primarily serves Victoria, but copies also sell in Tasmania, the Australian Capital Territory and border regions of South Australia and southern New South Wales. The result of his inquiries is the most comprehensive book ever written about the Exclusive Brethren. It details their origins in the United Kingdom in the nineteenth century, their fractious history, their extraordinary use of scripture to control members and dissidents, and their lucrative business and financial arrangements. It's a fascinating story of influence and power exercised across several continents. But it's a very human story, too – of damaged lives, of broken families, and of hurt and anger that stretches back decades.

Roger Olson in his blog, My Evangelical Musings, on the website Patheos (a non-denominational, non-partisan online media company providing information and commentary from various religious and nonreligious perspectives) commented:

> One of the questions I am asked most often is whether a specific religious church is a cult. Most often the questioner is not satisfied with my answer. That's because they want a simple yes or no and, is so often the case in matters religious (and other matters), there is usually no such simple answer. And a big part of that is the change in the meaning of the word cult in the past forty years – beginning especially with Jonestown in 1978.

Roger also included this in-depth remark:

> I have always had a keen interest in denominations–which is strange to many people who think we live in a post-denominational age. Actually, there are more denominations now (especially in the United States) than ever! Denominations are proliferating like crazy. However, many of them insist they are not a denomination.

Also reported by one of our researchers:

I recently heard a leader of a network of congregations call her Network a denominetwork. New word—at least for me (and I've been studying denominations for many years). So how many distinct denominations (including denominetworks) are there in the United States? Well, that's impossible to say. *Melton's Encyclopedia of American Religion* (8th edition) lists and describes well over a thousand. I seem to recall that someone once counted about 1,250 distinct religious bodies in the U.S. that have more than just two or three congregations. One of the most difficult denominations (although they insist they are not but are instead a movement) is the so-called Plymouth Brethren who call themselves Christian Brethren or just Brethren. So far as I can tell the 2012 *Yearbook of Churches* in the United States and Canada does not include them at all. The 2010 Religion Census includes a group called Christian Brethren but cites only 183 distinct congregations. I'm sure there are many more meetings than that among all the different groups scholars lump together as Plymouth Brethren.

This recent report from the *Huffington Post* states:

The Exclusive Brethren includes about 17,000 members across England. After their first bid for charitable status was rejected, the sect fought back with supporters writing thousands of letters to the Charity Commission, which regulates charities in England and Wales. The sect's leader is an Australian multimillionaire named Bruce Hales (followers call him the Prophet). Over 200 members of Parliament supported the Brethren's charity status. But new disclosures have changed the public image of the group. Eight former teachers have spoken to the media and described school buses segregated by gender, classroom racism and textbooks with pages on evolution, fossil fuels and sexual reproduction ripped out.

In her book *In the Days of Rain*, Rebecca Scott expresses the real feelings of many who have been enslaved in a cult. We hope that all of our readers learn something from this enlightening and revealing experience:

Like most Brethren children, I loved my parents and I was

scared of life outside. I used to hear the sound of Satan's hooves on the cobbles of our street or in the bushes of our garden, waiting to snatch us. Grown-ups were terrified of being thrown out, too. If someone was discovered with a radio, didn't give enough money to the collection or asked questions about the rules, they would be kicked out and they wouldn't see their family again. There were forced confessions, breakdowns and suicides. I knew I wasn't going to be saved in the Rapture because of the questions that constantly spun around my head: if radios were wicked, then why did my father keep one hidden in the back of his car and listen to the cricket on it? Did the Lord know about that? Was I supposed to denounce my father for the radio?

I worried about what I would do when the grown-ups disappeared in the Rapture. How would we get to high ground before the tidal waves came? How would we stay away from Satan's people? I began to steal and hide tins of corned beef and baked beans under my bed so I'd be ready for when the grown-ups would be taken up into the sky, leaving us to face the terrors of Armageddon.

When I was eight, my family left the Brethren. The elderly Brethren leader, called the Man of God, was found in bed with one of the married sisters, so 8,000 Brethren around the world, including my immediate family, left and formed a splinter group. Eventually, my parents left altogether and tried other churches. My father, at first anguished, soon discovered the joy of theatre, literature and music; he brought home a TV and took us to the cinema to see [a re-release of] Gone with the Wind. I remember stepping across the threshold of the cinema holding my mother's hand, certain the sky was going to fall. When I was 16 – the year before my father was arrested and sent to prison for fraud and embezzlement – he drove me all over the country to see plays. On those long car journeys we'd recite all the poetry we'd memorised, play the music we loved, argue about God, morality and Shakespeare. I finally got to ask him questions about the Brethren, but he was still struggling to understand what had happened, furious with himself for not having seen through it all, so he'd recite a poem by Yeats or Auden. I began to understand the world, and my family's history, for the first time.

When I went to university, I was forced to explain my early life with the Brethren so that certain things about me made sense to my friends. The fact that I'd stolen books from the school library when I was five, or that I had a compulsion to rescue people because I'd had dreams about being rescued myself. It's the reason I had a son in my second year of university – I wanted to start a family of my own that was safe. Growing up with the Brethren has made me skeptical of anyone who claims to have absolute answers, or of systems with absolute rules. Even now, I still have to remind myself that time isn't about to run out, that I'm not being watched and that the sky is not about to fall in on me. I've heard other ex-Brethren describe these feelings, too. I live in houses built on hills and I avoid watching TV footage of flooding; they remind me of the apocalyptic images the Brethren instilled in us. I now encourage my three children to think for themselves, to ask questions and to stand up when they see something unfair. According to Dr Stein, young people are particularly susceptible to cult recruitment. They might be living in a city away from home; many are lonely. They're looking for friends, family and structure – something that makes them feel secure.

My father died before he had answers to the questions that tormented him for decades: how did a group of decent, godly people turn into a cult? How did he get duped like that? In his last days, I promised him that I'd try to figure out our shared history, take his unfinished memoir and write my own book. I owed it to him, to my own children and to all the women currently living in a cult against their will to show that it's OK to talk. But I also owed it to the small girl in the headscarf with the plaited hair and endless questions she could never ask. Only after trying to find those answers have I been able to draw a line under my childhood and find closure.

Once an isolated Christian sect, the Exclusive Brethren has achieved a new and continuing prominence thanks to the continuing fall-out from a brief foray into politics last year in Australia. Martin van Beynenin in the *Religious News Blog* looks at who they are and what they believe.

Former Prime Minister Helen Clark calls them weird. Labour's energy minister David Parker has dubbed them the Christian version of the Taliban. The Exclusive Brethren's interpretation of the Bible has certainly resulted in more restrictions and prohibitions than the usual fundamentalist Christian sect. In a bid to practice separation from evil the brethren do not go to university, do not eat with outsiders and also banned are mobile phones, television, radio, internet, and films. Their homes and vehicles are free of the pipelines of media filth, the Exclusive Brethren's website says. The irony of having a website when internet usage is forbidden appears to have been lost on the sect. Women, who are not allowed to work outside their family businesses once married, must wear headscarves and must not cut their hair. No artificial birth control is allowed. Men must not wear shorts or ties. The group also eschews restaurants or venues of worldly entertainment. Members must marry within the fellowship although those that marry outside the brethren can be recovered as long as their spouses convert.

Exclusive Brethren have no monopoly over strict and seemingly odd beliefs. Most religions have practices which appear bizarre to outsiders and even disillusioned former brethren speak of the sect as comprising solid family people who run honest and efficient businesses and care for each other. Ngaire Thomas was born into an Exclusive Brethren family in Auckland in 1943, and did not leave with her husband and family until 1974. Her book *Behind Closed Doors* chronicles a life in the group spent fighting and beating what she describes as often silly, petty strictures imposed by sanctimonious hypocrites.

News reporter Martin van Beynen reported this interview with a past member of this cult:

> She says it is maddening for former members to find that activities such as the use of computers that could once earn expulsion are now acceptable. While the ban on computers and faxes appears to have been lifted, their use is still apparently strictly controlled by the church. Documents leaked to Australian media, show computers can be used in brethren - run businesses, as long as they are leased from a company run by senior members of the group. The equipment is said to be owned by an entity called National Office Assist which runs out of the same business address as the current worldwide leader of the brethren, multimillionaire Bruce D. Hales. While

it was true brethren were not allowed to bear arms, people should not overlook the fact hundreds of brethren men have been actively involved in the frontline duty in the great wars of the last century. This service has been in ambulance, medical and driving roles. Our stand from scripture is that we do not take life, so we have served in frontline, but non-combatant duty. We stand by the truth as it is in Jesus. We have nothing to be ashamed of. We seek to stand by the Cross of Jesus and the truth as set out in the Holy Scriptures.

Chapter Eight: Splinter Groups of the Main Cults

There have of course over the years been many breakaway groups from all cults and religions who objected to decisions made by their leaders, and especially is this highlighted in the case of the Mormons and the Watchtower Society. On reflection, the issue always came down to, who controls the purse strings?

In the case of the Watchtower Society, when Joseph Rutherford (1869-1942); being a very clever and shrewd lawyer, seized control of the headquarters of the Watchtower Society in Brooklyn, New York in 1916, despite the fact that the majority of the members of the then Governing Body opposed him taking over control from the late Charles Russell (1852-1916), the first President of the Watchtower Society. It was simply a case of who also controlled the printing presses to produce the literature and propaganda contained therein plus the already established network of distribution. In addition, Rutherford seized the properties purchased by Russell using the donated funds and profits from the sale of his many books and religious literature. These property holdings, plus later purchases and additions were used to house the headquarters and printing factories in Brooklyn, New York. Rutherford by use of his legal knowledge and cunning manipulation had arranged a court order to prevent any of the other dissenting members of the Governing Body and directors of the Watchtower Society to gain entrance into the headquarter buildings without his permission. This action by Rutherford of course created yet another splinter group which eventually faded away into oblivion.

Our source reflected that there have been other splinter groups and most have come to nothing, being simply crank groups. He quoted for example, Jesse Hemery who was appointed overseer of the Watchtower Society's British Isles branch office by Charles Russell in 1901, holding that post until 1946 when Welshman Pryce Hughes took over. Jesse Hemery and his wife had lived rent free and using Watchtower funds for many years while operating his clandestine scheme out of the Watchtower offices initially at 131, Gypsy Lane (later known as Green Street, Forest Gate in East London) and then ten years later, in 1911, transferred to Craven Terrace in Central London. Jesse Hemery, who had been privately writing his own literature, primarily against Rutherford and the changes he was making to erase or amend many of Russell's teachings, and Hemery went on and founded the Goshen Fellowship (now defunct) after he was personally disfellowshipped in 1951 by authoritarian President Nathan Knorr.

In 1962, The Watchtower controversially altered its long-standing doctrine (once again claimed under direction from God) on the meaning of the phrase related to being subjective to the superior authorities at Romans 13:1, identifying them as human governmental authorities rather than God and Jesus Christ as formerly believed. Many Witnesses in Romania rejected the change, and some suspected it was a communist fabrication intended to make them subservient to the state. After the Romanian ban was lifted, members and representatives of the Governing Body of Jehovah's Witnesses were able to meet thousands of long-separated Romanian Witnesses, but some Romanians still rejected certain changes and preferred their autonomy, forming The True Faith Jehovah's Witnesses Association in 1992.

Also when the Watchtower Society changed its interpretation about the superior authorities, some Jehovah's Witnesses in the USSR suspected that the change came from the KGB instead. This led to the formation of the Theocratic Organisation of Jehovah's Witnesses, which discontinued use of Watchtower Society publications printed after 1962.

In 1993, mathematician Gordon Ritchie requested baptism by Jehovah's Witnesses and almost immediately began advocating disagreements with their teachings. He claims he was expelled for apostasy in March 1996. Ritchie contends that Jehovah's Witnesses constituted the true religion up until 2004, but that his own group of the Lord's Witnesses is now the sole form of true worship on earth.

One other prominent breakaway group was formed by Paul Samuel Leo Johnson who was personal secretary, and in time also became the most trusted friend and advisor to Charles Russell, but he left the Watchtower Society when Joseph F. Rutherford, by legal manipulation took over its direction and control after Russell's death. P. S. L. Johnson then founded the Laymen's Home Missionary Movement in 1919, and served on its board of directors from 1920 until his death on October 22, 1950. He also was involved with the founding of the Bible Standard Ministries along with his colleague Raymond Jolly, which describes itself as, "We are an international, nonsectarian religious movement devoted to upholding the authenticity of the Sacred Scriptures".

According to *Wikipedia*:

> The Laymen's Home Missionary Movement, founded by Paul S. L. Johnson in 1919, is a non-sectarian, interdenominational religious organization that arose as an independent offshoot of the Watch Tower Bible and Tract Society after the death of its founder, Charles Taze Russell. In early 1917, a disagreement arose between the members of the Editorial Committee of the Watch Tower Bible and Tract Society (the Bible Student movement founded by Charles Taze Russell) over Russell's arrangements for the Editorial Committee outlined in his Last Will and Testament and the Society's official charter. This caused the Watchtower Society to splinter into many factions with over 25% of the original Bible students leaving the Watchtower Society by 1928 with many forming other independent groups and fellowships which included the Elijah Voice Society, The Pastoral Bible Institute (PBI) and others. The Laymen's Home Missionary Movement (LHMM) was formed by three former members of the Pastoral Bible Institute Committee which was formed by a large group of dissenting brethren in 1917 at the Fort Pitt Convention (Paul S L Johnson, Raymond G Jolly and Robert Hirsch). Today this group is slowly dwindling in numbers mainly caused by death of its members and further splits within the group and today has less than 15,000 adherents world wide.

The Dawn Bible Students Association is a Christian organization and movement, and a legal entity used by a branch of the Bible Student Movement. It was founded with the intention of becoming a publishing house to begin printing and distributing the first six volumes of the

Studies in the Scriptures series that were written directly by Charles Taze Russell, which the Watchtower Society had officially ceased publishing in 1927.

In 1966, the Dawn Group published "Oh, the Blessedness," a small booklet which rejected most of Russell's views of Bible prophecy and end time predictions resulting in numerous internal divisions. In 1928 Norman Woodworth, following intense personal disagreement with the new policies of the Watchtower Bible and Tract Society and actions of the Society's President, Joseph Rutherford, left to create the radio program, Frank and Ernest with the help of the Brooklyn congregation of Bible Students. He had previously been responsible for producing the same radio program for the Watchtower Society. The Frank and Ernest programs are still available today by means of streaming radio from this splinter group, Dawn Bible Student Association.

The Dawn Group was influential in re-gathering large numbers of the Bible Students who had ceased association with Watchtower Society between 1917 and 1928, and sponsoring the First Annual Reunion Convention of Bible Students in 1929. As a result, new congregations of Bible Students were formed in various countries worldwide and publishing their literature in various languages. Today the Dawn splinter group continues publication of Russell's *Studies in the Scriptures*, as well as booklets written by various Bible Students. They also produce radio and television programs. Current membership in America is difficult to estimate from the number of conventions. In the late 1980s they had a membership of about 60,000.

In recent years the Watchtower Society is now experiencing even more dramatic and bold steps by their members, not simply quitting as individuals but actually taking control of their local congregation and Kingdom Hall property, plus severing their ties as a group from the control of the dictatorial Governing Body. This letter was received by an individual interviewed by our research team:

> About 2 years ago an entire congregation in the UK had a
> meeting and decided that the Watchtower organization and
> its Governing Body had turned apostate after the whole child
> abuse scandal came to light and so they stopped reporting to

the organization, stopped sending their donations and stopped using their literature. They call themselves, Jehovah's True Witnesses [very unoriginal, I know]. The Jehovah's True Witnesses have almost exactly the same beliefs except they dropped the disfellowshipping and shunning rules. Cannot for the life of me recall where in the UK it was but I remember at the time that Bethel (headquarters) were more concerned that they were keeping the valuable property of the Kingdom Hall and the Watchtower Society couldn't take it by force because it was built using their own donations and with their own labour. They had lawyers involved and everything. The Jehovah's True Witnesses won.

Therefore, the question is now being asked, how many more local congregations of Jehovah's Witnesses throughout the world will see the light and take similar steps? Or is it too late in the day as the mother organization has now recently seized control and legal ownership of all the Kingdom Hall properties worldwide in order to prevent this occurring.

The Mormon Church has also experienced hundreds of splinter groups, the main one being, The Reorganized Church of Jesus Christ of Latter-Day Saints (RLDS) that was started in 1844 by Joseph Smith (Junior), the only surviving son of Joseph Smith. His father, also called Joseph who was murdered in 1844, but Joseph Jnr., was still under the influence of his powerful mother, widow of Joseph Smith, Emma Smith. The Smith family objected to the very dominant, influential new self-proclaimed leader of the LDS Church, Brigham Young, so as a result formed this breakaway group in 1844, which today claims to have about 250,000 members mainly based in Illinois, USA. On April 6, 1860, at a conference held in Amboy, Lee County, Illinois, Joseph Smith III was accepted and ordained as prophet, seer and revelator of the Church of Jesus Christ and the successor of his father. This group from 2001 is also now known as The Community of Christ. The president of the RLDS Church was always part of the Smith family. However, in 1995 W. Grant McMurray became the first RLDS president who is not a direct descendant of Joseph Smith (*Salt Lake Tribune*, June 29, 1996).

One splinter group from the main LDS Church was The House of Aaron. This group is less commonly known as the Aaronic Order or The Order of Aaron and is a religious sect that believes they are descendants of Aaron the older brother of Moses in the Bible and believe in the Aaronic writings. The sect is centered in Eskdale, Utah, a small farming community in Millard County, with additional branches in Partoun and Murray, Utah. The House of Aaron was founded in 1943 by Maurice L. Glendenning and has a membership estimated between 1,500 and 2,000. Our reporter interviewed a few of these members of this sect and found them to be one of the most open, humble and honest Christians he had ever met, although somewhat misguided in their claims of being the only true religion on earth today.

Maurice Glendenning was born 15 February, 1891 in Randolph, Kansas. He and his family were unfamiliar with the Latter-Day Saint movement and The Church of Jesus Christ of Latter-day Saints (LDS Church). However, as a boy, he confided in his father that he could hear heavenly music even when wide-awake. As a young teen, the heavenly music became interspersed with angelic voices uttering poetry, which he began to write down in notes he kept private out of fear of ridicule. As a young man, the angelic poetry evolved into doctrinal and philosophical statements, and he gradually began sharing the text of his messages with more and more friends and relatives. In 1928, Glendenning and his family moved to Provo, Utah, looking for employment. Counseled by LDS missionaries, Glendenning began to feel that a number of LDS doctrines, including the priesthood and proper authority, helped him understand his experiences and writings. Glendenning and his wife were baptized into the LDS Church on August 14, 1929.

On January 15, 1945, he was excommunicated because he was accused as the Instigator of the Aaronic Order. LDS Church General Authorities asserted that Glendenning was an apostate or heretic. While LDS members could receive divine inspiration for themselves, no one could receive authentic divine messages for the church as a whole, except the President of the Mormon Church. However, Glendenning claims not to have received divine messages for the LDS church as a whole; rather, he was accused of wrongdoing presumably because he had claimed to receive divine inspiration that, if true, would affect the validity of some of the teachings of the LDS Church.

The latest splinter group from the Mormons, one of the hundreds listed, was formed as recently as 2017, now called The Remnant, and led by a man called Denver Snuffer Jr. Of course, it was his account about a face-to-face meeting with Jesus Christ that branded him a prophetic figure in the first place. And his 2013 excommunication from the LDS Church for apostasy – arguing that after the death of Joseph Smith in 1844, the faith he founded no longer had the exclusive truth or divine authority – seems to have made Snuffer more popular with many segments of dissatisfied Mormons.

We must also be aware that America, the 'New World', was a recent, newly developing nation during the 18th and 19th centuries and had attracted many immigrants who were sickened by the established religions back in Europe. These immigrants included many disillusioned Christians who had belonged to organized religions in their home countries and they had arrived with free and open minds and they in turn created many new cults and religions, especially during the 19th century. Some of these religions have survived, for example, the Watchtower Society and the Mormons, but many others have simply dwindled into oblivion.

This was the basis of a new nation that promoted free thinking and liberty, plus is the primary reason for America today being the strongest and most liberal nation on earth. The issue of religious freedom has played a significant role in the history of the United States and the remainder of North America. Many Europeans came to America to escape religious oppression and forced beliefs by such state affiliated churches as the Roman Catholic Church and the Church of England. America proved to be a breeding ground for new religious ideas, many associated with the Adventist theme and the second coming of Christ and has been a religious hotbed, resulting in the emergence of multiple religious movements especially during the 19th century. Some of these new religions grew rapidly despite having such peculiar practices and doctrines, such as the Shakers, Father Divine, Christian Scientists, Millerites, and 7th Day Adventists, plus so many other strange and weird religious groups, many with restorational ideals, plus of course the two religions we have already highlighted; Jehovah's Witnesses and the Mormons.

Also included in the list of over 200 religious cults, recorded by the Cult Awareness Network, many other cult groups, some of which are simply crank groups (crank is a pejorative term used for a person who holds an unshakable belief that most of his or her contemporaries consider to be false) many with strange, weird beliefs and practices. But as one of our researchers who have looked into most cult groups, simply said, using the idiom, well it takes all sorts to make up the world. He also explained that most people belonging to a religion, does so because it makes them feel more secure and cared for, but also in contrast the atheist says religion is the opium of the people.

It was Karl Marx (1818-1883), who first used this expression. The full quote translates as: "Religion is the sigh of the oppressed creature, the heart of a heartless world, and the soul of soulless conditions. It is the opium of the people." Karl Marx also said "The abolition of religion as the illusory happiness of the people is the demand for their real happiness. To call on them to give up their illusions about their condition is to call on them to give up a condition that requires illusions." Marx believed that religion had certain practical functions in society that were similar to the function of opium in a sick or injured person: it reduced people's immediate suffering and provided them with pleasant illusions, which in turn gave them the strength to carry on.

Marx was a philosopher, economist, historian, sociologist, political theorist, journalist and socialist revolutionary. His political and philosophical thought had enormous influence on subsequent intellectual, economic and political history and his name has been used as an adjective, a noun and a school of social theory. Marx's theories about society, economics and politics – collectively understood as Marxism – hold that human societies develop through class struggle. In capitalism, this manifests itself in the conflict between the ruling classes (known as the bourgeoisie) that control the means of production and the working classes (known as the proletariat) that enable these means by selling their labor power in return for wages and protection.

The International Cultic Studies Association (ICSA) does not keep or maintain a list of so-called bad groups of religions, the reasoning behind this decision that the ICSA does not maintain a list, as they say it is up to the individual to decide what constitutes a cult or dangerous religion. They inform readers:

> We non-judgmentally list groups on which we have information. A listing on ICSA's web site does not mean that ICSA perceives the group named to be a cult, to practice coercive or destructive tactics, or to be in violation of any law. It simply means that ICSA has information on the group and/or has received inquiries from current and former members, their families, professionals, researchers, the media, or the general public. Groups listed, described, or referred to on ICSA's Web sites may be mainstream or nonmainstream, controversial or noncontroversial, religious or nonreligious, cult or not cult, harmful or benign.

Another organisation that offers help to individuals who have been enslaved by a cult is the Cult Information Centre (CIC), a charity based in London, England, providing advice and information for victims of cults, their families and friends, researchers and the media. CIC was founded in 1987 and became a registered charity (No. 1012914) in 1992. It was the first charitable organisation, established in the United Kingdom, focusing critical concern on the harmful methods of the cults. Cults use sophisticated mind control techniques that will work on anyone, given the right circumstances. Those who think they are immune are only making themselves more vulnerable. Remember the assault is on your emotions, not on your intellect, so we must be concerned about the use of deceptive and manipulative methods used by cults or religions to recruit and indoctrinate plus control unsuspecting members of society.

From records of history, religion has been responsible for wars and revolutions, causing the death of 100,000s of innocent lives. In their *Encyclopedia of Wars*, authors Charles Phillips and Alan Axelrod record 1,763 notable wars in world history and state this opinion, with which we agree:

> Wars have always arisen, and arise today, from territorial disputes, military rivalries, conflicts of ethnicity, and strivings

for commercial and economic advantage, and they have always depended on, and depend on even today, pride, prejudice, coercion, envy, cupidity, competitiveness, and a sense of injustice. But for much of the world before the 17th century, these reasons for war were explained and justified, at least for the participants, by religion.

The definition of a follower of a cult is "Any blind, unthinking, unquestioning follower of a philosophy." To a lesser degree we have other groups like the Moonies. Moonie is a pejorative term sometimes used to refer to members of the Unification Church. It is derived from the name of the church's founder Sun Myung Moon, and was first used in 1974 by the American media and believe it or not, is still now a popular religious cult in the USA being established in the 1960s.

The sole searching question related to the theme of our final chapter is, are the followers of these cults actually religious slaves, and if so, will these cults increase in number and also in power, influence and strength; or will they ever be exposed for what they really are. An enlightening article in the Atlantic in 2014, created a list of seven ways to recognize the difference between a sincere religious community and a cult. Written down, the signs seem clear:

1. Opposing critical thinking

2. Isolating members and penalizing them for leaving

3. Emphasizing special doctrines outside scripture

4. Seeking inappropriate loyalty to their leaders

5. Dishonoring the family unit

6. Crossing Biblical boundaries of behavior (versus sexual purity and personal ownership)

7. Separation from the Church

This quote by Gilbert Keith Chesterton (1874-1936) has a ring of truth regarding modern religion:

> The truth is, of course, that the curtness of the Ten Commandments is an evidence, not of the gloom and narrowness of a religion, but, on the contrary, of its liberality and humanity. It is shorter to state the things forbidden

than the things permitted: precisely because most things are permitted, and only a few things are forbidden.

Chesterton was an English writer, poet, philosopher, dramatist, journalist, orator, lay theologian, biographer, and literary plus art critic. Chesterton is often referred to as the prince of paradox. What is a paradox? It is a statement or proposition that seems self-contradictory or absurd but in reality expresses a possible truth, or proposition that when investigated or explained may prove to be well founded or true. Or it can refer to any person, thing, or situation exhibiting an apparently contradictory nature being an opinion or statement contrary to commonly accepted opinion. An example provided by an associate of the editor, the brilliant researcher and prolific Bible student, Rodney O******d, said it's a logical puzzle, and, to illustrate this, he said:

> Consider the following, can the Creator of the Universe, the all powerful, almighty God; create an object that is too heavy for him to lift? Try and work that out for yourself and if you can, you have found the secret and answer to life itself.

We again repeat a powerful message quoted earlier in our narrative, Therefore our observations and recommendation to our readers, is to carefully check by using a modicum of common sense that our personal religious beliefs and loyalties, plus that our Bible based conscience is not being manipulated or controlled by a religious organization or their leaders, who may try to dictate what you are to believe with respect to Bible doctrine and how your personal conscience is to react to certain given situations in life, in other words, avoid becoming a religious slave! If you cannot control this situation, then you simply break free.

This quote by the famous Hugh Cholmondeley, 2nd Lord Delamere of Vale Royal Abbey, Cheshire, England (1811-1887) is very true even today: "The most courageous act you can ever take as an intelligent human is still to think for yourself."

Conclusion

At this juncture and in the light of all the evidence presented in this book, why do people still join religious cults? Plus an even more serious scenario, why do people remain members of a religious cult when they know and have been made aware of the signs and dangers of a religion that operates like a cult? Somewhere down the line some people have become disillusioned with what they were taught in church and started looking for an alternative, others because circumstances in their life has made them turn to religion and they are looking for association that offers support or help from a close group environment.

Because Christian terminology is widely used in all religious cults, unwary and hopeless seekers of some other truth, get caught in the crossfire. Maybe also some are attracted to cults because they like to have their ears tickled, this describes individuals who seek out messages and doctrines that condone their own lifestyle or beliefs. The Bible warns us that over time some people won't be willing to hear or listen to sound and truthful doctrine. The Bible at 2 Timothy 4:3-4 declares: "For the time is coming when people will not put up with sound doctrine, but having itching ears, they will accumulate for themselves teachers to suit their own desires, and will turn away from listening to the truth and wander away to myths."

This Bible text was written by the Apostle Paul under the inspiration of the Holy Spirit and targeted directly to the disciple Timothy and the Christian congregation in the first century and contains a powerful warning, plus the principle is just as applicable today in the 21st century. It is a warning that some who profess to be Christians would apostatize from the true faith and not wanting to hear the truth of God's word, so we hope and pray that we are not amongst that group.

What has happened to the integrity of the leaders and masters of modern religion? Most of the individuals interviewed by our research team, no matter what religious affiliation they professed, expressed great concern that their shepherds and leaders must always display the important qualities of integrity and honesty. The definition of integrity is as follows, so we ask all of our readers to examine if their shepherds meet up to this standard. "Integrity is the practice of being honest and showing a consistent and uncompromising adherence to strong moral and ethical principles and values." In ethics, integrity is regarded as the honesty and truthfulness or accuracy of one's actions. Integrity can stand in opposition to hypocrisy, in that judging with the standards of integrity involves regarding internal consistency as a virtue, and suggests that parties holding within themselves apparently conflicting values should account for the discrepancy or alter their beliefs.

If you decide that the Watchtower Society, the Mormon Church, Scientology or any other cult, after reading this report does not meet this standard then it is your responsibility "holding your life in your hands", Psalms 119:109 and it behooves us to speak out and take the necessary action and tenaciously stick to your decision.

The Editor of *Patheos Evangelical News* observed:

> If we look at the definition of integrity, we can see the importance of such a virtue in society. To have integrity is to be trusted by others. After time, they know from experience that the person can be trusted, based upon their past. Integrity is the practice or habit of being an honest person before others; saying what you mean and meaning what you say; and doing that which was promised but in an honest manner. Having integrity is having a consistent and uncompromising adherence to ethical and moral principles. All of this is based upon honesty and truthfulness, and a person who has integrity is a person that is both honest and truthful in all their dealings with others, no matter how small or large the matter is.

Margaret Singer and Janja Lalich, in their book *Cults in Our Midst: The Continuing Fight Against Their Hidden Menace*, reported: "In the United States, there are at least ten major types of cults, each with its own beliefs, practices, and social mores. The list below is not exhaustive, but most cults can be classified under one of the following headings:

- Neo-Christian religious

- Hindy and Eastern religious
- Occult, witchcraft, and Satanist
- Spiritualist
- Zen and other Sino-Japanese philosophical-mystical orientation
- Racial
- Flying saucer and other outer-space phenomena
- Psychology or psychotherapeutic
- Political
- Self-help, self-improvement, and life-style systems

There are of course other cult groups not related to religion, but all cults are structured like the layers of an onion, with the most acceptable elements closest to the outside, followed by increasing layers of secrecy and abuse as recruits move closer to the centre. The following report from the BBC related a case in New York during June of 2019:

> Sex cult leader Keith Raniere, has been convicted in New York of charges including racketeering and sex trafficking. For 20 years, Raniere was the leader of Nxivm (pronounced nexium), which claimed to be a self-help group and to have thousands of followers. But during his trial, former members gave an insight into the reality of how the group was run. In the case of Nxivm, the outer layers saw seemingly harmless self-improvement programmes used to recruit members' friends, family and colleagues. But at its core, Raniere exerted extreme levels of control, allegedly culminating in sexual abuse, violence and the branding of his initials on female followers. They described being forced to break off previous relationships and of suffering physical and sexual abuse. Some were forced to have abortions. A slave and master system saw women forced to hand over collateral - often humiliating photographs - to show their commitment.
>
> The revelations have shocked many people and made headlines around the world. But, in reality, Nxivm reveals a great deal about how cults work. However, while cults tend to operate in a similar way, they exist at all levels of society and take a

wide variety of forms. Some are religious, political or self-improvement, but they can also be publically described as martial arts, yoga, business, UFO, and therapy groups. Arguably, many terrorist and extremist groups use similar isolating processes to recruit and indoctrinate members.

In *Unmasking the Cults*, Alan Gomes provides explicit descriptions regarding religious cults.

> Here is a concise definition of a cult of Christianity: A cult of Christianity is a group of people, which claiming to be Christian, embraces a particular doctrinal system taught by an individual leader, group of leaders, or organization, which (system) denies (either explicitly or implicitly) one or more of the central doctrines of the Christian faith as taught in the sixty-six books of the Bible.

Oliver Everhard of San Diego State University made this observation:

> Due to the increasing strength of the mainstream religions of the world (namely Christianity, Judaism, Islam, Hindu, Buddhism), cults has become something of a rarity in the modern world. Because almost all people either have strong ties with a religion (or lack of one), or find the idea of a cult to be scary, silly, or simply annoying, almost all new religious movements simply are unable to generate enough membership to *function*, let alone prosper. Because of this, I am fairly certain that cults, alternative religions, sects, and the like will, in this day and age, almost *never* be able to last.

In the *Guardian,* Rick Ross makes clear the dangers of being seduced by a cult:

> The word cult can be broadly defined as formal religious veneration, a system of religious beliefs and its body of adherents, a religion regarded as unorthodox or spurious. In addition it is a great devotion to a person or idea as well as persons united by devotion or allegiance to an artistic or intellectual movement or figure.

But the most salient concern to the general public, law enforcement and government officials today regarding groups called cults is what potential they might represent to do harm. Psychiatrist Robert Jay Lifton, who once taught at Harvard Medical School, wrote a paper titled "Cult Formation in the early 1980s." He delineated three primary characteristics, which are the most common features shared by destructive cults.

1. A charismatic leader, who increasingly becomes an object of worship as the general principles that may have originally sustained the group lose power. That is a living leader, who has no meaningful accountability and becomes the single most defining element of the group and its source of power and authority.

2. A process (of indoctrination or education is in use that can be seen as) coercive persuasion or thought reform (commonly called brainwashing). The culmination of this process can be seen by members of the group often doing things that are not in their own best interest, but consistently in the best interest of the group and its leaders.

3. Economic, sexual, and other exploitation of group members by the leader and the ruling coterie.

The destructiveness of groups called cults varies by degree, from labor violations, child abuse, medical neglect to, in some extreme and isolated situations, calls for violence or suicide. The following are some examples.

• Absolute authoritarianism without meaningful accountability.

• No tolerance for questions or critical inquiry.

• No meaningful financial disclosure regarding budget or expenses, such as an independently audited financial statement.

• Unreasonable fear about the outside world, such as impending catastrophe, evil conspiracies and persecutions.

• There is no legitimate reason to leave, former followers are always wrong in leaving, negative or even evil.

• Former members often relate the same stories of abuse and reflect a similar pattern of grievances.

• There are records, books, news articles, or broadcast reports that document the abuses.

- Followers feel they can never be good enough.
- The group/leader is always right.
- The group/leader is the exclusive means of knowing truth or receiving validation, no other process of discovery is really acceptable or credible.

An additional kind of cult is the category of commercial, multi-marketing cults. These are sustained by belief in attaining wealth and power, status, and quick earnings. The leader, who is often overtly lavish, asserts that he has found the way. Some commercial cults are crossovers to political and religious cults because they are based on ultra-conservative family values, strict morals, good health, or patriotism. Members are encouraged to participate in costly and sometimes lengthy seminars and to sell the group's product to others. This is especially true of the Mormon cult that promotes skin care and health products to the gullible females and their friends, the owners of these companies meanwhile have become multi-millionaires by benefitting from their scams and questionable business practices. These practices and influence techniques include deceptive sales skills; including guilt and shame, peer pressure, financial control, magical thinking, or guided imagery.

A final word was provided in the publication *Cult Watch* and serves as a warning to all of us.

> The cult leaders need to make you believe that there is no where else you can go and still be saved, and if you ever leave the one true church then you are going to hell. This is a fear-based control mechanism designed to keep you in the cult. It also gives the cult leaders tremendous power over you. If you really believe that leaving the group equals leaving God (or means you are leaving your only chance to succeed in life), then you will obey the cult leaders even when you disagree with them instead of risking being kicked out of the group. Exclusivism is used as a threat, and it controls your behavior through fear. Cult leadership is feared.

The religious cult leaders will claim to have direct authority from God to control almost all aspects of your life. To disagree with leadership is the same as disagreeing with God. Often some of the well-established cults have predicted the end of the world or changed their beliefs significantly; hence their older publications become a danger to them and encourage their followers to destroy these publications. This is a preemptive strike against the warnings from friends and family members whom they know will come. In fact some cults go as far to tell you that Satan will try and dissuade you by sending family members and friends to tell you it is a cult. When this tactic is used then often it is a warped form of logic that occurs in the recruits mind, the agents of Satan do come and tell them that it is a cult. So since the group predicted that would happen, the group therefore must be true! Basically if any group tells you that they are not a cult or that some people call them a cult, then for goodness sake find out why and think for yourself!

Image of Jesus Christ, our true master, courtesy of Truth Books, Jesusonian Foundation and Creative Commons

Appendices

Special Report No. 1: Philip David Morgan Rees

This real life, previously untold confidential report related to Philip Rees (1916-2000) is based on several private letters, numerous personal and private discussions with one of our researchers and illustrates the pros and cons of being able to think for ourselves and avoid becoming a victim and slave to a modern-day religion or cult.

These confidential letters were written by Philip to an unnamed private source, who was a personal friend, co-worker and confidant of Philip Rees for many years. Phil who had served as a loyal supporter of the Watchtower Society both in Australia and England for most of his life, quite freely volunteered his deep feelings and concerns. One of the private letters confirms the situation and reasoning, which personally troubled Philip deeply, that only members of the so-called unique remnant of the heavenly class, claimed to literally number 144,000 can be members of the Governing Body and the extreme steps and manipulations that have taken place by the Watchtower Society to make sure this so-called divine interpretation and revelation is complied with.

Also Philip seriously questioned this core teaching of the Watchtower Society that there are two separate and distinct groups of Christians, namely a special unique group of a literal 144,000 individuals, also known as the little flock or remnant who claim they are personally selected by God and invited to join Jesus Christ when they die, to sit at his right hand and rule the Universe with him in heaven as Kings and Priests and all other Christians are in the category as being classified as other sheep and their only hope for eternal life was on planet earth, if fortunate enough to be selected and resurrected with a new body. Philip had insisted that this personal information only be released after his death and the death of his wife. We are sad to report that Phil's much loved wife Maudie recently passed away aged in her late 90s, and our contact in the Australian Watchtower Branch Office confirmed the death of Maudie Rees but was unable or unwilling to give the exact date or location of her passing, claiming it was to be provided only to the next of kin, so we had to take this reply in good faith. After a prolonged period, our editor decided it was about time the facts, events and life of Philip Rees as a leading member of Jehovah's Witnesses be fully revealed, as this is what Philip Rees wished.

This report is not to be read as a gossip column or as a peek behind the screen or curtains of the secretive Watchtower Society, although it might appear like this to some of our readers, but this information is a brief glimpse into the life of a man; a sincere genuine Christian but who had spent his whole life as a slave to modern religion. After intense, serious reflection and discussions, the MTC International Foundation has decided to include this special report in this book about religious slavery, as they feel that the private and personal story of Philip Rees has to be finally told to the world, as this is what he truly desired. This is Philip's contribution to the story of Masters & Slaves of Modern Religion.

A sketch or cartoon indicating a peep behind the curtain or the screen and attempts to block the news and real facts, courtesy of the Library of Congress

The life of Philip David Morgan Rees began in Australia and being brought up by his paternal grandmother he was also introduced to the religion of Jehovah's Witnesses. After he left school at the age of 15 years, he volunteered or was more likely persuaded to work in the printing factory of the Australian Headquarters of the Watchtower Society, then based in Sydney, New South Wales. Apparently, he was not even baptized at that time in the early 1930s; and the Australian Branch of the Watchtower Society just wanted free labor. It appears that his grandmother was a personal friend of Alex MacGillivray and Philip was getting into all sorts of trouble as a youth so his grandmother reasoned that working in Bethel would sort him out. It was while he worked in Bethel that he met his future wife Maudie, the pretty, young and only daughter of the Branch servant (Manager) Alexander MacGillivray. Maudie was born and brought up in the Australian Bethel home and privately schooled by her mother. Phil admitted, what probably kept him in Bethel was his attraction for Maudie, but her father insisted he was baptized before they could start dating, so Phil was baptized at the age of 18 years in 1935, although he seemed a little confused about the exact date. All he could remember was the confusion at the time regarding the claim of either being one of the so-called anointed class or one of the other sheep. He also confessed that he was grateful that at least he was learning a trade of book binding and printing in a very efficient printing factory.

Alex MacGillivray, a very shrewd, brusque Scotsman had been sent to Australia as the new Branch servant by Joseph Rutherford, 2nd President of the Watchtower Society, after spending 10 years working in their New York headquarters. Alex had also become a very close personal friend of Joseph Rutherford and a secret whisky drinking partner. The Australian Branch office had been established as far back as 1904 by Charles Russell the 1st President of the Watchtower Society. Alexander MacGillivray, the father-in-law and mentor of Philip Rees died in 1942 at the comparatively young age of 52 years of cirrhosis of the liver, no doubt caused from his very heavy drinking as an alcoholic. He had been born on the Isle of Mull, Outer Hebrides, Scotland, before he moved to New York, America, in his early twenties.

Alexander MacGillivray and Alfred Greenlees (the father of Leo Greenlees, who later became a member of the Governing Body, but was asked to resign in 1984 as he was accused as a pedophile) and they went over much of Scotland on bicycles. According to the 1973 Year Book of Jehovah's Witnesses, they also worked as colporteurs the island of Orkney and the northern part of Britain. They distributed the bound books published by Pastor Charles Russell and the Watchtower Society and maintained themselves on the small margin the Society allowed them on the placement or sale of these publications. MacGillivray later became the branch overseer in Australia. The spread of Bible knowledge in Scotland may be measured by the fact that in 1903 there were seventy persons present to celebrate the Memorial of Christ's death.

This report from a reliable news website *Bravehost* lists over 200 legal cases related to the Watchtower Society that have occurred over numerous years and makes fascinating reading about the Australian branch of the Watchtower Society, while Philip Rees served there:

In January 1941, the Australian government temporarily outlawed the Watchtower Society, and ordered it's national and multiple state/regional headquarters locations seized and closed. A local reporter hurried to the Watchtower Society's national headquarters in Strathfield to get the Watchtower Society's side of the story. Upon arrival, that reporter discovered eight adult males armed with clubs guarding the front gate of the compound. When that reporter insisted on interviewing one of the Australian Watchtower Society's leaders, that reporter stated that he was seized and thrown into the street. That reporter later reported that he watched as more than 50 Jehovah's Witnesses attempted to empty the Watchtower Society's Australian national headquarters of its contents. Watchtower literature and other materials was carried to multiple waiting trucks and cars, which left the compound as soon as loaded, while some papers and documents was carried to an outdoor incinerator and burned. Days later, the Australian Watchtower Society's spokesperson publicly denied that any burning of documents had occurred.

However, six months later, on a Sunday night in July 1941, two of the Watchtower Society's appointed leaders in Australia, named Alexander MacGillivray and Philip David Morgan Rees, plus MacGillivray's wife, and an unidentified third adult male, attempted to secretly re-enter the Watchtower Society's national headquarters building located in Strathfield, Australia. The four Jehovah's Witnesses apparently were surprised to find two police officers guarding the premises. Alex MacGillivray assaulted the first police officer who challenged his presence on the property. The second police officer came to his partner's rescue, and struck MacGillivray on the shoulder with a baton. The two other Watchtower males then threateningly ran at the second officer, who pulled his revolver, and ordered them to halt. When the two men continued to advance toward the officers, the second officer fired a warning shot into the air. When even the warning shot did not stop the two advancing men, the officer finally fired a shot toward them – striking MacGillivray in the arm. Rees and the other unidentified male knocked that officer to the ground before he could fire any more shots; and began kicking him; and Philip D. Rees even allegedly choked the officer.

Philip Rees admitted that he had never, ever read the full press details about that court case in Australia back in 1941; ignorance is bliss Phil said while he chuckled, but he did confess that he had acted like an impetuous fool at times and it was possible they all had too much to drink that night. We must also remember that Philip's Welsh roots were based in the Brythonic Celtic people and warriors of ancient Briton, and he was very proud of his Welsh heritage. According to the *Sydney Morning Herald* of 8 July, 1941, it recorded that Philip David Morgan Rees was charged with assault and battery of Charles Hopton, Commonwealth Peace Officer and was released on bail of £80 pending trial at a later date.

Over the decades, the Watchtower Society has routinely labeled as religious persecution the foreseeable negative consequences resulting from bad judgments exercised by its Jehovah's Witnesses members and their leaders. Facts have been spun, changed, and even hidden to make incidents of violence against Jehovah's Witnesses appear to be proof that Satan and his human allies were intentionally targeting God's only true organization and the only remaining true worshipers left on planet Earth – the Watchtower Society and its Jehovah's Witnesses members.

Philip Rees confessed that the Watchtower Society, especially under the leadership of the manipulative Joseph Rutherford, often used Bible texts to justify his introduction of many unpopular teachings and doctrines in order to make it appear that members of the Watchtower Society religion were being persecuted for righteousness's sake and therefore were members of the true religion and no part of the rest of the satanic world. Using the Bible text, Matthew 24:9, "Then you will be arrested, persecuted, and killed. You will be hated all over the world because you are my followers." They also used this additional text at John 15:9, "If you were of the world, it would love you as its own. Instead, the world hates you, because you are not of the world, but I have chosen you out of the world."

It is most unusual and indeed very rare for a married couple to have a child, either planned or by accident, while still living and working in a Bethel home of the Watchtower Society, and then allowed to continue living there, as no one is indispensable and the rules are rules. But there have been rare exceptions, like the case already mentioned of Scotsman, Alex MacGillivray, personal friend of Joseph Rutherford and who was also apparently operating a very lucrative private engineering business while still serving as full-time branch servant in Australia, he and his family being supported by the voluntary donations of the sincere members of this religion. However, one of the most glaring examples of breaking the rules is the case of the late Albert Schroeder, a past very prominent, aggressive and dominant influential member of the Watchtower Society's Governing Body. In 1956, Albert Schroeder married Charlotte Bowin, a much younger, very sexually attractive girl according to existing photos; she was also a former student of the first class of the Gilead Missionary School that Schroeder headed and in 1958 their son, Judah Ben, was soon born. Schroeder and his wife were not requested to leave the Bethel, as all other married couples who had started a family while working and living in Bethel, as it was claimed by authoritarian Nathan Knorr, the 3rd President of the Watchtower Society, that Schroeder was absolutely necessary and indispensible, whatever that means, especially when you take into consideration their close personal friendship?

Also as pointed out by our research team, Schroeder was also a hypocrite of the first degree (a person who puts on a false appearance of virtue or religion or a person who acts in contradiction to his or her stated beliefs or feelings) as he along with the other members of the Governing Body, he had decried higher education as a pursuit by the rank and file of loyal members of this religion, yet his own son undertook higher learning by attending Columbia University and eventually qualified as a lawyer with a lucrative career and legal practice. One reporter asked our team of researchers. "I wonder how Schroeder could afford the very expensive college fees for his son when he only earned about $80 per month working full-time for the Watchtower Society. Who actually paid these college fees we would like to know?"

It is sad to note that because many young people turned down the opportunity of attending college or university in order to become slaves to the full-time service of the Watchtower Society, in later life they struggled to find suitable employment to provide for their families and most ended up having to take menial low caliber jobs with very poor pay. The Governing Body regularly discouraged higher education, for example this extract from one of their articles written over 50 years ago is typical of many:

> Many schools now have student counselors who encourage one to pursue higher education after high school, to pursue a career with a future in this system of things. Do not be influenced by them. Do not let them brainwash you with the Devil's propaganda to get ahead, to make something of yourself in this world. The world has very little time left! Any future this world offers is no future.... Make pioneer service, the full-time ministry, with possibility of Bethel or missionary service your goal. This is a life that offers an everlasting future! (*The Watchtower*, March 15, 1969, p. 17)

The Watchtower Society through its literature and lectures condemned seeking a decent education, this quote for example: "A university degree may or may not improve your employment prospects. But one fact is indisputable: The time left is reduced! (1 Corinthians 7:29). For all its presumed benefits, would four years or more in a university be the best use of that remaining time? (Ephesians 5:16). In view of these facts, many Christian youths have decided against a university education. Many have found that the training offered in congregations of Jehovah's Witnesses – the weekly Theocratic Ministry School in particular – has given them a real edge in finding employment." (*Awake!* May 8, 1989, pp. 13-14, "What Career Should I Choose?")

In answer to the obvious question, why does the Watchtower Society not approve of higher education? The following answer was submitted by one of our research team.

> The Watchtower Society has cleverly designed the condemnation of higher learning to benefit themselves through the continual recruiting of youth for the full-time service of selling and promoting their literature. Young members of the Witnesses are now replacing a beneficial college education with the door-to-door ministry and service to help fill the Worldwide Work donation box. Although financial gain is the predominant factor, the Watchtower Society also fears that

those who become well educated because it allows individuals to think for themselves and discuss Watchtower doctrine with other educated Biblical scholars who maybe will reveal the erroneous doctrines of the Watchtower Society. The Watchtower Society even today, still continually condemns pursuing worldly careers and education in their attempts to persuade loyal followers to become full time pioneers (Watchtower sales people) instead.

In addition to disapproving a decent education the Watchtower Society even discourages an individual from developing their true God given character and personality in order to advance their career or successful role in life and this is a very negative scheme or destructive tactic from these so-called shepherds of the flock. Why do they undertake this resistive approach?

We quote once again from the *Watchtower* magazine of 1963, which is a blatant manipulative attempt to justify this tactic and extreme control, plus displaying their mastery and their attempt to subjugate their followers:

> Clearly, not all dedicated and even mature Christian's possess the Holy Spirit to the same measure. There is no doubt that unselfishness, depth of devotion, self-control, humility, mildness of spirit, studiousness as regards God's word and zeal in God's service have a bearing on how much of the holy spirit we have. It also appears that inherited qualities have no small bearing on the extent to which we permit the Holy Spirit to have a free flow in our lives or tend to obstruct its activity. Therefore, the more colorful the personality; the more difficult for the Holy Spirit to saturate it fully. The colorful personality has more need of self-control and must in particular guard against the snare of creature worship. Richness of personality seems to work against spiritual-mindedness, as the colorful person tends to lean more on himself, even as those who are rich in material things tend to put their trust in them instead of Jehovah God. (*The Watchtower*, Feb.15, 1963, p. 108)

This article upset and deeply disturbed Philip Rees as he had been accused by certain members of the Governing Body that he had a colorful personality and was unsuitable for a leadership role in the organization. In the leaked confidential, personnel file of Philip, secured in the Branch Servant's locked files in the London Bethel, included a report from a visiting Zone Servant, representing the Governing Body and it was a report confirming this personal opinion of Philip Rees and that he could not always be trusted, was loose tongued and drank too much. The signature on this damaging and negative report is unmistakably that of Theodore Ted Jaracz, member of the Governing Body.

The anonymous writer of this article in the *Watchtower* magazine of 1963, representing the Governing Body of this religion about a colorful personality was obviously not a person who understood the nature and character of a true Christian who is made in the image of God; this writer was also clearly not qualified to make such a mental or emotional analysis of members of his religion. This article was written by an individual who fictitiously imagined himself as a brilliant psychologist or psychiatrist and really demonstrates the extent of the mind control that the Watchtower Society tries to hold over its subjective followers and he was certainly ignorant of the true power of God's Holy Spirit and how it operates in the life of a genuine Christian. This is truly another clear sign of a nefarious scheme by the manipulation of the leaders of a cult and their attempts in their mastery and the use of mind control to direct and slant the minds and character of their members plus also to subjugate or discourage them from confidently thinking for themselves or being, in their words, a colorful person. The definition of a colorful personality is tending to attract attention because of their exuberance, confidence, and stylishness. Synonyms are flamboyant, exuberant, confident, lively, animated or vibrant. These are all qualities that leaders of cults wish to crush, as this type of character tends to think for themselves.

After reviewing the 1983 *Year Book of Jehovah's Witnesses* our researchers also decided to reveal the following information about the work of the Watchtower Society in Australia, where Philip Rees started his career in the Watchtower Society's Bethel Home, in addition to the contents of his confidential letters and the many other private conversations. (The additional comment in italics were added verbally to the quote below by Philip Rees personally.)

Closely following the convention that year, an eviction notice
was delivered to the Bethel family on May 8, 1942, requiring
them to leave within 24 hours. The army was to occupy the
premises. Members of the Bethel family took up residence in
houses nearby. Shortly after the death of Brother Rutherford on
January 8, 1942, Brother Alexander MacGillivray also finished
his life course, on July 22, 1942. (*My father-in-law was only 52
years old when he died and used to claim he was of the anointed
class, up until 1935 and then for some reason he stopped taking the
emblems, but never told us why*). Philip Rees now carried on as
branch overseer. Then only 26 years of age (*I was actually only
25 years old at the time I took over.*) Brother Rees had been in
Bethel since he was 15. He knew the workings of the branch
thoroughly, having had constant contact with its development.
One of the reasons for Brother Rutherford's visit in 1938 (*Apart
from meeting up again with his former close friend, my father-
in-law Alex, plus also being his Scottish and whiskey drinking
partner*) was to examine complaints about certain commercial
activities that the Australian branch had developed to give
the local brothers employment (*including several farms and a
very large profitable engineering company, privately owned by my
father-in-law*). Rutherford was satisfied that these things were
not harming the preaching of the good news and commended
Brother MacGillivray (*his personal friend and boozing partner*)
on his initiative. However, later on these suspicious enterprises
were to bring big trouble and difficulty for the Witnesses in
Australia.

According to the 1983 *Yearbook of Jehovah's Witnesses* it is further
reported:

On one occasion when Brother MacGillivray was returning
home by car the usual guard at the front gate was missing.
He alighted and walked ahead of the car but was met by two
guards running from their office. Two shots were fired at him.
One of these pierced his shoulder. He was assisted into the
Bethel building, with blood pouring from his wound. Brother
MacGillivray made a good recovery, but six months later he
died. The authorities had restricted Australian branch overseer,
Philip Rees, to the town of Picton, where he was kept under
surveillance. Happily, the town was only 70 miles (110 km)

out of Sydney. Though he was not permitted to move out of that town, there was no restriction on other brothers visiting him there. Hence, two nights each week the brothers who were not restricted, and who were keeping things going, stoked up a charcoal-gas car and drove out to Picton to meet with Brother Rees in a secluded ravine.

The commercial activities operating out of the Australian Branch office over the previous five years now began to take their toll. During the years of war and ban, they had provided a means of supporting many former full-time servants who could not carry on their pioneer service because of the ban. However, the organization had actually gone too far by establishing commercial enterprises, and this had had a very disturbing effect on many brothers (many local members being stumbled and actually quit the organization). As soon as he was in a position to do so, Brother Rees took steps to liquidate these enterprises. But it was a very hard process, involving the lives of many who had accepted this kind of service in support of the organization. The adjustments were made, however, and by the time Brother Rees was called to the Watchtower Bible School of Gilead in 1946, the enterprises had been completely cleared out. Nevertheless, mistakes had been made over those years, and something was needed to clear the air. Then all the brothers could again press forward wholeheartedly in the all-essential work of Kingdom preaching. The first visit to Australia by the new Watch Tower president Nathan Knorr in March 1947 provided the occasion for this. Brother Knorr dealt forthrightly with the situation. Accompanied by the acting branch overseer, Brother Laurie Wills, he visited all the provincial capitals of the Australian states. He talked plainly to the brothers about the situation that had existed. Then he presented a resolution for their consideration and this ended the ongoing problem of personnel in the Bethel operating private businesses.

In a later discussion Philip expanded on those secret meetings that he held in the ravine outside Picton each week, mentioned in the 1983 Yearbook, as he was now supposed to be in complete charge of the activity of Jehovah's Witnesses in Australia. But there was very little he could do as most of the brothers had stopped attending meetings, no field service was allowed and most thought, including himself, that

Armageddon had already started based on the terrible news coming in from Europe. He was asked, what was discussed at these weekly private meetings you had with the two brothers from Sydney? And he honestly stated that he has no recollection and in their joint opinion everything was in the hands of the Lord. The only thing he could remember was that each time they had these short meetings it was a good excuse to have a thoroughly good booze-up, and they concluded the meeting with all of three of them being blind drunk. Of course this salient fact was not reported by the Watchtower Society in the 1983 *Yearbook*.

> *Editor's Note:* According to the Watchtower records (now sealed) a very serious situation had developed in Australia during World War II. (1939-1945) Many of the brothers, including those prominent in the Society's work, failed to maintain their neutral stand, but rather engaged in enterprises giving aid to the nation's war effort and were designed to provide lucrative material advantages for the local organization and some prominent individuals there in Australia, including the branch servant MacGillivray, Rutherford's personal friend. From another source it appears that MacGillivray's engineering company and a couple of others subsidiaries and subcontractors were actually manufacturing weapons of war under a secret contract with the Australian government.

Regarding the activities related to the commercial enterprises, these had been condoned and approved by Rutherford himself on his last visit to Australia in 1938 and nothing was done to stop these activities by the so-called hypocritical Governing Body based in the head offices of the Watchtower Society back in New York, not until Nathan Knorr (the new broom) took over total control in 1942. Phil reflected in one of his letters:

> I officially took over as branch servant later in 1942, the appointment letter signed by Nathan Knorr himself as the new President and I was only 26 years old, plus I was left with the hell of a job to sort out the mess left behind by Rutherford and my father-in-law Alex MacGillivray. Also I had to deal with the very serious complaints from many of the local brothers and the dreadful job of having to cut off the lucrative income for many of these brothers, including many who actually operated

their private businesses and enterprises out of the Bethel home and offices while still being supported by the donations of the local brothers, these donations supposedly being made as contributions to the Lord's work. I was being hammered from both sides and I must have aged an additional 25 years during that stressful period and I was eventually glad to get out of Australia and move with my darling wife Maudie to the London Bethel in England.

Phil never fully revealed what sorts of lucrative commercial enterprises were involved but another source informed our researcher that mainly it was related to the selling of war bonds. War Bonds (now called Treasury Bonds) the full title was Commonwealth of Australia War Savings Certificates, actually supporting the British government and commonwealth countries war efforts of the Second World War, but also it soon spread into other very lucrative, financial but somewhat unscrupulous business practices that had evolved and developed, thereby as masters using their privileged position and power in the ranks of the Watchtower Society, exploiting the local somewhat naïve sincere Witnesses, such as selling them worthless insurance policies.

We now quote from the somewhat watered down and misleading version of the official Watchtower Society History Book of 1993, *Jehovah's Witnesses: Proclaimers of God's Kingdom* (also known simply as the Proclaimers book).

> Problems arose in Australia starting in 1938 and escalated during the ban on the Society (January 1941 to June 1943). In order to care for what at the time seemed to be valid needs, the branch office of the Society got directly involved in a variety of commercial activities. Thus, a great mistake was made. They had sawmills, more than 20 Kingdom farms, an engineering company, a bakery, and other enterprises. Two commercial printeries provided a cover for continued production of the Society's publications during the ban. But some of their business operations got them involved in violations of Christian neutrality, the work being done on the pretext of providing funds and supporting the pioneers during the ban. The consciences of some, however, were deeply disturbed.

One of his last duties before leaving Australia and voicing some concern,

Philip Rees had commented in the annual report he had posted and sent to the New York headquarters for the 1946 *Yearbook*:

> The commercial activities of the previous five years now began to take their toll. During the years of war and ban, they had provided a means of supporting many former full-time servants who could not carry on their pioneer service because of the ban. However, the organization had actually gone too far by establishing commercial enterprises, and this had had a disturbing effect on many brothers.

Philip later admitted that he was so sickened by this whole episode in Australia that his wife Maudie, who was also very aware of all of this questionable, suspicious activity by some of the local leaders of this religion, it was Maudie who actually wrote the report as he was so depressed and was at a loss of what to declare and expose in the report. He said that as she was more focused, discreet and tactful with her expressions that she actually wrote most of that 1946 report sent to the Headquarters office, unknown to the all-male chauvinist Governing Body. Phil then added, "OK, it was fair-dinkum as they never knew the full truth about who wrote that report, and what the eye doesn't see, the heart doesn't grieve over."

Philip Rees did however comment that with Rutherford condoning this blatant unscriptural and unethical activity, also being corrupt in the opinion of many, and operated by some of the leading brothers in Australia with the full approval of Rutherford, one wonders what other issues and lucrative exploits Rutherford (plus other leading Watchtower officials) had conducted on his own account and justified as Kingdom Projects. Phil had met Rutherford back in 1938 and observed that Rutherford with his legal scheming mind was capable of anything during his period of serving as the all-powerful, narcissistic President of the Watchtower Society from 1916 to 1942. Philip had also just recently heard of the purchase and building of the palatial new mansion in San Diego, California, supposedly for the ancient worthies (princes of the old testament of the Bible, such as King David, Moses, Abraham, plus a whole list of others and their families we presume, who certainly could not all be accommodated in that property of only 12 bedrooms) These individuals were all due to be resurrected back to earth in 1925 or soon thereafter, according to Frederick Franz, the Watchtower prophet, and to reside on this beautiful estate, which Rutherford claimed as his own as custodian until they returned. These princes never did return back to earth of course and this was just another false and misleading claim made by the Governing Body of the Watchtower Society, then controlled entirely by Rutherford and their so-called divine revelations. Philip expressed that learning of the fiasco of this mansion and its occupation by Rutherford did deeply disturb him at the time and cause him to ask soul searching questions about his religion, but he was advised by a personal friend to put it behind him and look forward to the future, as all men are imperfect, he also added that Rutherford would not live forever, so why worry.

At a later date Phil revealed in more detail about his late father-in-law Alexander MacGillivray and wanted to put the record straight about some of the questionable relationships that he knew about, directly connected to men who were the leaders of this religion and that caused him great concern. Phil pointed out the low-key comment in the 1983 *Yearbook* that stated, "Brother Alexander MacGillivray also finished his life course, on July 22, 1942." We all knew, Phil said, that Alex had claimed to be of the anointed class of 144,000 since he was baptized as a Jehovah's Witness but then he suddenly stopped taking the bread and wine in 1935. He never explained to his family why, so we were puzzled, but it did explain the curt comment in the 1983 Yearbook. Some years later Philip's wife Maudie received a letter from her mother in Australia, written just before she died and both Maudie and Phil were truly shocked, as Maudie's mother told them that Maudie's father Alex, since 1935, had been involved in a clandestine affair with a young woman half his age who worked in the office of his engineering company. What made it even more shocking was that Alex and this young woman had an illegitimate son also called Alex, who was the half-brother of Maudie and this caused Maudie to go into a very deep depression and was morose for many weeks, as she was at a loss of what steps to take next. Maudie's mother died in the 1950s and no contact was ever made by this ex-girlfriend of her father, who was not a member of Jehovah's Witnesses or from the half-brother, so all was simply placed on the back burner.

One other troubling matter that Philip recalled was when Joseph Rutherford visited the Australian headquarters in 1938, he arrived by luxury liner and he was accompanied by a young woman named Berta, who it appears lived with Rutherford at his mansion in San Diego, being his personal dietician. Rutherford claimed Berta was his nutritionist and he requested adjoining, interlinking bedrooms so that in the evenings they could discuss the following days strict diet that his doctor recommended. Of course, this raised quite a few eyebrows in the Bethel, but what could we do, Phil opined; as he was the all-powerful President. In an interview with a now deceased elder from the Long Beach, California, congregation of Jehovah's Witnesses, who claims he personally knew Berta, he related that Berta had a bedroom adjoining Rutherford's in the train car they used in their travels, with a directly connecting door between the two rooms. He learned this when Berta met with the elders before she died and gave them a full confession and stated, "He was like a husband to me in every way."

The woman in question, a Mrs. Berta Peale, was a close friend of Bonnie Boyd, Rutherford's stenographer. She accompanied Boyd to a Watch Tower convention in Europe at some point in the mid or late 1930s. At that convention she evidently met Rutherford. Thereafter, in June 1938, she abandoned her non-Jehovah's Witness husband of fifteen years and moved to the Brooklyn Bethel where at least outwardly she became Rutherford's dietician and nurse. In November 1939, her husband, Albert Peale, filed for a divorce from her for adultery and desertion. It was granted in March 1940. Philip Rees was also aware that wild rumors were circulating that three members of the Governing Body, especially President Knorr and two others had recently been married to young vulnerable sisters in order to surreptitious hide from the public and the press that they were closeted homosexuals, and this also troubled him.

Philip empathized that his marriage to Maudie was a very happy and contented one for both of them, which was not true of many marriages amongst Jehovah's Witnesses, but there was a wild rumor going the rounds that Philip had an illegitimate son in the United States, who claimed that his mother had told him she had a brief affair with Philip Rees when he was on a trip to America. Philip did confess that when he attended the 1953 Watchtower Convention at Yankee Stadium, dated July 19-26' under the theme "New World Society of Jehovah's Witnesses" that Maudie could not accompany him as she was very ill with emotional and nervous depression and had to remain in England and Phil knew she was being well cared for in the London Bethel. Maudie's problem was basically caused by the several emotional shocks she had just received, her dear mother dying, being told about her father's infidelity, a man she really worshipped despite his violent temper and drinking problem, and then finding out she had a half-brother in Australia, who was her only living, fleshly relative and who was probably going to be destroyed at Armageddon, as he was not one of Jehovah's Witnesses. Maudie always had personality problems as she had been brought up as an isolated child in the closeted confines of the Australian Bethel with home schooling, with virtually no contact with other children and became involved with Philip Rees while they were both young teenagers; this obviously took its toll on her true development as a strong, confident individual.

There was also this wild rumor that Philip Rees had fathered a son who lived in America, and was probably started by some idiot who intensely disliked Philip. After the convention in New York, 1953 was over, Philip took two weeks sick leave and spent some time in New Hampshire and there he had met a young sister with whom he foolishly became very friendly, but he swears nothing serious happened and they did not have sex, at least from what he could remember, as he was sloshed most evenings along with a few of the local brothers, so he could not swear with his hand on the Bible that he was innocent. This young man had claimed that his mother informed him that after spending a wild weekend with Philip Rees in the 1950s that she became pregnant with Philip's child and he was the product of the relationship. Philip of course was now back home in England and was focused on his work on behalf of the Lord's organization and was comfortably entrenched and absorbed in his work as manager of the printing factory, a job he truly enjoyed, so he simply put the whole sordid episode out of this mind.

Philip Rees and his wife, Maudie (only daughter and child of Alex MacGillivray), eventually became members of the London, England, Bethel family with future plans by the Governing Body; now directly controlled by Nathan Knorr, who had privately planned and personally informed Phillip that he was to eventually take over from the current, but now rapidly ageing Branch Head, Alfred Pryce Hughes (1895-1978). According to one of Philip's private letters, this idea of becoming the Branch Servant of the British Isles was a dream of his, especially having Welsh roots (Phil never knew his mother or father and was brought up by his Welsh grandmother) and his wife also having Scottish roots, but as events unfolded this was not to be. Phil later verbally also added with emotion in his voice, that he and Maudie felt that they were coming home!

Photograph of Philip Rees and his wife Maudie taken in 1951 on their 10th wedding anniversary, courtesy of the late Maudie Rees from her family album

Philip never realized his dream of eventually becoming the Branch Servant of the British Isles as this position was abolished in 1976 and no longer did a branch of the Watchtower Society operate under the jurisdiction of an individual branch servant. In 1975, the Governing Body had unanimously approved one of the most significant organizational readjustments in the modern-day history of Jehovah's Witnesses and from February, 1976 each of the Branch Offices throughout the world was supervised by a Branch Committee appointed by the Governing Body. In the case of Britain, a committee of five men was appointed, including Philip Rees, the other four members being John Wynn, Jack Barr, Pryce Hughes and Wilfred Gooch. Phil served on this committee for a number of years until he was eventually removed because of his age and his ongoing drinking problem was causing some concern.

I asked Philip one evening, why did he drink so much? He simply pointed out that the Bethel in London received so much donated beer, wine and liquor, which was always very welcomed by the mentally and emotionally stressed-out leading members of the Bethel family (names that Phil refused to identify), after which he said, he simply could not refuse. Phil reminisced that when he worked in the Australian Bethel it was the normal way of life and the in-thing to drink beer or whiskey every evening until they were truly sloshed. He also pointed out; not to justify his drinking problem he emphasized, that his father-in-law, Alex MacGillivray and Joseph Rutherford were two of the most prolific drinkers of alcohol he had ever seen or experienced in his whole life.

Heavy use of alcohol by the workers in the various Bethel homes of the Watchtower Society was common knowledge and has been the source of causing stumbling to many genuine, sincere members of this religion. In his book, *Apocalypse Delayed*, Jim Penton states:

> Since Rutherford's death, drinking has continued to be common at Bethel and Watch Tower officials who can afford to do so will have cabinets well stocked with expensive liquors. Even the business-like no-nonsense Nathan Knorr is still renowned among Bethelites, Witness missionaries, and former personal friends for the twenty-year-old Bell's Scotch Whiskey, which he would serve to favoured guests. The use of alcohol therefore holds great social value at Bethel, and many workers, including high-up Watch Tower officials, drink regularly on a social basis. Also it is well known that several prominent Bethelites, including the wife of a member of the Governing Body and the wife of a senior member of the society's Service Committee, have had problems with alcoholism.

Philip very quickly changed the subject and I could see that this caused him some embarrassment, so he then went on to mention that one of the highlights of his life while serving the Watchtower Society was when he was invited by the Governing Body to speak at the famous international Divine Will convention, held at Yankee Stadium and the Polo Grounds in New York City, 27 July to 3 August, 1958, and was privileged to give the final talk of the evening on Monday, 28 July, called, "Be Quick to Obey". Phil then pointed to his head and made the gesture of spinning his pointed finger toward his brain while laughing out loud. I never did learn at that time, what he meant by that visual expression and gesture. I later drew my own conclusion from my own observation and research that this gesture, where you point at your head and make a circle with your extended first finger is to imply someone is crazy, a nutcase or off his mind and is screwy (to an Australian using slang, when you say or gesture that someone has a screw loose, you mean that they behave in a strange way and seem slightly mentally unstable.) Phil reflected that when he thinks of that material he covered in that lecture, "Be Quick to Obey,"it gives him the willies (an idiom meaning it makes you feel nervous or frightened.)

> *Editor's Note:* How did the term willies come into existence?
> Some historians point to productions of the ballet *Giselle*, which
> debuted in Paris in the 1840s. In it, a young heroine falls in
> love with a man pretending to be someone else. In reality, he's a
> scoundrel who's already engaged to another woman. When the
> heroine discovers the betrayal during a passionate dance scene,
> she dies of a broken heart and joins the Queen of the Wilis,
> who is accompanied by a host of female spirits who have also
> been scorned. Together, these ghosts – known collectively as the
> Wilis – seek revenge upon men they encounter in the haunted
> woods by dancing them to death. To see the Wilis appear as
> apparitions on stage probably was enough to give viewers a
> little fright, something that eventually led to the common term
> the willies.

Phil reflected that when he looks back at that Divine Will convention in 1958, plus the contents of that lecture and the notes he was compelled to read to the large audience, being a manuscript having been written, prepared and supplied by the Governing Body, it made him squirm, as the contents included the clear instructions that members of Jehovah's organization must display absolute obedience to the Lord's faithful and discreet slave without ever questioning or reasoning why. Phil added that since the events of 1975 and the incidents of Raymond Franz and Edward Dunlap, who were part of the headquarters staff in New York, and being disfellowshipped for sincerely and genuinely questioning the existing controversial doctrines and teachings of the Watchtower Society, Philip had personally experienced a tortuous time in his own private life.

Philip Rees continued his story and mentioned that he was proud of the day he was selected and nominated by Nathan Knorr to be a member (equivalent to a shareholder in legal terms) as part of the small, exclusive group of approximately 500 men (no women were allowed) classified as official members of the legal corporation, Watch Tower Bible & Tract Society of Pennsylvania, Incorporated, and Phil of course diligently and sincerely exercised his vote and authority in selecting the seven directors (who in those days operated as the Governing Body) and the three management officers of the corporation. Phil by being personally present at the annual General Meeting in Pittsburg, Pennsylvania, or by proxy, made him feel at that time he was of some value to the Lord's organization.

Philip later resigned as an official member of this legal corporation for personal reasons as he had now come to realize he had been nominated as a member by sycophant, Nathan Knorr, who was using this deceptive, calculated ploy to get Philip to eventually join the Governing Body and also publicly declaring and claiming to be one of the Lord's Anointed (Heavenly Chosen Ones) of 144,000. It seems that Knorr had an obsession of wanting guys from Australia; born there or had served in the Bethel there, being on his Governing Body. We wonder why? What did they have that we American men do not have? To our young reporter from Salt Lake City in Utah who asked this innocent, naïve question, I sarcastically replied, "I will tell you when you are 21 years old."

For the general enlightenment of our readers, we cover the basic legal setup of the Watchtower Society and its role, not as a Christian religion but rather a powerful, lucrative, legal, and commercial entity.

On December 15, 1884, the religion started by Charles Russell was incorporated as Zion's Watch Tower Tract Society of Pennsylvania as a non-profit, non-stock corporation with Charles Russell as president. The corporation was located in Allegheny, Pennsylvania. In its charter, written by Russell, the society's purpose was stated as the mental, moral and religious improvement of men and women, by teaching the Bible by means of the publication and distribution of Bibles, books, papers, pamphlets and other Bible literature, and by providing oral lectures free for the people. The charter provided for a board of seven directors, three of whom also served as officers; a president, vice-president and secretary-treasurer. The charter also stipulated that the officers be chosen from the directors and be elected annually by ballot. Board members would hold office for life unless removed by a two-thirds vote by shareholders. Vacancies on the board resulting from death, resignation or removal would be filled by a majority vote of the remaining board members within 20 days; if such vacancies were not filled within 30 days an appointment could be made by the president personally, with the appointments lasting only until the next annual corporation meeting, when vacancies would be filled by election.

An amendment to Article V was passed in 1945, detailing the qualifications for membership of the society. Each donation of $10 to the society funds had formerly entitled the contributor to one voting share; the amendment limited membership to, only men who are mature, active and faithful witnesses of Jehovah devoting full time to performance of one or more of its chartered purposes ... or such men who are devoting part time as active presiding ministers or servants of congregations of Jehovah's witnesses. The amended article stipulated that a man who is found to be in harmony with the purposes of the Society and who possesses the above qualifications may be elected as a member upon being nominated by a member, director or officer, or upon written application to the president or secretary. Such members shall be elected upon a finding by the Board of Directors that he possesses the necessary qualifications and by receiving a majority vote of the members. The amendment limited membership at any one time to between 300 and 500, including approximately seven residents of each of the 50 individual States of the USA.

An amendment to Article VIII was also passed in 1945, detailing the office holders of the society and the terms of office and method of appointment of officers and directors. A clause stating that board members would hold office for life was deleted. The new clause provided for board membership for a maximum of three years, with directors qualifying for re-election at the expiration of their term.

An example of the legally required annual General Meeting of the Watchtower Bible & Tract Society of Pennsylvania was the one held in 1954 at its newly built registered Head Office on Bigelow Boulevard, Pittsburg, Pennsylvania, and on 1 October, 1954, the Annual General Meeting was held there in this impressive new building for the first time. In attendance were the current 484 members of this legal corporation and included amongst them was Philip Rees, who was flown in from London by the Watchtower Society, and the comment that appeared in the *Watchtower* magazine (1954, pages 745-747) is of interest, plus very informative and truly telling from the viewpoint of the local humble members of this religion. "The corporate membership is truly representative of the world-wide New World society. Twenty-nine different nationalities are represented, serving in all forty-eight states of the United States and in a total of sixty-nine countries. They are mature and two thirds of them are of the remnant. Their average age is nearly 60 years and all but twelve have been in Kingdom service prior to 1940 and the majority for more than twenty-five years. Of course, being so widely scattered, most of them voted by proxy."

> *Editor's Note*: In this phrase that appeared in this *Watchtower* article no mention is made of the fact that they were all men and that no women were allowed to be members, in addition the misleading phrase is used, 'truly representative of the world-wide New World society.' This statement is a blatant, direct and deceptive lie, as at that time according to the now dysfunctional system of records cards, the membership of this religion was in fact made up of approximately 75% women.

The Watchtower Society files no publicly accessible financial figures, they are kept secret but reported in their official magazine of 2011 that it had spent more than $173 million that year in caring for special pioneers, missionaries and traveling overseers in their field service assignments. Donations obtained from the distribution of literature is a major source of income, most of which is used to promote its evangelical activities. Author James Beckford has claimed that the status of the all-male voting members of the society is also purely symbolic. He said they cannot be considered to be representatives of the mass of Jehovah's Witnesses and are in no position to challenge the actions or authority of the society's seven directors.

James Arthur Beckford, FBA (born 1 December 1942) is a British sociologist of religion. He is also Professor Emeritus of Sociology at the University of Warwick in Coventry, England, and a Fellow of the British Academy. In 1988/1989, he served as President of the Association for the Sociology of Religion, and from 1999 to 2003, as the President of the International Society for the Sociology of Religion. Apart from general writings on the sociology of religion, Beckford has been a prolific author of books and articles on new religious movements and society's responses to them. He has also researched and written about religious issues affecting prison inmates.

Philip Rees was a very experienced but somewhat, albeit limited knowledgeable Bible student, and his main attribute was that he had extensive skills in managing a Branch office and printing facility of the Watchtower Society. Plus, he also in the past had experienced first hand connections with influential Joseph Rutherford (1869-1942), in addition also with the 3rd President of the Watchtower Society, Nathan Homer Knorr (1905-1977) who had taken over complete and absolute control in 1942 and who also demonstrated his inherited and ruthless power as an autocrat, following the example of his predecessor and mentor Joseph Rutherford.

Philip was invited in 1961 and felt personally privileged to attend the initial class of a new ten-month long Special Gilead Course for branch overseers plus other special individuals who were viewed as prospective leaders when the new system of things was due to begin in the very near future. (This phrase was actually used in the confidential invitation letter sent to each prospective attendee.) The wives of the invited attendees (if married) had to sign a cleverly worded personal agreement drawn up by the Governing Body (their legal department) that they agreed to their husbands being absent for the year; a precaution so as not to violate scriptural standards, the covering letter stated. The contents of this agreement that these poor subjective wives had to sign; obviously prepared by a man, would blow your mind, as it clearly gave all protection to the husband and virtually no protection at all to the wife, who would meantime somehow have to cope with the absence of her husband for almost one year, while he was away on active service of the Lord. Phil said; while he laughed out loud, "It could have been drawn up by Rutherford himself, had he been alive."

Most of these individual men who attended these ten-month special Gilead courses from 1961-1964 (these courses were soon abandoned in 1964 as an utter failure and waste of time and money) are now dead or have been ex-communicated, like one notorious attendee, the so-called British leader District Overseer, Douglas Turnbull (who proclaimed himself as Daniel in the Lions Den, based on his appearance on a 3rd rate TV programme). Or these men have simply abandoned this religion or faded into the background because of being disillusioned by the many false and misleading promises. Plus, of course, in 2019, if any of these special individuals are still alive, which is very unlikely, we must remind ourselves once again that 60 years later this religion is still waiting for the imminent new system to arrive in the very_near_future, the place where these specially trained individuals using wasted funds from the regular donations of their followers and who were supposed to be taking over as prospective leaders in the New World.

During Phil's time in New York, while attending this special Gilead course, Nathan Knorr had called Philip into his private, penthouse office and surreptitiously suggested that Philip would be of great value and an asset to the Society if he eventually was invited to serve on the Governing Body, but the only way he could be invited is that he must display publicly that he partakes of the bread and wine, thus expressing to all that he was one of the heavenly, specially chosen ones by Jesus Christ and a member of this unique little flock of kings and priests mentioned in the book of Revelation. This deeply troubled Philip, as up until this time in his association with Jehovah's Witnesses he had always sincerely thought, and was personally satisfied according to the current Biblical interpretation of the organization that he was simply a humble member of the so-called earthly great crowd of other sheep and certainly not royalty, but rather to enjoy, sometime in the unknown future, with his treasured wife Maudie, and have a family of their own in the promised, soon to come, paradise on earth. But more about the outcome of this incident is covered later in our report.

When the name of Douglas Turnbull came up in our conversation, Phil's eyes lit up, as he had always personally felt that this man was one of the most dangerous, aggressive and arrogant individuals he had ever met. Turnbull had served as a prominent District Servant in England for many years; was also a graduate of the failed 10-month Special Gilead Course for special individuals and acted as though he was the self-appointed leader and spokesman of the Watchtower Society in Britain, which Phil honestly admitted; that he personally resented because of Turnbull's high-minded attitude. But Phil also humbly confessed that Turnbull's lectures at the conventions and local circuit assemblies were always very powerful and inspiring to the flock to do greater things in the name of Lord, so obviously he was well liked and admired by the organizational leaders and also by his audiences of local witnesses whenever or wherever he spoke, just like an American evangelist.

Phil also mused about the fellow subordinate of Turnbull, who was Turnbull's assistant, sometimes substitute and lackey for many years, namely Ronald Drage who also adopted the same arrogant mentality as Turnbull. Ron Drage had never lived in America, but in his daily vocabulary he used American slang and expressions with a pseudo accent in an attempt to impress his audience that he was an international celebrity, although he was just a simple working-class boy from the north-east of England. Drage was also one the most aggressive proponents of 1975 being the year when he served as a district servant in the British Isles, and he was also well known as a strict society man.

According to the informative website, Silent Lambs.org, which covers all cases of sexual and child abuse by the shepherds of the Watchtower Society, Ronald Drage was forced to resign in 2014 along with a fellow Bethel official called Jack Dowson, as a leading member of the managing committee of the Watchtower Society in London because of his involvement with the cover up of child molestation along with a personal fellow elder of his, a friend called Michael Porter. Porter had previously pleaded guilty to 25 cases of indecent assault on a male and committing gross indecency with or towards a child and was sent to prison, one of his victims was an 18-month-old baby. It is also reported that in recent years 26 key leading members of the Watchtower Society in England have also been convicted of child molestation.

Later in life, Ronald Drage denied that he ever believed or promoted 1975 as being the year and also stated that he never accepted the bold statements made by Frederick Franz of the Governing Body and his ridiculous prophetic claims related to that year of 1975. Phil commented that this claim by Drage was simply not true and his denial was total hogwash as there are tape recordings of lectures by Ronald Drage making these erroneous statements about 1975 being the year. These tapes include unquestionable statements in which he clearly makes excitable claims by the Governing Body (the faithful and discreet slave) about the important significance of 1975 being the end of the present system of things (end of the world) and that the brothers must now be obedient and making arrangements to change their life style and serve more fully in the preaching work, plus other totally silly, stupid and irrelevant remarks made without any scriptural basis whatsoever, emphasizing his claim as clearly recorded on tape, before the new system (the new world) begins in the very, very near future.

> *Editor's Note*: The Watchtower Society, after the failure of 1975, repeatedly claimed that the world's end would come before the year 2000 AD despite later denials; this is just one typical example of their lies and deceit, "The end of the world is expected to come before the end of the century." (*The Watchtower*, January 1, 1989, p. 12)

Many more private details of notorious cases of immoral wrongdoing and corrupt business dealings have also been revealed and exposed to our intensive and dedicated research team, especially regarding gross misconduct by leading members of the Watchtower Society; some being provided and leaked by a leading member of the Service Department in the London Bethel. But the management committee of the MTC International Foundation decided that these sordid, disgusting details of sexual perversion, even including animals, committed by these shepherds and leading members in the Watchtower Society, were not up-building to genuine Christians, many who still sincerely try to maintain their pure (Matthew 5:8 and 1 Timothy 1:5) and simplistic faith in God and Jesus Christ while at the same time remain associated with the Watchtower Society or the Mormon Church. Most of these x-rated details, out of respect for individual and human dignity, have been omitted from this report.

> *Editor's Note*: We strongly encourage that if any of our readers in the United Kingdom hear or have knowledge of child

sexual abuse by any member of the Watchtower Society, even if they are appointed elders or ministerial servants, work in the London Bethel or in fact are members of any other religious organization, cult or sect, plus any other social, welfare organizations or other public or private groups, that they immediately report this case to the British Home Office who are currently handling an Independent Inquiry into Child Sexual Abuse (See their web site at www.iicsa.org) that is very similar to the Australian Royal Commission (ARC). For readers in all other countries please check with your local police authorities or contact a firm of attorneys that specialize in these sordid cases.

Returning to the notorious case of the Watchtower official Douglas Turnbull, unfortunately the influential and impressive power he held eventually went to Turnbull's head and Phil recalled the time when Turnbull was caught with his pants down, don't forget Phil was an outspoken Australian. While Turnbull was acting as the Convention Overseer of the well-publicized Edinburgh International Convention of 1965, ironically called Word of Truth held at Murrayfield Rugby Stadium in Scotland, the first international convention held in Edinburgh for over 30 years and which over 40,000 members planned to attend. Phil recalls that Turnbull, during that time while he was serving as convention overseer, was also having an adulterous affair with an attractive young sister only half his age; she was supposedly to be acting as his private secretary. When it was discovered by Joan, his faithful wife of many years, she of course divorced him and he was later disfellowshipped and married this young attractive sister, whose name we will not reveal as she was simply a victim of a typical aggressive, dominant master in this religious cult, but she was also excommunicated according to the Watchtower regulations for her actions and conduct.

This observation regarding power going to one's head was made by a leading researcher at Penn State University. "The more power one has, the more they will have, and the more will go the way they want. Someone with misguided power can fail in their powerful position and become a very negative asset to a group. When someone attains power, their personality sometimes changes. Take for example when a person suddenly becomes famous. They do not act the same as they used to, because fame goes to their head. Something happens chemically in their brain that pushes them to act suddenly like a different person."

According to the now sealed files in the London Bethel offices of the Watchtower Society, Phil remembered this case was so notorious that it reverberated and sent shock waves through the ranks of the local Witnesses throughout Britain. Phil recalled, according to the notes submitted to the London office by the local judicial committee, that Turnbull at his judicial hearing was so arrogant, that in his defense for not being disfellowshipped, Turnbull had used the Biblical case and example of King David as recorded in the Bible at 2 Samuel, Chapter 11, who also committed adultery and murder, but was still approved and kept in his position of favor by God.

Turnbull lost his appeal of course and was eventually excommunicated in line with the Bible text at 1 Corinthians 5:1-5, "He who has done this be ... removed from among you," but in Turnbull's case it was for a minimum of ten years. See also the Bible texts at 1 Corinthians 5:9-13; 1 Timothy 5:19, 20 and 2 Thessalonians 3:6, 11, 13-15. We remind our readers that this rule of ten years expulsion is not recorded in the Bible, but based on instructions from the Governing Body and originally published as a series of three brochures issued over a period of several years but later included in the infamous secret text book of rules exclusively for elders called, Pay Attention to Yourselves and to all the Flock published in 1978 by the Watchtower Society. The Governing Body laid down the rule that if because of the notoriety involved, in certain cases ten years must elapse before one could ever again apply for reinstatement to the organization. This ten-year expulsion and restriction before one is forgiven of their sins is not in the Holy Scriptures (see and compare Ephesians 1:7 and 4:32, plus James 5:14-16) so we have no idea which individual in the Watchtower headquarters invented this arbitrary rule contained in this publication supposedly written under the guidance of the Holy Spirit, as it was certainly not Jesus Christ or Almighty God, Yahweh. But this revelation of the ten-year rule contained in that publication must have been proof-read and approved by the Governing Body. The Holy Scriptures are very clear about adding or taking away from the inspired word of God, for example the text at Proverbs 30:5, 6, "Every word of God proves true; he is a shield to those who take refuge in him. Do not add to his words, or else he will rebuke you, and you will be found a liar." (see also Deuteronomy 4:2; 1 Corinthians 4:6 and Revelation 22:18, 19)

One of our researchers who had spent several hours interviewing a past member of the writing department of the New York Watchtower Society headquarters told our researcher that he had spoken some time ago to one of the now deceased writers of this special book, *Pay Attention to Yourselves and to all the Flock*. This secret manual was not available to the general members of Jehovah's Witnesses but only to appointed local leaders in each congregation, especially the congregation service committee and they were instructed to not divulge the contents to anyone or make copies and to hand their copy of the manual back to the congregation servant if ever they ceased being a member of the service committee, as this manual was strictly the exclusive, supposedly secret property of the Watchtower Society. Needless to say this instruction was violated on numerous occasions with copies of the manual being sold openly on eBay and sections widely quoted on *Wikipedia* and other websites. Several court cases have resulted for violation of this instruction emanating from the very aggressive legal department of the Watchtower Society, who lost most of these cases in any event. It was reported by our source that when the final draft of this manual was submitted to the Governing Body for their signing off, it contained the instruction that if a case was notorious then a period of 25 years must elapse before the guilty party can apply for reinstatement.

According to the leaked minutes of the meeting of the Governing Body held in February of 1978, member Lyman Swingle, and this was confirmed by a relative of Swingle in Salt Lake City, he had raised the issue that he felt the Governing Body was overstepping their power by enforcing this 25-year rule as it appeared they were issuing a life sentence or perhaps even worse, a death sentence, rather than a simple restriction because of the notoriety of a case and this might stumble some of the brothers who understood that the forgiveness of Jesus Christ was limitless. The Governing Body as a result of the suggestion by Lyman Swingle must have felt uncomfortable about this statement and unanimously decided that such a length of time sounded more like a death sentence, so they instructed the writer to reduce the time period to ten years, as it eventually appeared in the final printed version of this secret manual.

This manual for Elders has now been recently replaced in 2010 by another publication by the Watchtower Society called *Shepherd the Flock of God* (also known simply as the Shepherd book) under the same terms and restrictions. In additional this fixed time period before one could apply for reinstatement and be forgiven after 10 years was also removed, plus the word notoriety and the phrase, brazen conduct. The most recent revised edition was released in April 2020. One such ludicrous addition to this secret manual, written by an individual in the writing department of the Watchtower Society is the following: "When the body of elders discusses a matter, Christ by means of the holy spirit can influence any elder to make an expression that contributes to a wise decision, one that may not have been reached if the elders had been consulted individually." The loyal, docile, slave like members of Jehovah's Witnesses are instructed by their Governing Body to actually believe this material or face dire consequences, illustrating once again how a cult operates and controls the minds of its followers.

Returning to the Turnbull case, Philip Rees pointed out that Turnbull later made an additional appeal in writing directly to the London branch office, with a copy sent to the Governing Body in New York and, in his letter, he claimed that the current decision by the local judicial committee to disfellowship him and including the ten-year restriction was not impartial but prejudiced against him, as one of the members of this five man committee so disliked him. Turnbull claimed this member was an ex-circuit servant who Turnbull in the past had to strictly counsel and reprimand because of certain unethical actions this man had taken while serving under the direction of Turnbull, when he was a leading district servant. This member of the judicial committee later admitted to a friend of one of our researchers that Turnbull had in fact destroyed his theocratic career with the Watchtower Society a few years ago and he was glad to see Turnbull finally fall from grace and receive his just deserts. Turnbull also claimed in his letter of appeal that this man, who obviously disliked and resented Turnbull, had negatively influenced the other four members of this committee against him, so their final decision was totally prejudiced and the hearing must be reheard by another group of alternate men whom Turnbull must approve in advance.

As recalled by Philip Rees and according to the leaked file in the London Bethel, the head of the service department at the time simply consulted with the branch servant and one of his assistants and then decided to completely ignore this written request by Turnbull to reopen the case, as he personally knew Turnbull and his truculent character, so to deal with this further appeal would only end up in a long protracted dispute, so the original decision stood and was enforced, the letter also being ignored, filed away and forgotten.

What sort of secret information does this exclusive manual for judicial committees contain? This very enlightening article, quoted below, made on the website Watchman Fellowship, written by Jason Baker after reviewing this secret manual, Pay Attention to Yourself and to all the Flock published by the Watchtower Society, reveals his feelings and opinion.

> The reason for the Society's intense secrecy regarding the manual can be explained in one word: power. The majority of Pay Attention... is devoted to the exercise of power within a congregation, instructing elders in the proper procedure for handling a wide array of punishable offenses. Power is also at issue because the Society has deliberately kept these regulations from becoming common knowledge amongst the organization, thus leaving Witnesses unprepared and without recourse should their elders accuse them of wrongdoing. The organization has deliberately kept its followers in the dark despite its professed dedication to publishing new light. Even though elders as a body exert tremendous power over the lives of individual Witnesses, Pay Attention ... shows that the office of elder has little inherent authority; all actions of any importance must be taken as a governmental body. Only a select set of actions may be taken on the individual elder's initiative: the Presiding Overseer may only deliver and post congregational announcements and schedule Service Meeting assignments, the Secretary may only organize files and write general letters of introduction and transfer for publishers, and the Service Overseer may only process magazine order changes

(*Pay Attention...*, p. 68). A significant limitation on the power of individual elders is that any counseling performed with Witnesses must be reported to the Presiding Overseer (p. 97) (This will be discussed in greater detail in the section below on judicial hearings.) The power of the elders as a body is also limited; any decision can be overruled by the Circuit Overseer (p. 67).

These restrictions on the elders have the positive effect of preventing any individual elder from accruing extensive power over the congregation and his fellow elders. Negatively, these restrictions result in absolute power being held by the Governing Body in Brooklyn. All decisions must be made according to the stipulations and ever-changing doctrines of the faithful and discreet slave and its agencies (*Pay Attention...*, p. 64; cf. p. 84), and even many minor actions are dictated from officials in Brooklyn. An important point for non-Witnesses to realize is that the power of the Society extends over not only the elders and Witnesses lower in the hierarchy; it can also intrude into the lives of non-Witnesses. A record is kept of each individual with whom the Witnesses speak, and the leaders in Brooklyn often order elders to call or visit specific individuals (*Pay Attention...*, p. 61). Non-Witnesses are thus placed in a network of Watchtower records with numerous people tracking their responses to Witness pressure. Regrettably, the Society has kept knowledge of such abuses of power secret from the majority of its followers. *Pay Attention...* outlines in detail the procedures for holding a judicial hearing.

The most significant rule affecting the accused is that he or she is not allowed any written or recorded documentation involving the proceedings (*Pay Attention...*, p. 110). Elders are also forbidden from sending any documentation stating the precise accusation being leveled against the Witness. If a written invitation to the hearing is necessary, the elders simply state the accused's alleged course of action, the time and place of the hearing, and a contact reference for rescheduling (p. 110). Similarly, the accused may bring neither outside observers, nor tape-recording devices into the hearing (p. 110). Verdicts are rendered orally (p. 121); the written documentation for disfellowshipping (Forms S-77 and S-79) are sent to Brooklyn

(p. 122). Controlling all the evidence concerning the events surrounding the hearing allows the Society to protect itself should a punished Witness resort to legal action against the Watchtower.

Most Jehovah's Witnesses who serve within the Watchtower bastion are largely unaware of the full arsenal of disciplinary weapons at the Society's disposal. They believe that the Society is opposed to accruing power through the almost total curtailing of personal freedom. The Watchtower has even derided others for abusing their authority, noting that worldly managers or bosses often show this attitude by surrounding themselves with yes-men, who offer no dissenting views and who do not challenge their superiors' worldly quest (greed) for power (*Watchtower*, August 1, 1993, p. 13). Unfortunately, the Governing Body engages in this same worldly quest (greed) for power by using its vast array of regulations and disciplinary measures to create yes-men, who offer no dissenting views and do not challenge their superiors. It is the responsibility of Christians to share with Jehovah's Witnesses God's evangel, the good news that "if the Son therefore shall make you free, ye shall be free indeed" (John 8:36). If *Pay Attention to Yourselves and to All the Flock* is proven to be an authentic elder's manual (the Society's allegation that posting this document on the Internet was a violation of copyright law, and their demand for its removal, strongly support its authenticity), Christians will have an unprecedented opportunity. Using this Watchtower literature, they can compare for Jehovah's Witnesses the bewildering morass of public and secret Societal restrictions and punishments with the freedom that Christians have in Christ.

An additional website called Witness Outreach also reviewed *Pay Attention to Yourselves and to All the Flock* and made the following comments related to the powerful control that the Governing Body of the Watchtower Society exercises over the members of this religion.

Individual congregations of Jehovah's Witnesses are overseen by designated men who are called 'elders'. To become an elder, a male member of the congregation must be approved for the position by the Watchtower Bible and Tract Society.

The arrangement of having a group of elders oversee the congregations began on October 1, 1972. (Prior to this, congregations were overseen by a Congregational Servant). In order to assist the elders in handling various congregational matters and situations, the Watchtower Society has published a manual that describes their approved protocols for handling the matters which arise. Elders are expected to adhere strictly to the manual as published. The current manual is titled *Shepherd the Flock of God*, released in 2010. This basically replaces the previous manual, which was titled *Pay Attention to Yourselves and to All the Flock* (1991).

Such manuals are intended to be for the Elders' eyes only; no other members are supposed to be privy to its contents. Therefore, elders are expected to keep their copies secured away from the eyes of others. As a result, a large number of the membership isn't even aware that the book exists. In fact, quite often, if a regular member mentions this manual to an elder the first question the elder will ask is something along the line of, "Where did you hear about this book?" This book is guarded so carefully that, if an elder ceases being an elder, he is required to return his copy of the manual to the congregation instead of keeping it. This is clearly stated in the beginning of the manual: A copy of this textbook is issued to each appointed elder, and he may retain it as long as he continues to serve as an elder in any congregation. At such time as he should cease to serve in that capacity, his copy of the book must be handed over to the Congregation Service Committee, since this publication is congregation property. No copies are to be made of any part of this publication.

Editor's Note: Although both of these articles quoted above imply that the rank and file of the members of Jehovah's Witnesses did not know of the existence of this secret manual is somewhat misleading, as in our research and interviews with hundreds of members and ex-members of this religion, every single one had heard and knew of the existence of this manual, some even showed photo-copies of relevant pages, so to try and call it a secret manual is laughable.

Referring back to the case of Douglas Turnbull, ironically in time after the ten years expired, he was reinstated and once again was restored to a good, honorable standing within the Watchtower organisation, but this incident meantime had set a very negative precedent, plus serious irreparable damage to many genuine, sincere Christians; totally innocent parties according to observers of this case. Phil also added in our tense conversation in an attempt to temper his severe anger and criticism of the disgusting and repulsive action of Turnbull that Phil still believed that all men, and women he quickly added, who have sinned still deserve the forgiveness and blessings of the Lord, without time limits being imposed by some official body, basically because of the inherited imperfection of mankind from the Creation and the original sin. So we today, no matter which religious view we claim to acknowledge or observe, cannot argue over that extremely profound and wise observation as presented by our dear friend, the late Philip Rees.

We encourage all of our readers to research the new book by the MTC International Foundation (partially written by the late Philip Rees) titled *Error 404 - The Mystery of the Man Who Never Was, or The Greatest Man Who Ever Lived?* This book covers the ministry and life of Jesus Christ and the fine example he displayed of how he forgave sinners and how he eventually gave his human life on behalf and in redemption of sinful mankind.

Over the years it is on record that other prominent men in the Watchtower Society did the same, identical thing as Turnbull; got rid of their no longer wanted wives, then they willingly accepted the official procedure of being disfellowshipped for a short period, then simply applied for reinstatement and some even became elders again (shepherds of the flock), to the disgust of Philip Rees, plus also many other sincere Christians who followed the notorious Turnbull case. The sad part of this account, Phil said, was twofold. Firstly, Turnbull's wife of many years, as a faithful and loyal Christian wife, was now very ill and a totally destroyed, childless woman, so Turnbull then had the audacity to send his wife off to stay with friends in Birmingham, England, and callously told her to contact her old friends and they would take care of her. Secondly, that there is on record many other cases of prominent men in the ranks of the Watchtower Society, also successfully doing exactly the same thing as Turnbull and also successfully using the same tactic that

Turnbull employed, in trying to avoid paying the consequences of their dirty deeds and then later being appointed again to senior positions within this religion.

Philip Rees had pointed out that Turnbull knew he would eventually have to face the music for throwing his middle-aged, now very sick wife to one side and moving into his recently purchased, very expensive, costly country house in a beautiful part of the midlands of England with his new young bride. So, Turnbull handed in his resignation as a district overseer of the Watchtower Society and hoped he could carry on in a local congregation of Jehovah's Witnesses as though nothing had ever happened. But what shocked many observers even more so, was the fact that Turnbull, who had been in the full-time service of the Watchtower Society for most of his life, since he was a teenager, receiving the usual very frugal monthly allowance; yet even though unemployed he now had the cash to buy a high-priced property and purchase an expensive, lucrative business venture. Phil in his usual dry humor said, "I also have been in the full-time service for approximately the same length of time and I could not even afford to buy a second-hand bicycle."

There was some suspicion by the Watchtower branch office in London after this incident became public, so they called in a recently converted member of Jehovah's Witnesses, a retired forensic official of the CID, Scotland Yard, London, to investigate the records and finances of the ill-fated Edinburgh convention of 1965, which had been controlled and personally managed by Turnbull, but nothing untoward could be proved. A rumor had existed that Turnbull had taken a massive kickback from a known corrupt government official who worked in the local British army depot related to the hiring of hundreds of large army tents, camp beds and blankets to set up a temporary camp site in a swampy field on the outskirts of the City of Edinburgh. It appears there was insufficient accommodation facilities for the now many expected families that were planning to attend this well advertised international convention in Scotland, and also use the event for private tourism of this beautiful country and its magnificent scenery.

This temporary camp site turned out to be a total fiasco, as the weather was so wet and cold that summer in Scotland that the field that had been rented was virtually under water, but the many visitors and users of this camp site still had to pay expensive accommodation fees to the convention administration, operated by the Watchtower Society. The brothers and their families who were assigned to this accommodation facility on this camp site were allocated two blankets per camp bed, which was totally insufficient for the cold and damp nights, but some bright spark in the convention administration, probably Turnbull or his subjective lackey; assistant convention servant Ron Drage, issued the rule that the brothers could have additional blankets, but at an extra fee per blanket, over and above the already expensive accommodation fees. The conditions at this camp site were so intolerable and unbearable that is was reported that many families simply had to return home before the convention was half over and also forfeit their money paid in advance to the Watchtower Society with no hope of a refund. With a sigh, Phil reflected, no crime was uncovered however; as Turnbull had made sure that he had covered his tracks very skillfully, if indeed he was guilty of any unethical or criminal practices.

A friend of one of our researchers, called Peter **** who was assigned by the Watchtower Society to assist in supervising this camp site recalled that during the nights, there was so much whining and wailing of children and their mothers because of the cold and dampness, plus many of the fathers appeared to be just walking aimlessly about the camp site in their top coats or wrapped in black plastic refuse bags all night, just to try and keep warm as they had lovingly sacrificed their blankets to other members of their family. Peter also said, "I had visions of this camp being very similar to the Nazi concentration camps of Belsen, Auschwitz or Dachau, and it took many months for me to mentally recover from this emotionally distressing and disturbing experience."

***

Returning to the personal experience of Philip Rees with the Governing Body of the Watchtower Society, we learn more about this incident and manipulative scheme of Nathan Knorr to encourage and persuade Philip to start taking the symbolic bread and wine at the annual memorial celebration, in order to establish his public claim that he was of the exclusive, special, so-called anointed chosen ones. The following year, after careful thought Philip did innocently and being very short-sighted, he decided to partake of the bread and wine to establish his outward public expression of the so-called holy spirits leading (promoted and introduced by Nathan Knorr, the autocratic, manipulative leader of the Watchtower Society) indicating publicly that Phil was now one of the special heavenly class. Phil also admitted that he stupidly thought that this would now further advance his career in the Watchtower Society and that he would soon be invited to join the Governing Body as hinted by Nathan Knorr.

Philip reflected and stated that he innocently and naively thought that this was the way the Lord communicated and informed one of the decision by Almighty God to those who had been selected as belonging to this unique heavenly class, being through the Governing Body or its chairman. Phil then quickly added "What a stupid fool I was to believe or be even considering such rubbish." His poor wife Maudie at the time was devastated at the thought of being left alone on earth and her dearly loved, handsome husband of many years; and had known since he was 15 years old, despite all of his dreadful faults, that Philip was to be taken away to heaven someday, when he died, to sit as a sexless king and priest at the right hand of Jesus Christ and she would never see him ever again.

Later however, Philip Rees eventually decided after deep thought, reflection and meditation that he was not going to partake of the bread and wine at any future annual Memorials, as calculatingly suggested by Nathan Knorr, so as a result he was obviously never invited to become a member of the Governing Body of the Watchtower Society.

Philip had recently learned through a friend of his in the New York Bethel, of the case of Nathan Knorr also persuading Milton Henschel (1920-2003), Knorr's private secretary and travelling companion for many years, who had been baptized in 1934 at the age of 14 years old, the same confusing year as Hayden Covington and for Henschel to now start partaking of the bread and wine in 1947 when he was 27 years old, despite previously thinking and also personally believing he was one the so-called other sheep class with an earthly hope when he became baptized back in 1934. This sudden turn-around appeared strange to say the least and also from comments made by fellow workers that Milton Henschel made this decision and changed his mind for undisclosed very personal and private reasons and refused to openly discuss the issue with any of his curious fellow associates in the Bethel headquarters. But Henschel also no doubt desired and was now compelled to publicly declare that he personally believed he was now one of the so-called heavenly class of 144,000 sexless Kings and Priests, plus had been chosen and selected by God himself to rule the Universe along with Jesus Christ. No doubt he was also privately motivated so that he could prepare himself to be invited to join the Governing Body, as was personally promised by his very close and intimate friend Nathan Knorr.

Henschel, as expected, was quickly appointed by Knorr later that same year in 1947 to the Board of Directors of the Watchtower Society, who also traditionally made up the Governing Body. Back in 1939, Henschel had been appointed by Rutherford as the private secretary to Nathan Knorr, apparently at the personal request of Knorr who was at that time still overseeing the production of the millions of books, Bibles and magazines in the Watchtower printery. When Knorr became president of the Watchtower Society in 1942 after the death of Rutherford, Henschel continued as his personal assistant and private secretary and regularly accompanied Knorr on his international travels, visiting at least 150 countries during this time. By 1945, Henschel was also a featured speaker at many international events despite the fact he was only 25 years old at the time.

It may be of interest to some of our readers who are aware of the disturbing rumors of homosexual activity in the various Bethel homes of the Watchtower Society throughout the world, or maybe this information is totally irrelevant to many others of our readers who accept same sex relationships as normal. Nathan Knorr insisted that he and Milton Henschel had adjoining bedrooms in the Bethel headquarters and this was confirmed by our research team from at least three ex-workers in the New York complex. Plus the same instruction was issued by Knorr related to having connecting bedrooms in the various hotels they stayed during their frequent and regular overseas travels.

Editor's Note: With due respect we must also point out, based on feedback from one of our sources in the New York headquarters of the Watchtower Society, who claims that some time ago he had spoken to an elderly sister who used to handle the travel arrangements for President Nathan Knorr. She stated that this request for connecting bedrooms was a genuine request based on the need for the convenience for President Knorr to review his speeches and talks with Milton Henschel for the next day of his duties and for no other clandestine reasons. In good faith we make this comment known to our readers in our quest for openness about our reporting, but our inside source could not locate any written records or memos in the archives of the Watchtower Society's travel office that would prove or disprove this claim. Also remember this was before Knorr or Henschel were married to their new brides in the 1950s in an attempt to cover over their homosexual tendencies.

Philip Rees spent the rest of his life working diligently in the London Bethel, firstly as the Factory Overseer and Assistant Branch Servant, plus he was later appointed at the end of 1961, after completing the 10-month Special Gilead Course, by Nathan Knorr and the Governing Body and spent two years, 1962 and 1963 as the instructor of the newly established, four-week long Kingdom Ministry School, primarily held for presiding congregation servants, plus a few outstanding special pioneers. This new school had been started in New York in 1959 but only introduced to the British Branch at the beginning of 1962. Phil said that Nathan Knorr had spoken to him privately during the same conversation that Knorr hinted about Phil making a public claim that he was one of the anointed and also dropped hints about him eventually being invited to join the Governing Body in New York. Knorr had told Phil that being appointed as the first instructor of the British Kingdom Ministry School, this would be good training for Phil to be more friendly, outgoing and communicative and not so much of a recluse or withdrawn personality. Phil laughed out loud about this observation by Knorr and commented how little Knorr knew about the real Philip Rees.

Philip always still lived with the hope that one day of still being appointed as the new Branch Servant of the British Isles upon the resignation or the removal of the now elderly; unfortunately, also now because of his age, a very inefficient fellow Welshman, Alfred Pryce Hughes. But this was never to happen, as Philip knew he had crossed swords with, and met the disapproval of the autocratic, ruthless Nathan Knorr, so the Governing Body, at that time totally controlled and manipulated by Knorr, appointed a British brother called Wilfred Gooch from the Nigerian Branch office as a stop gap and who served for a short time as Branch servant of Britain until his expected death.

In 1968, Gwen the wife and now widow of Wilfred Gooch presented her side of this event in an interview and said "Wilf received an invitation to attend a ten-month course of special instruction in Brooklyn, New York. After finishing it, he was unexpectedly assigned back to England. I had remained in Nigeria and was given only 14 days notice to meet Wilf in London. I left with mixed feelings, since Nigeria had been such a happy assignment. After serving 14 years abroad, it took time to adjust to life in England again. However, we were grateful to be close to our aging parents once more and to be able to help care for them. Tragically, my dear husband died and it was an especially hard blow to handle."

The day that Wilfred Gooch arrived at the London Bethel from New York in December of 1963, he was accompanied with a personal letter from the Desk of the President Nathan Knorr, dated 27 November, 1963, confirming his new appointment as Branch Servant to replace the elderly Pryce Hughes, who had served for almost 20 years. The whole procedure was done very quickly and also secretly, as no one in London Bethel was aware of this immediate change of personnel and only a couple of the members of the Governing Body were informed, namely Suiter and Henschel, that was the way Knorr operated. That morning at breakfast when Pryce Hughes read aloud this letter to the gathered London Bethel family it was still vivid in the memory of Phil Rees, and he said "It sent shudders down my spine." He and everyone else who worked in the London Bethel at that time had expected Philip to become the next Branch Servant but Phil had fallen foul of the powerful, dictatorial Nathan Knorr, so this was one of the greatest disappointments in Phil's life. Nathan Knorr was a very autocratic, ruthless individual and even though the Watchtower Society described itself as theocratic (God-ruled) it was in fact still run by an autocrat who was more like a German Nazi dictator than a humble servant of the Lord.

The Vice-President, Frederick Franz had virtually no involvement with the day to day running of the organization as he was closeted in his secluded penthouse office or exclusive private suite having visions and writing more of his extreme interpretations of the Bible and prophetic expectations, especially his theory of the coming year of 1975, plus creating mystical charts in order to prove that 1975 was the year and bring about Armageddon and the 1,000-year rule of Christ. (Revelation 20:4-10) The other members of the Governing Body subjectively, simply allowed Knorr his head, and continue as the existing, powerful, heavy handed, autocratic and apparently somewhat very frustrated, President of the Watchtower Society.

For those who were in the know it was common knowledge that Wilfred Gooch was a very sick man when he took over as Branch Servant of the British Isles in 1963, as he had experienced a very severe case of malignant tertian malaria while serving in Lagos, Nigeria, and for the past ten years had a very weak heart as a result, so he was not expected to last very long in his new demanding position and assignment. Nathan Knorr meantime was also fully conversant of the serious health condition and the dim prospects of poor Wilfred Gooch. As a result of Knorr's scheming mind and displaying the extreme power of his role as President, not long after Gooch was appointed in 1963 to his new assignment in London, replacing Pryce Hughes, Nathan Knorr also assigned an American brother to also serve in the London Bethel and he was to take over from Philip Rees as instructor of the four-week long Kingdom Ministry School and Philip was moved sideways to the position as factory overseer again.

This new brother, whom Knorr assigned to the London Bethel, was called David Ingold and he was a very skilled organizer and brilliant instructor but had little spiritual experience and a very limited knowledge of the scriptures. He had served in a senior position in the US Military but had taken early retirement with a lucrative government pension when he converted to the Watchtower religion, so he was a man of independent means and even though he was a member of this religion for only a few years he very quickly climbed the ranks of the organization. Many were very surprised when he received such a prominent role in the London Bethel, a direct assignment from his now close personal friend Nathan Knorr the President, that some felt he still came under the category of being a newly converted man. The full Bible text says at 1 Timothy 3:6 when discussing the qualification for being an elder, "He must not be a recent convert, or he may become puffed up with conceit and fall into the condemnation of the devil." But the autocratic Knorr simply ignored this biblical warning and felt otherwise, plus he was obviously prejudiced and thought he knew better than the wisdom of the Apostle Paul writing under the inspiration of the Holy Spirit, especially regarding his now personal friend and his new special appointment of David Ingold to a very senior position in the London Bethel.

Philip remembered that from day one in 1964, he and David Ingold clashed and although Ingold was originally assigned by President Knorr to the role of Kingdom Ministry School instructor to replace Phil in the London Bethel, he also acted as though he was the branch servant in waiting and this truly irritated and upset Philip Rees, as Phil was still having to deal with the personal humiliation of being stepped over as the new Branch Servant upon the replacement, removal or resignation of the elderly Pryce Hughes. Some who worked in the London Bethel accused Phil of having sour grapes, which Phil fervently denied, however it did not expunge the ongoing friction and jealousy between most of the leading, senior brothers in the London Bethel, which was now reaching an intolerable level and driving most of them to drinking alcohol without restraint to try and subdue their frustrated feelings and emotions.

Philip Rees did however comment that he had suspicions regarding the confidential discussion that President Nathan Knorr must have had with David Ingold in his private penthouse office in New York City regarding his new appointment in London, as Phil had also been through the exact same experience, procedure and type of private discussion some years earlier, when the all-powerful and manipulative autocrat Knorr tried to persuade Philip to join the Governing Body. No one today of course knows what was actually discussed between Knorr and Ingold at that private interview as they are both now long gone. However, in view of Wilfred Gooch probably only having an expected few years serving as the British Branch Servant because of his very poor health, Phil felt that David Ingold was Knorr's personal choice as the next Branch Servant to replace Gooch when poor Wilfred eventually had to resign from his assignment, either for health, family reasons or possibly his expected early death and once again overstepping Philip Rees being appointed as the next Branch Servant. Knorr's tactics as an autocrat were later confirmed in Phil's mind, especially when the news started the rounds and hit the Watchtower private news wires regarding the underhanded tactics used by Knorr in getting another personal friend of his; Theo (Ted) Jaracz, former Branch Servant of Australia being appointed on the Governing Body in 1974. There is an amusing but rather cynical phrase used by the many members of the Watchtower Society religion today regarding spreading gossip and important news; telephone or telegramme or Tell-a-Witness.

But Phil had not yet finished his story about David Ingold and his very attractive, glamorous wife. We will not reveal her name as she was simply another innocent victim of a cult. David Ingold was a very handsome and dynamic character, plus he had the looks of Cary Grant, the Hollywood actor. In addition, his wife had entered London Bethel along with her husband, as a very outstanding, glamorous, affluent looking woman, but she soon had to cope with working full-time as a female in Bethel and this took its heavy toll on her general appearance and demeanor. Much to the resentment and anger of David Ingold, who was now firmly entrenched as a leader and senior official in the London Bethel office, his wife had been assigned as a house maid by Pryce Hughes, the recently relegated Branch Servant but now the newly appointed house manager or butler of the Bethel home, who by this time was then well over seventy years of age and was displaying early signs of dementia. Pryce Hughes, who after being replaced by Knorr as the redundant Branch Servant, manager and overseer after 20 years of service was re-assigned in charge (with a few young very keen assistants) of the mundane duties of running the Bethel home at Watchtower House in London, including the gardens, cleaning and catering, and Pryce was now acting as Bethel house manager, better described as the butler according to Phil's sarcastic remark.

Philip also said that his second-best friend; Piyce Hughes reminded him every day; as Pryce, also as an unmarried man, faithfully and loyally carried out his duties in the Bethel home in London, and was very similar to the character, Mr. Stevens of (fictional) Darlington Hall portrayed in the film, Remains of the Day, serving as a dignified butler, which also was starring a fellow Welshman, Anthony Hopkins. This was one of Philips favorite films. He also reflected in our conversation that he also wished he could have met his own father from Wales whom he had never known, and who unfortunately had died in a mine accident before he was born, while working in the Kalgoolie gold mine shortly after he came to Australia many years ago. Philip Rees also stressed that even Pryce Hughes was also personally very disappointed that Philip, being his longtime friend of over 30 years was not appointed to succeed him as Branch Servant (manager) of the British branch office of the Watchtower Society by Nathan Knorr, as originally agreed by Knorr and the subjective Governing Body of seven members back in New York, as Pryce personally felt that he and Philip would have made a very good management team.

Referring back to the duties of the glamorous wife of David Ingold; she now being part of the team of house maids, who took care of the over 110 bedrooms and dormitories in the London Bethel; cleaning bathrooms, toilets, soiled bed sheets, carpets and blinds, etc., rooms occupied mainly by young single very healthy men who worked in Bethel and were not the cleanest or tidiest on the planet by any means. Whereas, Philip's wife Maudie; she worked in the office of the service department in a very comfortable office environment overlooking the beautiful front gardens of Watchtower House, occupying a job as secretary and typist. Ingold's wife, meantime, who also was a diligent, faithful and very sincere hard-working Christian woman, was assigned as a cleaner. She had come from a very wealthy family in America and up until now, had enjoyed the luxury of a large house with at least two Hispanic maids plus servants, and here she was now in the London Bethel (House of God), working as a char (British idiom meaning a cleaning woman) as her assigned dedicated service to the Lord.

Philip said, as he reminisced; but with a very sad, wistful look on his face, and thinking back on his many years working in the London Bethel, he saw this woman; the wife of David Ingold, deteriorate day by day, from being a glamorous, confident, attractive female to a tired, weary looking, exhausted old hag (an Australian slang word or idiom for a unattractive old woman) as a direct result of her tedious and very hard work as part of the Bethel home cleaning team at Watchtower House. Phil also expressed his personal feelings, as an earthy Australian guy naturally would, that he always admired healthy looking women, including, he continued, much to my surprise, also my own beautiful wife Pauline, who always kept herself in tip-top physical condition. This comment by Phil at first unnerved me but on reflection I later knew and understood what he genuinely meant by his bold remarks. It was not for any sexual reasons he was quick to add, but just to admire the personality and character of a woman who was focused in mind and body to display she was a creation of the Lord and also equal to men in every way possible. He was of course also now including, not just my own lovely and treasured wife Pauline, but primarily also referring to his long time, very much-loved best friend and his dear wife Maudie, whom he had known since he was 15 years old, and had kept Phil safe, secure and focused on his real purpose in life as a dedicated and caring Christian husband.

With regard to David Ingold, he continued to enjoy his new powerful role of seniority in the London Bethel, and his popularity in the many local London congregations, plus being an outgoing, over confident American, plus his very stylish speaking assignments throughout Britain were well liked by his enthralled audiences. Ingold especially was attracted to Scotland, which he seemed to visit on a regular basis, mainly because of its scenery. Apart from his love of Scotland as an American tourist he always stayed in top class hotels and never in the local homes of his humble fellow Witnesses. He always kept boastfully reminding his very impressed subjective audiences, while speaking with his genuine American-Texan accent that when he spoke, he was speaking on behalf of the Governing Body.

But it was not long, however, before Ingold became involved in an adulterous affair with a very wealthy attractive widow from one of the local London congregations, and one day he simply walked out of Bethel with his suitcases never to be seen again. His poor wife of course was forced to return to her home in Texas and also was never heard from again. Philip did not gloat regarding the misfortunes of the Ingolds' and simply emphasized again the risk of appointing a newly converted man to a senior position within the organization and he hoped that Nathan Knorr had learned something from this erratic, foolish and ultimately destructive experience and decision of his. But Phil also added sarcastically that from his own personal experiences with pigheaded (willfully or perversely unyielding) Nathan Knorr; but he very much doubted it.

Before Phil left this part of his story to move on to other personal issues, and he reminded me that one of the saddest moments in his life was when Pryce Hughes died in 1978, as he and Pryce had been the closest of friends for many years, from when Phil first came to the London Bethel as his assistant back in 1948. Also, they were both of Welsh background and roots, so that in itself created an even closer bond, which the Welsh readers of our report will understand and appreciate. He mentioned that his friendship with Pryce Hughes felt like what the Bible text states at Proverbs 18:24: "There exists a friend sticking closer than a brother." Also, Phil was very honest and also very open about his friendship with Pryce Hughes and admitted he was always grateful that although Pryce was the appointed Branch Servant for 20 years, being personally answerable to the Governing Body, he also had kept quiet and turned his back regarding Phil's personal struggle with his ongoing drinking problem. Pryce Hughes had left instructions requesting that Philip give the main eulogy at his funeral in the Mill Hill, Kingdom Hall upon his death and this was one of the greatest privileges that Philip ever experienced.

An additional great disappointment of Philip Rees was the outcome of the claim that the year 1975 was to be a major event in Bible prophesies, as promulgated by the Governing Body of the Watchtower Society, especially leading member Fred Franz. Philip had acted as spokesman for the British Branch office for a number of years even though he was not the officially appointed Branch Servant but served as the Assistant Branch Servant, owing the fact that Pryce Hughes had a very bad stutter and was camera-shy. Based on this fact, as a result Phil often appeared on the BBC news channel and was quoted in many news articles regarding the claimed coming events of 1975. He expressed his bitter disappointment in being used as an instrument or tool of having misled so many genuine, sincere people in believing the misguided Bible interpretation by the Governing Body (mainly Fred Franz), and he expressed his feelings that he could never put this error of judgment out of his mind and personally felt riddled with guilt. This of course did not help Phil with his growing dependence on alcohol and he confessed that he was now taking his morning coffee laced with a big dose of brandy.

***

Pryce Hughes along with fellow Bible Students, Frank Platt and Frank Healy, plus many others were imprisoned as conscientious objectors during World War I (1914-1918), and the treatment meted out by the prison guards, as recorded in the Defense Ministry archives was a disgrace to the British Government of the day. One such treatment was to tie them to the side wheels of a gun carriage while it was being fired in practice, and Pryce Hughes directly blames this treatment as being the cause of his bad nerves and stutter. In the *Manchester Guardian Weekly* of March 14, 1982, it recorded these horrendous acts, especially the use of the gun carriages, which was described in one of the letters to the editor, on page 2, under the title, "Inhuman Acts on Conscientious Objectors."

Philip Rees was also known for his outspoken comments and the tendency to speak before thinking, and he had on many occasions upset individuals and he openly admitted this personal flaw and fault in his character. In one of his private conversations, Philip Rees admitted that one of the most egregious errors in his whole career was while serving the Watchtower Society as an instructor in the Kingdom Ministry School; apart from his secret and dependent use of alcohol, which consoled him and kept him sane he claimed. And he quickly also pointed out, it was also practiced by many or probably most other leading stressed officials of the Watchtower Society, so he certainly was not alone coping with this problem of being dependent on alcohol.

Phil then went on to mention a very embarrassing incident that occurred when he was conducting one of his last classes in the recently introduced four-week long, Kingdom Ministry School held in the Bethel

476

at Watchtower House in Mill Hill, London. Philip commented that this unfortunate incident was one of his biggest faux pas when he was conducting his last class as instructor in December, 1963, consisting of a group of students, mainly congregation servants (presiding overseers) and a few outstanding special pioneers attending this one-month long Kingdom Ministry School conducted in the London Bethel. Amongst the students attending were two rather overweight females, with extremely large breasts, aged about 30 years old who were serving as special pioneers in Ireland, an almost solid Roman Catholic country; they had been recommended to attend this course by the Irish Branch office, which (according to our reporter) was operated and controlled by the two very strange, weird and peculiar physical half-brothers, Arthur and Dennis Mathews.

This branch office in Ireland has since been closed due to the severe cut back in expenses by the Governing Body, plus other serious problems related to so-called acts of apostasy at the Irish Branch Office that cannot be revealed as they are still under seal in blue envelopes held at the London and New York Bethel offices and our reporter could not gain access to the contents. According to the book by Edmund Gruss, The Four Presidents of the Watchtower Society, a major portion of the Witnesses in Ireland simply withdrew from the Watchtower Society, spearheaded by two local prominent Witnesses and appointed Elders, Martin Merriman and John May who had exposed the cruel treatment of Raymond Franz by the ruthless Governing Body. These two Witnesses actually visited the New York Bethel headquarters at their own expense to try and meet with members of the Governing Body but were refused an audience by these arrogant, aloof men and were simply told to go back home and write a letter.

One morning, as recalled by Philip, these two young women were late for class and as they entered; typically without thinking, he blurted out in his broad Australian accent, and said in full hearing of the class of about thirty; mainly all male students who all burst out with raucous laughter and that highly embarrassed Philip Rees, as he stated "at last, our two heavenly bodies have arrived." These two young women were of course highly offended and stormed out of the classroom and they reported Philip for his offensive remark and their personal humiliation and he was later severely reprimanded by a branch committee. These congregational Elders in the classroom obviously were very familiar with Hugh Hefner's centerfold page, Heavenly Bodies, portrayed in his popular magazine Playboy. Philip Rees denied at his enquiry before the special branch committee that he had ever seen or viewed this sex magazine but had heard of it, as it was regularly impounded and shredded from the various bedrooms in the London Bethel by the loyal female room cleaners.

To clarify the outcome of this incident, Philip reflected that he had actually known from the records that these two young women both publicly claimed they were part of the so-called special anointed heavenly class of 144,000 unique members of Jehovah's Witnesses selected to join Jesus Christ in heaven as kings and priests when they died, even though they were only young women, and he had just simply, momentarily forgotten this fact. A colleague from the Irish Branch Office of the Watchtower Society later informed our reporter and passed on the information that these two young women eventually turned out to be lesbians and at their hearing held by the judicial committee of their local congregation, they claimed innocence and had justified their sexual relationship being based on the Bible text, that members of the heavenly class were sexless like angels in heaven. They quoted from the Bible book of Matthew 22:30: "They neither marry, nor are given in marriage, but are as the angels of God in heaven."

How many more such relationships exist, especially between men, as homosexuals in the Watchtower Society, particularly in the almost all-male environs of the various Bethel homes throughout the world, under the same guise and excuse? Reports certainly point to this type of reasoning in the clear case of the man Ewart Chitty. While Chitty served in the London Bethel for many years and his relationships with other men while living there was well known and Chitty actually later became a leading member of the Governing Body of this religion when he moved to the New York headquarters. Chitty was eventually exposed and asked to resign from the Governing Body of the Watchtower Society on the weak excuse, because of reported incidents that he had homosexual tendencies. Of course, this unfortunate incident regarding the two young women from Ireland and the claimed insulting remark made by Philip Rees while he was acting as a senior member of the London Bethel Office, related to these two heavenly bodies, along with his other setbacks did not reflect well in his personnel records at Bethel. As recorded in the internal reports and files on Philip Rees, sealed and kept in the private offices (but leaked to our reporter by an unnamed member of the London office staff) of the Watchtower Society and it truly destroyed any hope of his future advancement in the official ranks of this religion.

As a result of this unfortunate experience, he was also replaced as the instructor of the Kingdom Ministry School in 1964, a role Phil truly enjoyed and really wholeheartedly wished to continue. However, Philip sadly entered into a more severe depression that eventually led to his becoming a full-blown alcoholic in order to drown his sorrows and his dreadful, awful disappointments in his personal life and depressing experiences with the Watchtower Society.

One summer evening Philip began to reminisce on the many years he had spent working and living in Bethel both in Australia and London, and with a nostalgic look on his face, he stared out of the lounge window down toward the orchard in the far distance, and he continued his story. He recalled how since he was 15 years old and had spent much of his life in Bethel, most of the time with no regrets but he had experienced some very serious issues on many occasions that deeply troubled and disturbed him. Philip was slowly becoming more and more of a recluse with little connection with other members of the Bethel family. He reflected also that many men in the London Bethel viewed him as a wowser (Australian slang for being strait-laced or a prude). It's amazing how a guy can talk when he has had a few glasses of whisky!

One of these same officials who was critical of Phil and who was also a leading member of the London Bethel, when he heard of this account regarding Philip Rees and his life experiences being published as part of this book by the MTC International Foundation about religious cults, he made this comment to a member of our research team. He stated, and falsely accused Phil: "Philip Rees was so intoxicated most of the time that he could not even remember what day it was, and he was only kept in the London Bethel because of his past years of service to the organization, but his story is a pure prevarication and a load of bunkum." This comment of course was the personal opinion of one individual who himself had become a very bitter, screwed up and a very disappointed man, even though he served in the House of God, because he had been overlooked so many times and not being promoted within the hierarchy of the Watchtower Society, which was a common problem amongst many of these power-seeking individuals. This man also carried a chip on his shoulders as Philip Rees had previously investigated, being part of a judicial committee, and had reported this individual for unethical behavior regarding trying to hide the conduct of a personal friend of his; an Elder in a local London congregation, who eventually was exposed, convicted and finally imprisoned for sexual abuse of a young child.

This type of bitterness, back-biting and scheming was common place in most Bethel homes throughout the world, plus the internal politics and pulling rank was the propensity and normal behavior of most of these ambitious, power seeking officials, but was unseen and unknown to most of the simplistic members of this religion who simply thought of the place called Bethel as being the symbolic House of God when they undertook their regular tours and listened to the BS provided by their tour guides.

Philip explained how on many occasions he was assigned to spend weekends visiting outlying congregations in the British Isles on speaking assignments, which both he and his wife Maudie thoroughly enjoyed; getting out of Bethel in congested London, and meeting the local brothers, spending time in their homes with their Christian families and seeing some of the more beautiful parts of Britain, including Wales and Scotland. One issue that deeply disturbed him was his experience of how, whenever they left their weekend assignment to return back to the Bethel in London, how many of the local brothers privately slipped him or his wife, envelopes containing money as a gesture of appreciation for his services. Phil was also fully aware that this was also experienced by most of the other leading brothers in Bethel, who were allocated these outside speaking assignments, but it was an unspoken and unwritten rule that no one ever mentioned, discussed or revealed and the lucrative, secret, personal perks they received. Also Philip speculated that this same practice by local brothers, privately handing envelopes containing cash to the various district and circuit servants; again secretly kept quiet as a private unspoken fringe benefit of the exclusive elite being in the full time work of the Watchtower Society.

This fact was later confirmed by more than one disillusioned ex-circuit overseer we interviewed, especially since they were forced to retire from the circuit work as they had reached the recently introduced compulsory 70-year age limit, due to new rules by their masters and they also had to reluctantly sacrifice and give up the benefit of these private perks. Some of these misguided individuals, especially in Britain are now having to actually live off welfare and charity as they never paid into the National Pension Fund for personal reasons, others receive a very small monthly allowance as infirm special pioneers paid to them by the Watchtower Society. Maybe they thought they would never reach retirement age because they were told by their masters, the Watchtower Society that the old world is ending and the new world was coming soon?

What disturbed Phil most of all though, was that many of the very sincere brothers and sisters also in the full time service of the Watchtower Society but who were assigned and tied to local congregations had to struggle to survive, some on the very small monthly allowance allocated by the treasury department at Bethel headquarters or had to engage in part-time work, mainly in menial jobs such as window cleaning, car washing, selling soap from door to door or bagging potatoes to sell from door to door. At least we in Bethel, Philip continued, received a small monthly allowance that was mainly spent by the young guys at the Adam & Eve pub up the road from Bethel, but we also had free bed and board in a very comfortable, brand new purposely built Bethel home in Mill Hill, an exclusive up-market area of London with food and services that matched the very same high standards of a well-established 4-star hotel.

Based on a report submitted by one of our researchers the following information was provided and also confirmed by an ex-circuit servant who was involved in this business of bagging potatoes, but will remain nameless to protect his family, as he is still an active member of this religion. This individual stated that this business venture was started with an honorable motive to provide part-time work of bagging and selling potatoes by the willing full-time pioneers, many desperate for part-time work to financially support themselves, and was under the control of a private registered company that was secretly owned by a consortium of very shrewd, enterprising and resourceful group of circuit servants in Britain, who were all supposed to be fully occupied in the full-time service of the Watchtower Society. This company also employed as supervisors in this business venture, ex-Bethel boys who had completed their required term of service in the London Bethel who were also now desperately looking for employment, and the company paid them a small salary plus a commission based on the number of bags of potatoes sold.

The owners of this private company; a syndicate of circuit servants, pocketed the large profits made and through their appointed representatives or managers, who in turn also supervised and made payment of the very small remuneration for these unsuspecting workers, namely the regular pioneers they employed who were struggling to survive while doing the Lord's work as book sellers for the Watchtower Society. These payments to these regular pioneers were made as cash under the table and were in direct violation of the regulations laid down by the British Government Ministry of Labor. Our source who revealed these facts also pointed out that when he received his share of the profits he simply sent the money to the London Headquarters of the Watchtower Society as an anonymous donation owing to the fact he felt so guilty over this unethical scheme and he also suspected some kind of illegal or underhanded financial transactions were involved, so he resigned from the syndicate as it seriously troubled his conscience. He also pointed out that he was not sure what his associates did with their share of the profits and did not want to speculate but he did have his suspicions. When Philip Rees heard of this troubling account he interjected: "Does this sort of conduct occurring in the 1970s remind you of other incidents in the history of the Watchtower Society especially related to Joseph Rutherford and my father-in-law and the disgraceful conduct and experiences of the senior personnel in the Australian Bethel back in the 1940s?"

Returning to the subject of the volunteer workers at the various Bethel homes, some available brothers were called to serve in Bethel, because they had some special skill or talent that the Watchtower Society could use or exploit, and these individuals, if they passed the strict screening process, quickly found a comfortable, secure niche and very rarely ever left their assignment, as they enjoyed their very luxurious, comfortable life style at Bethel and still felt satisfied in their conscience they were continuing in their full time service to the Lord. In addition, these men were usually of independent means so the very low pay and monthly allowance as a member of the Bethel family was of little concern to them. The longer they stayed in Bethel and individually displayed; plus showed absolute slave-like loyalty to the organization (being true society men was the phrase used), they slowly worked their way up the ranks and hierarchy to be officially appointed to new senior positions by the Governing Body. However, for the average recruit to Bethel, they were the lowly, sincere, dedicated and baptized young men, who had usually been persuaded by their parents or the local district or circuit servants to volunteer and work in Bethel.

There is a certain amount of glamour being a member of the Watchtower Bethel family, but it also could be a very lonely, frustrating and emotionally disturbing experience, as displayed by the conduct of some of these young men, who often developed unhealthy practices, "you know what I mean," Phil said, as he pointed to his crotch, conduct that was taboo under the strict code and instructions laid down by the very frustrated autocrat Nathan Knorr and the Watchtower Society, and some of these young men turned to drinking heavily to drown their deep emotional conflicts and feelings. These young recruits had to sign a legal written agreement guaranteeing their stay at Bethel for a determined number of years, so to quit and leave would have created a scandal, not only for themselves personally, but more importantly for their parents, so this was another trap that they had to face. Phil reflected that although it was not a regular occurrence, but it did happen from time to time that occasionally one of these frustrated young men simply walked out of the Bethel home and disappeared. Most of the others eagerly waited for the day that their agreement expired, so that they could simply get out of the place.

For most of these young men who worked in Bethel, it was an experience they survived for the required few years that they had committed themselves to serve, and it always looked impressive on their theocratic résumé, but for others it became a nightmare and many of them turned to alcohol. While again it was not a regular occurrence, it did happen from time to time that a young man could not bear his ordeal any longer and actually took his own life, some by hanging themselves in the bathroom or in the clothes closet of his room or sometimes by throwing themselves off the roof of the office building. The official files of the various branch offices around the world have many sealed records of these very sad and regrettable incidents. Of course, one of the senior members of the Bethel staff had the unenviable task of telephoning or contacting the parents or guardians of the now unfortunate victim of suicide and to request the parents to make arrangements to collect his body, now no longer one of Jehovah's Witnesses; member of the Bethel family or the religion of the Watchtower Society, which was now probably temporarily lying in the Bethel infirmary in a body bag. Also the other sad consequence of these dreadful incidents is that the poor victim was not even allowed a decent funeral in the local Kingdom Hall of his parents because of the strict policy of the Watchtower Society regarding suicide.

Most of these young volunteers who came to serve in Bethel were assigned menial tasks, which they willingly accepted, as they sincerely believed and was viewed as part of the Lord's Service, such as working in the laundry, kitchen, gardens or maybe in the printing room or shipping department; packing books and magazines into boxes all day. The day was also very long, tedious and often six days per week, and in the opinion of many it was nothing more than modern day slavery.

This personal sentiment that one of our researchers uncovered says a lot about the role of these young men that volunteered to serve in the Bethel homes and printing factories. One elder in my congregation, who had spent six years there, told me: "Bethel is no paradise, make no mistake. It's full of politics; homosexuality, stress, heavy drinking, and you're not likely to get the job you want. It was, for me, confirmation that Bethel was no utopia. While the female housekeepers were instructed to report any questionable music or reading material, such as *Playboy* magazine found inside the dorm-style rooms, bottles of whiskey and bourbon were left untouched. Alcohol was their coping mechanism.

I will add that the spirit of brotherhood and unity I expected to find there was non-existent. I encountered many burned-out, cynical adults who stayed for no reason other than they had no idea how they would survive in the outside world."

Philip continued relating his own personal experience while living in Bethel for most of his adult life and he pointed out that the Branch Office received many gifts and donations from the deceased estates of some obviously very sincere Witnesses, these donations included properties, cars, cash and jewelry, plus many other valuable items. He laughed out loud and with his broad Australian accent as he related a story, based on rumor he emphasized, that Grant Suiter (1908-1983), who was secretary-treasurer of the Watchtower Society for many years and a leading member of the Governing Body and the account was related to his young Italian wife Edith (née Rettos), who Suiter had married in 1956 when he was over 50 years old. Edith was rarely ever seen outside their private suite in the New York headquarters, but when she was sighted, she was decked out with so much donated jewelry that she looked like the Queen of Sheba! A report was also received from an ex-member who worked at the New York headquarters and had spent five years in the offices of the Governing Body at Bethel. He reported that they would occasionally pass down the ranks, boxes of expensive watches and jewelry that had been donated from the estates of deceased loyal members but only after firstly the individual members of the Governing Body and their wives had gratuitously chosen what they wanted.

Philip also added and mentioned that Grant Suiter, who he had met on several occasions and had enjoyed a tipple or two with him on many evenings when he regularly visited the London Bethel to meet up with his personal friend Ewart Chitty, but also pointed out that Suiter was a very moody and capricious individual. From established and known records, Suiter had a very serious, unexplained fall in his private suite in the New York Bethel in 1983 (rumored that he was blind drunk at the time) and he never recovered, eventually dying at the age of 75 years, the same year as his injuries. After the death of Grant Suiter, Edith his young widow left New York Bethel and remarried, eventually dying in England aged 84 in 2007. By the way if you are curious, she also took all the donated jewelry she had collected and hoarded while living in the New York headquarters of the Watchtower Society.

Phil said that although it was none of his business, he always thought it was very strange that these two men, both senior officials and directors of the Watchtower Society and leading members of the Governing Body, Suiter and Knorr, both had married much younger women and neither of these women claimed to be of the so-called heavenly class as their husbands did. So, Philip privately queried how these women could accept this reality and live with the knowledge, currently promoted by the official doctrine of this religion that one day they would be left on earth, when their much older husbands eventually died and supposedly joined Jesus Christ in heaven as part of the unique so-called 144,000 chosen ones, to be sexless Kings and Priests, as they personally claimed, while their wives would be left behind on earth to either stay single or remarry. Phil also sadly reflected how much of a trauma this created for his own wife Maudie when he told her of his then stupid decision back in 1961 that he would be compelled to partake of the bread and wine at the annual memorial as instructed by manipulative Nathan Knorr, so that Philip could eventually be allowed to join the Governing Body.

Nathan Knorr, President of the Watchtower Society, who married his much younger bride, Audrey Mock in 1953, had no doubt also influenced the decision of Grant Suiter, Secretary-Treasurer, who married his young Italian bride, Edith Rettos in 1956. Plus, Milton Henschel, another leading member of Governing Body who also married a much younger Lucille Bennett in 1956. In addition, leading member of the Governing Body, Lyman Swingle, also married a local sister in New York, called Crystal Waldrop in 1956, mother of two daughters. As a result of these marriages by members of the Governing Body, the rules of the Watchtower Society were conveniently changed to allow male members to marry and still keep their assignments in the various Bethel homes around the world under certain special conditions related to their experience, skills and years they had served to date, as approved by the Governing Body. Previously the official ruling was that, if a male member wished to get married, he was compelled to leave his assignment in the Bethel home unless he had accumulated of certain number of years of service. From our intensive research this change of rules created some very serious cases of men misusing this loophole, as some of these new wives were certainly not of the caliber one would expect who was now supposedly living and serving in the House of God.

This volte-face or change of rules regarding men in the headquarters and Branch offices being allowed to marry and remain in their positions did not create a throng of mass marriages similar to the Moonies Cult, but it did make a distinct uptick in the increasing number of single brothers working in the various Bethel homes throughout the world and their applications for permission to marry and still remain, along with their new wives, in their comfortable assignments and their lives plus life-style being financed by the voluntary donations of the loyal followers of this religion.

Phil observed, and please remember this was only his private and personal opinion, that some of these new wives were not of the caliber of being a modest and submissive wife as outlined in the Bible at Proverbs, Chapter 31, and were not always fitting examples of what a Christian wife should be. And, in his opinion, this changed the character and demographics of the various Bethel Homes and Bethel families throughout the world owing to the fact that these new wives were usually childless, unfulfilled women, and it also created tension and girlish gossip, plus jealousy and competition that in turn created additional frustration and friction in many cases. Also, these new marriages, if they were permitted under these new rules laid down by the Governing Body were also strictly controlled and limited (contrary to the Bible instructions of 1 Corinthians, Chapter 7) in that no children would be permitted or allowed to be born as long as their parents lived and worked in the Bethel homes of the Watchtower Society. Our researcher personally knew of many of these men who verbally disagreed with Philip Rees, primarily as they privately already had very attractive, desirable girl friends outside of Bethel who they met on their weekends off, and were just waiting for the day when Nathan Knorr would relax the rules especially after his own marriage and that of his fellow associate Grant Suiter, plus other members of the Governing Body.

Philip Rees was well qualified to make this observation about these new wives as he was a married man himself and was privileged on many occasions during the late 1950s and early 1960s to act as a modern-day Zone Servant to make visits to many Branch Offices of the European countries, besides being the Assistant Branch Servant for the British Isles and he saw first-hand some very glaring examples of this growing problem. The duty of a Zone Servant in those days and this hierarchal system is still functioning today, was that during the service year, members of the Governing Body or others assigned by them made zone trips to all the branches of the Watchtower Society. These zone servants were to hold discussions with members of the Branch Committees, as well as with local district and circuit overseers and other full-time servants. This enabled the members of the Governing Body or their representatives to obtain firsthand information as to the condition of each Branch Office and to discuss any problems that may have existed, so it involved an intense inspection of the Bethel Home, the Offices and the staff, both new and older members plus especially the printing factories, as this was the primary source of income for the organization. They were to make any suggested changes, improvements or identify specific problems directly to the Governing Body for their immediate action in order to keep the cash flowing in. This system was a perfect commercial method of exercising their hierarchal authority as masters of this religion.

What made the case of Nathan Knorr actually getting married to a young woman most amusing; if we can use that word, is the fact that Knorr had been the world's greatest proponent of men in the Watchtower organization remaining single and unmarried, plus his favorite Biblical text he used was from 1 Corinthians 7:32, "The unmarried man is anxious about the affairs of the Lord, how to please the Lord; but the married man is anxious about the affairs of the world, how to please his wife, and his interests are divided." Also, he had previously followed his mentor that women were nothing more than a bag of bones and hank of hair, as indoctrinated and promoted by his predecessor Joseph Rutherford. So something must have changed Knorr's mind, so we wonder what it could be.

So, as a result, the case of Nathan Knorr, who was then approaching 50 years of age and getting married in 1953 to a young sister almost

20 years his junior, in fact young enough to be his daughter, was kept very low profile and even hidden by the press office of the Watchtower Society for some years, primarily in order to avoid the many questions now being asked by some of the male members and also even curious female members of this religion, who failed to understand the sudden change of mind by their leaders. Many of these male members were left with the bitter disappointment of having turned down their own opportunity of getting married and perhaps having families as a result of being negatively influenced by President Knorr and the Governing Body, who were always emphasizing that the end of the world was coming soon and a new world was near at hand and making statements such as "Staying single was the desirable way to fully please and serve the Lord during these last days." (*The Watchtower*, 1 July, 1955) Also remember these misleading and false claims were made over 70 years ago and they still persist even today in 2019 by the masters of this modern religion.

Philip confessed that he was fully aware that during the 1950s there were serious problems of accusations being made regarding leading members of the Watchtower Society in New York were perhaps gay. Also, a number of saunas had been installed in the housing blocks of the New York headquarters to cater for the approximately 800 male volunteer workers and these became a great concern to the block supervisors because of claims of what was actually taking place in these saunas by the young, very physically healthy male workers and of course some older perverts. In an attempt to possibly diffuse these gay rumors and also perhaps being lonely, single, disappointed and delusional men, Suiter, Knorr and Herschel finally married, even though very late in life, and Philip also mentioned that these marriages were never consummated according to strong rumors from friends of his, emanating from the New York Bethel headquarters. Phil also stated that he could not confirm this claim and also he clearly emphasized that he had no personal knowledge of any accusations actually being made or proved against these three men as being homosexual in the all-male society of a Watchtower Bethel Home.

These four members of the Governing Body, all claiming to be of the heavenly class suddenly getting married within this short period of time raised many eyebrows, some being surprised and others disapproving, plus serious questions were being asked amongst the local members of this religion, especially when they slowly learned of these events through the grapevine. These marriages were certainly not announced in the Watchtower literature and attempts were clearly made by the Watchtower press office to keep them secret. Had these men suddenly decided to marry because they had met the right woman at last or was there some other surreptitious, clandestine motive behind this sudden change of mind from being single, unmarried men? Had they been watching too many romantic films on their televisions and suddenly realized what they were missing before they were finally called to heaven? Regarding the other three members of the Governing Body in the 1950s, Thomas (Bud) Sullivan (1888-1974) was already married to his wife Evelyn from Ireland when he entered the New York headquarters in 1924 and was invited to join the Governing Body by Rutherford in 1932. Hugo Reimer (1879-1965) who joined the Governing Body in 1923 was a confirmed bachelor and never married and Freddy Franz (1893-1992) who joined the Governing Body in 1945 was such an introverted eccentric that he was totally unaware that the female species actually existed?

Phil was positive along with many others who personally knew these men, Knorr, Henschel and Suiter, and who worked in the New York Bethel headquarters and were convinced that these marriages were just for convenience. A marriage of convenience is contracted for reasons other than that of the relationship of love. Instead, such a marriage is entered into for personal gain or some other sort of strategic purpose such as securing citizenship. Another common reason for marriages of convenience is to hide one partner's homosexuality. In modern times, the phrase has broadened into an opposition between marrying for love on the one side, and for some reason other than love, for example, expediency on the other side. Phil also reminded me and stressed that he only knew what was taking place in the London Bethel, as this was his area of influence and could not make any meaningful observations about what was going on and taking place in the New York headquarters.

Phil continued that he did know by actual experience, being the appointed Assistant Branch servant of the London Bethel that there were several cases of young men in the London Bethel who were under suspicion of perhaps being gay. He pointed out that to get around this serious, embarrassing problem these brothers were usually persuaded to marry unwitting local pioneer girls in the London area, who had been influenced to marry these men and then they were given special assignments outside of the London Bethel, usually as special pioneers where their suspected status in the organization could then be secretly hidden away, but they could still remain in good standing in the organization. I asked Philip if other branch offices of the Watchtower Society also had similar experiences and Philip unequivocally stated, "Yes, no doubt I know they did, especially in the Paris, Amsterdam and the German Bethel homes."

This very controversial subject, which has dogged the Watchtower Society for many years, plus also other religions such as the Anglicans, Catholic Church, the Mormons, and many others, related to some of their spiritual leaders being gay, homosexual or lesbian, and is covered in the new book currently being researched by the MTC International Foundation. In this new book, *Masters & Slaves of Modern Marriage*©, an entire chapter is devoted to this subject and is currently being written by a contributing editor who is a clinical psychologist with vast experience on this important topic. Questions will be answered, such as, is a person born gay; does he or she develop into being gay, perhaps because of overpowering parents or other extenuating circumstances and is there such a treatment as conversion therapy, which is the pseudoscientific practice of trying to change an individual's sexual orientation from homosexual or bisexual to heterosexual, using psychological or spiritual interventions?

The Watchtower publicly condemns homosexuality and child sexual abuse but it is a known fact that it was practiced and still is by many members in the various Bethel homes throughout the world and by many of their so-called spiritual shepherds outside of Bethel. This is a very worrying issue to this religion, but as we know today it was kept secret from the authorities but now known that 1,000s of cases of child abuse have been exposed in the press with serious financial consequences for the Watchtower Society. Quoting from the Watchtower Society's own literature, "True, some individuals may very well be prone to homosexuality... a Christian cannot excuse immoral behavior by saying he was born that way. Child molesters invoke the same pathetic excuse when they say their craving for children is innate. But can anyone deny that their sexual appetite is perverted? So is the desire for someone of the same sex." (*Awake!* Feb.8, 1995)

***

Philip Rees had a very sensitive conscience about life in general, and he and his treasured wife of many years Maudie; they both had decided to never have children of their own, both single-mindedly spending their entire lives in the service of the Watchtower Society. They had both agreed, he said, being influenced by the Watchtower teaching that the world's end was fast approaching and the new system would be here any time soon, and that the blessing of having a family of their own and enjoying the pleasure of bringing up children would come after Armageddon and their future life together in the 'new world'. But that dream was never, ever to be experienced by Phil and his wife, plus also by many other sincere, dedicated servants in the full time service of the Watchtower Society, who later displayed and actually stated with extreme bitterness, they had postponed having children or a family, as advised by the teachings of the Watchtower Governing Body, because of the promise of the impending, soon to come, end of the old system of things and this promised new world. Quoting once again from The Watchtower magazine, which is accepted as the inspired word of God by Jehovah's Witnesses. "Although Noah's three sons were all married, none fathered children until after the Deluge. While this does not imply that it is wrong to have children today, many Christian couples decline to have children so as to become more fully involved in the urgent work that Jehovah has given his people to do. Some couples have waited for a time before having children; others have decided to remain childless and consider the possibility of bearing children in Jehovah's righteous new world." (*The Watchtower*, August 1, 2000, p. 21)

Phil also confessed that when he lived in Australia as a young man, for relaxation at weekends he used to shoot rabbits out in the bush or outback. He said that later in life he deeply regretted this thoughtless action, as he admitted that he did it just for the sport and not for food and since then has always felt some measure of remorse and guilt about his stupid, reckless actions of deliberately destroying life; those helpless small rabbits being lovely, gentle creatures of the Almighty. He then repeated that he was also strongly opposed to the sports of hunting and fishing just for the excitement of the kill and especially boxing matches between two stupid men trying to bash the brains out of each other. And Phil stated that he knew of many members of various religions, including Jehovah's Witnesses who claim to accept the principles of the Bible and claiming to be peace loving Christians but yet were actually enthusiastic spectators of this blood sport without any conscience whatsoever and this deeply disturbed him.

Philip admitted this some years later, when we last met in 1983 at a district assembly in Bolton, England; this was the last time I ever saw Philip Rees and able to spend some precious time with him, because shortly thereafter he was sent back to Australia by the Watchtower Society and we eventually lost contact. Also, I was on permanent overseas assignments and our correspondence slowly diminished. Phil reminisced and confessed that he also had benefitted from many donated items to the Watchtower Society, as one day the London Bethel received a collection of donated desk top computers (from a liquidation sale) and one ended up in Phil's private suite in Watchtower House at Mill Hill in London. He also admitted he was an old fashioned sort of guy and had no knowledge of how to use the contraption, and again laughing out loud, he said it took him many months to learn how to use the computer and by that time he had learned at least one function and that was the button that he pressed on the front of the box, and Phil said, "lo and behold, it actually opened a small shelf" (it was the CD-Rom) he thought it was a shelf on which to place his glass of whisky!

British Headquarters of the Watchtower Society, courtesy of Philip Rees and Creative Commons (now recently sold by the IBSA & Watchtower Society to finance their new Temple Farm project in Chelmsford, Essex)

One other serious incident that Philip had recounted, which we are compelled to include in his life story, was his disapproval of his fellow, long time serving Bethel worker in London, namely Ewart Chitty (1898-1993), who was the official accountant and secretary of the International Bible Students Association (IBSA), this religions British equivalent of the Watchtower Bible and Tract Society of New York, Inc. (WTB&TS) and his extreme disappointment when Chitty was selected to be a member of the Governing Body in New York in the year 1974. Chitty was selected primarily because he claimed publicly that the Holy Spirit had personally informed him that Jesus Christ had privately selected him to be a King and Priest and rule at his right hand when he died as he was now a member of the exclusive, anointed, special chosen ones of the 144,000, heavenly class, described as Kings and Priests in the Bible book of Revelation. Plus of course it also helped in his selection to the Governing Body, was the fact that Chitty was a very close, personal friend of Grant Suiter (1938-1983), who was a prominent, influential member of the Governing Body of the Watchtower Society in New York and also its Secretary-Treasurer (one the three primary officials and directors of the WTB&TS), plus Suiter was also the Assistant Secretary under Chitty, of the IBSA in London. Grant Suiter, although he was a dominant force on the Governing Body he was also known as a very heavy drinker and it was reported that his young wife was a full-blown alcoholic, but they both remained in the New York headquarters up until his death, both being fully supported financially for many years by the voluntary donations of the sincere, world-wide Jehovah's Witness members.

It was common knowledge by many long-standing members of the London Bethel family that Chitty was a practicing homosexual but they never came forward with any proof or accusation, mainly because they were covered by the direct scriptural rule imposed by the Watchtower Society based on their interpretation of the requirement for the need of two witnesses. Plus, also another very important factor for remaining silent was to avoid a major personal clash with this man Chitty, if they ever accused him to his face regarding his so-called misconduct, so they lived in cowardly fear of this individual, as Chitty was a very aggressive, arrogant and influential person. We must remember he also had powerful, influential personal friends on the Governing Body of the Watchtower Society. In addition, these cowards did not step forward, as doing so they could also incense, rile or provoke the autocratic Governing Body, especially Nathan Knorr, who dominated and controlled the subjective Governing Body at that time. Also, to courageously step forward could possibly have serious consequences to their own theocratic career as they had already personally witnessed what had happened to Philip Rees and his career with the Watchtower Society and in the London Bethel.

Philip also remarked that Ewart Chitty had a reputation of also being a very heavy drinker, even worse than my problem, Phil added, "but it was an accepted fact that amongst many of us in the Bethel, and especially in the New York headquarters that excessive use of alcohol was the norm and this did not affect Chitty being chosen and appointed to the Governing Body by Nathan Knorr." Philip Rees also reluctantly and shamefully admitted that he too had acted like a coward and had never confronted Chitty regarding his homosexuality, as he also held back because Phil had already experienced one very serious run-in with obstinate Nathan Knorr in the past, and could not risk another conflict. Plus, Phil was battling with his own demons and he sadly stated with tears in his eyes, that he could not risk being forced out of Bethel after so many years as it had been his home since he was 15 years old and he had no other home to go to. Our reporter said "My heart went out to Philip Rees that day as I knew and understood what he truly meant."

This was reported in the blog Watchtower Observers:

> As to Chitty's alleged homosexuality, he certainly made some remarks in his 1963 life story in The Watchtower that leaned in this direction. By then he had roomed with the same man for 30 years.

This man and roommate of Chitty was Edgar Clay from Coventry who was a subjective, very small, demure, effeminate looking man, who had entered London Bethel, then located at 34 Craven Terrace, Central London, in 1926 as a linotype operator along with Pryce Hughes, who later became the Branch Servant. When Chitty moved to Brooklyn, New York, he seems to have preferred younger men as roommates. The actual charge brought to the Governing Body against Chitty was made by a former roommate and involved some sort of inappropriate conduct. The Governing Body concluded that Chitty had homosexual tendencies, whatever that means, and asked him to resign. Chitty could hardly do anything but comply with the rest of their wishes, since his only alternative would have been to leave Bethel at the age of 81 and after being there for 58 years. It may well be that the Governing Body did not view Chitty as guilty of actual homosexual activity, since he remained a Bethel member in Brooklyn and later in London up until his death in 1993, but it may also be that they made a private deal: Chitty would remain quiet about where the dead bodies (including financial and personal conduct of his fellow members of the Governing Body) were buried as long as the Society cared for him in his old age.

The un-named member of Jehovah's Witnesses who provided this information about Chitty and Greenlees also made the following comment:

> Please keep in mind that the evidence, while third-hand or circumstantial, is from a number of independent sources, and to

an objective observer has the ring of truth. Also keep in mind
that GB members don't just up and resign – they have to be
forced out. Note how Greenlees for instance, just disappeared
from mention in WTS literature after 1984, and a January 1,
1986 WT article (p. 13), soon enough after that to be extremely
suggestive, commented that: "Shocking as it is, even some who
have been prominent in Jehovah's organization have succumbed
to immoral practices, including homosexuality, wife swapping,
and child molesting." If someone calls the Watchtower
Society today and asks the Public Affairs Office about Chitty
or Greenlees, it's likely that the response will be, "we cannot
comment on such personal matters." Sources for the above
information include personal conversations with current and
former Bethelites, private emails, publicly posted information
and comments, plus the Watchtower literature. Those who have
revealed information privately will remain anonymous until
they want to go public themselves.

Edgar Clay (third from the right) at the dedication of a new local Kingdom Hall in
Coventry, England, along with members of the building committee and trustees,
courtesy of the *Coventry Evening Telegraph*©

The most personal distressing experience that Phil Rees had observed while in the London Bethel was the relationship that co-worker Ewart Chitty had developed with a new young recruit to the London Bethel family, called Andrew H*****. Andrew had recently been converted to the religion of the Watchtower Society when he lived in Dunstable, Bedfordshire, and he was the son of a very wealthy family who disowned him when he joined this religion. From recollection, Phil said Andrew was a most handsome and well endowed, physically built young man, and was a great asset in the printing department. It was not long before this young man after joining the Bethel family in London, that although he was only in his late twenties, and only recently been baptized, for some weird reason, he started to partake of the bread and wine at the annual memorial celebration, indicating that he personally believed (the holy spirit and Jesus Christ had informed him) that he was a chosen member of the remnant of the so-called little flock of 144,000 and one of the Lord's anointed to eventually live in heaven as a sexless High Priest at the right hand of Jesus Christ and rule the Universe. Phil commented that another close friend of Andrew's who worked with him in Bethel hinted that Andrew had somehow been influenced or persuaded by the very powerful, overbearing Ewart Chitty, for possibly, some personal ulterior motive to think that Andrew was of the heavenly class, and was now like an angel in heaven, as the Bible states at Matthew 22:30, "they neither marry, nor are given in marriage, but are as the angels of God in heaven.". Phil said with a sarcastic voice, "you can draw your own conclusion from those comments."

Philip went on to chat, but now in a very serious tone and explained that no one can ever question this personal claim to being one the exclusive so-called anointed class of 144,000 with heavenly hopes, as it was one of the basic core doctrines of the Watchtower Society. Also it is up to each individual to decide, but it did cause some serious ripples and a few raised eyebrows amongst the other leading members of the Bethel family in London and especially also many of the long time serving circuit and district servants in Britain regarding gossip about Andrew. It came to a head when Ewart Chitty was appointed by the Governing Body as Chairman for the world famous, eight day, 'Peace on Earth' convention that was held at the Wembley Stadium in London in 1969, which was addressed by visiting members of the Governing Body, especially Nathan Knorr, Fred Franz and Milton Henschel, plus several others.[27] Chitty assigned his new friend, as he had the authority to do so, the young 27-year-old Andrew to present one of the major lectures at the convention and this brought severe criticism and also extreme jealousy from many longer serving and older members in the full-time service of the Watchtower Society, including district and circuit servants and senior members of the London Bethel, who were not included on the programme. Plus this unusual experience also created personal embarrassment for Andrew; as he later confessed to one of his close friends, a very experienced, insightful, and compassionate congregation elder.

Our researcher, after he had discussed with Philip Rees, the serious issue of being called as a member of the remnant of this exclusive and strictly limited little flock of the literal number of 144,000 heavenly ones and also his personal experience related to Nathan Knorr and his manipulative attempts of trying to influence and persuade Phil to partake of the bread and wine at the annual memorial celebration so that he could join the Governing Body, our researcher recorded the following information as gleaned from Philip Rees, plus other additional sources. Philip then confidentially informed me of details of several additional serious cases that he uncovered during his extensive career spent in Bethel, both in Australia and London, most of which we have decided will not be revealed in this special report as they are too extreme in detail to expose and could well destroy the character and reputation of certain individuals who still continue and try, in complete sincerity, to live their personal lives as Christians, but unknowingly are also innocent victims of the manipulative leaders and masters of this cult.

While interviewing many existing Witnesses (plus many ex-Witnesses) our researcher informed us that he learned of at least one case where an individual sister, who was converted to the religion of the Watchtower Society back in the late 1930s and was a long serving, exemplary,

---

[27] This was the international convention that coined the phrase, which was then aggressively promoted, 'the blessings of Christ's Kingdom rule is just around the corner'. This was also the year they then started adding the subtle suggestion that maybe, just maybe the year 1975 is going to be the year.

dedicated Christian, and subjective woman all of her life. While this sister, who had associated with Jehovah's Witnesses most of her adult life and always believed; plus felt in her heart, that she was of the heavenly class, in other words, personally knew she was to live in heaven (paradise) after she died. But she always hesitated taking the emblems, as they are called, the unleavened bread and wine at the annual memorial celebration by Jehovah's Witnesses. She also had hesitated in view of the Governing Body's confusing and often contradictory teachings from 1935 onwards and also being subjected to the humiliating, derogatory remarks about females in the Watchtower organization (which included the thousands of faithful and loyal Christian sisters and women worldwide) remarks often made by Rutherford in his private and public speeches, that, a woman is nothing but a bag of bones and a hank of hair. This derogatory phrase was originally coined by Rudyard Kipling in his poem the "Vampire" (1897).

Watchtower President Joseph Rutherford was probably one of the most glaring examples of a practicing misogynistic individual on record, and this example has unfortunately influenced many more men in the Watchtower organization, an attitude that still prevails today. This unnamed sister was also fully aware of the general underlying cynicism by male members of this religion against women who partook of the emblems of the bread and wine, indicating that they personally believed they were future Kings and Priests to rule with Christ in heaven even though they are in the human form of a mere woman while living on earth. This fact was confirmed by the special pioneer sister who introduced this unnamed sister to the religion of Jehovah's Witnesses, who herself claimed she was one of the Lord's anointed ones of the remnant of the 144,000. And she did so with full knowledge and acceptance of this personal criticism of her partaking of the bread and wine her entire life since she became a member of this religion back and was baptized back in 1926.

Philip Rees, while speaking to our associate and referring back to the experience of this very sincere sister that was interviewed, she said once again, that later in her life she recalled and could not ignore this inner feeling she always had; of being a member of the so-called little flock as defined and currently taught by the Watchtower Society and the feeling that she rightfully belonged in heaven when she died. She once again discussed with a couple of leading, very prominent, visiting elders in the organization and she requested to partake of the bread and wine. Shortly before she died, they once again told her that the number of the 144,000 was already full, so it was impossible she could be a member, so they refused to allow her to share in the annual memorial celebration and partake of the emblems of bread and wine as she was now infirmed and house-bound. These same elders also added the iniquitous comments that for her to think this way, she was actually submitting to the wicked influences of Satan, and also as pointed out by her daughter, this sister was definitely not mentally or emotionally unbalanced as callously suggested by these same elders, as they proudly quoted from the *Watchtower* magazine article. This is the official doctrinal journal of the Governing Body that is often used as the ruling standard even above the Bible in most cases, which plainly stated: "A number of factors – including past religious beliefs or even mental or emotional imbalance – might cause some to assume mistakenly that they have the heavenly calling."

Draw your own conclusion from those remarks, made by these officially appointed shepherds and representatives of the Governing Body and try to conclude if being a member of the so-called little flock was a personal and private issue or not? In addition, this individual case once again illustrates just another example of how a cult operates, the masters of modern religion make their decisions and rules, and the slaves are compelled to simply obey and conform without question, plus also to ignore their own personal conscience or individual belief. We again quote from a previous paragraph earlier in our narrative defining a cult, as "a group or movement exhibiting a great or excessive devotion or dedication to some person, idea, or thing, and employing unethically manipulative techniques of persuasion and control designed to advance the goals of the group's leaders, to the actual or possible detriment of members, their families, or the community."

***

In later years, the Watchtower Society changed their policy by replacing the permanent, Presiding Overseer (Congregation Servant) of each congregation, with a rotating body of elders and the new Presiding Elder was to be replaced each year in rotation in each congregation of Jehovah's Witnesses. The individual congregations were instructed to hold a special meeting, where all existing appointed servants attended and they were assigned the egregious task of going through the record cards (which recorded their level of devotion to the Watchtower Society) and names of all baptised male members of the congregation to discuss and decide who should be recommended to the Branch office (representing the Governing Body) to make up this new body of elders; who also would now be the only ones allowed from now on to be teachers in the congregation. This disjointed; chaotic new system has been amended many, many times since it was introduced back in 1970 and in quite a number of congregations it produced unhealthy rivalry and jealousy.

Referring back to the individual and specific case of Andrew H*****, the intimate friend of Ewart Chitty. Andrew who was a member of a local London congregation, as were all members of the Bethel family, and the group of male appointed servants in his local congregation after going through the record cards of all men associated with their congregation, decided between themselves for reasons unknown, that in their personal opinion, young Andrew did not qualify as an elder or older man in terms of the scriptural requirements as listed in the Bible and the rules laid down in the instruction letter from the Watchtower Society, so he was not recommended to the Branch office as an elder in his local congregation. This truly devastated Andrew, according to Philip Rees, as Andrew suddenly realized that here he was, a publicly proclaimed member of the heavenly class; one of the Lord's anointed to eventually sit at the right hand of Christ as a King and High Priest to rule the universe, and he was not even considered worthy to be qualified as an elder in his local congregation in London.

Philip Rees recounted that one day later, after hearing the news of his rejection as not being qualified as an elder in his local congregation, and by this time Andrew was now one of Phil's very dependable and loyal personal assistants in the printing department, Andrew simply packed his bags and walked out of Bethel at Watchtower House in Mill Hill, London, for the last time, and he was never heard from again. However it was later rumored, based on our research team's investigation, that he went to a University in London and qualified as a Pediatrician, but also sadly that he later in life committed suicide, and if so, one can easily understand why; in view of his horrific experiences of belonging to this so-called true religion and under the control and manipulations of its masters. Phil said, with tears in his eyes, as he took another shot of his favorite Bell's whisky: "Andrew was a very needy guy and much misunderstood by many of his associates. Wherever you are dear Andrew, we are sorry that we could not help you more than we did." However, the life of Andrew was not in vain or a waste, as he set a clear example to the world of what happens when it comes to being a slave of modern religion and the consequences thereof.

At this time in his life, Philip Rees although being virtually brought up in this religion and spending most of his life from the age of 15 years old, working full time in one of the branch offices of Australia and later Britain, was also having serious misgivings regarding some of the core teachings of the Watchtower Society; teachings that go way back to the days of the founder Charles Russell. Phil had recently read the book written by ex-member of the Governing Body, Raymond Franz, *Crisis of Conscience*, even though it was against the unwritten official rules of the Watchtower Society but we know of many other senior members of this religion also had secretly read this book; probably for the sole reason to check if their names or names of their associates are mentioned or exposed in any derogative or disparaging way.

Phil admitted that he had met Raymond Franz on several occasions and he was very impressed by his honesty, candor and his character as being a genuine, true Christian and a courageous Bible student. Phil also admitted openly that he too was having a crisis of conscience, as he now questioned the basis for making 1914 a pivotal year in Bible chronology and the 144,000 mentioned in the book of Revelation as being a literal number as currently claimed by the Governing Body and not being a symbolic number as clearly understood by all other intelligent students of the Bible. Plus Phil also personally could not justify the current interpretation by the Watchtower Society of there being two separate and distinct groups in the religion, namely the exclusive anointed little flock treated like royalty (going to heaven to rule with Christ immediately when they died) and also the use of the contorted so-called Biblical description, the great crowd of other sheep for all other members of this religion (who would sleep in death and then maybe or possibly be resurrected, if they had been obedient to the organization, and then to live in a paradise on a new earth sometime in the unknown future).

In addition, Phil also once again confessed the burden he felt in his heart, for his role in promoting and the later failure of the 1975 debacle, which had caused so much pain, stress and bitter disappointment to so many genuine, sincere Christians who were still members of the world-wide congregations of Jehovah's Witnesses. Phil admitted that he was simply and blindly following the lead of the organization and the Governing Body such as this honest and accurate news article published in July of 1969 revealed. President Nathan H. Knorr addressed 81,000 Witnesses at Dodger Field in Los Angeles. "Why are we looking forward to 1975?" Knorr asked, and then he answered his question: "It is firmly maintained that by the autumn of the year 1975, the battle of Armageddon will have been fought and God's new world will have been established." (*Los Angeles Herald Examiner*, July 21, 1969)

The following is an extract from the script of the interview with Philip Rees, then current official spokesman for the Watchtower Society in Britain, by courtesy of the BBC. Philip kept a copy of this script and also he still had the actual voice recording on cassette tape, and he smiled ruefully and said in his broad Australian accent, "When I look back at this interview with the BBC, I feel like a b***** fool for making such stupid remarks." Yes, Phil did use colorful expletives from time to time.

1968, BBC interview with Phillip Rees, the Assistant to the Presiding Minister at Watchtower House, discussing 1975.

This interview took place after the BBC had recently interviewed the young brilliant soccer star, Peter Knowles (1945-?) after he publicly declared in 1960 he was quitting his lucrative contract with the successful and popular soccer club Wolverhampton Wanderers (The Wolves), as he had recently joined Jehovah's Witnesses and wanted to use the remainder of his life and his time serving the organization before the year of doom arrived in 1975, as he had been taught by the leaders of the Watchtower Society. Peter Knowles is also on record, when asked in a BBC interview, what happens if nothing takes place in 1975 as you claim? He replied "Then I will eat my Bible!" Of course nothing did happen in 1975, but also poor, misguided Peter Knowles had to swallow his words and as a point of interest to our curious readers, he never did *eat his Bible!*

> Journalist: I challenged him [Peter Knowles] that the threat of a year of doom, 1975, seemed to be a fairly wild and irresponsible surmise.
>
> Philip Rees: *er*, well, I don't accept your term the year of doom 1975, but we don't, *er*, put it as a threat. We firmly believe that in the near future this system of things is going to perish, because the Bible plainly says that all the way through it. But, *er*, we want people to appreciate that it is the prelude to the kingdom of God. You see you sweep away the old before the incoming of the new.
>
> Journalist: Well if the end does come in '75 will we all be dead?
>
> Philip Rees: Yes, *er, er, er*, Armageddon when it comes, it is going to mean a sweeping away of this system, and the system of things, of course, is built up of individuals. That's why we do not tire of telling the people, You must now come out of this system of things, Come out of Babylon the Great and take your stand for God's kingdom because that alone is going to survive.
>
> Journalist: What will happen to the rest of the people?
>
> Phillip Rees: The rest of the people will perish.
>
> Journalist: How?
>
> Philip Rees: By, *er*, the, *er*, by the forces of, *er*, God, just how I don't know, *er*, I don't know exactly how.

In a later interview with the BBC, recorded after the world's first heart transplant at the Groote Schuur Hospital, Cape Town, South Africa, in 1967, by the world-famous surgeon Chris Barnard (1922-2001), Phil was asked the question regarding the Watchtower's view on organ transplants? Phil replied to the BBC interviewer in line with what he had been instructed to say by the Governing Body, and simply said, "it is cannibalism." Of course, later on, the Watchtower Society did another about turn and from 1980 onward the interpretation of the matter of organ transplants is now being viewed as a personal matter for each individual member. Phil once again said, he felt such a fool when he looks back on his role in supporting the Watchtower Society all of his life and with a sadness in his eyes, he quoted Raymond Franz's book Crisis of Conscience, which Phil had highlighted in his personal copy:

> I have since come to appreciate the rightness of a quotation
> I recently read, one made by a statesman, now dead, who
> said: The great enemy of the truth is very often not the lie –
> deliberate, contrived and dishonest – but the myth – persistent,
> persuasive and unrealistic. I now began to realize how large a
> measure of what I had based my entire adult life course on was
> just that, a myth – persistent, persuasive and unrealistic.

Owing to Philip's long-standing problem of alcohol abuse, and as he was an Australian citizen; never having registered as a British National, he and his lovely, long-time supportive wife and best friend Maudie, were sent back to Australia by the Watchtower Society to end their lives there, under the supervision of a privately run care centre for elderly Jehovah's Witnesses. Philip would have preferred to remain in Britain for the remainder of his life as he had spent over 40 years living in the London Bethel, it was his home. He had left Australia behind back in 1946 but the local branch committee, under instructions from the Governing Body in New York, heartlessly decided he had to leave London and go back to Australia. A mutual friend who was a solicitor in London explained that they could have easily approached the British Government for Philip and his wife to remain in England and it would have been granted without question and the Watchtower Society also had the facilities to care for him in his declining years.

The London Bethel had such a facility staffed with volunteer nurses to care for the elderly and sick Bethel workers, in fact the disgraced, disreputable ex-Governing Body member Ewart Chitty was already housed in that facility until he died along with a number of additional infirmed ex-full-time workers of the Watchtower Society, all costs being paid for by the voluntary donations of the sincere members of this religion. But the unfeeling branch committee representing the Governing Body was not interested in Philip's plea or request to remain in London. Phil showed no resistance to this decision as he was now penny-less and the Watchtower Society was paying for the one-way ticket for himself and his wife to travel from Heathrow airport in London to Sydney, Australia and he knew that they would be taken care of by the socialist Australian government as he was still an Australian citizen. He was also reassured by the Governing Body as a special concession that he would not be required to repay the cost of the tickets after he settled, as was the usual practice for Gilead graduate missionaries who left their assignments and returned home.

> *Editor's Note:* The regulations enforced by the Watchtower Society regarding missionaries was that if a missionary left their assignment and returned home, they had to pay their own cost of the return trip. If the missionary could not afford to pay this expense and their parents or relatives could not help them, the Watchtower Society would lend them the money, which had to be repaid with interest, within a certain period of time and this caused extreme hardship in many cases, especially when they had been assigned to far distant lands.

A couple of weeks before Philip was due to leave for Australia, a mutual friend took Phil and his wife on a trip to the South Wales Valleys in Carmarthenshire and especially the beautiful Rhondda Valley, as this was a personal request of Philip's. He wanted to see for one last time the place where his grandparents had lived and where his father was born and lived working in the coal mines before moving to Australia. A small group of friends bought Philip an original copy of the best-selling book *How Green Was My Valley* (1939) by Richard Llewellyn, plus a copy of the video tape of the Hollywood award winning film released in 1941 by the same name, directed by John Ford and staring the young 13-year-old British actor Roddy McDowall. Phil said that this presentation was the most treasured gift he had ever received, as it was the story of the Morgan family and their struggles working in the filthy and dangerous coal mines of Wales. Don't forget that Philip's middle name was Morgan, which was his grandmother's maiden name, so Phil must have personally related to the fictitious family portrayed in this film and we are sure that as Philip watched this film many times during his last remaining years spent in the private care center in Australia, he must have compared the battles and struggles of the Morgan family in Wales with his own private life and his personal battles.

I was visiting Phil one weekend to discuss the manuscript for a soon to be published book about the life of Jesus, the greatest man who ever lived and what happened next was a truly devastating and an emotional, sobering experience for me personally, as Phil suddenly burst into tears and cupped his face in both hands and cried like a baby. All I could do was to place my arm around his shoulders and try to console him. It took several minutes before Philip could compose himself and he apologized for his emotional outburst. We then simply laughed; shared another scotch and soda and then decided to call it a day and we both retired to our rooms in the London Bethel. Before Philip parted that evening, he once again apologized for embarrassing me and I then convinced him that this was not the case at all, and reassured him that I was pleased that I was there for him no matter what happened.

Today, when I look back at this incident that took place on one of the last evenings I spent with Philip Rees, I realized that I had witnessed the climax of the life of a man who had given his entire existence in a genuine sincere attempt to serve his real master, the Lord, Jesus Christ, but was simply misguided as he sincerely and genuinely served a religious organization that he thought represented Almighty God, Yahweh, and which had demanded his entire being. I had witnessed a man whose life had been torn apart as a result of being enslaved, as though by chains in a religious cult, and I also learned that men are human and also have deep emotional needs, yes and that even real men sometimes cry. So, we hope all of our readers, including myself as editor, learn something from the life of Philip David Morgan Rees.

Phil never did quit this religion and continued his association until his death in 2000, despite his very serious misgivings regarding the claim made the Watchtower Society of being the only true channel between God and mankind. By this time he was physically helpless but he never lost his personal faith in God and Jesus Christ. Unconfirmed reports from our contact in the Australian Bethel suggested that he had dementia and pancreatic cancer, plus had reached an age when he was in constant need of physical care and attention. So, we say farewell Phil, you did the best you could, under the circumstances, so thank-you from all of us at the MTC International Foundation.

Philip Rees was a man of great faith and believed in the existence of an Almighty God, Creator of the Universe and knew him as a personal spiritual father by his name Yahweh (in Hebrew) or Jehovah (in English). Phil also believed in the existence of the only-begotten son of God, Jesus Christ and that Jesus had a pre-human existence known as Michael the Archangel, also that he came down to earth to live in the form of a perfect human being for a period of 33 years until the day he was executed by his enemies. He knew from the scriptures that Jesus as a perfect man who also gave his human life as a sacrifice for the benefit of all sinful mankind; was then resurrected and returned to his pre-human existence and is alive even today along-side his father Yahweh in the unseen heavenly realm. Philip Rees also believed in the unconditional, inspired words and promise of John 3:16, "For God so loved the world, that he gave his only Son, that whoever believes in him should not perish but have eternal life."

Philip also inspired the writing of a narrative based on the life of Jesus Christ, the greatest man who ever lived, a manuscript that is currently being sponsored, researched and written by the MTC International Foundation, a non-profit charity that hopes to have this inspiring book ready for release and publication in 2022. This new book *Error 404- The Mystery of the Man Who Never Was or The Greatest Man Who Ever Lived?©* in its acknowledgements states:

> This narrative is also in memory of the late Philip David Morgan Rees (1916-2000), one of the most genuine, sincere Christians who ever lived. Many of the editorial comments, explanations and remarks made about the various Bible texts quoted in this book, which we acknowledge are uniquely Philips that he provided to the editor, especially from the four gospels and Acts of the Apostles. These are based on the words, thoughts, both recorded and written by Philip Rees when this manuscript was originally being prepared by him over 35 years ago in cooperation with the editor, which unfortunately because of circumstances Philip never completed.

Philip Rees, like many others who still belong to the religion of Jehovah's Witnesses, an ever-increasing percentage based upon feedback obtained by our research team, have serious misgivings about the teachings and methods of control used by the Watchtower Society, but still continue as members. Why, you might ask? The main reason is that they feel a measure of the benefits and security, plus the protection and therapy of belonging to a group and to leave the group is simply too dramatic of a step and would create such a vacuum and serious disruption of their personal, family and private lives. They are afraid of rocking the boat (an idiom that means fearful of upsetting the status quo or bringing up controversial issues). They therefore simply accept peace at any price; however, this famous quote by Ève Curie (1904-2007) still resounds in the minds and hearts of many of the existing members: "We discovered that peace at any price is no peace at all...that life at any price has no value whatever; that life is nothing without the privileges, the prides, the rights, the freedom, the joys that make it worth living and also worth giving."

In *Sociology of Religion*, which goes into great depth of how a cult feeds upon itself, sociologist Ronald Lawson has suggested that it is the group's intellectual and organizational isolation – coupled with the intense indoctrination of adherents, rigid internal discipline and considerable persecution – that has contributed to the consistency of its sense of urgency in its apocalyptic message. Therefore, we have to face the fact that most leaders of religious cults demand complete, absolute obedience to their organizational rules because they claim that they themselves are the masters and the loyal members and followers are similar and viewed as obedient slaves and are not allowed to think for themselves; for their own personal protection they claim. No matter what reasons are put forward for such strict control, such as to keep the purity of their movement intact, we still remind our readers that there is only one master of our faith and religious beliefs who can demand our complete obedience and trust; that is Jesus Christ the Son of God.

We all abhor slavery. The idea of being a slave in chains or being treated like a slave in any circumstance, whether in a secular, personal, family or religious manner, it is abhorrent to all of us. Perhaps that is why we have such a difficult time understanding one of discipleship's most important lessons that Jesus teaches in this brief Parable of the Dutiful Servants. These words from our true Master Jesus Christ at Luke 17:5-10 should motivate us as Christians to do our duty, to make sure we live a life of integrity and honesty, plus where necessary reveal and expose the dishonesty, deceit, hypocrisy and unscrupulous conduct of those who knowingly operate and control religious cults as pseudo masters.

Also, the words of Isaac Watts (1674-1748), the English writer and hymnist, were an inspiration to Philip Rees, who privately confessed that he often secretly used to slip into a local Church in London to listen to the powerful and inspiring organ music and hymns being sung by the choir. We hope these words will also inspire all of our readers who try to practice the life of a true Christian as a follower of Jesus Christ, and not men, and render true worship and obedience to the one who alone deserves it, our heavenly father Almighty God, Yahweh.

> Were the whole realm of nature mine
> That were an offering far too small
> Love so amazing, so divine,
> Demands my soul, my life, my all.

Special Report No. 2: Brigham Young

Although it is recognized that the Church of Jesus Christ of Latter-day Saints (Mormons) was started by Joseph Smith back in 1830, but the most prominent and outstanding figure and character that steered its expansion and development was the brilliant, highly intelligent leader Brigham Young (1801-1877).

Of course, there is no one alive today that can provide personal information to our research team, so we have had to rely on the journals written by Young himself and also by some of his contemporaries. In addition, our research team also interviewed members of this Church who had ancestors who personally knew Brigham Young and had orally passed down important information about his character and accomplishments. This short report is not so much about his influence on the teachings of the Mormon Church but rather more of an intimate view of his personal life, plus his exemplary dedication to a cause and our research is also based on the many books that have been written about this colorful character. Some books however provide prejudiced and sometimes unauthenticated information, so our research team has diligently tried to weed out the real facts about this inspiring character Brigham Young and present it as honestly as possible.

Brigham Young in 1870, courtesy of Charles William Carter (1833-1918) and Creative Commons

No matter what we personally think about the most unusual and very difficult to believe story of young Joseph Smith having visions and receiving golden plates and the original establishment of this religion being chosen by God as the only true religion on earth, as do several other religions such as Jehovah's Witnesses. Most modern-day members of the Mormon Church that we interviewed, the majority do not personally believe this story about Joseph Smith, but they simply accept it because as they replied, it is simply a matter of a written article of our faith.

Brigham Young became the 2nd President of the LDS church in 1847, three years after the murder of Joseph Smith, the founder in 1844. The LDS Church headquartered in Salt Lake City is by far the largest branch of Mormonism. It has continuously existed since the succession crisis of 1844 that split the Latter-Day Saint movement after the death of founder Joseph Smith, Jr. But Brigham's most important and vital contribution to our modern world was the establishment of the beautiful city of Salt Lake City, which nestles at the foothills of the Wasatch Front Mountains of the Uinta Range. As one of the researchers into the Mormon religion and having lived in this beautiful city for many years said "I personally support this opinion of Salt Lake City being such an inspiring place to live. My favorite place, being Park City, which lies east of Salt Lake City in the western state of Utah." Framed by the craggy Wasatch Range, Park City is bordered by the Deer Valley Resort and the huge Park City Mountain Resort, both known for their ski slopes. In town, Main Street is lined with buildings built during a 19th century silver mining boom, a truly inspiring place. The Uinta Mountains are an east-west trending chain of mountains in northeastern Utah extending slightly into southern Wyoming in the United States. As a sub-range of the Rocky Mountains, they are unusual for being the highest range in the contiguous United States running east to west, and lie approximately 100 miles (160 km) east of Salt Lake City. The range has peaks ranging from 11,000-13,528 feet, with the highest point being Kings Peak, also the highest point in Utah.

The story goes that when Brigham Young and his party of pioneers approached the salt valley in present day Utah on 24 July, 1847, he looked across at the expanse and the huge lake beyond and simply said

"This is the place". For the tourist one can still enjoy this panoramic and inspiring view from the top of Emigration Canyon.

***

Before settlement by members of the LDS Church, the Shoshone, Ute, and Paiute tribes of Native Americans had dwelt in the Salt Lake Valley for thousands of years. At the time of Salt Lake City's founding, the valley was within the territory of the Northwestern Shoshone; however, occupation was seasonal, near streams emptying from canyons into the Salt Lake Valley. One local Shoshone tribe, the Western Goshute tribe, referred to the Great Salt Lake as Pi'a-pa, meaning big water, or Ti'tsa-pa, meaning bad water. The land was treated by the United States government as public domain; no aboriginal title by the Northwestern Shoshone was ever recognized by the United States or extinguished by treaty with the United States. The first American explorer in the Salt Lake area was probably Jim Bridger in 1825, although others had been in Utah earlier, some as far north as the nearby Utah Valley (the 1776 Dominguez-Escalante expedition were undoubtedly aware of Salt Lake Valley's existence). US Army officer John C. Frémont surveyed the Great Salt Lake and the Salt Lake Valley in 1843 and 1845. The Donner Party, a group of ill-fated pioneers, had traveled through the Great Salt Lake Valley in August 1846.

Salt Lake City c. 1880 by Carleton E. Watkins,
courtesy of Wikipedia & Creative Commons

The valley's first permanent settlements date from the arrival of the Mormons in July 1847. They had traveled beyond the existing boundaries of the United States into Mexican Territory seeking a secluded area to safely practice their religion away from the violence and the persecution they experienced in the Eastern United States. Their original target was either northern California or Oregon but upon arrival at the Salt Lake Valley, president of the church Brigham Young is recorded as stating, this is the right place, drive on. Brigham Young claimed to have seen the area in a vision prior to the wagon train's arrival. They found the broad valley empty of any human settlement.

Part of Main Street, Salt Lake City in 1890, courtesy of Wikipedia & Creative Commons

Four days after arriving in the Salt Lake Valley, Brigham Young, a brilliant planner, designated the building site for the Salt Lake Temple. The Salt Lake Temple, constructed on the block later called Temple Square, took 40 years to complete. Construction started in 1853, and the temple was dedicated on April 6, 1893. The temple has become an icon for the city and serves as its centerpiece even today. In fact, the southeast corner of Temple Square is the initial point of reference for the Salt Lake meridian, and for all addresses in the Salt Lake Valley. The wide roads of the new city were designed to allow for the full turn a wagon and oxen and are envied by many other newly developed cities in America. The story goes as written in one old journal we read, that Brigham Young, who led Mormon settlers to the West in 1847, directed

515

that the streets of Salt Lake City be made sufficiently wide so that a wagon team could turn around without resorting to profanity.

The pioneers then organized an additional State of America to be called the State of Deseret, and petitioned the American Government for its recognition in 1849. The United States Congress re-buffed the settlers in 1850 and established the Utah Territory, vastly reducing its size, and designated the small city of Fillmore as its capital city. Great Salt Lake City replaced Fillmore as the territorial capital in 1856, and the name was later shortened to Salt Lake City. (The city is also known as the gateway of the west.) The city's population continued to swell with an influx of converts to the LDS Church and Gold Rush gold seekers, making it one of the most populous cities in the American Old West.

In his book, *The Mormons of Yesterday & Today*, Rodman Paul observes:

> Joseph Smith was succeeded by one of the outstanding organizers of the 19th century, Brigham Young. If the circumstances of his life had worked out differently [he] might have become a captain of industry – an Andrew Carnegie or John D. Rockefeller or a railroad builder. Instead, this able, energetic, earthy man became the absolute ruler and the revered, genuinely loved father figure of all Mormons everywhere. During the 30 years between the Mormons' arrival in Utah in 1847 and [his death in] 1877, Young directed the founding of 350 towns in the Southwest. Thereby the Mormons became the most important single agency in colonizing that vast arid West between the Rockies and the Sierra Nevada.

As colonizer and founder of Salt Lake City, Young was appointed the territory's first governor and superintendent of American Indian affairs by President Millard Fillmore on February 3, 1851. During his time as claimed prophet, Young directed the establishment of settlements throughout present-day Utah, Idaho, Arizona, Nevada, California and parts of southern Colorado and northern Mexico. Under his direction, the Mormons built roads and bridges, forts, irrigation projects; established public welfare; organized a militia and issued an extermination order against the Timpanogos Indians and after a series of wars eventually made peace with these Native Americans. Young was also one of the first to subscribe to Union Pacific stock, for the construction of the First Transcontinental Railroad.[28]

After Young organized the first legislature and established Fillmore as the territory's first capital he also organized a board of regents to establish a university in the Salt Lake Valley. It was established on February 28, 1850, as the University of Deseret; its name was eventually changed to the University of Utah with an excellent Department of History that has been a major source of material for the publishers of this book by the MTC International Foundation, plus several other publications. As a great leader in the field of education, for which he was admired by many, on October 16, 1875, Young deeded buildings and land in Provo, Utah, to a board of trustees for establishing an institution of learning, ostensibly as part of the University of Deseret (U of U). Young said in his journal, "I hope to see an Academy established in Provo ... at which the children of the Latter-day Saints can receive a good education unmixed with the pernicious atheistic influences that are found in so many of the higher schools of the country." The school eventually broke off from the University of Deseret (University of Utah) and became Brigham Young Academy, the precursor to Brigham Young University (BYU) today one of the greatest centers of learning in the world.

To remind our readers, Brigham Young was an American religious leader, politician, and settler. He was the second president of The Church of Jesus Christ of Latter-day Saints (LDS Church) from 1847 until his death in 1877. He also served as the first governor of the Utah Territory. Young also led the founding of the precursors to the University of Utah and Brigham Young University. Young had many nicknames, among the most popular being American Moses (alternatively, the Modern Moses or Mormon Moses), because, like the biblical figure, Young led his followers, the Mormon pioneers, in an exodus through a desert, to what they saw as a promised land. Young

---

[28] You must read the account of this incredible story as published by the *Time Life* books dated 1973, titled *The Railroaders* and it will leave you breathless when you learn of the experiences of what happened during this magnificent accomplishment of the American spirit during this period of history. Promontory Point, Utah, was the site of the dramatic completion, on 10 May 1869, of the first transcontinental railroad, which linked the Union Pacific on the east and the Central Pacific on the west and known as the Golden Spike National Park, 66 miles outside Salt Lake City.

was dubbed by his followers the Lion of the Lord for his bold personality and was also commonly called Brother Brigham by Latter-day Saints. Being a polygamist, Young also had 55 wives. He instituted a church ban against conferring the priesthood on men of black African descent, and also led the church during the Utah War against the United States. In the book by Russell Nelson, *The Exodus Repeated,* he also reports, "Many instructive parallels exist between the exodus from Egypt of the Israelites under Moses and the exodus from the United States of the Latter-day Saint pioneers under Brigham Young."

This quote from one of Brigham Young's personal journals perhaps expresses best of all his inimitable drive and ambition to make Utah a prosperous and successful State.

> Go to the United States, into Europe, or wherever you can come across men who have been in the midst of this people, and one will tell you that we are a poor, ignorant, deluded people; the next will tell you that we are the most industrious and intelligent people on the earth, and are destined to rise to eminence as a nation, and spread, and continue to spread, until we revolutionize the whole earth. If you pass on to the third man, and inquire what he thinks of the Mormons, he will say they are fools, duped and led astray by Joe Smith, who was a knave, a false Prophet, and a money digger. Why is all this? It is because there is a spirit in man. And when the Gospel of Jesus Christ is preached on the earth, and the kingdom of God is established, there is also a spirit in these things and an Almighty spirit too. When these two spirits come in contact one with the other, the spirit of the Gospel reflects light upon the spirit which God has placed in man, and wakes him up to a consciousness of his true state, which makes him afraid he will be condemned, for he perceives at once that Mormonism is true. Our craft is in danger, is the first thought that strikes the wicked and dishonest of mankind, when the light of truth shines upon them. Say they, if these people called Latter-Day Saints are correct in their views, the whole world must be wrong, and what will become of our time-honored institutions, and of our influence, which we have swayed successfully over the minds of the people for ages.

With respect to the incredible building projects in Salt Lake City, spearheaded by Brigham Young, the construction of the temple in Temple Square comes up as number one. The location for the temple was first marked by LDS prophet Brigham Young, the second president of the church, on July 28, 1847, just four days after arriving in the Salt Lake Valley. In 1901 the apostle Anthon H. Lund recorded in his journal that it is said that Oliver Cowdery's divining rod was used to locate the temple site. The temple site was dedicated on February 14, 1853, by Heber C. Kimball. Groundbreaking ceremonies were presided over by Brigham Young himself, who laid the cornerstone on April 6 of that year. The architect was Truman O. Angell, and the temple features both Gothic and Romanesque elements.

Salt Lake Temple in Temple Square, Salt Lake City, Utah,
courtesy of Entheta and Creative Commons

The walls of this temple are quartz monzonite (which has the appearance of granite) cut from the Little Cottonwood Canyon, located twenty miles (32 km) southeast of the temple site. Oxen transported the quarried rock initially, but as the Transcontinental Railroad neared completion in 1869 the remaining stones were carried by rail at a much faster rate. The capstone – the granite sphere that holds the statue of the Angel Moroni was laid on April 6, 1892, by means of an electric motor and switch operated by Wilford Woodruff, the church's fourth president, thus completing work on the temple's exterior. The Angel Moroni statue, standing 12.5 feet (3.8 m) tall, was placed on top of the capstone later the same day. At the capstone ceremony it was proposed by Woodruff that the interior of the building be finished within one year, thus allowing the temple to be dedicated forty years to the day of its commencement. John R. Winder was instrumental in overseeing the completion of the interior on schedule; he would serve as a member of the temple presidency until his death in 1910. Woodruff dedicated the temple on April 6, 1893, exactly forty years after the cornerstone was laid. Sad to report, that Brigham Young had died in 1877, so he was unable to see the completed final work of this magnificent building that he started way back in 1853.

Brigham Young (or Pioneer Monument), a bronzed historical monument located on the north sidewalk of the intersection at Main and South Temple Streets of Salt Lake City, Utah, courtesy of Wikipedia & Creative Commons

There are many other remarkable buildings in Salt Lake City that were influenced by the acute and far-sighted Brigham Young, that also deserve mention and are now highlighted in our report. One such building is the Salt Lake Tabernacle, also known as the Mormon Tabernacle, constructed under the supervision of the visionary Brigham Young and is located on Temple Square in Salt Lake City. This incredible structure was a concept of Young and was built from 1864 to 1867 to house meetings for The Church of Jesus Christ of Latter-day Saints and was the location of the church's semi-annual general conference for 132 years and of course is now the home of the world-famous Mormon Tabernacle Choir. The roof of Salt Lake Tabernacle was constructed in an Ithiel Town lattice-truss arch system that is held together by dowels and wedges. The building has a sandstone foundation, and the dome is supported by forty-four sandstone piers. The overall seating capacity of the building is around 7,000, which includes the choir area and gallery (balcony).

Henry Grow, an LDS civil engineer, oversaw the initial construction of the Tabernacle, the domed roof being the most innovative portion of the building. Brigham Young, president of the LDS Church at the time, wanted the Tabernacle roof constructed in an elongated dome shape with no interior pillars or posts to obstruct the view for the audience. (the gallery was added later). When Young asked Grow how large a roof he could construct using the style of lattice that he had used on the Remington Bridge, Grow replied that it could be 100 feet wide and as long as is wanted. Eventually, Grow engineered the Tabernacle roof to be 150 feet across and 250 feet long. Skeptics insisted that when the interior scaffolding was removed, the whole roof would collapse. The roof structure was nine feet thick, formed by a Remington lattice truss of timbers pinned together with wooden pegs. Green rawhide was wrapped around the timbers so that when the rawhide dried it tightened its grip on the pegs. When the roofs structural work was completed, sheeting was applied on the roof, which was then covered with shingles. The interior was lathed and then plastered; the hair of cattle was mixed with the plaster to give it strength.

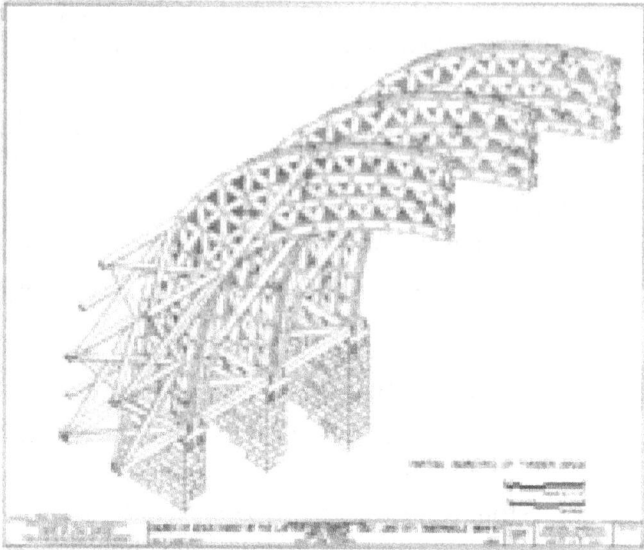

Civil Engineer Grow's design is notable because he built the roof with hardly any nails, the wooden pegs and beams were bound together by strips of rawhide, courtesy of the Library of Congress and *Wikipedia*

Construction of the Tabernacle began on July 26, 1864, but construction of the roof did not begin until 1865 when all 44 supporting sandstone piers designed by William H. Folsom were in place. Civil engineer Grow rapidly built the roof structure from the center out, but encountered difficulty engineering the semicircular ends of the roof. This difficulty dragged structural work on the roof into fall of 1866 even as other parts of the roof were being shingled. However, Grow finished and shingled the entire roof by the spring of 1867, before the interior of the building was finished. The Tabernacle was first used for the October, 1867 conference. The roof has lasted for over a century without any structural problems, though the shingles were replaced with aluminum in 1947. The structure was an architectural wonder in its day, prompting a writer for *Scientific American* to comment on the mechanical difficulties of attending the construction of so ponderous a roof. In 1882, while on a lecture tour of America, Oscar Wilde noted that the building had the appearance of a soup-kettle; he added that it was the most purely dreadful building he ever saw. Some visitors around the beginning of the 20th century criticized it as a prodigious tortoise that has lost its way or the Church of the Holy Turtle, but Frank Lloyd Wright[29] dubbed the tabernacle one of the architectural masterpieces of the country and perhaps the whole world.

The Tabernacle building has an international reputation as one of the most acoustically perfect buildings in the world; it is common for LDS missionary tour guides to demonstrate the acoustic properties of the Tabernacle by dropping a pin on the pulpit or tearing a newspaper there, which can be heard throughout the building. This feature all goes to the credit of Brigham Young and his appointed staff in the construction of this incredible structure.

The Salt Lake Tabernacle, photograph taken in the 1870s, showing granite blocks in the forefront to be used in the construction of the Salt Lake Temple, courtesy of Craig Pickup and *Wikipedia*

The organ in the Tabernacle has the organ case positioned at the west end above the choir seats, and is the focal point of the Tabernacle's interior. The original organ was made by Joseph H. Ridges in 1867 and contained 700 pipes. The organ has been rebuilt several times with the

[29] Frank Lloyd Wright (1867-1959) was an American architect, interior designer, writer, and educator, who designed more than 1,000 structures, 532 of which were completed. Wright believed in designing structures that were in harmony with humanity and its environment, a philosophy he called organic architecture.

total pipe count being 11,623, making the Tabernacle organ one of the largest pipe organs in the world and probably one of the most perfect organs ever built, according to Jack Bethards.[30] This brings us to the formation of the Mormon Tabernacle Choir. How did the choir come into being and eventually become one of the most famous choirs in the world?

The choir was founded in August, 1847; one month after the Mormon pioneers entered the Salt Lake Valley. Prospective singers must be LDS Church members between 25 and 55 years of age at the start of choir service, and live within 100 miles of Temple Square. The choir started out fairly small and rather undisciplined. In 1869, George Careless (1839-1932) composer and music director from London, England, was appointed as the choir's conductor and the Tabernacle Choir began to musically improve. Under George Careless, the first large choir was assembled by adding smaller choral groups, many from Wales in the UK, who had a world-renowned reputation of choral groups and harmonious voices, these singers were added to the main Salt Lake Choir. This larger choir, just over 300, sang at the church's October 1873 general conference. It was at this point that the choir began to match the size of the spacious Tabernacle. The formation of the incredible choir was again another feature of the creative vision of Brigham Young.

The world-famous Mormon Tabernacle Choir has inspired so many people over the years and in some cases even prevented suicide. For example, we quote from the brilliant book, *Zero Hour of the Apartheid Regime of Zuid Afrika.*

> Mentioning Chapman's Peak Drive reminds me of a private, personal story relating to a very close friend of mine, who I will call KP to hide his identity. He was a highly qualified professional person but he often felt very low in spirit and at one stage was suicidal as he witnessed and contemplated the deteriorating situation in South Africa in the 1990's and he tried very hard not to absorb, but rather deflect the way this

---

[30] Jack Bethards, is internationally known as a pipe organ consultant specializing in evaluating instruments and planning programs for renovations. Jack is a San Francisco Bay Area native and holds Bachelor's and Master's Degrees from the University of California at Berkeley. He has been a professional musician and is currently active in the American Guild of Organists.

beautiful country was heading. KP was not alone in this view of South Africa as many other genuine, sincere citizens, both white and non-white were becoming more distressed with the worsening situation. His answer and solution to his personal problem was to take a drive by himself along Chapman's Peak Drive to simply view and contemplate the majestic beauty of the Lord's creation; the powerful, magnificent South Atlantic Ocean, the lofty mountains and the wildlife that was prolific in this area, and he immediately felt his spirits lift. He also played on the tape deck in his car the music and lyrics of that glorious hymn, Lift Me Up sung by the Mormon Tabernacle Choir.

My friend's conclusion is that these words kept him sane, and he sincerely believed that the Good Lord would never abandon such a beautiful, awe inspiring country as South Africa, so whether you as our reader accept and believe that philosophy or not, it did at least save one person's life; that of my good friend KP. I am pleased to report that my friend still lives in South Africa and also in his own way, like many of the committed white people that still remain in the country, he still tries to make a positive contribution to up building the important positive vibes to both black and white citizens in maintaining a bright outlook for this beloved country. Of course the fact that my friend KP reached such a low level in his life was not unique, as many other members of the white citizens in South Africa also displayed symptomatic signs and were also living in daily dread and fear of the possible black uprising, with mobs of blacks led by violent left wing socialist leaders storming their homes, looting, seizing their property, raping of their women and possibly slaughtering them in the process of a new revolution, similar to the Mau Mau uprising in Kenya during the period 1952-1964.

Brigham Young had been born in Vermont and later moved to Kirtland, Ohio, after he converted to the Mormon religion. Repeated conflict led Young to relocate his group of Latter-Day Saints to the Salt Lake Valley, which was then part of Mexico. Young organized the journey that would take the Mormon pioneers to Winter Quarters, Nebraska, in 1846, then to the Salt Lake Valley. By the time Young arrived at the final destination, it had come under American control as a result of war with Mexico, although U.S. sovereignty would not be confirmed until 1848.

The eventual residence of Brigham Young in Salt Lake City was the Beehive House and was constructed in 1854, two years before the neighboring Lion House was built (also a residence of Brigham Young). Both homes are one block east of the Salt Lake Temple and Temple Square on South Temple Street in Salt Lake City, Utah. The home was designed by Young's brother-in-law and architect of the Salt Lake Temple, Truman Angell, who also designed the Lion House. It was constructed of adobe and sandstone. Young was a polygamist, and the Beehive House was designed to accommodate his large family. The Lion House also became his official residence as governor of Utah Territory and president of the LDS Church. Upon its completion, Young briefly shared the Beehive House with his senior (and only legally recognized) wife Mary Ann Angell (1803-1882), though she chose to make her home in the White House, a smaller separate residence on the property. Young's first polygamous wife, Lucy Ann Decker Young (1822-1890), possibly due to her seniority, became hostess of the Beehive House and lived there with her nine children.

Lion House, courtesy of Charles Savage and *Wikipedia*

Being a polygamist, Young ultimately fathered 57 children by more than two dozen wives, and also had many adopted, foster and stepchildren. He owned residences throughout Salt Lake City and Utah Territory, but many of his wives and children were housed in the Lion House. The house contains large public rooms on the ground floor with 20 bedrooms on the upper floors, and was home to as many as 12 of Brigham Young's wives. After the death of Young in 1877 the property came under the ownership of the LDS Church. In the 1920s, the Lion House housed the domestic science department of LDS University. In the 1930s, it was operated by the Young Women Mutual Improvement Association of the LDS Church as a social center for study and also for renting of rooms for social events. Today the bottom floor of the Lion House is a functional, cafeteria-style restaurant called The Lion House Pantry which is open to the public.

Special Report No. 3: Lucifer

There have been many religious questions presented to our research team related to this issue of Satan and his demonic influence over mankind. Is Satan or Lucifer a real spirit person, or a figment of our imagination? If real, when did he become such a wicked individual? Can he literally take over the mind and heart of a person? Were these outstanding characters of the past actually taken over and controlled by Satan, for example, Hitler, Mussolini, Idi Amin of Uganda, Saddam Hussein of Iraq, Bashar al-Assad of Syria, Ron Hubbard of the Church of Scientology, Joseph Smith founder of the Mormon Church, Fred Franz of the Watchtower Society and possibly Nathan Knorr and his mentor Joseph Rutherford, plus many others not mentioned, but still recorded in history? In addition, this issue arose because Hayden Covington claimed that Nathan Knorr was possessed by Satan when he blocked his appointment in becoming the 3rd President of the Watchtower Society as authorized by Joseph Rutherford. The sponsors of this book on cults, does not claim to be able answer these questions but are fully aware that no matter which religious affiliation one professes, these questions arise often in discussions and debates about the Bible, our personal faith and how to maintain our stand as true Christians and resist the powers of evil as personified in Satan the Devil.

We therefore present some material by kind permission of the Holypop Media Group, LLC, written by Dr. Elmer Towns who is a college and seminary professor, an author of popular and scholarly works, the editor of two encyclopedias, and a popular seminar lecturer. This written material attempts to explain what Hayden Covington must have felt and struggled to understand when he first hand witnessed and experienced the scheming, underhanded, devilish actions of Nathan Knorr in his personal quest to become the powerful 3rd President of the Watchtower Society as related in Chapter Three of our book. This extract is from the notes of Dr. Elmer Towns as presented in his famous lecture to the Liberty University on the subject of Satan:

There are two important passages in the Word of God concerning the origin and fall of Satan. The first passage relating to Satan's fall is found in Ezekiel 28:12-19 where Ezekiel describes the creation and judgment of a vile and vicious non-human creature whose name we find out later to be Lucifer. The second passage relating to Satan's fall is found in Isaiah 14:12-14 where the prophet Isaiah presents the origin and fall of Satan. With reference to a specific time in history when Satan fell from Heaven, it must be stated that there is no clear revelation as to exactly when Satan fell, but here are limits to the possible time which we may deduce from biblical evidence. Based upon information gleaned from a comparison of Ezekiel 28:12-19 with Isaiah 14, Jude 6, and 2 Peter 2:4, plus other passages, the following picture of Satan starts to emerge. Satan was created as one of the host of angelic beings, an anointed cherub, i.e., the captain of the cherubic hosts.

Sometime prior to the creation of the natural order, Satan became vain about his beauty and position, and his heart became rebellious against God. Apparently, he was able to secure a considerable following among the angels, resulting in their expulsion from Heaven (Luke 10:18; 2 Peter 2:4; Jude 6; Revelation 12:4). Since that day, Satan devotes himself to opposing the work of God in every way possible and to attempting to destroy all of the good that God has created in the natural order. He (Satan) is allowed to continue this way for a period but will ultimately be confined to Hell (symbolic lake of fire and sulfur) for eternity" (Revelation 20:10). If we assume that angels (including Satan) were part of the creation of Genesis 1:1, then their fall (including Satan's) follows that point in time. However, it may be that angels were created prior to the creation of the heavens and the earth. In either case, angels (including Satan) were present when God "laid the foundation of the earth" and "set its measurements" (Job 38:4, 5), for it was then that the morning stars sang together, and all the sons of God shouted for joy (Job 38:7). This involved all the angels rejoicing with God. Satan and his angels fell, then, sometime after the original creation of the heavens and the earth.

It is certain that Satan had fallen before Genesis Chapter Three was written, where the temptation of Adam and Eve is recorded. He fell before man fell; but whether he fell before or after man's creation, we cannot say for certain. Satan's fall was a direct result of his self-exaltation that was manifested in his pride, the first sin. (1 Timothy 3:6) Motivated by pride, Satan set out on an irrational course to seize for himself God's authority over the universe (Isaiah 14:12-14). Some commentators believe that this revolt of Satan towards God occurred after the creation week, but before the fall of man (Genesis 1:31; 3:1-6). It appears that the Devil became the prince of this world when he led man (Adam and Eve) to sins against God and thus brought the rulers of earth under his domination (Genesis 1:26; 3:1-6; John 12:31; Colossians 1:13; Acts 26:18). The ultimate desire of Satan was to take God's place. Lucifer's first attempt involved his ascent into the abode of God. The Bible identifies three heavens. The first heaven is the sky surrounding our planet, the atmosphere. The second heaven is the stellar heaven which is apparently the abode of angels. The third heaven is the dwelling place of God. When Lucifer determined to ascend into heaven, he sought to move into the third heaven, the dwelling place of God. Satan wanted to ascend above the position and place where he was created and assume the place of his Creator.

Satan sought authority over the other angels. Satan wanted to be exalted above the stars. The term star is often used in the Bible to identify angels. (Revelation 1:20; 12:4) Some commentators believe Satan ruled the angels as an archangel along with Michael and Gabriel. If this were the case, Satan then sought to expand his sphere of authority over Michael and Gabriel and those angels they ruled. This would make Satan the ultimate authority in heaven, perhaps taking the place of God over the angels. If this trinity of archangels exited before the fall of man, it may explain why a third of the angels fell with Satan (Revelation 12:4). Satan desired to "sit also upon the mount of the congregation, in the sides of the north" (Isaiah 14:13). The phrase "mount of the congregation" is an expression relating to ruling in the kingdom of God (Isaiah 2:1-4). Lucifer seemed to be saying, "I want a share in the kingdom." The problem was he wanted God's share. The "north side" is a term relating to God's presence in Scripture (Psalms 75:6, 7). During the millennial reign of Christ, Christ will rule this earth from the north (Psalms 48:2).

There can be no question that Satan was prepared to attempt a coup in heaven. His desire was not simply to get closer to God but to surpass God. "I will ascend above the heights of the clouds" (Isaiah 14:14). Clouds are often used to refer to the glory of God. In fact, 100 of the 150 uses of the word "cloud" in the King James Version have to do with divine glory. Satan sought glory for himself that surpassed the glory of God. Paul revealed the ultimate desire of Satan when he wrote, "who opposeth and exalteth himself above all that is called God, or that is worshipped, so that he as God sitteth in the temple of God, shewing himself that he is God" (2 Thessalonians 2:4. KJV) Satan sought the authority of God for himself. By becoming the most high, Satan would be the possessor of heaven and earth. By ascending into heaven, he would rule angels and ultimately enjoy a messianic rule. This attempt to be like God is similar to Satan's strategy today. All of Satan's plans in the universe are counterfeit to God's plans. One of the chief works of Satan today is imitating Christianity. He attempts to counterfeit all that God performs. The Christian needs to be certain he is not tricked into accepting a satanic counterfeit of God's best for his life.

An additional review of the above article was submitted by one of our experienced researchers of the Bible, from Cambridge University, and adds a few more helpful details that explain this serious and sometimes confusing issue related to Satan:

The devil was forcibly struck down to earth, like a lightning bolt, before the birth of Christ. Jesus revealed he witnessed the event when he said, "I was watching when Satan fell from heaven like lightning" (Luke 10:18). Lucifer was initially given the unique job of covering God's throne (Ezekiel 28:14). He carried out his duties so well that the Lord, in the only angelic promotion recorded in Scripture, rewarded him with a throne of responsibility over other spirits tasked with goals on the earth (Isaiah 14:13). God's greatest creation, however, filled himself with vanity and lust.

After turning himself into Satan the Devil he deceived those angels under his supervision into turning themselves into demons. The devil then mounted a sneak attack on God's throne (Isaiah 14:12 -14) His efforts perfectly failed, however, resulting in him and his demon army being thrown back to the vicinity of the earth (Revelation 12:4). This initial expulsion from heaven, seen by Christ, likely took place between the events of Genesis 1:1 and 1:2. In the near future, the devil's second (and final) attack of heaven will result in his permanent banishment from God's throne. This event will be the catalyst for starting the Great Tribulation period and Satan's rule over the earth through the Beast and False Prophet. (Revelation 12:7 - 12, 13:3 - 15)

Special Report No. 4: Hayden Covington and Nathan Knorr

These meaningful remarks were submitted by a fellow researcher, ex-Jehovah's Witness named John from Texas, and he reported the following. "Frederick Franz and Nathan Knorr were the polar opposites of the dynamic duo, Rutherford and Covington. These two, Knorr and Franz, would conspire to drive Covington out. Knorr intensely hated Covington to an unbelievable degree. Knorr was anti-intellectual and Covington disdained Knorr's lack of education. Both Rutherford and Covington were hard drinkers. Eventually, the drinking and bullying of Knorr would get Covington kicked sideways by Franz and Knorr and the excuse would be given that Covington would step down from the Vice-President position because he wasn't of the heavenly class. This is bullshit for an obvious reason: he never claimed to be of the anointed in the first place, and this was never an obstacle before."

These remarks made by ex-Jehovah's Witness, Jerry Bergman, Ph.D. researcher and writer, further expanded his experience when he interviewed Hayden Covington in 1974 a few years before his death:

> When I arrived, Covington was not home, so his wife went out to locate him. He was at a bar, drinking. When she brought him home, he was rather tipsy. This was disappointing to me because I was raised not to drink. Drinking was a problem among Witnesses, and I knew that it had been a problem with Covington and was part of the reason why he left Bethel. His being tipsy was good in one way because he was very open with me and willing to talk about almost everything I asked him, and I took notes. It became very clear that he idolized Rutherford. For example, I knew that Rutherford's wife had a stroke and that she wasn't in good health [she died in 1962] and I asked about the philandering rumors. Covington was laying down when I asked him about this and immediately sat up and was obviously very, very angry. He looked at me and said, "If your wife was paralyzed, what would you do?" I immediately knew

I better not pursue that line of questioning. He seemed to acknowledge that Rutherford did have paramours, but defended him to the hilt. I also asked him who wrote the articles in the Watchtower publications? He answered Rutherford, who had some help, but alone was responsible.

He kept calling N.H. Knorr, the president then, a cobra. When I asked him why he said this, he answered, "Do you know what a cobra does? They'll slither behind you, and they'll strike viciously." It became apparent that he detested Knorr. This could be because his problems with the society began when Knorr became president. Covington claimed that he, Covington, had the votes to become president, but Knorr connived him out of the presidency. I never had that much respect for Knorr, partly because Knorr only had a high school education but, as Covington talked; I had more respect for Knorr. A conflict clearly existed between Knorr and Covington so I openly asked him, "Why didn't you like Knorr? What was the problem?" He never gave definitive evidence that Knorr had a legitimate problem except Covington's personality was very much like Rutherford's and very much in contrast to Knorr's.

We found the contents and opinions of Hayden Covington expressed in this interview with Jerry Bergman both reasonable and acceptable when describing his relationship with Nathan Knorr, even though Covington was obviously inebriated at the time. In addition it even appears that Covington was quite obviously trying to mangle the reputation of Nathan Knorr, who had enjoyed such adoration and was almost idolized by the followers of the Watchtower religion during his lifetime. Although it must be noted that these millions of followers had no knowledge of the real persona behind the public profile that Knorr displayed. This material supplied by Jerry Bergman transcends everything that the Watchtower Society has ever revealed in their literature about the relationship between Covington and Knorr plus their personal battle for power, especially the deliberate lie that appeared in *The Watchtower* magazine that Covington, graciously declined to serve further as a member of the board of directors and as vice-president of the Watch Tower Bible and Tract Society of Pennsylvania.

The only comment that we take exception with and object to, is that portion of the interview when Covington tried to justify the revolting and scandalous immoral conduct of his personal friend Joseph Rutherford with his constant female companions, by using the disgusting excuse that Rutherford's wife Mary was an invalid and partially paralyzed so Rutherford was only doing what any normal man would have done. It is a known fact that Rutherford and his wife had lived completely separate lives ever since Rutherford became the President of the Watchtower Society back in 1916 and had virtually no contact whatsoever with Mary his wife, also little contact with his son and only child Malcolm. There is one instance that they may have met, and that was on the occasion when Rutherford picked up his son Malcolm and Malcolm's wife Pauline and took them on a very expensive world cruise that Rutherford regularly enjoyed, using the excuse, for health reasons. The tab for the cost of the luxury life style of Joseph Rutherford was picked up by the Watchtower Society as usual and paid for through the donations from the loyal flock of followers of this is religion. Also, in answer to the question, "who wrote the articles in the Watchtower?" Covington knew the answer but was very cagey in his reply, he knew firsthand that it was Freddy Franz and a few other ghost writers who wrote all of the material credited to Joseph Rutherford, but would not admit it.

Special Report No. 5: Hayden Covington and Muhammad Ali (Cassius Clay)

According to the book by Leigh Montville, Muhammad Ali sought the advice of attorney Hayden Covington, who had successfully represented Jehovah's Witnesses against draft boards. He was the most successful lawyer ever to go against the Supreme Court at the time, Montville tells the History magazine.

> Covington's success with the Jehovah's Witnesses was based on the contention that everyone who was a member was a minister, and the Jehovah's Witnesses were historically a very active religious group, ringing doorbells and proselytizing. Covington tried to make a case that Ali was a minster like that, and he was in a way, because he spoke at temples and was always talking about his religion.

> If there was one thing Ali could do better than box, it was talk, and his outspokenness put him at the center of countless arguments about race, religion, politics and war during the turbulent 1960s, particularly after he confirmed his conversion to the Nation of Islam the morning after he defeated Sonny Liston in 1964 to capture the heavyweight belt. Ali cited his religious beliefs against war as the reason he should be exempt from joining the 438,000 American troops in Vietnam. "I am a member of the Muslims and we don't go to no wars unless they are declared by Allah himself" Ali told Chicago Daily News sportswriter Tom Fitzpatrick. "I'm not going 10,000 miles from home to help murder and burn another poor nation simply to continue the domination of white slave masters of the darker people the world over" Ali said a week before his scheduled induction ceremony. "If I thought the war was going to bring freedom and equality to 22 million of my people, they wouldn't have to draft me, I'd join tomorrow."

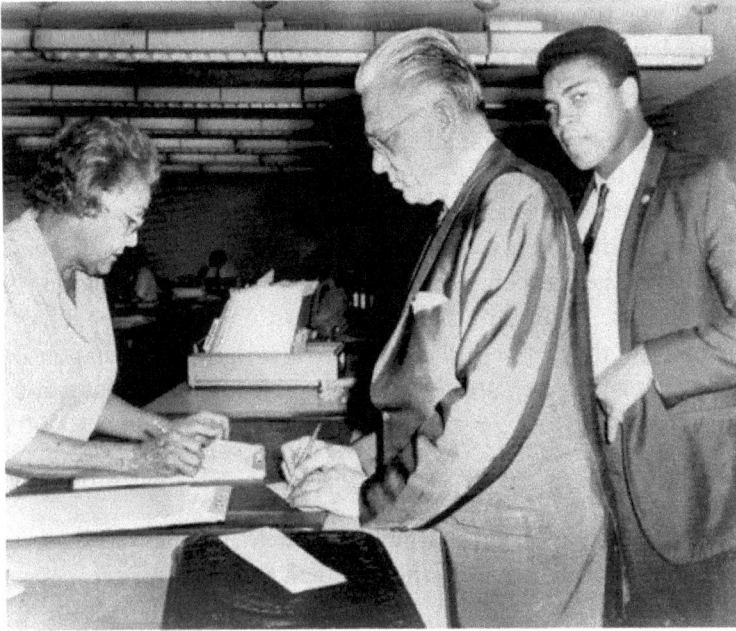

Muhammad Ali, formerly Cassius Clay aged 25 years old, with his attorney, Hayden Covington, files petition to halt induction into the Armed Services in 1967, courtesy of *History* magazine and Creative Commons.

The *History* magazine continued: Less than two months after Ali refused to step forward at the induction center, an all-white jury took just 21 minutes to find him guilty of draft evasion on June 20, 1967. The judge made an example of the high-profile defendant by handing down the maximum penalty for the felony offense – five years in jail and a $10,000 fine. It is too bad he went wrong. He had the makings of a national hero, lamented Washington Post columnist Shirley Povich. The New York Athletic Commission revoked the champ's boxing license while the World Boxing Association did what none of Ali's professional opponents had been able to do up to that point in stripping him of his title. Released on bail pending appeal, Ali lived for three years in exile from the ring. As public opinion began to turn against the war, however, it softened against Ali. In 1970 the New York State Supreme Court ordered his boxing license reinstated, and the following year the U.S. Supreme Court overturned his conviction in a unanimous decision. After 43 months away, Ali returned to the ring on October 26,

1970, and knocked out Jerry Quarry in the third round. Four years later, he regained the heavyweight belt after knocking out George Foreman in the Rumble in the Jungle.

It's interesting in how it all ended with the Supreme Court. Basically they just gave him a pass for being Muhammad Ali. If he had been a normal guy he would have been in jail two years before. In the end it was celebrity justice, Montville says. In the beginning he was penalized for being Muhammad Ali and in the end was let off for being Muhammad Ali, which probably shows you the course of the Vietnam War right there; that one guy saying the one same thing is interpreted two different ways in a matter of years.

In his book, *I Wept by the Rivers of Babylon*, Terry Walstrom records:

Hayden Covington cut short a legal presentation, a draft case for a JW brother from Oklahoma called Sam Salamy, cut short in 1967 mid-trial because he had received a phone call from Muhammad Ali's legal team who offered a quarter of a million dollars if he could get Muhammed Ali off in his Draft Dodging court case. Only JWs whose families had enough money could afford to hire Covington on reputation alone. Sam Salamy ended up paying Covington ten-thousand dollars and got convicted anyway. Hopping into the limelight, Lawyer Covington took the lazy way out suggesting Muhammed Ali should accept a guilty sentence and seek to make a deal with the prosecutor, Morton Susman, United States Attorney. In fact, he talked Ali into requesting that the Judge sentence him immediately! It was this tactic which frustrated and upset Ali's first-hired attorney, Quinnan A. Hodges of Houston. It is also the reason Ali's handlers refused to pay Covington when all was said and done. However Covington subsequently sued Ali to recover $247,000 in legal fees.

Muhammad Ali (Cassius Clay), left, laughs along with his attorney Hayden Covington in 1967. Covington represented Ali in his effort to obtain conscientious objector status. Photo is by kind permission of Associated Press and Creative Commons.

Special Report No. 6: Use of the word Paradise in the Bible

This report not only covers the correct interpretation of the word 'paradise' in the Bible but also includes reports and details never before revealed, information based on the research and notes of some very intelligent and courageous Bible students, particularly Raymond Franz, Edward Dunlap and Lyman Swingle, who were part of the five-man team that produced the excellent Bible encyclopedia, *Aid to Bible Understanding*, published by the Watchtower Society in 1969.

The opinion of Australian Paul Grundy based on his extensive research into the religion of Jehovah's Witnesses, and was also confirmed in our research that more and more members of Jehovah's Witnesses are tending toward the belief that paradise mentioned in the Greek scriptures (New Testament) is actually heaven and to be their ultimate reward as faithful and loyal Christians. In addition, many Jehovah's Witnesses are truly fed-up with repeated promises by their leaders, that the end is nigh and as members of the so-called other sheep class can only expect everlasting life in a promised new earth (paradise) sometime in the future, but only if they have been faithful and obedient to the Organization. Yet their leaders, the Governing Body claim that they will go immediately to heaven when they die, as personally promised by Jesus Christ.

In our research we also found that many members of this religion are slowly changing their belief from what the Watchtower Society has taught them, namely that their dead relatives and loved ones are not lying in the grave waiting for a future resurrection sometime in the future as claimed, but that the spirit or personage of their loved relatives is already in heaven waiting to welcome them when they die, plus they might at this very moment be looking down upon them here on earth. They also remind themselves of the words of Jesus, a promise to the evildoer at his side as he was dying, "You will be with me in paradise."

Strange as it may sound, some of those members of the so-called remnant of the 144,000 heavenly class today, including members of the current and past Governing Body, whose now dead beloved parents, husbands or wives, family members or other relatives who also had claimed to be members of the remnant of the anointed heavenly class in the past, and had been immediately raised to heaven upon their death. In their fervor, members of this anointed class have publicly and privately stated that they are looking forward to seeing them when they receive their reward in heaven. Some of the past members of this so-called remnant have also been known to proudly boast about their superior reward of going immediately to heaven when they die to join Jesus Christ as Kings and Priests, and they felt pity for the inferior members of this religion who were classified as the other sheep. Many followers of this religion want to know why there is such a difference in their rewards, one for the special anointed class that includes their leaders, and another one for the so-called earthly great crowd of other sheep, who by far make up the majority of the members of this religion.

This so-called heavenly class, believe from what they have been taught that when a member of the other sheep class dies, their bodies have to lie in the grave and the spirit of that person would not be allowed into heaven (Ecclesiastes 12:7) but had to wait and wait until some future time to be resurrected back on earth as humans, which is in accordance with the current teachings of their religion. As a result, the leaders of the Watchtower Society are now facing a critical dilemma as more and more of their followers are opting for the more traditional Christian belief of life after death and an immediate reward to life in a heavenly paradise as promised by Jesus, similar to the claimed members of this anointed class, their leaders the Governing Body, who currently believe and claim is their future reward. This is in contrast to the ongoing repeated and boring statements by the Watchtower Society and the existing repeated promise to members of the other sheep class, year after year, of their reward and only hope is that of an earthly paradise, the new world or new system of things, being just around the corner. This is in line with the current teaching of the Governing Body of the Watchtower Society, as a result of their erroneous belief, of there being two separate classes of Christians on earth today.

This current complex, disconcerting and contradictory issue now being faced by the Governing Body is reminiscent of the year 1935, which was also a very confusing time for this religion when many of the so-called remnant partaking of the bread and wine, being their claimed proof they were of the exclusive anointed class, which was the traditional understanding at the time. However, many decided to abandon their then current view and that they were not of this so-called heavenly class as they had previously been taught and to enjoy immediate life after death in heaven, but preferred to change their minds as to their future hopes and enthusiastically followed the new revelation by Joseph Rutherford and this religion that the great crowd was not a lesser or inferior spiritual class in heaven standing before the throne of God. But now this new teaching offered the chance to live forever in paradise on a new earth without pain or suffering, in line with Revelation Chapter 21, and this was far more desirable for many of these members.

Today it now appears to be a reversal and more and more followers of this religion believe that it is more alluring to accept immediate life after death, as promised in the Bible, and meet up again with their deceased, much loved family members rather than keep waiting for a promise that never seems to be fulfilled. They experience the emotion described in the inspired word of God, which speaks for itself without any twisting or private interpretation by the Watchtower Society; the words of Proverbs 13:12: "Hope deferred makes the heart sick." The Watchtower Society is now paying the penalty for not being open and honest about their teachings and the misleading of their followers, which once again is a clear sign of a religious cult.

When we look at the example of the past long-time serving member of the Governing Body, Lyman Swingle who served from 1945 until his death aged 90 in 2001, we learn of some interesting facts. Lyman is on record that, just before he died in 2001, he stated in the presence of his brother from Salt Lake City that he was so much looking forward to his death as he was excited about meeting up again with his mother and father, when he finally joined Jesus Christ and served at his right hand, as they would both be there waiting in heaven to welcome him. According to the announcement in the *Watchtower* magazine of July 1, 2001 under the title, He Endured to the End, the parents of Lyman

Swingle; his mother Minnie and father Leroy, were both members of the Bible Students from 1913 onward and had brought up Lyman and his siblings in their new religion founded by Charles Russell in 1879. They both also claimed they were of the so-called anointed class and when they died was presumed by Lyman to have immediately ascended to heaven, as taught by the Watchtower Society. Lyman knew this and he truly believed in immediate life after death in his case also. It is a known fact that at least one current member of the Governing Body, as revealed in a private conversation, has the identical emotional feelings and opinion as Lyman Swingle and also because of the same reason that his much-loved mother was a member of the so-called anointed class, he was excited about meeting her soon in heaven when he received his heavenly reward after his death, expected in a few short years. This man also believes in immediate life in heaven after death and no doubt so do all of the other members of current Governing Body.

Of course it is also known that if a current member of this religion is classified under the label, the great crowd of other sheep, they are not allowed to even think for themselves that they will enjoy immediate life after death or presume they will ascend to heaven or paradise when they die, and if they do make this claim, they are contradicting the teachings of the Governing Body and are subject to extreme discipline with the possibility of being expelled for apostasy. As explained in the Special Report, No.1, by Philip Rees, from his experiences he had on record, Philip recounts a case when a sister asked to partake of the bread and wine she was refused because these representatives of the Governing Body told her, to think this way she was subjecting herself to the influences and power of Satan, or she was mentally unbalanced.

According to the now archived records of the Watchtower Society, leaked to one of our researchers, Lyman Swingle was one of the Watchtower Governing Body members that sided with Raymond Franz and prevented him from being immediately excommunicated in 1980 and as a result Ray was only asked to resign and leave his position in the organization, along with the offensive offer of a cash settlement to keep him quiet. But later Lyman was compelled for reasons unknown to join his detractors on the Governing Body, especially now showing weakness of character, as he went along with and had agreed to the unanimous decision to excommunicate as an apostate the sincere Bible student Edward Dunlap, a fellow leading member of this religion. Lyman Swingle became downright morose and very depressed as a result of this incident and his melancholy also escalated after the death of his wife Crystal in 1998, the mother of two children, insinuated but unproved, by one critic of the Watchtower Society as having been fathered by Lyman. Crystal did not claim to be of the so-called anointed class and receive immediate heavenly life after death, as Lyman personally believed, so in his sick and confused mind he knew that he would never see his treasured wife or two children and grandchildren ever again, so he began drinking very heavily, according to eye witnesses of his sad life during his last few years in the New York Bethel.

At the Memorial Service for Lyman Alexander Swingle on Monday, March 19, 2001, Carey Barber, member of the Governing Body from 1977 until his death in 2007, gave the main eulogy. Carey himself died at the age of 101 in 2007 while he still lived in the New York Bethel. The following is a short extract and quote from the speech by Carey Barber and is in memory of this man Lyman Swingle from Salt Lake City, Utah. Lyman provided some valuable, insightful material to Chapter Three of this book about the Watchtower Society, ironically without him ever knowing it.

> Carey Barber read aloud the words of 1 Thessalonians 4:13-17: "Do not sleep in death…For since we believe that Jesus died and rose again, even so, through Jesus, God will bring with him those who have died." Lyman Alexander Swingle successfully completely his life course on earth and has gone on to unimaginable blessings and service. Not a time of sorrow for him but victory and joy. We can be glad he died with his boots on. He even went to work a week before passing at the age of 90. Brother Swingle was also known for his being approachable. He had an open-door policy. Whenever someone would come to see him, he would give them his full attention. He so loved children, and they always felt comfortable around him. They liked to go for his unique eye-brows and touch them. And Brother Swingle would let them! Another outstanding example of humility is how Brother Swingle would pray to Jehovah on

his knees even when in recent times it was very difficult for him to get up. But he would insist and say that's what knees are for. We can all rejoice with Lyman in his new heavenly assignment ... some of us hope to join him there soon. He leaves behind a sister, two brothers, two daughters, grandchildren and great-grandchildren.

The only clues that we could uncover regarding Lyman being the biological father of these two daughters of Crystal and also it is claimed to have been fully known, but quietly ignored by the rest of the members of the Governing Body and hidden, secreted or closeted away to avoid another public scandal of this magnitude, as they all knew that Crystal had been separated from her legal husband for many years during the time that Lyman had a close relationship with her and her two daughters were born. The Governing Body was only just recovering from the Rutherford years (1916-1942) and the era of his well-known infamous scandals related to his debauched lifestyle plus having a mistress known as Berta Peale, and they could ill afford another disgraceful spectacle so soon after Lyman Swingle was appointed to the Governing Body in 1945. Can you imagine that if this story about Lyman Swingle and Crystal is actually true and was leaked to the press that has the proclivity to expose scandals, what major headlines would have been displayed and exploited? "Top Jehovah's Witness Exposed: Discovered Having Scandalous Secret Love Affair With Married Woman, Fathering Two Illegitimate Children." This would have received more world-wide exposure than the recent case of a Roman Catholic Archbishop in Washington being defrocked because he confessed to having an illegitimate child with a nun.

This relationship between Lyman and Crystal had been frowned upon by some of the older, more conservative members of the Watchtower headquarters and they had privately warned Lyman of the risk and dangers involved. Also at the Memorial service upon the death of Lyman, the speaker Carey Barber referred to his two daughters, several grandchildren and great-grandchildren. Of course as pointed out by an avid supporter of the Watchtower Society and also defender of the memory of Lyman, who was a leading member of the Governing Body, the speaker Carey Barber could have meant, step-daughters, etc, but that is not what he stated. It could have been simply a slip of the tongue, but as Carey is no longer around to explain himself, we probably will never know the full truth of this incident.

In our research we could not locate the names of these two daughters of Crystal or the dates of their birth, as this could have confirmed or rejected this accusation that Lyman was their biological father or not. We do know however that Crystal was brought up a Catholic before she converted to Jehovah's Witnesses and her legal husband, probably also being a Catholic had refused to give her a divorce, thus the reason she had to wait until he died before she could marry Lyman Swingle in 1956. Although Carey Barber later did make the point and went out of his way toward the end of his eulogy at the funeral of Lyman, to mention, that in 1956, "Lyman married Crystal who had two daughters from a previous marriage. Lyman loved and treated these as his own daughters." We are not sure if this statement was necessary or not, so Carey Barber either knew this as a fact or he had been slipped a note during his eulogy and told by other members of the Governing Body to make sure and emphasize this claim to avoid further embarrassment, as they alone knew the real truth of this secret and clandestine affair between Lyman Swingle and Crystal Zircher. As we have learned, the Governing Body of this religion is not above lying when it comes to expediency and trying to protect their reputation. In addition, our usual source of information in Salt Lake City, a close blood relative of Lyman refused to even discuss this matter, which made our reporter even more suspicious and ask himself, was it just another skeleton in the family cupboard.

***

In using the word 'paradise' by Jesus Christ when being executed by the Roman soldiers, was he actually referring to the heavenly realm, the location where he lived in spirit form before becoming a human and taking the form and fashion of mankind? If correct, this will thus confirm the words of Jesus, when he said to the repentant evildoer (*thief*) at his side, while also being executed along with Jesus on Golgotha at Calvary, Jerusalem, and Jesus knowing that they would both be dead as human beings before the Jewish day ended at 6pm. "Jesus, remember me when you come into your kingdom." And he said to him, "'Truly, I say to you, today you will be with me in paradise. Then Jesus, calling out with a loud voice, said, 'Father, into your hands I commit my spirit!' And having said this he breathed his last" (Luke 23:42, 43, 46).

This verse in the Bible is difficult to interpret and as a result at least three opposing and contradictory views have developed as to what Jesus actually meant by his use of the word, 'today'. As there is no punctuation mark or comma in the original Greek manuscript, so depending on the personal doctrinal background and religious affiliation of the Bible scholar it is rendered in two distinct different ways. The mark of a comma used today is descended from a diagonal slash known as 'virgula suspensiva', used from the 13th to 17th centuries to represent a pause. The modern comma was first used by Aldus Manutius an Italian humanist, scholar, educator, and the founder of the Aldine Press. Manutius devoted the later part of his life to publishing and disseminating rare texts.

In the English version of this text the comma has been placed sometimes before the word 'today', as is indicated in the Westcott and Hort translation of this Greek manuscript of 1881. Thus reading "Truly, I say to you, today you will be with me in paradise." This implies that the very same day that Jesus and the evildoer were to die as human beings they both would leave their earthly existence and enter into the heavenly spirit realm. Of course one is then faced with the question of where the person, we know as Jesus was after he died that Friday evening (Good Friday) and his perfect earthly, but now sacrificed human body lay for most of three days decaying in the tomb provided by Joseph of Arimathea. This question is taken up later in this special report based on the research and records of the late Edward Dunlap, a brilliant Bible student. This personal sacrifice by Jesus Christ was in fulfillment of the arrangement by Jesus, when in his pre-human form that he made with his heavenly father, as Jesus had agreed to give up his heavenly life, to descend to earth, to be born as a human and then sacrifice his perfect human body as a ransom price for all sinful mankind.

Some Bible students' interpretation of the word 'today' in this statement of Jesus recorded in Luke, Chapter 23, has having no relevance to time, either that same day or a day some time in the future when the evildoer would enter Paradise. If this was the case then the text would have simply read, "Truly, I say to you, you will be with me in paradise." For example, the Watchtower Society in their literature says the use of the word today was inserted by Jesus, not to give the time or the day of the evildoer being welcomed into Paradise, but rather to call attention to the time period in history in which the promise was being made. This claimed use of the word 'today' if accepted in a general historical sense, as we would use the expression, today we live in the nuclear age. This raises an important issue as no one today, including the Watchtower Society, actually knows what Jesus had in mind by the use of the word today.

The Watchtower Society confidently states in their literature "It was the day (today) when Jesus had been rejected and condemned by the high-ranking religious leaders of his own people and was thereafter sentenced to die by the Roman authorities." This is basically claiming that Jesus used this word 'today' in a general historical sense only. There is absolutely no basis for this interpretation of the word 'today' by the Watchtower Society and is pure speculation on their part and without foundation. In addition the word 'today' in that context does not relate to the main subject of the sentence, namely, 'you will be with me in paradise.' In addition, the Bible gives a clear warning that we should "not go beyond the things written" (1 Corinthians 4:6) or "Do not add to his words, or else he will rebuke you, and you will be found a liar." (Proverbs 30:5, 6) The Watchtower Society regularly violates and ignores this scriptural warning, so these words of Jesus as recorded and written in the Holy Bible stand alone without adding any additional words and leaving the only issue to be resolved being, in which position should the comma be placed; before or after the word 'today'.

The Bible record states that Jesus was resurrected on the third day (Sunday) after his death and then appeared again in human form, often explained by some as visionary experiences, in which the presence of Jesus was felt or that what they saw was an illusion as Jesus displayed the holes in his hands and feet.[31] Jesus appeared to his disciples and

---

[31] In the controversial Bible commentary by Dr. Thomas Sheeham, the account of the resurrection is not to a literal, physical rising from the grave. Paul's understanding of the resurrection, and perhaps Peter's as well, is a metaphysical one,

others for a period of 40 days before he finally and actually ascended to heaven, presumably, according to the notes of renowned Bible student Edward Dunlap, after visiting heaven several times during those 40 days, as he was already a spirit creature with full access to the heavenly realm. Jesus left his disciples and the vicinity of earth for the very last time and ascended to rejoin his father in heaven for this final and spectacular event, doing so in full view of his eleven faithful disciples. "While He was blessing them, He parted from them and was carried up into heaven" (Luke 24:51). Read also Acts 1:9-11. There is no biblical proof that the actual physical dead body of Jesus, while he lived in human form for 33 years was actually seen by these disciples on its way to heaven but was rather only an illusion or a symbolic image of Jesus in human form.

According to the Bible text at John 20:19-29, "On the evening of that day, the first day of the week, the doors being locked where the disciples were for fear of the Jews, Jesus came and stood among them and said to them, "Peace be with you". When he had said this, he showed them his hands and his side. Then the disciples were glad when they saw the Lord." So Jesus had literally entered into a room that had locked doors and solid walls, how did he accomplish this? This comment recorded in the reference work Biblical Hermeneutics is made by one knowledgeable Bible student.

> Thomas' reaction because he saw the marks in the hands and felt a hole in Jesus' side with his hand, or was it a reaction to Jesus' presence and that Jesus knew Thomas doubted? Was the reaction more to do with Thomas' being humbled by his disbelief and less to do with Jesus' body? In both cases, being shown this materialized body seems to be the proof that he is their Lord, which would seem to imply there were marks to be seen. However, recognizing Jesus after his resurrection seems to involve more than just seeing or feeling him, like how he walked with the men on the road to Emmaus and he wasn't revealed to their eyes until afterward. Thomas' earlier statement could simply be an over-the-top claim. A loud denial exaggerating that he would need to feel Jesus' side. Thomas

---

with the stories of Jesus' (figurative) resurrection reflecting his triumphant entry into God's eschatological presence.

could see Jesus well, a man he knew and recognized, standing in front of him. Seeing his healed body when they knew it to be injured would almost be as much if not more proof of the power of his resurrection, than seeing a man with open wounds walking around.

If Jesus was raised up with a spirit body could he be seen at all? Spirit creatures can take on human form. Some angels in the past did this and they could even eat and drink just like a physical man does (Genesis 18:1-8; 19:1-3) but they were still spirit creatures and could sluff (discard) of the material form instantly. (Judges 13:15-21) After his resurrection, Jesus could do the same as those angels and materialize a temporary body. But as a spirit creature he too was able to appear and disappear suddenly (Luke 24:31; John 20:19, 26) and he appeared multiple times in different manifestations not always identical in appearance. That's why even close friends only recognized him by what he said or did. (Luke 24:30, 31, 35; John 20:14-16; 21:6, 7) So when Jesus appeared to Thomas he appeared with a materialized body that had wound marks to help Thomas who doubted his Lord could really be alive again. (John 20:24)

Returning to the text in the Gospel of Luke, the opposing view and opinion of this word used by Jesus, namely 'today', is that Jesus was in fact talking about the same day he was making this statement, namely that he and the evildoer were to be put to death that same day but that eventually, some time in the future after they both would give up their human existence that same day, but only enter into the spirit realm, paradise, at a later date. Thus, the text at Luke 23:43 reads in some translations of the Bible as follows, "Truly, I say to you today, you will be with me in paradise" thus implying possibly sometime in the future. If this is the correct rendering then the meaning of this text implies a totally different concept and thus the confusion experienced today by serious students of the Bible.

In the opinion of most reliable Bible students, it is certain that Jesus definitely entered into the spirit realm that same day he was executed and ended his human existence, and he was not left in limbo. Limbo 'Latin limbus, meaning edge or boundary' referring to the edge of Hell and is the religious viewpoint concerning the afterlife condition of those who die in original sin without being assigned to the Hell of the Damned. According to the words of the Apostle Peter it is probable that Jesus used those three days to perform an important duty during the time between his actual death as a human and the later disappearance of the human body from the tomb. He used this opportunity to proclaim judgment on the wicked spirit creatures that rebelled against God during some time before the flood and before Jesus came down to earth being born as a human. The written words of the Apostle Peter at 1 Peter 3:18-20 explains, "For Christ also died for sins once for all, the just for the unjust, so that He might bring us to God, having been put to death in the flesh, but made alive in the spirit; in which also He went and made proclamation to the spirits now in prison, who once were disobedient, when the patience of God kept waiting in the days of Noah, during the construction of the ark, in which a few, that is, eight persons, were brought safely through the water."

Jesus was put to death in the flesh but made alive in the spirit, so this means that death could not hold him. He was sinless and death is the wages of sin (Romans 6:23), but since Jesus never sinned, his spirit remained alive, even though he suffered death in the flesh. Some Bible scholars claim and believe that the evildoer did not enter the spirit realm that same day as Jesus did, but the Bible is silent as to what happened to this evildoer after his death as a human, apart from this verbal promise of Jesus Christ, so any other remarks made by Bible scholars is pure speculation.

Jesus was said to have made a proclamation, to the spirits now in prison. Nowhere in the Bible are humans referred to as spirits so this seems to refer to demon spirits that are bound in the abyss and these demons are the fallen angels who were permanently bound because of heinous and extreme wickedness. This comment is what John MacArthur's Study Bible (ESV) makes in its study notes: "This seems to also fit the Bible text of Jude 6-7 which says, "And the angels who did not keep their positions of authority but abandoned their proper dwelling – these he has kept in darkness, bound with everlasting chains for judgment on the great Day."

Based on the information provided by our researchers, you as the reader therefore have the choice of three possible variations of this powerful text in Luke, Chapter 23, and we encourage you to accept the version you prefer with an open mind and heart, as no one today can read the mind of Jesus Christ and what he actually meant when he used the word 'today' in this Bible text. However we offer a word of caution, that it is unwise to glibly accept the hidden interpretation of this word 'today' or the word 'paradise' from any religious body or religious leaders who claim to have exclusive authority from Almighty God to interpret the true meaning of the Bible, for example, the Watchtower Society or the Mormon Church.

This opinion piece below by Edward Dunlap and with which Raymond Franz concurred, refers to the early Christians also believing that upon death they would immediately be transferred to heaven. Although this is only a personal viewpoint by Edward, it does hold some validity as we remind ourselves that Jesus Christ was still human when he uttered these provocative, inspirational words recorded at Luke 23:43. Also the question has been raised, what did Jesus have in mind when he said to the evildoer, "you will be with me in paradise", and what did Jesus mean by his use of the word paradise? Most knowledgeable Bible students and Christian commentators over the centuries conclude that Jesus meant the heavenly realm, and even Charles Russell the founder of the Watchtower religion believed this was the case. However, some religions today, including the Watchtower Society currently state adamantly that Jesus was not referring to the heavenly realm by the use of his word 'paradise'.

The Apostle Paul expressed the same confidence that after death he would be with Christ: "My desire is to depart and be with Christ, for that is far better" (Philippians 1:21-26). So it is clear that we also, if we believe, and it is our desire, we will be with Christ after we die. That is in heaven, where Jesus is (Acts 3:21), where God is (Matthew 23:9), and where the angels are. (Matthew 22:30). The body we now have is just a 'tent' and when we die we go home to be with God and his son Jesus Christ. (2 Corinthians 5:1-8)

Editor's Note: In the appendix to the New World Translation (NWT) (*one volume, green back edition of 1963*) published by the Watchtower Society, on page 3591, which is also repeated in their *Interlinear Translation of the Greek Scriptures* of 1969, there is a feeble attempt to try and explain why the NWT renders the Greek word 'analysai' as 'releasing' at Philippians 1:21-26, when all other reputable translations use the English word 'depart' in this Bible verse. They also comment that Paul was actually not referring to his own death as a human being and departing thus from this life, but was making reference to the event of Christ's return in his second presence in 1914 and the releasing and rising of all those dead in Christ (the 144,000) from the first century to be with him forevermore in heaven, which took place according to the Watchtower literature in 1919. However, the verse makes quite clear that Paul was facing the dilemma of two choices only, between life and death, with absolutely no reference to a third choice, as suggested by the writer of the NWT in making reference that Paul is suggesting a third thing and this thing is what he really desires. In the Appendix of the *NWT* it clearly states, "There is no question about his desire, for this thing is preferable, namely, the releasing (at some future time) for then it means he will be with Christ in heaven." This is why many criticize the NWT because the Watchtower Society blatantly translates certain verses to suit their own private interpretation of doctrine and teachings. To anyone possessing even a cursory knowledge of Greek grammar the translation, "but what I do desire is the releasing" (verse 23) signifies either a woeful ignorance of the rudiments of the language or a deliberate, calculated perversion of terminology for a purpose or purposes most questionable. – *Kingdom of the Cults*, p. 77, (1985)

In their literature the Watchtower Society clearly states the following. "As to the identification of the Paradise of which Jesus spoke, it is clearly not synonymous with the heavenly kingdom of Christ." They also state that, "likely the paradise familiar to the Jewish malefactor to whom Jesus spoke was the earthly paradise described in the first book of the Hebrew Scriptures, the paradise of Eden. His promise to the evildoer would therefore give assured hope of a resurrection of such an unrighteous one an opportunity to life again in that restored paradise (on earth)" (*Aid to Bible Understanding*, p. 1269) They also state in their publication, *The Greatest Man Who Ever Lived*, Section 125. "This promise (of paradise) will be filled when Jesus rules as King in heaven and resurrects this repentant evildoer to life on earth in the paradise that Armageddon survivors and their companions will have the privilege of cultivating."

The point made by Edward Dunlap when discussing this issue, was that Jesus was never going to return to earth again as a human, as claimed by some religions, so if the evildoer was being promised a future life as a human in an earthly paradise similar to the Garden of Eden yet to come, then he certainly would not be with Jesus, as Jesus was living in heaven as a spirit being and had no plans or need of returning to earth as a human ever again. Therefore, the words by Jesus, "you will be with me in paradise" are meaningless if related to the earth and can only mean one thing that paradise is actually heaven. One member of the team working with Edward and Raymond after reviewing this text and the word paradise made a point that he personally believed, along with Raymond Franz, the evildoer would be living in an earthly paradise after his resurrection from the dead, along with millions of other Armageddon survivors and resurrected ones, so he possibly could be with Jesus in paradise 'figuratively' speaking. But this is not what Jesus said, Jesus plainly stated, "you will be with me in Paradise," so it is pure conjecture on behalf of any Bible student to try and explain this in any other way.

This opinion was also presented by Raymond Franz: "The system of punctuation we are used to in the English language – which includes quotation marks, commas, semicolons, etc. – was not used in the Greek language that the Gospel of Luke was written and recorded. As a result, English translators of the Bible had to place punctuation into the Bible based on the context of the translation. While they have generally done an accurate job with this, their lack of understanding of the timing of the resurrections and their belief in non-biblical doctrines such as the immortality of the soul led them to incorrectly punctuate Luke 23:43. So what did Jesus mean? A common phrase of Jesus' day was the emphatic, "I say to you today," with which Jesus prefaced his statement that "you will be with me in Paradise." Raymond added "Christ wasn't saying, "You will be with me in Paradise today," but rather, "Today I'm telling you, you will be with me in Paradise." Also quoting from the Westcott and Hort transliteration of the Greek text that adds more confusion, it renders this verse, "And he said to him Amen to you I am saying today with me you will be in the paradise."

In addition, Edward Dunlap quoted and referred to the Weymouth New Testament that renders this verse as, "I tell you in solemn truth", replied Jesus, "that this very day you shall be with me in Paradise." The editor of this translation, Ernest Hampden-Cook added a footnote that reads "Since it is towards afternoon and the Jewish day ended at sunset the interval may have been one of only a few hours. Nay more, just as a heavenly ecstasy has come to many a martyr at the stake, in the very midst of the flames, so doubtless even while the Saviour was uttering the promise – a foretaste of Paradise came to the heart of this penitent robber."

> Editor's Note: The *Weymouth New Testament* (WNT), otherwise known as, *The New Testament in Modern Speech* or *The Modern Speech New Testament*, is a translation of the New Testament into nineteenth century English by Richard Francis Weymouth. It was based on the text of The Resultant Greek Testament. The text was produced by Weymouth. It was what resulted from his compilation of readings from Stephens (1550), Lachmann, Tregelles, Tischendorf, Lightfoot, Ellicott, Alford, Weiss, the Bâle edition (1880), Westcott and Hort, and the Revision Committee of London. Where these editions differed, Weymouth selected the reading favored by the majority of editors. The text was prepared for final publication by his secretary, Reverend Ernest Hampden-Cook, after Weymouth's death in 1902.

Based on an interview with one of the past members of the research team involved with writing *Aid to Bible Understanding*, released by the Watchtower Society in 1969, there was a heated debate between Raymond Franz and Edward Dunlap over the use of the word paradise in the Bible. The issue and argument was over the explanation behind the word 'paradise' mentioned in Luke 23:43. Raymond Franz argued and theorized that Jesus meant by his use of this word that he was referring to a future earthly paradise that Jesus would establish after the Battle of Armageddon, soon to take place, and the beginning of the 1,000 years of peace as promised in the book of Revelation.

On the other hand, Edward argued and hypothesized that Jesus was referring to a heavenly paradise that he and the evildoer would enjoy immediately after their death as humans and he pointed out that the word paradise is used three times in the New Testament (Greek Scriptures) at Luke 23:43; 2 Corinthians 12:4 and Revelation 2:7, and on each occasion implies a heavenly location. Of course, as we know today, Raymond Franz overruled Edward Dunlap and appeared to win the argument and explanation of the word 'paradise' as he understood it, and later explained in this publication, the Aid book, and being that of an earthly paradise. In this case, according to most knowledgeable students of the Bible, this diligent and very sincere Bible student Raymond Franz was incorrect in his opinion of what Jesus meant by the word paradise. This incorrect explanation has been carried forward in every piece of literature the Watchtower Society has ever published since this release of the Aid book, even though the majority of Christians, religions and Bible students believe that Jesus was referring to a heavenly paradise.

Of interest to our readers, we quote from the leaked, archived confidential notes of the debate between Raymond Franz that influenced his interpretation of this word paradise and the retort made by Edward Dunlap, to support his argument regarding paradise being heaven, as used by Jesus Christ in Luke 23:43. Remember these words and the intense discussion were between two of the most courageous Bible students who ever lived, but we also need to remind ourselves that they were both imperfect, were not inspired of God and prone to error, and they are both now categorized as apostates and both have been excommunicated by the 'Holier than Thou', Watchtower Society.

Even though he had been warned not to be influenced by any current Biblical interpretations that appeared in the Watchtower publications over the years, Raymond Franz had noted that in the original writings of Charles Russell in 1909 that Russell had tried to explain the word paradise. This was some years before the claimed prophetic date of 1914 when Russell forecast that Jesus Christ would return in his second coming. Russell had questioned the correctness of the word 'today' and also the word 'paradise' in this controversial statement by Jesus Christ and Russell had written in *The Watchtower* magazine of 1909:

> The thief asked the Lord a special request saying: 'Lord, remember me when thou cometh into thy Kingdom'. Our Lord has not come into His Kingdom yet, and hence the time when that thief wished to be remembered has not yet come. We are still praying 'Thy Kingdom come, etc.' The Lord answered the thief's request just as he requested. The word rendered "verily" (truly) means the same as "amen," meaning "so be it", 'I will remember you *when* I come into my Kingdom'.

Russell in his writings was obviously referring to the future year of 1914 when he personally believed that Christ would return invisibly for his second coming or presence to set up his Kingdom in October of that year 1914, and at that future time the thief (evildoer) would then be received into the Kingdom, heavenly paradise.

Edward Dunlap pointed out to Raymond: "Yes Ray, I agree with some of what you say, but remember that is what Russell sincerely believed at that time, of course he was wrong about 1914 being the date of Christ's return as we both know today, but he was partially correct in his interpretation, in that the evildoer was promised a life in paradise after his death and that was a heavenly paradise in the Kingdom of God." Of course, Raymond objected to this remark by Edward and remained stubbornly fixed in his viewpoint that paradise is the future earthly paradise after Armageddon. Raymond also put forward the same argument as Russell had done in 1909 and was obviously influenced by Russell's incorrect opinion, to quote Russell's words in the 1909 *Watchtower* magazine:

> When our Lord died he did not go to paradise but he went into the tomb. We read that God raised Christ from the dead, he was dead and rose from the dead on the third day, and he did not come back from paradise.

Russell also stated in this same article and took the liberty of adding three extra words:

> When he did rise from the dead, one of the Marys clasped Jesus by the feet, but he said to her, 'detain me not for I have

not yet ascended to my Father and to your father, and to my
God and your God. What our Lord did say, in effect was this, 'I
say unto you today, notwithstanding that I am hanging on the
cross and it looks as though I was a deceiver or criminal, etc.,
yet I say unto you today, <u>this dark day</u>, thou shalt be with me in
paradise." (Underlining is ours)

Edward Dunlap vehemently argued the point, according to the archived
notes, and he reminded Raymond of one of the most powerful lectures
that Edward ever gave while he was the main instructor at the Gilead
Missionary School, and these comments were confirmed by two friends
of the editor, one being the late Philip Rees, one time Branch Servant
of Australia, and the other being at this time unnamed, so as to avoid
embarrassment, as he still lives a sad and disappointed life in the London
Bethel of the Watchtower Society. He requested this anonymity as he
didn't want to be identified, as he is the source of sensitive information
used in our research and also material that he anonymously placed on
Wikipedia and he may subsequently be disfellowshipped if identified.
These two individuals, Philip Rees and our unnamed friend, had also
attended this special 10-month course two years before Raymond
had been a student, and both referred to their notes regarding this
outstanding lecture by Edward Dunlap. Raymond Franz along with
Lloyd Barry, who both later became members of the Governing Body
of the Watchtower Society were in the last class of 1964, being this
failed venture of a special 10-month Gilead course for Branch servants
and other special individuals to be prepared and trained to become
leaders in the soon to be expected new world or new system of things,
which of course the Watchtower Society is still waiting for 56 years
later, in this year of 2020.

The following comments on the remarks by Edward Dunlap may
appear to be very speculative to some of our readers as they relate to
the relationship between Jesus Christ and his heavenly father and it
is very difficult for us humans to envisage two spirit beings having a
conversation, but it does happen according to the Bible. Of course,
Edward had no first-hand knowledge of these events and was not
speaking under inspiration of the Holy Spirit, as some writers of the
Watchtower material often claimed, but he described these events based

on his deep knowledge of the scriptures as he felt this gave him some license to reflect on the scriptures he had intensely studied for most of his life, and Raymond was reminded and basically agreed with this fact.

Edward pointed out in his lecture that Jesus must have had access to the heavenly realm from the very moment he died as a perfect human, his life force having been transferred back to a spirit creature again immediately upon his death as a human, as pre-arranged with his father and was active as a spirit person from that time onwards. The first priority of Jesus was probably to immediately meet up with his much-loved Father once again to discuss matters of great importance, as Jesus had been in human form for 33 years and they had been separated and Jesus had been strictly limited in his face-to-face contact with his heavenly Father, they had totally depended on the power of prayer for communication, as we do today as humans. Both Jehovah and Jesus (now being the archangel Michael once again) would have so much to discuss now that the first major step had been successfully completed, that of the sacrifice of a perfect human life to redeem mankind from their inherited sin from the first man Adam.

> *Editor's Note*: According to the notes of Edward Dunlap he also points out the following. There are three occasions that the voice of God was actually heard by Jesus while he was on earth in human form, these were: Firstly, at the time of Jesus' baptism when God's voice declared, "You are my Son, the Beloved; with you I am well pleased." (Luke 3:22) Secondly, at the transfiguration of Jesus when a similar expression was heard but this time also by the apostles Peter, James and John, "This is my Son, my Chosen; listen to him!" (Luke 9:35) And thirdly, the event shortly before the last Passover shared by Jesus with his apostles when God responded to the request by Jesus that God glorify his name, and God replied, "A voice occurred from heaven, "I both gloried it and will glorify it again." (John 12: 28, 29)

The notes from Edward's thought provoking lecture continue: Now that this first step was complete they would have probably now discussed the next important step to take for the benefit of the now redeemed humankind, namely what to do about Satan and his demon followers, who were the real cause of the original downfall of mankind and who had meantime been placed under severe restriction as spirit creatures and restrained plus confined in an unknown location somewhere in the wide unseen Universe, but in some translations of the Bible identified as the abyss. Jesus under instructions from his father then would immediately undertake the next important step and he probably used these three days between his death as a human being and before his return as a spirit being, to the vicinity of the earth again, as he was required under instructions from his father to preach or make a proclamation to the spirits in prison, as recorded in 1 Peter 3:18-20. The Greek word translated proclaimed or preached means to publicly declare or to herald. If the spirits are demons, then Peter says that Jesus went to the Abyss and proclaimed his victory to the fallen angels imprisoned there. They had lost, and he and his Heavenly Father had won.

An additional comment received from a fellow Bible student made the following observation that supports the opinion of Edward Dunlap.

> The spirits in prison are mentioned in the context of what the resurrected Jesus did in the time between his death as a human, his life being resurrected into a spirit form and his later return to the vicinity of earth. First Peter 3:18-20 says, "He was put to death in the body but made alive in the Spirit. After being made alive, he went and made proclamation to the imprisoned spirits – to those who were disobedient long ago when God waited patiently in the days of Noah while the ark was being built." Note that Jesus' human body was now dead and awaiting a resurrection or removal, namely to prove to Jesus' disciples that Jesus Christ was still alive, but he was already spiritually alive, but unknown to his disciples, during the time that this decaying human body was lying in the grave for those three days.

Jesus Christ also had the pressing need to return to the vicinity of the earth to complete and finalize the establishing of the Christian congregation, once again as pre-arranged with his father, which would occur on the day of Pentecost of 33 AD. Edward Dunlap then read to the class the moving passage from the Act of the Apostles, Chapters One and Two, in which it describes this important meeting when the eleven faithful apostles and an additional, estimated 120 disciples who all received the gift of the Holy Spirit, which allowed them to speak in foreign tongues that enabled the Good News about Jesus Christ to be spread world-wide. Edward was such an emotive and dramatic speaker that it is reported that a large number of the all-male members of the student body had tears rolling down their cheeks as they intensively listened to these words spoken aloud by Edward Dunlap during his gripping and inspiring lecture.

Edward Dunlap also confirmed that along with most serious students of the Bible, the fact that the decaying human body of Jesus had simply disappeared from the tomb before the end of the third day. Ed then presented three possible reasons or explanations for this fact. Firstly, the foes and enemies of Jesus stole the body. If they did (and they never claimed to have done so), they surely would have produced the body to stop the successful spread of the Christian faith in the very city where the death of Jesus occurred. But they could not produce it. Secondly, Jesus' friends stole the body. This was an early rumor and recorded in Matthew 28:11-15. Is it probable or even possible that this bribe paid to the guards by the Jewish religious leaders to spread this rumor would succeed? Could these friends of Jesus have overcome the guards at the tomb? More important, would they have begun to preach with such authority that Jesus was raised, knowing that he was not? Would they have risked their lives and accepted beatings for something they knew was a fraud? Thirdly, that Jesus was not dead, but only unconscious when they laid him in the tomb and that he awoke, removed the stone, overcame the soldiers, and vanished from history after a few meetings with his disciples in which he convinced them he was resurrected from the dead. Even the foes of Jesus did not try this line. He was obviously dead; the Romans soldiers had made sure of that. The stone could not be moved by one man from within who had just been stabbed in the side by a spear and spent six hours nailed to a tree or stake.

According to our source, who was at one time a member of the writing department of the Watchtower Society, Edward then enthusiastically continued to enforce his sound research and resumed his argument and discussion with Raymond Franz. It was not Jesus, per se, who was lying in the tomb, it was simply a dead corpse that at one time used to contain the personage of Jesus when he was in human form, and now being simply a corpse and was in the process of returning to dust as all dead bodies do; returning to the elements of the earth. The Bible however reveals that the human body of Jesus had simply disappeared; also, most students of the Bible feel this was probably an act of Almighty God, as he alone knew the fickleness of man and their tendency to worship objects or people. God knew what his once chosen people, the Israelites had done when Moses was on the Mountain of Sinai received the ten commandments from him, the Israelites on the plains below could not wait for his return so they molded a Golden Calf to worship instead. (Exodus 32:4)

All that remained in the tomb that Sunday around 2000 years ago were some bandages, plus the garment, cloth or shroud that was used to wrap around the dead body or corpse that used to contain the personage of Jesus. Even this object, the linen cloth, later became an object of worship as today the Shroud of Turin, also called the Holy Shroud is a length of linen cloth bearing the negative image of a man. Some claim the image depicts Jesus of Nazareth and the fabric is the actual burial shroud in which he was wrapped after his execution, and is displayed in a prominent place in the Cathedral of Saint John the Baptist, Turin, Italy. It still remains even today as an important religious symbol for Christians around the world and an object of worship, but this is another story and beyond the scope of this report to analyze.

Returning to the debate between Edward Dunlap and Raymond Franz, Ray in turn pointed out that if this was the case that the dead body of Jesus had disappeared, possibly removed by God, then how was it that the eleven faithful apostles saw Jesus ascending to Heaven, forty days later. The logical answer that Edward gave, based on his extensive knowledge of the scriptures, was that this was simply an apparition or optical illusion to illustrate and convince these eleven faithful men that Jesus was already a spirit being and had been going backwards and forwards from the heavenly spirit realm (paradise) and had been doing so since his death forty days earlier and he was not literally on that day before Pentecost ascending to heaven for the first time. This miraculous event was simply an act of compassion on the part of Jesus to help his disciples to cope with the future, as they were being left alone on earth by their Lord and Master at a critical time and the promise that

Jesus had made that he was going to his Father to arrange for a helper (John 15:26-27) to come to their needs, namely the Holy Spirit, which in fact did occur ten days later at Pentecost. It appears that Raymond had to take a few days off in order to meditate over this very valid argument by Edward Dunlap before the writing committee came to a final conclusion.

As all sensible and reasonable Bible students concur, Raymond Franz and Edward Dunlap agreed to differ but Raymond, being the editor-in-chief of the Aid book, insisted his view of the word paradise in Luke 23:43 was made the official view and that became set in concrete for the future benefit of the Watchtower Society and their publications and teachings. Both of these courageous Bible students are now dead and buried, but we wonder on reflection if they were alive today on earth, if perhaps they might have changed their minds about this serious conflict of opinion.

So, once again, as we don't actually know what Jesus had in his mind when he spoke the words, 'you will be with me in paradise', during those last few minutes of his earthly life, so it is pure speculation for any Bible student today to assume his intent and meaning of the use of the word paradise? What we do know however is that Jesus during his last few minutes of life as a mortal human and was hanging there nailed to a stake or cross and enduring great pain and suffering inflicted by his fellow men, he knew that in the next few minutes he would be released from this excruciating pain and suffering on behalf of mankind as pre-arranged with his heavenly father. He knew also that immediately he died as a human being, which would be very soon; within hours on that same day in fact, he would be changed in a blink of an eye and that he who is mortal must put on immortality also as pre-arranged with his heavenly father before he came down to earth as a human sacrifice. Jesus already knew in his mind that he would be changed from a mortal human to an immortal spirit being, and would resume his divine role once again in the heavenly realm or kingdom. (1 Corinthians 15:1-58)

Edward Dunlap did not want to speculate what Jesus had in his mind while hanging there in great pain and suffering, but he could have been visualizing that very soon, probably within minutes and at least before

6pm on that Friday, 14 Nisan, 33 AD, that he would die as a human being but would immediately be restored again to his pre-human existence and glorious life as a spirit being. He knew that he would immediately be able to rejoin his beloved father Yahweh and resume sitting at his right hand again; he also knew that he would be resuming his role as Michael the Archangel and being reunited again with all of his friends in the angelic heavenly host. All of these very positive and up-building facts and details would probably be swirling around in the mind of Jesus Christ during those last few minutes on earth as he prepared for death as a mortal human. This could have been what Jesus meant when he used the word paradise, as the definition of paradise is the following; 'paradise is a place of exceptional happiness and delight, a place of contentment.' Knowing this fact, Jesus, who we must remember was a perfect man, could have been mentally and emotionally reacting to the thought of what he was about to experience before that day ended and what was about to occur in the next few minutes; meeting his father again, etc., and these thoughts flowing through his mind as being like paradise, a place of exceptional happiness and delight, a place of contentment. Based on this assumption, many students of the Bible feel confident that Jesus was correct when he assured the evildoer at his side that he would also be dead as a human that very same day, putting an end to his suffering and would be joining Jesus Christ as a resurrected spirit being in paradise, the heavenly realm or kingdom.

A fascinating report was submitted by one of our research team regarding this Bible text at Luke 23:43 and a little background to this report will be of interest to our readers. This controversial report was originally written in 1967 over 50 years ago, and some time before the Aid book was finally published that had been mainly written and edited by Raymond Franz and we have extracted some relevant details of this account for the edification of our readers. This written report was mailed and submitted to the Watchtower Society in 1967 for the attention of Raymond Franz, as it was already known from an inside contact that he was involved with this question, along with Edward Dunlap, related to the correct interpretation of the word paradise in this Bible text. This report and its contents were never utilized by the Watchtower Society or Raymond Franz for one of the following reasons. Firstly, it is possible that as the Watchtower Society receives hundreds of letters each day from concerned Christians, that this letter containing this important document was simple viewed as junk mail and disposed of without ever being opened or forwarded to Raymond Franz as requested.

Secondly, that Raymond did receive this report from this unknown Bible student, but was so distracted at the time to even open it or read its contents and perhaps just filed it away to read later. It was known that during the year of 1967, Raymond Franz was so stressed out with the results of his research while preparing the Aid book he was having sleepless nights, as he somehow had to find the courage and strength to present and inform the Governing Body with the results of his findings that he along with his fellow researchers had uncovered about the more serious discrepancies and errors of the many current doctrines and teachings of the organization. These serious issues involved their findings that the so-called gentile times or appointed times of the nations of 2,500 year from 607 BC to 1914 AD was a totally erroneous belief and that Jerusalem was only destroyed many years after 607 BC, and this of course now brought into question this absolute date of 1914, which had been a core teaching of this religion since it was founded back in 1879. As one leading member of the Governing Body had said, they would never, ever change that absolute date of 1914, so how would they react when they found out that 1914 has no significance in Bible prophecy. The issue of the current doctrine of the great crowd of other sheep and the anointed little flock classes was also now discovered from their intense research to be an error and false teaching, and they are not two separate classes of Christians as currently taught, and there was only one flock under Jesus Christ.

Raymond had to face the Governing Body with these discoveries and he knew these men personally, he also knew what their reaction would be to these vital necessary changes of doctrine, so it is no wonder that Ray was having sleepless nights and was so stressed out. So perhaps he can be forgiven for not reading this report sent to him that covered a seemingly less important issue of the interpretation of a single Bible text. What actually happened to this report we will never know and it probably ended up in the waste paper basket, but what we do know is that Raymond Franz as editor-in-chief, even after his being excommunicated from this religion, stuck to his private interpretation of Luke 23:43. An acquaintance of Raymond confirmed that he stubbornly and perversely stuck to his interpretation and never changed his mind for the rest of his life, being that when Jesus used the word paradise in Luke 23:43, he was referring to an earthly paradise sometime in the future, after the Battle of Armageddon and that Jesus was definitely not referring to that of a heavenly paradise.

We are fortunate today that our editor has in his possession an old copy of this controversial written report and with the approval of its author our readers will now be privy to its contents, as we have reviewed this report and we highlight the major relevant issues brought to the attention of the Watchtower Society and Raymond Franz back in 1967:

> These words at Luke 23:42, 43 were written by the disciple Luke and he was not an actual witness to these words of Jesus, they had been passed down to him by someone who was actually standing close to Jesus as he hung there on Golgotha. Luke only became a disciple some years after the death of Jesus and his Gospel was only written in about 56 AD while he was in Caesarea. Although Luke is nowhere named as the writer, most Bible scholars agree that from internal evidence of the book it strongly points to Luke as being the author. Luke also wrote the Acts of the Apostles in about 61 AD while he was in Rome with the Apostle Paul who was awaiting his appeal to Caesar. As Luke's gospel is the only one that mentions these profound words that record this brief conversation between Jesus and the evildoer while hanging there at Calvary, where did Luke obtain the details of this conversation that he recorded in his gospel under inspiration of the Holy Spirit, as he was not an eye witness? Who did Luke know who had been present when this conversation took place back on 14 Nisan, 33 AD? We find it strange that these final and important words of Jesus Christ, the very last words he ever spoke as a human being, are not confirmed and recorded in the other gospels as they are known as the synoptic gospels.

> One Bible critic even suggested that Luke invented these final words of Jesus to make his gospel more exciting, as after all, this critic claimed, the Bible shows that Luke was a clever well-educated man, far superior to his more simplistic associates and fellow believers, also a doctor to cap it all? The only ones

present as eye witnesses to the last few minutes of the life of Jesus Christ and possibly could have heard these final words of Jesus, were Jesus' mother Mary, his mother's sister, Mary the wife of Clophas (or Cleophas), and Mary Magdalene. The disciple who was also present is simply identified only as the disciple whom Jesus loved and this is generally accepted as being the Apostle John. So where in fact did Luke obtain this vital information regarding these final words of Jesus just before he died? It could have been from any one of these individual eye witnesses, if they were still alive when Luke wrote his gospel, or even from the notes of the Apostle James that he had recorded, as James was a very active, fiery and zealous follower of Jesus, and also the deceased older brother of the Apostle John who we know from the Bible was a witness to these final words. James was later beheaded in Jerusalem by King Herod Agrippa acting as Governor of Judea for the Roman Empire around the year 44 AD. This was because of the zeal of James for his Lord and Master, Jesus Christ and the Christian congregation. (Acts 12:1-2)

Continuing with the private written notes from our research partner and please remember these comments are only speculative as no one actual knows what Jesus fully meant by the words, today or paradise.

When the evildoer asked Jesus, please remember me when you come into your Kingdom, this man knew full well that this kingdom could not be a literal new kingdom or government to be established on earth at that time, as was feared by the non-Christian Roman authorities. This evildoer could plainly see that Jesus was soon to die and his human life was at an end, as was his own. This man was being executed because he was convicted as a thief and was paying the consequences of the Roman law at that time, which was an execution, a death penalty. He was tied by ropes to his cross while Jesus was actually nailed, by his hands and feet, because it was claimed he was being executed as a result of a greater crime, which was supposedly trying to overthrow the Roman government of the day. This evildoer, as he was now repentant of his criminal life had possibly listened in the past to some of the sermons of this man Jesus hanging at his side, and was now convinced that this man was really the Messiah, the son of God and was totally innocent of any charges against him. (Luke 23:41) He may also have been a witness to the many powerful miracles that Jesus had performed in the local area, even raising people from the dead, so he was fully aware of what Jesus could do under the power of the Holy Spirit. He could have heard Jesus plainly state at his trial before Pontius Pilate. "My kingdom is not from this world. If my kingdom were from this world, my followers would be fighting to keep me from being handed over to the Jews. But as it is, my kingdom is not from here." (John 18:36) This evildoer could easily read the small sign nailed above the head of Jesus being in three different languages, Hebrew, Latin and Greek (John 19:20) which read, "INRI" and stems from the Latin phrase, *Iesus Nazarenus Rex Iudaeorum* meaning 'Jesus of Nazareth, King of the Jews' and this could have possibly confused him.

***

If there is any portion in the whole of this book that we should remember, it is this one, as it embodies the very core of what it means to be a Christian and not be a slave to modern religion. Regarding the background and contents of the Bible text at Luke 23:43, we know very little about this unnamed man, who is simply described as the evildoer, and who was hanging there and slowly dying at the side of Jesus Christ. We don't know his parentage, his race, the color of his skin, if he was married and possibly had children, but the one thing we do know is that he was a repentant individual and sorry for all the wrongdoing he had committed to his fellow man and also breaking the laws laid down by Almighty God. Edward Dunlap during one of his last lectures at the Bible School of Gilead, under the theme Paradise, he succinctly paraphrased those final few seconds of conversation between this unnamed individual and Jesus Christ, being the very last words that Jesus spoke as a human on earth and based on Edward's deep knowledge of the scriptures everyone was paying very close and undivided attention.

These are the comments taken from the notes of Edward Dunlap, one of the most courageous Bible students who ever lived; comments he made without changing or misinterpreting the true meaning of this all-important Bible text.

When the repentant evildoer looked across at Jesus hanging
at his side that sad day, he knew instantly that in view of the
physical state of Jesus and his quickly deteriorating condition
that he was very close to death and only had a few minutes
of life remaining. He also knew that he himself would be
dead before the day was out, so he was motivated to ask Jesus
a direct question in view of their impending death. But he
still courageously and in good faith asked Jesus to remember
him when he came into his kingdom, not when he set up his
kingdom some time in the future, so the evildoer must have
understood this to mean a heavenly kingdom, especially from
what he had heard, and not a kingdom on earth as imagined
by the Roman government. In modern terminology the
conversation could have been as follows: Jesus knew that this
man was now a repentant individual and he was now a believer
in Jesus as being the Messiah and if he was given the chance, he
would from now on have lived a life as a dedicated and devout
Christian.

Jesus gave a straight forward answer to this unambiguous
request regarding Jesus soon re-entering or coming into his
heavenly kingdom once again, as Jesus must also have noted
that this evildoer was now truly repentant of his past life and
not just using meaningless hypocritical words. In effect Jesus
was saying after the request made by the evildoer, 'remember me
when you come into your kingdom', his reply was substantially,
don't worry my friend, of course I will remember you, I am
making this promise to you here and now, but please carefully
listen to me, as I make this true statement to you today, you will
be dead before the day ends, as I will, but don't be concerned,
keep your hope alive as I am, as you will be with me in paradise
before this day is completed, namely with me in my heavenly
kingdom that I share with my father. It is quite clear that the
use of the word 'kingdom' by the evildoer and the reply by Jesus
using the word 'paradise' are both referring to one and the same
location and subject at hand.

Editor's Note: We thank Edward Dunlap for his very clear
and insightful explanation of this important Bible text.
Edward Dunlap as we know passed away in the 1980s and
notwithstanding the travesty of a judicial hearing and the

malicious, false accusation by the Watchtower Society that he was an apostate (meaning to disclaim or abandon one's belief in God) we believe that Edward today is in paradise alongside Jesus Christ and the unnamed so-called evildoer.

The issue of Jesus being resurrected on the third day, namely the following Sunday, as recorded in the Bible, Jesus was already an immortal spirit being, having been so since the Friday evening, therefore when the disciples visited the tomb it was empty, the now dead human body left behind by Jesus Christ had simply been removed from the tomb and no record is made of what happened to that corpse. It did however by its disappearance prove to the disciples of Jesus that he had been resurrected and was now able to support them from his newly restored position in the heavenly realm.

In review of the extensive research undertaken and based on his notes, Edward Dunlap claimed to have clearly established the following:

- That when Jesus Christ died that Friday evening his life as a human ended and he was immediately transferred to that of a spirit, a heavenly creature once again.

- That the use of the word paradise in the Christian Greek scriptures always refers to the heavenly realm.

- That the evildoer at the side of Jesus also died that same day and his life was transferred to the heavenly realm that same day or soon thereafter.

- That to claim that this evildoer was to simply lie in the grave until a future time and he would then be resurrected along with millions of others of the human race, to live in a restored paradisiacal park-like earth similar to the Garden of Eden was incorrect.

As a point of interest, in the Mormon confusing theology, paradise also usually refers to the spirit world, the place where spirits dwell following death and awaiting the resurrection to a higher level. In that context, paradise is the spirit state of the righteous ones after their death. In contrast, the wicked and those who have not yet learned the gospel of Jesus Christ (or joined the Mormon Church) await the resurrection in a spirit prison. After the universal resurrection, all persons will be assigned to a particular kingdom, planet or degree of glory. This may also be termed paradise. The Mormon Church also believe that after the resurrection, all men and women – except the spirits that followed Lucifer and the sons of perdition – would be assigned one of three degrees of glory. Within the highest degree, the celestial kingdom, there are three further divisions, and those in the highest of these celestial divisions would become gods and goddesses through a process called exaltation or eternal progression. The doctrine of eternal progression was succinctly summarized by LDS Church leader and 5th President of the LDS movement, Lorenzo Snow (1814-1901): "As man now is, God once was: As God now is, man may be." In Mormonism, the concept of divinity centers around an idea of exaltation and eternal progression and mortals themselves may become gods and goddesses in the afterlife, be rulers of their own heavenly kingdoms, have spirit children, and increase in power and glory forever. Mormons also claim and understand according to their prophet that there is a Heavenly Mother, but not to be worshiped like the Heavenly Father.

This official document issued by the Mormon Church was uncovered by our researcher in Salt Lake City, under the title *Mother in Heaven* and issued in 2015.

> The Church of Jesus Christ of Latter-day Saints teaches that all human beings, male and female, are beloved spirit children of heavenly parents, a Heavenly Father and a Heavenly Mother. This understanding is rooted in scriptural and prophetic teachings about the nature of God, our relationship to Deity, and the godly potential of men and women. The doctrine of a Heavenly Mother is a cherished and distinctive belief among Latter-Day Saints. While there is no record of a formal revelation to Joseph Smith on this doctrine, some early Latter-day Saint women recalled that he personally taught them about a Mother in Heaven.

> The earliest published references to the doctrine appeared shortly after Joseph Smith's death in 1844, in documents written by his close associates. As with many other truths of the gospel, our present knowledge about a Mother in Heaven is limited. Nevertheless, we have been given sufficient knowledge to appreciate the sacredness of this doctrine and to comprehend

the divine pattern established for us as children of heavenly parents. Church leaders have affirmed the existence of a Mother in Heaven. In 1909, the First Presidency taught that all men and women are in the similitude of the universal Father and Mother, and are literally the sons and daughters of Deity. Susa Young Gates, a prominent leader in the Church, wrote in 1920 that Joseph Smith's visions and teachings revealed the truth that, the divine Mother, is side by side with the divine Father.

According to Joseph Smith's King Follett discourse,[32] God the Father once passed through mortality as Jesus did, but how, when, or where that took place is unclear. The prevailing view among Mormons is that God once lived on a planet with his own higher god. According to Mormon scripture, the Earth's creation was not *ex nihilo* (Latin phrase which means out of nothing) but organized from existing matter. The Earth is just one of many inhabited worlds, and there are many governing heavenly bodies, including the planet or star named Kolob, which is said to be nearest the throne of God. Kolob is a star or planet described in the fictitious Book of Abraham, but viewed as sacred text by the Latter-Day Saint movement. Several Latter-Day Saint denominations hold the Book of Abraham to have been translated from an Egyptian papyrus scroll by Joseph Smith, the founder of this religious movement.

Our readers will notice that the loyal members of the Mormon Church are very similar to the followers of the Watchtower Society and both religions demand complete, blind obedience and belief in whatever their religious leaders declare as being true and based on Holy Scripture, no matter how extreme and outrageous these interpretations appear. This is another clear sign of how a cult operates.

***

Returning to the account of Raymond Franz and Edward Dunlap,

---

[32] The King Follett discourse, or King Follett sermon, was an address delivered in Nauvoo, Illinois, by Joseph Smith, president and founder of the Church of Jesus Christ of Latter-Day Saints, on April 7, 1844, less than three months before he was murdered by a mob. It is so named after the funeral service of church official, Elder King Follett. This information is viewed by the Mormons as a divine revelation, exactly the same way as the followers of the Watchtower Society believes in their dogma.

they had both worked under the clear instructions of the combined Governing Body of the Watchtower Society that the material for this new Bible encyclopedia, the Aid book, was to be based purely on known established facts and accurate research, including outside, so-called worldly sources and not necessarily influenced by any current Biblical interpretations that appeared in the Watchtower publications over the years. This request by the Governing Body was untested at the time and little did they know what a can of worms they were opening and what the final outcome and consequences of this decision was to bring. It was later admitted by all concerned that it was impossible to not be influenced by the previous or current writings of the Watchtower Society, as all of these men involved in the research for this new publication had been unwittingly indoctrinated with the teachings of this religion for most of their lives and could not help but be influenced by previous teachings, as Raymond Franz clearly showed and demonstrated when he argued about Charles Russell's writings in the *Watchtower* of 1909 regarding paradise. Raymond also admitted this in Crisis of Conscience and stated unfortunately with a tinge of hypocrisy as he used the words, "not taking some previously held view." The full quote taken from Raymond's book, reads, "I began to appreciate more than ever before how vitally important context was in discerning the meaning of any part of Scripture, and that realization seemed to be true of others of the group who were working regularly on the Aid project. We also came to realize the need to let the Bible define its own terms rather than simply taking some previously held view or letting an English dictionary definition control."

The new understanding and so-called clarification of the terms, overseers and elders in the Bible was claimed to have been uncovered by Raymond Franz and his research team, and was quickly accepted and adopted as being new light or a revelation by the Governing Body and was immediately introduced and implemented in 1972, creating one of the most dramatic changes to the organizational structure of the Watchtower Society. This change of their interpretation of elders or overseers suited most of the members of the Governing Body and fitted into their already secret plans of how to change the structure of the Chairman and Presidency within the organization without creating too much of a reaction from the rank-and-file members. However, the many other more serious issues uncovered by this research team could not or would not be accepted at that time by the Governing Body for fear of the resulting devastating consequences that could cause many members abandoning their religion and created a sudden drop in donations.

> *Editor's Note*: Lyman Swingle confessed to his then Jehovah's Witness relative in Salt Lake City and conveyed to our reporter that the primary reason they (the Governing Body) were quick to accept this new light on the elder arrangement as they also saw the opportunity to change the internal structure of the Governing Body itself, the authority of the Chairman and to restrain the power of the Presidency. Lyman admitted that they had been looking for some time how to subdue Nathan Knorr, as the members were becoming more and more concerned about the narcissistic and arrogant manner of Nathan Knorr and his refusal to consult with other members of the Body over major decisions and this so-called new light appeared to be the perfect solution.

The other more serious subjects were shelved especially related to the 'gentile times' of 2,500 years starting in 607 BC and the so-called absolute date of 1914, the definition of two separate classes of Christians making up the organization, one being labeled anointed and the other being labeled the great crowd of other sheep, and particularly the meaning of the term 'this generation' used in Matthew 24:34. This research and the extensive notes had now being passed on to the Governing Body for their review as instructed. Most of these topics that Raymond Franz, Edward Dunlap and their team uncovered and revealed in their deep research were too extreme for the Governing Body to handle, so the Governing Body were forced to simply closet them away until they could decide how to deal with these major issues and the now obvious uncovered contradictions to their existing doctrines and teachings, as to implement those dramatic changes at that time would be catastrophic and threaten the very survival of this religion. Of course this pathetic group of religious leaders is still struggling with these very same issues even today, as they experience a stagnant growth of their sect, the shrinking funds, plus the growing dissatisfaction of their frustrated followers. Because of the two-group classification currently promoted by the Watchtower Society, there are two different rewards for the faithful, but who knows what new revelations will be released by the Watchtower Society in the coming years, that is if they survive as a religion that long, especially when this erroneous teaching of there being two classes of Christians that make up this religion has to be finally abandoned.

What the Governing Body did not realize at the time, was that these men assigned to undertake this requested research did not become apostates of their own volition as claimed, but they were unknowingly created and then labeled as so-called apostates by the Governing Body itself, as a direct result of their clear mandate to this team of Bible researchers, especially such men as Raymond Franz and Edward Dunlap who simply obeyed the organization, right or wrong, as they had been carefully taught over the years. This decision by the Governing Body to try and identify these men as being apostates was primarily to cover over their own embarrassment, as by this time they had deeply regretted their joint decision to initially launch this research project for the Aid book in the first place, which was primarily Nathan Knorr's idea and the rest of the members of the Governing Body later tried to pass all the blame onto him; poor Nathan Knorr became the fall guy. The Governing Body also inexcusably bears the blood guilt of having to later carry out the act of figuratively flogging and executing these two courageous men, Edward and Ray as a result of them simply obeying the direct instructions of their masters, the Governing Body itself. Yes indeed, without doubt, the Governing Body has blood on their hands.

Based on our research into the notes and audio recordings of both Edward Dunlap and Raymond Franz, plus interviews with some of the unnamed support team who worked in the New York Bethel, assigned by the Governing Body to assist Raymond Franz in preparing the new publication, *Aid to Bible Understanding*, there were clear indications that all were not in total agreement with the recommendations for the change in doctrines to eventually be placed before the Governing Body of the Watchtower Society. For example, what became a very serious issue was the definition of there being two classes of Christians, one being the immortal anointed heavenly class, including the Governing Body, who will all immediately go to heaven when they die, and the other group being a great crowd of other sheep with the only hope of everlasting life on earth sometime in the future. This division and conflict of opinion between Raymond and his support team did not prevent their overall agreement that what they had discovered so far is that the Watchtower Society was in fact promoting numerous false doctrines and many wrong interpretations of the Bible.

In *Crisis of Conscience*, Franz described his experiences at the world headquarters this way: "What I saw, heard and experienced during the next fifteen years had a great impact on me. Whether the reaction of the reader will coincide with mine, I have no way of knowing, but one thing is certain and that is that no one could understand what brought me to a crisis situation without knowing these developments. The proverb is apt: 'When anyone is replying to a matter before he hears it that is foolishness on his part and a humiliation'." (p. 20)

When Raymond Franz was invited to work in the Watchtower New York headquarters in 1965 he was assigned to the writing department. A few months later, Raymond was given the direct assignment by Nathan Knorr himself, the task of collaboratively writing the *Aid to Bible Understanding* – the first religious encyclopedia published by Jehovah's Witnesses. Franz wrote: "A few months after our arrival and after I had done some work in writing, President Knorr showed me into an office containing a table piled high with stacks of typed papers and asked me to undertake the development of a Bible dictionary. Others shared intermittently for varying periods but the five individuals mentioned carried the project through until the 1,696-page reference work, called *Aid to Bible Understanding*, which was completed five years later." – *Crisis of Conscience*, p. 21

Editor's Note: The five individuals mentioned were Lyman Swingle; now deceased but remained an inactive, confused member of the Governing Body despite his many unanswered questions. Edward Dunlap; disfellowshipped as an apostate and now deceased, Reinhard Lengtat; quietly withdrew from this religion in 1980, John Wischuk; currently still an active JW working as a 'helper' to the Governing Body and still hopes to make major changes from within the organization, plus of course the editor-in-chief Raymond Franz; disfellowshipped and now deceased. As Raymond learned the inner workings of the Governing Body, he became deeply concerned that the focus was more on preserving the image of the Organization rather than on sound Biblically based decisions.

We must remember that Raymond Franz (1922-2010) personally believed at that time, and had done so since the date of his baptism in 1939, despite the claim by Rutherford that the number 144,000 was already filled by 1935, Ray always claimed he was one of the so-called heavenly class and expected immediate life in heaven upon his death as a human, and for eternity to rule the universe with Jesus Christ as a sexless King and Priest. Based on a comment by a personal friend of Raymond Franz, Ray admitted that he publicly partook of the emblems, claiming he was one of the special anointed class, although being only 17 years of age, as he had been advised to do so by his manipulative, domineering father who was a zealous, ambitious member of the Watchtower Society, being baptized himself in 1913 and he also claimed to be one of the so-called anointed class and was also a personal friend of Charles Russell the founder of this religion.

In addition, Ray's father was also a personal friend of Joseph Rutherford and had extensive knowledge of the inner workings of the Watchtower Society. Ray's scheming father apparently had privately told him that if he wanted to get on and advance in the organization it would be to his advantage to claim he was of the anointed class, as that was the best and most successful way he could climb the ranks of the hierarchy and eventually get onto the Governing Body. Plus having an influential uncle on the inside would also be a definite advantage, as Uncle Freddy was hand in glove with President Rutherford and later Nathan Knorr. Ray privately admitted this personal experience to a couple of his friends who were fellow students in the 1944 Gilead School along with Raymond when he was only 22 years old. This was some years before he married his wife Cynthia Marie Badame of Italian background in 1959, when Ray was aged 37 and Cynthia was 13 years his junior. Cynthia had graduated from the 28th class of Gilead, a missionary school for Jehovah's Witnesses, in 1956 and she did not profess to be one of the so-called anointed class as did Raymond, but at this time it was not frowned upon as several members of the Governing Body had also done the same thing during the 1950s by getting married to much younger women and who were not members of the heavenly class (see pages 325-326). Cynthia's first assignment was in Puerto Rico and while a missionary, she met her future husband Raymond Franz in 1957. Raymond had graduated from the 3rd class of Gilead back in 1944 and had been in Puerto Rico since 1946 serving as the Branch servant, a very senior position for such a young man of 24. When Ray was directly asked this question during an interview about his being of the so-called anointed class of 144,000 and being influenced by his late father, he visibly squirmed and refused to answer, except to say it was a personal matter between him and the Lord.

> *Editor's Note*: Ray's father, Albert Franz, who was a very successful businessman in his own right and made substantial donations to this religion, clearly being a straight-forward unequivocal case of quid pro quo [you scratch my back and I'll scratch yours], plus he had the skill of using tactics to climb the hierarchy of this rapidly growing religion as he had already persuaded Joseph Rutherford to recruit his eccentric younger brother Frederick, who was baptized in 1914. From archived private letters, it appears Albert Franz informed Rutherford that his brother Fred would be useful in the writing department of the Watchtower Society as he had a flair for writing religious articles and he claimed Fred was deeply spiritual, plus he had studied fine arts at the University of Cincinnati while making plans to be a Presbyterian minister, but quit after two years when he joined the Bible student movement. As a result, Frederick entered the Watchtower Society's New York headquarters in 1920 at the personal invitation of Joseph Rutherford, he being no doubt influenced by Ray's father, the older brother of Frederick. By 1926 Frederick was head of the writing department and already ghost-writing Rutherford's books, commencing with the *Harp of God*. By 1945 Frederick was appointed as Vice-President of the Watchtower Society, replacing Hayden Covington and eventually replaced Nathan Knorr as Chairman of the Governing Body in 1976 and reaching the pinnacle of his career by being appointed President of the Watchtower Society in 1977 at the age of 84 and remained in that position until his death in 1992 at the age of 99 years.

According to one of our researchers based on his review of
this beautifully written book, Harp of God, it was published
in 1927 by the Watchtower Society, but blazoned with the
name of Joseph Rutherford as the author. In the introduction
it refers to the ten-string harp that David used in the Psalms;
that this would seem to picture how Jesus used the antitypical
harp along with his followers. "The ten springs of the harp
represent the ten basic doctrines and the divine plan. When
one understands these fundamental truths…it will bring joy to
his heart and fills his soul with sweet music. We will we now
consider each one of these ten fundamental truths, each one
represented by a sting of the harp."

This new book definitely had an intense spiritual content and it
is of interest to note, according to our researcher that these very
same almost identical words, plus some of the subject material
was used in a sermon given in 1913 by a Presbyterian Minister
when giving a lecture at the Columbia University. Was this a
clear sign of Freddy Franz using his skill as a ghost writer for
Rutherford or the start of using plagiarism in his writings, as
Freddy certainly did later in his Watchtower articles when he
plagiarized much of the material written by Herbert Armstrong
in his popular magazine, *The Plain Truth* (see pages 60 and 180-
184 of Chapter Three). There is no way that Rutherford wrote
this book despite the false claim of being the Author, as he was
one of the least spiritual individuals known to mankind, he was
simply a straight-forward money grabbing manipulator.

Raymond was also the beneficiary of his father's influence in
the Watchtower Society hierarchy, as Ray himself soon climbed
the ranks even though he was a very shy, reticent, withdrawn
young man, according to those who knew him, and by 1944
was a graduate of the Watchtower Bible School of Gilead and
received a senior appointment in the Caribbean. In 1965 he was
invited by Knorr to work in the New York headquarters and
appointed to be editor-in-chief of the new Bible encyclopedia
and by October of 1971 was invited to join the exclusive
Governing Body by Nathan Knorr. It was a known fact that this
advancement in the ranks of the hierarchy of the Watchtower
Society was as a direct result and influence of his late father
and his Uncle Freddy, and this privately troubled Raymond

apart from his internal struggle with some of the erroneous doctrines of a religion that he was supposed to be a leading figure. Raymond was also aware of accusations of nepotism by some jealous members in the headquarters, but Ray never publicly admitted that he knew of this insinuation except maybe once, privately, to a couple of his close friends, but he makes no reference in his two books, either intentionally or by forgetfulness, related to this incident. Neither does he mention in his books that his rapid advancement in this religion was perhaps due to his father and Uncle Freddy's influence. In 1964 Ray had met Edward Dunlap, a prolific Bible student and they were soon exchanging and comparing notes about some of the possible incorrect doctrines of the Watchtower Society, especially the 'appointed times of the nations' theory of 607 BC, plus the date 1914 AD, and the rest is history.

As further clarified in our Report No.7 related to Edward Dunlap (1904-1988?), Edward publicly professed and believed since his baptism in 1935 that he was a member of the earthly other sheep class, but suddenly in 1979 he changed his mind and then claimed he was one of the so-called little flock of 144,000 heavenly anointed class, although understanding at the same time, he candidly admitted, was a symbolic number only, which on the surface appears confusing to say the least. Whether Edward made this change of mind perhaps in the hope of being invited to join the Governing Body is unclear, as many others doing so had this clear ulterior motive, men such as Theo Jaracz (1925-2010) Philip Rees (1916-2000) and most of the current members of the Governing Body. We could not establish from the other members of this support team working on the *Aid* book, as to whether they claimed they were of the other sheep class or the anointed class, but most were excommunicated from the Watchtower religion in any event because of their remarks and opinions that they did not agree with many of the current policies and doctrines of the Governing Body based on their extensive research and resultant findings.

One fact we did establish, was that most of the individual researchers working on the *Aid* book project supported Edward Dunlap and his later private view and opinion that there is no such thing as a biblical doctrine of two classes of Christians today, especially in the light of his correct interpretation of the Bible text at Romans 8:12-17 and this claim of there being two classes of Christians was an entirely false and concocted teaching by the Watchtower Society inherited from the Rutherford days. Raymond Franz was still sitting on the fence and was not really sure of the correct interpretation of Romans 8:14, "For all who are led by the Spirit of God are children of God." Ray was also unsure about the explanation of the words of Jesus, "I have other sheep not of this fold" recorded in the gospel of John 10:16. Ray must have still believed there were two classes of Christians, the so-called other sheep and the anointed little flock, because when the *Aid* book was published, being editor-in-chief he worked under the instructions that this encyclopedia was to avoid details of religious doctrines and dogma if possible, but simply present facts and definitions of topics mentioned in the Bible.

The title page of the *Aid* book states "Containing historical, geographical, religious and social facts concerning Bible persons, peoples, places, plant and animal life, activities and so forth." In the foreword, pages 5 and 6, it also explains that over 250 researchers in more than 90 countries contributed to this work. At least ten of these contributors were personal friends of the editor of this book that you are currently reading; only one is still alive today, of the other nine men, eight quit this religion or were excommunicated and all nine are now deceased and almost forgotten.

The foreword of the *Aid* book goes on to state "The editors were not influenced solely by what is simply the presently "popular view" especially among religious commentators, especially since such popular views often fail to harmonize with the Bible account. Yet even such contrary views are not entirely ignored, and the reasons for rejecting them are often presented. This…is not intended to be a doctrinal commentary or an interpretive work. However, many words are employed in the Bible in both a literal and figurative sense. The figurative usage is often more important to understanding than the literal meaning, as in the prophetic symbolisms in the books of Daniel and Revelation."

In the light of this claim by this team of five editors, many readers asked if these men were perhaps unwittingly influenced by their personally held private views on certain topics covered in this helpful volume and the remarks made were perhaps clouded and prejudiced and this problem could not be avoided. With due respect, these five editors they did not claim that they were directly inspired by Holy Spirit as the 39 writers of the Holy Bible were, and that this volume was not an inspired work of God as is the Holy Bible, (2 Timothy 3:16) but simply an Aid to Bible Understanding. It has been noted however that at least three of these editors claimed they were of the so-called 'anointed class' of the 144,000-little flock of spirit begotten ones and their role in editing this book was in line with their 'calling'.

Therefore as a result of this explanation, in this Bible encyclopedia there is no category listed, 'Little Flock' or 'Other Sheep' but a single short reference is made on page 1484 under the heading, 'Sheep' and the prophetic and figurative use thereof: "That Jesus' sheep, both the 'little flock' and the 'other sheep' that follow his lead and are well cared for." By trying to connect these two isolated and unrelated Bible phrases and texts in this manner, Luke 12:32 and John 10:16, shows a clear attempt to try and relate them as an established irrefutable fact and Bible teaching, but in line with the instructions of the Governing Body the *Aid* book does not provide a doctrinal interpretations. No further attempt is made in the *Aid* book to explain the text, "I have other sheep not of this fold" and that the two groups referred to in John 10:16 are in fact the Jews and their Gentile companions back in the first century, both groups of mankind making up one flock as Christians under Jesus Christ as their shepherd. The word 'sheep' is used over 500 times in the Bible but only once is the term 'little flock' used and that is in Luke 12:32 in reference to the small group of Jewish Christian disciples of Jesus during his earthly ministry. This reference on page 1484 of the *Aid* book clearly indicates that the material used was in fact influenced by the current false doctrines of the Watchtower Society, despite their blatant denial.

Under the category 'Anointed' on page 83, it does make some reference to this group of anointed ones and includes some highly interpretive remarks, but does not use the actual number 144,000. However, on page 1404, under the topic 'Revelation to John' it insinuates that this could be an actual physical number and yet in this same vision of the

Apostle John he describes in symbolic terms and clearly portrays from the context of Revelation, Chapters 7 and 14 that this number is purely symbolic and not literal. In addition, the *Aid* book on page 855 under the subject 'Israel of God' clearly states that "Jesus revealed the number of this spiritual Israel of God to be 144,000, bought from among mankind." Again, surreptitiously implying in the opinion of the editors, it is a literal physical number, which is a unique religious doctrine that is primarily promoted by the Watchtower Society. The *Aid* book states on page 83:

> Like Jesus, his footstep followers who have been spirit begotten and anointed by Holy Spirit can be spoken of as anointed ones. (2 Corinthians 1: 21, 22) ... So Jesus was anointed directly by Jehovah and his congregation of spiritual brothers received their anointing as a body of people through Jesus Christ. (Acts 2:1-4, 32, 33) They have thereby received an appointment from God to be Kings with Jesus Christ in the heavens. (2 Corinthians 5:5; Ephesians 1:13, 14; 1 Peter 1:3, 4; Revelation 20:6)

This scripture at Luke 12:32 is one that is difficult to interpret, especially the term 'little flock' so this once again has resulted in several attempted explanations, the most bizarre and egregious one being by the Watchtower Society. They claim in their literature that the term 'little flock' that occurs only once in the Bible is a direct reference by Jesus to the group described as the 144,000 mentioned in the book of Revelation and claim that this number is a literal number, whereas all other Bible students know without doubt it is purely symbolic. The Watchtower Society claims that the 144,000 being a literal number is in fact a 'little flock' when compared to the millions of the members of their followers who are supposedly of the 'great crowd of other sheep'. Of course they cannot substantiate this claim and without any evidence to support this interpretation they expect their follows to accept this opinion without question. Without any scruples they then take these isolated Bible texts, Luke 12:32 and Revelation 14:1 and 7:4; combine the two terms or words and create a new so-called scriptural term or expression, for example, "the little flock of 144,000" and then blatantly use this phrase throughout their literature under the pretext it is a direct quote from the Bible, which of course it is not, but this is the way cults operate.

Many other students of the Bible claim that by the use of the term 'little flock' Jesus was using this expression simply as words of endearment and reassurance, and he was not making any specific reference to the size of this group of faithful Jewish disciples. Jesus was promising this small Jewish group of Christians that, if they followed his teachings, they would receive the reward of the heavenly Kingdom. He also reassured them that even if they sold all their belongings and joined him in the work of making disciples and converting more Jewish Christians, God would take care of them and the remainder of Luke Chapter 12 explains how this would be accomplished.

A third opinion is that Jesus could have perhaps been drawing attention to the size of this group or flock of Jewish disciples knowing that it was small (or little) at that time of his ministry. But Jesus knew it would be expanded to a much larger number with the help of his Jewish disciples and Christianity would eventually expand throughout the whole earth after Pentecost, when all nations (Gentiles) would be joining this original small group of Jewish Christians as further explained in John 10:16. The word 'little' in Ionic Greek (Ionic Greek was a sub-dialect of the Attic–Ionic or Eastern dialect group of Ancient Greek) or in the actual Ancient Greek language itself, μῑκκός (mīkkós) simply means small or insignificant but in a broader meaning can also refer to being unique, delicate or precious.

After his expulsion from the Watchtower Society, Raymond Franz wrote and published a second book in 1992 titled, *In Search of Christian Freedom.* This book does not provide many more details of the inner workings of the Watchtower Society as revealed in his first book, or his personal experiences while a member of the Governing Body but rather concentrates on the need for people who believe in and love the resurrected Christ, love God and treat others as they want to be treated themselves. He covers the basic core of Christianity, the central or most important part of living a life as a Christian and the need for accepting the Grace of Jesus. "And the Word became flesh and lived among us, and we have seen his glory, the glory as of a father's only son, full of grace and truth." ~ John 1:14

Raymond does not clarify in his second book if he was still personally convinced, averred or believed in there being two separate classes of Christians today. One of our fellow researchers tried several times to interview Raymond and ask him this direct question, if he still believed in these two separate classes of Christians promoted by the Watchtower Society; and if he accepted that the 144,000 was not a literal number but purely symbolic, but was unsuccessful in his attempts. Raymond passed away in 2010 and we still don't know if he ever changed his mind and eventually agreed with his fellow courageous Bible student Edward Dunlap.

> *Editor's Note*: In the vision recorded by the Apostle John, "The revelation of Jesus Christ, which God gave him to show his servants what must soon take place; he made it known by sending his angel to his servant John." In the Bible book of this Revelation, sent to John by Jesus through his angel messenger, numerology could certainly be in play for the usage of the number 144,000 in Chapter Seven and Fourteen. The number twelve is utilized to symbolize completeness, perfection, and God's power throughout the Bible, i.e. 12 tribes of Israel and 12 disciples of Jesus. The number twelve is found 187 times in the Bible, and makes a special appearance in Revelation, the number being used at least 22 times, showing the authority and perfection of God's kingdom. The use of the figure twelve is highlighted at Revelation 21:14 "And the wall of the city has twelve foundations, and on them are the twelve names of the twelve apostles of the Lamb." Revelation 21: 21, "The twelve gates are twelve pearls, each of the gates is a single pearl, and the street of the city is pure gold, transparent as glass." Revelation 22:2, "Through the middle of the street of the city, on either side of the river is the tree of life with its twelve kinds of fruit, producing its fruit each month; or the leaves of the tree are for the healing of the nations." Plus, at James 1:1, when writing to the Christian congregation, "James, a servant of God and of the Lord Jesus Christ, to the twelve tribes in the Dispersion." Reference in the Old Testament is also highlighted, "Take the finest flour and bake twelve loaves of bread … This bread is to be set out before the Lord regularly, Sabbath after Sabbath, on behalf of the Israelites, as a lasting covenant." (Leviticus 24:5-9) Also in the natural cycle of things, mankind has followed the lead of the Bible and our year is divided into 12 months that it takes the earth to circle the Sun.

In reference to the figure 144,000, twelve is multiplied by itself and then again by a thousand, indicating completeness and perfection to the ultimate degree. The figurative use of the whole number 1,000 is common in Old Testament usage and the word thousand, appears 521 times in the King James Version Bible. This number evokes a very long time according to most Bible passages. It is often used in scripture also to specify an indefinite quantity or number. For example, "May the Lord, the God of your ancestors, increase you a thousand times more and bless you, as he has promised you." (Deuteronomy 1:11) "Know therefore that the Lord your God is God, the faithful God who maintains covenant loyalty with those who love him and keep his commandments, to a thousand generations." (Deuteronomy 7:9) "For every wild animal of the forest is mine, the cattle on a thousand hills." (Psalm 50:10) "For a day in your courts is better than a thousand elsewhere." (Psalm 84:10) "He is mindful of his covenant forever, of the word that he commanded, for a thousand generations." (Psalm 105:8)

According to the notes of Edward Dunlap, he wrote, "So what do the scriptures reveal about the number 1,000? It is a number that typically signifies the idea of immensity, fullness of quantity or multitude. This number can represent a large number or extended period of time." In addition, this large symbolic group of Israelites, now likened to spiritual Israel in John's vision in the book of Revelation, would include such men as Abraham, Isaac, and Jacob, as confirmed in Matthew 8:11, which states, "And I say unto you, That many shall come from the east and west and shall sit down with Abraham, and Isaac, and Jacob, in the kingdom of heaven."

In his Commentary on the Bible, Adam Clarke (1762-1832) a brilliant student of the Bible, which took him 40 years to complete, he made the following observation that the book of Revelation is highly symbolic and not literal. In the use of the number of 144,000 are included all the Jews converted to Christianity; symbolically 12,000 out of each of the twelve tribes: but this must be only a certain for an uncertain number; for it is not to be supposed that just 12,000 were converted to Christianity out of each of the descendants of the twelve tribes. The Apostle John goes on to describe a great multitude and this appears to mean the Church of Christ among the Gentiles, for it was different from that collected from the twelve tribes; and it is here said to be of all nations, kindreds, people, and tongues, all clothed with white robes, being both symbolic and emblems of innocence and purity. They are described as having palms in their hands, in token of victory gained over the world, the devil, and the flesh. This observation of Adam Clarke is confirmed by the Apostle John in his gospel at Chapter 10, when he explains that Jesus had other sheep (the Gentiles) that were to join the already gathered Christian Jewish people, together making up one flock or group of Christians.

Edward Dunlap and Raymond Franz had carefully read the Bible Commentary by Adam Clarke, plus many others on a similar vein and all of them clearly made the point that this number of 144,000 was definitely symbolic in its meaning and not a literal number. However, Edward and Raymond had to contend with the fact that this theory of it being a literal number as promoted by the early Bible students under the direction of Charles Russell was the very core of the Watchtower doctrine and beliefs. They both realized to make a recommendation of such a dramatic change of this nature would have brought about serious repercussions, so they thought at the time is was more expedient to keep it under wraps for the time being and carry on with their other research. From our interviews with past members of this research team involved with the *Aid* book, Edward finally made up his mind that the 144,000 was definitely symbolic, but Raymond apparently was unsure. As already pointed out in Chapter Three of this book, the Watchtower Society is the only recognized leading religious sect that believes this number of 144,000 in the Bible is a literal number and is formulated as part of its official dogma. Based on our research, we have discovered that many intelligent members of this religion have privately questioned this doctrine and personally believe that it must be a symbolic number only, especially in the light of the context. This questioning even includes several current members of the confused Governing Body, plus a number of their so-called spirit-appointed 'helpers' but to openly and publicly express their private misgivings would be catastrophic to the very foundations and survival of this religious cult, plus of course their privileged positions.

Based on a review of this second book by Raymond Franz, In Search of Christian Freedom, we learn the following:

> Members of The Governing Body further claim that they are the last members in a chain of faithful and discrete slaves that have handed down their special status from generation to generation since the first century. All religious organizations have leaders and many of these leaders claim to have a special connection to God. The Watchtower Society claims its authority must be honored because its leaders have been chosen by Christ as his faithful and discreet slave class. The book explains how cult-like organizations can be identified and he is adamant that true Christians should read the Bible, independent of literature provided by external sources. Mr. Franz does not identify any religion as being the correct one. To him, true Christians are people who believe in and love the resurrected Christ, love God and treat others as they want to be treated themselves. As a result, In Search of Christian Freedom leaves many questions unanswered.
>
> Mr. Franz does not steer his readers into what he considers to be the true religion, because he finds fault with all of them. His honest and documented history of this period when he was a Jehovah's Witness is not only helpful in understanding the inner workings of this group, but it is a revealing study in what happens when absolute power corrupts the thinking of good people. However, he gives his readers outstanding information on how they can take responsibility for their own salvation by reading the scriptures, independent of conclusions reached by others. This narrative is an intelligently written analysis of Christianity and what it means to be free as a Christian and not a slave of a particular denomination.
>
> Before we leave this drama of the expulsion of Raymond Franz and Edward Dunlap from the Watchtower Society, one member of our research team who was determined to leave no stone unturned, interviewed a now deceased ex-member of the writing department of the Watchtower headquarters and he revealed details of a private conversation he had one evening with John Wischuk. Apparently, it was a tense but very revealing discussion over a few drinks they enjoyed together, and the subject of Raymond Franz, Edward Dunlap and

Lyman Swingle, plus their role in the *Aid* book project was covered. Remember that Wischuk was one of the team of five who worked on the *Aid* book project under Raymond Franz for over five years. Our informant was shocked to learn that Wischuk told him that Edward Dunlap had decided to start taking the bread and wine at the 1979 memorial to prove he was of the anointed class with the clear intension of being invited to join the Governing Body, as his two associates on the editorial committee, namely Raymond Franz and Lyman Swingle were already members and could perhaps pull a few strings. Between themselves they hoped that the three of them would have the clout to bring about the necessary changes to certain teachings of the Watchtower Society that were obviously incorrect, especially the date 1914 and the so-called 'appointed times of the nations' and bring about much needed major reforms regarding these teachings.

It appears that Albert Schroeder, who by this time in the late 1970s and early 1980s was the man holding the power in the hierarchy of the organization, Knorr having been sidelined in 1976, although officially Knorr was still the President and Freddy Franz his Vice-President was not interested in the workings of the Governing Body but was closeted in his private rooms supposedly having visions. Someone tipped Schroeder off regarding this plan by Raymond Franz, Lyman Swingle and Edward Dunlap using their influence on the Governing Body and their secret arrangement to try and change the 1914 doctrine. It was at this time that Schroeder gave his famous speech in 1977, including the words, "there was a campaign going on both inside the organization and from outside to have the Society's 607 BCE (before our Common Era)-1914 CE (Common Era) chronology and the understanding of the 'last generation' be overthrown. The Society, however, had no intention of ever, ever abandoning it." Schroeder's reaction to this scheme or campaign as he put it, by these three leading members of the organization was to immediately take steps to block this plan and to personally act against Raymond Franz that eventually resulted in him being forced to resign from the Governing Body in 1980 and leave the headquarters, and later in 1980 Schroeder had Edward Dunlap expelled as an apostate. Strange at it seems, no action was taken against Lyman Swingle who was in total agreement with the finding of Raymond

Franz and Edward Dunlap about 1914 and some of the other existing erroneous teachings of the Watchtower Society. Why? What was the basis for Lyman Swingle escaping the axe as he was just as guilty as Raymond and Edward in expressing his thoughts about these false teachings of the Watchtower Society uncovered in their research?

We must also remember that Lyman Swingle and Raymond Franz had both raised this possible error of the year 1914 some years earlier at one of the weekly meetings of the Governing Body. Lyman, who had already spent about 20 years and Raymond from 1965, were both working in the writing department in the early 1970s and from their research it appeared that Charles Russell, who was the original source of this date 1914, was probably mistaken, as much clearer and more reliable information had come to light in recent years.

Raymond Franz had just recently joined the Governing Body in 1971 and according to the recorded minutes during his first year he and Lyman Swingle put forward a resolution that a closer examination be made regarding the current teaching of the 'gentile times' and the accuracy of 1914. They claimed that based on current research it was quite probable the date 607 BC and the destruction of Jerusalem was not correct and was much later and this would then throw out the whole issue of 1914 AD being the invisible second return of Jesus Christ to earth. According to the report by Lyman they were quickly outvoted by the rest of members, and Knorr who was the Chairman, urged on by Schroeder and the rest of the Governing Body threw out this resolution requesting the re-examination of the date 1914. It was rejected not because it could possibly be right or wrong; that appeared to be of the least concern, despite the brief but very clear and powerful argument presented by Raymond Franz. The primary concern according to Lyman Swingle was that the majority of the Governing Body expressed the opinion that to make such a dramatic change to this core doctrine would be a dangerous step to take with disastrous financial consequences, as this could create a serious fall in the membership of the organization resulting in a severe drop in contributions and sale of the literature.

We do know that Raymond Franz after he was expelled from the Governing Body in 1980 that he was going to spill the beans sooner or later regarding his experiences and expose the inner workings of a group of men who had such ruthless power over the sincere humble followers of this religion. Everyone who was following his case, especially those who worked in the Watchtower headquarters expected a book to be eventually published as he would not be silenced by the attempted pay-off by means of the cash settlement offered by the Watchtower Society. Raymond although an introverted, quiet and reserved man, was an excellent writer and this was his forte, so he certainly did not disappoint his readers when his book was published in 1983 under the title, *Crisis of Conscience*. Schroeder and the Governing Body were not too concerned about Edward Dunlap as he was already showing signs of dementia and old age, plus his recurring illness, and probably would be harmless after his expulsion in 1980, but why did they not take any action against Lyman Swingle who was also intricately involved in this strategy to expose these erroneous teachings of the Watchtower Society, especially the 1914 doctrine?

From our research and based on discussions with the relatives of Lyman Swingle from Salt Lake City, Lyman had worked in the Watchtower headquarters for 71 years from 1930 and had been on the Governing Body since 1945, plus he had extensive knowledge of the inner workings and behind the scenes activity of this religion. Lyman had worked in the treasury for a number of years so he knew where the money was going, he knew of the debauched lifestyle of Joseph Rutherford and his corrupt dealings, he knew of the scandalous conduct of Hayden Covington and Nathan Knorr regarding their disgusting power struggle for the presidency back in 1942, he knew of the fraudulent activities of Freddy Franz and his plagiarizing of material for Rutherford's books and articles in the Watchtower magazine, he also knew of the homosexual activities of certain members of the Governing Body. Last but not least, he alone knew the full truth as to whether he was the father of two illegitimate daughters and that the Governing Body at the time decided to help him cover over this fact to avoid a major scandal. In fact, he had more knowledge and information that could harm or destroy the reputation of this religion than Raymond Franz and Edward Dunlap combined, so if Lyman Swingle ever publicly revealed these facts he would be the real enemy of the organization. But Schroeder and the Governing Body did absolutely nothing. They obviously knew the truth of the saying, "keep your friends close but your enemies closer," so they adopted this strategy and expediently decided to allow Lyman to remain a member of the Governing Body, but in a very low-key capacity with no official duties.

In order to buy his silence, they allocated Lyman Swingle a luxury suite with full room service in the New York headquarters and provided him with two full-time nurses to help him care for his very sick wife. The only conditions were that he would not speak out publicly or privately about his experiences with Raymond Franz and Edward Dunlap, and secondly, he was to create the image of loyalty to the organization and attend the weekly meetings of the Governing Body so that they could meet the legal requirements of having his name recorded in the official minutes. Lyman faithfully carried out and complied with the terms of his agreement with the Governing Body even though during the final few months of his life he was in a wheelchair and under heavy sedation, and he could neither speak or hear what was discussed when he attended this weekly meeting. This is another clear example of the hypocrisy of this religion, they are only concerned about their image and prestige; truth and honesty have very little significance in their modus operandi, functions or decisions.

This was the lifestyle of Lyman Swingle from the 1980s onward and he had to carry this depressing knowledge and burden in his mind and heart for the rest of his life and at the same time remain silent about what he knew regarding this religion and live the life of a hypocrite, as he had personally agreed with the Governing Body. This continued until he had a complete mental and emotional breakdown, primarily as a result of the death of his wife in 1998, plus no doubt also having to carry this knowledge of his experiences in this religion for so many years until his own death on 14 March, 2001. Perhaps the experience and life of poor Lyman Swingle may prove to be a reminder to us today that if we allow ourselves to be enchained like a slave to a religious cult and we do not break free, then the price we will eventually pay is almost unimaginable.

We tried to secure an answer from John Wischuk, who is still active in the Watchtower headquarters, as we believed he was more open minded than most officials of the Watchtower Society and he had worked closely with these three men for over five years as part of the *Aid* book project. We simply wanted him to either confirm or deny this claim that he divulged this confidential information regarding the motives of these three men especially Edward Dunlap, but he refused our frequent requests for an interview.

Special Report No. 7: Edward Dunlap

This account and report regarding the traumatic experiences of Edward Dunlap is adapted from the two-hour long audio tape recordings by Edward Dunlap made after he was excommunicated for apostasy, in which he reviews his life and experiences with the Watchtower Society. Although we must confess these audio tapes are sometimes difficult to follow, primarily because of the advanced age of Edward they appear to be somewhat confusing in certain sections. We have also used authentic material from the book, *Crisis of Conscience*, written by the late Raymond Franz, which is described as the story of the struggle between loyalty to God and loyalty to one's religion, information that is now in the public domain. However, we thank the publishers and copyright owners of this book by Raymond Franz for their permission to quote and use some of this material for the sole purpose of revealing the inner workings of the Watchtower Society. In addition, we thank David Henke who adapted this account by Raymond Franz into his articles, portions of which are quoted below in English, including some of his personal observations on the life of Edward Dunlap and his final years as a member of Jehovah's Witnesses. David Henke founded the Watchman Fellowship in Columbus, Georgia in 1979, focusing on new religious movements, cults, the occult and the New Age. The copyright of the book, Crisis of Conscience was inherited by Cynthia, the widow of Raymond Franz, after his untimely death on June 2nd, 2010. She in turn transferred the copyright to her close personal friend of many years, Deborah Dykstra and today is jointly owned by Deborah and the publishers Commentary Press, who all gave their verbal permission to quote some details from this excellent and highly recommended book by Raymond Franz, one of the most courageous students of the Bible who ever lived.

According to Dr. Joseph F. Zygmunt, Associate Professor, Department of Sociology, University of Connecticut, after reading this book by Raymond Franz made the following comments.

This is a candid and uniquely informative view of the authority structure and inner workings of the religious organization known as Jehovah's Witnesses. This is also a poignant personal document, reaffirming the value of 'freedom of conscience' and inviting renewed attention to the classic problem of how this value is to be kept alive in the face of the perennial resurgence of bureaucratic and authoritarian structures.

Raymond Franz also stated in his introduction to *Crisis of Conscience*:

> What this book contains is written out of a sense of obligation to people whom I sincerely love. In all good conscience I can say that its aim is to help and not to hurt. If some of what is presented is painful to read, it was also painful to write. It is hoped that the reader will recognize that the search for truth need never be destructive of faith, that every effort to know and uphold truth will, instead, strengthen the basis for true faith.

The following special report consists of extracts and material from all three sources; audio recordings by Edward Dunlap; the book by Raymond Franz, and also the articles by David Henke. In addition, we have used extracts from the booklet written by the late Jon Mitchell, Where is the Great Crowd Serving God? Jon Mitchell was a former secretary to the Governing Body and is an account of Jon's observations and his personal research from 1980 to 1981 while serving at Brooklyn Bethel in New York. We have made this material available in this special report in our efforts to advance the understanding of the issues of educational, environmental and humanitarian significance. We believe this constitutes fair use of any such material as provided under Section 107 of the US *Copyright Law* of 1976.

> Edward Alexander Dunlap was the registrar and instructor of the only school of Jehovah's Witnesses for missionaries, the Watchtower Bible School of Gilead, and also one of the main contributors to the Bible dictionary of the organization, Aid to Bible Understanding, released in 1969. He was also the writer of the only biblical commentary of the Watchtower Society, named, Commentary on the Letter of James, released in 1979. He expressed having some difference of opinion on some points of doctrinal character in private conversations with his friends of many years. In the spring of 1980 a committee of five

men, none of them a member of the Governing Body of the organization, met with him in secret session for several hours, questioning him about his views on certain biblical issues. After more than forty years of association and having contributed to the writing of numerous articles in the Watchtower magazine as well as several books, Dunlap was eventually fired from his job and from his home at the international headquarters of Jehovah's Witnesses in New York and expelled from the organization.

The traumatic events that were experienced by this man Edward Dunlap are almost unbelievable if they were not true, but are now accurately recorded for posterity. He experienced such emotionally disturbing incidents in his life that were inflicted by the ruthless Governing Body of this religion, who acting as a tightly-knit group, that could only have come from the minds of individuals who were fiendish and wicked plus displayed a mephistophelian contempt and they flouted the very principles of true Christianity. What these so-called shepherds did to this man in the name of the Lord is inexcusable in any circumstances. They also vilified the good name of Edward, and tried to destroy his reputation as a courageous, honest student of the Bible and his good standing as a loyal Christian and follower of his master Jesus Christ.

One eyewitness to this dreadful account of Edward being excommunicated wrote this message to one of our fellow researchers and illustrates the dramatic, emotional trauma created when a loved one is disfellowshipped from this religion. "I vividly remember the day Edward Dunlap was going to be disfellowshipped (or at least announced as such). I was at my table in the dining room at the New York Bethel. I was literally shaking, and as a table head that was unnerving to me. I wondered if anyone else knew what I felt. My heart was pounding like a drum. My pulse could be seen in my arm. I was so paranoid I thought I was going to pass out. I looked around, but everyone was preoccupied with the announcement. I don't even remember who the jackass Governing Body member was who read out the announcement. People were weeping, it was surreal. Never before in five years of Bethel service had I seen this. Tom Cabeen, [who was later also disfellowshipped for apostasy in 1982 but passed away in 2020. You can read his life story on this website at TowerWatch.com] had told me the night before that they were going to read off his disfellowshipping letter. So I knew it would be big. After that it was really hard for me to go to breakfast, as I couldn't eat. What was fun and clever, being Martin Luther at the Wittenberg Cathedral door, was suddenly real life, and I witnessed people were being destroyed and killed."

A fellow worker of Edward Dunlap said, "Nathan Knorr totally ignored the medical needs of Edward, consigning him to labor in the factory as punishment for being ill." It should be noted that the editor and several members of our research team knew some of these men on a personal level who were part of the Governing Body in the 1950s to the 1970s, and all agreed in recognizing that when acting as individuals they mainly portrayed an image of being humble, sincere, genuine and compassionate Christians, even though often misguided. But as soon as they came together and acted as a group they changed their decorum or propriety and appeared to have been mentally possessed and taken over by some unseen force of personality and acted in a pernicious or deleterious manner, to their detriment.

A somewhat amusing experience, and it would be laughable if it were not so serious, was related by our reporter, which he had read in the book by Raymond Franz. A long standing member of the Governing Body, Thomas Sullivan (1888-1974) would often fall asleep during the important weekly meeting of the Governing Body, and when it came time to render his vote on a serious issue, sometimes very serious issues related to life pertaining matters and decisions that would affect and influence the personal lives of millions of followers of this religion. Sullivan's fellow member on the Governing Body, (Milton Henschel, it is reported) would nudge him and waken him up and whisper to this half-asleep man and get his, "yes, vote for Knorr", and thus making the decision unanimous, which was the ruling in those days, then this man Bud Sullivan, now in his eighties would simply fall asleep again until the end of the meeting. To reassure our readers that Raymond Franz was not exaggerating this story in order to make mockery of the Governing Body in some sort of retaliation for being excommunicated, as suggested by one of our readers, this identical account was also reported by Lyman Swingle, also a member of the Governing Body, and he confidentially but unethically reported a similar account to his relative in Salt Lake City some years earlier.

From the time that the reference book *Aid to Bible Understanding* was finally completed by the Watchtower Society, Raymond Franz had developed a close association with Edward Dunlap as they both had scrupulously worked on the intensive research involved preparing this excellent Bible encyclopedia in their quest for truth, along with additional assistance from other members of the Writing Department. Raymond continues his story:

> I met him (Edward Dunlap) in 1964 while I was attending a ten-month course at the Gilead School. At that time he was the registrar of the school and one of the four instructors. Our class (the 39th) consisted of about a hundred people, mostly men from the overseas branches of the Watchtower Society. It can be affirmed with truth that most of them considered Dunlap's classes by far the most instructive in what had to do with acquiring understanding of the Scriptures. Lloyd Barry who later became a member of the Governing Body was also in this class and made similar comments on more than one occasion. I doubt that any student of Ed has ever doubted his love and deep knowledge from the Scriptures. Originally from Oklahoma, somewhat shabby looking, and despite an ordinary education, Ed had the ability to take very difficult and complex topics and put them in simple form and language, whether the subject of the functions of the Mosaic Law or scientific study of genetics. However, the most important thing for me was the lack of pretension. Apart from his preference for brightly colored ties, he was basically - in size, speech and behavior - a simple person, without ostentation. No matter what responsibility was assigned to him, he remained the same.

> He had always been completely dedicated to the organization; the record of his full-time service matched mine in length. Another circumstance that says something about him is related to a condition that developed in the late 1960s. Commonly called tic douloureux (French term meaning painful spasm), the medical term for this is trigeminal neuralgia, which is inflammation of a large facial nerve, the trigeminal branch is

in three parts, and is capable of producing some of the most painful humanly known diseases. The stinging and blinding pain can be caused by anything, a gentle breeze, the touch that excites the nerve, and as the disease worsens, the victim becomes increasingly difficult to do normal things such as combing ones hair, brushing teeth, or even eating, without risking an attack. Some thus afflicted go so far as to commit suicide. Ed suffered with this for at least seven years.

During that time, the president, Nathan Knorr, for some reason took the opinion (perhaps based on comments from others) that this was something emotional on Ed's part and not a genuine physical problem. One day he talked with Ed about his ailment, inquiring about his married life and other related matters. Ed assured him that one had nothing to do with the other, which he could be enjoying a good day's vacation and an attack would come on without warning. The president, however, gave no weight to Ed's explanation and informed him that he had decided to send him to the factory for some time to get some exercise. He was then assigned to go and work in the bookbinding department. Ed, then in the late sixties, had been for some time taking potent medications – prescribed by the doctor in the central offices to suppress these painful attacks, and sometimes had been in bed for days and even for a whole week, with his ailment. But now he was sent to the bookbinding department and assigned to supply a machine in the binding line. He did it for months and took great pains to carry out this theocratic assignment as well as possible. But as he told me confidentially, this experience made him realize for the first time of the absolute control that the organization exercised over one's life. His attempts to explain were overlooked and against all good sense, he was placed in this situation that was totally undesirable for someone who suffered from such an ailment. He did not expect any apology from the organization for this serious error of the organization in the infliction of his trial, nor for the way they had considered and handled his distressing problem, and none was offered.

Since our workplaces, both during the Ayuda Project (a UNO project for the hungry and displaced residents in the World) and thereafter, were very close to each other, we talked often, sharing interesting points that we found during our investigations. The Drafting Committee of the Governing Body assigned us to work together on a number of projects, such as the Commentary on the Charter of Santiago (published by the United Nations regarding human rights). In our conversations we did not always agree on all points, but it did not affect our friendship or mutual respect. I mention all this because Edward Dunlap was one of the few people who knew how deep my concerns were in relation to what I saw in the organization, and in particular, what I saw in the Governing Body. He shared such concern. Like me, he came to feel that way because he could not harmonize much of what he saw, heard and read with the Scriptures. Although he was associated with the organization since the early 1930s, during much of that association he did not consider himself as part of the anointed ones. I talked to him about it one day in the late 1970s and he told me that when he began to associate with the Watchtower Society, he pointed out that there were two classes that would inherit the heavenly life: the elect (composed of the 144,000) and the great crowd or great company of Revelation chapter seven. The great company was said to be Christian but of a lesser faith than that of the elect and therefore, though equally destined for heavenly life, the great company would not be among those who would rule with Christ as kings and priests.

Since Edward Dunlap had been taught by the Watchtower Society that of these two classes, one was superior and the other inferior, Edward typically assumed, being a very modest and humble man that he belonged to the lower class, the great company or great crowd of other sheep, as he had been baptized around that very confusing time when the number claiming to be the elect, the remnant of 144,000, the little flock, was now being exceeded by the increasing numbers joining Jehovah's Witnesses. This same issue was also demonstrated by Hayden Covington and Milton Henschel, both of them when they were baptized around 1935 and accepted they could only be members of the great crowd of other sheep. Both of these men eventually became members of the Governing Body and their story is referred to in this book, Chapter Three. It came about in 1935 that Joseph Rutherford, at the Washington D.C. assembly, announced the newly revealed truth (supposedly coming directly from God by means of his Holy Spirit) that those of the great company were biblically living today, not in heaven, but on earth.

Edward had said openly that he had always harbored the hope of heavenly life, and he felt that there could be nothing more wonderful than serving in the presence of God and in the company of his son Jesus Christ. But because of the announced change in the organization's position and change in the interpretation of Revelation 7:9, he cushioned those hopes and accepted what he was told of his hope, as part of the great crowd of Revelation 7:9. It was not until 1979 that he came to the personal decision that no human organization could change the invitation found in the Scriptures, in effect setting a date for a change in the hope presented in the Bible itself as open to any person embracing such hope. So, forty-five years after 1935, being the year that Rutherford announced this new interpretation of Revelation 7:9, Edward began to participate in sharing the emblems, the bread and wine, in the annual Lord's Supper (Memorial Celebration), something that only the anointed class from among the Jehovah's Witnesses is permitted to do.

Edward Dunlap also believed that Chapter 8 of the letter to the Romans was not about two classes of Christians divided by their hope, one heavenly and the other earthly, as claimed by the Watchtower Society, but that it deals with two kinds of people: those guided by the spirit of God and those ruled by sinful flesh. The contrast that the Apostle Paul presents is not between life in heaven or life on earth, but between life and death itself, between friendship with God, or at enmity with Him. As Ed noted, the apostle did not say to just some, but ALL who are led by the spirit of God are his children (verse 14). Referring back to the words of Raymond Franz in his book, "suffice it to say that Edward Dunlap shared with me the same basic concerns, particularly those related to dogmatism and the authoritarian spirit that was manifesting itself by the Governing Body. His point of view, like mine, was that human authority, when taken beyond its proper limits, inevitably ends up taking away the merit of Christ Jesus as head of the Christian congregation."

Quoting once more from the book by Raymond Franz, we read:

> Four weeks after I started my period of absence, while I was
> still in Alabama, I received a phone call from Ed Dunlap. After
> a general conversation he told me that two members of the
> Governing Body, Lloyd Barry and Jack Barr, had come to his
> office and questioned him for three hours about his personal
> beliefs. At one point Ed asked them, "What is the purpose of
> this judicial interrogation?" They assured him that this was not
> the case, but simply wanted to know how he felt about some
> issues. They did not give him any explanation about what had
> motivated his interrogation. Although they pretended to make
> people believe that the discussion was only of an informative
> nature, for Ed this gave clear indications of the principle of an
> action on the part of the organization that would prove to be
> inquisitorial and punitive. The questions asked were about the
> point of view regarding the organization, about the teachings
> regarding the year 1914, the two classes of Christians, the
> heavenly hope, and similar points. Regarding the organization,
> he told his interrogators that his biggest concern was the lack of
> Bible study on the part of the members of the Governing Body;
> that he felt that it was the obligation of the brothers to consider
> the study and research of the Scriptures as their first priority,
> instead of allowing the concern for office work and other
> matters to lead them away from Bible study. I saw Ed Dunlap
> standing in front of one of the buildings in the headquarters.
> He had to meet that day with one of the judicial committees.
> Ed was then sixty-nine year's old.
>
> The previous year, in 1979, he had commented that he was
> seriously considering leaving central offices. He knew that he
> had been the target of attacks, both in the weekly sessions of
> the Governing Body, and also outside of these. On one occasion
> he asked the Drafting Committee (of the Governing Body)
> to relieve him of the harassment being experienced. When at
> the end of 1979 I informed Ed of our thoughts about leaving,
> he said that he had weighed the idea but had come to the
> conclusion that such a step was not possible. Considering his
> advanced age and economic situation, it was difficult to see
> how he and his wife could reasonably maintain themselves. By
> staying, they would have at least a place to live, with food and

medical attention. So he had decided to stay and added, "If they bother me a lot in the Editorial Department, I'll ask them to transfer me to the carpentry shop or any other job."

Less than a year later he was summoned to a hearing with a judicial committee. The day I saw him he said, "I'm going to be very frank with them, it's against my nature to be evasive." He added that he had very little doubt as to what the committee would do. After the initial visit of Lloyd Barry and Jack Barr with him, for almost six weeks none of the members of the Governing Body went to Edward Dunlap to discuss the matter, to reason with him or to discuss the Word of God with this man who had been associated for almost half a century, he had spent some forty years in the service to the organization, who professed the heavenly hope, and who was now about seventy years of age. They themselves are witnesses that this is true. How different from the pastor (the shepherd) who leaves the ninety-nine to go in search and to help the one lost sheep. The Judicial Committee was tasked with judging Ed Dunlap, this five-man committee was selected from the headquarters staff. The Governing Body remained in the background. All the five men assigned were younger than Ed; none (at that time) professed to be of the anointed ones.

After deliberating for a single day they came to their decision. Quite typical of the attitudes shown are the following expressions: When asked about his point of view regarding the organizational teaching of two classes of Christians, Ed pointed out the words of Romans 8:14, which say: "ALL who are led by the spirit of God" are children of God. Fred Rusk, who also had served as an instructor at the Watchtower School of Gilead School for several years while Ed was the Registrar said, "Oh, Ed, that's just your interpretation of the passage." Ed asked, "So, how else can you explain it?" Fred Rusk's reply was, "Look, Ed, it's you who's being judged, not me."

As extracted from the audio tape by Edward Dunlap, when he was asked about the rules of the organization, he emphasized that the Christian is not under rules or laws, Mosaic or modern day, but under the undeserved kindness (or grace) of Jesus Christ. He added that faith and love were superior forces in regard to justice than the rules could ever be. Robert

Wallen, who was a member of this Judicial Committee said, "But Ed, I like to have someone tell me what I have to do." Ed replied, "Robert, you should be bearing in mind the words of Hebrews 5:13, 14, that says Christians should not be like babies but be as mature people, who by means of use have their perceptive faculties trained to distinguish both right and wrong." Ed also added to his remarks, "Then you have to read your Bible more." Robert Wallen smiled and said, "Me and two million others." Ed replied, "The fact that they do not do it does not excuse you from doing it." Edward Dunlap emphasized that this was the biggest problem, the brothers simply did not study the Bible; they depended on the Watchtower publications; their consciences were not genuinely biblically trained. The judicial committee wanted to know if he would speak in the future about these points with other people. Edward replied that he had no intention of campaigning among the brothers. But he also said that if some people came privately to him, asking for help, he would, because he would feel the obligation to help them. Surely this was the determining factor. Such freedom for the discussion and private biblical expression was not acceptable, but seen as heretical, as a dangerous attempt against the order of the organization.

One of the statements presented by these so-called spiritually qualified men on this judicial committee seemed particularly paradoxical. Ed had told them clearly that he had no desire to be expelled, that he enjoyed the company of the brothers and did not contemplate or desire to be separated from them. The committee encouraged him to put his trust in the organization and have patience, saying, "Who knows? Maybe in five years many or all of the things you're saying will be published and (openly) taught." These men already knew the fluctuating nature of the teachings of the Watchtower Society and knew about the many serious issues that Raymond Franz and Edward had put forward to the Governing Body based on their research for the Aid book, but had been shelved for fear of the consequences of radically changed doctrines and beliefs, so without a doubt this was what also motivated them to express themselves like they did. But, according to this statement, how far did their conviction come from the correctness of these teachings and their solid biblical basis? If they were willing to accept the possibility that the teachings of the organization on these points in question were subject to change and not more solid and lasting than what was said, how was it possible then for them to use these same teachings to determine if this man Edward Dunlap was a loyal servant of God or an apostate?

If they considered that such teachings were so subject to change to the extent that it would be worth waiting and seeing what the next five years would bring, why would it not then also be appropriate to postpone all judicial action against this man who had given, not five years, but half a century of service to the organization? The logic of such reasoning can be understood only if one accepts and sustains the premise that the interests of the person - including his good name, the reputation forged with effort, the years of life offered in service – are disposable if they interfere with the objectives of an organization. We are sure that each of the men on that judicial committee recognized that Edward Dunlap had a deep love for God, for Jesus Christ and for the Bible – and yet they felt they had to take action against this man. Why? They knew the prevailing character in the Governing Body, expressed through its Committee of the Presidency. Loyalty to the organization required such action on their part, since this man neither accepted nor could accept all the pretensions and interpretations coming from that organization.

When the Judicial Committee of five Bethel elders had finished doing what was required, they passed the file onto the Governing Body and it was their turn to finish the job and they finally met with Edward Dunlap and informed him of their decision to expel or excommunicate him. Ed replied and said: "Okay, if that's your decision. But do not say or put in writing that it is because of apostasy. You know that apostasy means rebellion against God and Jesus Christ, and you know that this is not true of me." So, ignoring his special request they expelled Edward Dunlap for apostasy and asked him to leave what had been his home in the headquarters in Bethel for so many years. He returned to Oklahoma City where he had grown up and where, at about 70 years of age, he began earning a living for himself and his wife, wallpapering walls, a job he learned before beginning his forty years of full service as a representative of the Watch Tower Bible & Tract Society. Raymond Franz commented about this dreadful and callous decision to excommunicate Edward Dunlap from the religion that he had spent most of his adult life supporting and promoting. "It is difficult for me to understand how those who were responsible – genuinely and primarily responsible for this entire disfellowshipping process can approach God in prayer at night and say, Show us mercy as we have shown mercy to others."

After this callous, unfeeling and ruthless expulsion from the Watchtower Society headquarters in New York, by the Governing Body of this religion, Edward Dunlap went through Alabama on his way to Oklahoma City and his new beginning, now being free from the chains and slavery of a religious cult. When Raymond Franz spoke with Ed, his close friend and fellow Christian, he told him, "It seems to me that the only thing you can do is try to live a Christian life and helping people in whatever sphere of influence one normally has, the rest is in the hands of God." Both Raymond Franz and Edward Dunlap survived this spiritual crisis in their lives. How did they accomplish this? They both still believed in the existence of Almighty God and his beloved son Jesus Christ, plus the ransom sacrifice he had made, and they continued to believe in the inspired written word of God and allowed it to speak for itself. They were both fully aware and trusted the words at 2 Timothy 3:16, "All scripture is inspired by God and is useful for teaching, for reproof, for correction, and for training in righteousness." Both Edward and Raymond were also familiar with the words of Psalms 119:109, "I hold my life in my hand continually, but your law (words or reminders) I have not forgotten."

Selected Bibliography

Anderson, Barbara. *Eyewitness to Deceit*. Phoenix, Arizona. Ghost River Images Publishers. 2018.

Appel, Willa. *Cults in America*. New York, N.Y. Holt, Rinehart & Winston Publishers. 1983.

Aron, Raphael. *Cults, Terror & Mind Control*. Richmond, California. Bay Tree Publishing. 2009.

Bachelard, Michael. *Behind The Exclusive Brethren*. Victoria, Australia. Scribe Publications. 2008.

Barker, Eileen. *New Religious Movements: A Practical Introduction*. London, England. HMSO Publishers. 1991.

Beckford, James A. *The Trumpet of Prophesy*. New York, N.Y. John Wiley & Sons Publishers. 1975.

Bergman, Jerry R. *The Criterion: Religious Discrimination in America*. Richfield, Minneapolis. Onesimus Publishing. 1984.

Bergman, Jerry R. *Jehovah's Witnesses and the Problem of Mental Illness*. Clayton, California. Witness Inc. Publishers. 1992.

Bergman, Jerry R. *Jehovah's Witnesses and Kindred Groups*. New York. Garland Publishing. 1984

Bergman, Jerry R. *Jehovah's Witnesses: A Comprehensive and Selective Annotated Bibliography*. Westport, Connecticut. Greenwood Press. 1999.

Besier, Gerhard & Staklosa, Katarzyna. *Jehovah's Witnesses in Europe: Past and Present. (Two Volumes)* Newcastle, England. Cambridge Scholars Publishing. 2016.

Beverley, James A. *Crisis of Allegiance*. Burlington, Ontario. Welch Publishing Company. 1986.

Bjorling, Joel. *The Churches of God, Seventh Day*. New York, N.Y. Garland Publishing Inc. 1987.

Botting, Gary & Botting, Heather. *The Orwellian World of Jehovah's Witnesses*. Toronto, Canada. University of Toronto Press. 1984.

Bowman, Robert M. Jnr. *Understanding Jehovah's Witnesses: Why They Read the Bible the Way They Do*. Grand Rapids, Michigan. Baker Book House. 1991.

Brown, J.A.C. *Techniques of Persuasion; From Propaganda to Brainwashing*. London, England. Penguin Books. 1963.

Buchner, J.L.F. *Armstrongism Bibliography*. Sydney, Australia. University of Western Sydney Press. 1983.

Butters, Alan. *No Room to Move: The Bizarre World of the Watchtower Society*. St. Ives Media, Melbourne, Australia. 2013

Butterworth, John. *Cults & New Faiths*. St. Catherines, Ontario. Lion Publishing. 1981.

Cameron, Don. *Captives of a Concept*. Morrisville, North Carolina. Lulu Press. 2013.

Casarona, Keith. *New Boy-Life & Death at the World's Headquarters of Jehovah's Witnesses*. Portland, Oregon. The Oregonian Press. 2019.

Cather, Willa & Georgina Milmine. *The Life of Mary Baker G. Eddy & The History of Christian Science*. Lincoln, Nebraska. University of Nebraska Press. 1993.

Cetnar, William. *Questions for Jehovah's Witnesses*. Phillipsburg, New Jersey. P & R Publishing. 1983.

Chidester, David. *Salvation & Suicide: Jim Jones, the Peoples Temple, and Jonestown*. Bloomington, Indiana. Indiana University Press. 1988.

Chryssides, George. *Historical Dictionary of Jehovah's Witnesses*. Lanham, Maryland, USA. Rowman & Littlefield. 2008.

Chryssides, George. *The A to Z of Jehovah's Witnesses*. Plymouth, UK. Scarecrow Press. 2009.

Chryssides, George. *Jehovah's Witnesses: Continuity and Change*. Farnham, England. Ashgate Publishing. 2016.

Chrnalogar, Mary Alice. *Twisted Scriptures: a Path to Freedom From Abusive Churches*. Chattanooga, Tennessee. Control Techniques Inc. Publishers. 1997.

Clark, Elmer T. *The Small Sects in America: An Authentic Study of Almost 300 Little-Known Religions*. Gloucester, Massachusetts. Peter Smith Publishers. 1937. (Revised 1981)

Clarkson, Frederick. *Eternal Hostility: the Struggle Between Theocracy & Democracy*. Monroe, Maine. Common Courage Press. 1997.

Clemens, Clara. *Awake to a Perfect Day - My Experience With Christian Science*. New York, N.Y. Citadel Press. 1956.

Cole, Marley. *Jehovah's Witnesses the New World Society*. New York, N.Y. Vantage Press. 1955.

Cole, Marley. *Triumphant Kingdom*. New York, N.Y. Criterion Books. 1957.

Collins, John J. *The Cult Experience: an Overview of Cults, Their Traditions & Why People Join Them*. Springfield, Illinois. Charles Thomas Publishers. 1991.

Corydon, Bent. *L. Ron Hubbard: Messiah or Madman?* Fort Lee, New Jersey. Barricade Books, Inc. 1992.

Court Systems & Records. *The Douglas Walsh Trial: The Watchtower Bible and Tract Society Takes the Stand*. Infinity Publishers, New York, N.Y. 2007.

Covington, Hayden. *Defending & Legally Establishing the Good News*. New York, N.Y. Watchtower Society. 1950.

Cowan, Douglas. E & David G. Bromley. *Cults & New Religions: A Brief History*. Hoboken, New Jersey. Blackwell Publishing Ltd. 2008.

Crompton, Robert. *Counting the Days to Armageddon*. Cambridge, England. James Clark Publishers. 1996.

Chretien, Leonard. *Witnesses of Jehovah*. Eugene, Oregon, Harvest House Publishers. 1988.

Darlington, Christina. *Documented Facts the Watchtower Society Doesn't Want You to Know*. Colorado Springs. Create Space Publishing. 2012.

Dawson, Lorne L. *Comprehending Cults: The Sociology of New Religious Movements*. Oxford, England. Oxford University Press. 1998.

Decker, Ed & Dave Hunt. *The God Makers: A Shocking Exposé of What the Mormon Church Really Believes*. Eugene, Oregon. Harvest House Publishers. 1984.

Deikman, Arthur J. *The Wrong Way Home: Uncovering the Patterns of Cult Behaviour in American Society*. Boston, Massachusetts. Beacon Press. 1990.

Duggar, Gordon E. *Jehovah's Witnesses: Watch Out for the Watchtower*. Grand Rapids, Michigan. Baker Book House Publishing.1989

Edmonds, Anthony. *Muhammad Ali: A Biography*. Houston, Texas. Greenwood Publishing. 2006.

Enroth, Ronald. *A Guide to CULTS & New Religions*. Downers Grove, Illinois, USA. InterVarsity Press. 1983.

Eskridge, Larry & Mark A. Noll. *More Money, More Ministry: Money & Evangelicals in Recent North American History*. William B. Erdmann Publishers. 2000.

Evans, Lloyd. *The Reluctant Apostate: Leaving Jehovah's Witnesses Comes at a Price*. London, England. JLE Publishing. 2017.

Ferngren, Gary. *Science and Religion: A Historical Introduction*. Baltimore, Maryland. John Hopkins University Press. 2002.

Franz, Raymond. *Crisis of Conscience*. Atlanta, Georgia. Commentary Press. 1983.

Franz, Raymond. *In Search of Christian Freedom*. Atlanta, Georgia. Commentary Press. 1992.

Fraser, Caroline. *God's Perfect Child: Living and Dying in the Christian Science Church*. London, England. Picador Press. 1999.

Furuli, Rolf. *The Role Of Theology and Bias in Bible Translation*. Christian Publishing House, Cambridge, Ohio, USA. 1999.

Furuli, Rolf. *My Beloved Religion – And The Governing Body,* Norway. Awatu Publishers. 2020.

Gottlieb, Robert & Peter Wiley. *America's Saints*. New York, N.Y. G.P. Putnam's & Sons. 1984.

Gray, Daniel. *Terminal Visions: Apocalyptic Thought of Jehovah's Witnesses and the Stella Group*. Champaign, Illinois. Illinois University Press. 1986.

Gruss, Edmund. *Jehovah's Witnesses: Their Claims, Doctrinal Changes and Prophetic Speculation*. Florida, USA. Xulon Press (Salem Press). 2001.

Gruss, Edmund. *The Four Presidents of the Watchtower Society*. Oregon, USA. Xulon Press. 2003.

Hamilton, Marci. *God vs. The Gavel: Religion and the Rule of Law*. London, England. Cambridge University Press. 2005.

Harrison, Barbara Grizzuti. *Visions of Glory, History & Memory of Jehovah's Witnesses*. New York, N.Y. Simon and Schuster. 1978.

Harrod, Allen F. *Deception by Design. The Mormon Story*. Kearney, Nebraska. Printed in the USA by Morris Publishing. 1998.

Hassan, Steven. *Releasing The Bonds: Empowering People to Think for Themselves*. Newton, Massachusetts, USA. Freedom of Mind Press. 2000.

Hassan, Steven. *Freedom of Mind: Helping Loved Ones Leave Controlling People, Cults, and Beliefs.* Newton, Massachusetts, USA. Freedom of Mind Press. 2002.

Hassan, Steven. *Combating Cult Mind Control*. Rochester, Vermont, USA. Park Street Press. 1988.

Haworth, Ian. *Cults: A Practical Guide*. London, England. Cult Information Centre Publishers. 2001.

Hebdon, Geoffrey. *The Delamere Saga-The Untold Story of Vale Royal Abbey*. Queensland, Australia. Glass House Books. 2020.

Heftmann, Erica. *Dark Side of the Moonies*. Sydney, Australia. Penguin Books. 1982.

Heiser, Michael. *The Unseen Realm*. Bellingham, Washington, Lexham Press. 2019.

Henderson, Jennifer, Jacobs. *Journal of Church and State, Vol. 46*. Oxford, England. Oxford University Press. 2004.

Henry, Matthew. (New edition of 2009 in 6 volumes) *Bible Commentary of the Old and New Testaments.* Peabody, Massachusetts. Hendrickson Publishers. 2009.

Hewitt, Joe. *I Was Raised a Jehovah's Witness*. Grand Rapids, Michigan.

Kregel Publications. 1997.

Hexham, Irving & Karla, Poewe. *Understanding Cults & New Religions*. Grand Rapids, Michigan, USA. William B. Erdmann Publishing Company. 1986.

Hexham, Irving; Stephen Rost & John W. Morehead II. *Encountering New Religious Movements: Holistic Evangelical Approach*. Grand Rapids, Michigan, USA. Kregek Publications. 2004.

Hoffer, Eric. *The True Believer: Thoughts on the Nature of Mass Movements*. New York, N.Y. Harper and Row. 1951.

Jenkins, Philip. *Mystics & Messiahs. Cults and New Religions in American History*. Toronto, Canada. Oxford University Press. 2000.

Johnson, David & Van Vonderen, Jeff. *The Subtle Power of Spiritual Abuse*. Minneapolis, USA. Bethany House Publishers. 1991.

Johnson, Phillip E. *Reason in the Balance: The Case Against Naturalism in Science, Law & Education.* Downers Grove, Illinois, USA. InterVarsity Press. 1995.

Johnson, Sonia. *From Housewife to Heretic*. Albuquerque, New Mexico. Wildfire Books. 1989.

Jones, Leslie. *What Pastor Russell Taught*. Chicago, Illinois. Dr. Leslie Jones Publisher. 1919.

Russell, Charles Taze. *What Pastor Russell Said*. Chicago, Illinois. Bible Students Book Store. 1922.

Jonsson, Carl Olof. *The Gentile Times Reconsidered*. Atlanta, Georgia, USA. Commentary Press. 1998.

Judah, Stillson J. *The History & Philosophy of the Metaphysical Movements in America*. Philadelphia, Pennsylvania. The Westminster Press. 1967.

Kaplan, Jeffrey. *Radical Religion in America: Millenarian Movements from the Far Right to the Children of Noah*. Syracuse, New York, N.Y. Syracuse University Press. 1997.

Kaufman, Robert. *Inside Scientology: How I joined Scientology and Became Superhuman*. London, Great Britain. The Olympic Press Ltd. 1972.

Keiser, Thomas W. & Jacqueline L. Keiser. *The Anatomy of Illusion: Religious Cults and Destructive Persuasion*. Springfield, Illinois, USA. Charles C. Thomas Publishers. 1987.

Kephart, William M. & William W. Zellner. *Extraordinary Groups: An Examination of Unconventional Life-styles*. New York, NY. St. Martin's Press, Inc. 1994.

Kant, Immanuel (Translated by T. K. Abbott, 1988). *Fundamental Principles of the Metaphysical of Morals*. Amherst, New York, N.Y. Prometheus Books. 1785.

Kant, Immanuel (Translated by Werner Pluhar, 2009) *Religion Within the Limits of Reason Alone*. Indianapolis, Indiana. Hackett Publishing Company. 1793.

Kilduff, Marshall & Ron Javers. *The Suicide Cult: The Inside Story of the Peoples Temple Sect and the Massacre in Guyana*. New York, N.Y. Bantam Books. 1978.

Kostelniuk, James. *Wolves Among Sheep: The True Story of Murder in a Jehovah's Witness Community*. Toronto, Canada. Harper Collins Canada. 2000.

Knox, Zoe. *Jehovah's Witnesses and the Secular World.* London, England. Macmillan. 2017.

Kroeger, Otto & Roy M. Oswald. *Personality Type and Religious Leadership.* Washington (D.C). The Alban Institute, Inc. 1992.

Lamont, Stewart. *Religion Inc.: The Church of Scientology*. London, England. Harrap Publishers. 1986.

Larson, Bob. *Strange Cults in America*. Carol Stream, Illinois. Tyndale House Publishers, Inc. 1986.

Lewis James R. *Odd Gods: New Religions & the Cult Controversy*. Amherst, N.Y. Promotheus Books. 2001.

Lewis, James R. *Doomsday Prophecies: A Complete Guide to the End of the World*. Amherst, N.Y. Prometheus Books. 2000.

Lingle, Wilbur. *What the Watchtower Society Doesn't Want You to Know.* Port Washington, USA. CLC Publications. 2009.

Lofland, John P. *Doomsday Cult: a Study of Conversion, Proselytization, & Maintenance of Faith*. New York, N.Y. Irvington Publishers, Inc. 1977.

MacHovec, Frank J. *Cults & Personality*. Springfield, Illinois. Charles C. Thomas Publishers. 1989.

Magnani, Duane. *Who is the Faithful & Wise Servant? A Study of Authority Over Jehovah's Witnesses.* Clayton, CA, USA. Witness Inc., Publishers. 1992.

Martin, Walter. *Jehovah of the Watchtower*. Bloomington, Minneapolis, USA. Bethany House Publishing. 1981.

Martin, Walter. *The Maze of Mormonism*. London, England. Morgan, Marshall & Scott Publishers. 1963.

Martin, Walter. *Rise of the Cults*. Los Angeles, CA. Vision House Publishers. 1978.

Martin, Walter. *The Christian and the Cults*. Grand Rapids, Michigan, USA. Zondervan Publishing House. 1956.

Martz, Larry & Ginny Carroll. *Ministry of Greed: the Inside Story of the Televangelists and Their Holy Wars*. New York. Weidenfeld & Nicholson Publishers. 1988.

McElveen, Floyd. *The Mormon Illusion*. Grand Rapids, Michigan, USA. Kregel Publications. 1997.

Macmillan, Alexander. *Faith on the March*. New York, N.Y. Prentice-Hall. 1957.

McMinn, Mark R. & James D. Foster. *Christians in the Crossfire: Guarding Your Mind Against Manipulation and Self-deception*. Newberg, Oregon. Barclay Press. 1990.

Meerloo, Joust A.M. *The Rape of the Mind: The Psychology of Thought Control, Menticide, and Brainwashing*. New York, N.Y. Grossett & Dunlop Press. 1956.

Miller, Maryann. *Coping with Cults*. New York, NY. Rosen Publishing Group, Inc. 1990.

Millar, Ralph. *Jehovah's Witness-Victims of Deception*. New York. Comments from the Friends Press. 1995.

Miller, Timothy, (Editor). *America's Alternative Religions*. New York, N.Y. State University New York Press. 1995.

Mooney, Annabelle. *The Rhetoric of Religious Cults*. New York, NY. Palgrave MacMillan. 2005.

Moore-Emmett, Andrea. *God's Brothel: The Extortion of Sex for Salvation in Contemporary Mormon & Christian Fundamentalist Polygamy*. San Francisco, CA. USA. Pince-Nez Press. 2004.

Montville, Leigh. *Sting Like a Bee: Muhammad Ali vs. The United States of America, 1966-1971*. New York, N.Y. Random House Publishing. 2017.

Needleman, Jacob. *The New Religions*. New York, N.Y. The Crossroad Publishing Company. 1984.

Nelson, Russell Marion. *The Exodus Repeated*. Provo, Utah. LDS Publishing. 1999.

Oakes, Len. *Prophetic Charisma: The Psychology of Revolutionary Religious Personalities*. New York, NY. Syracuse University Press. 1997.

Paddock, William & Paul. *World Famine 1975*. Washington, USA. Little, Brown & Company Publishers. 1967.

Paul, Erich Robert. *Science, Religion and Mormon Cosmology*. Urbana, Illinois. University of Illinois Press. 1992.

Penton, M. James. *Apocalypse Delayed: The Story of Jehovah's Witnesses*. Toronto, Canada. University of Toronto Press. 1985.

Penton, M. James. *Jehovah's Witnesses and the Third Reich*. Toronto, Canada. University of Toronto Press. 2004.

Porterfield, Kay Marie. *Blind Faith: Recognizing and Recovering From Dysfunctional Religious Groups*. Minneapolis, Minnesota. CompCare Publishers. 1993.

Prichard, Denise and Ackerman, Raymond. *Hearing Grasshoppers Jump: The Story of Raymond Ackerman*. Seattle, Washington. Philips Publishing. 2001.

Reed, David. *Index of Watchtower Errors, 1879-1989*. London, England. Baker Publishing. 1990.

Reed, David. *Blood on the Altar: Confessions of a Jehovah's Witness Minister.* Amherst, N.Y. Prometheus Books. 1996.

Rhodes, Ron. *The Culting of America*. Eugene, Oregon, USA. Harvest House Publishers. 1994.

Reiterman Tim. *Raven: The Untold Story of the Rev. Jim Jones and His People*. Boston, Massachusetts. Dutton Publishers. 1982.

Roberts, Robert. *Dr. Thomas, His Life and Work.* Birmingham, England. Christadelphian Press. 1873.

Robertson, Irvine. *What the Cults Believe*. Chicago, Illinois. Moody Press. 1991.

Rodriguez, Daniel. *The Watchtower's Coming Crisis*. Oregon, USA. Chick Publications. 2009.

Rodriguez Orlando. *When Dinosaurs Fall: The Age Of Extinction Of Jehovah's Witnesses*. Florida, USA. Self-Published.

Schnell, William J. *30 Years a Watch Tower Slave*. Grand Rapids, Michigan. Baker Book House. 1971.

Scorah, Amber. *Leaving the Witness: Exiting a Religion and Finding a Life*. London, England. Penguin Books. 2019.

Shupe, Anson D. *The Darker Side of Virtue: Corruption, Scandal and the Mormon Empire*. Buffalo, N.Y. Prometheus Books. 1991.

Streissguth, Thomas. *Charismatic Cult Leaders*. Minneapolis, Minnesota. The Oliver Press. 1995.

Thompson, Damian. *The End of Time: Faith and Fear in The Shadow of the Millennium*. Hanover, N.H. University Press of New England. 1996.

Thrupp, Sylvia L. *Millennial Dreams in Action: Studies in Revolutionary Religious Movements*. New York, N.Y. Schocken Books. 1970.

Tobias, Madeleine Landau & Janja Lalich. *Captive Hearts, Captive Minds: Freedom & Recovery From Cults and Abusive Relationships*. Alameo, California. Hunter House, Inc. 1994.

Twain, Mark. *Christian Science*. Amherst, New York, N.Y. Prometheus Books. 1993.

Verdier, Paul A. *Brainwashing & The Cults.* Hollywood, California. Wilshire Books Company. 1977.

Vicky, J. *Sex in the Sect.* Melbourne, Australia. Essien Publishing. 1995.

Walstrom, Terry. *I Wept by the Rivers of Babylon.* New York, N.Y. Random House Publishing. 2013.

Ward, Vicki. *Kushner, Inc: Greed, Ambition, Corruption.* New York, N.Y. St. Martins Press. 2019.

Watters, Randall. *Thus Saith...The Governing Body of Jehovah's Witnesses.* Manhattan Beach, CA. USA. Bethel Ministries. 1987.

Watters, Randall. *Refuting Jehovah's Witnesses.* Manhattan Beach, CA, USA. Bethel Ministries. 1990.

Watters, Randall. *The Occultic Origins of the Watchtower.* Manhattan Beach, CA, USA. Bethel Ministries. 1992.

Watters, Randall. *The Truth Will Set You Free.* Manhattan Beach, CA, USA. Bethel Ministries. 1995.

Webber, Max. *Sociology of Religion.* Boston, USA. Beacon Press. 1963.

Whalen, William, J. *Armageddon Around The Corner: A Report on Jehovah's Witnesses.* New York, N.Y. John Day Publishers. 1952.

Wilson, Bryan. *When Prophecy Failed.* London, England. SCM Press. 1978.

Wilson, Bryan. *Magic and the Millennium.* New York, N.Y. Heinemann Publishers. 1973.

Wilson, Diane. *Awakening of a Jehovah's Witness. Escape from the Watchtower Society.* Amherst, N.Y. Prometheus Books. 2002.

Zahn, Gordon. *German Catholics and Hitler's Wars; A Study in Social Control.* New York, N.Y. Sheed and Ward. 1962.

Zieman Bonnie. *EXiting the JW Cult: A Healing Handbook: For Current & Former Jehovah's Witnesses.* Charleston, South Carolina. Create Space Publishing. 2015.

About the Editor

Geoffrey Hebdon

Geoffrey Hebdon was born and brought up in Lancashire, England, in the heart and region of the cotton industry. After leaving college, having studied textile engineering, he embarked on the vocation of education, including lecturing, teaching and evangelical work. He and his wife Pauline lived and served in various parts of the United Kingdom, including Scotland, Yorkshire, Cheshire, Warwickshire, Northamptonshire, Cambridgeshire, Bedfordshire and Buckinghamshire.

After starting a family in the 1970s, Geoffrey and his wife decided to relocate to Southern Africa and for almost 30 years were based in Cape Town. While working in Cape Town, Geoffrey, a dedicated educationalist, along with a business partner, decided to open a private, non-profit Academy with campuses in Bellville, the northern suburbs of Cape Town and also in Central Cape Town, with plans to open a third campus in the African township of Khayelitsha in the Western Cape, to offer career training courses, including, business management, computers, travel and tourism, journalism, plus health and beauty. This private academy later expanded its scope to the more disadvantaged students of Southern and Eastern Africa, with the help of the Department of Education plus generous private subsidies and sponsorships.

In 2000, Geoffrey and his wife Pauline relocated their family to the United States of America and lived in Salt Lake City, Utah, for eight years before moving to the Los Angeles area of California, where his family is currently based. Even though semi-retired, Geoffrey is still involved with research, reporting and writing.

www.ingramcontent.com/pod-product-compliance
Lightning Source LLC
Chambersburg PA
CBHW060420100426
42812CB00030B/3245/J